D1453461

Before the Deluge

Before the Deluge

PUBLIC DEBT, INEQUALITY, AND

THE INTELLECTUAL ORIGINS OF

THE FRENCH REVOLUTION

Michael Sonenscher

PRINCETON UNIVERSITY PRESS

PRINCETON AND OXFORD

COPYRIGHT © 2007 BY PRINCETON UNIVERSITY PRESS

PUBLISHED BY PRINCETON UNIVERSITY PRESS, 41 WILLIAM STREET, PRINCETON,
NEW JERSEY 08540

IN THE UNITED KINGDOM: PRINCETON UNIVERSITY PRESS, 3 MARKET PLACE,
WOODSTOCK, OXFORDSHIRE OX20 1SY

ALL RIGHTS RESERVED

LIBRARY OF CONGRESS CATALOGING-IN-PUBLICATION DATA

SONENSCHER, MICHAEL.

BEFORE THE DELUGE:

PUBLIC DEBT, INEQUALITY, AND THE INTELLECTUAL ORIGINS OF

THE FRENCH REVOLUTION / MICHAEL SONENSCHER.

P. CM.

INCLUDES BIBLIOGRAPHICAL REFERENCES AND INDEX.

ISBN-13: 978-0-691-12499-5 (HARDCOVER : ALK. PAPER)

ISBN-10: 0-691-12499-X (HARDCOVER : ALK. PAPER)

1. FRANCE—HISTORY—REVOLUTION, 1789–1799—CAUSES. I. TITLE.

DC138.S57 2007

944.04—DC22   2006016623

BRITISH LIBRARY CATALOGING-IN-PUBLICATION DATA IS AVAILABLE

THIS BOOK HAS BEEN COMPOSED IN JANSON TYPEFACE

PRINTED ON ACID-FREE PAPER. ∞

PRESS.PRINCETON.EDU

PRINTED IN THE UNITED STATES OF AMERICA

1 3 5 7 9 10 8 6 4 2

For Elizabeth

CONTENTS

CONTENTS

ACKNOWLEDGEMENTS

I AM grateful to the Provost and Fellows of King's College, Cambridge for the many different resources that they have made available to me over the years, and, more particularly, to my colleagues Stephen Alford and Melissa Lane for their kindness in taking on my usual administrative responsibilities while I was writing this book. I am also greatly indebted to the Arts and Humanities Research Council and, in its former incarnation, the British Academy for the financial support that enabled me to collect much of the material referred to in what follows. I have relied very heavily upon the goodwill and active help of the many librarians and archivists responsible for the collections on which I have drawn, and I am most grateful to them all. I would also like to thank the Hackett Publishing Company for allowing me to use passages from the introduction to my translation of *Sieyès: Political Writings* (Indianapolis, Hackett, 2003), and the editors and publishers of the following previously published articles or chapters for their generosity in allowing me to reproduce passages from them: "The Nation's Debt and the Birth of the Modern Republic: The French Fiscal Deficit and the Politics of the Revolution of 1789," *History of Political Thought* 18 (1997): 64–103, 267–325; "Fashion's Empire: Theories of Foreign Trade in Early Eighteenth-Century France," in Robert Fox and Anthony Turner, eds., *Innovation and Markets in Eighteenth-Century France* (London, Hambledon Press, 1998); and "Property, Community and Citizenship," in Mark Goldie and Robert Wokler, eds., *The Cambridge History of Eighteenth-Century Political Thought* (Cambridge, Cambridge University Press, 2006).

I have learned a great deal over the years from conversations with Keith Michael Baker, John Dunn, Bianca Fontana, Raymond Geuss, Ross Harrison, Bernard Manin, Pasquale Pasquino, Munro Price, Emma Rothschild, Gareth Stedman Jones, and Richard Tuck. I have also benefited from conversations with Maxine Berg, Lesley Millar, and Katie Scott about the arts and the luxury trades in the eighteenth century. One intermittent conversation, with my friend Colin Jones, now extends over thirty years. As another friend, Anna Hont, has often reminded me, I have been lucky in many ways and particularly so for having been able to enjoy his unfailingly generous intellectual and personal companionship over so many years. I am grateful, too, to Edward Castleton, Rachel Hammersley, Béla Kapossy, Ruth Scurr, and Richard Whatmore for many helpful discussions about some of the topics addressed in this book and for the items of information that, from time to time, they were kind enough to pass on to me. Jacques Guilhaumou kept me regularly informed of his own publications on Sieyès, while Loïc Charles and Catherine Larrère did the same with their publications on eighteenth-century French political and economic thought. I have also gained a great deal from supervising the work of Stephen Butler, Andrew Glencross, Isaac Nakhimovsky, and Jaikumar Ramaswamy. It may be a dangerously double-edged gesture to say that I genuinely could not have written a book like this without the years of conversation that I have had with my friend and colleague Istvan Hont. It should be taken to refer to what he taught me to think about and aim for, not to what, in the end, I may have managed to do. I am particularly indebted to him and to Elizabeth Allen, Richard Bourke, William Doyle, Colin Jones, and Béla Kapossy for their comments on parts or all of earlier drafts of the text, to Keith Michael Baker and Ed Hundert for their very helpful, initially anonymous, readers' reports after the text was submitted, and to Ian Malcolm at the Princeton University Press for his editorial guidance and commitment in turning the typescript into a book. It is also a real pleasure to thank Lauren Lepow at Princeton for her professional skill, attention to detail, and invariably helpful guidance in preparing the text for publication. I am grateful, as well, to Amelia Jackson at the British Museum for her invaluable help in locating the image used on the dust jacket, and to Richard Bourke for his advice on translations of Greek and Latin terms. Thanks, too, to various individuals at Thomson Gale who were kind enough to allow me to have more or less uninterrupted access to their on-line database, ECCO, before it became generally available to British universities under the terms of an agreement that will, I hope, be a precedent for making other electronic databases nationally accessible for research. I also owe a debt to John Robertshaw and Michael Thompson (not, I hope, literally) both for what they have taught me about eighteenth-century French books and, especially, for what passes for polite repartee in the book trade. Thanks, too, to the personnel of Walter Purkis & Sons of Muswell Hill for both the fish and the songs. All this should make it clear that the many remaining faults in this book really are my own.

Before the Deluge

INTRODUCTION

THE phrase *après moi, le déluge* ("after me, the deluge") is sometimes attributed to Louis XV, France's penultimate eighteenth-century king. It seems, however, to have been coined by his mistress, Mme de Pompadour, and she seems to have used it to refer to "us," not "me" (as in *après nous, le déluge*).[1] The phrase, and the various attitudes towards intimations of disaster that it might have been intended to express (shocked recognition, grim resignation, or selfish heedlessness, for example), have often been associated loosely with the French Revolution, even though Mme de Pompadour died in 1764, and even though it is not entirely clear what kind of equivalent of a biblical flood she may have had in mind.[2] Curiously, however, the phrase was current, even before 1789, and it did mean something like what it is now usually taken to mean (selfish heedlessness, rather than shocked recognition or grim resignation). In this usage, it was connected directly to the subject-matter of this book, because it was applied to public debt. This, for example, is how it was used in a book entitled *Entretiens d'un jeune prince avec son gouverneur* (Conversations between a Young Prince and His Governor) published in 1785 by Victor Riqueti, marquis de Mirabeau, the father of the better-known revolutionary orator Honoré-Gabriel Riqueti, comte de Mirabeau. Part of the content of the book had actually been written nearly two decades earlier and first appeared in instalments in the monthly periodical the *Ephémérides du citoyen* (The Citizen's Ephemeredes) in 1769.[3] Mirabeau applied the phrase to the practice of government borrowing and, more particularly, to the practice

---

[1] See [Jean-Baptiste-Denis Desprès], "Essai sur la marquise de Pompadour," in Nicole du Hausset, *Mémoires de Madame du Hausset, femme de chambre de Mme de Pompadour*, ed. Quintin Crauford (Paris, 1824), pp. xix–xxxviii (p. xix). Unless stated otherwise, translations of this and subsequent quotations from French texts are my own. I have usually dropped eighteenth-century capitalisations of words like "nation" or "republic" and have modernised the original punctuation.

[2] See, for example, Evelyn Farr, *Before the Deluge: Parisian Society in the Reign of Louis XVI* (London, Owen, 1994), although she did not actually examine the phrase itself.

[3] They began to appear, under the title of "Dialogues entre un enfant de sept ans & son mentor, par Mr B," in the sixth part of the *Ephémérides du citoyen* in 1769. The "Mr B" in question may have been the first editor of the *Ephémérides*, the abbé Nicolas Baudeau, but this may still mean that Mirabeau was the author, if not the actual writer, of the articles. In keeping with the practice of more or less collective authorship that was one of the features of Physiocracy, the book-length version of the *Entretiens* was also the work of another of Mirabeau's collaborators, Charles Grivel, just as Mirabeau was the author of several ("une cinquantaine," he wrote) of the articles that Grivel contributed to the volumes on *Economie politique* in the *Encyclopédie Méthodique* (see Musée Arbaud, Aix-en-Provence, Fonds Mirabeau, 20, Mirabeau to Longo, 30 September 1783; fol. 147, 11 October 1784; fol. 176, 27 February

of using life annuities to fund the costs of government debt. Life annuities, he wrote, were the quintessence of what he called "that misanthropic sentiment (*ce sentiment ennemi*), *après moi, le déluge*."[4] In the milder English-language equivalent of the phrase, they were a way of drawing bills on posterity. Like all forms of public credit, Mirabeau argued, they consumed wealth before it was produced and, because of this, could erode the resources required for new production, leaving a state that placed its future in the hands of capitalists (the eighteenth-century French word for investors in the public funds) with the possibility of having to face that future without the accumulated assets that it might need to maintain its long-term domestic prosperity and external security. Public debt, Mirabeau warned, could, quite literally, destroy what, in 1756, he had been the first to call "civilisation."[5]

This is a book about how this kind of vision of the future was registered in eighteenth-century thought, and, more specifically, about how it can be connected to the political thought of the period of the French Revolution. Its argument, outlined in what follows in this introduction, can be summarised quite briefly. It is that the modern idea of representative government,

---

1785; and see A. Dauphin-Meunier, "Les dernières années du marquis de Mirabeau," *Le Correspondant*, January 1913, p. 258).

[4] Victor Riqueti, marquis de Mirabeau, *Entretiens d'un jeune prince avec son gouverneur*, 4 vols. (London and Paris, 1785), 2:525. A life annuity was a form of government borrowing that came to be widely used in the eighteenth century, particularly in France. At its simplest, it was stock that carried a rate of interest for the lifetime of the lender. A combination of an increasingly sophisticated capacity to calculate life expectancy (notably that of a sample of young Genevan women, the famous *trente demoiselles de Genève*) and the syndication of state-backed loans among a large number of international banking houses turned life annuities into a major, but controversial, source of state credit in the second half of the eighteenth century. For the broader background, see Herbert Lüthy, *La banque protestante en France de la révocation de l'édit de Nantes à la Révolution*, 2 vols. (Paris, 1959–61); James C. Riley, *The Seven Years War and the Old Regime in France: The Economic and Financial Toll* (Princeton, Princeton University Press, 1986); and the more detailed bibliography on p. 38, n. 40, below.

[5] On the eighteenth-century concept of "civilisation," see Jean Starobinski, *Blessings in Disguise; or the Morality of Evil* [Paris, 1989], trans. Arthur Goldhammer (Cambridge, Polity Press, 1993), pp. 1–35; Bernard Plongeron, "Affirmation et transformations d'une 'civilisation chrétienne' à la fin du xviiie siècle," in Jean-René Derré, Jacques Gadille, Xavier de Montclos, and Bernard Plongeron, eds., *Civilisation chrétienne. Approche historique d'une idéologie xviiie-xixe siècle* (Paris, 1975), pp. 9–21 (p. 17); Bernard Plongeron, "Bonheur et 'civilisation chrétienne': une nouvelle apologétique après 1760," *Studies on Voltaire and the Eighteenth Century* 154 (1976): 1637–55; Bernard Plongeron, "Echec à la sécularisation des lumières? La religion comme lien social," in Michel Mat, ed., *Problèmes d'histoire du christianisme* (Brussels, 1984), pp. 91–126; Joachim Moras, *Ursprung und Entwicklung des Begriffs der Zivilisation in Frankreich, 1756–1830* (Hamburg, 1930); and, for a general overview, Jörg Fisch, "Zivilisation, Kultur," in Otto Bruner, Werner Conze, and Reinhart Koselleck, eds., *Geschichtliche Grundbegriffe*, 8 vols. (Stuttgart, 1972–97), 7:679–774. On Mirabeau's use of the term, see below, chapter 3.

notably the one developed by the abbé Emmanuel-Joseph Sieyès, owes rather more than it may now seem to the type of future-oriented speculation about public debt that, among other things, was captured by the phrase *après moi, le déluge*.[6] To see why it does, two aspects of public credit need, in the first instance, to be distinguished from one another. Public credit may, as several historians have argued, entail constitutional government and economic growth.[7] But public credit was also a product of war and continuous preparations for war. The practice of borrowing money against the state's future tax revenue to fund the costs of the large, permanent array of armed forces required for modern warfare began in a durable way during the period of the Wars of the League of Augsburg and the Spanish Succession in the late seventeenth and early eighteenth centuries, and has continued ever since.[8] These two aspects of public credit were easier to distinguish in the eighteenth century than they are now, mainly because expenditure on warfare, not welfare, was then responsible for almost all government borrowing.[9] Together, they served to give public credit, or

[6] Two gestures at the direction of this argument can be found in Michael Sonenscher, "The Nation's Debt and the Birth of the Modern Republic: The French Fiscal Deficit and the Politics of the Revolution of 1789," *History of Political Thought* 18 (1997): 64–103, 267–325; and "Republicanism, State Finances and the Emergence of Commercial Society in Eighteenth-Century France—or from Royal to Ancient Republicanism and Back," in Martin Van Gelderen and Quentin Skinner, eds., *Republicanism: A Shared European Heritage*, 2 vols. (Cambridge, CUP, 2002), pp. 275–91. Full bibliographical details on Sieyès's life and thought can be found in the notes to chapter 1.

[7] See, particularly, the work of Douglass C. North, from his *The Rise of the Western World: A New Economic History* (Cambridge, Cambridge University Press [henceforth CUP], 1973) to his *Institutions, Institutional Change, and Economic Performance* (Cambridge, CUP, 1990), and, in more detail, Douglass C. North and Barry Weingast, "Constitutions and Commitment: The Evolution of Institutions Governing Public Choice in Seventeenth-Century England," *Journal of Economic History* 49 (1989): 803–32. For a generalisation of North's argument, see Niall Ferguson, *The Cash Nexus: Money and Power in the Modern World 1700–2000* (London, Allen Lane, The Penguin Press, 2001). Two other recent books deal with the same subject: see James Macdonald, *A Free Nation Deep in Debt: The Financial Roots of Democracy* (New York, Farrar, Straus and Giroux, 2003), and, from a more sceptically analytical standpoint, David Stasavage, *Public Debt and the Birth of the Democratic State: France and Great Britain, 1688–1789* (Cambridge, CUP, 2003). On the bearing of institutional economics on the historiography of the French Revolution, see the works referred to below, p. 56, n. 105.

[8] See notably P.G.M. Dickson, *The Financial Revolution in England: A Study in the Development of Public Credit, 1688–1756* (London, Macmillan, 1967), and, more recently, John Brewer, *The Sinews of Power: War, Money and the English State, 1688–1783* (London, Collins, 1989).

[9] On the wider issues surrounding warfare and welfare as these were construed in the eighteenth century, see, classically, Jacob Viner, "Power versus Plenty as Objectives of Foreign Policy in the Seventeenth and Eighteenth Centuries" [1948], reprinted in his *Essays on the Intellectual History of Economics*, ed. D. A. Irwin (Princeton, Princeton University Press, 1991), and, for overviews of early modern public finance, see Richard Bonney, ed., *The Rise of the Fiscal State in Europe: 1200–1815* (Oxford, Oxford University Press, 1999), and Charles Tilly,

what came to be called the modern funding system, a distinctly Janus-faced appearance. On the one hand, it seemed to be established most firmly in countries like Britain and the United Provinces of the Netherlands where economic prosperity and political representation were strongly entrenched. On the other hand, it seemed to be responsible for some, if not most, of the scale, scope, and frequency of eighteenth-century warfare. The urgency underlying the way that Mirabeau used the phrase *après moi, le déluge* grew out of this Janus-faced aspect of public credit. It implied that the very properties of public credit that favoured prosperity and stability might also favour the kind of social collapse that could be represented by the image of a biblical flood. At the limit, Mirabeau suggested, public credit could destroy what it had been established to preserve. This, a generation earlier, had been the reason why the philosopher David Hume had written, "either the nation must destroy public credit, or public credit will destroy the nation."[10]

The two faces of public credit go some way towards explaining why, in the eighteenth century, thinking about politics could sometimes take place under the sign of a biblical flood. This strand of thought may look like the other side of the Enlightenment, but it did, in fact, form part of the context that gave that well-worn word much of its original theological and teleological charge. Referring to enlightenment, *lumières*, or *Aufklärung* (although the French and German usually require the definite article) implied making some kind of claim about what, ultimately, human society was supposed to be for, despite the often hideous appearance of the world as it was, or the even more terminally catastrophic prospect that its future could appear to hold.[11] Getting behind that appearance could, in the eighteenth century, take the form of a theodicy, or an argument that was designed to explain how the all-too-visible existence of evil and injustice in the world could, under more careful inspection, be reconciled with the idea of a good,

---

ed., *The Formation of National States in Western Europe* (Princeton, Princeton University Press, 1975) and his *Coercion, Capital, and European States AD 990–1990* (Oxford, Oxford University Press, 1990).

[10] David Hume, "Of Public Credit" [1752], in David Hume, *Essays: Moral, Political and Literary*, ed. Eugene F. Miller (Indianapolis, Liberty Press, 1985), pp. 360–1. The phrase "to draw bills upon posterity" was Hume's: see p. 352. On the essay and its argument, see Istvan Hont, "The Rhapsody of Public Debt: David Hume and Voluntary State Bankruptcy," in Nicholas Phillipson and Quentin Skinner, eds., *Political Discourse in Early Modern Britain* (Cambridge, CUP, 1993), pp. 321–48, now reprinted in his *Jealousy of Trade: International Competition and the Nation-State in Historical Perspective* (Cambridge, Mass., Harvard University Press, 2005), pp. 325–53.

[11] The description can, I think, be reconciled with the more polemical argument in John Robertson, *The Case for the Enlightenment: Scotland and Naples 1680–1760* (Cambridge, CUP, 2005).

just, and omnipotent God.[12] In a less obviously spiritual way, it could also take the form of a more secular, but still philosophical, examination of human history and the reasons underlying the more directly visible arrangements of the world as it was.[13] As the mixture of biblical and financial connotations in the phrase *après moi, le déluge* suggests, the subject-matter of this book straddles these two kinds of concern. Its focus is almost entirely historical, but this does not mean that the more theological dimension of its subject-matter was totally absent from thinking about both the promise and the menace of public debt. "I do not blame anyone if political evils make him begin to despair of the welfare and progress of mankind," wrote the philosopher Immanuel Kant in 1798. "But I have confidence in the heroic medicine which Hume prescribes, for it ought to produce a speedy cure."[14] Here, it was the menace of public credit that loomed largest. For Sieyès, however, it was its sheer unavoidability, which meant that coming to terms with the system of modern war finance had to involve finding a way to deal with Hume's stark alternatives. This, too, had a speculative dimension. As for many of the post-Kantian German idealists who were intrigued by his thought, God, for Sieyès, was simply the *ultra-mètre*, the ultimate measure that lay beyond even the grandest of achievements that human history might display and the ever-receding symbol of a not entirely consoling intimation that there was more still to come.[15] A great deal of Sieyès's interest in the details of social organisation and how they could be fitted together to form something systematic was connected to this radically open-ended historical vision.

Generally, however, it was the more immediately menacing aspect of public credit that dominated speculation about the future. It supplied much of the content of a way of thinking about eighteenth-century power politics

[12] For a helpful way into the subject of theodicy in eighteenth-century thought, see Susan Neiman, *Evil in Modern Thought: An Alternative History of Philosophy* (Princeton, Princeton University Press, 2002).

[13] A good way into eighteenth-century philosophical history is Duncan Forbes, *Hume's Philosophical Politics* (Cambridge, CUP, 1975), along with his introduction to Georg Wilhelm Friedrich Hegel, *Lectures on the Philosophy of World History* (Cambridge, CUP, 1975) and the following articles: "Sceptical Whiggism, Commerce and Liberty," in Andrew S. Skinner and Thomas Wilson, eds., *Essays on Adam Smith* (Oxford, Oxford University Press, 1975), pp. 179–201; "Natural Law and the Scottish Enlightenment," in Roy H. Campbell and Andrew S. Skinner, eds., *The Origins and Nature of the Scottish Enlightenment* (Edinburgh, John Donald, 1982), pp. 186–204.

[14] Immanuel Kant, *The Conflict of the Faculties* [1798], trans. and ed. Allen W. Wood and George Di Giovanni (Cambridge, CUP, 1996), p. 308. I have preferred the translation in Immanuel Kant, *The Contest of the Faculties*, in Immanuel Kant, *Political Writings*, ed. Hans Reiss (Cambridge, CUP, 1991), p. 189.

[15] The text is published in Jacques Guilhaumou, "Fragments d'un discours sur Dieu: Sieyès et la religion," in *Mélanges Michel Vovelle* (Aix-en-Provence, Publications d'Université de Provence, 1997), pp. 257–65.

and, more specifically, of a peculiarly explosive concept of revolution that have both been largely forgotten.[16] Both predated the events of the French Revolution by some considerable time and, after 1789, soon came to be overshadowed, first by its real social, political, and military history and then by the strongly teleological claims about its wider historical significance embedded in the philosophies of history of Hegel, Comte, and Marx in the nineteenth century. Before then, however, the related subjects of war, debt, and revolution helped to give the theme of decline and fall a resonance that went beyond the way that, at least in the Anglophone world, it came to be transmitted to posterity by Edward Gibbon.[17] They did so because they lent themselves to a new and alarming variation on the well-established parallel between the modern world and its ancient counterpart. Chronologically, the modern world was its heir. What came to matter in the eighteenth century was whether it might also have its fate. The details of this possibility were certainly cloudy, but its content was still quite determinate.[18] In this version of the parallel, eighteenth-century Europe might have to face the prospect of a replay of the ancient cycle of decline and fall under modern conditions of war and debt. Here, the threat to established power and prosperity was not so much the inequality and luxury that, according to a long-standing tradition of political and historical analysis, had been responsible for earlier cycles of decline and fall, but the new financial instruments and fiscal resources that had accompanied the transformation of warfare during the seventeenth and eighteenth centuries.[19] The revolution that was anticipated surprisingly frequently in the eighteenth century was, it was claimed, likely to be a product of the huge standing armies and the intense financial pressures that had come to dominate the great power politics of the modern world coupled with the violent conflict between the rich and the poor that had been one of the features of the politics of the ancient world. Together, they were taken to be likely to lead, suddenly

---

[16] See, however, Hont, "The Rhapsody of Public Debt."

[17] On Gibbon and the wider theme of decline and fall, see now J.G.A. Pocock, *Barbarism and Religion*, 4 vols. to date (Cambridge, CUP, 1999–2005).

[18] On broader eighteenth-century concepts of revolution, see, particularly, Reinhart Koselleck, *The Practice of Conceptual History* (Stanford, Stanford University Press, 2002), chs. 5–10, 12–4; and Pocock, *Barbarism and Religion*, vol. 3, *The First Decline and Fall* (2003), chs. 14–6. The interrelationship of public debt, power politics, and political upheaval described in chapter 1 below supplies part of the content of the concepts of revolution discussed in these works.

[19] On the political dimensions of the themes of inequality and luxury, see, classically, J.G.A. Pocock, *The Machiavellian Moment: Florentine Political Thought and the Atlantic Republican Tradition* [1975], 2nd edition (Princeton, Princeton University Press, 2003). See also the comments by Istvan Hont in his "The Rhapsody of Public Debt" on J.G.A. Pocock, "Hume and the American Revolution: The Dying Thoughts of a North Briton," in his *Virtue, Commerce, and History: Essays on Political Thought and History, Chiefly in the Eighteenth Century* (Cambridge, CUP, 1985), pp. 125–41.

and brutally, to the emergence of a highly militarised dictatorial regime equipped with a capacity to destroy much of the civility, culture, and liberty that had been built up in Europe since the age of the Renaissance. From this perspective, the eighteenth century appeared to have created the conditions that might, once again, favour the emergence of either a Caesar or a Spartacus.

In this concept of revolution, the modern system of war finance would make most types of private property the property of the state and, by doing so, would give the state itself despotic power. Here, the Janus-faced quality of public credit was the crucial ingredient. Public credit might well give rise to economic prosperity and constitutional government, but economic prosperity and constitutional government could, in their turn, give rise to new political risks. Adding a debt to a state could either make it easier to embark upon an ill-judged foreign adventure or might make it more difficult to take preemptive action against a less constitutionally constrained enemy. Borrowing money could make it easier for a government to avoid raising taxes, but could also make it difficult to avoid subsequent conflict over the distribution of the resulting tax burden. Public credit could give a government more financial latitude, but could then leave it with less room for manoeuvre in political decision-making, either because of a state's dependence on other powers for the trade required to generate the tax revenue needed for debt service, or because of its need to observe constitutional proprieties in meeting its commitments to its creditors, or because of the political divisions produced by a debt-generated tax burden. In all these ways, adding a debt to a state introduced a new dimension of uncertainty into political life, raising the possibility that, in conditions of international rivalry, orderly constitutional politics might switch quite suddenly into a hectic scramble for survival. The result was something like a political double-bind. The very constitutional and institutional arrangements that helped to make public credit secure could begin to look like obstacles to the wider security of the state as a whole. The dynamics of power politics and the intensity of the debt-driven financial pressure generated by what, in the German-speaking world, was already called "nationalism" could, it was claimed, lead to a state of affairs in which a government might either have to choose, or might simply be forced, to sacrifice the interests of its creditors to the imperatives of national survival.[20] In these circumstances, it would simply default on its debt and, since it still had a tax base but now paid no interest, it would be in position to use the resources that it now had available to promote war on a massive scale. The future-oriented

---

[20] On "nationalism" in the eighteenth century, see, particularly, Istvan Hont, "The Permanent Crisis of a Divided Mankind: 'Nation-State' and 'Nationalism' in Historical Perspective," in his *Jealousy of Trade*, pp. 447–528 (at, specifically, pp. 499–504).

speculation of the eighteenth century was a product of this dilemma because it seemed to indicate that all roads led to state bankruptcy.

This was the prospect raised by the phrase *après moi, le déluge*. The combination of a public debt, an existing tax base, and an established administrative system meant that if, for one reason or another, a government opted for a voluntary debt default, it might be stronger, not weaker, because it would, de facto, be in possession of much of the available wealth of society. The result was a political paradox. Constitutional government might make public credit secure, but once public credit really was secure, it could give rise to conditions in which constitutional government might have to go. And, if one state were to apply the sponge (the eighteenth-century metaphor for a voluntary state bankruptcy), the rest would have to follow. An absolute government might be able to default more easily than one with a less centralised system of political decision-making, but if the chain-reaction were ever to start, then every type of government would have to suspend constitutional propriety. Necessity, as the ancient Roman republican maxim put it, had no law (*necessitas non habet legem*). The imperatives of survival would force every state to use the resources generated by the modern funding system to fight for hearth and home (*pro aris et focis*) because, as yet another celebrated Roman republican maxim had it, the public safety had to be the supreme law (*salus populi suprema lex esto*).[21] From this perspective, one that was more familiar in the eighteenth century than it is now, modern economics appeared to have paved a way for a revival of ancient politics. From a parallel perspective, the modern funding system appeared to have produced a range of fiscal and administrative institutions capable of equipping a republic with something like the same command structure as an absolute government without, however, requiring it to have an absolute monarch. Well before the Bastille fell, the eighteenth century already had something like a prospective history of the violent political trajectory that was to lead, first to Maximilien Robespierre and the revolutionary government of the Year II of the first French republic, and then to Napoleon Bonaparte's imperial regime.

The broad aim of this book is to describe some of the ways by which this sort of projection can be connected to both the history and historiography of the French Revolution and, more particularly, to the political thought of the abbé Sieyès. By doing so, it is intended to show what the French Revolution might begin to look like in the light of a detailed historical examination of the range of ideas and more ambitious political theories

---

[21] On these themes in the history of European political thought, see the classic Friedrich Meinecke, *Machiavellism: The Doctrine of Raison d'Etat and Its Place in Modern History* [1924], trans. D. Scott, ed. W. Stark (London, Routledge, 1957), and, more recently, Richard Tuck, *The Laws of War and Peace* (Oxford, Oxford University Press, 1999).

that, directly or indirectly, can be associated with the menace underlying the phrase *après moi, le déluge*. This, in the first instance, means reversing the perspective that the sequence of events of the French Revolution came to pass on to posterity. From the vantage point of 1740 or 1780, an image of the type of regime now associated with the Terror was already in existence well before any of the political conflicts that preceded and followed the fall of the Bastille. "We are poor," wrote Montesquieu in *The Spirit of Laws* in 1748, "with the riches and commerce of the whole world; and soon, by thus augmenting our troops, we shall all be soldiers, and be reduced to the very same situation as the Tartars."[22] This was the prospect raised by the modern system of war finance. From this perspective, the Terror came first. It may not have been associated with France (the "we" in Montesquieu's sentence referred to Europe's "three most opulent powers"), but it imposed a firmly limited horizon of expectation upon the future. Taking that idea seriously may help to throw a new, but historically more accurate, light upon the very elaborate set of constitutional and institutional arrangements that Sieyès envisaged in 1789. These were designed to secure public credit's promise, but to avoid its menace. This is what this book is about.

Its more immediate historiographical starting point is, perhaps, best indicated by a question raised by François Furet and Ran Halévi in one of the last books that Furet published before his death. As they put it, the French Revolution has presented two classic problems to posterity: the causes of 1789 and the causes of the Terror. The second, they went on to suggest, may now be less intractable than the first, because, they continued, it may now be easier to explain the radicalisation of the revolution after 1789 than the radicalism of 1789 itself.[23] The radicalisation of the revolution, Furet famously wrote, was a largely unforeseen effect of the unitary sovereignty of the nation established in 1789 and the way that it opened up towards an increasingly strident sequence of competing claims about the location and purposes of sovereign power.[24] This, he argued, was why the initial radicalism of 1789, or the unilateral seizure of power by the representatives of the French Third Estate as a National and Constituent Assembly, had so problematic a significance, and why the question of the interrelationship of reform, revolution, and the financial problems of the eighteenth-century French monarchy was still a subject of real historical interest. Although the claim may, in fact, presuppose too much about the

[22] Charles-Louis de Secondat, baron de Montesquieu, *De l'esprit des lois* [1748], bk. 13, ch. 17. I have used the reprinted edition of the eighteenth-century English translation by Thomas Nugent, entitled *The Spirit of Laws*, ed. Franz Neumann (New York, Hafner Publishing Company, 1949) and abbreviated it to *SL* (here, *SL*, bk. 13, ch. 17, p. 217).

[23] François Furet and Ran Halévi, eds., *Orateurs de la révolution française*, (Paris, Gallimard, 1989), p. xcv.

[24] François Furet, *Interpreting the French Revolution* [1978] (Cambridge, CUP, 1981).

politics of Jacobinism, it does highlight something genuinely historically puzzling about the revolution of 1789. Right from the start, the strong claims about sovereignty made by what was soon to be the French National and Constituent Assembly and the controversial rejection of an English-style system of mixed or balanced government that accompanied those claims provoked a mixture of enthusiastic acclaim, puzzled surprise, and horrified indignation.[25] Even if some of the details of the argument set out in Sieyès's famous pamphlet *What Is the Third Estate?* can be found in many other contemporary publications, the one-word answer—"everything"—that, at the very beginning of his pamphlet, he gave to the question it posed is an indication of the radicalism to which Furet and Halévi referred.[26] Even if, too, much of the boldness of that answer may, perhaps, have had its origins in Sieyès's private life or in his unarticulated ideological allegiances, its theoretical point and wider political and institutional ramifications still have to be explained.[27]

The suggestion developed here is that what Furet and Halévi called the radicalism of 1789, or, more simply, the difference between revolution and reform, is best understood in the light of the Janus-faced quality of public credit and the theoretical and practical difficulties involved in separating its promise from its menace. Modern historiography has focused largely on its promise. The eighteenth century focused largely on its menace. The system of representative government that Sieyès conceived was the first systematic attempt to address the question of how to have the one without the other. Although Sieyès was an important political actor both in 1789 and in 1799, it has only begun to become clear relatively recently, now that his own unpublished papers have begun to be more widely studied, that he was a more significant political thinker than he was taken to be for much of the nineteenth and twentieth centuries.[28] Since, however, he published nothing of a comprehensively theoretical character, it is still quite hard to see what the system of representative government that he envisaged might have looked like. One of the effects of putting back eighteenth-century speculation about Europe's future into the prehistory of the French Revolution is to help to make that system clearer. The key move that Sieyès

---

[25] For these assessments, see below, chapter 1.

[26] Emmanuel-Joseph Sieyès, *What Is the Third Estate?* [1789], in *Sieyès: Political Writings*, ed. Michael Sonenscher (Indianapolis, Hackett, 2003), p. 94.

[27] For the claim about Sieyès's ideological allegiances, see William H. Sewell, *A Rhetoric of Bourgeois Revolution: The abbé Sieyès and "What Is the Third Estate?"* (Durham, N.C., Duke University Press, 1994).

[28] On Sieyès's political thought, see, particularly, Paul Bastid, *Sieyès et sa pensée*, 2nd ed. (Paris, Hachette, 1970); Murray Forsyth, *Reason and Revolution: The Political Thought of the Abbé Sieyes* (Leicester, Leicester University Press, 1987); and Pasquale Pasquino, *Sieyès et l'invention de la constitution en France* (Paris, Editions Odile Jacob, 1998).

made was to see that adding a debt to a state required more than a purely constitutional solution to produce a durably stable social and political outcome. The corollary of that move was a renewed interest in what, in the eighteenth century, was usually called the distinction of ranks. Adding a debt to a state certainly called for constitutional government to make public credit secure. But it also called for rethinking the whole organisation of society and the various economic and social hierarchies that it housed in order, by extension, to make the constitution itself secure. In the context of 1789, this meant revolution, not reform.

Sieyès's initial move was predicated upon a recognition that a constitution might well secure a public debt, but, by doing so, it might also give rise to problems that threatened the security of the state itself. In this sense, adding a debt to a state created something like a prefiguration of what, in the nineteenth century, came to be called the "social question" (even though the latter was a question about the propertied and the propertyless and not, as in this case, about the owners of different types of property).[29] As with the later social question and its concern with the tension between legal equality and economic inequality, the right kind of constitutional and institutional arrangements could give rise to the wrong kind of social and political divisions. It could do so because of the two different claims about justice that the government of a state with a debt had to meet. The first arose from the state's obligations to its creditors, while the second arose from its obligations to society as a whole. The two types of obligation could pull quite strongly against one another. Raising taxes to pay interest could clash with demands to reduce economic and social inequality. Covering interest payments to investors in the public funds could clash with demands for emergency expenditure in times of economic hardship or war. The relatively high levels of taxation secured by political representation, coupled with the way that state-backed government bonds could be used to fund the costs of private transactions, could make it easier to avoid a trade-off between public and private prosperity. But the fact that public credit could, in this way, spill over quite quickly from its initial use as war finance to become a more deep-seated part of the whole economic and social fabric could either narrow down the range of policy options to something like a single track or generate so many different policy options that no broad consensus would be easy to reach. The interest of the owners of government stock might serve the interests of the state, but it might equally be-

[29] For helpful starting points on the literature on the "social question," see Giovanna Procacci, *Gouverner la misère: la question sociale en France (1789–1848)* (Paris, Seuil, 1993); Donald R. Kelley and Bonnie G. Smith, "What Was Property? Legal Dimensions of the Social Question in France," *Proceedings of the American Philosophical Society* 128 (1984): 200–30, and their introduction to Pierre-Joseph Proudhon, *What Is Property?* [1840] (Cambridge, CUP, 1994).

come an interest in its own right. Ambiguities like these meant that even if public credit and constitutional government went hand in hand, the likely outcome of the combination remained, at best, indeterminate and, at worst, might threaten the survival of constitutional government itself.

This type of double-bind called for something more comprehensive than a purely constitutional solution. It called for detailed examination of all the components of modern political societies as these had emerged from Europe's ancient, feudal, and absolute pasts, and for thinking about how they could be put together to give a political society the allegiance of most of its members for most of the time. This was the intellectual setting in which Sieyès's system took shape. It was, in a real sense, a system. Its start- ing point was the modern economy and the array of occupations, activities, and social distinctions that had come into being over the previous several hundred years. But its aim was to establish a further level of political and social distinction above those generated by wealth, birth, or connection. Sieyès called the kind of theoretical enterprise that this involved "social science" or "social mechanics," meaning that it had much the same kind of concern with a limited array of fundamental principles as the natural jurisprudence of the seventeenth and eighteenth centuries had done, but that it also had a historical dimension that pointed as much towards natural outcomes as towards natural foundations.[30] Its starting point was a radical reformulation of the idea of representation so that it referred, initially, to something more basic than was usually implied by established legal or po- litical usage.[31] In Sieyès's usage, anyone acting on someone else's behalf was acting as that person's representative, even if the action in question amounted to no more than doing something that someone could have done all by himself (or, as Sieyès also indicated, herself). Someone who made your shoes, he noted, was, in this sense, acting as your representative.[32]

This simple idea meant that representation was built into even the most rudimentary social and economic transactions, irrespective of the existence of separate political societies. Representation was simply the division of labour in another guise. From this perspective, political representation was a particular species of this broader genus, and, since it was, it had to have

---

[30] On these aspects of Sieyès's thought, see Sieyès, *Political Writings*, ed. Sonenscher, pp. ix, xiv, xlvi, 4–5, 15, 39, 50, 115, 131–2, 134. On natural jurisprudence, see Richard Tuck, "The Modern Theory of Natural Law," in Anthony Pagden, ed., *The Languages of Political Theory in Early Modern Europe* (Cambridge, CUP, 1987); "Grotius and Selden," in J. H. Burns and Mark Goldie, eds., *The Cambridge History of Political Thought, 1450–1700* (Cambridge, CUP, 1991); and his *Philosophy and Government, 1572–1651* (Cambridge, CUP, 1993).

[31] For a starting point on the idea of representation, see, classically, Hannah Fenichel Pitkin, *The Concept of Representation* (Berkeley and Los Angeles, University of California Press, 1967).

[32] Sieyès, *Political Writings*, ed. Sonenscher, p. xxix, note 47.

attributes that were consonant with the initial idea. In a generic sense, representation was stateless. In a particular sense, it was what gave government its right to rule. Combining the two, or fitting politics and the economy together, involved finding a way to integrate the two types of representation into a single system, but one that would still have a capacity to keep them distinct, so that both the initial and the modified ideas of representation could each exist, even under conditions of war and debt. This was what the system of representative government that Sieyès envisaged was designed to do. It was intended to produce a new, meritocratic level of social distinction out of the mixture of economic and political representation to be found in a large, developed nation like France and, once it was in place, to allow the merit-based inequality involved in this kind of social distinction to act as a moral counterweight to both economic and political inequality. What Sieyès called a "monarchical republic" was designed to produce an extra level of social distinction above the property- or office-based hierarchies involved in economic, political, and administrative life. The further level of social distinction that this entailed would, in addition, make it easier to build a bridge between the multiple and unitary forms of political representation involved in republican and royal systems of rule. Sieyès (anticipating more recent political science) called the first a polyarchy and the second a monarchy.[33] The first, he argued, could be combined with the second through the use of a constitutionally specified mixture of election and eligibility as a filtering mechanism to produce a single head of state. The outcome would be a system of government that would join the unity of monarchy to the pluralism of a republic and, by doing so, would bypass the need to have to make a choice between the two.

The result was a framework for thinking about how to add a debt to a state in a way that was compatible with all the various political and nonpolitical forms of representation that Sieyès had identified. A constitution and the fundamental principles that it embodied could secure a separation of powers between the legislative, executive, and judicial functions of the state and, by doing so, could supply the conditions required for keeping the public faith. But it could not, in itself, prevent the possibility of the damaging political conflicts or the wider political risks that keeping the public faith might involve. This was why the vertical separation of powers involved in constitutional government had to be complemented by a horizontal separation of different levels of political and administrative responsibility, on the one hand, and of different levels of social distinction and moral authority, on the other. The system of representative government that Sieyès envisaged was designed, in this sense, to have two distinct parts, a political part that would be elected and a nonpolitical part that, although

---

[33] For this opposition, see Sieyès, *Political Writings*, ed. Sonenscher, p. 172.

it would also be elected, would play no part at all in the way that the government itself worked. It would, however, play a vital part in giving the whole system its moral authority, so that, if conflicts or hard political choices were to arise, the system as a whole would retain its legitimacy, however divisive or contentious any particular issue might prove to be. The ingenious aspect of Sieyès's system was the way that it was designed to bypass every actually existing social hierarchy and to subsume them all within a broader, dual hierarchy of political power and moral authority. As Pierre-Louis Roederer, one of Sieyès's closest political allies, put it in 1804, the whole system was intended to rely on both a balance of powers and what he called "the artifice of hierarchies."[34] It was designed, in the first place, to segment the many different types of inequality built into economic and social life and prevent any one of them from dominating political power. But it was also designed, in the second place, to integrate them all within a broader system of political and moral representation. It was intended to secure public credit, but to prevent it from becoming a threat to either the internal or external security of the nation as a whole. In this sense, Sieyès's idea of representative government is, perhaps, best characterised as a daringly modernist answer to the eighteenth century's often lurid speculations about modernity's future.

Sieyès had no illusions about the way that public credit could produce what, in 1795, he was to call a *ré-total* (as against a *ré-publique*), but was still prepared to accept the fact that public debts were an unavoidable part of modern political societies and the multiple forms of representation that they housed.[35] The system of government that this entailed was one that was not mixed in the sense that the eighteenth-century British or American systems of government could be said to be mixed, but still did not have the kind of single centre that was built into the absolute governments of the eighteenth century. Sieyès called it a monarchical republic, as against a republican monarchy. In the first, sovereignty began from below (hence its republican nature) but would give rise to a form of government with many of the attributes of a monarchy. In the second, sovereignty began from above (hence its monarchical nature) but would give rise to a form of government with many of the attributes of a republic. Paradoxically, it was the monarchical structure of the first, not the republican structure of second, that, according to Sieyès, was best able to maintain the very inclusive idea of sovereignty

[34] Pierre-Louis Roederer, "De l'hérédité du pouvoir suprême dans le gouvernement français" [an xiii/1804], reprinted in *Oeuvres du comte P. L. Roederer*, ed. A. M. Roederer, 8 vols. (Paris, 1852–9), 7:269. For further details, see below, chapter 1.

[35] Sieyès introduced the neologism in his *Opinion de Sieyès sur plusieurs articles des titres IV et V du projet de constitution de l'an III* (Paris, 1795). On the coinage, see Pierre-Louis Roederer, "Du néologisme de Sieyès" [1795], reprinted in his *Oeuvres*, 4:204–5.

on which the whole system was based.[36] The mechanisms of political representation that the system housed were designed to produce a single, largely symbolic, head of state and a multiple set of political representatives. They were also intended to work in a way that would keep the single representative of the whole nation quite separate from the multiple representatives of its members. Sovereignty and government would, in short, be kept as far apart as possible. To accomplish this, the system of representation that Sieyès envisaged was based on a mechanism that its advocates called "graduated promotion" or "gradual election."[37] This was not simply a form of indirect election but, as its name indicates, a hierarchical system of eligibility for election to office. The idea underlying the system was to ensure that, however well-provided with all the goods of fortune (wealth, birth, or connection) anyone might be, the eligibility requirements built into the system would require everyone to start at the bottom of the political pyramid and work their way, step by step, all the way up to the top. Ultimately, it would leave just one eligible candidate for the office of head of state. The shape of the whole system would be monarchical, but its republican nature would be based on eliminating inheritance from all of its constitutionally specified parts. It was intended to be compatible with every aspect of an economically developed society and the many different types of division of labour that it might house, but it was also intended to generate a further, nonpolitical and meritocratic hierarchy based on public service. This was the original idea underlying what, in 1802, became the French Legion of Honour.[38] The result, if the system had ever been implemented fully, would have been the formation of two distinct types of social hierarchy. One would have been property-based, but the other would have been service-based, with the moral authority of the second acting, in conjunction with free public discussion, as a barrier against the emergence of either an oligarchy or a plutocracy out of the first. Over time, the system of gradual election and the limitations on inheritance imposed on the membership of the service-based hierarchy would prevent this higher level of social distinction from being reabsorbed by the property-based hierarchy.

The corollary of Sieyès's initial insight into the double-bind that could be produced by securing public credit by purely constitutional means was a strong interest in the part played by multiple forms of social distinction in maintaining political stability. This, in part, was connected to the way that public credit could intensify the kind of symbiosis of land, money, and office that Sieyès was to highlight in some of the more vitriolic passages of

---

[36] See Sieyès, *Political Writings*, ed. Sonenscher, pp. 163–73.

[37] On this idea of political representation, see below, chapter 1.

[38] On this aspect of the system, see below, chapter 1.

the pamphlets that he published in 1788 and 1789.[39] There, the French nobility was presented as either a parasitic aristocracy or a plutocracy, a class of titled mendicants feeding on the resources supplied by a court-centred absolute government and a burgeoning public debt. But Sieyès's interest in different types of social distinction and the various, and often incommensurable, kinds of public or private good with which they could be associated had a further, more positive, dimension. As the future-oriented speculation of the eighteenth century indicated, adding a debt to a state gave rise to a particularly vivid case of the more general problem of identifying and fixing the limits of state power. One way of establishing such limits was provided by the mechanisms involved in constitutional government. But the double-bind that these could produce required a further layer of moral and political constraint to make the constitution itself secure. This, for Sieyès, was why the multiple goods associated with a variety of different types of social hierarchy mattered. Although they might all, in the last instance, still have to be subordinate to the state and might all still have to give way to its final role in preserving the public good, their very variety and incommensurability could set powerful limits on what the content of that ultimate value might be. The multiple goods and services supplied by a complex commercial and industrial society meant that preserving the public good would still have to leave room both for the kind of instrumental trade-offs involved in comparing one type of good against another and for the less instrumental and more aesthetic attractions of social diversity itself. Different types of good might not have much in common, but their very incommensurability and the pluralistic set of values that this entailed could play a part in making a whole social and political system acceptable, however much it might fall short at one time or another or frustrate the interests of one or other of its component parts.

Here, the promise of public credit could begin to outweigh its menace. What had begun as war finance could also be used to promote the public welfare. In part this was an effect of the protean character of public credit and the way that part of the revenue raised through the issue of state-backed debt would feed back into the economy either because of government expenditure or because of the way that interest-bearing paper could be used as security for private credit. In a larger measure, however, it was an effect of the power supplied by the combination of permanent taxation

---

[39] Notably in his *Essay on Privileges*, in Sieyès, *Political Writings*, ed. Sonenscher, pp. 68–91. Compare to Hilton L. Root, *The Fountain of Privilege: Political Foundations of Markets in Old Regime France and England* (Berkeley and Los Angeles, University of California Press, 1993), which, in other respects, relies on the literature on institutional economics and public choice referred to in note 7 above and, in a weaker sense, on the kind of characterisation of the English constitution described in Montesquieu's *The Spirit of Laws*. For Montesquieu's own views, see below, chapter 2.

and permanent influence over the money supply that public credit produced. The combination gave government real leverage over economic and social life. Here, too, Sieyès was uncompromisingly on the side of the moderns. He opposed all the monetary schemes developed to eliminate the nation's debt during the period of the revolution, including the decision to confiscate the property of the French church in November 1789 and all the increasingly ambitious debt-reduction programmes to which that decision gave rise.[40] He was attacked very strongly for doing so, mainly because it was easy to claim that his view had been shaped by his clerical allegiances. There is no reason, however, to think that this was the case. Instead, his position followed quite logically from his disabused acceptance of the fact of public credit and the permanent capacity for social and economic leverage that adding a debt to a state entailed. If there could be no taxation without representation, the opposite also applied. In a world made up of many states, war was always a possibility, and, if there was war, there would also be debt. Just as there could be no taxation without representation, there also had to be no representation without taxation and, in the absence of perpetual peace, a government that was strong enough to be able to do both. It is the kind of government that we have. It may not be quite like the kind of government that Sieyès envisaged, but the state-funded combination of welfare and warfare that is one of its most deep-seated features was what, instead of the deluge, came next.

Sieyès sometimes claimed that he had thought of most of the features of what he usually called the representative system well before 1789. He did so most pointedly in the public debate that he had with the Anglo-American republican Tom Paine in 1791.[41] Much of the content of this book is intended to explain why it is not particularly surprising that Sieyès should have made that claim. It is, accordingly, arranged in a way that is designed to show how the system of representative government that he envisaged went with the grain of a great deal of thinking about domestic and international politics in the second half of the eighteenth century and, in particular, with the interest in different types of social hierarchy and their relationship to political power that developed in the wake of the publication of Montesquieu's *The Spirit of Laws* in 1748. Montesquieu associated one type of hierarchy with what he called the English system of government and another with what he called the "monarchies we are acquainted with," or the absolute monarchies of the European mainland.[42] He also hinted that the second, not the first, might be more able to withstand the combination

---

[40] For his alternative to confiscating the property of the church, see Sieyès, *Political Writings*, ed. Sonenscher, p. xliv.

[41] Sieyès, *Political Writings*, ed. Sonenscher, p. 172.

[42] Montesquieu, *SL*, bk. 11, ch. 7, p. 162.

of military and financial pressure that was one of the hallmarks of the modern world, because the kind of hierarchy that it sustained was outside, not inside, the formally political part of the whole system of government and could, therefore, form a real obstacle to the untrammelled exercise of state power. The purpose of the initial chapter of this book is, first, to show how this suggestion was registered and, second, to explain how the related subjects of war, debt, and revolution formed the historical and analytical context in which it came to be assessed. The starting point of the whole chapter is the concept of revolution that, in the eighteenth century, could be associated with the phrase *après moi, le déluge*. Setting Sieyès's political thought in this context may make it easier to see what it was designed to forestall as well as what it was intended to achieve, and how, in this setting, it can also be seen to be the most elaborate (but certainly not the last) of a number of different attempts to think about how to preserve modernity's potential for prosperity, culture, and civility while avoiding its potential for collapse. The system of representative government that he envisaged is perhaps best described as a point-by-point reworking of Montesquieu's conception of monarchy, using a different version of the now largely forgotten idea of representation on which that concept was based.[43] Where Montesquieu's idea of monarchy was a single system made up of two parts, based respectively on the inheritance of property and the inheritance of thrones, Sieyès's idea of a republic was a single system that was also made up of two parts, but where election, not inheritance, filled the hierarchy of positions in the whole social machine.

Several moves were required to get from Montesquieu to Sieyès. Looming over them all was the idea of a unitary, but representative, sovereign state set out in the seventeenth century by the English political philosopher Thomas Hobbes.[44] "The error concerning mixed government," Hobbes had written in his *Elements of Law*, "hath proceeded from want of understanding of what is meant by this word *body politic*, and how it signifieth not the concord, but the union of many men."[45] A political society, in Hobbes's terms, involved union, not simply concord. But public credit seemed to require something like the opposite. It required, on the one hand, investments made severally by banks or individuals with capital at their disposal either at home or abroad and, on the other hand, interest payments made severally to all the various owners of government stock both at home and

---

[43] On this idea of representation and the part that it played in Montesquieu's conception of monarchy, see below, chapter 2.

[44] On this aspect of eighteenth-century thought, see, particularly, Reinhart Koselleck, *Critique and Crisis: Enlightenment and the Pathogenesis of the Modern Society* (Cambridge, Mass., M.I.T. Press; Leamington Spa, Berg Press, 1988).

[45] Thomas Hobbes, *Elements of Law Natural & Politic* [1640], ed. Ferdinand Tönnies, introd. M. M. Goldsmith (London, Cass, 1969), pt. 2, ch. 8, sec. 7, pp. 173–4.

abroad. The whole idea of keeping the public faith presupposed concord. The state that was best equipped to maintain it was likely to be the winner in the international capital markets and to reap the reward of lower interest rates and the virtuous circle of public and private prosperity that they brought in their wake. But the double-bind to which this could lead also seemed to call for union. Concord might be required for keeping the public faith, but union might still be required for unleashing state power. Hobbes's theory of political representation lent itself very well to this latter purpose but left very little room for the former. Adding a debt to a state seemed to call for both. It seemed to require the concord that Hobbes associated with mixed government without, however, actually having a system of government that was really mixed. The political crisis that developed over the French monarchy's financial deficit in 1787 made the sequencing issue clear. Union had to come first, so that concord could then have a chance to take root. *What Is the Third Estate?* spelled out the message. First the nation had to exercise sovereign power; then, under the aegis of the system of representative government that Sieyès had in mind, private and public prosperity could work together.

The next three chapters describe how this outcome acquired its shape in the sequence of moves that, in a not particularly stylised way, can be said to have led from Montesquieu to Sieyès. The thread connecting them is the subject of inequality, both within and between states. It was central to Montesquieu's conception of monarchy, described in chapter 2, and to the various replies to that concept produced by Rousseau, the Physiocrats, and the members of the Gournay group, described in chapter 3. The focus of chapter 4 is on the political and economic thought of a number of individuals, beginning with Claude-Adrien Helvétius and ending with Jean-Baptiste Say, who began to show how it might be possible to move beyond the binary opposition between equality and inequality dominating discussions of modern political societies in the third quarter of the eighteenth century. This interest in the origins of different forms of inequality and the various types of social hierarchy that they could generate pointed towards a range of claims about the compatibility between an English-style system of balanced government and many of the most fundamental features of the modern world. But it was also particularly exposed to the equally powerful claims about the dangers of public credit and the kind of double-bind to which it could expose a system of mixed or balanced government. The dilemma pointed back towards the comparison that Montesquieu had made between monarchy and the English system of government. But the intervening interest in the multiple origins of different types of inequality and the composite character of the distinction of ranks opened up a way to avoid the double-bind. This, effectively, was what Sieyès did. The idea of both political and nonpolitical representation that this involved amounted to the superimposition of a radically modified version of Montesquieu's conception of monarchy upon an English-style commercial society. The final chapter of this book picks up the subject of the relationship between representation and different types of inequality as it was discussed at the time of the formation of the first French Empire. It ends by examining some of the dilemmas that these revealed (and may still do) by describing how the kind of future-oriented speculation that had occurred before the French Revolution was carried through into the first three decades of the nineteenth century in both Europe and the United States of America to form a more open-ended counterpoint to the better-known philosophies of history of Hegel, Comte, and Marx.

The theme of inequality and its political implications that runs through this book forms a further connection between its subject-matter and the historiography of the French Revolution. If the debt problem supplies a context for establishing a clearer historical understanding of what François Furet and Ran Halévi called the radicalism of 1789, it also forms a link between two long-standing interpretations of the French Revolution itself. A generation ago there used to be a "social" interpretation of the French Revolution and a "political" one.[46] This is a book about the bridge between the two. In less metaphorical terms, it is about the social and political dimensions of the future-oriented speculation associated with the phrase *après moi, le déluge* and the light thrown by them both on what was at stake in 1789. The content of this book may, perhaps, make it easier to see why both types of retrospective characterisation of the French Revolution make partial sense, and why, therefore, there is no need to have to opt for either the one or the other, because the real historical question is, rather, to try to identify how they could be taken to be connected. Its content may also, perhaps, form a further bridge to other, more recent, developments in the historiography of the French Revolution, notably the rediscovery of eighteenth-century French Jansenism, the renewal of real historical research into the high politics of the French monarchy, and the broader revival of interest in the content of eighteenth-century thought.[47] The picture of the

---

[46] See, famously, Alfred Cobban, *The Social Interpretation of the French Revolution* (Cambridge, CUP, 1964); George V. Taylor, "Non-capitalist Wealth and the Origins of the French Revolution," *American Historical Review* 72 (1967): 469–96. For a modified version of the "social" interpretation, see Colin Jones, "The Great Chain of Buying: Medical Advertisement, the Bourgeois Public Sphere and the Origins of the French Revolution," *American Historical Review* 101 (1996): 13–40. For general overviews and recent discussions, see William Doyle, *Origins of the French Revolution*, 3rd ed. (Oxford, Oxford University Press, 1999), and Peter R. Campbell, ed., *The Origins of the French Revolution* (London, Palgrave, 2006).

[47] On these developments, see, on Jansenism, Dale Van Kley, *The Jansenists and the Expulsion of the Jesuits from France, 1757–65* (New Haven, Yale University Press, 1975); *The Damiens Affair and the Unraveling of the Old Regime* (Princeton, Princeton University Press, 1984); "Pierre Nicole, Jansenism, and the Morality of Enlightened Self-Interest," in Alan Charles

French Revolution presented here is not very like those that can be extrapolated from these recent historiographical developments, but this does not mean that they are mutually incompatible. Much of the difference arises from the way that this book begins. Its starting point is not what the French Revolution was, or how or why it occurred. It begins, instead, with a revolution that, at least in the first instance, was simply predicted. But this does not mean that it had no bearing upon the French Revolution. What follows is designed to show how it did.

Kors and Paul J. Korshin, eds., *Anticipations of the Enlightenment in England, France and Germany* (Philadelphia, University of Pennsylvania Press, 1987); "The Jansenist Constitutional Legacy in the French Pre-revolution," in Keith Michael Baker, ed., *The Political Culture of the Old Regime* (Oxford, Pergamon Press, 1987), pp. 169–201; "The French Estates-General as Ecumenical Council," *Journal of Modern History* 61 (1989): 1–52; *The Religious Origins of the French Revolution* (New Haven, Yale University Press, 1996); "Christianity as Casualty and Chrysalis of Modernity: The Problem of Dechristianization in the French Revolution," *American Historical Review* 108 (2003): 1081–103; and Dale Van Kley, ed., *The French Idea of Freedom* (Stanford, Stanford University Press, 1994). On the high politics of the eighteenth-century French monarchy, see John Hardman, *French Politics 1774–1789: From the Accession of Louis XVI to the Fall of the Bastille* (London, Longman, 1995); Julian Swann, *Politics and the Parlement of Paris under Louis XV* (Cambridge, CUP, 1995); and, particularly, Munro Price, *The Fall of the French Monarchy* (London, Macmillan, 2002). On the broader intellectual history of eighteenth-century France, see, most notably, Keith Michael Baker, *Inventing the French Revolution: Essays on French Political Culture in the Eighteenth Century* (Cambridge, CUP, 1990).

∾1∾

FACING THE FUTURE

THREE DESCRIPTIONS OF THE FRENCH REVOLUTION

THE revolution began with deep divisions at the royal court. The first signs of political instability took the form of a number of vicious personal disputes among members of both the royal family and the high nobility over the status and character of the reigning queen. She, it was said, had succeeded in building up a party of her own, barely disguising her indifference to the established institutions and formal procedures of the kingdom's government in her eagerness to promote the interests of her favourites and clients. Her foreign origins and the aura of religious scepticism that surrounded her circle served to arouse the resentment of patriots and to awaken the anxieties of the devout, giving the growing number of her enemies many easy opportunities to add fuel to rumours of libertinism at home and treachery abroad. Relaxation of the censorship laws added to the sense of unease. Wave upon wave of satirical, libellous, or crudely pornographic pamphlets, prints, and songs, concerned as much with the queen's sexual affairs as with the political, economic, and moral damage done to the kingdom by a widely hated minister, caused political legitimacy to crumble. As it did, royal legislation became easier to challenge and more difficult to enforce, turning even minor infractions of the law into opportunities for theatrical legal trials and florid appeals to public opinion. The drift towards disaster was marked by growing hostility in the face of a series of controversial reforms to the kingdom's military, legal, and fiscal establishments, hostility that was reinforced by widespread suspicion of an unprecedented set of changes to the kingdom's traditional system of diplomatic alliances. The sequence of events that led to the final explosion took place quite slowly, filling the better part of three tense years. But when the crisis at last occurred, things were all over in a matter of days. "It is surely," wrote one contemporary, "one of the most rare revolutions that history can offer for our observation."[1]

The revolution in question was not the French Revolution of 1789 but the Danish Revolution of 1772. The queen was not Marie Antoinette but Caroline Matilda, the sister of Britain's King George III and wife of the

---

[1] [S. O. Falkenskjold], *Mémoires authentiques et intéressans, ou histoire des comtes Struensee et Brandt* (London, 1789), p. 142.

very much more irretrievably insane Danish king Christian VII. The minister was not Charles-Alexandre de Calonne, or Etienne-Charles Loménie de Brienne, or even Jacques Necker, but Johann Friedrich Struensee, the court physician who became the queen's lover and, until his grisly death in January 1772, the most powerful man in Denmark.[2] The Danish Revolution was not the French Revolution. But, as a number of historians have recently shown, the French Revolution began where it might have been expected to begin—in the high politics of an eighteenth-century monarchy and in the many dimensions of indeterminacy involved in political decision-making and choice.[3] In this respect, the parallel is not entirely fanciful. Knowing something about the Danish Revolution of 1772 makes it easier to see why events in France were registered in the way that they were in the diplomatic correspondence dispatched from Versailles and Paris to Vienna, St. Petersburg, Berlin, London, Venice, or Philadelphia between 1787 and 1789. From the perspective of eighteenth-century political science, the French Revolution of 1789 could, and still does, look a bit like the Danish Revolution of 1772. It could, and still can, be taken to be something like the type of revolution generic to the kind of absolute monarchy that both the French and Danish monarchies were.

By the first decade of the nineteenth century, however, it had become clear that the French Revolution was not at all like the Danish Revolution of 1772. Instead, it became usual to describe it as a different kind of revolution, one generated not by the vagaries of factional infighting under an absolute government, but by a deadly combination of international power politics, war finance, and republican government. This characterisation of the French Revolution also owed something to eighteenth-century political science. Many years before 1789, wrote an American commentator on political affairs named Robert Walsh in 1810, "it was predicted 'that the

---

[2] For English-language publications on the Danish revolution, see H. Arnold Barton, *Scandinavia in the Revolutionary Era 1760–1815* (Minneapolis, University of Minnesota Press, 1986), and a number of articles by John Christian Laursen: "David Hume and the Danish Debate about Freedom of the Press in the 1770s," *Journal of the History of Ideas* 59 (1998): 169–72; "Spinoza in Denmark and the Fall of Struensee, 1770–1772," *Journal of the History of Ideas* 61 (2002): 189–202; "Luxdorf's Press Freedom Writings: Before the Fall of Struensee in early 1770s Denmark-Norway," *The European Legacy* 7 (2002): 61–77. For a description of Struensee's religious scepticism (and an interesting bibliographical guide to moderate Protestant responses to the works of Rousseau and Helvétius), see D. Munter, *A Faithful Narrative of the Conversion and Death of Count Struensee, late Prime Minister of Denmark* (London, 1773). On the vast literature on the cultural origins of the French Revolution, distinguished by the works of Roger Chartier, Robert Darnton, Lynn Hunt, Sarah Maza, and Mona Ozouf, see the recent compilation edited by Ronald Schechter, *The French Revolution* (Oxford, Blackwell, 2001).

[3] See, most vividly, Munro Price, *The Fall of the French Monarchy* (London, Macmillan, 2002).

continent would be speedily enslaved should a nation, with the resources of France, break through the forms and trammels of the civil constitutions of the period; shake off fiscal solicitudes by a general bankruptcy; turn her attention exclusively to military affairs and organize a regular plan of universal empire.' "[4] That prediction, whose words Walsh quoted, had been made in 1772 by a precociously talented French writer on military affairs named the comte de Guibert, whose *Essai général sur la tactique* (A General Essay on Tactics) was published when Guibert was little more than twenty years old. Walsh immediately went on to quote another prediction of revolution that, he claimed, also amounted to a remarkably accurate description of the French Revolution. This one was to be found in the Scottish Jacobite Sir James Steuart's *Inquiry into the Principles of Political Economy*, a book that had been published in 1767. In it, Steuart had outlined a speculative scenario to show how the modern system of war finance had the potential to revive what he called "the most perfect plan of political oeconomy . . . anywhere to be met with, either in ancient or modern times," namely, the political economy of the republic that Lycurgus had founded in Sparta.[5] It was "perfect" because everything in Sparta was done for the service of the state, leaving no room at all for any sort of private interest.

At first sight, Steuart had written, the prospect of reviving the ancient Spartan political economy in the modern world appeared to be extremely far-fetched because it seemed to call for the wholesale renunciation of landed possessions and every other kind of private property. But if, he continued, "that supposition should appear too absurd," there was still no reason to rule it out. All that was needed to reestablish the "most perfect plan of political economy" was for a prince "to contract debts to the value of the whole property of the nation; let the land-tax be imposed at twenty shillings in the pound, and then let him become bankrupt to the creditors."

> Let the income of all the lands be collected throughout the country for the use of the state; let all the luxurious arts be proscribed; and let those employed in them be formed, under the command of the former land proprietors, into

---

[4] [Robert Walsh], *A Letter on the Genius and Dispositions of the French Government, including A View of the Taxation of the French Empire*, 3rd ed. (Philadelphia, 1810), pp. 10–1. On Walsh, whom John Quincy Adams described as "a political fanatic against Bonaparte and subsequently a federalist of the highest color," see Drew R. McCoy, *The Last of the Fathers: James Madison and the Republican Legacy* (Cambridge, CUP, 1989), pp. 86, 105–13; Arthur P. Whitaker, *The United States and the Independence of Latin America, 1800–1830*, 2nd ed. (New York, Norton, 1964), pp. 338–42, 351, 357; M. Frederick Lochernes, *Robert Walsh* (New York, 1941); and Paul Y. Hammond, "The Political Order and the Burden of External Relations," *World Politics* 19 (1967): 443–64.

[5] Sir James Steuart, *An Inquiry into the Principles of Political Oeconomy* [1767], ed. Andrew Skinner (Edinburgh and Chicago, 1966), bk. ii, ch. xiv, p. 218.

a body of regular troops, officers and soldiers, provided with everything necessary for their maintenance, and that of their wives and families at the public
expence. Let me carry the supposition farther. Let every superfluity be cut off;
let the peasants be enslaved, and obliged to labour the ground with no view of
profit to themselves, but for simple subsistence; let the use of gold and silver
be proscribed; and let all these metals be shut up in a public treasure. Let no
foreign trade, and very little domestic be encouraged; but let every man, willing to serve as a soldier, be received and taken care of; and those who either
incline to be idle, or who are found to be superfluous, be sent out of the country. I ask, what confederacy among the modern European Princes, would carry
on a successful war against such a people? What article would be wanting to
their ease, that is, to their ample subsistence? And what country could defend
itself against the attack of such an enemy?[6]

From the vantage point of the first decade of the nineteenth century, there
was enough similarity between the course taken by events in France and
Steuart's projection—one that he had called a "relaxation to the mind, like
a farce between the acts of a serious opera"—for Robert Walsh to be able
to cite it as evidence both of the devastating political and military power
of the resources made available by the modern funding system and of how,
deliberately or inadvertently, the French had managed to tap that power
in an utterly unprecedented way.[7] The French Revolution was Steuart's
"farce" made real. "Nothing, indeed," Walsh commented, "but a total revolution in the internal constitutions of the other states could have prepared
them to meet France on equal terms."[8]

This kind of prescience is now usually associated with Edmund Burke (a
writer whom Walsh also greatly admired) and his grim prediction in the
penultimate paragraph of his *Reflections upon the Revolution in France*, published three years before the Jacobin Terror of 1793–4, that the new French
regime might have "to be purified by fire and blood" before the form of
its government came to "its final settlement."[9] But for all its vivid power,
Burke's prediction belonged to a form of speculation about the nature and
future of the modern world that was quite common in eighteenth-century
thought. Burke himself had published conjectures of a similar sort well
before 1790. Nearly twenty years before the French Revolution, he had

---

[6] Steuart, *Inquiry*, bk. ii, ch. xiv, pp. 226–7 (cf. Walsh, *Letter*, p. 11).

[7] The passage describing the projection as a "farce" appears at the beginning of the following chapter. See Steuart, *Inquiry*, bk. ii, ch. xv, p. 227.

[8] Walsh, *Letter*, p. 18.

[9] Edmund Burke, *Reflections on the Revolution in France* [1790], ed. J.G.A. Pocock (Cambridge, Mass., and Indianapolis, Hackett, 1987), p. 218. See, too, the more recent editions,
edited by J.C.D. Clark (Stanford, Stanford University Press, 2001) and Frank M. Turner
(New Haven, Yale University Press, 2003).

made another, equally striking prediction in the wake of the royal coup against the French parlements in 1771 and the partial debt default that preceded it. "In a word," he wrote in the *Annual Register* of 1772, after reporting that the indications of an accommodation between the French royal government and the princes of the royal blood signalled the end of all serious opposition to Maupeou's coup,

> if we seriously consider the mode of supporting great standing armies, which becomes daily more prevalent, it will appear evidently that nothing less than a convulsion, that will shake the globe to its centre, can ever restore the European nations to that liberty by which they were once so much distinguished. The western world was the seat of freedom, until another, more western, was discovered; and that other will probably be its asylum when it is hunted down in every other part. Happy it is, that the worst of times may have one refuge still left for humanity.[10]

The prediction followed the same logic as Steuart's. "The mode of supporting great standing armies," as Burke put it, supplied them both with the starting point for their respective projections about both Europe's and France's future and the bleak probability that it would consist either in liberty's being "hunted down," or in "a convulsion that will shake the globe to its centre," or in "the most perfect plan of political economy," or simply in "fire and blood." From the point of view of a strong admirer of Burke like Robert Walsh, writing in the light of the events of the previous twenty years, the terms were almost interchangeable.

But the terms also have a more interesting historical and historiographical significance. They suggest that, from the vantage point of eighteenth-century political speculation, the Terror came first. This aspect of eighteenth-century political thought has been largely forgotten by modern historiography, partly perhaps because many of the intimations of revolution that it contained soon found their way into royalist indictments of the new French regime and were carried through into the early nineteenth century in the works of critics of the Restoration settlement like Antoine Ferrand, Alphonse de Madrolle, Joseph de Maistre, Charles-Louis de Bonald, and the Swiss political theorist Karl Ludwig von Haller, or on the

---

[10] *The Annual Register, or a View of the History, Politics and Literature for the Year 1772* (London, 1773), p. 79. Attribution of the article to Burke was made by Sir James Mackintosh in his essay entitled "The Administration and Fall of Struensee," originally published in the *Edinburgh Review* of 1826 and republished in Sir James Mackintosh, *Miscellaneous Works* (London, 1851), p. 470. The spelling and punctuation in the quotation have been modernised. The assumption that Burke was the author of the *Annual Register* articles on foreign affairs published in that year is also accepted in Jonathan Haslam, *No Virtue like Necessity: Realist Thought in International Relations since Machiavelli* (New Haven, Yale University Press, 2002), p. 105.

now largely unread pages of *Le Catholique* and the *Gazette de France*.[11] There, they were subsumed into an increasingly nostalgic historiographical subgenre centred upon the putative failure of the French monarchy to avert a widely predicted catastrophe, with the accompanying message that its restored counterpart could not afford to make the same mistake again. The dark side of eighteenth-century political speculation thus came to have a more narrowly French focus than it had originally had, and, as it did, its content came to be associated more emphatically with a distinctively Francophone characterisation of what, in the nineteenth century, came to be known as the Enlightenment, the substantive noun (or, in the twentieth century, project) that replaced the weaker, usually theologically derived, eighteenth-century concept of enlightenment.[12] In this new, postrevolutionary guise, the broad range of eighteenth-century concerns with the nature and future of the modern world (including its enlightenment), and the possibility that it might repeat the cycle of decline and fall that had destroyed the ancient world, gave way to a number of more strongly future-oriented forms of political and historical speculation, generated in large measure by the ongoing argument over the causes and historical significance of the French Revolution itself. As it did, the concept of revolution underlying eighteenth-century speculation about the future gradually disappeared from historical view.[13]

[11] See, in particular, Antoine Ferrand, *L'esprit de l'histoire, ou lettres politiques et morales d'un père à son fils*, 3rd ed., 4 vols. (Paris, 1804), and the compilation of eighteenth-century predictions of revolution in Karl Ludwig von Haller, *Restauration de la science politique ou théorie de l'état social naturel*, 4 vols. (Paris and Lyon, 1824–61), vol. 4, chs. 6 and 7. See also Edmond Lerminier, *De l'influence de la philosophie du xviiie siècle sur la législation et la sociabilité du xixe siècle* (Brussels, 1834), p. 10; Pierre-Edouard Lemontey, *Histoire de la régence et de la minorité de Louis XV* [1816], 2 vols. (Paris, 1832), p. 301; Ferdinand, baron d' Eckstein, "De l'influence des doctrines matérielles sur la civilisation moderne," *Le Catholique* 3 (1826): 237–8; Alphonse de Madrolle, *La sagesse profonde et l'infaillibilité des prédictions de la révolution qui nous menace* (Paris, 1828); Honoré de Lourdoueix, *De la restauration de la société française*, 3rd ed. (Paris, 1834).

[12] On the nineteenth-century origins of the modern concept of the Enlightenment, see James Schmidt, "Inventing the Enlightenment: Anti-Jacobins, British Hegelians and the *Oxford English Dictionary*," *Journal of the History of Ideas* 64 (2003): 421–43. According to John Robertson, *The Case for the Enlightenment: Scotland and Naples 1680–1760* (Cambridge, CUP, 2005), p. 10, note 24, Schmidt's article is "an object lesson in the dangers of relying on a dictionary for a definition of a concept." As I read it, however, its aim was to distinguish one concept (enlightenment) from another (the Enlightenment). Despite its title, the content of Robertson's book shows that he is too good a historian to have opted consistently for the latter.

[13] It has, however, begun to reappear: see Reinhart Koselleck, *The Practice of Conceptual History* (Stanford, Stanford University Press, 2002), chs. 5–10, 12–4, and J.G.A. Pocock, *Barbarism and Religion*, vol. 3, *The First Decline and Fall* (Cambridge, CUP, 2003), chs. 14–6. See, too, Geoffrey Barraclough, "Europa, Amerika und Russland in Vorstellung und Denken des 19. Jahrhunderts," *Historische Zeitschrift* 203 (1966): 280–315.

The concept of revolution in question referred to a volatile combination of ancient republican politics and modern war finance. The ancient part of the combination was made up of evocations of the conflicts between the rich and the poor that had heralded the onset of decline and fall in the Athenian, Spartan, and Roman republics. Here, the history of the Gracchi in the Roman republic served as an enduring emblem of the dilemmas involved in reconciling political power with social justice once states began to grow. The modern part was connected to the military, financial, and commercial resources that had come to govern the destinies of sovereign states in the wake of the long reign of Louis XIV. The revolution that gripped political imaginations in the eighteenth century involved a fusion of the two. Well before the Bastille fell, something that looked very like the Jacobin phase of the French Revolution was the revolution that the eighteenth century had long foretold. "Through the whole of the last century," wrote an American diplomat named Alexander Hill Everett in 1820, "there prevailed among the reflecting men in France, not a vague conjecture, but a settled conviction, which may be now found in a thousand passages of their writings, that the existing institutions could not stand." There was, therefore, no reason to be surprised that, as he put it, "the period in which we live" was "naturally to be looked to as the *Age of Revolutions*."[14] Everett's remark, made at the beginning of a survey of the situation and future prospects of the major European powers after the Napoleonic Wars, captures something of the generic quality of the predictions by Guibert and Steuart that Robert Walsh rehearsed. As it suggests, eighteenth-century anticipations of revolution are not hard to find. The best known, and the one that gave Everett the phrase that he used to describe the age, was Jean-Jacques Rousseau's claim, published in his *Emile* in 1762, that "we are approaching the state of crisis and the century of revolutions," because, he added in a note, it was "impossible for the great monarchies of Europe to last much longer."[15] It was a claim that he repeated in his *Considerations on the Government of Poland* of 1772. "I see," he wrote there, "all the states of Europe rushing to their ruin. Monarchies, republics, all those nations with all their magnificent institutions, all those fine and wisely balanced governments, have grown decrepit and threaten soon to die."[16] Nor was Rousseau's prediction unusual. "The singular revolution with which Europe is

---

[14] Alexander Hill Everett, *Europe: or a General Survey of the Present Situation of the Principal Powers; with Conjectures on their Future Prospects* (Boston, 1822), pp. 18–9.

[15] Jean-Jacques Rousseau, *Emile, ou de l'éducation* [1763], ed. Michel Launay (Paris, Garnier Flammarion, 1966), Bk. III, p. 252. See Everett, *Europe*, p. 19, for an allusion to the passage.

[16] Jean-Jacques Rousseau, *Considérations sur le gouvernement de Pologne* [1772], ed. Barbara de Negroni (Paris, 1990), p. 164. I have slightly modified the translation given in Jean-Jacques Rousseau, *The Social Contract and Other Later Political Writings*, ed. Victor Gourevitch (Cambridge, CUP, 1997), p. 178.

threatened," wrote the journalist Simon-Nicolas-Henri Linguet in 1777, either would result in the total collapse of modern civilisation or would throw up "some new Spartacus" to establish an "absolute division of the goods of nature" after destroying the "murderous and deceitful" system of laws and government underlying the property-based regimes of the modern world. "One or other of these two calamities," Linguet warned, "is inevitable."[17]

The outcome of this race towards ruin was not expected to be positive. From the marquis de Mirabeau's warning that the "necessary consequence" of the modern "social revolution" would be a massive, modern version of the Mosaic Jubilee, to the Scottish philosopher Adam Ferguson's observation that the "boasted refinements of the polished age" would serve simply to "prepare for mankind the government of force," to the abbé Gabriel Bonnot de Mably's prediction that the modern world was "nearer than one might think to the revolution that Asia underwent," so that "the time may not be too far away when Europe will languish under the splendour and misery of despotism and slavery," claims about decline and fall, leading to crisis, revolution, and a despotic, highly militarised republican regime, were a feature of eighteenth-century thought, particularly in the four decades between the end of the War of the Austrian Succession in 1748 and the beginning of the French Revolution.[18] The American Revolution added a further dimension of uncertainty to an already problematic future. "North America is become a new *primary* planet in the system of the world," wrote Thomas Pownall, the former governor of Massachusetts, in 1780, "which while it takes its own course, in its own orbit, must have effect on the orbit of every other planet, and shift the common centre of gravity of the whole system of the European world."[19] Speculation about the revolution's possible repercussions ranged from a modern replay of the internecine warfare that had dogged the history of ancient republican confederations like the Achaean League (as the political economist and Anglican dean of Gloucester Josiah Tucker predicted), to the creation of an

[17] Simon-Nicolas-Henri Linguet, "De la société en général. Révolution singulière dont l'Europe est menacée," *Annales politiques, civiles et littéraires du dix-huitième siècle* 1 (1777): 83–103 (pp. 83 and 103). For an English-language compilation of Linguet's conjectures, see Simon-Nicolas-Henri Linguet, *Political and Philosophical Speculations on the Distinguishing Characteristics of the Present Century* (London, 1778).

[18] Victor Riqueti, marquis de Mirabeau, *Entretiens d'un jeune prince avec son gouverneur*, 4 vols. (Paris, 1785), 3:234, 318; Adam Ferguson, *An Essay on the History of Civil Society* [1767], ed. Duncan Forbes (Edinburgh, 1966), pt. V, sec. iv, pp. 231–2; Gabriel Bonnot de Mably, *Notre gloire ou nos rêves* [1779] in his *Oeuvres*, 15 vols. (Paris, 1794–5), 13:396.

[19] [Thomas Pownall], *A Memorial most humbly addressed to the Sovereigns of Europe, on the Present State of Affairs between the Old and New World*, 2nd ed. (London, 1780), p. 4. On Pownall, see Peter Miller, *Defining the Common Good: Empire, Religion and Philosophy in Eighteenth-Century Britain* (Cambridge, CUP, 1994), pp. 202–8.

Anglo-American commonwealth of independent states or "Grand British League and Confederacy" (as the English parliamentary reformer Major John Cartwright hoped), to a further round of Franco-British hostilities (driven by the formation of a pro-French republic on America's eastern seaboard and a pro-British republic in the American West), to the total subordination of a largely agricultural American republic to a revived French empire (with Spain's northernmost colonial possessions in Louisiana and Florida acting as a French Trojan horse), to the formation of a huge American monarchy covering both North and South America if Spain's empire were ever to meet the same fate as its British counterpart. Many of the arguments deployed by the authors of *The Federalist* were designed to show how to counter possibilities like these.[20]

One of the most lurid, and most widely noticed, examples of the range of conjecture produced by the American Revolution could be found in the abbé Guillaume-Thomas Raynal's *Histoire philosophique et politique des établissements et du commerce des européens dans les Deux Indes* (A Philosophical and Political History of the Settlements and Trade of the Europeans in the East and West Indies), a multivolume, multiauthored work, whose commercial success (it was reprinted fifty-five times and translated into every major European language in the last quarter of the eighteenth century) owed a great deal to the "gunpowder passages," as one of its readers called

---

[20] Some of these scenarios are presented in Louise Burnham Dunbar, "A Study of 'Monarchical' Tendencies in the United States from 1776 to 1801," *University of Illinois Studies in the Social Sciences* 10 (1922): 1–164. The earlier compilation by Charles Sumner, *Prophetic voices concerning America* (Boston, 1874), published in anticipation of the centenary of the American Revolution, contains a range of such predictions. See also the introduction to the recent edition of Alexander Hamilton, John Jay, and James Madison, *The Federalist*, ed. J. R. Pole (Indianapolis, Hackett, 2005), p. xxii. On Tucker and Cartwright, see Robert Livingston Schuyler, *Josiah Tucker: A Selection from His Political and Economic Writings* (New York, Columbia University Press, 1931), pp. 328, 366, 384, and his *The Fall of the Old Colonial System* (Oxford, Oxford University Press, 1945), pp. 59–60. See, too, Worthington Chauncey Ford, ed., *The Writings of John Quincy Adams* (New York, 1913), pp. 133, 156–7, 184, 212–6, 234–5, 272, and Frederick Jackson Turner, ed., *Correspondence of the French Ministers to the United States 1791–1797*, 2 vols. [Washington, 1904] (New York, Da Capo Press, 1972). On the idea of a *translatio imperii* from Britain to North America, see Laurence Dickey, "*Doux-commerce* and Humanitarian Values: Free Trade, Sociability and Universal Benevolence in Eighteenth-Century Thinking," *Grotiana*, n.s., 22–3 (2001–2): 271–317 (especially pp. 305–8). See, too, Antoine-Marie Cerisier, *Le destin de l'Amérique, ou dialogues pittoresques dans lesquels on développe la cause des événements actuels, la politique et les intérêts des puissances de l'Europe relativement à cette guerre et les suites qu'elle devrait avoir pour le bonheur de l'humanité* (London, 1780), and the texts published in Hans-Jurgen Lusenbrink and Alexandre Mussard, eds., *Avantages et désavantages de la découverte de l'Amérique: Chastellux, Raynal et le concours de l'Académie de Lyon de 1787* (Saint-Etienne, Université de Saint-Etienne, 1994). On the diplomatic background to the Louisiana purchase, see the documents printed in F. P. Renaut, *La question de la Louisiane 1796–1806* (Paris, 1918).

them, written for it by Denis Diderot.[21] Raynal's *Philosophical History* set out an elaborate account of the causes responsible for driving the New World apart from the Old and a vivid prediction, similar to the one that Burke had made in 1772, that without corrective action, the future would belong entirely to the New World and not at all to the Old. The American Revolution, Raynal wrote, was capable of igniting a chain of insurrections in the slave-based European colonies in the Caribbean. These, he claimed, could well destroy the combination of sugar and slavery that was one of the pillars of metropolitan prosperity and, under the aegis of a new Spartacus, give liberty a new abode in America, leaving Europe exposed to run through the whole devastating cycle of decline and fall. "The plains of America," Raynal warned (in a passage that Haiti's founder Toussaint Louverture was later to notice), "will suck with transport the blood which they have so long expected, and the bones of so many wretches, heaped upon one another, during the course of so many centuries, will bound for joy."[22] The "crimes of kings and the sufferings of the people," he predicted, "will render universal this fatal catastrophe, which must detach one world from another," and, in the longer term, might well create a situation in which "Europe may some day find its masters in its children."[23]

Events in France lent themselves to speculations of a similar kind. One that came to seem particularly prescient was to be found in a pamphlet entitled *La Voix du citoyen* (The Voice of the Citizen) published early in 1789. Its author, Charles-François Lebrun, had been the confidant of the French chancellor René-Nicolas de Maupeou during the last great demonstration of royal authority in France in 1771 and was later to become duke of Piacenza and, as governor of Liguria and then Holland, one of the high dignitaries of Napoleon's empire.[24] His pamphlet was intended to be a warning about what might happen if a solution to the monarchy's financial problems could not be found. It was possible, Lebrun wrote, that the repre-

[21] See Henry Redhead Yorke, *Letters from France in 1802*, 2 vols. (London, 1804), 2:299.

[22] Guillaume-Thomas-François Raynal, *A Philosophical and Political History of the Settlements and Trade of the Europeans in the East and West Indies*, trans. J. O. Justamond, 6 vols. (reprint, New York, 1969), 4:128–9. More generally, see Robin Blackburn, *The Overthrow of Colonial Slavery* (London, Verso, 1988); Christine Holbo, "Imagination, Commerce and the Politics of Associationism in Crèvecoeur's *Letters from an American Farmer*," *Early American Literature* 32 (1997): 20–46, and Christopher Iannini, " 'The Itinerant Man': Crèvecoeur's Caribbean, Raynal's Revolution, and the Fate of Atlantic Cosmopolitanism," *William and Mary Quarterly* 61 (2004): 201–34.

[23] Raynal, *Histoire philosophique et politique des établissements européens dans les Duex-Indes* [1772] (Geneva, 1781), 6:427–8; bk. xviii, ch. 52.

[24] On Lebrun, see Louis Laisney, "Un Normand qui a influé sur les destinées de la France de Louis XV à Louis XVIII. Charles-François Lebrun (1739–1824)," *Revue du département de la Manche* 15 (1973): 121–240. On Lebrun, see, most recently, Valérie Chrétienne, *Charles-François Lebrun (1739–1824)*, 2 vols. (Lille, Atelier national de reproduction de thèses, 1998).

sentatives of the nobility and the clergy at the forthcoming Estates-General might refuse to accept fiscal equality, leaving the Third Estate to shoulder the burden of the debt alone. But the Third Estate might well refuse to do so and precipitate a bankruptcy. Its effects, Lebrun emphasised, would be catastrophic. Either a bankruptcy would destroy public power, leaving no social ties and no nation at all, or, if France did manage to survive, the weak and divided state in which she would be left by the collapse of public credit would make her the most insignificant of all the European powers.[25] Yet, Lebrun continued, in this final extremity, patriotism would find its appointed place and, adopting the ancient republican maxim that the public safety should be the supreme law (*salus populi suprema lex esto*), would do whatever was necessary to preserve the French state. It would sacrifice both the nobility and the clergy to the "tumultuous equality" of democracy. And if democracy were in turn to fail, France would still find a way to ensure that she was not effaced from among the European powers. A "determined *leveller*" would emerge from within the Third Estate and found a new constitution upon the ruins of the old.[26] This new constitution would set the true scale of society's needs and fix the true level of public contributions. Not content with the destruction of the nobility and the clergy, this "audacious leveller" would summon the citizenry to even greater liberty and prosperity. But he "would lack the authority needed for his beneficent views."[27] At every step, perpetual meetings would distract the people from industry, agriculture, and commerce, producing a general desire (*voeu général*) to entrust him with all public power. A legal despotism, as Lebrun put it, would ensure that "our common chains would be riveted to the trunk of legislation," allowing a new kind of monarchy to rise up on the ruins of the old social order.[28] The whole sequence was quite an accurate prediction of the future course of events in France (so much so that Lebrun chose to reissue it after Napoleon's rise to power). Nor was it unique. "Societies become corrupt as they grow old," the abbé Mably's literary executors informed Thomas Jefferson well before the Terror began, "and torrents of blood have to be spilled to regenerate them."[29] Set in this context, Burke's prediction of "fire and blood" in 1790 was simply one of a much larger number of eighteenth-century anticipations of Armageddon.

But the revolution of 1789 was not like the revolution that Guibert, Steuart, Rousseau, Ferguson, Mirabeau, Linguet, Raynal, Lebrun, or Mably had imagined. Nor, however, was it like the Danish Revolution of

[25] Lebrun, *La voix du citoyen* (Paris, 1789), p. 83.

[26] Lebrun, *Voix*, p. 84.

[27] Lebrun, *Voix*, p. 85.

[28] Lebrun, *Voix*, p. 85.

[29] The abbés Chalut and Arnoux to Thomas Jefferson, 20 May 1791, in Thomas Jefferson, *Papers*, ed. Julian P. Boyd, vol. 20 (Princeton, Princeton University Press, 1982), p. 428.

1772. If it shared some of the characteristics of both, it was also legal and constitutional in character. It began in 1787 and 1788 with the French parlements' refusal to accept any solution to the monarchy's financial problems without the prior approval of the Estates-General. It acquired a more obviously political dimension in the winter of 1788–9 with the campaign to double the representation of the Third Estate and abolish the system of voting by order in the revived Estates-General. It became a real revolution in ten hectic weeks in the summer of 1789, beginning with the unilateral decision by the representatives of the Third Estate to proclaim themselves to be a National and Constituent Assembly on 17 June 1789, and ending with the proclamation of the Declaration of the Rights of Man on 26 August 1789.[30] Between the two dates, the combination of the Tennis Court Oath of 20 June 1789, the Parisian insurrection that led to the fall of the Bastille on 14 July 1789, and the National Assembly's proclamation of the abolition of feudalism on the night of 4 August 1789 brought the old system of absolute royal government to an end. These events made the French Revolution a different kind of revolution from both the palace revolution that took place in Denmark in 1772 and the "total revolution" described by Robert Walsh in 1810. They made it, instead, a revolution based upon claims about national sovereignty, political representation, the rule of law, and the rights of man. In this guise, it had little or nothing to do with events in Denmark or memories of Lacedemonia because its normative principles belonged to a long tradition of political thought, beginning in either fifteenth-century Florence or sixteenth-century Holland, continuing in seventeenth-century Britain, and culminating in the United States of eighteenth-century America, in which the conceptual foundations of modern politics were laid.[31] However much its immediate ideological origins might have been connected to a distinctively "French idea of freedom" associated with the legal institutions of the French monarchy and the austere Catholicism of the French admirers of the seventeenth-century Belgian theologian Cornelius Jansen, and however much its immediate constitutional and administrative achievements were to be overshadowed by the brutality of the Jacobin Terror and the carnage of the Napoleonic Wars, the events of 1789 gave the French Revolution a political and constitutional dimension that it has never lost.[32] From this point of view, it could still,

---

[30] The clearest account of the sequence of events is to be found in William Doyle, *The Oxford History of the French Revolution* (Oxford, Oxford University Press, 1989).

[31] See, most comprehensively, Quentin Skinner, *The Foundations of Modern Political Thought*, 2 vols. (Cambridge, CUP, 1978), and his *Visions of Politics*, 3 vols. (Cambridge, CUP, 2002).

[32] On Jansenism and the putative "French idea of freedom," see Dale Van Kley, ed., *The French Idea of Freedom* (Stanford, Stanford University Press, 1993). For some reservations, see Michael Sonenscher, "Enlightenment and Revolution," *Journal of Modern History* 70 (1998): 371–83.

even in 1989, look something like the kind of revolution that was most compatible with the government and politics of the modern world.[33]

THE TERROR AND ITS CAUSES

The three descriptions of the French Revolution are not, in any sense, mutually exclusive. But the way in which they have been connected has had a considerable bearing upon both French revolutionary historiography and the broader subject of how the government and politics of the modern world might best be understood. The usual procedure has been to describe a causal sequence that follows the historical sequence of the dynamics of revolutionary politics as these unfolded between 1789 and 1794. The interconnection of the three descriptions thus runs from the first (Danish-style, palace revolution) to the second (Jacobin-dominated, total revolution) by way of the third (constitutional and political revolution), making the political and constitutional dimension of the French Revolution the pivot on which the sequence turned. From this perspective, the key component of the sequence, and the one sometimes charged with ultimate responsibility for turning high political infighting into armed republican force, was to be found in the most famous pamphlet published in 1789, the abbé Emmanuel-Joseph Sieyès's *What Is the Third Estate?*. The one-word answer—"everything"—that Sieyès gave to his question and the reasons that he added to support the claim pointed the way, it has often been suggested, towards the revolutionary government of the Year II.[34] The Third Estate, Sieyès argued, was "a complete nation," equipped with all the means, both economic and political, that a nation needed to survive and prosper.[35] This, in the first instance, was simply a matter of numerical fact. The members of the Third Estate were responsible for doing everything needed to make France the kind of nation that it was. They carried out all the work involved in agriculture, industry, trade, and the professions and performed all the real military, fiscal, administrative, and legal tasks involved in government. But, Sieyès emphasised, the numerical fact went along with a theoretical

[33] See, most emphatically, Francis Fukayama, *The End of History and the Last Man* (New York, Free Press, 1992).

[34] The claim is now associated with François Furet, *Interpreting the French Revolution* [1978] (Cambridge, CUP, 1981), although Furet's argument seemed to suggest that the unitary principle of national sovereignty that came to be enshrined in article 3 of the Declaration of the Rights of Man of 1789 had its origins in the conception of sovereignty underpinning the absolute monarchy. The point was made more clearly by Lucien Jaume in *La Révolution française et le Jacobinisme* (Paris, Fayard, 1989).

[35] Emmanuel-Joseph Sieyès, *What Is the Third Estate?* [1789], in Emmanuel-Joseph Sieyès, *Political Writings*, ed. Michael Sonenscher (Indianapolis, Hackett, 2003), p. 96.

truth. A nation was a single entity, not simply a large number of people bound together by all the things involved in a common way of life. It was a union, not an aggregation or a multitude. Although its individual members were certainly many, the nation itself was still one. Either it existed as it did, or it was something else. The kind of nation that the French nation was—one that contained both a large, populous society and a big, complicated government—was, Sieyès argued, the work of the Third Estate alone. The nobility and clergy might, independently, exist as nations in their own right. But they would not be France. Without the Third Estate, there would be no French nation at all. It followed that the right to decide how France should be governed belonged straightforwardly to the Third Estate.

Almost every evaluation of the French Revolution, whether by conservatives, liberals, or socialists in the nineteenth century or by marxists or revisionists in the twentieth, has taken its cue from the tension between the one and the many built into Sieyès's claim.[36] A nation might be one, but it was still made up of many different people. Some were rich and others poor. Some were men and others women. Some lived in cities and others in villages. Applying a unitary concept of a nation to the multiple interests making up any actual nation seemed, even at the time, to entail a radical lack of fit, opening the way to exactly the kind of ferociously competitive political struggle to speak or act for the nation that took place in France between 1789 and 1794. As several of Sieyès's contemporaries pointed out, it looked like an almost perverse indifference to social and political reality. "It seems to me," wrote one of these, a Swiss writer named Jacques-Henri Meister, in a pamphlet entitled *Des premiers principes du système social* (On the First Principles of the Social System) published in February 1790,

> that by wanting to talk about the rights and the powers of the nation, one can get lost in such abstract ideas that by dint of pretending to seek the original titles of its independence, one ends up with propositions that, though they may have a very republican air, are nonetheless as unintelligible to me as the oracular pronouncement that Louis XV is supposed to have made in some sort of a reply to the remonstrances of the parlements: namely, "I am the nation; the nation is wherever I am."
>
> Our philosophers have made the nation a kind of absolutely metaphysical power; and when I wish to try to realise this chimera in my imagination, all I can see is a hydra with twenty million heads, as incapable of willing as of obeying, of acting as of thinking.
>
> A great nation, understood as a collective being in which supreme power resides, will never be anything other than a speculative being (*un être de raison*),

---

[36] The best introduction to this long tradition of controversy can be found in William Doyle, *Origins of the French Revolution*, 3rd ed. (Oxford, Oxford University Press, 1999).

the most sublime, but perhaps also the most frivolous of all political hypotheses. Only by bringing back so vast and vague an idea to infinitely simple terms might it be possible to arrive at a real result. The nation really exists only among an elite of men chosen from among the different classes who compose it, chosen freely on the trust of public opinion or of those who have acquired the right to guide it.[37]

Meister's charge was echoed late in November 1790 by Edmund Burke. "You might if you pleased," he wrote in his *Reflections on the Revolution in France*, "have profited of our example and have given to your recovered freedom a correspondent dignity."

> Those opposed and conflicting interests which you considered as so great a blemish in your old and in our present constitution interpose a salutary check to all precipitate resolutions. They render deliberation a matter, not of choice, but of necessity; they make all change a subject of *compromise*, which naturally begets moderation; they produce *temperaments* preventing the sore evil of harsh, crude, unqualified reformations, and rendering all the headlong exertions of arbitrary power, in the few or in the many, for ever impracticable. Through that diversity of members and interests, general liberty had as many securities as there were separate views in the several orders, whilst, by pressing down the whole by the weight of a real monarchy, the separate parts would have been prevented from warping and starting from their allotted places.[38]

This failure to deal with the financial problems of the French monarchy by building a broad variety of different interests into a decision-making system containing the kind of checks and balances to be found in the British system of government after 1688 was the basis of the most famous of all Burke's indictments of the new French regime.

> But now all is to be changed. All the pleasing illusions which made power gentle and obedience liberal, which harmonized the different shades of life, and which, by a bland assimilation, incorporated into politics, the sentiments which beautify and soften private society, are to be dissolved by this new conquering empire of light and reason. All the decent drapery of life is to be rudely torn off. All the superadded ideas, furnished from the wardrobe of a moral imagination, which the heart owns and the understanding ratifies as necessary to cover the defects of our naked, shivering nature, and to raise it to dignity in our own estimation, are to be exploded as a ridiculous, absurd, and antiquated fashion.[39]

---

[37] Jacques-Henri Meister, *Des premiers principes du système social appliqués à la révolution présente* (Paris, 1790), pp. 49–50.

[38] Burke, *Reflections*, ed. Pocock, p. 31.

[39] Burke, *Reflections*, ed. Pocock, p. 67.

The charge has echoed down the ages. The "new conquering empire of light and reason" still stands accused of defaulting into conquest, pure and simple. France was first made subject to the Jacobin conquest of Paris and then proceeded to subject Europe to Napoleon Bonaparte's conquering power.

The mistake seems so elementary that the only question it seems to suggest is how it was made at all. But both the charge and the accompanying prognosis of "fire and blood" look less conclusive when set against the eighteenth century's many other anticipations of Armageddon. These add a different dimension to the political arguments that began in France in 1787 because they introduce a range of causal considerations and conjectures into what might otherwise seem to have been no more than the flat assertion of irreconcilable principle. In imaginative terms, 1794 came before 1789. If this was the case, then taking the principles proclaimed in 1789 as the pivot that (however inadvertently) set revolutionary politics on course for the Terror may not be quite right. The principles themselves may need more careful examination, because they may have had to include the subject of averting Armageddon as much as they also, more obviously, involved overturning absolute government. They may, therefore, have to be set alongside a broader range of causal claims both about the properties of a world made up of sovereign states, standing armies, and public debts and about the kind of political system able to withstand its putative potential for catastrophe. This makes the sequence more complicated. It does so not just because it opens up more of a space for a lower level of causal inevitability and a greater amount of more historically contingent political argument and choice, but also, more importantly, because it makes the question of the alternative to absolute government a matter of real historical and analytical significance. The name of that alternative is well-enough known. It is called constitutional government, representative government, or simply democracy. But the thing itself is still surprisingly opaque.

One reason for this opacity is the staggered emergence of those systems of government that now seem most compatible with the modern world. Some, like those of the United Provinces, Great Britain, or the United States of America were already in existence before 1789. Most, however, were established in the nineteenth and twentieth centuries. It is easy to assume a fairly substantial amount of constitutional continuity between the two. Between them, however, lay not so much the events of 1789 as the financial and fiscal problems that preceded the French Revolution itself. It is not clear, against this background, whether it is entirely safe to assume a broad constitutional continuity stretching from the seventeenth to the twentieth century, not only in the light of the eighteenth century's problem of funding the costs of war but also in the much more lurid light of the eighteenth century's nightmare vision of a revolution driven by the modern system of war finance itself. The first of these subjects has been studied very fully.[40] The second has barely been studied at all.[41] In the eighteenth century, however, the two were often taken to be inseparable. Before the French Revolution many of the eighteenth century's best-known political theorists argued, as Burke did, that "the mode of supporting great standing armies which becomes daily more prevalent" left little political and constitutional room between the Scylla of Armageddon and the Charybdis of absolute government. Eliminating the threat of the former meant relying on the power of the latter, just as undermining the power of the latter meant risking the threat of the former. At different times, both have actually occurred—not only in France after 1789, but in many other parts of Europe before and after the First World War and, in the second half of the twentieth century, in many South American, Asian, and African countries. But, however recurrent these economic and political catastrophes may have been, it is still fairly clear that the modern world has managed to find a way to avoid both Scylla and Charybdis. What is less clear is whether it has done so by reverting to the eighteenth century and the English model of constitutional government that Edmund Burke commended to the French, or whether it has done so by devising something new.

This, as indicated, is what this book is about. It is about eighteenth-century conceptions of the future and, in particular, the future of a world made up of sovereign states with public debts. One conception of that

[40] See John Brewer, *The Sinews of Power: War, Money and the English State, 1688–1783* (London, Collins, 1989); Lawrence Stone, ed., *An Imperial State at War* (London, Routledge, 1993); Richard Bonney, ed., *Economic Systems and State Finance* (Oxford, Oxford University Press, 1995); and Richard Bonney, ed., *The Rise of the Fiscal State in Europe* (Oxford, Oxford University Press, 1999). For recent discussions, see Philip Harling and Peter Mandler, "From 'Fiscal-Military' State to Laissez-Faire State," *Journal of British Studies* 32 (1993): 44–70, and Patrick K. O'Brien, "Fiscal Exceptionalism: Great Britain and Its European Rivals from Civil War to Triumph at Trafalgar and Waterloo," *Working Paper 65/01*, Department of Economic History, London School of Economics (October 2001). On the French dimensions of the subject, see Bailey Stone, *The Genesis of the French Revolution: A Global-Historical Interpretation* (Cambridge, CUP, 1994), and *Reinterpreting the French Revolution: A Global-Historical Perspective* (Cambridge, CUP, 2002). As Stone acknowledges, the argument underlying the two books builds on Theda Skocpol, *States and Social Revolutions* (Cambridge, CUP, 1979). Recent guides to the large literature on the technical problems generated by funding the costs of war can be found in Kathryn Norberg, "The French Fiscal Crisis of 1788 and the Financial Origins of the Revolution of 1789," in Philip T. Hoffman and Kathryn Norberg, eds., *Fiscal Crises, Liberty, and Representative Government 1450–1789* (Stanford, Stanford University Press, 1994), pp. 253–98, and David Stasavage, *Public Debt and the Birth of the Democratic State: France and Great Britain, 1688–1789* (Cambridge, CUP, 2003). As Stasavage points out (see notes 105 and 107 below), this literature still leaves open the question of why democratic states are committed to their commitments.

[41] See, however, Istvan Hont, "The Rhapsody of Public Debt: David Hume and Voluntary State Bankruptcy," in Nicholas Phillipson and Quentin Skinner, eds., *Political Discourse in Early Modern Britain* (Cambridge, CUP, 1993), pp. 321–48, now reprinted in his *Jealousy of*

future, most famously set out by the Prussian philosopher Immanuel Kant, involved keeping sovereign states, but abolishing public debts as the way towards perpetual peace. A second, set out by his philosophical and political critic Johann Gottlieb Fichte, involved keeping public debts in order to eliminate the commercial rivalry driving sovereign states to war.[42] But the modern world still has both. Whether this means that the ironic leitmotif of Alexis de Tocqueville's *Ancien Regime and the French Revolution* should be applied to the post–French revolutionary world with still greater force than even Tocqueville may have intended is not entirely clear. Nor is it clear whether there is any substantive difference between Tocqueville's retrospective claim about the durability of the old regime and the bold prospective view set out by the Scottish philosopher David Hume at the beginning of his mid-eighteenth-century essay "Of Civil Liberty." "Having intended in this essay to make a full comparison of civil liberty and absolute government," Hume announced, "and to show the great advantage of the former above the latter,"

> I began to entertain a suspicion that no man in this age was sufficiently qualified for such an undertaking; and that whatever any one should advance on that head would, in all probability be refuted by further experience, and be rejected by posterity.[43]

Time, Hume warned, might reveal that judgements about the gulf between absolute governments and free states might, like those made about politics two centuries earlier by the Florentine political theorist Niccolò Machiavelli, turn out to be judgements informed by the experience of "having lived in too early an age of the world to be a good judge of political truth."[44]

Time has certainly passed since Hume made this remark, but it may not have passed long enough for "political truth" to have become entirely self-evident. At the least, Hume's scepticism about evaluating the difference between free states and absolute governments raises two real historical and analytical questions. The first is whether the modern alternative to absolute government was, as Burke argued, already in existence well before 1789. The second is whether a real alternative, as Sieyès argued, had yet to be established, and, once it was, whether, as Hume guessed and Tocqueville

---

Trade: International Competition and the Nation-State in Historical Perspective (Cambridge, Mass., Harvard University Press, 2005), pp. 325–53.

[42] Immanuel Kant, *Toward Perpetual Peace* [1795], in Immanuel Kant, *Practical Philosophy*, trans. and ed. Mary Gregor (Cambridge, CUP, 1996), p. 319; Johann Gottlieb Fichte, *Der geschlossen Handelstaat* [Stuttgart, 1800], trans. as *L'état commercial fermé* (Lausanne, L'Age d'homme, 1980).

[43] David Hume, "Of Civil Liberty" [1741], in Hume, *Political Essays*, ed. Knud Haakonssen (Cambridge, CUP, 1994), p. 52.

[44] Hume, "Of Civil Liberty," ed. Haakonssen, p. 51.

claimed, it owed rather more than might seem to be the case to the old regime. The two questions have a particular bearing on the subject of sovereign states with public debts. Thinking about the rise and fall of states and their governments did not begin in the eighteenth century. A large and impressive body of historical scholarship has shown how one, particularly capacious way of addressing the subject, beginning with Polybius and running through the works of Machiavelli and Harrington, continued to supply the eighteenth century with a range of resources for thinking about decline and fall, and the related problem of reform.[45] The eighteenth century gave the subject a number of additional dimensions. Some were connected to trade and the problem of the relationship between rich countries and poor countries under conditions of international competitiveness. Others were connected to empire and the question of the kind of government capable of ruling both a metropolis and its colonies. Yet others were connected to morality and the values and behaviour underlying different systems of property-based rule.[46] These were the topics that were present in every eighteenth-century discussion of reform, motivating many of the uses to which the rich conceptual resources of Europe's Greek, Roman, and Christian pasts could be put, and many of the arguments about historical continuity and discontinuity underlying different conceptions of reform. Public credit added a further dimension to the subject because it raised a question about sovereignty and the purposes for which sovereign power might be used.

Investing in a state's debt presupposes political stability, but the range of interests underpinning that stability may, at best, limit a government's capacity to govern and, at worst, undermine its ability to act to maintain the independence and external sovereignty of the state. Burke himself was well aware of how narrow this left the range of choice. In his famous speech on economical reform to the House of Commons on 11 February 1780, at the height of the war with France over the American Revolution, he warned his audience how mistaken it would be to assume that the institutional foundations of a system of state finance based on public credit would always be more readily and reliably available in Britain than in France. "Credit," he stated, "cannot exist under the arm of necessity."

> Necessity strikes at credit, I allow, with a heavier and quicker blow under an arbitrary monarchy than under a limited and balanced government; but still necessity and credit are natural enemies, and cannot be long reconciled in any

---

[45] See, particularly, J.G.A. Pocock, *The Machiavellian Moment: Florentine Political Thought and the Atlantic Republican Tradition* [1975], and his afterword to the 2nd ed. (Princeton, Princeton University Press, 2003), pp. 553–83, as well, of course, as his subsequent *Barbarism and Religion*.

[46] On these themes, see Hont, *Jealousy of Trade*, introduction, for a wide-ranging overview.

situation. From necessity and corruption, a free state may lose the spirit of that complex constitution which is the foundation of confidence. On the other hand, I am far from being sure that a monarchy, when once it is properly regulated, may not for a long time furnish a foundation for credit upon the solidity of its maxims, though it affords no ground of trust in its institutions. I am afraid I see in England and in France, something like a beginning of both these things. I wish I may be found in a mistake.[47]

Governments still act for reasons of necessity. To do so, they often make use of public debt (which was why Kant argued that perpetual peace would have to go hand in hand with eliminating public debt). But public credit is no longer simply a way to fund the costs of war. It is now a component part of the complex financial arrangements underpinning modern systems of welfare and is used to fund government expenditure on health, education, transport, and pensions as well as the costs of external defence. The proportions may vary, but public credit has become necessary for them both. But the two kinds of necessity seem to pull against one another. The one seems to point to the "limited and balanced government" that Burke associated with the British political system after 1688, the other to a government able to strike with "a heavier and quicker blow," as Burke described the "arbitrary" monarchies of the eighteenth century. Modern representative governments seem to be able to do both. Trying to see how and why they can, particularly under conditions of war and debt, may throw some light on the question of whether the modern alternative to absolute government is really a thing or merely a word, and, if it really is a thing, how and why it might still be a different kind of thing from the system of government that Burke admired. This, in turn, may go some way towards identifying the attributes of the system of representative government that the abbé Sieyès envisaged.

BALANCED GOVERNMENT AND THE ENGLISH CONSTITUTION

Stripped of its rich and not entirely rhetorical ornamentation, the description of the system of government that Burke commended to the French in 1790 owed more than a little to two famous chapters of Charles-Louis de Secondat, baron de Montesquieu's *De l'esprit des lois* of 1748. Montesquieu's description was, however, strikingly Janus-faced. If, on the one hand, the English nation was "passionately fond of liberty" because that liberty was both "real" and, in its political guise, even "extreme," England

---

[47] Edmund Burke, *Speech on presenting to the House of Commons on the 11th February, 1780 a plan for the better security of the independence of Parliament, and the economical reformation of the civil and other establishments*, in Edmund Burke, *Works* (London, 1899), 2:275–6.

was also likely, Montesquieu warned, to become "one of the most servile nations upon earth" if that liberty were ever to be lost.[48] This ambiguity was connected to the odd nature of the English system of government. It was, as Montesquieu put it, "a republic, disguised under the form of monarchy."[49] Montesquieu also made it clear that it was not the disguised republican part of the system that favoured the long-term survival of civil and political liberty. In fact, something like the opposite was the case. "Democratic and aristocratic states," he wrote, "are not in their own nature free."[50] This was because the properties that gave republican systems of government their nature (whether they were democracies or aristocracies) also made it difficult to prevent all or part of the people from exercising the legislative, executive, and judicial powers as a single body. This was how the republics of the ancient world had been ruled and, as Montesquieu noted, was also how the Italian republics were governed in his own time. There, he wrote, the "whole power is united in one body," leaving the citizens of these republics with "less liberty than in our monarchies."[51] The underlying republican features of the modern English system of government provided for the same possibility, most importantly because it contained no extraconstitutional arrangements able to prevent politics from acquiring the unitary character that Montesquieu took to be the hallmark of both republican and despotic forms of rule. "Abolish the privileges of the lords, the clergy and cities in a monarchy," he wrote, "and you will soon have a popular state, or a despotic government."[52] But this, he suggested, was broadly what had happened in seventeenth-century England. "The English," Montesquieu observed, "to favour their liberty, have abolished all the intermediate powers of which their monarchy was composed."[53] Since the English nobility had "buried themselves with Charles I under the ruins of the throne," England's monarchy was now based on republican foundations.[54] The real liberty that the English enjoyed thus depended heavily on the constitution. This, Montesquieu suggested, was

---

[48] Charles-Louis de Secondat, baron de Montesquieu, *The Spirit of Laws*, trans. Thomas Nugent (London, 1750), ed. Franz Neumann (New York, Hafner Publishing Company, 1949), bk. xix. ch. 27, pp. 309–10; bk. xi, ch. 6, p. 162; bk. ii, ch. 4, p. 17. I have preferred to use this edition of the eighteenth-century translation by Thomas Nugent rather than the more recent translation edited by Anne Cohler, Basia Miller, and Harold Stone (Cambridge, CUP, 1989). Henceforth references to the Nugent translation will be abbreviated as Montesquieu, *SL*, followed by the book, chapter, and page numbers.

[49] Montesquieu, *SL*, bk. 5, ch. 19, p. 68.

[50] Montesquieu, *SL*, bk. 11, ch. 4, p. 150.

[51] Montesquieu, *SL*, bk. 11, ch. 6, p. 152.

[52] Montesquieu, *SL*, bk. 2, ch. 4, p. 16.

[53] Montesquieu, *SL*, bk. 2, ch. 4, p. 17.

[54] Montesquieu, *SL*, bk. 8, ch. 9, p. 115.

why they had "a great deal of reason to be jealous of this liberty."[55] If the constitution were to fail, there was nothing to prevent a republic disguised as a monarchy from defaulting into despotism.

Montesquieu was consistently suspicious of sovereign power.[56] Its unitary character and untrammelled force made it a uniquely dangerous component of every political society. The chapter on the constitution of England, as Montesquieu headed chapter 6 of book 11 of *The Spirit of Laws*, took the problem of sovereignty as its starting point. He began the chapter by describing the three sorts of power (legislative, executive, and judicial) to be found in "every government" and the way that, as one of his early commentators put it, "perfection" consisted of "the separation of the three, balancing powers."[57] He then went on immediately to define what he called "the political liberty of the subject." This, he wrote, was "a tranquillity of mind arising from the opinion each person has of his safety." To have it, he continued, "it is requisite the government be so constituted as one man need not be afraid of another."[58] Since Montesquieu began *The Spirit of Laws* by stating that man "in a state of nature" would "feel nothing in himself but impotency and weakness . . . trembling at the motion of a leaf and flying from every shadow," this kind of security had to be the effect of a very artfully constructed set of institutional arrangements.[59] Fear would not be eliminated if the legislative and executive powers were "united in the same person, or in the same body of magistrates"; nor would it disappear if "the judiciary power" were joined to either the legislative or the executive power.[60] Uniquely, the constitution of the English system of government provided for clear distinctions among the three. It did so, moreover, not because it had been deliberately designed to meet that end, but because, through a series of historical accidents, it had come to resemble the ancient German system of government from which it had first begun. "In perusing the admirable treatise of Tacitus *On the Manners of the Germans*," Montesquieu famously observed, "we find it is from that nation that the English borrowed the idea of their political government. This beautiful system was invented first in the woods."[61]

---

[55] Montesquieu, *SL*, bk. 2, ch. 4, p. 17.

[56] On the sparing use of the concept of sovereignty in Montesquieu's entire oeuvre, see the list of citations in Jean Ehrard, "Actualité d'un demi-silence: Montesquieu et l'idée de souveraineté," *Rivista di storia della Filosofia* 4 (1994): 9–20.

[57] François Véron de Forbonnais, *Extrait du livre de "l'Esprit des loix"* (Amsterdam, 1753), p. 176.

[58] Montesquieu, *SL*, bk. 11, ch. 6, p. 151.

[59] Montesquieu, *SL*, bk. 1, ch. 2, pp. 3–4.

[60] Montesquieu, *SL*, bk. 11, ch. 6, pp. 151–2.

[61] Montesquieu, *SL*, bk. 11, ch. 6, p. 161.

But Montesquieu's description of the English constitution was also curiously elegiac. Immediately after making the association between England's "beautiful system" and the German woods, he went on to announce that it was one that was bound to die. "As all human things have an end," he wrote, "the state we are speaking of will lose its liberty, will perish. Have not Rome, Sparta and Carthage perished? It will perish when the legislative power shall be more corrupt than the executive."[62] The "prophecy" (as it was sometimes termed) was widely noticed.[63] Rousseau, for example, endorsed it publicly.[64] As one early commentator on the passage put it, Montesquieu was "like Tacitus who, several centuries beforehand, foresaw the causes of the fall of the Roman empire."[65] According to Burke's German translator, Friedrich Gentz, it played some part in determining French involvement in Britain's conflict with the American colonies.[66] Montesquieu's warning about where the cause of the danger was most likely to be found was also widely noticed. One of the first to see his point was David Hume, who, early in 1749, wrote to the French magistrate sending him "several thoughts," as he put it, "designed mainly to confirm the more the principles upon which your system is based."[67] He was particularly im-

---

[62] Montesquieu, *SL*, bk. 11, ch. 6, pp. 161–2.

[63] See, for example, Arthur Young, *Political Essays Concerning the Present State of the British Empire* (London, 1772), p. 60; Francis Stoughton Sullivan, *Lectures on the Constitution and Laws of England: with a Commentary on Magna Charta, and Illustrations of Many of the English Statutes* (London, 1776), p. 178; Joseph Pollock, *Letters of Owen Roe O'Nial* (Dublin, 1779), p. 33; [Anon.], *A letter to Lord North, on his Re-Election into the House of Commons* (London, 1780), p. 20; M. Desaubiez, *Système de finances et d'économie publique applicable aux divers gouvernements de l'Europe et du Nouveau Monde* [London, 1780] (Paris, 1826), p. 202; John Andrews, *An Essay on Republican Principles and on the Inconvenience of a Commonwealth in a Large Country and Nation* (London, 1783), pp. 88, 92; Christopher Keld, *An Essay on the polity of England: with a view to discover the true principles of government, what remedies might be likely to cure the grievances complained of, and why the several provisions made by the legislature, and those recommended by individuals have failed* (London, 1785), pp. 188–9; *Monthly Review* 34 (1783): 125, 201; William Mitford, *The History of Greece*, 3rd ed., 6 vols. (London, 1795), 4:373–4; Henry Maddock, *The Power of Parliaments Considered, in a Letter to a Member of Parliament*, 2nd ed. (London, 1799), pp. 3–4.

[64] In the English translation of his *Extrait du projet de paix perpétuelle*, published in the same year as the original, Rousseau wrote, "it is easy to foresee that in twenty years from this time, England, with all its glory, will be ruined and have lost the remainder of its liberty": Jean-Jacques Rousseau, *A Project for Perpetual Peace* (London, 1761), p. 16. See also Rousseau, *Oeuvres complètes*, 5 vols. (Paris, Pléiade, 1959–1995) (henceforth, Rousseau, *OC*, followed by the volume and page numbers), here 3:573, note.

[65] Stefano Bertolini, "Analyse raisonné de *l'Esprit des lois*" [1754], in Montesquieu, *Oeuvres posthumes* (Paris, 1798), p. 347.

[66] Friedrich Gentz, *Essai sur l'état actuel de l'administration des finances et de la richesse nationale de la Grande Bretagne* (London, 1800), p. 3.

[67] Hume to Montesquieu, 10 April 1749, in *The Letters of David Hume*, ed. J.Y.T. Greig, 2 vols. (Oxford, 1932, reprint, 1969), vol. 1, letter 65, p. 133.

pressed by Montesquieu's "new and striking observation" that the English, to favour liberty, had removed all the intermediate powers that had once formed their monarchy, leaving them with the prospect of becoming "one of the most servile peoples on earth" if, as *The Spirit of Laws* warned, they were ever to lose their liberty.[68] As Hume noted sardonically, the British government's response to the Jacobite rebellion of 1745 displayed a blissful ignorance of the danger that Montesquieu had identified. "You will not perhaps be displeased to know," he wrote,

> that the English Parliament, finding, after recent events, that the Scottish na-tion was not sufficiently republican, concluded that this violent penchant for monarchical government was an outcome of the nobility's continued posses-sion of gothic, feudal jurisdictions; which is why, two years ago, Parliament abolished them. This goes to show how consistent and consequential the En-glish have been in their manner of reasoning on this subject. The consequences which you predict would certainly arrive were there to be a revolution in our government.[69]

Orthodox Whigs were more dismissive. "Against the assertions of Montes-quieu," noted the barrister Francis Plowden, stood "the principles of free-dom, of justice, and safety" invoked by the Duke of Newcastle's nephew, Charles Yorke, in his *Considerations on the Law of Forfeiture*, written, like Hume's letter, in the aftermath of the '45. "The English constitution," Yorke had written, "is formed upon them. Their reason shall subsist as long as the frame of it shall stand: and being maintained in purity and vigour will pre-serve it from the usual mortality of government."[70] But Hume was not alone in highlighting the tension between the disguised republican foundations of the English monarchy and the complicated intricacies of its constitution as a genuine problem for liberty's long-term survival. The problem gave his compatriot Adam Ferguson, professor of moral philosophy at the University of Edinburgh, much of his life's work, beginning with his *Essay on the History of Civil Society* of 1767 and continuing into his *History of the Progress and Termination of the Roman Republic* of 1783. By then, the repercussions of the American Revolution had given Montesquieu's prophecy a renewed sa-lience. "The sun of her glory," wrote Thomas Jefferson of England in 1781, "is fast descending to the horizon. Her philosophy has crossed the Channel, her freedom the Atlantic, and herself seems passing to that awful dissolution, whose issue is not given human foresight to scan."[71]

---

[68] Montesquieu, *SL*, bk. 2, ch. 4, p. 19.

[69] Hume to Montesquieu, 10 April 1749, in *The Letters of David Hume*, 1:134.

[70] Francis Plowden, *The Constitution of the United Kingdom of Great Britain and Ireland, Civil and Ecclesiastical* (London, 1802), p. 4 and footnote.

[71] Thomas Jefferson, *Notes on the State of Virginia* [1781], ed. William Peden (Chapel Hill and London, University of North Carolina Press, 1982), p. 65.

The road to dissolution continued to follow the direction that Montesquieu indicated. "I admire the form of our government as much as any
body," wrote the Scottish philosopher James Beattie in 1784, "but I have
long thought the democratical principal rather too predominant; and if
it continue to gather strength, as it has done for these twenty years past,
the independence of the other branches of the legislature will be nothing
but a name."

> Several of our ancient statesmen were of opinion that England could never be
> ruined but by a parliament; and Montesquieu says, this will happen, whenever
> the legislative power shall become more corrupt than the executive. From the
> executive, at present, I think we have nothing to fear; and I am persuaded, that
> the majority of the nation is of the same opinion.[72]

As Beattie's remark suggests, ruin was likely to be the result of a dangerous
intensification of partisan popular politics leading, ultimately, to the death
of the constitution. The causal mechanisms underlying the process could
be found in Edmund Burke's *Thoughts on the Cause of the Present Discontents*
of 1770 and the attack that it contained on the ultrapatriot policies pro-
moted by the new king George III's principal minister, Lord Bute. "When
the people conceive that laws, and tribunals, and even popular assemblies,
are perverted from the ends of their institution," Burke wrote, "they find
in those names of degenerated establishments only new motives to discon-
tent."[73] An intense campaign for patriotic political reform would, he
warned, serve only to undermine the institutions that needed reform, leaving nothing beneath them but a bitterly divided society and the looming
prospect of violent social conflict. This, Burke argued, would be the effect
of misguided attempts to follow the principles of patriotic political moralists like the high Anglican cleric John Brown in adopting "an affected terror
of the growth of an aristocratic power, prejudicial to the rights of the crown
and the balance of the constitution" (this had been one of the themes of
Brown's *Estimate of the Manners and Principles of the Times*, a work that had
enjoyed great popularity during the period of the Seven Years War).[74] A
fiercely patriotic campaign against "faction" as outlined both in Brown's
Estimate and in the late Viscount Bolingbroke's earlier *Idea of a Patriot King*
would, Burke warned, be self-defeating. "Fierce licentiousness begets vio-

---

[72] James Beattie to the Hon. Mr Baron Gordon, Aberdeen, 7 March 1784, in Sir William
Forbes, *An Account of the Life and Writings of James Beattie*, 2 vols. (Edinburgh, 1806), 2:134.

[73] Edmund Burke, *Thoughts on the Cause of the Present Discontents*, in Edmund Burke, *Works*,
12 vols. (London, John C. Nimmo, 1899), 1:483. For corroboration of Burke's argument, see
Philip Connell, "British Identities and the Politics of Ancient Poetry in Later Eighteenth-
Century England," *Historical Journal* 49 (2006): 161–92.

[74] Burke, *Thoughts*, p. 457.

lent restraints. The military arm is the sole reliance; and then, call your constitution what you please, it is the sword that governs."[75]

Montesquieu himself had been much more circumspect in identifying the possible causes of the constitution's death. When asked to do so in 1749 by William Domville, the man responsible for overseeing Thomas Nugent's English translation of *The Spirit of Laws*, he drafted a surprisingly sanguine reply.[76] The very openness of English political corruption, he argued, was a kind of guarantee against its most damaging potential effects. Modern Britain, he added, was not republican Rome. There, "the people formed a single body and when the people became corrupt, corruption inevitably had its effect."[77] But in England the people was not a single body. In constitutional terms, it was made up of the residents of the counties and boroughs because these were the units responsible for electing representatives to the Commons. As a result, corruption was always likely to be local, not general. Inversely, the general character of English opulence was both an obstacle to excessive concentrations of patronage and power and a relatively self-sustaining source of the kind of social mobility that was compatible with a politically stable hierarchy of ranks. Echoing his own assessment of the positive effects of English commercial prosperity and partisan politics in chapter 27 of book 19 of *The Spirit of Laws*, Montesquieu outlined an unusually bullish assessment of England's future. "Never compare your riches with those of Rome, nor those of your neighbours," he wrote in the draft letter to Domville. "Instead, compare the sources of your riches with the sources of the riches of Rome and the sources of the riches of your neighbours." Absolute wealth was less significant than the means by which it was acquired. Where Rome's wealth was based on "tributes" and "pillaging conquered nations," Britain's was based on "commerce and industry." The growth of the former was a zero-sum game. But the growth of the latter added to general prosperity, limiting the dangers of a polarisation of society into the extremely rich and the extremely poor. For "as long as the sources of great riches remain the same," Montesquieu wrote, "and are not spoiled by the greater resources supplied by other riches," Britain's future was secure.[78]

---

[75] Burke, *Thoughts*, p. 484.

[76] The text can be found in Charles-Louis de Secondat, baron de Montesquieu, *Pensées*, ed. Louis Desgraves (Paris, Robert Laffont, 1991), pp. 598–601 (*pensée* 1960), and has been translated by Donald Desserud, "Commerce and Political Participation in Montesquieu's Letter to Domville," *History of European Ideas* 25 (1999): 135–51.

[77] Montesquieu to Domville (May 1749), trans. Desserud, "Commerce and Political Participation," p. 147.

[78] Montesquieu to Domville (May 1749), trans. Desserud, "Commerce and Political Participation," pp. 148–9 (I have slightly modified Desserud's translation).

Montesquieu's confidence was based on a strong claim about the difference between the ancient and the modern worlds. "The ancients," he wrote at the head of chapter 8 of book 11 of *The Spirit of Laws*, had no "clear idea of monarchy."[79] As he indicated immediately, the idea in question included both the absolute monarchies of the European mainland and the British monarchy. "The ancients had no notion of a government founded on a body of nobles, and much less on a legislative body composed of the representatives of the people."[80] Monarchy, Montesquieu asserted, was modern, not ancient. "The ancients," he added in the next chapter, "who were strangers to the distribution of the three powers in the government of a single person, could never form a just idea of monarchy."[81] Although there were substantial differences between the British monarchy and "the monarchies we are acquainted with" (as Montesquieu headed the seventh chapter of book 11 of *The Spirit of Laws*), both shared a key common element. Both were more complicated than the word "monarchy" and the corresponding idea of rule by a single person seemed to imply. The "monarchies we are acquainted with" included "a body of nobles" as part of their nature, while the British monarchy encompassed a "legislative body composed of the representatives of the people" as well as a House of Lords and a king. Neither was a single, sovereign system. Both, instead, contained several distinct parts, making it easier to see whether a change in one of them might alter the nature of the government as a whole. This built-in checking mechanism matched the abiding suspicion of unified sovereign power that was one of the most deep-seated features of Montesquieu's political thought. "Union in a body politic," he wrote in his *Considerations on the Causes of the Greatness of the Romans and Their Decline* in 1734, "is a very equivocal term":

> true union is such a harmony as makes all the particular parts, as opposite as they may seem to us, concur to the general welfare of the society, in the same manner as discords in music contribute to the general melody of sound. Union may prevail in a state full of seeming commotions; or, in other words, there may be an harmony from whence results prosperity, which alone is true peace, and may be considered in the same view, as the various parts of this universe, which are eternally connected by the action of some and the reaction of others.[82]

---

[79] Montesquieu, *SL*, bk. 11, ch. 8, p. 161.

[80] Montesquieu, *SL*, bk. 11, ch. 8, p. 161.

[81] Montesquieu, *SL*, bk. 11, ch. 9, p. 164.

[82] Charles-Louis de Secondat, baron de Montesquieu, *Considérations sur les causes de la grandeur des Romains et de leur décadence* [1734], ed. Françoise Weil and Cecil Courtney (Oxford, Voltaire Foundation, 2000), ch. ix, p. 157. The citation is from the English translation, published as *Reflections on the Causes of the Rise and Fall of the Roman Empire* (Oxford, 1825), pp. 105–6.

The planetary metaphor was one that Montesquieu used quite frequently, always with reference to monarchy. It was one that was less readily applicable to republican governments (whether democratic or aristocratic) because of the absence of anything outside a republic's membership to maintain the balance between too much concord and too much discord that Montesquieu took to be the basis of "true union." Instead of the action and reaction that gave stability to a dual system like the sun and its planets, a unitary system had to rely entirely upon its own internal properties to maintain its stability. Generating the requisite motivation to do so called for a level of self-denial (or political virtue) that was feasible only in very simple, egalitarian societies. This, Montesquieu had argued, was why the key to understanding Rome's historical trajectory was its inability, despite its imperial government and the massive amount of wealth and power at its command, to escape from its republican origins and become a monarchy in anything like the modern sense. Imperial Rome remained, at bottom, republican, and it was this that proved to be its nemesis. Under the Roman emperor Commodus, Montesquieu wrote, "what was called the Roman empire, in this century, was a kind of irregular republic, much like the aristocracy of Algeria, where the army, which has sovereign power, makes and unmakes a magistrate called the Dey. And perhaps it is a rather general rule that military government is, in certain respects, republican rather than monarchical."[83] Monarchy, whether modified by "a body of nobles" or "a legislative body composed of the representatives of the people," had a built-in capacity to avoid either the tumultuous conflict of too much discord or the deadly silence of excessive concord.

The key question raised by what Montesquieu had written about the British and European monarchies was which of the two was most able to resist the pressure towards union, with its potentially despotic outcome. Even after the French Revolution the answer was not entirely clear (it is often forgotten that Benjamin Constant's famous public lecture in 1819 on ancient and modern liberty was the second in a course of lectures on the English constitution).[84] Before 1789, it was even less apparent. Here, the elegiac assessment of the future prospects of English liberty to be found in *The Spirit of Laws* soon received powerful support from David Hume. In a late addition to his *History of England* in 1778 Hume picked up the theme of the letter he had written to Montesquieu nearly three decades

---

[83] Montesquieu, *Considérations*, ch. xvi, pp. 219–20; *Reflections*, pp. 160–1. On the whole subject of Rome's significance in eighteenth-century political thought, see Pocock, *The First Decline and Fall*, pt. V.

[84] See Alain Laquièze, "Benjamin Constant et les lectures à l'Athénée royal consacrées à la constitution anglaise," *Annales Benjamin Constant* 23–4 (2000): 155–71. More generally, see Edouard Tillet, *La constitution anglaise, un modèle politique et institutionnel dans la France des lumières* (Aix-en-Provence, Presses Universitaires d'Aix-Marseille, 2001).

earlier to make the paradoxical point that modern Britain was in greater
danger of slavery than England had been under the absolute government
of Elizabeth I.

> England (he wrote) though seemingly it approached nearer, was in reality more
> remote from a despotic and eastern monarchy, than the present government
> of that kingdom, where the people, though guarded by multiplied laws, are
> totally naked, defenceless, and disarmed, and besides, are not secured by any
> middle power, or independent powerful nobility, interposed between them and
> the monarch.[85]

Although he did not know that it existed, Hume's reasoning converged
with the warning about the need to prevent anything from eclipsing industry and trade as the basis of Britain's prosperity that Montesquieu had issued at the end of his draft letter to Domville. The alternative to industry
and trade was to be found in the modern system of war finance and the
investments in the public funds that had come to be used to support the
massive increase in the size and cost of standing armies. This, too, was
something that Montesquieu had written strikingly about. "A new distemper has spread itself over Europe," he wrote in chapter 17 of book 13 of
The Spirit of Laws.

> Each monarch keeps as many armies on foot as if his people were in danger
> of being exterminated; and they give the name of peace to this general effort
> of all against all. Thus is Europe ruined to such a degree that were private
> people to be in the same situation as the three most opulent powers of this
> part of the globe, they would not have necessary subsistence. We are poor with
> the riches and commerce of the whole world; and soon, by thus augmenting
> our troops, we shall all be soldiers, and be reduced to the very same situation
> as the Tartars.[86]

A generation later, the words were turned back upon him by one of Edmund Burke's most forceful early critics. "It was the apprehension of Montesquieu," wrote Sir James Mackintosh in his *Vindiciae Gallicae* of 1791,
"that the spirit of increasing armies would terminate in converting Europe
into an immense camp, in changing our artisans and cultivators into military savages, and reviving the age of Attila and Genghis."[87] Events in
France, Mackintosh announced with a confidence that he would come to
regret, served to show how wrong Montesquieu had been.

---

[85] David Hume, *The History of England*, 6 vols. (London, 1778), 4:370. On the date of
the addition of the phrase after "disarmed," see Duncan Forbes, *Hume's Philosophical Politics*
(Cambridge, CUP, 1975), pp. 178–80.
[86] Montesquieu, *SL*, bk. 13, ch. 17, p. 217.
[87] James Mackintosh, *Vindiciae Gallicae* (London, 1791), p. 55.

As Mackintosh later acknowledged, he had failed to identify the real source of the danger (his early admiration for the work of one of his teachers at the University of Aberdeen, William Ogilvie, the author of an *Essay on the Right of Property in Land*, took his argument in exactly the opposite direction).[88] This was not the arms race itself but the system of public borrowing on which it had come to depend. In his essay *Of Public Credit* (published first in 1752), Hume set out the connection between the public debt and the future of England's constitution in a way that Montesquieu had only hinted at in the last part of his letter to Domville.[89] The essay set out three scenarios generated by recurrent cycles of war and debt. The first highlighted the difficulties of trying to eliminate a public debt by relying on public credit itself, a procedure that Hume described as the "euthanasia" of public credit because, he argued, the procedure involved too many uncertainties to be manageable and was, as he put it, more likely to kill the debt at the hands of the doctor than to treat the problem successfully. The South Sea Bubble and the French Mississippi scheme of the period of the Regency were both examples of how an ambitious debt-reduction scheme would lead to ruin, not recovery. The second scenario described what Hume called the "natural death" of public credit. It amounted to a voluntary declaration of insolvency, destroying both the income and capital value of money invested in the public funds. The third scenario amounted to the "violent death" of public credit. It would occur, Hume argued, if the interests of investors in the funds were to become so deeply entrenched in the political system that no funds would be available to meet the costs of external defence. This was the reason why Hume began his essay with the blunt warning that "either the nation must destroy public credit or public credit will destroy the nation." The "natural death" scenario was, he argued, the only expedient that would allow Britain to match the combined financial and political power of absolute monarchies like France and escape from a possible "violent death" of public credit at the hands of a foreign power. As he had pointed out in his earlier essay "Of Civil Liberty," "as an absolute prince may make a bankruptcy when he pleases, his people can never be oppressed by his debts."[90]

Hume insisted that this was an option that had to be faced in Britain too. But its implications were grim. In the additions that he made to the

[88] On Ogilvie, see my "Property, Community and Citizenship," in Mark Goldie and Robert Wokler, eds., *The Cambridge History of Eighteenth-Century Political Thought* (Cambridge, CUP, 2006).

[89] In this section, I follow Hont, "The Rhapsody of Public Debt."

[90] David Hume, "Of Civil Liberty" in Hume, *Essays: Moral, Political and Literary*, ed. Eugene F. Miller (Indianapolis, Liberty Press, 1985), p. 96. The essay was also published in French translation in 1754 and reprinted in edited form in Condorcet's *Bibliothèque de l'homme publique*, vol. 1, no. 2 (Paris, 1790) (p. 99 for the passage in question).

essay in 1764 and 1770, he shifted away from appearing to commend a patriotic coup against the nation's creditors as a necessary, but relatively benign, way to preserve England's free constitution, and moved significantly closer to the pessimistic assessment of the prospects for English liberty to be found in Montesquieu's *Spirit of Laws*. Continued government borrowing, Hume now pointed out, was capable of raising the level of public indebtedness to equal the entire taxable revenue of the kingdom, making the annuitants the indirect owners of all the national wealth. This was the scenario that was to supply Sir James Steuart with his "farce." Hume's description of its implications fitted the warning that he added to his *History of England*. Opting for the "natural death" of public credit would also herald the end of English liberty. Once a public debt had grown to equal the entire taxable revenue of the kingdom (and Hume thought that it would), and a government was faced, in emergency, with a choice between paying interest on the debt and raising additional revenue for defence, it would have to opt for the latter and a coup against the state's creditors. But the result of such a coup would not favour liberty. It would mean that "the whole income of every individual in the state must lie entirely at the mercy of the sovereign," leading to a "degree of despotism which no oriental monarchy has ever yet attained."[91]

ENGLAND'S FUTURE IN A FRENCH CONTEXT

Edmund Burke's prediction of "fire and blood" in his *Reflections on the Revolution in France* combined Montesquieu's "prophecy" about the death of the English constitution with Hume's description of how that death would occur, and applied them both to France. "The legislators who framed the ancient republics," Burke wrote, "thought themselves obliged to dispose their citizens into such classes, and to place them in such situations in the state as their peculiar habits might qualify them to fill."[92] But the "new modern legislators" of the French National and Constituent Assembly had taken "the directly contrary course." They had "levelled and crushed together all the orders which they have found, even under the coarse unartificial arrangement of the monarchy, in which mode of government the classing of the citizens is not of so much importance as in a republic."[93] They had, in effect, established a republic disguised as a monarchy. They had also vastly magnified the size of the French public debt by confiscating the property of the church and by issuing a paper currency based upon the

---

[91] David Hume, "Of Public Credit" [1752], in *Essays*, ed. Miller, p. 359.
[92] Burke, *Reflections*, ed. Pocock, p. 162.
[93] Burke, *Reflections*, ed. Pocock, p. 163.

anticipated sale of the newly nationalised land to fund the ongoing costs of government, now including those previously met by the church. Just as Montesquieu had emphasised that the English constitution would have to stand or fall without the assistance of any type of intermediate power, and Hume had warned that the growth of the British debt would leave every individual's income at the mercy of the sovereign, so, according to Burke, these were the dangers that now faced the new French regime.

> For want of something of this kind, if the present project of a republic should fail, all securities to a moderated freedom fail along with it; all the indirect restraints which mitigate despotism are removed; insomuch that if monarchy should ever again obtain an entire ascendancy in France, under this or any other dynasty, it will probably be, if not voluntarily tempered at setting out, by the wise and virtuous counsels of the prince, the most completely arbitrary power that has ever appeared on earth. This is to play a most desperate game.[94]

There is something slightly paradoxical in the warning. Burke's prescience involved recasting England's nightmare as France's future. Yet his prudence seemed to call for France to adopt England's political institutions. The paradox raises two further questions. The first is mainly historical, while the second is more historiographical.

The historical question concerns Burke's own explanation of British political stability. For all his admiration of the English constitution, he was quite explicit that its stability was an effect of a deeper set of underlying causes. The famous lament ("But the age of chivalry is gone. That of sophisters, economists and calculators has succeeded; and the glory of Europe is extinguished forever.") that he issued immediately after describing how he had once seen Marie Antoinette, "glittering like the morning star," when he had visited Versailles, transferred Montesquieu's remark about liberty and the German woods to a later, more morally charged, historical epoch and, by doing so, added a stronger political content to Montesquieu's own remarks about gallantry.[95]

> This mixed system of opinion and sentiment had its origin in the ancient chivalry; and the principle, though varied in its appearance by the varying state of human affairs, subsisted and influenced through a long succession of generations even to the time we live in. If it should ever be totally extinguished, the loss I fear will be great. It is this which has given its character to modern Europe. It is this which has distinguished it under all its forms of government, and distinguished it to its advantage, from the states of Asia and possibly from those states which flourished in the most brilliant periods of the antique world.

[94] Burke, *Reflections*, ed. Pocock, p. 163.
[95] Montesquieu, *SL*, bk. 28, ch. 22, p. 119.

It was this which, without confounding ranks, had produced a noble equality and handed it down through all the gradations of social life. It was this opinion which mitigated kings into companions and raised private men to be fellows of kings. Without force or opposition, it subdued the fierceness of pride and power, it obliged sovereigns to submit to the soft collar of social esteem, compelled stern authority to submit to elegance, and gave a domination, vanquisher of laws, to be subdued by manners.[96]

For all its rhetorical imagery, Burke's proposition was quite simple. The moral foundations of the modern world were laid well before the modern age began. Without the moral afterlife of "ancient chivalry," there would be nothing but "sophisters, economists and calculators." This, combined with a strong emphasis upon the English common-law principle of prescription as the ultimate source of the legitimacy of private property, brought Burke's political theory more firmly into line with the conventions underlying British political practice than Montesquieu's had ever been.

Burke's critics took a different position. "Our constitution and our commerce have grown up together," wrote one of them, a Liverpool merchant named James Currie, in 1793. "Our very habits and manners, and the structure of society among us, are founded on this union."[97] Burke's own explanation of political stability, Currie claimed, was based upon a deep-seated prejudice towards trade and manufacture, nurtured, he suggested rather nastily, by his education at the Jesuit college of St. Omer.

> Early education, natural taste, and peculiar sublimity of imagination have made, I presume, the detail and the exactness of commerce disgusting to Mr Burke; and have furnished his mind with those grand and obscure ideas, that associate with the lofty manners of chivalry and the Gothic gloom of a darker age. Hence probably (since time, by extinguishing ambition, has restored the original habits of his mind), we are to explain his strong preference of the feudal relicks of our constitution, and his dread of the progress of commerce, as leading to innovation and change.[98]

But Currie also shared Hume's fears about the public debt, arguing (in a way that inadvertently echoed Hume's "violent death" scenario) that the huge size of Britain's debt made the current war against France a dangerous folly. "Fifty years ago," he wrote,

> Mr Hume, treating on the effects of public credit, observed that it must either destroy the nation or the nation must destroy it. 'I must confess', says this

---

[96] Burke, *Reflections*, ed. Pocock, pp. 66–7.

[97] [James Currie], *A Letter, Commercial and Political addressed to the Right Honourable William Pitt: in which the Real Interests of Britain in the Present Crisis are Considered, and Some Observations are Offered on the General State of Europe*, 3rd ed. (London, 1793), p. 31.

[98] [Currie], *A Letter*, p. 32.

profound observer, 'when I see princes and states, quarrelling amidst the debts, funds and public mortgages, it always brings to my mind a match of cudgel-playing fought in a china shop'.[99]

Now, Currie warned, not only the china, but the shop itself would come down about the ears of a government that went to war. All that stood between Britain's commercial prosperity and financial ruin was the "progress of knowledge of the useful arts" and the increased sources of public revenue that they had served to create. These, he argued, were what needed to be protected by a sustained period of peace.

> The surprising advances of chemistry, and the effects of its application to manufactures; the wonderful combinations of chemistry and mechanics, for the reduction of labour—these are the happy means by which bankruptcy has been hitherto averted. . . . Britain has grown prosperous in spite of the wretched politics of her rulers. The genius of Watt, Wedgwood and Arkwright has counteracted the expense and folly of the American war.[100]

Others from the opposite side of the late-eighteenth-century political divide took Currie's argument very much further. The real foundation of British political stability, argued Currie's opponent George Chalmers, in 1794, lay in the "active enterprise and prudent oeconomy" of the whole nation, not in the genius of a handful of individuals. It "has been ably debated in our own times," Chalmers went on to point out, "whether a rich and industrious people can be overpowered or emulated in trials of manufacture, of traffic and adventure by a poor and idle people. And the golden prize was awarded, by universal suffrage, to the most wealthy and diligent people."[101] This general prosperity, Chalmers argued, also explained why Currie's rehearsal of Hume's warning about public credit was entirely unwarranted. "Hume," he wrote, "saw every body busy about him, yet did not perceive that they moved."[102] The scale of that movement was best measured by the facts and figures registering the growth of Britain's population, the size of her merchant fleet, the volume of her foreign trade, and the massive increase in her government's income from customs and excise dues. These made it clear that Britain's power and prosperity rested on very much more solid foundations than the achievements of "a chemist in Birmingham, a potter in Stafford and a millwright in Manchester."[103] "The business of life does not admit of fantastical causes for its prosperity

---

[99] [Currie], *A Letter*, p. 30.

[100] [Currie], *A Letter*, pp. 6–7.

[101] George Chalmers, *An Estimate of the Comparative Strength of Great Britain During the Present and Four Preceding Reigns*, 2nd ed. (London, 1794), p. xci.

[102] Chalmers, *Estimate*, p. x.

[103] Chalmers, *Estimate*, p. xxiv.

or decline," Chalmers concluded flatly. Simple numerical facts showed that Britain's stability was an effect of "our having a greater number of people who are better instructed and more industrious, who employ greater capitals to more profitable purposes, who derive an energy from the constitution and place a confidence in their rulers."[104]

These different explanations of constitutional stability ("ancient chivalry," inventive "genius," or "active enterprise") raise a second question about Burke's imaginative recasting of England's nightmare as France's future. This latter question is more historiographical than historical. There is now quite a large literature on the origins of modern democratic politics and the combination of political institutions and financial resources that give modern governments their legitimacy and power. Much of its analytical content is quite similar to the two chapters on England in Montesquieu's *The Spirit of Laws*. As with Montesquieu, the combination in question is usually taken to consist of an elected government, constitutional decision-making, and some kind of separation of powers, on the one hand, and a tax system, public expenditure, and a public debt, on the other. The two, as Montesquieu also pointed out, tend to go together because of the way that limited government serves to reduce the costs of public borrowing, lowers the risks of debt default, and stimulates economic activity, thus creating a virtuous circle of domestic prosperity and external security.[105] But it is less clear what makes limited government limited, or why it is now so much less prone to the kind of fate that Montesquieu and Hume predicted of England and which Burke transposed to France. A government that is strong enough to provide the kind of security that Montesquieu called the political liberty of the subject is also strong enough to destroy that liberty (as both the first French republic and Napoleon Bonaparte did). This latter problem has come to form the subject-matter of a second historiographical tradition, centred mainly on the question of whether democracy and capitalism (to describe the combination most succinctly) really depend on a deeper set of moral values, similar to those generated by either "ancient chivalry" or "active enterprise," for a stability that even the best-designed of constitutions

---

[104] Chalmers, *Estimate*, p. xxv.

[105] For an overview, see Niall Ferguson, *The Cash Nexus: Money and Power in the Modern World 1700–2000* (London, Allen Lane, The Penguin Press, 2001). As Ferguson emphasises (p. 15), his work builds upon the institutional economics of Douglass C. North, *Institutions, Institutional Change, and Economic Performance* (New York, 1990). Two other recent books deal with the same subject: see James Macdonald, *A Free Nation Deep in Debt: The Financial Roots of Democracy* (New York, Farrar, Straus and Giroux, 2003), and, more sceptically, Stasavage, *Public Debt and the Birth of the Democratic State*. See also Norman Schofield, " 'The Probability of a Fit Choice': American Political History and Voting Theory," in Keith Dowding, Robert E. Gooding, and Carole Pateman, eds., *Justice and Democracy* (Cambridge, CUP, 2004), pp. 59–78. For a recent assessment of some of the causal claims underlying the "new institutionalism," see Adam Przeworski, "Institutions Matter?" *Government and Opposition* 39 (2004): 527–40.

and institutional arrangements cannot supply.[106] The two historiographical traditions both deal with the same subject, namely, the somewhat counterintuitive capacity that the combination of political democracy and capitalist society seems to have acquired for committing itself to its commitments. According to the one historiographical tradition, the explanation is largely a matter of institutional design. According to the other, it is largely a matter of morality and manners. But even the best of modern political science has found it hard to explain how or why the two preconditions have ever happened to coincide.[107]

But setting the two historiographical traditions alongside one another also raises a further question. This is not just a question about which of the two (the political institutions or the morality) came first, but also about whether that initial question really matters. One reason why it may not (or not as much as might seem) has to do with a development that belongs to a third historiographical tradition. This has been rather less concerned with the financial stability and institutional design of modern governments, or with their underlying moral and legal foundations, than with the size and scale of states themselves. There are, as was already clear in the late eighteenth century, a great deal fewer of them now than was the case in 1300 or 1500.[108] Those that exist are, however, of a size and scale matched only by the great colonial empires of the past. But there is a difference between an empire and a huge federal state like the one formed by the United States of America or, perhaps, by the European Union (or, even more speculatively, by something analogous in Asia). The one is centralized; the other is not. An imperial government can accommodate a separation of powers of a vertical sort, with separate agencies taking responsibility for the legislative, executive, and judicial functions. But a horizontal separa-

[106] See Albert O. Hirschman, *Rival Views of Market Society and Other Recent Essays* (New York, Viking, 1986); *The Passions and the Interests: Political Arguments for Capitalism before Its Triumph* (Princeton, Princeton University Press, 1977); *Essays in Trespassing: Economics to Politics and Beyond* (Cambridge, CUP, 1981), pp. 287–306. Jon Elster, *Alchemies of the Mind: Rationality and the Emotions* (Cambridge, CUP, 1999).

[107] The problem forms the subject-matter of Stasavage, *Public Debt and the Birth of the Democratic State*. "Whether and when checks and balances make a difference," he concludes, "depends on the nature of distributional conflicts in society and on the balance of forces between the political parties that form to represent different groups" (p. 176).

[108] "The tendency of Europe is so manifestly towards consolidation that, unless it should suddenly and unexpectedly take a different turn, in a few years there will be not more than four or five sovereign states left of the hundreds which covered this quarter of the globe": John Quincy Adams to Thomas Boylston Adams, 14 February 1801, in John Quincy Adams, *Writings*, ed. Worthington Chauncey Ford (New York, 1913), 2:500. See, helpfully, Charles Tilly, ed., *The Formation of National States in Western Europe* (Princeton, Princeton University Press, 1975), and Charles Tilly, *Coercion, Capital, and European States AD 990–1990* (Oxford, Oxford University Press, 1990).

tion of powers, with separate levels taking responsibility for different functions, necessarily entails the end of empire.[109] In the vocabulary that Montesquieu used in *The Spirit of Laws*, it would no longer have the same nature.

This possibility can also be found in eighteenth-century political speculation. As well as the "farce" to which the American political commentator
Robert Walsh referred in 1810, Sir James Steuart's *Inquiry into the Principles
of Political Oeconomy* also contained a second, rather different set of speculations about the potential effects of a large public debt. He called this second
conjecture a "rhapsody."[110] It appeared in two different places in his *Inquiry*,
the first in a chapter dealing with the "general consequences resulting to a
trading nation, upon the opening of an active foreign commerce," and the
second in a book dealing with public credit itself. The "rhapsody" began
with a description of the development of foreign trade and then went on
to examine the implications of one of the properties of public credit that
set it apart from other ways of funding the costs of war. Borrowing money
to fund the costs of war does not take as much money out of circulation as
taxation or building up a cash reserve will do because government stock
also functions as a source of private credit. Steuart's "rhapsody" took this
property as far as it could go and used it to show how it could become the
basis of what he called "an endless path" in which borrowing and lending
would turn into taxing and spending, all within a single common market,
free of trade imbalances and payments deficits.

At the outset, he suggested, when societies were much simpler than they
had come to be, trade with foreigners would have been based solely upon
natural differences and absolute advantages in different kinds of natural
endowment. "In one part," he wrote,

> I see a decent and comely beginning of industry; wealth flowing gently in, to
> recompense ingenuity; numbers augmenting, and every one becoming daily
> more useful to another; agriculture proportionally extending itself; no violent
> revolutions; no exorbitant profits; no insolence among the rich; no excessive
> misery among the poor; multitudes employed in producing; great oeconomy

---

[109] The distinction between a "vertical" and a "horizontal" separation of powers is discussed
in Alberto Postigliola, "En relisant le chapitre sur la constitution de l'Angleterre," *Cahiers de
Philosophie Politique et Juridique* 7 (1985): 7–28 (10–1). As Postigliola indicates, the distinction
can be found in Norberto Bobbio, *La teoria delle forme di governo nella storia del pensiero politico*
(Turin, 1976), p. 148, who, in some sense, took it from Montesquieu. On the large and rather
diffuse literature on the idea of the separation of powers in Montesquieu's thought, see Alberto Postigliola, "Sur quelques interprétations de la 'séparation des pouvoirs' chez Montesquieu," *Studies on Voltaire and the Eighteenth Century* 154 (1976): 1759–75.

[110] Steuart, *Inquiry*, ed. Skinner, bk. ii, ch. ix, p. 182. This aspect of Steuart's thought is still
taken to be an indication of his precocious "Keynesianism" rather than a reply to Hume. See,
however, Walter F. Stettner, "Sir James Steuart on the Public Debt," *Quarterly Journal of
Economics* 59 (1945): 451–76.

upon consumption; and all the instruments of luxury, daily produced by the hands of the diligent, going out of the country for the service of strangers; not remaining at home for the gratification of sensuality.[111]

But this state of affairs, he continued, could not last. Sooner or later, the harmonious relationship between foreign trade and the domestic economy would break down. Interruptions to circulation abroad would give rise to stagnation of production at home. Domestic consumption would then have to take up the slack and, when it did, it would increase out of all proportion to the size of foreign trade.

> Upon this cities swell in magnificence of buildings; the face of the country is adorned with palaces, and becomes covered with groves; luxury shines triumphant in every part; inequality becomes more striking to the eye; and want and misery appear more deformed, from the contrast; even fortune grows more whimsical in her inconstancy; the beggar of the other day now rides in his coach; and he who was born in a bed of state, is seen to die in an alms-house. Such are the effects of great domestic circulation.[112]

The "lustre of private wealth" now "eclipsed" the wealth of the government, forcing the statesman (the figure for whom the whole *Inquiry* was written) to "avail himself of art and address as well as of power and authority." This, according to Steuart, was where government borrowing would begin to have its effect.

> By the help of cajoling and intrigues, he gets a little into debt; this lays a foundation for public credit, which, growing by degrees, and in its progress assuming many new forms, becomes, from the most tender beginnings, a most formidable monster, striking terror into those who cherished it in its infancy. Upon this, as upon a triumphant war-horse, the statesman gets astride, he then appears formidable anew; his head turns giddy; he is choked with the dust he has raised; and at the moment he is ready to fall, he finds, to his utter astonishment, and surprise, a strong monied interest, of his own creating, which, instead of swallowing him up as he apprehended, flies to his support. Through this he gets the better of all opposition, he establishes taxes, multiplies them, mortgages his fund of subsistence, either becomes a bankrupt, rises again from his ashes; or, if he be less audacious, he stands trembling and tottering for a while on the brink of the political precipice. From one or other of these perilous situations, he begins to discover an endless path, which, after a multitude of windings, still returns into itself, and continues an equal course through this vast labyrinth.[113]

---

[111] Steuart, *Inquiry*, ed. Skinner, bk. ii, ch. ix, pp. 180–1.
[112] Steuart, *Inquiry*, ed. Skinner, bk. ii, ch. ix, p. 181.
[113] Steuart, *Inquiry*, ed. Skinner, bk. ii, ch. ix, pp. 181–2.

Steuart took up "the rhapsody" again in the fourth book of his *Inquiry* by suggesting that repeated cycles of government borrowing really could amount to an "an endless path, which, after a multitude of windings, returns into itself."[114] This further development picked up the theme of the potentially destabilising effects of foreign trade on a trading nation, but dealt with it from a rather different point of view. Instead of showing how public credit could enable a government to coexist with the large amount of private wealth generated by domestic markets as these latter took up the slack left by interruptions to foreign trade, Steuart set out to show how public credit could give a government a remarkable capacity to promote the rotation and redistribution of wealth. He did so by rehearsing the idea that he had taken over from Hume's essay *Of Public Credit* and used in his "farce," where the tax revenue needed to service a public debt was allowed to run up to the total size of annual national income. Although, he admitted, "the notion of actually imposing 20 shillings in the pound upon the real value of all the land-rents of England, appears to us perfectly ridiculous," there was no way of showing why it had to stop at any number below the maximum.[115] In real life, of course, there were a number of offsetting factors. The alternative to taxing income was to use excise duties or a sales tax to tax consumption dependent upon foreign trade. Income from the latter would offset income from the former, making a 100 percent income tax unnecessary. But foreign trade, Steuart argued, was not as fundamental to a political society as domestic trade because it had, in the last analysis, to involve the import and export of superfluities. Foreign trade was also a matter of boundaries and currencies and mattered only in a world of separate nations and relative wealth. If, Steuart continued, there was no foreign trade because trade was purely domestic, "I perceive no limit to which I can confine the extent of proportional taxes."[116] The effects of this rise in taxation to the maximum possible would, he suggested, be quite unusual. The first would be "that the state will then be in possession of all that can be raised on the land, on the consumption, industry and trade of the country; in short of all that can be called income, which it will administer for the public creditors." This, in the second place, would have the effect of eliminating debts or, more precisely, of transferring all debts to the public creditors.

> When this comes to be the case, debts become extinguished of course; because they come to be consolidated with the property: a case which commonly happens when a creditor takes possession of an estate for the payment of debts equal to its value.[117]

[114] Steuart, *Inquiry*, ed. Skinner, bk. iv, pt. iv, ch. viii, p. 647.
[115] Steuart, *Inquiry*, ed. Skinner, bk. iv, pt. iv, ch. viii, p. 646.
[116] Steuart, *Inquiry*, ed. Skinner, bk. iv, pt. iv, ch. viii, p. 646.
[117] Steuart, *Inquiry*, ed. Skinner, bk. iv, pt. iv, ch. viii, pp. 646–7.

But this would not be all. In contradistinction to the scenario that he set out in his "farce," Steuart went on to present a different scenario. A government that was now the owner of all the income of the country would not need to take possession of all that it owned.

> Government then may continue to administer for the creditors, and either retain in its hand what is necessary for the public expence of the year; or if it inclines to shew the same indulgence for this new class of proprietors as for the former, it may limit the retention to a sum equal only to the interest of the money wanted; and in this way set out upon a new system of borrowing, until the amount of taxes once more extending to the amount of the public revenue be transferred to a new set of creditors.[118]

The cycle was, in theory, endlessly renewable, an "endless path," as Steuart called it, "which, after a multitude of windings, returns into itself."[119] Although, as he readily acknowledged, the "whole of this hypothesis" was "destitute of all probability," it did have a point. It was designed "to disprove the vulgar notion, that by contracting debts beyond a certain sum, *a trading nation which has a great balance in its favour*, must be involved in an unavoidable bankruptcy. To say that a *nation* must become bankrupt to itself is a proposition which I think implies a contradiction."[120] Nations could and did default on their debts to other nations and their citizens. But they could not become bankrupt to themselves. Instead, they simply redistributed resources from one part of society to another by way of taxation and expenditure.

In purely numerical terms Steuart's "rhapsody" was just like his "farce." The difference between the two was not a matter of the amount of government borrowing or its ultimate outcome in a tax regime equal to the entire national income. It was, instead, a matter of the way that a trading nation would avoid the kind of pressures generated by unfavourable trade and payments balances if all its trade were domestic. If this were the case, borrowing and lending would simply turn into taxing and spending before the cycle started again. Everything would depend on how the government behaved. The "farce" consisted of a government that set out to conquer the world by using the nation's whole income to build up and deploy a massive military force. The "rhapsody" consisted of a government that limited the use of its income to cover the cost of the interest payments needed to pay for the capital costs of public expenditure over a year, leaving the rest of the national income to be used as its owners saw fit. It would be a limited government of a very specific kind. It would be at the beginning,

---

[118] Steuart, *Inquiry*, ed. Skinner, bk. iv, pt. iv, ch. viii, p. 647.
[119] Steuart, *Inquiry*, ed. Skinner, bk. iv, pt. iv, ch. viii, p. 647.
[120] Steuart, *Inquiry*, ed. Skinner, bk. iv, pt. iv, ch. viii, p. 647.

not the end, of the road because it would be able to tax the new owners of property in just the same way as before. In the "farce" public credit would destroy private property. But in the "rhapsody" the opposite would be the case. The proprietors would change, but property would remain. The new cycle would again involve paying interest and raising taxes. Property would again have to be used productively, resulting in further cycles of foreign and domestic trade, government borrowing, and rising taxation before the next climacteric was reached.

This potentially "endless path," Steuart argued, was why it was a great mistake to think that equality and wealth could not go hand in hand. "The patrons therefore of Agrarian laws and of universal equality," he wrote, "instead of crying down luxury and superfluous consumption, ought rather to be contriving methods for rendering them more universal."[121] The subject, he continued, was usually discussed in two apparently different, but actually rather similar, ways. Some claimed that "an equality of fortune would banish luxury and superfluous consumption." Others, however, argued that equality and luxury were perfectly compatible, provided that luxury was equally distributed. It was true, Steuart agreed, that an equal distribution of luxury would reduce the consumption of some and increase that of others. But it did not follow from the equal availability of luxury goods that the effects of inequality would disappear. Doubling the quantity of ribbands that a country girl could buy, he pointed out, would still not make her richer than the haberdasher who sold them to her. She might be richer and he might be poorer, but they would still not be equal because the world as it was would already be there. For real equality to exist, property and consumption would have to be levelled down to what was absolutely necessary for physical survival. This, Steuart had shown, was not absolutely impossible, even in the modern world. But if the "farce" showed that public credit could be used in this way, the "rhapsody" pointed in a different direction. The "endless path" of borrowing and taxation meant monetising everything and promoting a gradual circulation of goods and services of every kind, so that nothing in society would be fixed. As some rose and others fell, there would, he claimed, still be a point midway between the two at which equality would occur.

> Absolute equality, *de facto*, is an absurd supposition, if applied to a human society. Must not frugality amass, and prodigality dissipate? Those opposite dispositions are of themselves sufficient to destroy, at once, the best regulations for supporting equality; and, when carried to a certain length, must substitute in its place as great an inequality as the quantity of circulation is capable to produce.[122]

[121] Steuart, *Inquiry*, ed. Skinner, bk. ii, ch. xxvi, p. 316.
[122] Steuart, *Inquiry*, ed. Skinner, bk. ii, ch. xxvi, p. 317.

A public debt, Steuart argued, was a sort of social gyroscope that would keep society stable despite the fact that all of its individual parts were constantly moving. If, he wrote, some people save and others spend, "what scheme can be laid down for preserving equality, better than that of an unlimited industry equivalent to an universal circulation of all property, whereby dissipation may correct the effects of hoarding, and hoarding those of dissipation?"

> This is the most effectual remedy both against poverty and overgrown riches; because the rich and the poor are thereby perpetually made to change conditions. In these alterations in their respective situations, the parties who are changing by degrees, must surely in their progress towards a total alteration, become, at one time or another, on a level, that is, to an equality; as the buckets in a well meet, before they can pass one another.[123]

It is, perhaps, a somewhat odd notion of equality. But if the alternatives are either a physical minimum or an unlimited abundance, it may be the only kind of equality within reach.

Steuart's "rhapsody" was more than a reply to Hume's speculation about the despotic potential of government borrowing. It was also an investigation into the properties of states. For all its unfamiliar vocabulary, Steuart's "rhapsody" is quite like a rather blurred version of the world as it is (Friedrich List, the early-nineteenth-century German political theorist, took it to be the starting point for thinking about how national prosperity and independence could be established and maintained).[124] It is a description of a world made up of sovereign states with perpetual debts, but with little or no foreign trade. This latter feature was, as Steuart presented it, not the result of an underdeveloped economy with a limited amount of industry and trade, but of a huge domestic market and a single common currency. States would be big and prosperous, but largely self-sufficient. If the whole world really were just like that, then, as Steuart envisaged, borrowing and lending would simply turn into taxing and spending. Governments borrow huge sums of money, but the money that they borrow is never repaid. Public debts are perpetual. What matters for those who invest in them is the rate of interest that they bear and a government's ability to fund the cost of its interest payments out of its tax revenue. Interest rates vary not only in terms of a government's expenditure and ability to tax but also in terms of a country's trade and payments balances. High government expenditure coupled with trade and payments imbalances is likely to generate upward pressure on interest rates and magnify financial risks. But some of these pressures can be reduced by the creation of common markets and

---

[123] Steuart, *Inquiry*, ed. Skinner, bk. ii, ch. xxvi, p. 318.
[124] On List's indebtedness to Steuart, see Hont, *Jealousy of Trade*, p. 151 (and note 269).

single currencies. If, as a result, most trade were to become domestic, it is not nearly so clear what the limit on government borrowing might be. Without a world made up of separate states and interdependent national economies, a government that borrowed at a rate of interest equal to total national income (or 100 percent) would simply be transferring resources from one part of society to another. If it could not pay this astronomical rate of interest on its debt, it would, in a sense, be bankrupt. But in another sense it would simply have taxed one part of society for the benefit of another. All the funds that it had borrowed would still be there, available to be used again. Some would undoubtedly suffer. But others would also gain. What would be certain, however, is that, whether they won or lost, they would all be subject to the decisions of a government ruling over so big an economic area that the distinction between what was domestic and what was foreign would no longer matter at all. What would matter instead would be the legitimacy and power of a government like that.

We do not know what a government like that would look like, or how, with such vast financial resources at its disposal, it might have been able to maintain a durable balance between consumption and production without, as several of Steuart's critics pointed out, exercising the most despotic power. Nor did Steuart's "rhapsody" supply much guidance. As one of his late-eighteenth-century admirers acknowledged, most of the available language of political theory was mired so deeply in metaphor and analogy that it was almost analytically unserviceable.[125] But it is plausible to suggest that the question of what a government like that might have looked like was as alive in the eighteenth century as it might be now. The "union of Great Britain with her colonies" that Adam Smith canvassed on the eve of the American war in the fourth and fifth books of his *Inquiry into the Nature and Causes of the Wealth of Nations* was a clear reply to Steuart's "rhapsody" and only one of a number of speculative descriptions of what the outcome of a possible *translatio imperii* from Britain to North America might be.[126] Although Smith took issue with the credit-driven process of promoting prosperity that Steuart had described, he was still prepared to contemplate the possibility of dealing with the problem of funding Britain's debt by extending the British system of taxation to the whole British Empire. The modern "idea of representation," he argued, made this a possibility that had not been available to republican Rome. Its long-term outcome, he suggested, might be a shift of the "states-general of the British empire"

---

[125] David Williams, *Egeria, or Elementary Studies on the Progress of Nations in Political Oeconomy, Legislation and Government* (London, 1803), p. 64. The whole book is a discussion of how to give practical application to Steuart's thought. On Williams, see J. Dybikowski, *On Burning Ground: An Examination of the Ideas, Projects and Life of David Williams*, Studies on Voltaire and the Eighteenth Century, 307 (Oxford, Voltaire Foundation, 1993).

[126] On these conjectures, see the works listed in note 20 above, especially Dickey, "*Doux-commerce* and Humanitarian Values."

from England to North America to match the changing balance of resources within the new transatlantic state. "Such a speculation can at worst
be regarded as a new Utopia," he acknowledged, "less amusing certainly,
but not more useless and chimerical than the old one."[127]

Speculations like these suggest that nobody in late-eighteenth-century
France needed to wait until Burke had published his *Reflections on the Revolution in France* to find out about the dangerous properties of sovereign
states with public debts. The political precipice was quite easy to see.
"Dined today," the English political commentator Arthur Young noted in
Paris on 17 October 1787, "with a party, whose conversation was entirely
political." "It is very remarkable," he continued,

> that such conversation never occurs, but a bankruptcy is a topic; the curious
> question on which is, *would a bankruptcy occasion a civil war, and a total overthrow
> of the government?* The answers that I have received to this question appear to
> be just; such a measure, conducted by a man of abilities, vigour and firmness,
> would certainly not occasion either one or the other. But the same measure,
> attempted by a man of a different character, might possibly do both.[128]

Young was no stranger to the topic under discussion. In 1769 he had published a warning to his compatriots about the dangers of complacency in
the aftermath of the triumphs of the Seven Years War. If, he wrote, it was
true that "England is the most prosperous" of the two nations, France
remained "the richest and most powerful."[129] This was not simply a matter
of France's massive territorial and human endowments, which, if fully developed, might overwhelm the more limited riches available to Britain.
France's more immediate advantage lay in her system of absolute government and the power of her rulers to cancel (or "spunge," i.e., "expunge")
their debts. The Seven Years War, Young argued, had gone well for England only because the French had failed to use their political advantage
as lethally as they might have done.

> Had they by the most regular punctuality lulled all Europe into an opinion
> of their funds, until they had encreased them as much as their utmost possibil-
> ity would bear, and then spunged the whole into mere life annuities to the

---

[127] Adam Smith, *An Inquiry into the Nature and Causes of the Wealth of Nations* [1776], ed.
R. H. Campbell, A. S. Skinner, and W. B. Todd, 2 vols. (Indianapolis, 1981), bk. IV. vii. c, pp.
624, 625–6; bk. V. iii, pp. 924, 933–4. The editors, in a note at p. 924, associate Smith's
comments about "one author" who had "represented" the "public funds of the different indebted nations of Europe, particularly those of England," as "the accumulation of a great
capital superadded to the other capital of the country" with the French writer Jean-François
Melon. The content of Smith's description makes it more likely that the writer in question
was Steuart and his "rhapsody."

[128] Arthur Young, *Travels in France* [1792], ed. Constance Maxwell (Cambridge, CUP,
1929), 17 October 1787, pp. 84–5.

[129] Arthur Young, *Letters on the French Nation* (London, 1769), p. 442.

then possessors alone, they would have added infinitely to the strength and power of the state, and lost very little more of their credit than they have done without such a conduct—There is nothing so pernicious to a ministry, and even to a kingdom at large, if under an arbitrary government, as their being knaves by halves.[130]

Young's account of political conversation in Paris in the autumn of 1787 followed the logic of that earlier warning. As he presented it, there were two possible outcomes to the problem of the deficit: either the crisis would be resolved by a royal coup against the state's creditors or, if it were not, continued vacillation would lead to an involuntary default and civil war. Interestingly, Young failed to foresee what did, in fact, occur. While his first scenario postulated a bankruptcy and *no* revolution, and his second a bankruptcy *and* a revolution, what actually happened in 1789 was a revolution and no bankruptcy.

It was not long, of course, before one of the two scenarios that Young *did* predict actually came to pass. By late 1790, when Burke published his *Reflections*, it was not hard to foresee that France would have both a revolution and a bankruptcy. But it may still be worth trying to understand the political and constitutional dimension of the revolution of 1789 from the vantage point of what Young did not foresee. From this perspective, the political and constitutional part of the French Revolution might best be seen as the last of a number of eighteenth-century attempts to think about how to devise a way to avert Armageddon and, by doing so, to enjoy the benefits of what, in the second half of the eighteenth century, had come to be known as "civilisation."[131] This is why it is worth paying some attention to the eighteenth century's many imaginative anticipations of the Terror. Putting the imaginative sequence ahead of the actual sequence (which also

---

[130] Young, *Letters*, p. 418. Young's warning captures the style of eighteenth-century realpolitik thinking remarkably well. For another, equally fascinating glimpse of this kind of speculation (verging on the insanity to which he eventually succumbed), see Roch Pellissery, *Le Caffé politique d'Amsterdam, ou entretiens d'un françois, d'un hollandois et d'un cosmopolite sur les divers intérêts économiques et politiques de la France, de l'Espagne et de l'Angleterre*, 2 vols. (Amsterdam, 1776): "Je vous ai déjà dit qu'en matière d'état, quand on se met au dessus des formalités ordinaires . . . il faut se justifier par de plus grands crimes. . . . En système d'état rien n'est crime, dès que l'on peut se justifier par l'utilité publique" (1:74, 77). On this basis, he suggested that Britain, during the Seven Years War, should have defaulted on her debt and used the extra revenue to foment revolt in the Spanish colonies, creating a client Mexican monarchy and extending her empire to the whole American continent. On Pellissery's subsequent history, see his *Lettres de M. de Pellissery, prisonnier onze an et deux mois à la Bastille et treize mois à Charenton* (Paris, 1792) and Jean-François Labourdette, *Vergennes. Ministre principal de Louis XVI* (Paris, Editions Desjonquières, 1990), pp. 144–5.

[131] On the eighteenth-century concept of "civilisation," see Jean Starobinski, *Blessings in Disguise; or the Morality of Evil* [Paris, 1989], trans. Arthur Goldhammer (Cambridge, Polity Press, 1993), pp. 1–35, and the earlier secondary works referred to there.

means following the real historical sequence) may help to throw new light on what the political and constitutional dimension of the revolution of 1789 was designed to do. From one perspective, the prospect of catastrophe that was so much a part of eighteenth-century political speculation highlighted the need to draw back from a world that, it could be claimed, was already far too dangerously modern, and to revert instead to something like the more balanced or mixed political system that Burke was by no means alone to recommend. But from another perspective, the imminence of disaster could be seen as an opportunity to establish a regime that could face the possibility of Armageddon in a way that no actually existing system of government might be able to do. This makes the political and constitutional dimension of the French Revolution more problematic, because it is not clear what the properties of a regime like that might be. Sieyès, the individual taken by most of his contemporaries to have been its chief theoretical architect, sometimes called it a "monarchical republic" or, more usually, "a system of representative government." But the details of the system were never laid out in a single, authoritative text.

SIEYÈS AND HIS CONTEMPORARIES

One reason for this is the collective character of political life in any period, not just the French Revolution. Just as *The Federalist* had a number of authors—as, more comprehensively, did the American Constitution as a whole—so, too, was almost everything official that was published in France a matter of collaboration, compromise, and collective agreement. But a second reason is that Sieyès himself published almost nothing of a purely theoretical character. None of his publications (with the partial exception of his draft Declaration of the Rights of Man of 1789) displays the strong theoretical concern with the causal mechanisms underlying human association and collective decision-making to be found in the works of his contemporary Condorcet, or the equally strong theoretical concern with morality and religion to be found in the works of his later critic Benjamin Constant. Unlike many of the works of Kant, Hegel, Bentham, or even James Madison, almost everything that Sieyès published was connected directly to the politics of the day. And, in keeping with the provisions of the constitution that he played a major part in designing (the constitution of 1799, or the Year VIII of the first French republic), Sieyès never published anything at all after he became a senator in 1800. Some gaps can be filled from his own surviving papers.[132] Others can be covered, perhaps more tendentiously, by

---

[132] Selections from these can be found in Emmanuel-Joseph Sieyès, *Des Manuscrits de Sieyès*, ed. Christine Fauré, Jacques Guilhaumou, and Jacques Valier (Paris, Honoré Champion,

the publications of his admirers and critics, although both their assorted predilections and his own personality made the distinction quite unstable. One contemporary portrait captures his intellectual presence quite well. It was published in 1797 by Jacques-Henri Meister, whose earlier *Des premiers principes du système social* anticipated many of Burke's later premonitions about the course that the revolution would take.

Meister first referred to Sieyès's political writings in a work published in 1795, comparing their impact in France in 1789 to the success of the Anglo-American revolutionary Tom Paine's *Rights of Man* in Britain three years later, but noting that "Paine's dialectic," as he put it, was not as "profound or precise" as that of Sieyès.[133] Two years later, in a long footnote on Sieyès published in an account of a return visit he made to Paris in the aftermath of the Terror, Meister paid striking tribute to "the power of his dialectic, the profound penetration of his views and the haughty intrepidity of his plans," and, somewhat more ironically, to the prophetic vision inherent in so acute an intellectual power. He was particularly struck by the tension between Sieyès's unusually bold intellectual prescience and his real political failure.

> I have never seen anyone analyse an idea, establish a principle, develop a long series of reasonings with a firmer or more precise logic. In this respect, I have often found myself listening to him with extreme pleasure even when he was upholding an opinion that was the exact opposite of my own sentiments. . . . Weak and timid when it comes to action, none of the consequences of his principles, none of the results of his projects seems to astonish his thought, still less frighten his sensibility.[134]

This was the man, Meister commented, renowned for having said early in June 1792 that "the revolution will be over only when there is a road running directly between the rue Saint-Honoré and the rue du Bac" (which was Sieyès's metaphor for putting an end to social and political segregation); that "property has to stay, but the proprietors will have to change"; and that "it is said that the nobility has been destroyed, and yet there are still nobles." This, he added, was the man who, late in 1788, had already

---

1999), and Emmanuel-Joseph Sieyès, *Emmanuel Joseph Sieyès, Ecrits politiques*, ed. Roberto Zapperi (Montreux, Editions des archives contemporaines, 1989). The best biography of Sieyès is by Jean-Denis Bredin, *Sieyès. La clé de la Révolution française* (Paris, Editions de Fallois, 1988). On Sieyès's political thought, see, particularly, Pasquale Pasquino, *Sieyès et l'invention de la constitution en France* (Paris, Editions Odile Jacob, 1998); Paul Bastid, *Sieyès et sa pensée*, 2nd ed. (Paris, Hachette, 1970), and Murray Forsyth, *Reason and Revolution: The Political Thought of the Abbé Sieyes* (Leicester, Leicester University Press, 1987).

[133] Jacques-Henri Meister, *Souvenirs de mes voyages en Angleterre*, 2 vols. (Zurich, 1795), pp. 29, 274, note 2.

[134] Jacques-Henri Meister, *Souvenirs de mon dernier voyage à Paris* [Paris and Zurich, 1797], reprint, ed. Paul Usteri and Eugène Ritter (Paris, 1910), pp. 154–5, note 1.

said, "[L]et us stake out the terrain of the Republic." But this, he concluded, was also the man who, at the time of the confiscation of the property of the church, had already begun to see that things were starting to go wrong, saying, "[T]hey want to be free, yet they do not know how to be just."

> If there is anyone entitled to boast of having foreseen just where the revolution would take France, that honour undoubtedly belongs to the abbé Sieyès. Since he did not make everything happen, nor happen in quite the way that his logic had arranged and conceived of it, although he had more or less of a part in everything, I doubt whether there is any man in France, even among the most violent aristocrats, who, within himself, is more displeased with everything than the abbé Sieyès.[135]

The mixture of foresight and bitterness, and the accompanying suggestion of an opportunity that had been lost or squandered, was a recurrent feature of many contemporary assessments of Sieyès's thought. The comte de Mirabeau, the dominant figure in the French National Assembly in 1789 and 1790, came to a similar view. "The abbé Sieyès is a man of genius whom I revere and love tenderly," he wrote in a note in 1790 to Pierre-Louis Roederer, one of Sieyès's most long-lasting intellectual and political allies.[136] As Mirabeau informed Sieyès himself in February 1789, he was "called to serve us as a guide in the National Assembly that will fix our destiny." In July 1790, he secretly proposed Sieyès to the king and queen as his preferred candidate for entry into a new royal ministry. Gradually, however, the tone changed. "Do not let the poor, tiny handful of good— and inflexibly good—citizens that we are become divided," Mirabeau wrote to Roederer in 1790. "In the end, my friend, my imagination will grow dark and my heart grow ill if you do not come, along with our dear master, to whom I have dispatched a patrician ambassador to touch his *aristocratic* heart—which found itself unable to resist such powerful magnetism."[137]

---

[135] Meister, *Souvenirs*, ed. Usteri and Ritter, pp. 154–5, note 1.

[136] Archives Nationales [hereafter, A. N.], Paris, 29 AP 12, fol. 80ᵛ (Mirabeau to Roederer). The letter is printed in Pierre-Louis Roederer, *Oeuvres du comte P. L. Roederer*, ed. A. M. Roederer, 8 vols. (Paris, 1853–9), 4:172. On Roederer, see the introduction to Pierre-Louis Roederer, *The Spirit of the Revolution of 1789 and Other Writings of the Revolutionary Epoch*, ed. Murray Forsyth (Aldershot, Scolar Press, 1989). On Roederer and Sieyès, see Forsyth, *Reason and Revolution*. Roederer is the source of the last piece of information about Sieyès, when, after the 1830 revolution, Sieyès returned to France from his exile in Brussels. Some time after his return, he was invited to resume his position as a member of the French Institute. Sieyès declined. "Enfin," he said, "je ne sais plus parler, ni" (after a pause), "ni me taire": Henry, Lord Brougham, *Historical Sketches of Statesmen who Flourished in the Time of George III*, 6 vols. (London, 1843), 5:142–3.

[137] A. N., Paris, 29 AP 12, fol. 83. This letter is not published in Roederer's *Oeuvres*. The final phrase is an allusion to Sieyès's interest in mesmerism and animal magnetism. The letter from Mirabeau to Sieyès of 23 February 1789 is reprinted in Charles-Augustin Sainte-Beuve, *Causeries de lundi*, 12 vols. (Paris, 1852–7), 5:163. On Mirabeau's proposal for Sieyès's entry

The anxious jocularity was a hint of the disenchantment that was to come. "It is not surprising," Mirabeau was reported to have said,

> that someone who not only had not worn out his mind, but had enriched it with useful reading and reasoned conversation over a space of thirty years, someone who can grasp a subject strongly, meditate upon it, deepen it, see it from every aspect and draw it out in all its force was likely to attract a following. Novelty is inviting and the vivid explosion of a talent that had been hidden for so long before revealing itself in all its lustre produced a sensation that won every vote. M. Sieyès has all that is needed to please the common reader: a staccato style, a decisive tone, bold assertions and new ideas; opinions that were so well suited to the taste of the day managed both to arouse the curiosity and assuage the anxieties of most of his readers.

But, Mirabeau continued, "those brilliant qualities" had not been matched by the kind of measure that was essential in political affairs. "Without it," he concluded, "one can gamble a kingdom for double or quits."[138]

By Mirabeau's death in 1791, it was clear that the gamble had failed. But the sense of unrealised possibility remained alive. It was a feature of several assessments of Sieyès's thought published by Roederer after the Terror. It surfaced, too, in publications by visitors to France, particularly from Switzerland and the German states, where several of Sieyès's admirers sought to arrange some kind of public intellectual collaboration between him and Kant, to the embarrassment, it seems, of them both.[139] "Ensure

---

to the ministry, see Munro Price, "Mirabeau and the Court: Some New Evidence," *French Historical Studies* 29 (2006): 37–75 (pp. 47, 68–9). On Mirabeau's early view of Sieyès, see also his speech to the National Assembly on 18 August 1789 commending Sieyès's draft Declaration of the Rights of Man (*Archives Parlementaires*, 8:453). See also Stanislas Girardin, *Discours et opinions. Journal et souvenirs*, 4 vols. (Paris, 1828), 3:95–6, and the further sources listed in note 159 below.

[138] Pierre-René Auguis, *Les révélations indiscrètes du xviiie siècle* (Paris, 1814), pp. 333–6 (the original in the translated passage reads, "Sans cela, on joue le royaume à pair ou non").

[139] On these attempts, which, among others, involved the Prussian philosopher Wilhelm von Humboldt, see François Azouvi and Dominique Bourel, *De Königsberg à Paris. La Réception de Kant en France (1788–1804)* (Paris, 1991), pp. 77–83, 102–12, and Jan Goldstein, *The Post-Revolutionary Self: Politics and Psyche in France, 1750–1850* (Cambridge, Mass., Harvard University Press, 2005), pp. 123–9. It is worth noting, too, that the German philosopher Johann Gottlieb Fichte was responsible for overseeing the publication of a German-language compilation of Sieyès's writings in 1796. Discussion of the publication project began in the summer of 1794, but the book was published only two years later, as *Emmanuel Sieyès. Politische Schriften*, ed. Konrad Engelbert Ölsner (n.p., 1796). On this episode, see Ives Radrizzani, ed., *J. G. Fichte. Lettres et témoignages sur la révolution française* (Paris, Vrin, 2002), pp. 46, 48–9, 281. Although there is no evidence that Sieyès knew of, or subscribed to, the Rousseau-inspired theory of a "closed commercial state" that Fichte was to set out in 1800 in his *Der Geschlossen Handelstaat* (a more appropriate parallel would be with Hegel, rather than Fichte), the similarity between Fichte's theory and the early-nineteenth-century French concept of "industrialism" (which owed something to Sieyès) was noticed by at least one observer:

that the new constitutional charter expresses the primary and secondary goals of every political association," wrote one of them to Sieyès, "the man whom I have always regarded as the true founder of representative governments," shortly after the coup d'état of the 18 Brumaire.

> Be sure to stipulate expressly that the primary goal is to guarantee the rights of man, or his freedom, and that the second is to promote the development and rule of morality; and that every vague idea about happiness, public safety, prosperity, etc.—dangerous, double-edged weapons in the hands of tyranny and licence—are banished from the preface to the social code.[140]

Some of these assessments echoed the theme of Hume's mid-eighteenth-century essay "Of Civil Liberty" and its suggestion that the apparently clear-cut division between free states and absolute government might turn out to be less categorical than it seemed. "I am a republican out of principle, but very much in the manner of the abbé Syeyes [sic]," wrote an English correspondent of the future Girondin leader Rabaut Saint-Etienne in the summer of 1791, after reading the public debate between Sieyès and Tom Paine that took place in the wake of Louis XVI's flight to Varennes.[141] The subject-matter of that debate resurfaced six years later in an assessment of Sieyès's thought published by Roederer in his *Journal d'économie publique* in the summer of 1797. As Roederer presented him, Sieyès stood at the end, not the beginning, of a long period of moral and political argument that was now almost over.

Roederer set out to illustrate the point in an article entitled "Entretien de plusieurs philosophes célèbres, sur les gouvernements républicain et monarchique" (A Conversation between Several Celebrated Philosophers on Monarchical and Republican Governments).[142] The philosophers in question were Thomas Hobbes, John Locke, Pierre Bayle, Voltaire, Helvétius, Montesquieu, Jean-Jacques Rousseau, and Sieyès himself. The conversation began with an argument between Voltaire and Hobbes over

---

see Sieyès, *Political Writings*, ed. Sonenscher, p. xii. On Sieyès's views on foreign trade, see the note (apparently from 1781) published by Christine Fauré, "Sieyès, lecteur problématique des lumières," *Dix-Huitième Siècle* 37 (2005): 225–41 (p. 236), where Sieyès commented that unlimited free trade should not be allowed to jeopardise the viability of landed units operating at the very lowest levels of agricultural productivity, a position that can, however, be aligned with what Jean-Baptiste Say was later to write about foreign trade and redistributive taxation. On Say's rather neutral position on the merits of foreign trade, as against the earlier views of the Gournay group, see below, p. 340.

[140] A. N. 284 AP 16, dossier 3, P. A. Stapfer to Sieyès, 30 Brumaire an VIII.

[141] A. N., F⁷ 4774⁸⁶ (unsigned letter, dated 27 July [1791] addressed to Rabaut St Etienne). For the debate between Sieyès and Paine, see Sieyès, *Political Writings*, ed. Sonenscher, pp. xxvi–xxviii, 163–73.

[142] Pierre-Louis Roederer, "Entretien de plusieurs philosophes célèbres, sur les gouvernements républicain et monarchique," *Journal d'économie publique*, 20 Prairial an 5 (8 June 1797), reprinted in Roederer, *Oeuvres*, 7:61–71.

which of the two forms of government was the more natural. Voltaire, in keeping with the moral theory to be found in all his publications, argued that republican forms of government fitted the communal character of the simplest human societies. Hobbes, also in keeping with his own moral theory, took the opposite tack, arguing that what Voltaire took to be a society was no more than a horde or multitude. The only genuinely natural society, he insisted, was the family, and every family, he pointed out, had a head. Locke then interrupted the dispute to point out that there was a difference between a family and a people. Families were held together by natural affections, but it was not obvious that anything comparable applied to relations between kings and their peoples. At this point, Sieyès broke into the argument. The dispute could not be resolved, he announced, unless the subject of what was natural was clarified. The word "natural" could mean something in its original, primary state, before anything had been added to it, or it could mean something compatible with nature, but that did not necessarily have to come first. The first usage raised a question of fact that could be settled by historical research, but the second sense of the word raised a theoretical question that had to be answered by reason. Nor, Sieyès continued, did a positive answer to the first question have a bearing on the answer to the second. Whatever the more natural form of government in the first sense might be, it did not follow that a barbarous people was closer to reason than an enlightened people might be.[143]

Sieyès's intervention provoked some surprise. Voltaire asked Bayle in a whisper who he was. Bayle looked inquiringly towards Locke, Montesquieu, and Rousseau, who all looked blank. But the intervention served to turn the conversation to the second of Sieyès's two definitions of what was natural. Here, Helvétius offered a step forward by proposing that the answer to the question had to be the form of government in which the people were happiest. But this, Montesquieu pointed out, might vary with the size, climate, and situation of a state. Rousseau (as he had done in his *Social Contract*) agreed. But Hobbes, Bayle, and Sieyès all rejected this ultra-sceptical view. Every government, they asserted, ought to guarantee liberty and property, irrespective of the size, population, or geographical position of a state. This narrowed the question to a discussion of the respective properties of the two kinds of government and turned the conversation towards the subject of the degree of damage to liberty and property that each type of government might do. Here Voltaire came out strongly against monarchy and the abuse of power to which centralised government was prone, while Bayle and Hobbes argued that the more general threat to both liberty and property was more likely to arise in a republic. Rousseau

---

[143] Roederer, "Entretien," in Roederer, *Oeuvres*, 7:62.

sided with Voltaire, arguing that a property-based system of government could not rely on the ultimate power of a person as sovereign to keep liberty intact. The conversation then began to degenerate into an exchange of rival examples until Montesquieu interrupted again to emphasise that the degree of security of liberty and property in republics and monarchies could not be settled unless a distinction were made between different types of republic and between monarchy and despotism. This latter distinction also served to blur the difference between republican and monarchical forms of government because, according to Montesquieu, the fundamental laws that served to distinguish monarchy from despotism were the work of the people and, being its work, could not be contrary to that people (Roederer was an unusually perceptive reader of Montesquieu's account of the origins and mutations of the fundamental laws underlying modern monarchy). This gave Sieyès his cue for a second, concluding, intervention. Montesquieu, he said, had been right to emphasise the difference between monarchy and despotism, as well as that between democracy and aristocracy. But, he went on to say, there were still many more possible distinctions, within republics as well as within monarchies. There were real differences, he argued, between democracy and ochlocracy (or mob rule), between democracy in a big state and democracy in a small one, between hereditary monarchy and monarchy for a period of time, and between hereditary aristocracy and what he called a representative aristocracy. But these differences, he continued, were not the place to begin. The principal question was the one that had been posed by Helvétius, namely, which of the two forms of government was better able to realise the happiness of the people.[144] This, Sieyès continued, still recapitulating the earlier discussion, had to be understood as the full enjoyment of liberty and property. If this was the end, then the question of the means depended on deciding which form of government was best able to reach it. But this latter question, he insisted, could not be answered solely on the basis of an examination of every actually existing system of government. It also called for consideration of every possible form of government, including those that did not exist at all. There was no reason, Sieyès suggested, to accept a bad government unless it could be shown that it really was impossible to establish one that was simply good. The answer to the question about monarchical and republican forms of government might, therefore, turn out to be a form of government that had never yet existed.

The form of government that Sieyès had in mind was never set out in a single text. It is well known that he was not a strong admirer of the English system. It was, he acknowledged in *What Is the Third Estate?*, "an astonishing piece of work at the time when it was established." But, despite its

---

[144] Roederer, "Entretien," in Roederer, *Oeuvres*, 7:63, 70.

qualities, that "much-vaunted masterpiece" could not withstand "an impartial examination based on the principles of a genuine political order." "I would still dare to submit," he wrote, "that instead of displaying all the simplicity of good order, it rather reveals a scaffolding of precautions against disorder."[145] As an early-nineteenth-century German commentator noticed, it was an assessment that chimed very well with Montesquieu's earlier "prophecy."[146] But the alternative that Sieyès envisaged is considerably less well known. To his critics, he had no alternative at all. "Abbé Sieyès," wrote Burke derisively in 1796,

> has whole nests of pigeon-holes full of constitutions ready made, ticketed, sorted and numbered; suited to every season and every fancy; some with the top of the pattern at the bottom, and some with the bottom at the top; some plain, some flowered; some distinguished for their simplicity; others for their complexity; some of blood colour; some of *boue de Paris*; some with directories, others without a direction; some with councils of elders, and councils of youngsters; some without any council at all.[147]

The taunt has stood the test of time rather better than Sieyès's own, more elaborate, constitutional system. This latter is best understood in the light of the concept of revolution that predated the French Revolution itself. That concept of revolution was made up of a combination of acute social instability and intense political conflict generated by the impact of the modern system of war finance upon existing levels of economic stratification and property ownership. In the nineteenth and twentieth centuries, the two parts of the combination were separated off from one another, forming what, in the late twentieth century, came to be known as the "social" and the "political" interpretations of the French Revolution.[148] But in the eighteenth century both were taken to be part of a single problem. Borrowing money to finance war meant raising taxes to pay interest on the state's debt. Raising taxes served in turn to reinforce existing economic and social inequalities by directing resources away from taxpayers to the owners of investments in the public funds, or "capitalists," as they came to be

---

[145] Sieyès, *What Is the Third Estate?*, ed. Sonenscher, p. 131.

[146] Friedrich Murhard, ed., "Europa im Jahre 1823," *Allgemeine Politische Annalen* (Stuttgart and Tübingen, 1823), 10:3–142, citing Sieyès (pp. 73–9) and Montesquieu (p. 80) on the English constitution. I owe the reference to F. Gunther Eyck, "English and French Influences on German Liberalism before 1848," *Journal of the History of Ideas* 18 (1957): 313–41 (p. 323), although Eyck did not highlight the similarity between Sieyès and Montesquieu on the English constitution that Murhard noticed.

[147] Edmund Burke, *A Letter to a Noble Lord* [1796], in Edmund Burke, *Further Reflections on the Revolution in France*, ed. Daniel E. Ritchie (Indianapolis, 1992), p. 316.

[148] See, famously, Alfred Cobban, *The Social Interpretation of the French Revolution* (Cambridge, CUP, 1964), and, for a historiographical overview, Schechter, ed., *The French Revolution*.

known in eighteenth-century France. The result was a potentially fatal tension between legality and morality as the obligation to maintain public credit pulled against the unequal distribution of goods in society at large, setting the needs of the state against the needs of its members and making the partiality of inherited or acquired advantage increasingly difficult to justify or disguise. Nor was the domestic dilemma the only one. If public credit was vital for a state's external security, it was also capable of generating an interest that might turn out to be incompatible with its long-term survival. The revolution anticipated in the eighteenth century lay at the confluence of these potentially irreconcilable pressures. Rising public borrowing might generate a powerful lobby favouring short-term financial stability above long-term external security. Recurrent cycles of war, debt, and taxation might ratchet up economic resentment and social envy until the spring finally snapped. But using state power to block the escalating cycle of political and social division might simply destroy the liberty and property that states were supposed to maintain.

True Monarchy, or the Idea of a Modern Republic

Barring an end to war, the dilemmas pointed towards a stark choice between Hume's "natural death" scenario and Steuart's "rhapsody," with the looming possibility of either Hume's "violent death" or Steuart's "farce" lying in the background. There is no reason to think that Sieyès was unfamiliar with either pair of possibilities.[149] He even outlined a scenario of his own pointing in the same direction as did both Steuart and Hume. In a manuscript note, he laid out a "bizarre agreement" (*une convention bizarre*) containing his own version of the effects of massive government borrowing. In this thought experiment ten producers, in a society of one hundred individuals, would agree to exempt the other ninety from having to work but would still, in contradiction to any notion of justice, allow them to have their share of the annual product. However bizarre such an "original convention" might seem, Sieyès noted, this was exactly what would happen if the spiral of debt, interest payments, and taxation were allowed to run its course, generating a society made up of "ten slaves feeding ninety masters (or eighty if the political class continues to do its duty)." It was, he warned, worth taking care:

---

[149] Although his papers contain no trace of an interest in Steuart comparable to the sustained interest that he showed in Adam Smith's *Wealth of Nations*, the title, in English, of Steuart's book can be found in Sieyès's early bibliographical notes, written in the 1770s: A. N. 284 AP 1, dossier 3 (Sieyès, who read English, noted the title, along with the English titles of works by Francis Hutcheson and the *chevalier* Ramsay, many years before Steuart's

public credit, investments in the funds, etc., will lead our societies to that fatal term by a thousand different routes; if, for example, the landowners alienate their land, reserving an annual revenue for themselves, once that revenue reaches 80 [percent of the annual product] we will have reached the fatal moment.[150]

The note pointed in the direction of debt default. But, in the context of 1789, this was to play into the hands of the royal government. The strategy that Sieyès set out in the *Views of the Executive Means Available to the Representatives of France in 1789* (written in the summer of 1788) was explicitly designed to prevent a patriotic coup against the nation's creditors by either the royal government or the Estates-General itself. Avoiding the scenarios that Hume and Steuart had set out, while still insulating the state from the possible effects of the spiral of debt, implied opting for something that was not to be found in any actually existing system of rule.

The new course pointed towards a system of government that was able to limit its ability to swallow up private property but was still powerful enough to tax and spend without, either deliberately or inadvertently, allowing any single type of interest or property to have a status that was likely to bring existing economic and social arrangements into disrepute or compromise the stability and external security of the state. Three features of the system of government that Sieyès envisaged can be singled out in this context. The first was the intensely political distinction that he made between what he called a constituting and a constituted power. The second was an elaborate electoral system as the basis of a properly constituted representative government. The third was an equally elaborately institutionalised meritocracy as a nonpolitical counterpart to the political system. Events, and Sieyès's own failure as a practical politician, pushed the first of these three features to the fore, giving his political thought the aura of hard-edged political realism that was to become the basis of his reputation as the ideologist of the Third Estate or, later, the bourgeoisie or, in the early twentieth century, of whoever, historically, happened to hold the constituting power.[151] But the two other features of Sieyès's thought pulled in

---

Inquiry appeared in French translation in 1790). For some of Sieyès's comments on Smith, see *Ecrits politiques*, ed. Zappieri.

[150] A. N. 284 AP 2, dossier 12 (a note headed "finances").

[151] The most recent description of Sieyès as the ideologue of a bourgeois revolution can be found in William H. Sewell, *A Rhetoric of Bourgeois Revolution: The Abbé Sieyès and "What Is the Third Estate?"* (Durham, N.C., Duke University Press, 1994). For an account of the compatibility between this aspect of Sieyès's thought and the political theory of Carl Schmitt, see Frederick E. Dessauer, "The Constitutional Decision: A German Theory of Constitutional Law and Politics," *Ethics* 57 (1946): 14–37 (20), and, more recently, Duncan Kelly, "Carl Schmitt's Political Theory of Representation," *Journal of the History of Ideas* 65 (2004): 113–34.

the opposite direction. They were designed to establish as dense a set of obstacles as possible against the dangerously unpredictable effects of unleashing sovereignty that, in times of political stasis, recourse to the nation's constituting power might produce. As Roederer noted, Sieyès also made a further distinction in private conversation between a "constituting power" and what he called "revolutionary power" (or what is now usually called emergency power, the power once associated with the office of dictator in the ancient Roman republic). Both were applications of sovereignty. But the one, Sieyès insisted (as, Roederer pointed out, Jean-Jacques Rousseau had also done), ought never to be exercised at the same time, still less by the same body, as the other.[152]

The two features of Sieyès's system that were designed to block the need to have recourse to sovereign power are considerably less well known than the distinction between constituting and constituted powers that was his version of the difference between sovereignty and government. The first was presented to the French National Assembly in December 1789 but emerged into full view only after 1799, in the wake of the military coup that brought Napoleon Bonaparte to power. This was what its advocates called a system of graduated promotion, or gradual elections. The system did not involve indirect election in the ordinary sense of the term but instead involved a system of promotion still currently in wide use in bureaucracies all over the world, where eligibility for promotion depends on having served in the office immediately below. Sieyès's conception of representative government involved coupling this criterion for eligibility to an elective mechanism and generalising it to every aspect of public life. It meant that all citizens, no matter how rich or otherwise well favoured they might be, would have to go into politics at the bottom and work their way up, step by step, perhaps to the top. The result was a pyramid-shaped system of political representation, one with a comprehensively democratic foundation but with an internal structure made up of a number of increasingly narrow levels of eligibility as the hierarchy rose to a peak. As Sieyès emphasised in his public debate with Tom Paine in the summer of 1791, the usual conception of a republican system of government was platform-shaped, with an elected set of political representatives electing a ministry responsible for the day-to-day business of government. The system of government produced by this procedure would, he wrote, be a "polyarchy."[153] His own conception involved turning the inverted triangle formed by an

---

[152] Pierre-Louis Roederer, *Cours d'organisation sociale*, in Roederer, *Oeuvres*, 8:262. For an example of (and, perhaps, a warning about) the way that the one could be conflated with the other, see Pierre-Louis Lacretelle, *Sur le Dix-Huit Brumaire. A Sieyès et à Bonaparte* (Paris, an VIII).

[153] Sieyès, *Political Writings*, ed. Sonenscher, pp. 169–70, 172.

absolute monarchy right side up, so that it would come to form a pyramid. Sovereignty would be placed on its proper, democratic foundation, but the process of gradual election would reduce the number of eligible candidates for the position at the top of the apex to no more than one. As the nineteenth-century Hungarian political philosopher József Eötvös put it, Sieyès's system was like a process of distillation by which "the whole French people would be sublimated through several retorts until it finally became a single 'great elector.' "[154] The result, as Sieyès suggested to Paine, would be a system that was able "to unite all the advantages attributed to *hereditary* (monarchy), without any of its inconveniencies, and all the advantages of election, without its dangers."[155] Instead of a republican monarchy, it would be a monarchical republic.

The second feature of the system was also first adumbrated in 1789 but again only came fully into view more than a dozen years later. This one, however, still exists. It is the French Legion of Honour, which was first established in 1802.[156] The choice of name may not have been Sieyès's own (the legislation that established it was presented to the French Legislature by the republic's minister of the interior, Lucien Bonaparte), but the purpose of the institution was very much in keeping with the system of gradual elections, or graduated promotion. It was intended to have some 6,000 members, divided into 15 different cohorts, each made up of 350 legionnaires, 30 officers, and 20 commanders, based in 15 different cities within what, in 1802, was still officially the first French republic. It would be headed by a seven-member great council consisting of the three consuls of the republic, together with one member elected from each of the republic's four other great institutions of government, the Council of State, the Senate, the Tribunate, and the Legislature. The great council would elect the legion's members, choosing from among those who were already distinguished in civil or military life. As with the broader political and adminis-

---

[154] József Eötvös, *The Dominant Ideas of the Nineteenth Century and Their Impact on the State* [1851–4], trans. D. Mervyn Jones, 2 vols. (Boulder, Colo., Social Science Monographs; Highland Lakes, N.J., Atlantic Research and Publications Inc.; distrib. Columbia University Press, 1996 and 1998), 1:251–2.

[155] Sieyès, *Political Writings*, ed. Sonenscher, p. 170.

[156] Nineteenth-century discussions of the subject of finding a way to establish alternatives to existing economic, political, or moral hierarchies have been examined in a number of fine studies of the history of nineteenth-century French political thought: see, particularly, Pierre Rosanvallon, *Le Moment Guizot* (Paris, Gallimard, 1989), and Lucien Jaume, *L'Individu effacé, ou le paradoxe du libéralisme français* (Paris, Fayard, 1997). For a recent discussion, see Annelien De Dijn, "Aristocratic Liberalism in Post-Revolutionary France," *Historical Journal* 48 (2005): 661–81. On earlier discussions of merit, see Jay M. Smith, *The Culture of Merit: Nobility, Royal Service, and the Making of Absolute Monarchy* (Ann Arbor, University of Michigan Press, 1996), and Rafe Blaufarb, *The French Army 1750–1820: Careers, Talent, Merit* (Manchester, Manchester University Press, 2002).

trative system, members of the legion would rise up its ranks by way of a system of graduated promotion to form a nonpolitical counterpart to the political hierarchy. Unlike the political hierarchy, however, its geographical distribution would give it a decentralised character that the political hierarchy was not designed to have. Entry into the legion would be the work of a central electing agency, but its membership would be dispersed all over the republic's territory, so that it would come to form a kind of exemplary local elite, distinguished by previous public service, sitting alongside the local political system.

Together, the two sets of institutions amounted to an ambitious attempt to create a largely artificial, but meritocratic, social hierarchy that could be distinguished quite clearly from all the various types of social hierarchy generated by property, industry, or inheritance (Sieyès, like Roederer, always held the view that property, particularly the private ownership of land, was more of a necessary evil than a moral good).[157] The most important feature of the meritocratic hierarchy, however, was that it would complement, not replace, those generated by property, industry, and inheritance. It would be natural in the second of the two senses that Roederer imputed to Sieyès in the imaginary conversation that he published in 1797 because it would be compatible both with those human qualities associated with admiration or respect and with all the ordinary economic and social arrangements likely to arise in a state of natural liberty. It would leave every kind of quasi-natural social hierarchy intact and form another, largely artificial hierarchy alongside of them, keeping a door permanently open for entry from the former to the latter, but blocking off any possibility of exit from the latter to the former by making membership of the artificial hierarchy elective and purely personal. As Roederer pointed out in the last of the truncated course of public lectures on "social organisation" that he gave at the Parisian Lyceneum in May and June 1793 (when the French Convention was concluding its debates on the constitution of the republic), the pyramidal shape of the system fitted both Montesquieu's conception of monarchy and Sieyès's conception of a republic.[158] But while the former was based on inheritance (both of the crown and of noble titles), the latter

---

[157] See, for example, the irritated annotations made by the abbé André Morellet to the edition of *Qu'est ce que le tiers état?* published in Paris in 1822.

[158] "On peut présenter ces réflexions de Montesquieu sous la même figure qui a servie à Emmanuel Sieyès pour comparer la monarchie à la république. Le gouvernement monarchique est solide parce qu'il finit en pyramide; . . . sur la *plate-forme* républicaine, au contraire, on se bat pour savoir à qui elle demeurera; on se bat au pied de la pyramide pour y arriver, on se bat encore en y montant. Si la monarchie était *cylindrique* et non pyramidale, le cylindre debout au milieu de pierres basses et égales, qu'il surpasserait toutes également en grandeur, serait en prise à tous les vents . . . et chancellerait bientôt sur ses fondements": Roederer, *Cours d'organisation sociale*, in Roederer, *Oeuvres*, 8:303.

was not. Merit and inheritance were kept firmly apart. Having two hierarchies instead of one was designed to make it easier to deal with the moral
and political difficulties posed by the relationship between private property
and the state and to reduce the potential for conflict between different
social interests over the distribution of taxation and expenditure. It was
also designed to provide public opinion with two different points of reference—one moral and personal, the other constitutional and legal—for as-
sessing the effects of policy choices on the nature of the system as a whole.
The dual hierarchy was, in short, designed to strip social envy of its potential for political conflict without, however, depriving the state of its financial resources. It meant that however much the quasi-natural social hierarchy might get entangled with the financial and fiscal requirements of the
state, there would still be another to moderate the tension between morality and legality that a purely property-based hierarchy might produce. The
ownership of private property might change, but the state and its government would be given a buffer to insulate them both from clashes between
property-based interests of every kind.

Sieyès played no public part in promoting either of these two sets of
institutions, but there is enough evidence to indicate that he was the source
of them both.[159] Benjamin Constant certainly took it for granted that Sieyès
was the system's architect, writing to him immediately after Bonaparte's
coup on the 18 Brumaire of the Year VIII to assure him that his own earlier
career in office would make him eligible for a position in the new legislative
assembly, which, he assumed, would be elected on the basis of graduated
promotion.[160] This, however, was not the first occasion on which the idea

[159] Sieyès published an outline of a system of gradual elections in his *Quelques idées de constitution applicable à la ville de Paris en juillet 1789* (Paris, 1789). Two sets of his papers (A. N., 284
AP 2, dossier 15, cahier iv and 284 AP 4, dossier 2) contain several drafts of a system of graduated promotion based upon a pyramidal system of electoral lists. Internal evidence (e.g., passages referring to "the national assembly" or to "landowners who, up to now, have been decor-
ated with the title of *seigneur*") indicates that they were written during the constitutional debates
in the National Assembly in the winter and spring of 1789–90. For the surviving evidence of
Sieyès's collaboration with Mirabeau in 1789, see the letters from Mirabeau to Sieyès in A. N.,
284 AP 8, dossier 4, and, more generally, Bredin, *Sieyès*, pp. 117–8, 188–90, as well as Bastid,
Sieyès et sa pensée, pp. 73–5, 90, 105–7. See also Jean Martin, "Quatorze billets inédits de Mirabeau à Etienne Dumont et à Du Roveray," *La Révolution française* 78 (1925): 289–311 (pp. 293–
5, on Mirabeau's role in October 1789 in promoting Sieyès's plan for a constitutional provision
to mark entry into active citizenship by an annual public ceremony and inscription on a civic
register, an idea that foreshadowed the proposal to establish the system of graduated promotion
in December 1789 that Mirabeau, supported by Roederer, presented to the National Assembly.
On the latter, see Martin, "Quatorze billets," pp. 297–300).

[160] For Constant's assumption about the authorship of the system of graduated promotion,
see Norman King and Etienne Hofmann, "Les lettres de Benjamin Constant à Sieyès avec
une lettre de Constant à Pictet-Diodati," *Annales Benjamin Constant* 3 (1988): 89–110, and
Constant's letter to Sieyès of 15 November 1799 (24 Brumaire 8) in Benjamin Constant,

appeared. It was first presented to the French National Assembly early in December 1789 by the comte de Mirabeau. Nearly half a century later, however, shortly after the revolution of 1830, Pierre-Louis Roederer ascribed its authorship to Sieyès, arguing that it should now become the basis of political representation in the newly established July monarchy. "The idea of this system belongs to Sieyès, to the man who was the first to say that the Third Estate is the Nation," he wrote in an addition to the third edition of his *De la propriété considérée dans ses rapports avec les droits politiques* (On Property, Considered in Relation to Political Rights), a work that he had first published in 1819.[161] This was the last of four attempts to introduce the system. Mirabeau's initial proposal met with a hostile reception in the National Assembly and was adjourned indefinitely. A second, equally unsuccessful attempt to make it a reality occurred in 1795 during the constitutional debate that preceded the formation of the Directory.[162] Roederer himself was responsible for the system's third, most substantial, incarnation when he presented a modified version of it to the two legislative bodies established by the Constitution of the Year VIII in 1801. He was also largely responsible for managing the legislative process creating the Legion of Honour in 1802, a much more elaborate version of a system of civic recognition that Sieyès had tried but failed to establish in 1789 to complement his own, non-property-based distinction between active and passive citizenship ("It was a great error in France," Sieyès told John Quincy Adams, the American ambassador in Berlin in 1798, not to have adopted "the many public ceremonies" to be found in the United States).[163] Although Roederer later (in 1830) came to describe the Legion of Honour as a device designed by Napoleon to undermine the system of graduated election by establishing a court-based system of royal patronage (according to another contemporary, Napoleon's changes turned the Legion from "the only instituted distinction that policy could admit" into a "monarchical order"), the arguments that he used in 1801 and 1802 to support the two proposals were very similar.[164] The two sets of institutions, he claimed,

---

Oeuvres complètes. Correspondance générale III, ed. C. P. Courtney, Boris Anelli, and Dennis Wood (Tübingen, Max Niemeyer Verlag, 2003), p. 457.

[161] Pierre-Louis Roederer, *De la propriété*, 3rd ed., reprinted in Roederer, *Oeuvres*, 7:348. The final section of this edition was an addition to the earlier, 1819, edition. See, for this edition, British Library (henceforth B. L.) 1141. h. 25 (13), *De la propriété considérée dans ses rapports avec les droits politiques* (Paris, 1819).

[162] For more details on these attempts, see the introduction to Sieyès, *Political Writings*, ed. Sonenscher, pp. lix–lx.

[163] Adams, *Writings*, ed. Ford, 2:333, note 1. For evidence of the very elaborate system of ceremonies that Sieyès envisaged, see Forsyth, *Reason and Revolution*, pp. 163–4, 205–6.

[164] For Roederer's view of the Legion of Honour in 1830 and the way in which, as he put it, it had substituted "une notabilité toute monarchique à la notabilité nationale," see his *De la propriété*, in Roederer, *Oeuvres*, 7:348, 352–3. On the transformation of the legion into "un

were both designed to block the influence of wealth and inheritance on competition for office and, by doing so, to give the political system a moral dimension that the social system on its own was unable to supply.

The claim echoed the one that Mirabeau had used in December 1789. As he informed the National Assembly then, the system of graduated promotion was intended "to prevent the degeneration of a class that, in every country in the world (with some, all the more honourable, exceptions) seems to fall proportionally down the moral order as it rises up the social order." By requiring every candidate to have been elected first to municipal and then departmental office before being eligible to stand for national office, the system's aim was to "annihilate" that "unhappy prejudice which, on the ruins of former distinctions, will not fail to raise up new forms of distinction and, out of the debris of the old classes and orders, will establish new classes and orders out of the electoral system itself and the inevitable differences between municipalities, departmental administrations, and the national assembly that it contains."[165] The argument was reinforced by an article by Jeremy Bentham's future collaborator, the Genevan exile Etienne Dumont, in Mirabeau's journal, the *Courier de Provence*. The system of graduated promotion, or "gradual elections" as Dumont put it, was the only one in which "the influence of the rich" would not, in the long term, become "redoubtable."

> The character of the rich, even in free states, is to want to get hold of everything (*de vouloir tout ravir*). In their licentious youth, they wish to be deprived of nothing, wanting to render no account at all to the people for their talents, their manners, or their opinions. . . . By subjecting them to a series of degrees in order to rise up to the most distinguished social functions and by requiring a new certification of their popularity at each step of the way, you will be offering a most eminent service both to them and to the people. You will be creating a link between the rich and the poor, making public opinion always necessary, and imprinting respect for the people, the source of every virtue, in every heart.[166]

---

ordre monarchique," see Charles-Jean-Baptiste Bonnin, "Sur l'établissement d'une noblesse" [1808], reprinted in his *Doctrine sociale ou principes universels des lois et des rapports de peuple à peuple déduit de la nature de l'homme et des droits du genre humain*, 2nd ed. (Paris, 1821), pp. 195–204 (p. 196). See also B. L. 1141. h. 25 (1), [Anon.], *La légion d'honneur en 1819. Par un membre de l'ordre*, 2nd ed. (Paris, 1819), and Prosper de Barante, *Des communes et de l'aristocratie* (Paris, 1821), pp. 60–1: "Il n'y a de vrai dans la noblesse que ce qui est indépendant de la volonté du monarque; il n'appartient pas à un pouvoir humain de conférer à personne, soit la gloire et la considération personnelles, soit la magie des souvenirs. . . . La noblesse impériale n'était qu'une émanation du pouvoir absolu, une marque de sa faveur actuelle."

[165] Mirabeau's speech is reprinted in M. J. Mavidal, E. Laurent, and E. Clavel, eds., *Archives Parlementaires*, vol. 10 (Paris, 1878), pp. 496–7, 577–9.

[166] *Courier de Provence* 79 (14–5 December 1789): 11–2. For Dumont's later account of the system's origins (which he attributed to himself, but based on a reading of Rousseau's *Social*

Graduating eligibility, Dumont argued, would impose a barrier upon the ambition of both the prince and the demagogue, neutralising the electoral system's vulnerability to subversion by either the rich or the poor without, however, encroaching directly upon the established social hierarchy.[167] Roederer's argument, a decade or so later, was almost the same (he had, in fact, also spoken in support of Mirabeau's proposal in 1789). The purpose of the system, he stated, was to ensure that what he called a *notabilité instituée* would not find itself in opposition to the *notabilité naturelle*, or the *notabilité politique* to the *notabilité morale*.[168] The terminology referred to the same problem that Roederer had described in a chapter inserted into a pamphlet published by one of his protégés, Adrien Lezay, in 1796. There, Roederer had highlighted the difficulty of giving legitimacy to majority rule. Elections produced what Roederer called a "legal majority." But that majority might not fit what he called the "natural majority" formed by the many gradations of wealth, interest, and status in society at large. The need, therefore, was to find a way to reconcile the one with the other, producing what Roederer called a "national majority" to underpin the purely numerical differences generated by the electoral system.[169] The pamphlet earned Roederer a vicious attack by the Jacobin poet and playwright Marie-Joseph Chénier in his *Épître sur la calomnie* (Epistle on Calumny). Wherever he went, Chénier wrote, "Trissotin Roederer calls himself Montesquieu." It was followed by a further onslaught in Chénier's *Docteur Pancrace*, published in December 1796 (where Roederer's prose was compared to Montesquieu's verse).[170] The association with Montesquieu was made quite often. A review of Lezay's pamphlet, published in *Le*

Contract and his *Observations on Poland* [*sic*]), see Etienne Dumont, *Recollections of Mirabeau and of the two first legislative assemblies of France* (London, 1832), pp. 192–4. Dumont did not mention any of the subsequent attempts to establish the system.

[167] *Courier de Provence* 79 (14–5 December 1789): 23.

[168] *Gazette national, ou Le Moniteur universel*, 22 Pluviôse an 9, no. 142, p. 592.

[169] Adrien Lezay, *De la faiblesse d'un gouvernement qui commence et de la nécessité où il est de se rallier à la majorité nationale* (Paris, an V). Roederer's text can now be found in Lucien Jaume, *Echec au libéralisme* (Paris, Kimé, 1990), pp. 98–105 (see also his commentary, pp. 55–7).

[170] Marie-Joseph Chénier, *Épître sur la calomnie* (Paris, an V/1796), p. 6 (the line in question was "Plus tolérant encore je souffre qu'en tout lieu Trissotin Roederer s'appelle Montesquieu," which can be translated roughly as "an even greater indication of my tolerance is my willingness to put up with Trissotin Roederer's calling himself Montesquieu wherever he goes"). "Trissotin" is an allusion to the character in Molière's *Femmes savantes*. See, too, Marie-Joseph Chénier, *Le Docteur Pancrace* (Paris, an V/1796), p. 5. Roederer, in his equally vicious reply to Chénier (suggesting that "if he was not a follower of Marat, he was his apologist, and if he was not the murderer of his brother, he was the friend of his murderers"), modified the wording of Chénier's poem to "everywhere I am called a Montesquieu" ("en tout lieu on m'appelle un Montesquieu"): see Pierre-Louis Roederer, "Lettre de Roederer à Adrien Lezay sur Chénier," *Journal d'économie publique* 2, no. 13 (10 Nivôse an 5/ 21 December 1796): 175–86 (p. 176).

Véridique in June 1796, accused him of substituting "affectation and obscurity" for Montesquieu's "extreme precision," while another review published a few days later in the *Nouvelles politiques nationales et étrangères* repeated Voltaire's dismissive joke about Montesquieu—that he was Grotius dressed up as Harlequin—and applied it to Lezay's rather ornately abbreviated style. Both reviews did, however, single out Roederer's contribution for its originality. The *Nouvelles politiques*, in particular, encouraged him to develop his definitions in a clearer conceptual language (as, it suggested, Lavoisier had done for chemistry).[171] Roederer duly did so in the modified version of the pamphlet's argument that he presented in 1801 and 1802, substituting the word "notability" for "majority" and giving the idea of a national majority a real institutional form. The combination of graduated promotion and the Legion of Honour, he now argued, would produce a notability that would exist as a moral institution alongside both the political notability produced by the electoral system and the natural notability generated by the social distribution of wealth. The result, he claimed, would be "the final blow against the old patriciat and an obstacle towards the birth of a new one."[172]

As Mirabeau had done in 1789, Roederer identified the system of graduated promotion with the political thought of Jean-Jacques Rousseau. Rousseau, Roederer stated, had described three types of aristocracy in his *Social Contract*: a "natural aristocracy" based upon physical endowments, with age being the most usual; an "elective aristocracy" made up of citizens elected by others; and a "hereditary aristocracy," where privileges were transmitted from one generation to the next. Rousseau's term, elective aristocracy, Roederer pointed out, was simply a synonym for representative democracy.

> It ought to be said, at the risk of causing deep chagrin to those modern politicians who believe themselves to be the inventors of representative government, that the elective aristocracy that Rousseau spoke about over fifty years ago is what today we call *representative-democracy*. No more than a little attention is needed to see the identity between the ideas contained by these different words. . . . *Elective aristocracy* and *representative democracy* are therefore one and the same thing.[173]

In its details the system was both more precise than, but also somewhat different from, the one that Mirabeau had proposed in 1789. Mirabeau's proposal was based on the electoral assemblies that were the hallmark of

---

[171] *Le Véridique, ou Courier universel*, 1 Messidor an IV (19 June 1796). *Nouvelles politiques nationales et étrangères*, 5 Messidor an IV (23 June 1796).

[172] *Moniteur*, 15 Ventôse an 9, no. 165, p. 689. The text is reprinted in Roederer, *Oeuvres*, 7:135–45.

[173] *Moniteur*, 15 Ventôse an 9, no. 165, p. 689.

electoral life in France before and after the elections to the Estates-General. In 1801, the electoral assemblies were abolished. Each citizen would simply draw up a list of up to thirty candidates and, after the lists drawn up by a series of citizens had been collated, those with the most votes would form a list of notables available for election to office at the lowest level of the system. That list would then become a new electorate, responsible for producing a list of candidates for election to departmental office. The departmental notables would in turn become a further new electorate, producing a final, national list of candidates eligible for the highest national legislative and executive offices. The result would be an elective aristocracy, not one that was either natural or hereditary. Each citizen, Roederer claimed, would end up with a mandated representative of his choice. "Since," he argued, "obeying one's mandatory really amounts to obeying oneself, and since obedience to oneself is always the most assured because it is the easiest, one could say that the character of representative government is to be both the most free and the most absolute, the most gentle and the most strong."[174]

The claim was vaguely redolent of the somewhat Jesuitical argument about political representation made by the seventeenth-century English political philosopher Thomas Hobbes (Roederer had in fact begun to translate Hobbes's *De Cive* while in hiding during the period of the Terror). It was also substantively quite similar to a passage in Rousseau's mid-eighteenth-century *Discourse on Political Economy*.[175] As the political economist Pierre-Samuel Dupont de Nemours noted from his exile in America, it meant that France, as he put it, had "reverted to something like an absolute monarchy, one more absolute than its predecessor." But, he continued, "the elective nobility that has just been established" was still preferable "to the hereditary nobility that we formerly had."[176] The two parts of the new system of political representation were intended to complement one another. Unitary sovereignty was to be offset by moral authority. As Roederer put it, the purpose of the new elite was to inject a moral dimension into

---

[174] *Moniteur*, 22 Pluviôse, an 9, no. 141, p. 592. The passage can also be found (in quotation marks, but without an indication of its author) in Charles-Jean-Baptiste Bonnin, *Considérations politiques et morales sur les constitutions* (Paris, 1814), p. 41, a pamphlet that follows Roederer quite closely and suggests that Sieyès's system also had some kind of presence in the constitutional discussions surrounding the end of Napoleon's empire.

[175] "[T]he most absolute authority is one that reaches into a man's innermost being and concerns itself as much with his will as with his actions": Jean-Jacques Rousseau, *Discours sur l'économie politique* [1755], ed. Bruno Bernardi (Paris, Vrin, 2002), p. 52.

[176] "Vous voilà revenus en France à une monarchie à peu près absolue et plus absolue que ne l'était l'ancienne. Mais je préfère de beaucoup la noblesse élective qui vient d'être établie à la noblesse héréditaire que nous avions auparavant": Pierre-Samuel Dupont de Nemours to Pierre-Paul Gudin de la Brenellerie, Good Stay, near New York, 10 Floréal an 8 (21 April 1800). Hagley Museum and Library, Delaware, Winterthur Mss. Group 2, Box 2, 574.

political life by founding "the sentiment of republican honour in our civil manners, a sentiment that is quite different from that feudal honour that was the lever of the monarchy."[177] That claim transferred the mantle of theoretical authority from Rousseau to Montesquieu, implying a degree of theoretical compatibility between the two that has often been overlooked (while suggesting, at the same time, that Chénier's satirical remark in 1796 was quite well aimed).[178]

The move had been foreshadowed in an article that Roederer had published in 1796 analysing the complexities of the word "honour" as it had been used by Montesquieu and Voltaire (Montesquieu, he argued, had used only one of the five different meanings of the word, although he had done so with a consistency that Voltaire had not recognised).[179] It was underlined by the carefully worded modifications to Montesquieu's usage that punctuated Roederer's speech in the subsequent debate on the Legion of Honour. The Legion, he said, "would efface those pseudonoble distinctions (*distinctions nobiliaires*) that set inherited glory above acquired glory and the descendants of great men above great men." It would, he continued, be a "moral institution" designed to add strength and activity to that "mechanism of honour" that moved the French nation so powerfully. It would also be a "political institution," placing "intermediaries in society" to relay "acts of power" to public opinion and, inversely, to relay opinion back to power, without partiality or malevolence. Finally, it would be a "military institution" that would encourage French youth to resist the seductions of afflu-

---

[177] *Moniteur*, 15 Ventôse an 9, no. 165, p. 690.

[178] Nor was it a late development. *The Spirit of Laws*, Roederer wrote in 1787, was to "the science of civil and political government" what Adam Smith's "excellent" *Wealth of Nations* was to the "science of public economy": Pierre-Louis Roederer, *Questions proposées par la commission intermédiaire de l'assemblée provinciale de la Lorraine, concernant le reculement des barrières, et observations pour servir de réponse à ses questions* [1787], in his *Oeuvres*, 7:455. The putative opposition between Montesquieu and Rousseau has not always been taken for granted. As the early-twentieth-century German constitutional theorist Egon Zweig put it, "Sieyès applied Montesquieu's terminology to Rousseau's ideas and thereby substantially disorientated the world of political conceptions" (Egon Zweig, *Die Lehre vom Pouvoir constituant* (Tübingen, 1909), p. 137, cited by Mark Vishniak, "Justifications of Power in Democracy," *Political Science Quarterly* 60 (1945): 351–76 (p. 361). Compare to Norman Hampson, "The Origins of the French Revolution: The Long and the Short of It," in David Williams, ed., *1789: The Long and the Short of It* (Sheffield, Sheffield Academic Press, 1991), p. 30: "The constitutional debates of August–September 1789 were dominated by what everyone saw as the choice between *De l'esprit des lois* and *Du contrat social*, however they chose to interpret either of these works."

[179] Pierre-Louis Roederer, "Querelle de Montesquieu et de Voltaire sur les deux principes du gouvernement monarchique et du gouvernement républicain," *Journal d'économie publique*, 10 Nivôse 5 (30 December 1796), reprinted in Roederer, *Oeuvres*, 7:55–61.

ent indolence and opt instead for military service.[180] It would, in short, generate a republican equivalent of the more morally unsavoury principle of honour that Montesquieu had associated with monarchy, forming a non-property-based bridge between the "legal" and "natural" majorities. By doing so, Roederer argued, "republican" honour would block "feudal" honour and would form the strongest possible barrier against the revival of hereditary distinctions and the "old patriciat."[181] Importantly too, the new set of distinctions would coexist alongside those generated simply by wealth. A nation could not prevent these from developing, Roederer emphasised, without affecting "property or industry." But it did not follow that the "inevitable distinction" that wealth produced should be the only one, or that "money" should have the sole right to be the focus of attention and the object of respect.[182] The new institution would create "a money of a quite different coin from the one issued by the public treasury."[183]

There were many other parts of the system of representative government that Sieyès imagined. Most of them were submerged by the hectic course of events that began in the late summer of 1788 when Sieyès wrote his *Views of the Executive Means Available to the Representatives of France in 1789*. There, he laid out a strategy in which the Estates-General as a whole would function as a constitutional convention. But events, as Sieyès acknowledged in the penultimate chapter of *What Is the Third Estate?*, turned the Estates-General into a great deal more, even before it began to meet. The decade of political conflict that followed meant that many of the system's details emerged briefly only ten years later, before disappearing once again under Napoleon's imperial rule. The graduated electoral mechanism was designed to produce a single elected head of state—a great elector, as Sieyès sometimes called the office—as well as a senate with a membership elected for life, with no legislative responsibility but instead with responsibility for what is now known as judicial review. The great elector was responsible for forming a ministry that, in turn, was accountable collectively to a legislature made up of two chambers, responsible respectively for discussing and voting on legislation initiated by the ministry itself. Members of the

---

[180] *Moniteur*, 26 Floréal an 10, no. 236, p. 961. The text of the speech can also be found in Roederer, *Oeuvres*, 7:228–35. A prefiguration of the idea can be found in Rousseau's discussion of what he called "a court of honour" in his *Lettre à M. d'Alembert sur les spectacles* of 1758. As Rousseau noted, in an acknowledgement of Montesquieu's typology of governments, "it is very doubtful whether such an institution would succeed, because it is entirely contrary to the spirit of monarchy": see Jean-Jacques Rousseau, *A Letter from M. Rousseau of Geneva to M. d'Alembert of Paris concerning the effects of Theatrical Entertainments on the Manners of Mankind* (London, 1759), p. 93.

[181] *Moniteur*, 1 Prairial an 10, p. 993.

[182] *Moniteur*, 1 Prairial an 10, p. 993.

[183] *Moniteur*, 26 Floréal an 10, p. 961.

legislature would be elected by the senate from the national lists of eligible
candidates, while membership of the senate would be at the disposal of
the great elector who would choose from a field made up of the outgoing
membership of the legislature. The system would also, Sieyès stated publicly in 1795, house two political parties, one associated with the ministry,
the other with the opposition.[184] Its fiscal powers, too, were intended to
be very broad (Sieyès was not at all sympathetic to the French National
Assembly's confiscation of church property in 1789 and the debt-reduction
scheme to which it led, arguing instead for a tax regime that would impose
a heavy burden on landed income and supporting the "portfolio tax," or
stamp duty on financial instruments like bills of exchange that Roederer
tried, unsuccessfully, to introduce late in 1790).[185] It would finally, as Sieyès
indicated in his public debate with Paine, have a built-in capacity for exercising emergency power without having to rely on collective decision-making or a Committee of Public Safety. Privately, Sieyès was more ambitious
still. Almost half of existing public expenditure, he noted, went on debt
service. If and when that proportion could be reduced, a vastly expanded
sum would be available for public works.

> The funds employed for public works could be distributed, and the work itself
> organised, in such a way as to be extremely easy to convert into war expendi-
> ture (*dépense de guerre*). My own decided view is that it is essential to be on a
> war footing to always have peace, as well as to increase general production to
> an infinite degree by means of such substantial public advances.[186]

Another "equally decided view" was to use the funding system to lend
money to the recently created departmental administrations to cover their
projected annual expenditure, making them accountable for the use of the
funds and responsible, too, for raising the taxes needed to cover the costs
of interest payments.[187] "In addition to public works," he also noted, "there
are public guarantees and insurance. These sorts of concern with supervision (*surveillance*) and useful speculation are no less necessary in a society
going to its proper goal (*qui va à son but*)."[188] Instead of the military-fiscal

---

[184] More detailed descriptions of these aspects of Sieyès's system can be found in the introduction to Sieyès, *Political Writings*, ed. Sonenscher, pp. xxx–xxxiii.

[185] On Sieyès's alternative to the confiscation of church property in November 1789, see
Sieyès, *Political Writings*, ed. Sonenscher, pp. xliii–xliv. On a portfolio tax, see Kenneth
Margerison, "P. L. Roederer: Political Thought and Practice during the French Revolution,"
Transactions of the American Philosophical Society 73 (1983): vii–166 (pp. 35–40).

[186] A. N., 284 AP 2, dossier 15, sheet entitled "Idée de la dépense publique."

[187] A. N., 284 AP 2, dossier 15, sheet entitled "Idée de la dépense publique."

[188] A. N., 284 AP 2, dossier 15, sheet entitled "Action en général du philosophe et du
gouvernement." (Internal evidence—a phrase referring to "une année de son revenu prêtée
aux grandes villes du royaume, ou aujourd'hui aux départements"—suggests that both notes
were written in late 1789 or early 1790.)

state of the eighteenth century, the system that Sieyès imagined looks somewhat more like the welfare-warfare state of more recent times.

Its most significant feature, however, was the double social hierarchy, the one more natural, the other more artificial, on which it was intended to be based. Roederer sometimes compared it to the mandarinate in China, the closest actually existing approximation, he stated in a paper to the French Institut in 1798, to the gradual system of promotion to public office commended by Rousseau and Mirabeau.[189] The idea of a double social hierarchy may now seem rather strange, but it corresponds quite closely to the distinction that the German philosopher Georg Wilhelm Friedrich Hegel was to make in the early nineteenth century between civil society and the state.[190] In Hegel's version, civil society was grounded upon all the activities involved in domestic and economic life. Morality, however, was grounded upon political institutions and the state. Sieyès's idea of a representative system followed the same logic.[191] Its aim was to offset the instability of what Hegel was to call civil society by setting a meritocratic hierarchy above the quasi-natural hierarchy generated by economic life. The quasi-natural hierarchy that was one part of Sieyès's system was property-based, or "real" in the language of the law. The more artificial, meritocratic hierarchy that made up the other part was purely nominal, or "personal" in legal language. Natural property might be used for any of the purposes of economic life, but all the property that those at the apex of the artificial hierarchy might enjoy (and Sieyès envisaged that they would enjoy a great deal) would revert to the state when they died. The gradual, but one-directional, movement of individuals from one part of the system to the other, coupled with the diffuse pressure of public opinion on the workings of both parts of the system, would give the artificial part of the system a higher status than the natural part, making it easier for a government to tax and spend without having to rely on any particular type of property or interest to maintain its legitimacy and power.

---

[189] Pierre-Louis Roederer, "Premier mémoire sur la constitution politique de la Chine," in Roederer, Oeuvres, 8:97–104 (pp. 102, 104 for the comparisons in question). This and two subsequent papers were prompted by the account by Sir George Staunton, whom Roederer knew, of Lord McCartney's mission to China.

[190] For a helpful bibliographical introduction to the literature on Hegel's concept of civil society, see Rolf-Peter Horstmann, "The Role of Civil Society in Hegel's Political Philosophy," in Robert B. Pippin and Otfried Höffe, eds., Hegel on Ethics and Politics (Cambridge, CUP, 2004), pp. 208–40 (at p. 237, note 42). More generally, see Frederick Neuhouser, Foundations of Hegel's Social Theory (Cambridge, Mass., Harvard University Press, 2000), pp. 114–74.

[191] A starting point for a fuller examination of the subject (but one that does not deal with Sieyès's version of a dual hierarchy) can be found in Jaume, L'Individu effacé, pp. 281–7. For an initial comparison, see Jean-François Kervegan, "Souveraineté et représentation chez Hegel," in Jean-Pierre Cotten, Robert Damien and André Tosel, eds., La représentation et ses crises (Besançon, Presses Universitaires Franc-Comtoises, 2001), pp. 243–62.

The distinction between the two kinds of hierarchy that Sieyès envisaged became the subject of two kinds of evaluation during the nineteenth century. The better-known is the one made by Karl Marx. As Marx described them, one hierarchy was simply the public facade of the other, the state-centred superstructure that masked the real dynamics of power and exploitation holding the capitalist mode of production (temporarily) in place. The second was made later in the nineteenth and early twentieth centuries as the focus of theoretical attention shifted towards organised political parties, mass electorates, and politics as a vocation. Here, in the tradition of sceptical political analysis established by Michels, Pareto, Weber, and Schumpeter, the evaluation was reversed, with the structure, composition, and authority of several, more or less differentiated types of hierarchy coming to be seen as the key to understanding the origins and nature of modern political power.[192] A great deal of the twentieth-century historiography of the French Revolution grew out of one or other of these evaluations, and it is not clear how much further forward more recent historiography has been able to get. In historiographical terms, taking a nineteenth-century evaluation of a solution to an eighteenth-century problem has made the problem itself less easy to see. The problem in question was not simply a matter of thinking about how to reconcile domestic political freedom and social justice with external power and security, however any of these might have been construed. It centred, more alarmingly, on the possibility that, under modern conditions of war and public finance, the one might turn out to be entirely incompatible with the other. This, disconcertingly, was how the problem came to be seen in the eighteenth century. If Sieyès's largely unimplemented solution makes historical and analytical sense in this intellectual setting, its recurrent short-term failures have made the setting itself all the more difficult to see.

Quite a large number of the individuals who addressed the problem were mentioned in the course of the debates that, between 1789 and 1830, accompanied the various proposals to establish the system of representative government that Sieyès envisaged. Perhaps surprisingly, the one invoked most frequently was Rousseau. "On every occasion," Mirabeau informed the National Assembly in 1789, "the immortal author of the *Social Contract*

---

[192] For a recent bibliographical guide to this literature, see Giorgio Sola, "Classe dominante, classe politica ed élites," *Il Pensiero politico* 36 (2003): 464–84. See also Quentin Skinner, "The State," in Terence Ball, James Ball, and Russell L. Hanson, eds., *Political Innovation and Conceptual Change* (Cambridge, CUP, 1989), pp. 90–131. The revival of interest in the work of the pre–First World War French historical sociologist Augustin Cochin is one, relatively recent, example of the continuity. On the return to Cochin's work and the extent to which it really did manage to escape from the Marxist historiography that it was used to attack, see Michael Sonenscher, "The Cheese and the Rats: Augustin Cochin and the Bicentenary of the French Revolution," *Economy and Society* 19 (1990): 266–74.

gave the highest praise to the graduated system that I now have the honour of submitting to you. In Rome's finest days, he says, it was necessary to pass through the praetorship to attain the consulate. Nothing, he also observes, had more integrity than the quaestors of the Roman army because the quaestorship was the first step towards attaining curial office."[193] Stanislas Girardin, the son of Rousseau's last patron during his time at Ermenonville, associated it with Mably as well as with Rousseau in his speech supporting Roederer's motion to establish the system in 1801.[194] Roederer, in the same debate, added Voltaire to the list, while still highlighting the identity between Rousseau's "elective aristocracy" and "representative democracy." Girardin quoted Montesquieu during the later debate on the Legion of Honour.[195] "It seems to me," Montesquieu had written in the eighty-ninth of his *Persian Letters*, "that we seem to extend our existence when we make it remembered by others. We seem to acquire another life, one that becomes as precious to us as the one we received from heaven." Only "a brilliant sophism," Girardin added, had later allowed Montesquieu to separate honour from public virtue.[196] His more orthodox republican opponents in the debate simply reversed the evaluation, arguing that the combination of graduated promotion and social distinction amounted to exactly the kind of hierarchy that Montesquieu had identified with monarchy. Sieyès himself was never mentioned at all.

The names may well have been mentioned mainly to lend a mantle of authority to political expediency (as, in another sense, may claims about the system's novelty). But the range itself is also indicative of something more. It suggests the absence of an authoritative solution to a generic problem, one produced by the military, fiscal, and financial resources on which eighteenth-century states had come to rely, and, by extension, by the difficulties involved in thinking, both causally and evaluatively, about the combination of economic prosperity, social stability, and political power on which they had also come to depend. One way of beginning to see its dimensions is to go back to the works of some of the individuals whose names were used to give Sieyès's system its rather uncertain theoretical pedigree. This, in the first instance, may help simply to explain how, as Mirabeau was said to have put it, that "vivid explosion of a talent that had been hidden for so long" could, in terms of the political theory that it came to articulate, have occurred. It may also make it easier to avoid some of the overdrawn antinomies and typologies that continue to survive

---

[193] Mavidal, Laurent, and Clavel, eds., *Archives Parlementaires*, 10:496–7, 577–9.
[194] *Moniteur*, 13 Ventôse an 9, no. 163, p. 676.
[195] *Moniteur*, 15 Ventôse an 9, no. 165, p. 689.
[196] *Moniteur*, 15 Ventôse an 9, no. 165, p. 689; 1 Prairial an 10, no. 241, p. 995 (the passage was omitted by Girardin's editor in his edition of the speech in Girardin, *Discours et opinions*, 1:154–71).

in the historiography of eighteenth-century political thought. It is not usual to find Montesquieu, Voltaire, Rousseau, and Mably set alongside one another in modern Enlightenment historiography, still less to find them all associated with a system of representative democracy that is both quite like, but still very unlike, any existing system of representative democracy anywhere in the world. The juxtaposition suggests a range of different ways of thinking about the same thing. They may, ultimately, have been incompatible, but they could also be used, in conditions of political advocacy, to point towards a consensus where no conclusive solution could be found.

Sieyès's system never really got off the ground. As Jacques-Henri Meister commented, the real tragedy of his political career was the mixture of acute foresight and resigned impotence that marked him out from the start. His surviving papers go some way towards confirming Meister's view. No one wrote more vividly about the promise that the future might hold, but no one also wrote more despairingly about how difficult it might be to get there. The more meritocratic aspect of his system lived on in some of Pierre-Louis Roederer's late historical works. There, in the oddly anachronistic descriptions of the reign of Louis XII and the polite society of the seventeenth-century Hôtel Rambouillet that he produced, Roederer applied Sieyès's notion of gradual promotion to the decentralised salon society of early-seventeenth-century France, a world that, Roederer argued, had been destroyed by the centralised royal court at Versailles. These late historical works played some part both in establishing Roederer's reputation as "Montesquieu's pupil" and in the formation of a view of French history that was to have some bearing on the elegiac quality of Tocqueville's political thought.[197] It is unlikely that Sieyès would have liked the association with Montesquieu that became part of the afterlife of his system. Its more strongly political aspect lived on in nineteenth- and early-twentieth-century Germany, where the hard-edged element of his distinction between a constituting and a constituted power fitted fairly readily into early-twentieth-century German discussions of the problematic interrelationship of democracy, political representation, and sovereign power.[198]

---

[197] The characterisation of Roederer—"En politique, il était élève de Montesquieu, et sur quelques points de Rousseau"—can be found in François Mignet, "Eloge historique de M. le comte Roederer," *Mémoires de l'académie royale des sciences morales et politiques de l'Institut de France*, vol. 2 (Paris, 1839), pp. lv–xclxxxix (p. lix). Mignet modified the wording slightly (turning Roederer into a "follower" of Montesquieu and, in part, of Rousseau) when he republished it in his *Notices et mémoires historiques*, 2 vols. (Paris, 1843), 1:29–67 (p. 34). For Roederer's application of the concept of the "gradualité des emplois publics" to the polite society of the Hôtel Rambouillet, see Roederer, *Oeuvres*, 2:387.

[198] Heinrich von Treitschke's remark that Sieyès "combined the fire of Rousseau's theory of popular sovereignty with the water of Montesquieu's doctrine of tripartite authority" was

But the connection between the political and nonpolitical parts of the system gradually disappeared from historical view. It may now be the case that a solution to the eighteenth century's concern with the debt problem really has been found, and that the many anticipations of revolution that it generated really were laid to rest once the French Revolution was over. Modern democratic governments may, perhaps, really have acquired a capacity to be committed to their commitments in ways that neither the absolute monarchies nor, ultimately, the free states and balanced governments of the eighteenth century were thought to be. But the emphasis upon the period of the French Revolution as a major turning point in European history has not made it easy to identify either the changes or the continuities that might have locked that capacity into place.

Sieyès himself claimed repeatedly that he had thought of all the features of his conception of a system of representative government well before the French Revolution began. He even drafted a review of his own of *What Is the Third Estate?* to highlight the claim.[199] It may be worth trying to take him at his word. Doing so may make it possible to build more of a bridge between his own political thought and that of the eighteenth century, and, more specifically, between his conception of representative government and the problematic future that, according to some of its best-known political theorists, the eighteenth century was expected to have. As this kind of future-oriented speculation indicates, the use of public credit to fund the costs of war raised new questions not only about the nature and purposes of sovereign power but also about the relationship between different types of economic and social inequality and the array of moral values that, at least officially, states and their governments had been established to maintain. By the time of the French Revolution both types of question had a long history. The first phase of that history began quite early in the eighteenth century and reached one kind of climacteric with the publication of Montesquieu's *The Spirit of Laws* late in 1748. Getting something like the measure of what Sieyès's system was designed to achieve calls, in the first instance, for getting something like the measure of Montesquieu's conception of monarchy. The former was by no means the same as the latter. But

---

something of a nineteenth-century commonplace. See Heinrich von Treitschke, *History of Germany in the Nineteenth Century*, trans. Eden and Cedar Paul, 7 vols. (London, 1916), 2:357, and Zweig, *Die Lehre vom Pouvoir Constituant*, p. 116.

[199] For these claims, see Sieyès, *Political Writings*, ed. Sonenscher, pp. viii, xxix, 172, and below, chapter 4. In his *Causeries de lundi*, vol. 5 (Paris, 1853), p. 153, Charles-Augustin Sainte-Beuve printed part of what Sieyès called a "*roman*" written in 1772 and describing an "analytical picture" of the formation of a human society. As Sainte-Beuve noticed, the "romance" contains a passage about the distinction between the physical and human sciences that Sieyès published in his *Views of the Executive Means* seventeen years later (*Political Writings*, ed. Sonenscher, p. 15). I have not come across the manuscript in question in Sieyès's papers.

their common concern with maintaining unitary sovereignty but limiting state power, and with endorsing inequality but trying to find ways to circumvent its more divisive effects, gave their respective conceptions of government a kind of family resemblance that could be exploited quite readily, either positively or negatively, during the period of the French Revolution. The central feature of both conceptions was the idea of a single system made up of two distinct parts. For Montesquieu, the bifurcating mechanism was supplied by property. For Sieyès, but more particularly for his republican critics, the question was whether the type of alternative that he envisaged could be prevented from defaulting into the kind of political system that Montesquieu had called monarchy.

⁓2⁓

MONTESQUIEU AND THE IDEA OF MONARCHY

THE TROGLODYTES AND THE MORALITY OF MONARCHY

THE system of representative government that Sieyès envisaged was an ambitious attempt to graft a new moral and political hierarchy onto an established set of property arrangements. It was designed to avoid direct interference with the existing property regime and to rely instead upon the machinery of representation itself to generate an extra level of power and authority to neutralise property's potentially divisive effects. The individual whose thought best registered some of the dilemmas that this involved was Montesquieu, because it was Montesquieu who first showed how sovereignty could be limited without being divided, but it was Montesquieu, too, who indicated that the price to be paid for doing so would have to be an elaborate hierarchy of ranks. The combination was something of a theoretical novelty. Usually, hierarchies of wealth, birth, status, or privilege (as between different estates and orders, or patricians and plebeians, or nobles and commoners) went along with mixed or balanced systems of government. But neither Sieyès's conception of a republic nor Montesquieu's conception of monarchy was mixed or balanced in this older, composite sense. Both made clear provision for the existence of a unitary sovereign power that, somehow, was still limited. What was less clear, at least to his critics, was whether Sieyès's version of limiting power could be prevented from defaulting into Montesquieu's and, by doing so, finding itself exposed to something more seriously damaging. "Just as monarchy came to be formed out of the debris of feudalism," warned Jacques-Henri Meister early in 1790, "so may we come to see the hydra of feudalism reborn out of the debris of monarchy."[1] "Montesquieu's idea of monarchy," noted Antoine-Joseph Barnave, the most forceful critic of the system of gradual election during the constitutional debates of the winter of 1789, "points towards either military despotism or organised monarchy," meaning by the latter something quite different from Sieyès's conception of a republic.[2]

Montesquieu's intellectual legacy came, accordingly, to cast something like a malign spell over the aura of novelty projected by its admirers upon

---

[1] Jacques-Henri Meister, *Des premiers principes du système social appliqués à la révolution présente* (Paris, 1790), p. 42.

[2] Antoine-Joseph Barnave, "Introduction à la révolution française," in his *Oeuvres complètes*, ed. Bérenger de la Drôme, 4 vols. (Paris, 1843), 1:63.

Sieyès's system. No one, least of all Sieyès himself, was ever prepared to claim *The Spirit of Laws* for inclusion in the system's intellectual pedigree. "Like Montesquieu," wrote one of Sieyès's opponents late in 1789, echoing one of Rousseau's assessments of Montesquieu himself, "you argue from fact to right and for this he is rightly to be faulted."[3] Nor was Rousseau's authority necessarily any the more sufficient. He, too, it could be claimed, had also succumbed to Montesquieu. As the abbé François-Jean-Philibert Aubert de Vitry, the author of a pamphlet entitled *Jean-Jacques Rousseau à l'assemblée nationale* (also published late in 1789), commented quite acutely, the fourth book of *The Social Contract* had been "spoiled by reading *The Spirit of Laws*," with the result that "it could not but fail to be infected, in certain places, by the venom of aristocratism."[4] The association continued to dog Sieyès's system all the way through to 1799 and beyond. If, as Pierre-Louis Roederer claimed in 1801, representative government was just another name for Rousseau's elective aristocracy, and if, as Aubert de Vitry suggested, Rousseau's elective aristocracy was simply a republican version of Montesquieu's concept of monarchy, then, as many of Sieyès's opponents concluded, representative government was really monarchy in another guise.

The hierarchical structure of both the political and nonpolitical parts of the system was an open invitation to insinuations of political apostasy or, in the recurrently murderous context of the first French republic, of something more comprehensively sinister. At most, all that could be offered in its defence was, as Stanislas Girardin proposed, a fulsome endorsement of the concept of honour in the young Montesquieu's *Persian Letters* and an easy qualification, quickly made, in the light of the "brilliant sophism" underlying the older Montesquieu's modification of the same concept in *The Spirit of Laws*. But, as Marie-Joseph Chénier's vicious attack on "Trissotin" Roederer and his young disciple Adrien Lezay in 1796 suggests, and as the later opposition to both the system of gradual election and the Legion of Honour indicates, Montesquieu's shadow fell heavily over every attempt to establish Sieyès's system.[5] From the outset, Sieyès's critics relied on Montesquieu's critics—notably Adam Ferguson, Jean-Louis Delolme,

---

[3] Armand-Benoît-Joseph Guffroy, *Lettre en réponse aux observations sommaires de M. l'abbé Sieyès sur les biens ecclésiastiques* (Paris, n.d. [but late 1789 from internal evidence]), p. 40, note 1. The phrase repeated what Rousseau, in his *Emile*, had written about Montesquieu. He was, Rousseau wrote, "le seul moderne en état de créer cette grande et inutile science eut été l'illustre Montesquieu. Mais il n'eut garde de traiter des principes du droit politique; il se contenta de traiter du droit positif des gouvernements établis, et rien au monde n'est plus différent que ces deux études": Jean-Jacques Rousseau, *Emile* [1763], bk. V, in Jean-Jacques Rousseau, *Oeuvres* (Paris, Pléiade, 1969), pp. 836–7.

[4] [Louis Aubert de Vitry], *Jean-Jacques Rousseau à l'assemblée nationale* (Paris, 1789), p. 220

[5] For these episodes, see above, pp. 83–4.

Claude-Adrien Helvétius, the abbé Gabriel Bonnot de Mably, and, more ambiguously, Jean-Jacques Rousseau—for many of the arguments that they used to oppose the system of representative government, applying many of the same, mainly moral, objections that had been made to Montesquieu's conception of monarchy to Sieyès's conception of a republic. The charge that Montesquieu's reputation could still carry, nearly two generations after the publication of *The Spirit of Laws*, is an indication of something deeply divisive in his thought. It is something that now sits somewhat uncomfortably with the image of irenic moderation usually associated with the constitutional theorist, advocate of the separation of powers, and intellectual progenitor of many of the most significant features of the American Constitution.[6] This latter image is not entirely false. But it misses one of the most important aspects of Montesquieu's political thought, one that served to set it apart from almost the whole of the very broad theoretical spectrum covered by both the critics and supporters of absolute government in eighteenth-century France. This was his very sophisticated, but very comprehensive, justification of inequality.

The theme first appeared in Montesquieu's allegorical discussion of the relationship between morality and politics in his *Persian Letters* of 1721. Letters 11 to 14 contained his *History of the Troglodytes*, "one of the most beautiful and finished pieces of moral painting that ever was exhibited," according to the preface to a self-standing English translation of the four letters that was published in 1766.[7] The *History* was an answer to the question of "whether men are made happier by the pleasure and satisfaction of the senses or by the practice of virtue," which Mirza had asked Usbeck in the tenth letter.[8] Montesquieu's answer was, initially, straightforward. At the outset, the Troglodytes were certainly "strangers to justice and human-

---

[6] See, standardly, William B. Gwyn, *The Meaning of the Separation of Powers: An Analysis of the Doctrine from Its Origin to the Adoption of the United States Constitution*, Tulane Studies in Political Science, 9 (New Orleans, 1965); M.J.C. Vile, *Constitutionalism and the Separation of Powers*, 2nd ed. (Indianapolis, Liberty Fund, 1998); Jean Starobinski, *Montesquieu par lui-même* (Paris, Seuil, 1956), p. 15; and, more historically, David Wootton, ed., *The Essential Federalist and Anti-Federalist Papers* (Indianapolis, Hackett, 2003), which summarises his "Liberty, Metaphor and Mechanism: 'Checks and Balances' and the Origins of Modern Constitutionalism," in David Womersley, ed., *Liberty and American Experience in the Eighteenth Century* (Indianapolis, Liberty Fund, 2006).

[7] Charles-Louis de Secondat, baron de Montesquieu, *The History of the Troglodytes* (Chelmsford, 1766), pp. i–ii (from which subsequent citations have been taken). A full, scholarly edition can now be found in Montesquieu, *Lettres persanes*, in his *Oeuvres complètes*, vol. 1, ed. Jean Ehrard and Catherine Volpilhac-Auger (Oxford, Voltaire Foundation, 2004), letters 11–4, pp. 161–72. (Henceforth this edition of the *Lettres persanes* will be abbreviated to *LP*.) Reference will also be made to the English translation of Montesquieu, *The Persian Letters*, trans. George R. Healy (Indianapolis, Hackett, 1999).

[8] Montesquieu, *LP*, letter 10, p. 159; *Persian Letters*, trans. Healy, letter 10, p. 22.

ity" and, in keeping with their selfish disposition, cultivated their land solely for the purpose of self-preservation. But variations in natural fertility, as well as localised droughts and heavy rainfall, soon made some need the assistance of others. Every appeal for help, however, turned out to be vain, as, too, was every attempt to settle disputes over women, the ownership of land, the price of subsistence goods, or the provision of medical care. Injustice brought the Troglodytes to the edge of extinction. Two families, however, survived. Unlike the other Troglodytes, the heads of these two families "were awake to the dictates of justice," living in a "retired but happy spot" that "yielded a cheerful plenty to their virtuous industry." They loved their wives and brought up their children to recognise "that the interest of individuals is involved in the interest of the public," and "that these interests cannot subsist separate and at variance." The two virtuous survivors gave the Troglodytes a second chance. Population grew and the seasonal rhythms of the agricultural year gave rise to a natural religion with regular festivals in honour of the gods, so that religion "cooperated with nature to soften and polish their manners." In this second incarnation, the Troglodytes were a pastoral people. Their flocks fed in common and "were so blended that it was difficult for anyone to know his own property; and this was a matter too of so much indifference." In the evenings, when their sheep were in their folds and their oxen had been released from their yokes, they would "assemble in parties and close the day with a frugal repast and festive or moral song." Justice at home went along with a strongly patriotic attitude towards threats from abroad. The Troglodytes' willingness to serve their country made them fierce and resolute fighters. Not "a man but was fired with the enthusiasm of a patriot, to die for his country. For the Troglodyte people was the in eyes of every man, glorious and desirable."[9]

But for all their love of their country, the Troglodytes' communal way of life did not last. When they "became numerous, they were seized with an inclination to choose a king," nominating a particularly virtuous patriarch for the task. He wept as he accepted the office, not with gratitude, but with sadness.

> Ambition, riches and pleasure begin to have charms for you; and you long to be placed in a situation in which you may court these vain delusions, in which you may aspire to be great, may pursue wealth or indulge in luxury, in which you may lay aside the solicitude after virtue, provided you are cautious to avoid open and dangerous crimes.[10]

[9] Montesquieu, *History of the Troglodytes*, pp. 2, 3–8, 9–14, 18–9; *Persian Letters*, trans. Healy, letters 11–3, pp. 23–9.

[10] Montesquieu, *History of the Troglodytes*, p. 22; *Persian Letters*, trans. Healy, letter 14, pp. 29–30.

What, he asked, his eyes streaming with tears, "is the nature of the office that you impose upon me? To command? Whom or what shall I command? Am I to command a Troglodyte to be virtuous?"[11] But that, sadly, was the point. Greatness and wealth set limits on how far virtue could go.

Montesquieu never published the sequel to the story that he wrote. He consigned it to his notebooks, commenting, "this was my idea" of how it would have continued. In this further letter, the virtuous patriarch soon died, worn out by the "secret anxiety" caused by the office he had accepted. The Troglodytes elected another king, "the wisest and most just" member of the same family. Towards the end of his reign, the Troglodytes' growing surplus of wealth led them to decide to introduce commerce and the arts into their community, preferring, as their new king put it when the proposal was presented to him at an assembly of the nation, wealth instead of virtue. But one of those present argued that the two were not necessarily incompatible. Everything, he suggested, depended on the example set by the king. If he chose to place wealth above virtue, his subjects would do the same, just as they would if he appointed someone rich, not virtuous, to his council. A further solution was to keep avarice and prodigality under tight control by making every citizen accountable for the use to which he put his goods and by punishing anyone not producing "an honest subsistence" as severely as if he had misappropriated his children's patrimony. The king agreed but warned that if the Troglodytes really did opt for wealth, then he would have to do the same.

> In your present state, I simply need to be more just than you. This is the mark of my royal authority and I cannot find any that is more august. If, however, you were to seek distinction in mere wealth, which is nothing in itself, then I will have to distinguish myself by the same means and, not to remain in a state of poverty that you will despise, I will have to load you with taxes and you will have to devote a large part of your subsistence towards maintaining the pomp and splendour that will make me respected.[12]

Once trade was established, Montesquieu suggested, then the survival of virtue as a ground for distinction would depend on the combined effects of moral example and a rigorous system of censorship (the census, it is worth remembering, was an ancient Roman moral and political institution). But if, Montesquieu warned, distinction came to be based solely on wealth, it would have to be counterbalanced by a draconian fiscal system.

It is not known when Montesquieu wrote this sequel. Nor is it clear whether he had any particular reason for not publishing it, although he

---

[11] Montesquieu, *History of the Troglodytes*, pp. 22–3; *Persian Letters*, trans. Healy, letter 14, p. 30.

[12] Montesquieu, *LP*, pp. 602–3 [*Pensée* 1616].

continued to revise the *Persian Letters* up to his death in 1754. The more
general reasons are, however, very clear. Between the publication of the
Persian Letters in 1721 and the appearance of *The Spirit of Laws* late in
1748, Montesquieu had two significant changes of mind.[13] The first change
preceded the publication of his *Considerations on the Causes of the Greatness
of the Romans and Their Decline* in 1734. The second occurred at some time
between the publication of the *Considerations* and the publication of *The
Spirit of Laws*. The two changes are best described in sequence because
they involved two different ways of thinking about the question raised by
the unpublished sequel to the Troglodyte history. The first change was
quite visible in the *Considerations*, but the broader analytical setting to
which it belonged was set out more fully in two other works that Montesquieu wrote at the same time. Together, the three works seem to have been
conceived as a trilogy, with only the first, the *Considerations*, finally being
released for public scrutiny. The second of the three works was the *Reflections on Universal Monarchy in Europe*, a work that Montesquieu planned to
publish alongside the *Considerations*, but then decided to withdraw from
the press while it was still in page proof. The third was an essay on the
English system of government, an essay that finally appeared as the famous
sixth chapter, "Of the Constitution of England," of the eleventh book of
The Spirit of Laws. Together, they amounted to a strong argument against
the sequel to the Troglodyte history and a correspondingly strong endorsement of the compatibility between wealth and virtue that the Troglodytes'
king had denied.

The three works were connected by the theme of commerce and the
promise of peace and prosperity that it appeared to offer to the modern
world. In different ways, each of them presented a facet of the broader
argument about the differences between the ancients and the moderns that
now made the warning of the unpublished sequel to the Troglodyte history
redundant. The first, the *Considerations*, was an examination of the conditions underlying Rome's rise to universal monarchy in the ancient world.
The second, the *Reflections*, was an account of the reasons that ruled out
universal monarchy among the moderns. The third, the future chapter on
the English constitution, was a description of the internal checking mechanisms contained in the English system of government. Together they added
up to an integrated argument about the differences between conquest and
commerce, on the one hand, and between ancient republics and modern

---

[13] The fullest discussions of the first of these changes of course can be found in Melvin
Richter, *The Political Theory of Montesquieu* (Cambridge, CUP, 1977), pp. 41–5, and, more
fully, in the important article by Paul A. Rahe, "The Book That Never Was: Montesquieu's
Considerations on the Romans in Historical Context," *History of Political Thought* 26 (2005): 43–
89. For further precision, see Istvan Hont, "Luxury," in Mark Goldie and Robert Wokler,
eds., *The Cambridge History of Eighteenth-Century Political Thought* (Cambridge, CUP, 2006).

monarchies, on the other. As Montesquieu presented them, each side of the two pairs went together. The Roman republic was a society organised for war. This was the reason for both its rise to greatness and its ultimate decline. The switch from republic to empire had not been matched by a corresponding switch from conquest to commerce because the Roman Empire had not been able to evolve into anything like a modern monarchy. This system of government, now best exemplified by the English constitution, could accommodate distinctions based on wealth more easily than Rome had been able to do. Wealth and the means to acquire it were also more easily transferable from one setting to another than the combination of Roman military organisation, patriotism, and political institutions had been. These, Montesquieu could argue, were the reasons why universal monarchy was ancient, not modern.

This change of mind brought Montesquieu very near to the parallel argument about the differences between the ancients and moderns that could be found in Voltaire's epic poem, the *Henriade* of 1723, and, more belligerently, in his *Letters concerning the English Nation* of 1733. There, Voltaire highlighted the differences between Roman slavery and Roman conquest, on the one hand, and English liberty and English commerce, on the other. "The fruit of the civil wars at Rome," he wrote, "was slavery, and that of the troubles of England, liberty."

> The English are the only people upon earth who have been able to prescribe limits to the power of kings by resisting them; and who, by a series of struggles, have at last established that wise government, where the prince is all powerful to do good, and at the same time his hands are tied against doing wrong; where the nobles are great without insolence and vassals; and where the people share in the government without confusion.
>
> The House of Lords and that of the Commons are the arbiters of the nation, and the king is the super-arbitrator (*sur-arbitre*). The Romans had no such balance. The patricians and plebeians in Rome were perpetually at variance and there was no intermediate power to reconcile them. The Roman Senate who were so unjustly, so criminally proud as not to suffer the plebeians to share with them in anything, could find no other artifice to keep the latter out of the administration than by employing them in foreign wars. They considered the plebeians as a wild beast whom it behoved them to let loose upon their neighbours, for fear that they should devour their masters. Thus the greatest defect in the government of the Romans raised them to be conquerors. By being unhappy at home, they triumphed over and possessed themselves of the world, till at last their divisions sunk them to slavery.[14]

[14] I have used the texts in François-Marie Arouet de Voltaire, *Lettres philosophiques* [1734], ed. Raymond Naves (Paris, Garnier, 1962), letter 8, pp. 34–5, and relied for the translation on Voltaire's original English version, now in Voltaire, *Letters concerning the English Nation*

The argument was not quite the same as Montesquieu's, but it pointed to the same conclusion. So, too, did the antithesis between conquest and commerce. Rome's greatness was based on the former, while modern Britain's was based on the latter. "As trade enriched the citizens of England," Voltaire wrote, "so it contributed to their freedom, and this freedom on the other side extended their commerce, whence arose the grandeur of the state."[15]

By 1748, when Montesquieu published *The Spirit of Laws*, his position had changed again. The effect of this change was to make *The Spirit of Laws* part of a three-sided argument about the interrelationship of commerce, government, and the distinction of ranks that was to continue into the period of the French Revolution and beyond. The first change involved a move away from the sequel to the Troglodyte history and its presentation of the relationship between wealth and virtue as something deeply problematic. That move was also a move away from the concept of monarchy contained in one of the eighteenth century's most enduringly popular works. This was *The Adventures of Telemachus, Son of Ulysses* by François de Salignac de la Mothe-Fénelon, archbishop of Cambrai until his death in 1715. Voltaire made the same move in his *Letters concerning the English Nation* (or *Philosophical Letters*), deliberately repeating Fénelon's description of virtuous rule ("the prince is all powerful to do good, and at the same time his hands are tied against doing wrong") and applying it, provocatively, to the government of modern Britain.[16] Montesquieu's second change of course, a change that took place between the publication of the *Considerations on the Romans* and the appearance of *The Spirit of Laws*, was a move against Voltaire. It was not, however, a reversion to Fénelon. The most obvious indication of the difference was in the location of what Voltaire, in his presentation of the English system of government, had called an "intermediate power."[17] Unlike the Romans, he argued, the English had a monarch who was able to act as an arbiter between the Commons and the Lords, or their equivalent of Rome's patricians and plebeians. Montesquieu transferred the idea to the system of ranks itself. "Intermediate, subordinate and dependent powers," he famously wrote in *The Spirit of Laws*, "con-

---

[1733], ed. Nicolas Cronk (Oxford, Voltaire Foundation, 1994), letter 8, pp. 33–4. I have modernised capitalisation and punctuation.

[15] Voltaire, *Lettres*, ed. Naves, letter 10, p. 45; Voltaire, *Letters*, ed. Cronk, letter 10, p. 42.

[16] Voltaire, *Lettres*, ed. Naves, letter 8, p. 34; Voltaire, *Letters*, ed. Cronk, letter 8, p. 34. Compare to François de Salignac de la Mothe-Fénelon, *The Adventures of Telemachus, Son of Ulysses* [1699/1715], ed. trans. Patrick Riley (Cambridge, CUP, 1994), bk. 5, p. 60. The phrase was also used by France's regent, the duc d'Orléans, in his address to the Paris parlement on 2 September 1715, the day after Louis XIV's death: see Colin Jones, *The Great Nation: France from Louis XIV to Napoleon 1715–99* (London, Allen Lane, 2002), p. 38.

[17] Voltaire, *Lettres*, ed. Naves, letter 8, p. 34; Voltaire, *Letters*, ed. Cronk, letter 8, p. 34.

stitute the nature of monarchical government, that is, of the government in which one alone governs by fundamental laws," adding almost immediately that "the most natural intermediate, subordinate power is that of the nobility."[18] The shift may appear to be small, but it opened up a three-sided argument that was to run all the way through the eighteenth century. In a typological sense it was an argument about the various conceptions of monarchy to be found in Fénelon, Voltaire, and Montesquieu. More analytically, it was an argument about the nature and location of the real limits on sovereign power, particularly under conditions of war and debt.

The conception of monarchy that Montesquieu set out in *The Spirit of Laws* also made the question of merit- versus wealth-based social and political distinctions redundant. The underlying stabilising principle of monarchy was honour, not virtue, and did not need to rely on the possibility that the prince might be "all powerful to do good" but whose hands were tied "against doing wrong," as Fénelon had put it. Montesquieu also defined honour in a way that (as Roederer's later struggle with the concept was to show) bypassed the warning about wealth and power that he had issued at the end of the unpublished sequel to the Troglodyte history. "A monarchical government," he now wrote, "supposes, as we have already observed, pre-eminences and ranks, as likewise a noble descent," and, "since it is the nature of honour to aspire to preferments and titles, it is properly placed in this government." Nor were these "pre-eminences" a result of moral distinction. The truth about monarchy, Montesquieu acknowledged, was "that philosophically speaking, it is a false honour that moves all the parts of the government; but even this false honour is as useful to the public as true honour could possibly be to private persons."[19] From the perspective set out in *The Spirit of Laws*, inequality was not a regrettable, potentially reversible development in most modern European societies (which considered action by a reforming government might aim to reduce), but was instead what made monarchy, uniquely, the type of government it was, giving it, as Montesquieu put it, its *nature*. This made the alternatives outlined in the unpublished sequel to the Troglodyte history irrelevant and, at the same time, also ruled out Voltaire's idea of a royal sovereign as an intermediate power. Monarchy, with its moorings in preeminence and ranks, was the real alternative both to Voltaire's meritocracy and to the tears of the soon-to-be-royal patriarch that brought the published version of the Trog-

[18] Charles-Louis de Secondat, baron de Montesquieu, *The Spirit of the Laws* [1748], ed. and trans. Anne Cohler, Basia Miller, and Harold Stone (Cambridge, 1989), bk. 2, ch. 4, pp. 17–8. I have usually preferred to follow the original English translation by Thomas Nugent, reprinted as Montesquieu, *The Spirit of the Laws*, ed. Franz Neumann (New York, Hafner Publishing Company, 1949), which, in subsequent notes, will be referred to as Montesquieu, *SL*, ed. Neumann, followed by book, chapter, and page numbers.

[19] Montesquieu, *SL*, ed. Neumann, bk. 3, ch. 7, p. 25.

lodyte history to a close. Having to opt between moral example and fiscal activism to keep virtue alive no longer mattered, because virtue (at least in its political guise) had simply fallen out of the picture. Monarchy, as Montesquieu presented it in *The Spirit of Laws*, could accommodate distinctions based on wealth without having to rely on either moral example or punitive taxation. "Ever since anyone began writing about governments," commented one of Montesquieu's early critics, "this is undoubtedly the first time that anyone has presented anything like this idea of monarchy."[20]

Three aspects of the conception of monarchy that Montesquieu set out in *The Spirit of Laws* underpinned its broader message of indifference towards having to make a choice between a merit- or a wealth-based social hierarchy. All of them were compatible with the decentralised system of public finance to which he remained committed all his life.[21] The first was Montesquieu's unusual insistence upon the importance of a noncommercial nobility. "In a monarchical government," he wrote in book 20, "it is contrary to the spirit of commerce that any of the nobility should be merchants." It was also, he added a sentence later, "contrary to the spirit of monarchy to admit the nobility into commerce. The custom of suffering the nobility of England to trade is one of those things which have there mostly contributed to weaken the monarchical government."[22] Forcing the French nobility to trade, he asserted, "would be the means of destroying the nobility, without being of any advantage to trade."[23] The second was Montesquieu's even more unusual endorsement of venal offices. Venality, he stated, was not at all compatible with despotic government, "where the subjects must be instantaneously placed or displaced by the prince." But "in monarchies," he continued, "this custom is not at all improper, by reason that it is an inducement to engage in what, as a family employment, would not be undertaken through a motive of virtue." Public service might be appropriate for "a republic founded on virtue"; monarchy, however, was based not on virtue but on honour. "In short," Montesquieu concluded, "the method of attaining to honours through riches inspires and cherishes industry, a thing extremely wanting in this kind of government."[24]

---

[20] Claude Dupin, *Observations sur un livre intitulé "De l'esprit des lois"*, 3 vols. (Paris, 1750), 1:105. For some indication of the scale of the reaction to Montesquieu's work, see John Pappas, "La Campagne des philosophes contre l'honneur," *Studies on Voltaire and the Eighteenth Century* 205 (1982): 31–44, and Céline Spector, *Montesquieu. Pouvoirs, richesses et sociétés* (Paris, Presses universitaires de France, 2004), pp. 64–5.

[21] Charles-Louis de Secondat, baron de Montesquieu, "Mémoire sur les dettes de l'état" [1717], in Montesquieu, *Oeuvres*, ed. Roger Caillois, 2 vols. (Paris, 1949), 1:66–71, and, on his later position, see pp. 166–72, below.

[22] Montesquieu, *SL*, ed. Neumann, bk. 20, ch. 21, 1:327.

[23] Montesquieu, *SL*, ed. Neumann, bk. 20, ch. 22, 1:327.

[24] Montesquieu, *SL*, ed. Neumann, bk. 5, ch. 19, 1:69.

He was, however, quite explicit in emphasising the undesirability of extending the same principle to the fiscal system, arguing that the English system of using government commissions, like the Excise, to manage tax collection was highly preferable to the French system of tax-farming. When tax-farming becomes "a post of honour," he stated flatly, "the state is ruined" ("financiers support the state," he was also reported to have said, "as rope supports a hanged man").[25] The third aspect of Montesquieu's conception of monarchy (one that it shared with "trading countries" like the Netherlands) was its capacity to maintain a system of publicly funded welfare for the poor. "The riches of the state," he wrote, "suppose great industry." But the vagaries of trade meant that "it is impossible but that some must suffer, and consequently the mechanics must be in a momentary necessity."[26] In these circumstances, Montesquieu wrote, "the state is obliged to lend them a ready assistance, whether it be to prevent the sufferings of the people or to avoid a rebellion." Here, "hospitals or some equivalent regulations" were necessary. Despite their shortcomings, "wealthy nations have need of hospitals, because fortune subjects them to a thousand accidents." But it was also important to prevent them from generating the kind of culture of dependency found in pre-Reformation England or modern Rome. "Transient assistances," Montesquieu suggested, were better than "perpetual foundations." "The evil is momentary; it is necessary therefore, that the succour should be of the same nature, and that it be applied to particular accidents."[27]

These aspects of monarchy had no place in either the Troglodyte history or its sequel. In the unpublished sequel, stability would depend on either royal example, moral censorship, or punitive taxation once trade and industry had been introduced. Nor, as with Voltaire, did stability depend on the part played by the monarchy itself in maintaining a balance among the assorted components of the social hierarchy. In the concept of monarchy set out in *The Spirit of Laws*, stability would depend upon the maintenance of a clear distinction between a trading and a nontrading sector, with the existing system of venal offices functioning as a bridge between the two, both to stimulate trade and industry and, by doing so, to generate the resources needed to offset the evils associated with infirmity, ignorance, old age, or unemployment. The honour-based principle upon which monarchy depended for its stability implied maintaining a noncommercial, but still open, elite above a thoroughly commercial society. Montesquieu may have

[25] Montesquieu, *SL*, ed. Neumann, bk. 13, ch. 19, 20, 1:218–9, 220. The remark attributed to Montesquieu about financiers can be found in Manon Roland, *Appel à l'impartiale postérité*, 2 vols. (London, 1795), 2:146.

[26] Montesquieu, *SL*, ed. Neumann, bk. 23, ch. 29, 2:25, 26.

[27] Montesquieu, *SL*, ed. Neumann, bk. 23, ch. 29, 2:26.

been reluctant "to examine the justice" of "purchasing honour with gold" and "of thus bartering for money the price of virtue," but he had no hesitation at all in stating that there were "governments where this may be very useful."[28] The prime example was France. The fact that "for two or three centuries" France "has been incessantly increasing in power" was, he wrote with uncharacteristic directness, not to be attributed to fortune, "but to the goodness of its laws."[29] The conclusion (at the end of a chapter entitled "A Singular Reflection") is an indication of the gulf that he had opened up with both of his earlier assessments of the relationship between wealth and virtue. The first followed the line of argument contained in Fénelon's *Telemachus*. The second paralleled Voltaire's evaluation of the English system of government. In *The Spirit of Laws*, Montesquieu opted against both. The best way to see how far he had moved is to follow the gradual emergence of his own conception of monarchy.

Montesquieu's first move was to turn away from the conception of monarchy to be found in Fénelon's *Telemachus*. This idea of monarchy came to be associated very closely with the question of the kind of revolution that the eighteenth century might expect. "Bear in mind, Telemachus," Fénelon had written, "that there are two things which are pernicious to the government of peoples and to which no remedy is almost ever supplied. The first is an unjust and excessively violent authority among kings. The second is luxury, which corrupts manners." The first was treatable, even if the remedy itself had its dangers. Only "a sudden and violent revolution" was capable of restoring a "power that had burst its banks" to "its natural course," even if a "coup" designed to moderate an excess of power "might destroy it completely." But, Fénelon warned, luxury was "almost incurable." Kings, he wrote, might be poisoned by excessive authority, but luxury "empoisons a whole nation."[30] This was why a root-and-branch programme of moral and social reform was needed to eliminate its effects. The detailed programme that Fénelon envisaged was one that continued to resonate right up to the period of the French Revolution and beyond. "One day" in 1793, a former member of the French Convention noted in 1795 with some degree of malice, Robert Lindet (the member of the Committee of Public Safety responsible for overseeing the workings of the maximum imposed on the price of grain and other subsistence goods) was giving a carefully prepared speech to the Convention. "Robespierre, who was sitting beside me, said to me, 'that man there (meaning Lindet) is the Fénelon of the revolution.' "[31] Whether or not Robespierre really did say it, the remark

---

[28] Montesquieu, *SL*, ed. Neumann, bk. 20, ch. 22, 1:327.

[29] Montesquieu, *SL*, ed. Neumann, bk. 20, ch. 22. 1:328.

[30] Fénelon, *Telemachus*, ed. Riley, bk. 17, p. 297.

[31] Michel-Edmé Petit, *Le procès des 31 mai et 2 juin, ou la défense des 71 représentants du peuple* (n.p., n.d., but Paris, 1795), p. 29. The anecdote appears in L. Boivin-Champeaux, *Notices*

was clearly intended to be a compliment. Others were less persuaded. "Louis XIV, with his despotism and his wars, never did as much harm as the counsels of the good Fénelon, the apostle of virtue and human well-being, could have done," wrote the political economist Jean-Baptiste Say a generation later.[32] Both, in their different ways, were still dealing with the question about the relationship between morality and politics that Fénelon had passed on to Montesquieu.

Montesquieu's Troglodyte history was a rehearsal of both Fénelon's presentation of the question and, in the unpublished sequel, of Fénelon's answer.[33] The first, virtuous, Troglodyte community corresponded to Fénelon's description of the pastoral community of Betica. The second, property-based, society corresponded to Fénelon's description of the reformed kingdom of Salentum. The combination of royal example, moral censorship, and punitive taxation contained in the unpublished sequel echoed the drastic reform programme that Fénelon had presented as the only way to revive Salentum once luxury and inequality had taken root. Montesquieu's decision not to include the sequel in the *Persian Letters* was, clearly, a rejection of this kind of programme of reform. But the decision not to publish it may also have been confirmed by his subsequent investigation of the English constitution (interestingly, in its obituary notice on Montesquieu, the British *Annual Register* described the whole published version of the Troglodyte history as "a representation of England").[34] The picture of English luxury, ferocious party-political conflict, and a tax regime beyond the power of any despot that Montesquieu presented in the famous twenty-seventh chapter of book 19 of *The Spirit of Laws* was a graphic illustration of what the conflict between wealth and virtue might look like if it came to be played out in real life. There, however, the peculiar intricacies of the English constitution supplied one kind of solution to the tension between inequality and morality that the unpublished sequel raised, making, as Montesquieu emphasised publicly, a great deal depend on the survival of an uncorrupted Parliament. From this perspective, dropping the sequel meant opting against trying to emulate English society (as

---

historiques sur la Révolution dans le Département de l'Eure (Évreux, 1868), p. 161, and Amand Montier, *Robert Lindet* (Paris, 1899), pp. 72, 244, as well as François Pascal, *L'économie dans la terreur: Robert Lindet 1746–1825* (Paris, SPM, 1999), p. 365. None indicate its source in Petit's pamphlet, which seems to have been signalled for the first time in an anonymous notice in *Annales révolutionnaires* 4 (1911): 385.

[32] Jean-Baptiste Say, *Mélanges et correspondance d'économie politique*, ed. Charles Comte [1834], reprinted in Jean-Baptiste Say, *Cours complet d'économie politique pratique* (Paris, 1843), p. 666. For a fuller examination of Fénelon's presence in eighteenth-century French thought, see the monumental study by Albert Chérel, *Fénelon en France au xviiie siècle* (Paris, 1916).

[33] On the use to which Montesquieu put Fénelon in the Troglodyte history, see Richter, *Political Theory of Montesquieu*, pp. 40–3.

[34] *Annual Register* (1758), p. 240.

Voltaire advocated in his *Philosophical Letters*) without having England's system of government. It meant, instead, opting for a different concept of monarchy, one that was not to be found either in the mythical kingdom of Salentum or in modern Britain. This concept of monarchy was neither a meritocracy tempered by a closely regulated system of private property, nor a frenzied struggle for public favour tempered by an elaborately structured political constitution. It was, instead, a system of government made up of three distinct parts: a king, a set of subordinate, dependent and intermediate powers, and a body of fundamental laws. Together, according to Montesquieu, they had come to make it unnecessary either to have to make a choice between wealth and virtue or to stake political and social stability upon a constitution.

Law's System, the Abbé de Saint-Pierre, and the Grand Design

The underlying assumption—that wealth and virtue pulled in opposite directions—had a long pedigree in ancient and Christian thought. From the point of view that Montesquieu came to adopt, monarchy alone could accommodate the tension between the two. Since, as he also argued, monarchy was modern, this meant that he lined himself up with the supporters of the moderns in the ongoing European culture wars between the ancients and the moderns. But from another perspective, Montesquieu's position was more ambiguous. Here, it was not so much ancient Greece or Rome and the values that they symbolised that stood at odds with Montesquieu's conception of monarchy, but a range of claims about the potential for improvement of modernity itself. In this second argument, Montesquieu was rather less committed to the side of the moderns.[35] *The Spirit of Laws* was, therefore, the product of an engagement with two different arguments, one with the supporters of the ancients, against the idea of reviving the ancient moral virtues and the conditions on which they were based, but another with the supporters of the moderns, against the idea that the modern, postfeudal world of trade and industry housed an unprecedented capacity for promoting human well-being. In the nineteenth century, the two lines of argument were both subsumed under the catchall label of the Enlightenment. But, although the two lines of argument converged on equality as their common outcome, the means that they proposed were still quite different.

[35] The ambiguity was captured quite well, if a bit strongly, by the Prussian minister Bielfeld: "Ce subtil, ce judicieux politique, qui semble n'oser se déclarer ouvertement contre le luxe et l'opulence, ne laisse pas en quelques endroits de son ouvrage, de lancer de traits qui font voir assez qu'un penchant naturel l'entraîne vers le sentiment des anciens à cet égard." Jacob Friedrich von Bielefeld, *Institutions politiques* [1760], new ed., 3 vols. (Leiden and Leipzig, 1768), 1:260.

Put crudely, the first involved levelling down, while the second involved levelling up. If Fénelon's reform programme, with its draconian sumptuary laws and strict agrarian, was the most famous example of the first, Voltaire's many literary works, from the *Henriade* to the *Anti-Machiavel* of 1741, were the most striking example of the second. Neither had any immediate or direct connection with public credit, but aspects of the system devised by the Scottish financier John Law during the period of the Regency lent themselves to both. Law's system was, in the first instance, a debt-reduction scheme that was intended to eliminate the mass of interest-bearing paper issued during the wars of the last years of the reign of Louis XIV. In that sense, it was designed to level down. But the paper currency established by the system was also intended to increase effective demand. In this sense, it was also designed to level up. The system's twin objectives served both to highlight the power available to a government with control over the money supply and to magnify its attractions not only to those (like Fénelon) who took France's postfeudal order to be too modern but also to those (like Voltaire) who took it to be not modern enough. Nor was either side's vision confined to domestic social and political arrangements. As both recognised, these could not be disassociated from the broader subject of international relations.

The "rhapsody" that Sir James Steuart presented in his *Inquiry into the Principles of Political Oeconomy* was the next generation's synthesis of the two lines of argument. It accepted the modernist endorsement of industry and trade, but was designed to confine them to a massively scaled-up version of the reformed kingdom of Salentum. As with Fénelon's original, Steuart's "rhapsody" was a description of a property-based society that was largely self-sufficient because all the resources that it needed to maintain its wealth and power came from within its own territory. Since it did not depend on foreign trade, it was able to avoid the pressure to compete in foreign markets or acquire colonial possessions to maintain domestic prosperity. It would trade for its convenience, not for its survival. Fénelon's disciple, the *chevalier* Andrew Michael Ramsay, spelled out the broader implications of the idea in the preface to the first posthumous edition of *Telemachus*, published in 1715, just after the long War of the Spanish Succession had come to an end. *Telemachus*, he wrote, was a reply not only to the "injustice and irreligion" of Machiavelli and Thomas Hobbes but also to the "more moderate" systems of Hugo Grotius and Samuel Pufendorf.

> It is true, these two modern Philosophers design'd their Labours for the Good of Society, and referr'd almost every Thing to the Happiness of Man, consider'd in a civil Respect. But the Author of *Telemachus* is original, in having join'd the most perfect Politicks to the Ideas of the most consummate Virtue: His grand Principle, which he makes the Foundation of all he teaches is, that the

Whole World is nothing but an universal Republick, and each Nation, as it were, a large Family. From this beautiful and luminous Idea grow what the Politicians call the *Laws of Nature and of Nations*; equitable, generous, and full of Humanity. We no longer look upon each Country as a Part independent of the rest; but upon Mankind as an indivisible Whole.[36]

Ramsay's vision of a world made up of nations, but free from conflict between states, also owed something to an essay by Fénelon on the balance of power, posthumously published in 1719. States whose resources and population were able to grow at home, Fénelon argued there, would be able to increase in influence and power without having to grow abroad. The balance of power could be changed as much from within as from without.[37] Since, as Fénelon also argued in his earlier *Demonstration of the Existence and Attributes of God*, the land was capable of yielding a hundred times more than what was put into it, a productive and populous society would be able to add to the range of resources at its disposal without having to compete with other nations abroad.[38] All these themes reappeared in Ramsay's own *Travels of Cyrus* (first published in 1727), a larger-scale version of *Telemachus* that came to form a bridge between Fénelon's original model and Steuart's later "rhapsody." As Benjamin Franklin's protégé Benjamin Vaughan put it in 1788, "the seeds of all the sentiments, if not all the doctrines of modern political oeconomy," could be found in the precepts contained in *Telemachus*.[39]

The second of the two sets of arguments that *The Spirit of Laws* was designed to counter involved a more positive endorsement of public credit. This set of arguments could be found not only in Voltaire's many works, but also in those produced during the 1730s by a cluster of like-minded writers, including Jean-François Melon, the abbé Jean-Baptiste Dubos, the

[36] Andrew Michael Ramsay, "Discours de la Poésie Épique et de l'Excellence du Poème Télémaque," in Fénelon, *Télémaque* (Amsterdam, 1725), pp. xxxviii–xxxix. This translation is taken from a contemporary English translation, Fénelon, *The Adventures of Telemachus, the Son of Ulysses*, 3rd ed., 2 vols. (London, 1720), pp. xlii–xliv.

[37] See the contemporary translation of [François de Salignac de la Mothe-Fénelon], "Sentiments on the balance of Europe," in *Two Essays on the Balance of Europe* (London, 1720).

[38] François de Salignac de la Mothe-Fénelon, *Démonstration de l'existence de Dieu, tirée de la connaissance de la nature* (Paris, 1713). For the claim about the productivity of the land, see the contemporary English translation, *A Demonstration of the Existence and Attributes of God* (London, 1720), p. 15.

[39] [Benjamin Vaughan], *New and Old Principles of Trade Compared* (London, 1788), p. vii, note. On the superficial similarity between Franklin's thought and Physiocracy, indicative of a common concern with the kind of healthy economy advocated by Fénelon, see Jessica Riskin, *Science in the Age of Sensibility: The Sentimental Empiricists of the French Enlightenment* (Chicago, University of Chicago Press, 2002), pp. 112–6, 134–7.

marquis d'Argenson, and the abbé de Saint-Pierre.[40] Here, the emphasis fell not so much on promoting peace by way of self-sufficiency as upon generating commercial reciprocity under the aegis of a comprehensive system of international agreements and a stable balance of power. If *Telemachus* was an epic that extolled the merits of the ancients, Voltaire's *Henriade* was an epic extolling the merits of the moderns. As Voltaire presented him, France's first Bourbon king had laid the foundations of the territorial, religious, and political stability that had become the platform for the unprecedented spurt in manufacturing and trading capacity that took place in France under the aegis of Louis XIV's minister Colbert.[41] In the vision of the future that Voltaire outlined in the seventh canto of his poem, unified territorial monarchies and the huge potential for trade and industry that they housed were Henri IV's lasting legacy to the modern world. Voltaire drove the message home some fifteen years later in his *Anti-Machiavel*. The fact that it was published under the name and authority of Prussia's king Frederick the Great gave an unusual prominence to its claim that the modern world had an unparalleled capacity to substitute "the spirit of commerce" for "the spirit of conquest."

The juxtaposition of the two phrases first appeared in one of the most influential books about trade published in eighteenth-century France, the *Essai politique sur le commerce* (A Political Essay on Commerce) by Jean-François Melon, published in 1734.[42] Montesquieu had no difficulty in endorsing it, and the fashion-driven concept of trade on which it was based (he and Melon were personal friends, but so, too, were Voltaire and Melon, with Voltaire calling him affectionately "Colbert-Melon" in his correspondence, describing him, too, as "one of the men of the world I respect the most").[43] But he came to have very considerable reservations both about

---

[40] On these individuals, see the various studies by Merle J. Perkins, *The Moral and Political Philosophy of the Abbé de Saint-Pierre* (Geneva, Droz, 1959); "Voltaire's Concept of International Order," *Studies on Voltaire and the Eighteenth Century* 36 (1965); and "Montesquieu on National Power and International Rivalry," *Studies on Voltaire and the Eighteenth Century* 238 (1985): 1–95; Lionel Rothkrug, *Opposition to Louis XIV: The Political and Social Origins of the French Enlightenment* (Princeton, Princeton University Press, 1965); Alfred Lombard, *L'abbé Dubos, un initiateur de la pensée moderne* (Paris, 1913); Thomas E. Kaiser, "The Abbé Dubos and the Historical Defence of Monarchy in Early Eighteenth-Century France," *Studies on Voltaire and the Eighteenth Century* 267 (1989): 77–102; Jean-François Melon, *Opere*, I and II, ed. Onofrio Nicastro and Severina Perona (Sienna and Pisa, 1977 and 1983); Jean-Claude Perrot, *Une histoire intellectuelle de l'économie politique* (Paris, Ecole des Hautes Etudes en Sciences Sociales, 1992), pp. 38–56.

[41] Voltaire, *La Henriade* [1723] (Paris, Garnier, n.d.), canto 7, p. 155.

[42] Jean-François Melon, *A Political Essay upon Commerce* [1734], trans. David Bindon (Dublin, 1738), pp. 138–9.

[43] See Voltaire to Thieriot, 18 November 1736, 4 February 1737, 25 January 1738, in Voltaire, *Correspondance*, ed. Theodore Besterman, 13 vols. (Paris, Pléiade, 1964), 1:797, 841, 997.

Melon's theory of public credit, and about its bearing on his broader theory of trade, when these came to be coupled with a further, even more ambitious, set of claims about modernity's capacity for peace and prosperity. The most wide-ranging version of this latter set of claims was to be found in the voluminous works of Charles-Irénée de Castel, abbé de Saint-Pierre. The length and repetitiveness with which the abbé de Saint-Pierre pursued his theoretical objectives (as well as his commitment to his own, phonetic, system of orthography) have sometimes made it hard to see how much of a connection there was between his system and the less wide-ranging, but more aesthetically or analytically attractive works produced not only by Voltaire and Melon, but also by two other members of the same circle: the abbé Jean-Baptiste Dubos, whose *Histoire critique de l'établissement de la monarchie française dans les Gaules* (A Critical History of the Establishment of the French Monarchy in Gaul) of 1734 was to be one of the targets of *The Spirit of Laws*; and René-Louis de Voyer, marquis d'Argenson, whose *Considérations sur le gouvernement ancien et présent de la France* (Considerations on the Present and Former Government of France) was written at the same time as Voltaire was writing the *Anti-Machiavel*, although it was published only a quarter century later. Together, they amounted to as ambitious and as comprehensive a case for a new European order as Physiocracy was to be a generation later.

The emblem of the new European order was Henri IV's Grand Design.[44] This was a plan devised by the French king and his minister Sully in the early seventeenth century to reorganise the territorial boundaries of the European states in the wake of the Dutch revolt and the failure of Spain's late-sixteenth-century attempt to establish political and religious hegemony in Europe. Its aim was to reduce Europe's many tiny principalities and city-states, particularly in Germany and Italy, to a much smaller number of roughly equally sized and equally endowed territorial states. The result would be a stable international balance of power. With this precondition established, the way would be open to create a permanent system of international arbitration based upon a European Diet made up of representatives of all the redesigned powers. This was the model that the abbé de Saint-Pierre spent his life promoting during the quarter century after the end of the War of the Spanish Succession. By guaranteeing the territorial boundaries and internal political arrangements of all the European states, and by subjecting disputes between them to a system of international arbi-

---

[44] The starting point for a full study of the cult of Henri IV and Sully in the eighteenth century is Marcel Reinhard, *La Légende de Henri IV* (Paris, 1935). I have learned a great deal about the political thought of the 1730s from the work of Isaac Nakhimovsky, "Voltaire, Frederick the Great, and the *Anti-Machiavel* in Historical Context" (M.Phil. diss., Cambridge University, 2002).

tration, it was designed, as the title of Voltaire's book indicated, to put an end to the Machiavellian politics of the past two hundred years and, by doing so, to give the European states a peace dividend that would entrench commerce, not conquest, into their domestic and foreign affairs. The most obvious obstacle to putting the plan into effect was the political character of the process of implementation. No single state had an interest in being the first to sign up to the plan. But the more deep-seated obstacle to its implementation lay in the unequal distribution of territory and resources among the existing European states. Here, it could be argued that the composite structure of the Holy Roman Empire of the German nation was the most formidable obstacle to a stable European balance. The many different parts of which it was made up and the many different legal principles—some Roman, some feudal, some customary—determining the right to rule both the empire itself and any of its single components were open invitations to turn every vacant succession into an occasion for instability. Montesquieu's second change of course was connected to this problem. To Voltaire and his circle, however, the problem itself was an opportunity.

The crisis that developed during the 1730s over the succession to the Holy Roman Empire quickly came to look like a way to overcome the obstacles standing in the way of a peaceful international system. To its critics, the Pragmatic Sanction proposed by the emperor Charles VI to enable his younger daughter, Maria Theresa, to succeed to the imperial throne was an unprecedented departure from established law. Quite apart from the problems that it seemed likely to store up by allowing the throne to pass to a female line and the complications about future imperial marriages and inheritance that this was likely to produce, it also appeared to violate the composite character of the empire itself by presupposing that it was a single unitary entity to be disposed of at its sovereign's will. Well before the War of the Austrian Succession began, it was quite easy to argue that this was an obvious breach of legality.[45] The shaky grounds on which the Pragmatic Sanction rested made the impending crisis look like a golden opportunity to realise Henri IV's Grand Design. This, certainly, was how the abbé de Saint-Pierre welcomed the publication of the *Anti-Machiavel* in 1740. "If, in commenting on the reflections against Machiavelli by Charles Frederick, king of Prussia," he wrote in an extended review of the book,

> I may have cast my eyes on him as most worthy and capable of undertaking and successfully carrying out the marvellous project of Henri IV, king of France, to make peace perpetual, it is simply because I have been able to see the range

---

[45] See, for example, [Anon.], *Réflexions d'un allemand impartial sur la demande de la garantie de la pragmatique impériale* (n.p., 1732), and [Anon.], *Réflexions d'un cosmopolite* (n.p,. n.d.).

and precision of his mind . . . and the goodness and solidity of his maxims in politics and morality.[46]

Events may well have raised a question mark about his judgement, but the abbé de Saint-Pierre was by no means alone in thinking that the Austrian succession crisis was an opportunity to promote regime change in Germany and, by doing so, to move towards a new European order. If the *Anti-Machiavel* of 1740 was the modernising manifesto of the opposition to France's ageing chief minister, Cardinal Fleury, the same idea appeared in François Boureau Deslandes's *Essai sur le commerce et la marine* of 1742 (published, with a lurid preface, in English translation as *An Essay on Maritime Power and Commerce*) and, more memorably, in the marquis d'Argenson's *Considerations on the Present and Former Government of France*. Although it was published only in 1764, d'Argenson wrote it before the beginning of the War of the Austrian Succession. As Voltaire informed him in May 1739, the work was a great improvement upon "the chimerical projects of the good abbé de Saint-Pierre" and far superior to Fénelon's Salentum, "where there were no pastry cooks and only seven styles of clothing." In his eyes, d'Argenson's proposals amounted to an adaptation of the best features of Britain's government to the French system of absolute rule.

> The king with his parliament is the legislator, just as he is here with his council. All the rest of the nation governs itself according to municipal laws, as sacred as those of parliament itself. Love of the law becomes a passion for the people because each individual is interested in its observation. All the highways are kept in good repair, hospitals established and maintained, while commerce flourishes without any need for a decree by the royal council.[47]

Appended to the first and second (1765) editions of the work (but dropped from the third, 1784, edition) was a short essay, programmatically entitled "Essai de l'exercice du tribunal européen pour la France seule. Pour la pacification universelle appliquée au temps courant." The title echoed the wording of the Grand Design, while the essay itself set out to show that France had a unique potential to become the kind of disinterested European hegemon that Henri IV and Sully had envisaged, with the ability to act as "an armed tribunal free from all fear of attack, content with her well-being and concerned solely with that of others."[48] Of all the powers, d'Argenson asserted,

---

[46] Charles-Irénée Castel, abbé de Saint-Pierre, "Réflexions sur l'Anti-Machiavel de 1740," in his *Ouvrajes de politique et de morale*, 16 vols. (Rotterdam, 1739–41), 16:536.

[47] Voltaire to d'Argenson, 8 May 1739, in Voltaire, *Correspondance*, ed. Besterman, 2:173. See also Voltaire to d'Argenson, 21 June 1739, in Voltaire, *Correspondance*, 2:191.

[48] René-Louis de Voyer, marquis d'Argenson, *Considérations sur le gouvernement ancien et présent de la France* (Amsterdam, 1764), p. 318. These first two, posthumous, editions were

only France today is able to play the fine role of universal arbiter. . . . She is in possession of the empire of taste and arts, an advantage she has obtained without seeking it. What other laws is she yet able to give, if not those of wisdom and politics? That is the true universal monarchy. To judge is to govern; to decide with equity should be the sole empire over men.[49]

The phrase sometimes used in private correspondence to describe the kind of international transformation envisaged by the cluster of French modernisers associated with the abbé de Saint-Pierre was "the German revolution."[50] Over a century was to pass before it occurred.

The change of course in Montesquieu's political thinking that took place between the appearance of the *Considerations on the Romans* and the publication of *The Spirit of Laws* was a response to this confident endorsement of modernity's potential. Two features of *The Spirit of Laws* can be taken as indices of the change. Both were highlighted in two of the many summaries of *The Spirit of Laws* that Montesquieu singled out for approval. One was by a Bordeaux merchant named François Risteau. Its concern was to explain Montesquieu's theory of trade and justify his endorsement of Cicero's opinion that the same people should not be both the lords and the factors of the whole earth.[51] To do so, he went about explaining what Montesquieu had meant by dividing trade into two different types, one based on economy and the other based on luxury, and also what he had meant by arguing that trade based on luxury was uniquely suited to monarchy. Risteau's summary (described in the final section of this chapter) points towards the connection between Montesquieu's conception of monarchy and the system of government that the advocates of Physiocracy were later to call "legal despotism." The second account of *The Spirit of Laws* was by a high-placed Florentine administrator-cleric named Stefano Bertolini. It points towards the connection between Montesquieu and Rousseau. "Our author," Bertolini wrote, "seems only to have written his work to oppose the opinions (*sentiments*) of the abbé de Saint-Pierre, just as Aristotle wrote his *Politics* solely to refute Plato." According to Bertolini, the core of the difference between them consisted of their radically different conceptions

---

followed in 1784 by a third, substantially enlarged edition incorporating further material from d'Argenson's unpublished manuscripts. In subsequent footnotes, references to particular editions are indicated by the dates in parentheses.

[49] Argenson, *Considérations* (1764), p. 327.

[50] "Je viens de recevoir dans ce moment une lettre d'un ministre. La révolution de l'Allemagne approche." Nieder-Sachsische Staatsarchiv, Zimmermann papers, MS XLII, 1933, AII, 83, I, fol. 128, Georg-Ludwig Schmid d'Auenstein to Zimmermann, 26 April 1757. See also the letter of 3 May 1757 from Schmid to Zimmermann: "Nous avons prévu une révolution, et je vous avoue que cette prévision m'a fait quitter l'Allemagne."

[51] Montesquieu, *SL*, bk. 20, ch. 4, p. 318.

of the international system. For Montesquieu, it was inconceivable that the system of international arbitration envisaged by Saint-Pierre could work unless its membership consisted of states with the same nature, "especially" he added, "of the republican kind."[52] This principle, Bertolini pointed out, "was entirely the opposite of the abbé de Saint-Pierre's plan for a European Diet."[53] Bertolini himself disagreed with Montesquieu's assessment, presenting a copious list of reasons to support Saint-Pierre's claim that improvements in law, philosophy, political science, the cultural prestige of the French, and the way that "the spirit of commerce" had "extinguished the spirit of conquest" all offered good grounds for thinking that the time for drafting the preliminary articles of a general peace settlement could not be far off.[54] Montesquieu's view lowered the horizons of expectation substantially. It took the world as it was, with its separate sovereign states and an attenuated capacity for avoiding war.

On several occasions Montesquieu singled out Law's system as the common element in the two arguments to which his own political theory was opposed. It was, he indicated, as central to Fénelon's reform programme as to the abbé de Saint-Pierre's peace project. He chose to give the name of Betica, the pastoral community that Fénelon had used as an emblem of a virtuous society with no private property, to the setting of what, in the 142nd of his *Persian Letters* (letter 136 in the first edition), he called "a fragment from an ancient mythologist," but that, in reality, was a satirical account of France's first experiment with a centralised system of public credit. In the satire, Law, here presented as the son of a union between Aeolus, god of the winds, and a Caledonian nymph, had been taught by his father how to capture the wind in bags. Since demand for wind in his own country was not very great, the enterprising bagpiper had travelled to Betica, where, as in Fénelon's mythical community, he found gold glistening everywhere. He embarked upon a campaign to persuade the people of Betica to substitute "the empire of the imagination" for "base metals" and, by doing so, to acquire "riches that will astonish you."[55] But the imagination of the people of Betica was not up to the task, which made coercion and severe punishments necessary to persuade them that wind really was wealth. These, too, turned out to be fruitless. In the end, all that the Caledonian enchanter could accomplish was to make three-quarters of the wealth of Betica disappear altogether.

Putting the Scottish bagpiper in Betica also had a political point. Although there is no reason to think that Fénelon himself ever entertained

---

[52] Montesquieu, *SL*, bk. 9, ch. 2, p. 127.

[53] Stefano Bertolini, "Analyse raisonnée de *l'Esprit des lois*" [1754], published in Montesquieu, *Oeuvres posthumes* (Paris, 1798), pp. 315–6.

[54] Bertolini, *Analyse*, pp. 316–8.

[55] Montesquieu, *LP*, letter 136, p. 515; *Persian Letters*, trans. Healy, letter 142, p. 246.

the project, it was quite usual, particularly in Protestant Europe, to read
Telemachus as a very pointed political allegory and to take the reformed
kingdom of Salentum as a model applicable both to France and to Britain
under a restored Stuart monarchy.[56] Properly reformed, the two countries
would be able to coexist peacefully because most of the causes of conflict
between them would have fallen away. From this perspective, public credit,
as Law envisaged its use, also complemented plans to revive Henri IV's
Grand Design. Its power to stimulate trade and industry, in conjunction
with a more stable international balance, pointed towards the more comprehensive system of commercial reciprocity envisaged by the abbé de
Saint-Pierre (the overlap also occurred in his and the *chevalier* Ramsay's
membership of the famous Entresol Club that met in Paris between 1724
and 1731).[57] Montesquieu never displayed any interest in this kind of project. Where Voltaire played a very active part in promoting French involvement in the War of the Austrian Succession (even drafting the French manifesto supporting Charles Edward Stuart at the time of the Jacobite rising
of 1745), Montesquieu was appalled by French policy.[58] It was, he wrote
privately, "a war that I detest and which the princes of Europe would soon
end, if they were prepared to listen to the requests of their faithful subjects."[59] In his eyes, the strongest supporters of the war—headed by Marshal Belle-Isle, the future war minister and protégé of Cardinal Fleury's
enemy, the keeper of the seals and foreign minister, Germain-Louis
Chauvelin, whom Fleury had succeeded in having dismissed in 1737—were
aiming, grandiosely, to take advantage of the disputed Austrian succession
and use French arms to create a more unified German state as a first step
towards a new European order modelled upon Henri IV's Grand Design.[60]
Belle-Isle, Montesquieu commented in 1742, "is to war what Law was to

---

[56] The connection between Salentum, James II as its misguided ruler Idomeneus, and the
Jacobite cause as the vehicle for carrying out the reform programme commended by Minerva
to Idomeneus was, for example, made explicit in the Rotterdam, 1719, edition of *Telemachus*:
see the scholarly edition of the text, edited by Albert Cahen, 2 vols. (Paris, 1927), 1:xlvi, xlix,
xcviii–xcix and 2:488, note 2.

[57] On this, still mysterious, club, see Nick Childs, *A Political Academy in Paris, 1724–1731:
The Entresol and Its Members* (Oxford, Voltaire Foundation, 2000).

[58] See Laurence L. Bongie, "Voltaire's English, High Treason and a Manifesto for Bonnie
Prince Charles," *Studies on Voltaire and the Eighteenth Century* 171 (1977): 7–29.

[59] "Ne sachant comment faire . . . à cause de ce malheureux embarras de cette guerre, que
je déteste, et que les princes de l'Europe finiraient bientôt, s'il voulaient entendre les requêtes
de leurs fidèles sujets": Montesquieu to Cerati, 19 April 1746, printed in Robert Shackleton,
"Montesquieu's Correspondence," *French Studies* 12 (1958): 330–1.

[60] On Belle-Isle's projections, see François Labbé, "La Rêve Irénique du Marquis de la
Tierce. Franc-maçonnerie, lumières et projets de paix perpétuelle dans le cadre du Saint-
empire sous le règne de Charles VII (1741–1745)," *Francia* 18 (1991): 47–69.

finance."[61] The comparison was not intended to be a compliment. "Mr. Law," he observed in *The Spirit of Laws*, "through ignorance both of a republican and monarchical constitution, was one of the greatest promoters of despotism ever known in Europe."[62] The remark was the direct opposite of Voltaire's claim in 1738 that if the system had succeeded, "the state had certainly been the most vigorous and powerful in the whole world," and, despite its failure, that all the more recent signs of French commercial prosperity were a product of the system. "Though we owe them all to him," Voltaire commented, "we are exceedingly ungrateful to the memory of our benefactor."[63]

Law developed the theory that lay behind his eponymous system at a time when the possibility of a Franco-Spanish union raised the threat of a Bourbon stranglehold upon the medium of international trade. "National Power and Wealth," he announced at the beginning of his *Money and Trade, Considered with a Proposal for Supplying the Nation with Money* (1705),

> consists in numbers of People, and Magazines of Home and Foreign Goods. These depend on Trade, and Trade depends on Money. So to be Powerful and Wealthy in proportion to other Nations, we should have Money in proportion with them; for the best laws without Money cannot employ the People, Improve the Product, or advance Manufacture and Trade.[64]

But control of the existing medium of circulation, gold and silver, lay in the hands of the nations of southern Europe. "Considering the present state of Europe, France and Spain being Masters of the Mines. The other Nations seem to be under a necessity of setting up another Money."[65] That other money, Law claimed, could be generated by the credit of the state rather than possession of mines. Transplanted to France, in the wake of the War of the Spanish Succession, it became the basis of his system.

Law's system was based upon two giant enterprises, a state-backed trading company and a state bank, each with a role in the debt-reduction scheme. The bank would buy all the outstanding interest-bearing debt and issue shares to an equivalent amount. These shares would be available for

---

[61] Montesquieu to Barbot, secretary of the Bordeaux Academy, 9 July 1742, in his *Oeuvres complètes*, 3 vols. (Paris, Editions Nagel, 1950–55), vol. 3, letter 300, p. 1020. Subsequent citations will use the abbreviation Montesquieu, ed. Nagel, followed by the volume, letter, and page number references.

[62] Montesquieu, *SL*, bk. 2, ch. 4, p. 19.

[63] Voltaire, "Of John Law, Melon and Dutot. On commerce and luxury" [1738], reprinted in Voltaire, *Dialogues and Essays, Literary and Philosophical* (Glasgow, 1764), pp. 183–93 (pp. 184–5 for the phrases cited). See, too, Henry C. Clark, ed., *Commerce, Culture, and Liberty: Readings on Capitalism before Adam Smith* (Indianapolis, Liberty Fund, 2003), p. 277.

[64] John Law, *Money and Trade, Considered with a Proposal for Supplying the Nation with Money* [1705] in his *Oeuvres complètes*, ed. Paul Harsin, 3 vols. (Paris, 1934), 1:80.

[65] Law, *Money and Trade*, pp. 104–6.

sale to holders of gold and silver coin and could be used to buy shares in the trading company, which, importantly, could not be bought with metal coin. Consequently two circulating mediums would emerge: gold and silver coin, which could be used to buy bank shares; and the paper of the bank itself, denominated in livres, sous, and deniers, the standard money of account, which would be the only way to buy shares in the trading company. Since the paper of the bank would also be used to pay interest on the debt, owners of debt would be forced to choose either to invest their interest payments in the trading company or to convert their paper back into gold or silver coin. But since the royal government itself no longer had to pay interest on its debts, its need for tax revenue would fall. Consequently, a larger amount of gold and silver coin would remain in circulation, causing a rise in the price of traded goods relative to the metallic currency.

This change in relative values would have two effects. The greater quantity of coin in circulation would produce a rise in the price of traded goods and cereals in particular, generating rising agricultural output and higher living standards. At the same time, the fall in the relative value of gold and silver coin would make conversion from bank paper (denominated in the money of account of livres, sous, and deniers) to coin (consisting of gold and silver louis and écus) run at a loss. But, since shares in the trading company could be purchased with bank paper at par, they would be insulated from the change in the relative values of the metallic currency and traded goods. There was, therefore, a powerful incentive to convert interest payments paid in bank paper into shares in the trading company. Since rising demand for shares in the trading company would increase their value, and since these shares were directly convertible into bank shares, it would then be possible to use the higher-priced shares in the trading company to redeem the bank's paper and gradually liquidate the debt. The system would, thus, work in several, mutually compatible ways. In the first place, it would force the owners of *rentes* and other forms of government debt to become traders, leading, in the long term, to a gradual levelling-out of the social hierarchy in a manner that was a modern (and much less painful) equivalent of an agrarian law. Additionally, by uncoupling the domestic monetary system from the gold and silver coin used in international trade, it would make it easier to escape from the need to put pressure upon the producers of agricultural and manufactured goods to hold down prices and wages at home to maintain the price competitiveness of internationally traded goods abroad. The result (it could be claimed) would be a stable system of free trade purged of the twin banes of self-interested government tampering with the metallic content of the medium of exchange, on the one hand, and of the ruthless regulatory pressure to hold down grain prices in order to maintain low wage costs, on the other. Nations would not find themselves forced to beggar their neighbours; public credit would, instead, allow each nation to become more self-sufficient and to rely on foreign trade purely for the transfer of products that were locally superfluous. Trade would be uncoupled from national survival, leaving nations to compete with one another in a substantially less lethal fashion. Although there might still be winners and losers, the losers would be better off, while the winners' position would be a just measure of their size, population, technical proficiency, and social fairness, so that the resulting world order would rest upon a tight fit between the natural and political endowments of nations.

Law made the point of the system clear by juxtaposing two different "estates," an "estate in annuities" and an "estate in money." An "estate in annuities" served to lock monetary circulation into a vicious circle of interest payments and taxation where the land was simply a form of security, setting a ceiling upon the upper limits of government borrowing. But land was a potential source of great wealth if its products could be drawn into a system of trade.

> One of the first Laws of Government, which is founded on Credit and Circulation, is, to have nothing in a State, at least as the principal Object of its Revenues, but Land and Trade. I look even upon land, not like those who distrust the public, as a safe Harbour in case of Shipwreck, but as one of the Fountains of Commerce, because of its product. An Estate in Annuities is directly opposite to this Principle. The lender stipulates, that his Money shall not be employed in any part of Trade, but settled upon a particular estate in land.[66]

An "estate in money" would unlock the resources of the land by magnifying the scale and intensity of the circulation of its products. By encouraging the state's creditors to opt for a paper currency out of fear and greed (fear of the losses caused by converting interest payments in bank paper into depreciating gold and silver coin, and greed generated by the ease of converting bank shares into the inflated assets of the trading company), the system would leave metallic money to circulate where it was needed (among those who produced the nation's wealth) and transform the kingdom into a rich and powerful nation. "An Estate in Money," Law emphasised, "does not grow by words, but an Estate in Credit increases by it wonderfully."[67] For Montesquieu, however, words were wind, and Law's idea of using public credit to promote prosperity was, as the collapse of the system demonstrated, wind of a terrifying power. His own conception of monarchy was designed to specify the properties of a political system that could be compatible with the modern world without having to rely on either the morality of the ancients or the financial resources of the moderns.

---

[66] [John Law], *The Present State of the French Revenues and Trade, and of the Controversy betwixt the Parlement of Paris, and Mr. Law* (London, 1720), p. 38.

[67] Law, *The Present State of the French Revenues*, p. 42.

FROM *THE PERSIAN LETTERS* TO *THE SPIRIT OF LAWS*

Three of the subjects addressed in *The Persian Letters* suggest the origins of Montesquieu's conception of monarchy. The first was the simple matter of the survival of France's reigning king. "I have seen the young monarch," Rica informed Ibben in the 104th letter. "His life is most precious to his subjects, and no less so to Europe as a whole because of the great troubles which his death might produce."[68] The allusion was to the five-year-old Louis XV, who had inherited the French throne in 1715 after the death of his great-grandfather, Louis XIV. The reason why his death might produce "great troubles" for the whole of Europe was a product of the rules governing the succession to the French throne. These were based upon the principle of what was called representative succession.[69] As the Dutch jurist Hugo Grotius put it in his *Laws of War and Peace* (1625), the French crown was successoral, lineal, and agnatic, thus making the royal succession "representative."[70] The idea of representative succession meant that the heir to the throne could not be chosen by the incumbent king, nor could he be a deceased king's brother, cousin, or uncle (nor, as the pronoun indicates, a woman) but instead had to occupy the appropriate position in the line of succession, coming to the throne either as the first direct male descendant of the previous king or, if there was no direct male heir to the throne, as the first direct male descendant, or representative, of the last deceased heir in the line of lineal, agnatic descent, so that, in legal terms, he was held to be exactly the same person as the previous king.[71] As a legal memorandum of 1716 put it, "in matters of succession, it is not he who is nearest to the throne who succeeds, but he who represents it."[72] But the rules of representative succession created a problem when Louis XIV died. This problem was also the reason why Louis XIV went to such lengths in trying to le-

[68] Montesquieu, *LP*, letter 104, p. 424; *Persian Letters*, trans. Healy, letter 107, p. 179.

[69] The modern historiography of the rules of the royal succession, either in France or elsewhere in Europe, is not very large. By far the most valuable study (but one that does not take the subject into the eighteenth century) is Ralph E. Giesey, "The Juristic Basis of Dynastic Right to the French Throne," *Transactions of the American Philosophical Society*, n.s., 51 (1961): pt. 5. See, too, André Lemaire, *Les lois fondamentales de la monarchie française* (Paris, 1907); Sarah Hanley, ed., *Les Droits des femmes et la loi salique* (Paris, Indigo, 1994); and, for comparison, Paul Sutter Fichtner, *Protestantism and Primogeniture in Early Modern Germany* (New Haven and London, Yale University Press, 1989).

[70] Hugo Grotius, *De jure belli ac pacis* [1625], trans. Jean Barbeyrac as *Le Droit de la guerre et de la paix* (Amsterdam, 1724), bk. II, ch. vii, §§12–37.

[71] Grotius, *De jure belli ac pacis*, trans. Barbeyrac, bk. II, ch. vii, §30, note 7.

[72] "Car en fait de succession, ce n'est pas celui qui est plus proche du trône qui y succède, mais celui qui le représente": B. L., FR 1, *Maximes du droit et d'état, pour servir de réfutation au mémoire qui paraît sous le nom de Monsieur le duc du Maine, au sujet de la contestation qui est entre lui et Monsieur le Duc, pour le rang de prince du sang* (n.p., 1716), p. 12.

gitimise his bastard sons (even being willing to countenance the argument that polygamy, not monogamy, was the natural human state, thus giving the sovereign, not nature, the right to determine a child's legitimacy). As Rica's letter presupposed, the rules of representative succession meant that if the boy king Louis XV were to die without an heir, then the French throne would go to Philip V of Spain (1683–1746), the second son and only surviving representative of Louis de France (1661–1711), Louis XIV's dead son and heir, thus reopening the prime cause of the War of the Spanish Succession, the huge European war with which the eighteenth century had begun.

The subject of war came immediately before Rica's observation about Louis XV. "In one of your letters," wrote Rhedi to Usbeck in the 102nd letter, "you have said much of the sciences and the arts cultivated in the west. You may regard me as a barbarian, but I am not convinced that the utility drawn from them compensates men for the evil purposes to which they are continually put."[73] Applying both the sciences and the arts to war had brought the age of urban militias to an end. No citizen-militia, Rhedi continued, was likely to be able to hold out against the "bombs" used in modern warfare, while the "large bodies of regular troops" on which princes had come to rely had also given them a new power to suppress their subjects. As Rhedi described them, the broader implications of these developments foreshadowed the later assessment of the "new distemper" that had spread over Europe that Montesquieu was to set out in chapter 17 of book 13 of *The Spirit of Laws*. The combination of bombs, standing armies, and defunct militias had, Rhedi wrote, "taken freedom away" from all the peoples of Europe, while gunpowder's ability to ensure that even the most heavily fortified emplacements could still be overrun meant that no place could be said to be an asylum from injustice and violence. "I still tremble," Rhedi concluded, "at the thought that ultimately someone will succeed in discovering some secret that will make it even quicker to kill men by destroying whole peoples and nations."[74]

If Rhedi's speculations look as if they may have given Rousseau his cue for his first major publication, the ninety-seventh letter supplied the connection between the two subjects. "Who would think," Rica informed Rhedi, "that a kingdom which is the most ancient and powerful in Europe would be governed for over ten centuries by laws that had not been made for it? If the French had been conquered, this would not be difficult to understand. But the French themselves were the conquerors. They have abandoned the old laws made by their first kings in the general assemblies of the nation and, what is even more peculiar, the Roman laws that they

---

[73] Montesquieu, *LP*, letter 102, pp. 416–7; *Persian Letters*, trans. Healey, letter 105, p. 174.
[74] Montesquieu, *LP*, letter 102, p. 416; *Persian Letters*, trans. Healey, letter 105, pp. 174–5.

adopted in their place were partly made already or were partly drafted by emperors who were contemporary with their own legislators."[75] They had then gone on to add a "new kind of servility" to this deference to the outside world by adopting all the papal constitutions and making them a further part of their law. When Montesquieu wrote *The Persian Letters*, the thorny question of Philip V's right to the French throne if Louis XV were to die without an heir was the most striking example of this strange process of legal osmosis. For the idea of representative succession was usually taken to be Roman in origin, even if it could also sometimes be associated with scripture. In this latter rendition, the right of representation was a right that God had given to Adam to continue, sexually, the work of creation.[76] More usually, however, it was taken to be a product of the Roman law and the way that a Roman custom designating a patrician by his (or her) right to be represented by a funeral image had come to be associated with the inheritance rights of a more or less extensive number of kin who, because of the funeral custom, were the literal representatives of the defunct. Although the right of representation looked as if it favoured equality, it could also be claimed that it worked in the opposite way ("the ideas of the *sameness* of the person of the *successor* and the *deceased* among the Romans, along with that of *inheritance*, were fatal to equality," wrote the Neapolitan republican Vincenzio Russo in 1799).[77] What was certain, however, was that originally it had nothing to do with monarchy. It was a legal fiction that, under different interpretations during the period of the Roman Empire, had been applied to any number of potential heirs, either direct or collateral, in both the male and female lines.[78] It had no intrinsic connection either to the French royal succession or, still less, to indivisible inheritance in an exclusively male line, the principle that was the cornerstone of the famous French Salic laws. But centuries of legal scholarship and recurrent polemic had consecrated both as distinctive features of the French monarchy, serv-

---

[75] Montesquieu, *LP*, letter 97, p. 404; *Persian Letters*, trans. Healey, letter 100, p. 167.

[76] In this, vaguely Christian, rendition, the "droit de représentation" was an individual natural right "que les hommes ne peuvent mettre en commun dans la masse des pouvoirs qui résultent de l'association" because it was a right that "la première créature humaine reçut de son auteur lorsqu'il la substitua à sa place pour propager cette espèce qu'il venait de créer": Louis-Ramond de Carbonnières, *Opinion énoncée à la société de 1789 sur les loix constitutionnelles* (Paris, 1791), p. 18.

[77] Vincenzio Russo, *Pensieri politici* [1799], reprinted by the Biblioteca Nazionale Vittor Emmanuele III and the Fondazione Giangiacomo Feltrinelli (Naples and Milan, 2000), pp. 52–3.

[78] See the presentation of the concept in the context of French customary and civil law in François Guyne, *Traités de la représentation du double lien et de la règle "Paterna Paternis, Materna Maternis" par rapport à toutes les coutumes de la France* [1698] (Paris, 1773).

ing to make it, as it was standardly described, successoral, lineal, and ag-natic.[79] But quite why it had acquired these qualities was not entirely clear.

Montesquieu's interest in the French afterlife of the Roman law was a recurrent theme of all his subsequent major works, including *The Spirit of Laws*. It led, ultimately, to his unusual conception of both the nature and principle of monarchy and, by extension, to an explanation of why inequal-ity was, in a fundamental sense, built into monarchy in a way that was not the case in either a republic or a despotism. In the final analysis, it was this that served to separate Montesquieu from Voltaire. Montesquieu's explana-tion of how monarchy and inequality had come to be connected seems to have developed out of thinking about the potentially perverse effects of the rules governing the French royal succession during the period of the Regency and the possibility that these might give rise to a major European war. This, highly fortuitous, possibility was the exact opposite of what the rules in question were supposed to achieve. The great advantage of the rules governing the French royal succession was that they took the right to nominate a successor out of the hands of the reigning sovereign and, at the same time, eliminated the possibility of conflict between rival claimants to a vacant throne. If an incumbent king were to die without a direct male heir, the principle of representation made it possible to identify a single rightful candidate to fill his place. As a result, the French monarchy was free from the kind of succession conflict that recurrently bedevilled the politics of many other European states, particularly in the elective monar-chy of Poland, but also in the despotic monarchy of Russia, where the reigning czar had the right to nominate his or her own successor.[80] But the advantage became a major problem in the peculiar circumstances created by Louis XIV's death. If the young Louis XV were to die without an heir, then, according to the rules of representative succession, Philip V of Spain was his only eligible replacement. This, however, had been emphatically ruled out under the provisions of the Utrecht peace settlement of 1713. The potential for war raised by this possibility formed the background to a number of related conflicts during the period of the Regency of the duc d'Orléans between 1715 and 1723. The danger of a possible replay of the War of the Spanish Succession (as a War of the French Succession) raised the question of whether it might be necessary to drop the rules governing the royal succession if Louis XV were to die. But this raised the further question of who had the right to decide to do so, and, if the established

[79] See Giesey, "The Juristic Basis of Dynastic Right," pp. 24–5 and passim.

[80] The case of Russia was an indication of the problems that might arise if, as Hobbes had argued in his *Leviathan*, ch. xix, the incumbent sovereign could nominate his or her successor. On this aspect of Hobbes's thought, see Thomas Hobbes, *Writings on Common Law and He-reditary Right*, ed. Alan Cromartie and Quentin Skinner (Oxford, Oxford University Press, 2005), especially at pp. 171–3.

rules no longer applied, what the alternatives might be. The cluster of conflicts that erupted in France after 1715—over the provisions of Louis XIV's last will and testament; over the standing of the dukes and peers (including the princes of the royal blood) in the parlement of Paris; over the rights and powers of the parlements themselves; over the financial legacy of Louis XIV's wars and John Law's debt-reduction system; and over the source of the rights and powers associated with the office of the Regency itself—were all connected to this explosive issue.[81] The welter of pamphlets to which they gave rise soon showed how difficult it was to find an authoritative solution.

The practical and theoretical questions generated by the succession problem came to a head at the time of the Cellamare conspiracy of 1718. This conspiracy (named after its somewhat distracted prime mover, Antonio Joseph del Guidice, prince de Cellamare, the Spanish ambassador to France) was an unsuccessful attempt by a number of highly placed nobles, mainly belonging to the circle associated with the duchesse du Maine— the wife of one of Louis XIV's two surviving bastard sons—to organise an armed insurrection against the Regent. This rebellion, the conspirators hoped, would begin in the province of Brittany and, with Spanish support, would spread over enough of the kingdom to force the duc d'Orléans to resign the Regency, leaving the way open for an assembly of the Estates-General of the kingdom to put an end to the Quadruple Alliance of France, Britain, the United Provinces, and the Empire, and to make Philip V of Spain Regent of France. Thus, in the event of a vacant succession, Philip would be able to secure his legitimate right to the French throne.[82] The conspiracy—and the year-long war with Spain that it precipitated—raised a number of questions about the rules governing the royal succession because of the wider implications of the four related issues from which it arose. The first was whether Philip V had lawfully renounced his rights to

---

[81] Despite many more recent publications, the best history of the Regency is still, in many respects, Pierre-Édouard Lémontey, *Histoire de la régence et de la minorité de Louis XV* [1816], 2 vols. (Paris, 1832). The best recent overview of the period can be found in Jones, *The Great Nation*, ch. 2.

[82] The conspirators' proclamations were reprinted in Jean-Baptiste-René Robinet, *Dictionnaire universel des sciences moral, économique, politique et diplomatique, ou Bibliothèque de l'homme d'état et du citoyen*, 30 vols. (London, 1772–83), vol. 11 (London, 1779), pp. 93–9. On the conspiracy, see Jean-François Marmontel, *Oeuvres posthumes. Régence du duc d'Orléans*, 2 vols. (Paris, 1805), 1:400–1, 406–18; 2:101–54; Henri Leclercq, *Histoire de la Régence pendant la minorité de Louis XV*, 3 vols. (Paris, Honoré Champion, 1923), 2:255–69, 326–48; and, most recently, James D. Hardy, Jr., *Judicial Politics in the Old Regime: The Parlement of Paris during the Regency* (Baton Rouge, Louisiana State University Press, 1967), pp. 145–6; Harold A. Ellis, *Boulainvilliers and the French Monarchy: Aristocratic Politics in Early Eighteenth-Century France* (Ithaca and London, Cornell University Press, 1988), p. 117.

the French throne.[83] The second was whether the status of certain French provinces, notably the province of Brittany, meant that the provisions of the Utrecht treaty had no standing without ratification by the French Estates-General. The third was whether one of the clauses of Louis XIV's last will and testament legitimating his two surviving bastard sons, the duc du Maine and the comte de Toulouse, had any standing as a law of the state.[84] The fourth was whether the nation, represented by the Estates-General, had a right to determine the answer to the first three questions if Louis XV were to die before he had produced an heir. This last issue—the question of who, in the last analysis, had the right to decide how the succession might be determined—intersected with the separate but related matter of French policy towards the Stuart Pretender's claims to the British throne because of the obvious parallel between Philip V's putative rights to the French throne and the Jacobite challenge to the British Parliament's decision to transfer the succession to the United Kingdom's throne to the house of Hanover. Encouraged by the new star of Spanish diplomacy, Cardinal Alberoni, and aiming to feed upon the hardship and rancour associated with the Utrecht peace treaty, the Cellamare conspirators seem, in their wilder moments, to have hoped that all these questions could be settled in a way that amounted to a reverse replay of Louis XIV's dream of a union of the Bourbon crowns of France and Spain, with a revived Estates-General restored to its traditional place within the government of the kingdom and with a revitalised French monarchy standing at the head of a huge colonial empire, turning a rich, powerful, politically regenerated France into the secular guardian of a Catholic Europe.

If the Utrecht settlement ruled out applying the rules of representative succession should Louis XV die, the Cellamare conspiracy ruled out recourse to the Estates-General as an alternative source of a legitimate decision about the future possession of the French throne. This left open the question of who had the right to decide a solution and, if a decision were needed, where the ultimate source of political legitimacy and obligation was to be found. One answer was to refer the decision to the parlement of Paris.

---

[83] On the background to the question, see Joseph Klaits, *Printed Propaganda under Louis XIV: Absolute Monarchy and Public Opinion* (Princeton, Princeton University Press, 1976), pp. 246–72; Kaiser, "The abbé Dubos and the Historical Defence of Monarchy."

[84] On the background to this issue, see Claire Saguez-Lovisi, *Les lois fondamentales au xviiie siècle. Recherches sur la loi de dévolution de la couronne* (Paris, Presses universitaires de France, 1983); Henri Morel, "Les 'droits de la nation' sous la régence," in *La Régence*, Centre aixois d'études et de recherches sur le dix-huitième siècle (Paris, Armand Colin, 1970), pp. 249–62; Sarah Hanley, "The Monarchic State in Early Modern France: Marital Regime, Government and Male Right," in Adrianna E. Bakos, ed., *Politics, Ideology and the Law in Early Modern Europe: Essays in Honor of J.H.M. Salmon* (Rochester, University of Rochester Press, 1994), pp. 107–26.

"Would you deny," wrote the author of one pamphlet, "that the parlement of Paris, made up of its magistrates and the peers and princes of the blood, is not like the representative body of the nation and that it cannot decide both the Regency and the Crown?"[85] If this was a rather parochial solution to a problem that had as much to do with international relations as with French domestic politics, the alternative was to invoke the rights of mankind. "Is it not more fitting to nature and right reason," wrote the author of another pamphlet, "to consider ourselves to be one single family, in which, unhappily, the vices and diversity of opinions have indeed caused some small divisions." Since these were not strong enough to put an end to "all friendship and commerce," the arrangements made in "smaller particular associations" were "still relative to the general society of all mankind."[86] It followed from this that humanity's right to peace had to prevail over Philip V's claim to the French throne. A third answer injected a further, more spiritual dimension into the argument, emphasising the special status of monarchy and the providential order to which all governments belonged.

> Europe once, for a long time, rightly feared that the house of Bourbon or the kings of Spain aspired to universal monarchy. God separated and spread the house of Bourbon to make it serve against itself to establish a just balance in Europe, turning the evil that alarmed all Europe into one of the principal foundations of public security and general peace.[87]

This strong emphasis upon divine providence (a prominent feature of the political theory of the Jansenist circles in which the pamphlet originated) made it easier to argue that human laws were subject to what the pamphlet's author called the "spirit of the laws." From this perspective, claims that Philip V had renounced the French throne without the opportunity to freely consider his obligations to the French people, or that his renunciation failed to cancel his natural place in the line of the succession, were irrelevant. Specifying the rights and obligations of princes, the pamphlet argued, was not simply a matter of asserting that "princes never keep bourgeois accounts," or that it is "unworthy of them to act for lucre or damages,

[85] [Guillaume Plantavit de la Pause de Margon], *Lettres de Monsieur Filtz-Moritz sur les affaires du temps et principalement sur celles d'Espagne sous Philippe V et les intrigues de la princesse des Ursins, traduites de l'anglois par Monsieur de Garnesai*, 2nd ed. (Amsterdam, 1718), p. 291.

[86] Claude Thémiseul de Saint-Hyacinthe, *Entretiens dans lesquels on traite des entreprises de l'Espagne, des prétentions de Mr. Le chevalier de Saint George et de la renonciation de sa majesté catholique* (The Hague, 1719), pp. 284–5.

[87] "L'Europe avoit craint avec sujet autrefois, et pendant longtemps que la maison de Bourbon, ou les rois d'Espagne, n'aspire à la monarchie universelle. Dieu a séparé et répandu la maison de Bourbon pour la faire servir contre elle-même, au juste équilibre de l'Europe; et du mal dont toute l'Europe étoit alarmé, il en a fait un des principaux fondements de la sûreté publique et de la paix générale": [Pierre Secret], *Conférences d'un anglois et d'un allemand sur les lettres de Filtz-Moritz* (Cambrai, 1722), p. 43.

like ordinary individuals," or that "they always give with open hands every time it is necessary to supply the needs of the state."[88] However true all these princely qualities might be, they served merely to describe rather than explain the status of kings. The reason why it was possible to say, "as the poet said, that 'their state is their son and their crown is their daughter' " was that the crowns held by princes came to them by way of laws. "It is not nature and blood that gives right to the crown of France or to any other thing that is in the world. . . . Nature makes all men equal. The law raises some and abases others."[89] The efficacy of a law was a result of the broader, providential system to which it belonged. Putting it this way, the pamphleteer emphasised, meant taking the law according to "the spirit of the law" and accepting the fact that, in the exceptional circumstances that might be created by Louis XV's death, the ordinary rules governing the succession to the French throne could not be applied.[90]

The phrase reappeared as the title of Montesquieu's most famous book. But it did so without the strongly providential undertone, based on the words of 2 Corinthians 3:6, that gave the phrase its resonance in Jansenist biblical scholarship (God, the passage ran, "hath made us able ministers of the New Testament; not of the letter, but of the spirit; for the letter killeth, but the spirit giveth life").[91] A number of further reasons kept the related subjects of the royal succession, law, and war alive well after it had become clear that Louis XV was likely to live long into adulthood. Of these, the most important was the looming dispute over the succession to the Holy Roman Empire and the pressure that it seemed likely to generate in France to embark upon a war leading to the implementation of Henri IV's Grand Design. "If one looks at the history books," Montesquieu wrote in his *Reflections on Universal Monarchy*, "one can see that for four hundred years it has not been war that has made the great changes in Europe, but marriages, successions, treaties, edicts; in short, Europe changes and has changed by virtue of civil arrangements."[92]

The recurrent domestic and international conflicts generated by the succession problem, and the wide but inconclusive range of answers given to

---

[88] [Secret], *Conférences*, pp. 152–3.

[89] [Secret], *Conférences*, p. 177.

[90] [Secret], *Conférences*, p. 178.

[91] For an example of Jansenist usage, see chapter xi of Jean Domat's prefatory *Treatise of Laws* entitled "Of the nature and spirit of laws and their different kinds": Jean Domat, *The Civil Law in its Natural Order*, 2 vols. (London, 1722), 1:xxvii.

[92] "Si l'on se rappelle les Histoires, on verra que ce ne sont point les guerres qui depuis quatre cents ans ont fait en Europe les grands changements; mais les Mariages, les Successions, les Traités, les Édits; enfin, c'est par des dispositions civiles que l'Europe change et a changé": Montesquieu, "Réflexions sur la Monarchie Universelle" [1734], in his *Oeuvres complètes*, ed. Caillois, 2:19–38 (p. 21).

the questions about political allegiance and entitlement that arose both during the period of the Regency in France and in the later wars of the Polish and Austrian successions, form a bridge between Montesquieu's description of the problem in the *Persian Letters* and the broader subject-matter of *The Spirit of Laws*. Repeated clashes between civil and political laws, or between domestic legal arrangements and the wider panoply of international treaties and alliances to which states were also, in some sense, subject, raised obvious questions about the nature and content of the generic term "law." Events could always give rise to exceptional cases. The difficulty was to find a way to deal with them without either obliterating established distinctions between different kinds of law or running the risk of the perverse effects produced by applying the wrong kind of law to the case at hand. The fact that the death of a human being (like Louis XV) could have a bearing on something that was not human (like a state), or that laws pertaining to the inheritance of property could have quite different effects when it came to the inheritance of thrones, made the problem of identifying and disentangling the different kinds of cases to which different kinds of law might apply a matter of more than purely theoretical interest. From this perspective, it might be possible to claim that *The Spirit of Laws* was simply an elaborate exercise in casuistry or, perhaps, an extended application of the Ramist logic often used to identify the kind of case to which a particular type of entity could be said to belong, and what, in the light of this, the appropriate course of action ought to be.[93] But the almost frantic determination that the old, nearly blind Montesquieu displayed in bringing his last major work to an end, and the care that he took to ensure that the published version would include two, hastily written, final books, both dealing with what he called the "theory of the feudal laws among the Franks" (completed only in the summer of 1748 after the rest of the manuscript had been finished and corrected for publication), are indications of something more. Even if, as Montesquieu wrote despairingly, shortly before he came to the end of the whole twenty-year odyssey, his book "could survive without them," the final struggle to complete the last two books of *The Spirit of Laws* points towards something fundamental about the historical dimension of the whole massive intellectual enterprise.

One clue to the significance of this historical dimension can be found in two quotations from the work of an early-eighteenth-century Neapolitan jurist, Gian Vincenzo Gravina, that Montesquieu gave in the third chapter

---

[93] For indications of the significance of Ramist logic in eighteenth-century thought, see Stephen H. Daniel, *The Philosophy of Jonathan Edwards: A Study in Divine Semiotics* (Bloomington, Indiana University Press, 1994), and his "The Ramist Context of Berkeley's Philosophy," *British Journal for the History of Philosophy* 9 (2001): 487–505.

of the very first book of *The Spirit of Laws*.[94] Montesquieu chose to para-
phrase Gravina's *Origines Juris Civilis* very prominently in his initial description of states as entities made up of both a union of strengths and a
union of wills. "The united strength of all individuals," he reported Gravina as having "well" observed, "constitutes what we call the body politic."
"The strength of individuals," he added a few lines further on, "cannot be
united without a conjunction of all their wills. The conjunction of those
wills, as Gravina again very justly observes, is what we call the civil state."[95]
At first sight, it is not clear why Montesquieu should have chosen to use
Gravina to make a point that could be found in almost any contemporary
treatise on civil or natural jurisprudence, including what was probably the
best-known work of them all, Jean Barbeyrac's French translation of Samuel Pufendorf's *Law of Nature and Nations*.[96] But what Montesquieu seems
to have noticed was that Gravina, in his *De Romano Imperio* (published as
part of his *Origine Romani Juris* in 1713), had assigned the two types of
unity to two separate agencies, the emperor and the Senate, so that the
government of the Roman Empire could be said to have consisted of a
single system made up of two distinct parts. This, according to Gravina,
was the reason why the government of the Roman Empire was different
from the unitary power of an absolute monarch.

> For the Romans there was a great difference between creating a king and an
> emperor, specifically that an emperor draws his majesty from the people while
> a king takes it away.[97]

Creating a king, he stated, entailed "directly conferring all the power of
the people and the whole public will" upon him, making him an "absolute
and independent master." But this concentration of power was, Gravina
argued, inherently unstable. "If the people wants to be rid of him, it is
obliged to overturn the whole civil state and found a new republic."[98] The
position of an emperor was not the same. "Since they are cloaked in the
majesty of the Senate and the people, without taking it away from them, it
was always possible to take away the empire or their lives if they were to

[94] Montesquieu's notes on Gravina have, regrettably, disappeared. He seems to have read
him in the late 1720s or early 1730s as part of his preparation for writing the *Considerations*:
see Françoise Weil, "Les lectures de Montesquieu," *Revue d'histoire littéraire de la France* 57
(1957): 494–514.

[95] Montesquieu, *SL*, bk. 1, ch. 3, p. 8; ed. Neumann, 1:6.

[96] "C'est de cette union de volontés et de forces que résulte le corps politique": Samuel
Pufendorf, *Le Droit de la nature et des gens*, trans. Jean Barbeyrac, 2 vols. (Amsterdam, 1712),
VII, ii, 5, 2:230, as noticed by Mark H. Waddicor, *Montesquieu and the Philosophy of Natural
Law* (The Hague, Martinus Nijhoff, 1970), p. 96, note 99.

[97] This citation is from the French translation, published as Jean-Vincent Gravina, *Esprit
des loix romaines*, 3 vols. (London, 1766), 2:271–2.

[98] Gravina, *Esprit des loix romaines*, 2:272.

abuse their power. This could be done without any change to the republic."[99] As an account of Gravina's work published in 1762 in the *Journal Encyclopédique* stated, Gravina had elaborated on a phrase—*Imperator erat in Republica*—used by the fifteenth-century French civil jurist Nicolas Cujas to show how the authority and majesty of the Roman republic continued under the empire, investing imperial power with a stability and durability that it would not otherwise have had. As Gravina had put it,

> Augustus, in uniting in his person the power of the Tribunes, the Pontificate, the Censorship, the title of Prince and Father of the country, as well as the right of relations with the Senate, took to himself, but did not take away (*de sumpserat, non assumpserat*) the majesty of the Senate and Roman people.[100]

As a result, "the title of Emperor was a purely military title" enabling its holder "to act against the external enemies of the state," while "all the civil power" continued to be available to the magistracies with which the emperor had been invested, but that existed independent of his person. This, Gravina claimed, meant that "the authority attached to the title of Emperor had nothing in common either with that given by the title of dictator . . . or that given by royalty."

> In a word, the Prince *was* in the Republic, whose existence, authority and powers were independent of the Prince who, for that reason, never swore an oath on his assumption of the Empire.[101]

This "political paradox," as the author of Gravina's intellectual biography put it in 1762, equipped the Roman emperors with a "double majesty" made up of both the authority of the republican magistracies and the military force of the imperial army.[102] Together they amounted to the union of wills and the union of strength that, in *The Spirit of Laws*, Montesquieu was to associate with Gravina.

The Inheritance of Property and the Inheritance of Thrones

Montesquieu repeated Gravina's dualism but dropped its association with Rome. If, according to Gravina, the government of the Roman Empire was made up of two distinct parts, then Rome's history seemed to indicate that the relationship between a residual republican government and armed imperial force was a source of weakness, not strength. But the idea of a

---

[99] Gravina, *Esprit des loix romaines*, 2:273.
[100] *Journal Encyclopédique*, December 1762, p. 17.
[101] *Journal Encyclopédique*, December 1762, p. 18.
[102] *Journal Encyclopédique*, December 1762, p. 18.

single system made up of two distinct parts could be applied to the moderns in a rather different way. As Montesquieu went on to show, much of the difference had to do with hereditary property and the part that it played in giving monarchy its distinctive nature. This insight allowed Montesquieu to transfer Gravina's idea to the Germanic peoples who had destroyed the Roman Empire and whose initial social, legal, and military arrangements were the real source of modern monarchy. He seems to have decided to do so by the time that he had finished writing his own Roman history and had begun to turn his attention to Rome's northern conquerors.[103] He had already made it clear, in his *Considerations on the Causes of the Greatness of the Romans and Their Decline*, that the Roman system of government during both the republic and the empire was, in fact, a unitary system, and that it was this that was the ultimate cause of the empire's failure to become a proper monarchy once the republic began to grow. The idea was given particular prominence in a review of the work written by one of Montesquieu's friends, the Jesuit Louis-Bertrand Castel, which he submitted to Montesquieu for correction before its publication in the *Journal de Trévoux* in 1734. As Castel informed Montesquieu in a letter accompanying the draft of his review, "I reduced everything to the idea of a centre, which I certainly felt was what had guided you everywhere."[104] The review itself underlined the point. "A centre is no more than a point to a political as well as to a speculative thinker," it announced, "but it is an energising point, like the focal point of all the rays spreading outwards from the most vast circumference." Rome had been such a focal point from its very foundation. "Romulus, in founding it, established a single centre for the whole universe," a centre that was aptly immortalised by the two words *urbis et orbis*.[105] But the unity that was the cause of Rome's greatness ultimately became the source of its downfall. As the republic gave way to the empire, the centre not only began to lose its purchase over the periphery, but also began to change into a "vague and shapeless chaos, a tumultuous mixture of every mind, every idea, every sort of manner, all the vices and all the follies of all of the universe" until it began to disappear itself.[106] As Castel concluded, "like an overextended vortex, it could only revert back into a multitude of vortices" until, as the centre of the empire shifted from province to province, it came to form "no more than a sequence of short-

---

[103] "Le seul reproche qu'on puisse faire à M. de Montesquieu est d'avoir voulu tout expliquer par la conquête," noted one of Napoleon's house intellectuals, Joseph Fiévée, quite perceptively in 1809: see Joseph Fiévée, *Des intérêts et des opinions pendant la révolution* (Paris, 1809), p. 19.

[104] Castel to Montesquieu (May 1734), in Montesquieu, ed. Nagel, vol. 3, letter 244, p. 965.

[105] *Journal de Trévoux* 134 (June 1734): 1030–67 (1031–2)

[106] *Journal de Trévoux* 134 (June 1734): 1054–5.

lived vortices, presaging permanent scission and absolute excentricity," before disappearing altogether, just as the Rhine, in Montesquieu's words,
disappears into the ocean like a tiny stream.[107]

If, according to Montesquieu, Rome's centralised system was the cause
of both its rise to greatness and its ultimate failure to evolve into a proper
monarchy, the system of government that had developed out of the fall
of the Roman Empire had a less unitary character. He made it clear, in
the *Considerations*, that there was a radical difference between the Roman
Empire and the disaggregated system of fiefs out of which the monarchies
of modern Europe had developed. "It might perhaps be objected," he
stated, "that empires founded on the laws of fiefs have never been durable
or powerful."

> But nothing in the world is more different from one another than the plan of
> the Romans and that of the Barbarians. To put it in a word: the former was the
> work of strength; the latter of weakness. In the first, subjection was extreme; in
> the second, independence was just as pronounced. In the countries conquered
> by the German nations, power was in the hands of the vassals; right alone was
> in the hands of the prince. It was exactly the opposite with the Romans.[108]

The paradoxical implication was that an empire founded on the law of fiefs
(where "power was in the hands of the vassals, right alone in the hands of
the prince") had a potential for durability and power that rivalled, if it did
not surpass, the Roman Empire because, unlike the latter, it genuinely did
house a capacity for avoiding the dangers of centralised decision-making
that, as Montesquieu was to emphasise in *The Spirit of Laws*, was common
to both republican and despotic forms of rule.

Montesquieu's characterisation of monarchy involved three elements: a
monarch, a number of intermediate powers, and a set of fundamental laws.
At first sight, it is not easy to see how any of the three could have come
into being without having been created by one of the others. It is also
clear, however, that claiming that one of the three was responsible for the
existence of the other two would undermine the delicate combination of
the whole. The explanation had, therefore, to be historical. This was what
Pierre-Louis Roederer seems to have noticed in the *Conversation between
Several Celebrated Philosophers on Monarchical and Republican Governments*
that he published in 1797. In it, he had "Montesquieu" claim that the fundamental laws that served to distinguish monarchy from despotism were
the work of the people.[109] Montesquieu himself, however, never made any-

---

[107] *Journal de Trévoux* 134 (June 1734): 1056, 1062.

[108] Montesquieu, *Considérations sur les causes de la grandeur des romains et de leur décadence*
[1734], ed. Jean Ehrard (Paris, Garnier-Flammarion, 1968), ch. 6, p. 69.

[109] "Dans la monarchie, un seul commande, il est vrai, mais suivant des lois fondamentales,
qui, étant l'ouvrage du people, ne peuvent lui être contraires": Pierre-Louis Roederer,

thing like so blunt an assertion in *The Spirit of Laws*. But the claim can be substantiated through a tracking of the sequence of changes that, according to Montesquieu, led to the transformation of the original Salic laws from a set of customary arrangements affecting the ownership and inheritance of small plots of land adjoining the mud-and-wattle huts belonging to the Frankish shepherds into the combination of rules affecting the inheritance of fiefs and the inheritance of thrones that served to give monarchy its nature. From this perspective, Roederer was right. The fundamental laws that made monarchy different from despotism were the work of the people. But they were not, originally, fundamental to monarchy in any obvious sense. They had, instead, acquired their character during the course of a complicated sequence of historical turning points that led, ultimately, towards the more recognisably modern incarnation of the Salic laws as the basis of the hereditary, lineal, and successive character of the French monarchy in an exclusively male line. The same kind of piecemeal historical causation applied to monarchy as a whole.

At some time between the completion of the *Persian Letters* and the publication of *The Spirit of Laws* Montesquieu seems to have come to see how to assign a discrete set of origins to each of the component parts of his conception of monarchy. By doing so, he was able to avoid committing himself either to a unitary model of political society or to a single starting point as the ultimate source of the attributes and capabilities of modern monarchy. The result was that he was able to circumvent the rival accounts of the origins and nature of royal authority that had been set out in 1727 by the comte de Boulainvilliers in his *Histoire de l'ancien gouvernement de la France* (A History of the Ancient and Former Government of France) and in 1734 by the abbé Jean-Baptiste Dubos in his *Histoire critique de l'établissement de la monarchie française dans les Gaules*.[110] Both, in their different ways, were comprehensive programmes of reform (Dubos's analytically sophisticated and powerfully argued *History* relied on the same office-based conception of monarchy as that used by Saint-Pierre, d'Argenson, and Voltaire). But each was based upon a unitary model of the origins, nature, and purposes of the French monarchy. Where Boulainvilliers highlighted the

---

"Entretien de plusieurs philosophes célèbres, sur les gouvernements républicain et monarchique," *Journal d'économie publique*, 20 Prairial an 5 (8 June 1797), reprinted in Roederer, *Oeuvres*, 7:69.

[110] The classic study of the subject remains Elie Carcassonne, *Montesquieu et le problème de la constitution française au xviiie siècle* (Paris, 1927). See, too, Catherine Volpilhac-Auger, "Tacite et Montesquieu," *Studies on Voltaire and the Eighteenth Century* 232 (1985), and her "Tacite en France de Montesquieu à Chateaubriand," *Studies on Voltaire and the Eighteenth Century* 313 (1993). On Boulainvilliers, see, most recently, Diego Venturino, *Le Ragioni della tradizione, nobilità e mondo moderno in Boulainvilliers (1658–1722)* (Turin, 1993). On Dubos, see Lombard, *L'abbé Dubos*.

merits of a decentralised system of fiefs as a more efficient alternative to the waste and corruption of the court-based system of venal offices, *partisans*, and *intendants* established during the reign of Louis XIV, Dubos highlighted the merits of an elaborate, but ultimately centralised, system of royal administration as a more efficient alternative to the fragmented and divisive remains of the old feudal system of government. Both looked to the past for models of political reform, but where Boulainvilliers looked back to the fief-based system of the original Frankish monarchy, Dubos looked back to Rome and its office-based system of government. Montesquieu diverged from them both.

Montesquieu's characterisation of monarchy allowed him to bypass the partisans of both the *thèse nobiliaire* and the *thèse royale*. It also enabled him to claim that, in contradistinction to the English system of government, monarchy could rely on a checking mechanism whose existence was not, itself, dependent on the political system.[111] By assigning a discrete set of origins to the combination of a single person and a number of intermediate, subordinate, and dependent powers held together by a set of fundamental laws, Montesquieu was able to present monarchy as a dual system, bearing a family resemblance to both absolute monarchy and mixed government, as well as to the constitutional arrangements underpinning the English system, but differing fundamentally from all three because of the separate origins and functions of its component parts. As he presented it, this dual system was made up of two sets of rules: the first affecting the succession to the throne, the second affecting the inheritance of property. By identifying the way in which the one set of rules had come to be locked into the other, he was able to show how the two parts of a monarchy had come to form a unified (but not a unitary) system without having had a common origin. This, in turn, enabled him to claim that it was possible to make a genuine, rather than a purely verbal, distinction between a state and its government, and, by doing so, to explain why the institutions responsible for maintaining the state could be distinguished from those responsible for maintaining justice and legality. It was this distinction, he suggested, that set modern monarchy apart from both the ancient republics of the past and the despotic governments of the East and allowed him to claim, too, that despotism was not, as his critics argued, simply a pathological form of monarchy, but a distinct species of government. "I cannot agree with you about despotism," he wrote in 1751 to François Risteau, the Bordeaux merchant who had written a *Réponse aux Observations sur l'Esprit des Loix*, defending

---

[111] On the theme of checks and balances in Montesquieu's thought, see Bernard Manin, "Checks, Balances and Boundaries: The Separation of Powers in the Constitutional Debate of 1787," in Biancamaria Fontana, ed., *The Invention of the Modern Republic* (Cambridge, CUP, 1994), pp. 27–62.

Montesquieu from one of his clerical critics. "A government that is both the state and the prince seems chimerical to you; I think, on the contrary, that it is very real and believe that I depicted it from truth."[112]

Montesquieu's starting point in explaining the origins of the distinction between the prince and the state seems to have been the remark that he made about the curious afterlife of the Roman law in the ninety-seventh of his *Persian Letters*. It was not obvious how the combination of representation and primogeniture that had come to determine the transmission of rights (particularly property rights) from one person in one generation to another person in the next had come to be lodged at the core of the political societies of modern Europe. By analysing how the peculiar institution of primogeniture had arisen and how it had come to be connected so tightly to the inheritance of thrones, Montesquieu was able to make a number of significant moves. The first of these was to identify a difference between the various mechanisms informing systems of inheritance and to explain why this difference had a crucial bearing on the powers and responsibilities of governments. This difference lay in whether property transfers from one generation to the next were effected directly or indirectly, either by the living themselves or by a higher authority responsible for imposing the will of the dead upon the community of the living. This idea enabled Montesquieu to come up with a new set of categories for political science and to replace variations on the Aristotelian typology of governments as consisting of either the one, the few, or the many by a new typology based upon the distinctive attributes of republics, despotism, and monarchy. Where the will of the living directly determined the transfer of property between the generations, stable property relations had to be an effect of either a high level of consensus about social and political values (if the wills in question were many) or of a massive amount of force (if the will in question was one). This, according to the typology of governments that Montesquieu devised, was why the fundamental principle of a republic had to be virtue, and why fear was the logical corollary of a system in which the transmission of property was subject to the will of a single living individual. But where the transmission of property was determined not by the will of the living but by that of the dead (so that the power of the living simply enforced the will of the dead), government had a correspondingly lower level of responsibility to discharge. Making the dead the authors of some of the actions of the living had the effect of establishing a clearer distinction between a state and its government. If government was responsible for the affairs of the living, responsibility for maintaining the bridge between the living and the dead was the prime duty of a state. This had the further effect of ensuring that

---

[112] Montesquieu to Risteau, 19 May 1751, in Montesquieu, ed. Nagel, vol. 3, letter 605, p. 1382.

the government had no direct concern with the mechanisms determining the social distribution of wealth and the property arrangements underpinning the hierarchy of ranks. As a result, Montesquieu could argue that monarchy housed certain fundamental laws, and could claim that hereditary royal government and a stable hierarchy of ranks were complementary features of a single type of political society in which, in his vocabulary, the prince and the state were separate, but related, entities.

Montesquieu's examination of the origins of this distinction was spread diffusely over virtually all thirty-one books of *The Spirit of Laws* but was connected by three key passages in Tacitus's *Germania*, one of the standard sources of information about the original relationship among the Germans, the Romans, and the Gauls. The best-known of them—*Nec regibus infinita aut libera potestas* ("the power of the kings is neither unlimited nor arbitrary") and *De minoribus rebus principes consultant, de maioribus omnes* ("minor affairs were submitted for discussion to the chiefs; major affairs were discussed by all")—appeared in the famous description of the English constitution set out in chapter 6 of book 11 and reappeared in chapter 30 of book 18, dealing with the relationship between the laws and the nature of the soil. Both had a long pedigree in mixed-government and monarchomach theory and were among the cornerstones of Boulainvilliers's *Histoire de l'ancien gouvernement de la France*. The third passage—*Reges ex nobilitate, duces ex virtute sumunt* ("in the choice of their king they were determined by his noble extraction and in that of their leader by his valour")—had also been used by earlier writers as evidence of the elective and hereditary character of the Frankish monarchy. But Montesquieu seems to have noticed that it could mean something different. He referred to the passage on three occasions in his *Pensées*, the third in a note about a passage in Dubos's *Histoire critique de l'établissement de la monarchie française dans les Gaules* in which Dubos had claimed that no Roman emperor before Constantine or any other foreign king had separated their officials into two classes responsible, respectively, for military and civil functions. As Montesquieu pointed out, the passage in Tacitus undermined Dubos's claim. It also meant, he added, that Dubos had been wrong to assert that the Merovingian kings of France had followed the usage of their nation in combining the civil and military powers because (as he paraphrased him) that usage did not allow for "the method of separating sovereign authority between two representatives in the same country." This, Dubos claimed, meant that the distinction between the civil and the military powers had been established relatively late in French history, by Louis XII. According to Montesquieu, this was simply not true.

> He cannot be unaware of what Tacitus rightly says about the difference among the Germans between the functions of the king, who had the civil authority,

and the functions of the duke, which the warriors had, which is the key to the beginnings of the French monarchy.[113]

The reason why it was "the key to the beginnings of the French monarchy" was that when it was combined with the two other features of German society which Tacitus had described and applied—not to the original German peoples who did not cultivate the land, but to the conquering German peoples who had all the land of Roman Gaul at their disposal—it became the basis of a type of monarchy that was neither mixed nor absolute, but modern. It was remarkable, Montesquieu commented, "that the corruption of the government of a conquering people should have formed the best kind of government men have been able to devise."[114]

The passage in Tacitus describing how the Germans chose their kings (*reges*) "according to nobility" and their leaders (*duces*) "according to valour" enabled Montesquieu to do three things. It allowed him, first, to drop the idea of indivisible, unitary sovereignty informing most accounts of the origins of political authority and, more specifically, the two rival characterisations of the origins and attributes of the modern French monarchy written by Boulainvilliers and Dubos. This move enabled him to explain the emergence of both a sovereign king and a number of "intermediate, subordinate, and dependent powers" in the form of the nobility without having to show that the one had developed at the expense of the other (either, as Boulainvilliers had argued, by the growth of the power of the monarchy at the expense of the original rights of the nobility, or, as Dubos replied, by a combination of royal grants and noble encroachments upon the original sovereign power acquired by the Frankish successors to the Roman emperors). Instead of a sort of historical zero-sum game, in which the rights and power of the king varied inversely with the rights and power of the nobility, Montesquieu presented the relationship between the two in terms of a history of role-switching. This third move enabled him to show that the dual system of authority which was the hallmark of the ancient government of the Germans was a mirror image of the government of modern France, making the transition from the one to the other the product of a peculiar switch in the location of military and civil power. While the Frankish kings had no power but had the right to judge, modern French kings had absolute power but had no right to judge. As Montesquieu noted in the brief remark he made about the government of the Franks in the *Considerations of the Causes of the Greatness of the Romans and Their Decline*, "power was in the hands of the vassals; right alone was in the hands of the prince." In the monarchies "we know," he wrote in *The Spirit of Laws*, "the prince has the

---

[113] Montesquieu, *Pensées*, ed. Louis Desgraves (Paris, Robert Laffont, 1991), no. 1906, p. 584.

[114] Montesquieu, *SL*, bk. 11, ch. 8, pp. 167–8.

executive and the legislative power, or at least a part of the legislative power, but he does not judge."[115] The switch from the former to the latter, giving power to the king and the right to judge to the nobility, was the basis of modern "moderate government," that "masterpiece of legislation," as Montesquieu put it, "which chance rarely makes and which prudence is rarely allowed to produce."[116]

The source of this switch was the way that the system of representative succession had developed, as Montesquieu indicated, "out of the corruption of a conquering people" to produce the hierarchy of "intermediate, subordinate, and dependent powers" that gave modern monarchy its nature.[117] The significance of the process was highlighted by the epigraph (one of the few at the head of any of the thirty-one books) taken from Ovid's *Metamorphoses*—"My imagination brings me to speak of forms changing into new bodies"—that Montesquieu placed at the beginning of book 28 of *The Spirit of Laws*, entitled "On the Origin and Revolutions of the Civil Laws among the French."[118] Its starting point was Montesquieu's earlier presentation of the original features of the Frankish system of government in book 18, where he had used Tacitus to describe the "great liberty" of a people who did not cultivate the land. In it, Montesquieu denied that there had been any original connection between the French monarchy and the hallowed Salic laws. The absence of landed property, he argued, made it inconceivable that the Salic laws had originally had anything to do with the transmission of land, the royal succession, or, a fortiori, with the exclusion of women from the throne. "The Salic law," he wrote,

> had not in view a preference of one sex to the other, much less had it a regard to the perpetuity of a family, a name, or the transmission of land. These things did not enter into the heads of the Germans; it was purely an oeconomical law, which gave the house and the land dependent thereon, to the males who should dwell in it, and to whom it consequently was of most service.[119]

Its original function was to prevent married women from inheriting the tiny plots of land surrounding the Germans' huts (known, Montesquieu stated, as Salic land, meaning land belonging to the *Sala*, or house) because, if they were allowed to inherit, the land would then become the property of another household. These little plots were the only land that the Germans owned because, as Tacitus and Caesar had shown, all the other land was

---

[115] Montesquieu, *Considérations*, p. 69; *SL*, bk. 11, ch. 11, p. 169.

[116] Montesquieu, *SL*, bk. 5, ch. 14, p. 63.

[117] Montesquieu, *SL*, bk. 11, ch. 8, pp. 167–8; bk. 2 ch. 4, p. 17.

[118] Montesquieu, *SL*, bk. 28, p. 532.

[119] Montesquieu, *SL*, bk. 18, ch. 22, p. 298; cross-references are made, too, under the following notes to the 1823 two-volume reprint of the Nugent translation, identified as "Nugent," as here: Nugent, 1:288.

available for cultivation or pasture for no more than a year, after which time it reverted to the common. The purely "oeconomical" purpose of the original Salic law became obvious, Montesquieu pointed out, after the Franks invaded Gaul. Then, married women were allowed to inherit property because there was more available land, which was why, he explained, the Franks introduced the custom of allowing a father to recall his daughter and her children into his household to have a share of his property after his death. "After what has been said," he concluded, "One would not imagine that the perpetual succession of males to the crown of France should have taken its rise from the Salic law. And yet this is a point indubitably certain."[120]

As Montesquieu commented in a private note, "a little change in the civil laws often produces a change in the constitution," adding, in the following note, a more general declaration of intent: "I plan to deal with the relationship of the civil laws to the political laws, something that I do not know if anyone has done before me."[121] The change in question, involving exactly the sort of sequential shift from the civil to the political laws to which he attached such significance, concerned the formation of hereditary fiefs. It was not the Salic law that led to the establishment of fiefs by setting restrictions upon the succession of women but, instead, the establishment of hereditary fiefs that placed limits upon women's right to inherit. This, he added dryly,

> was not the only case in which the political law of the Franks gave way to the civil. By the Salic law, all the brothers succeeded equally to the land, and this was also decreed by a law of the Burgundians. Thus, in the kingdom of the Franks, and in that of the Burgundians, all the brothers succeeded to the crown as (a few acts of violence, murders and usurpations apart) was also the case with the Burgundians.[122]

The setting in which these modifications took place formed the subject-matter of book 28. There Montesquieu set out to show how the "excessive independence" of the Germans—"a free and martial people, who lived without any other industry than that of tending their flocks, and who had nothing other but rush cottages to attach them to their lands," and who ordinarily "waged war with each other to obtain satisfaction for murders, robberies or affronts"—came to be subjected to a durable institutional hierarchy as a variety of ecclesiastical, seigneurial, and royal courts gradually took over responsibility for settling disputes.[123]

[120] Montesquieu, *SL*, bk. 18, ch. 22, p. 301; Nugent, 1:291.
[121] Montesquieu, *Pensées*, ed. Desgraves. nos. 1769, 1770, p. 553.
[122] Montesquieu, *SL*, bk. 18, ch. 22, p. 301; Nugent, 1:291–2.
[123] Montesquieu, *SL*, bk. 28, ch. 17, p. 552; Nugent, 2:191; bk. 30, ch. 12, p. 630; Nugent, 2:266.

This transformation involved a sequence of steps that developed out of the way that the German peoples originally settled conflicts. Initially, according to Montesquieu, there had not been a uniform system. Among most of the German tribes, disputes were settled by what he called negative proof, meaning that anyone accused of a crime could challenge his accuser to justify the charge and fight him to bring the matter to an end. Victory was taken to be a sign that right was on the side of the victor, just as the innocence of a woman was taken to be proved by her ability to withstand torture, ducking, or burning. Unusually, the Salic Franks (who supplied France with her first kings) did not allow the custom of negative proof. Instead, anyone charged with an offence had to be positively proven to have committed the act in question before he or she could be found guilty. But, in the short term, this system was swept aside in the turmoil of the invasion of Gaul. Trial by combat became the norm because of the many new opportunities for conflict caused by disputes over the possession of landed estates. As it became more general, trial by combat was endowed with a primitive set of rules. This, Montesquieu pointed out, served to explain the origins not only of the duel, but also of "the marvellous system of chivalry."[124] But however well-regulated fighting became, it had the disadvantage of allowing no redress. Once the fight was over, there was either no appeal because one of the contenders was dead or there was a further round of fighting, making the feud or vendetta a logical corollary of trial by combat. Gradually, therefore, trial by combat gave way to a more peaceful system of appeal to a higher authority, a procedure that necessarily led to the reemergence of the Salic Franks' system of positive proof as the way to draw a line under a dispute. In this way, the ancient German system of fighting to prove their innocence was grafted on to the system of fiefs.

The next step was to show how the system of dispute settlement was connected originally to a non-property-based social hierarchy, and to track the changes that took place when a military hierarchy turned into a landed hierarchy. Book 28 of *The Spirit of Laws* was mainly an account of how the manners and mores of the German peoples were the basis of a recognisably French system of honour in which "a challenge decided by blood" had been transformed progressively into "a paper quarrel" that was subject to the rules of a codified legal system.[125] But this account of the transformation of the German system of justice into a legal system based upon positive proof and an established process of appeal was somewhat incomplete, notably because it presupposed the existence of the system of fiefs, the mechanism by which the transformation of trial by combat into legal argument took place. Without the system of fiefs, it was hard to explain why trial by

[124] Montesquieu, *SL*, bk. 28, ch. 22, p. 562; Nugent, 2:201–2.
[125] Montesquieu, *SL*, bk. 28, ch. 27, p. 569; Nugent, 2:208.

combat did not degenerate into an endless cycle of revenge. There had therefore to be a further explanation of the origins and development of the feudal system. Montesquieu took up the question in the last two books of *The Spirit of Laws*, both entitled "Theory of the Feudal Laws among the Franks" and completed, in extremis, only in the summer of 1748. He began by rehearsing the descriptions of German society made by Caesar and Tacitus. These, he concluded, showed that

> among the Germans, there were vassals, but no fiefs; they had no fiefs, because the princes had no lands to give; or rather their fiefs consisted in horses trained for war, in arms, and feasting. There were vassals, because there were trusty men who being bound by their word engaged to follow the prince to the field, and did very near the same service as was afterwards performed for the fiefs.[126]

Vassals, accordingly, were originally what Tacitus called *comites*, a word that Montesquieu translated as *compagnons*, adding that they were also described in the Salic laws as "men who have vowed fealty to the king" and, in other sources, as "the king's *Antrustios*" or "*Leudes*, faithful and loyal" or, later, as "vassals and lords."[127] Insofar as they were heads of the tribes and companions of the king, their property was "regulated rather by the political than by the civil law, and was the share that fell to an army, and not the patrimony of a family." It was, Montesquieu added, variously known as "fiscal goods (*fiscalia*), benefices, honours and fiefs."[128] Possession of these goods was conditional upon the performance of military and judicial service, so that "the duty of a vassal towards his lord was to bear arms, and to try his peers in his court."[129]

This characterisation of the status and functions of the vassals allowed Montesquieu to build upon his earlier description of the German system of justice and explain why it was able to prevent trial by combat from degenerating into an endless cycle of vendetta, retribution, and blood feuds. According to Tacitus, he wrote, there were only two capital crimes among the Germans: "they hanged traitors and drowned cowards." All other injuries led to a demand of satisfaction from the injured party and his or her family, initially by the mutual agreement of the parties and later by a more general system of graduated fines, known as compositions. This system of conflict resolution fitted the distinction between natural society and natural government that Montesquieu had made at the very beginning of *The Spirit of Laws*. As he now pointed out in a remark on a law of the Frisians, the vendetta or blood feud was the logical corollary of natural society,

---

[126] Montesquieu, *SL*, bk. 30, ch. 3, p. 621; Nugent, 2:257–8.
[127] Montesquieu, *SL*, bk. 30, ch. 16, p. 640; Nugent, 2:275.
[128] Montesquieu, *SL*, bk. 30, ch. 16, p. 640; Nugent, 2:276.
[129] Montesquieu, *SL*, bk. 30, ch. 18, p. 645; Nugent, 2:280.

leaving the people in that situation in which every family at variance was in some measure in the state of nature, and which being unrestrained by a political or civil law, they might give a loose to their revenge, till they had obtained satisfaction.[130]

The system of compositions took the process of obtaining satisfaction out of the hands of the injured party. "By the establishing of those laws," Montesquieu commented, "the German nations quitted that state of nature, in which they seem to have lived in Tacitus' time."[131]

As Montesquieu presented it, vassals were responsible for enforcing the system of compositions as part of their duty to the various Germanic kings. They tried their peers in their courts, using the various systems of positive or negative proof that served to establish the guilt or innocence of the accused. In return for the right to be tried, those accused of an injury were required to pay a duty to the court, known as a *fredum*. The system of compositions thus meant that when disputes occurred, the courts supervened to protect the criminal from the injured party so that, in effect, the criminal bought the right to a composition to settle the dispute. This, Montesquieu argued, was "the origin of the jurisdiction of the lords."[132] It enabled him to conclude that the administration of justice was an intrinsic feature of the fief rather than a later royal grant or seigneurial usurpation. It was, as he put it, "a right inherent in the very fief itself, a lucrative right which constituted a part of it."[133] It was also a right that had nothing originally to do with the ownership of land because the Germans owned no land (other than the plots around their huts) until they invaded Gaul. But the massive expansion of opportunities for plunder and booty opened up by the invasion served to change the character of the fief. Originally, as Montesquieu explained, a fief was simply a right to a share of plunder, given at will rather than for any more determinate period in return for military and judicial service. But with so much plunder at stake and so large an amount of land available for plunder, both the kings and their vassals had a strong incentive to tamper with the way that fiefs were given, either by revoking grants that had already been made or by using bribery and corruption to obtain additional fiefs. The resultant anarchy led to "that famous revolution in French history" when a rebellion headed by Clotharius II

[130] Montesquieu, *SL*, bk. 30, ch. 19, p. 647; Nugent, 2:282.
[131] Montesquieu, *SL*, bk. 30, ch. 19, pp. 647–8; Nugent, 2:283.
[132] Montesquieu, *SL*, bk. 30, ch. 20, p. 652; Nugent, 2:287.
[133] Montesquieu, *SL*, bk. 30, ch. 20, p. 653; Nugent, 2:288. He added, to explain why the administration of justice could not have been a usurpation by the lords, that usurpations of the rights of princes were hardly a peculiarity of the Germans. "We are sufficiently informed by history, that several other nations have encroached upon their sovereigns, and yet we find no other instance of what we call the jurisdiction of the lords. The origin of it is therefore to be traced in the usages and customs of the Germans" (p. 653); Nugent, 2:289.

and supported by Warnacharius, mayor of Burgundy, broke out against the Frankish queen Brunhilda to defend their fiefs from her exactions. Until then, Montesquieu emphasised, the mayor was no more than the king's officer, responsible for the management of the king's household. But the mayor of Burgundy extracted a promise from his coconspirator Clotharius II that he would keep his office for life, and, when he died, Clotharius invited "the lords assembled at Troyes" to choose his successor. This, Montesquieu pointed out, made the mayor a different sort of vassal from the rest because he was now "independent of the regal dignity" and responsible for maintaining the security of the fiefs. After several further rounds of fighting the office of mayor of the palace became a permanent feature of the Frankish government of Gaul. "The nation thought it safer to lodge the power in the hands of a mayor whom she chose herself, and to whom she might preserve conditions, than in those of a king whose power was hereditary."[134] This dual system of authority was, Montesquieu emphasised, entirely consonant with the original attributes of the Frankish system of government.

> The Franks were descended from the Germans, of whom Tacitus says, that in the choice of their kings, they were determined by his noble extraction; and in their choice of their leader, by his valour. This gives us an idea of the kings of the first race, and of the mayors of the palace; the former were hereditary, the latter elective.[135]

When the Germans were a wandering, plundering people, the two functions were generally embodied in the same person. "By the regal dignity, our first kings presided in the courts and assemblies, and enacted laws with the national consent; by the dignity of the duke or leader, they undertook expeditions and commanded the armies."[136] But when the two functions became separate, the regal dignity was subordinated to the power of the mayor, resulting in the system of the mayors of the palace, who governed the kingdom in the name of an invisible, usually incarcerated, king. Since the mayors of the palace were elected to maintain the security of the fiefs, fiefs began to be given for life and soon started to become hereditary. This change led to two changes of dynasty and to two further additions to the attributes of the monarchy. In the first, Pepin, son of Charles Martel, used his control of the political government of the fiefs to combine the titles of king and mayor of the palace, replacing the Merovingian kings by the new Carolingian line and joining the elective principle governing the office of

---

[134] Montesquieu, *SL*, bk. 31, chs. 1–5, pp. 669, 670–1, 675, 677; Nugent, 2:304, 305–6, 310, 312.

[135] Montesquieu, *SL*, bk. 31, ch. 4, p. 677; Nugent, 2:312.

[136] Montesquieu, *SL*, bk. 31, ch. 4, p. 677; Nugent, 2:312.

mayor of the palace to the hereditary principle ruling the succession to the throne.[137] In the second, the most powerful feudal lord—in the person of Hugh Capet—overthrew the dynasty that had emerged from the holders of the office of mayor of the palace, replacing the Carolingian kings by the Capetians, uniting, as Montesquieu put it, the crown "to a great fief" and, by doing so, adding the principle of primogeniture to the elective and hereditary attributes of the monarchy.[138]

This addition was a result of the survival of the original attributes of the fief. The owners of fiefs were still required to bear arms and try their peers in their courts. This, according to Montesquieu, explained why the principle of primogeniture came to be attached to the inheritance of fiefs. Since ownership of a fief entailed performing military and judicial service, there had to be a system of inheritance able to produce an owner capable of doing his duty. When fiefs were held at will or for a lifetime, their owners' goods could be inherited by all his children, just as, during the Merovingian and Carolingian dynasties, the crown could be inherited by all the king's sons.

> But as soon as the fiefs became hereditary, the right of seniority was established in the feudal succession; and for the same reason in that of the crown, which was the great fief. The ancient law of partitions was no longer subsisting; the fiefs being charged with a service, the possessor must have been enabled to discharge it. The right of primogeniture was established, and the reason of the feudal law was superior to that of the political or civil institution.[139]

When Hugh Capet became king, the principle of primogeniture, or representative succession, was incorporated into the monarchy. As Montesquieu concluded triumphantly,

> When the fiefs were become hereditary, the law relating to the order of succession must have been relative to the perpetuity of the fiefs. Hence this rule of the French law, *estates of inheritance do not ascend* (*Propres ne remontent point*) was established in spite of the Roman and Salic laws. It was necessary that service should be paid for the fief; but a grandfather or a great-uncle would have been too old to perform any service; therefore this rule took place at first only in regard to the feudal tenures.[140]

The sequence that Montesquieu tracked served to make the French crown a combination of three elements: a king, a mayor of the palace, and a feudal

[137] Cf. Montesquieu, *Pensées*, ed. Desgraves, no. 1548, p. 497: "LES GERMAINS: '*Reges ex nobilitate, duces ex virtute sumunt*' dit Tacite, *De Moribus Germanorum*. C'est ce qui fit la différence du pouvoir des maires et des rois, et de leurs différents titres. Cela fut cause que les rois de la seconde race furent électifs, parce que la couronne fut jointe à la mairie du Palais."
[138] Montesquieu, *SL*, bk. 31, ch. 32, p. 717; Nugent, 2:352.
[139] Montesquieu, *SL*, bk. 31, ch. 33, p. 718; Nugent, 2:353.
[140] Montesquieu, *SL*, bk. 31, ch. 34; p. 722; Nugent, 2:357.

lord. As king, its owner had the right to make laws. As mayor of the palace, he held the highest executive office. As the owner of the greatest fief, he was entitled to rule by right of the principle of representative succession that governed the inheritance of fiefs. Once the sequence had taken place, the switch was complete. Kings had absolute power, but the nobility still had the original attributes of the fief, namely, the duty to serve the king by bearing arms and dispensing justice. Monarchy had acquired the three elements—a king; a nobility as the "most natural" of intermediate, subordinate, and dependent powers; and a set of fundamental laws governing both the succession to the throne and the inheritance of fiefs—that formed its nature and served to give it a built-in difference from both despotism and democracy. "The sovereign," as one of Montesquieu's later readers put it, "possesses by way of his empire what each of his subjects possesses by way of his domain."[141] Its unusual feature, however, was that it was possession by dominion that set limits upon possession by empire.[142] The way that this had occurred was, Montesquieu himself wrote, "an event which happened once in the world and which will never perhaps happen again."[143]

The point was underlined a few years after the publication of *The Spirit of Laws* by a Scottish jurist, Sir John Dalrymple, whose *Essay towards a General History of Feudal Property in Great Britain* of 1757 had, he wrote, been "revised by the greatest genius of our age," whom he identified in a note as "President Montesquieu."[144] As a description of the sequence of steps by which the original "situation of the Germans" was transformed into "a system of laws, without the plan of a legislator," it was a remarkably accurate elaboration upon the last two books of *The Spirit of Laws*.[145] Dal-

---

[141] [Le Roy de Barincourt], *Principe du droit fondamental des souverains*, 2 vols. (Geneva, 1788), 1:.

[142] See, helpfully, Yoshie Kawade, "La liberté civile contre la théorie réformiste de l'état souverain: le combat de Montesquieu," in Caroline Jacot Grapa, Nicole-Jacques Lefèvre, Yannick Séité, and Carine Trevisan, eds., *Le Travail des Lumières. Pour Georges Benrekassa* (Paris, Champion, 2002), pp. 203–23.

[143] Montesquieu, *SL*, bk. 30, ch. 1, p. 619; Nugent, 2:255.

[144] John Dalrymple, *An Essay towards a General History of Feudal Property in Great Britain* [London, 1757]. Citations in this and in subsequent notes are to the second (London, 1758) edition, pp. iv, ix. It is not entirely clear whether Dalrymple meant that he had revised his text in the light of Montesquieu's book or whether Montesquieu himself had revised his (Dalrymple's) book, as the passage does suggest. Substantively, the difference does not greatly matter. It is possible that Dalrymple did have some contact with Montesquieu through his own connections with Charles Yorke and Henry Home, Lord Kames, even though there is no trace of any correspondence between them (at least in Montesquieu's published surviving correspondence). For further information on Dalrymple, see Colin Kidd, *Subverting Scotland's Past* (Cambridge, CUP, 1993); David Lieberman, "The Legal Needs of a Commercial Society: The Jurisprudence of Lord Kames," in Istvan Hont and Michael Ignatieff, eds., *Wealth and Virtue* (Cambridge, 1983), pp. 203–34.

[145] Dalrymple, *Essay*, pp. 4, 6.

rymple began by repeating the use to which Montesquieu had put Tacitus's distinction between the German kings and their chiefs to make an identical sequence of switches. The first switch was a product of the transformation of fiefs into hereditary goods. It took the power (but not the right) to leave property out of the hands of its owner and transferred it to a higher authority. This separation of what Dalrymple called property from superiority had the effect, he went on to explain, of making it seem that "when I see the will of a person lying on a table, he seems present with me, and commanding me as if he was alive."

> This strikes the senses, and assists the imagination in transferring property to a living, from a dead person, by the will of the deceased. Thus it comes to be law, because it is every body's interest that it should be law, that men may name heirs by testament as they please: nor is this all, for men being fond of power, and letters expressing the exertion of that fondness, they name heirs to these heirs. Thus substitutions come into law; and *fidei commisses*, conditions, entails, and many other effects of pride, refinement, and an extended idea of property accompany them.[146]

As Montesquieu had shown, the switch that enabled the living to enforce the will of the dead entailed a further switch, in which the king, as a feudal lord and owner of the greatest fief, became the head of the elaborate system of law enforcement inherent in the ownership of fiefs, so that the administration of justice passed out of the hands of the monarchy and into those of the nobility. As Dalrymple pointed out, both these switches had the effect of eliminating the distinction between hereditary and elective monarchies.

> It is no objection to tracing such rules of succession, that in the earlier ages of Europe, the crowns were generally given by election; for if the rules of that election were properly established, and generally followed, they were properly rules of succession. The dispute is merely about words; the only difference between these words, is, that in the last case, the rule of law points out the succession in a law book; whereas, in the other case, the rule of law, in an assembly of the lawmakers, did the same.[147]

But the substitution of one rule of law for another (or inheritance for election) had the effect of preventing the succession problem from interfering with the continuity and stability of the state and, in exceptional circumstances, the additional effect of supplying a new set of criteria for deciding how to deal with some of the unforeseen, potentially perverse effects of hereditary rule. As Montesquieu himself emphasised, his historical account

[146] Dalrymple, *Essay*, p. 127.
[147] Dalrymple, *Essay*, pp. 173–4.

of the origins and nature of modern monarchy allowed him to approach the succession problem in terms of the need to maintain the dual system that gave monarchy its nature. "When that political law which has established in the state a certain order of succession, becomes destructive to the body politic for whose sake it was established," he wrote in book 26 of *The Spirit of Laws*, "there is not the least room to doubt but another political law may be made to change this order; and so far would this law be from opposing the first, it would in the main be entirely conformable to it, because both would depend on this principle, that the safety of the people is the supreme law."[148]

Montesquieu made no reference to any putatively ancient right of the French parlements or the dukes and peers to determine the succession, or to the rights of the nation, either as represented by an Estates-General or as embodied in the procedural life of the institutions of the kingdom, or to the general rights of mankind as the ultimate court of appeal in cases of disputed successions. His approach instead was bluntly realistic. Princes, he pointed out, "live not among themselves under civil laws" and could not be considered to be free in the way that the citizens "governed by civil laws" were free. They "are governed by force, and they may continually force or be forced." A prince who objected to the terms of a treaty he had been forced to sign was simply making a category mistake. "This," Montesquieu commented, "would be to complain of his natural state; it would seem as if he would be a prince with respect to other princes, and as if other princes should be subjects with respect to him; that is, it would be contrary to the nature of things."[149] The need to preserve stability had to come first. As Montesquieu put it, "when, by some circumstance, the political law becomes destructive to the state, we ought to decide by such a political law as will preserve it, which sometimes becomes a law of nations."[150] It was not difficult, in the light of passages like these, for one of Montesquieu's later readers to claim, with some exaggeration, that "this great work, in all its entirety," could be subsumed under the ancient republican maxim of the *salus populi*.[151] If it could, it also stripped that notion of some of its indeterminacy by supplying an additional set of criteria for making political judgements. In a situation like the one that had seemed possible at the time of the Regency, the ordinary rules governing the succession to the throne had to give way to those governing the inheritance of fiefs, giving, as had been the case at the time of Hugh Capet, "the owner of the greatest fief" the right to rule. Retrospectively, this amounted to an endorsement of the duc

[148] Montesquieu, *SL*, bk. 26, ch. 23, p. 516; Nugent, 2:159.
[149] Montesquieu, *SL*, bk. 26, ch. 20, pp. 514–5; Nugent, 2:157.
[150] Montesquieu, *SL*, bk. 26, ch. 23, p. 516; Nugent, 2:159.
[151] [Barincourt], *Principe du droit fondamental*, 2:288.

d'Orléans's claim to the French throne if Louis XV had died. Since military and judicial service had been the original title to the ownership of fiefs, and since the capacity to meet these obligations ruled out absentee ownership, the owner of the greatest fief would, necessarily, be an inhabitant of the kingdom rather than a foreign king. If the ordinary rules of succession threatened to produce a perverse effect, there was still a way to identify only one eligible candidate for succession to the throne.

The Problem of Sovereignty and the Nature of Monarchy

Montesquieu's demonstration that the monarchies of modern Europe were German, not Roman, in origin, and that the nature of monarchy itself was a product of a peculiar mutation of the Roman-law idea of representation, set his conception of monarchy at odds with almost every other description of royal government to be found before and after the publication of *The Spirit of Laws*. Two, in particular, had an enduring presence in eighteenth-century French thought. The first derived from Jansenist ecclesiology and, especially, from Jansenist claims about the position of the pope in the government of the Catholic Church. The second derived from the concept of monarchy in Fénelon's *Telemachus*. Jansenism has acquired a considerable prominence in the recent historiography of the French Revolution. Fénelon's intellectual legacy has been studied less fully.[152] Neither, however, made the strong analytical distinction between republican and monarchical forms of government that was one of the most innovative features of *The Spirit of Laws*. As Montesquieu recognised, it was this distinction that most disconcerted his early readers. In the foreword that he added to the edition of his book published in 1757, he went to some lengths to reply to their criticisms.

> For the better understanding of the first four books of this work, it is to be observed that what I distinguish by the name of *virtue*, in a republic, is the love of one's country, that is, the love of equality. It is not a moral, nor a Christian, but a *political* virtue; and it is the spring which sets the republican government in motion, as *honour* is the spring which gives motion to a monarchy. Hence it is that I have distinguished the love of one's country, and of equality, by the appellation of *political virtue*. My ideas are new, and therefore I have been obliged to find new words, or to give new acceptations to old terms, in order to convey my meaning.[153]

[152] See, however, Chérel, *Fénelon en France*, and for, more recent bibliographical information, F-X. Cuche and J. Le Brun, eds., *Fénelon Mystique et Politique (1699–1999)* (Paris, Honoré Champion, 2004).

[153] Montesquieu, *SL*, ed. Neumann, p. lxxi.

The novelty was not so much the ascription of love of country and of equality to a republic, but the glaring omission of them both from the concept of monarchy set out in *The Spirit of Laws*. The omission served to establish a clear line of demarcation between the two, so that in a sense the modern distinction between republics and monarchies could be said to have begun with Montesquieu. Before then, it was still quite usual to follow Aristotle, Cicero, and Polybius and to assume, first, that monarchy, aristocracy, and democracy were all different species of the genus *res publica*, and, second, that a mixture of all three was most likely to suit a republic made up of several different levels of wealth or privilege. Jean Bodin's *Six livres de la république* (Six Books of a Commonweal) of 1576, with its strong endorsement of monarchy as the most suitable form of government for a republic, simply followed this long-established usage (differing only by highlighting the compatibility between the unitary character of monarchy and the indivisible nature of sovereignty in governing the *res publica*). So, too, but in a very different sense, did most of Montesquieu's critics. What separated them from Montesquieu himself was not simply their reluctance to accept his strong analytical distinction between republican and royal forms of government, but, more fundamentally, their equally considerable reluctance to adopt his solution to the practical and theoretical problems generated by the modern concept (and fact) of sovereignty. It was this, ultimately, that made established usage analytically untenable, and it was Montesquieu who saw it first.

Politics, wrote Philippe Hay, marquis du Châtelet towards the end of the seventeenth century, "is the art of governing states." The ancients had called politics "a royal and a most divine science, surpassing in excellency and superior to all others," occupying the same position of "precedence in practical learning" as metaphysics and theology "in the speculative." The "means prescribed for politics," he continued, were

> an exact observance of religion, a doing justice in all cases, a providing that the people be protected in times of peace and war; and a preserving the state in a just and laudable mediocrity, by exterminating the extremes of poverty and of riches.[154]

To these broadly Christian and Aristotelian themes, Hay du Châtelet added another, centred on the more recent concept of sovereignty.

Politics, he wrote, has three principal branches, "namely the three sorts of regular government in which men live under the authority of the laws." These, he continued, were monarchy, aristocracy, and democracy. Monarchy was a system of government in which "one only prince doth command

---

[154] [Philippe Hay du Châtelet], *The Politics of France*, 2nd ed. (London, 1691), ch. 1, pp. 1–2.

for the public good"; in aristocracy "the honestest and wisest persons, being elected out of all the subjects, have the direction of public affairs"; while democracy was a government "in which all deliberations and orders are held and do pass by the agency and vote of the people." There were, he added, two sorts of monarchy. "The first of these is entitled the *Lacedemo-nian*, in which the king hath but a limited authority. The second *oeconomical* in which the king hath a sovereign and absolute power in his kingdom, as a father of a family hath in his home."[155] This latter form of government, Hay stated, was actually "the best government." This, he explained, was not just because this kind of monarchy "represents the authority which a father exercises in his house," but also, he emphasised, because monarchy "also necessarily occurs in an aristocracy and in democracy itself."[156]

> For both in the one and the other of these states, the sovereignty is entirely one, so that no single person can possess any the least parcel of it. In an aristocracy, no one of the senators is a sovereign, but the whole senate being united of one accord, is king. In a democracy, no one of himself hath power to make the least ordinance; the people assembled are the monarch.

Since sovereignty was unitary, even a government made up of many individuals had to have this feature. Monarchy, however, had it by nature. Thus, Hay concluded, "everywhere appears an indivisible sovereignty, so conform to the laws of nature is monarchy."[157] The kind of royal government that Hay du Châtelet called *oeconomical* was the physical embodiment of sovereignty itself.

This conception of sovereignty has sometimes been associated with the political thought of Thomas Hobbes. It has also been associated with the French Revolution. Putting the nation in place of the king (it has sometimes been claimed), but keeping the same conception of absolute, sovereign power, served to open up the space that came to be filled by the competitive struggle to speak for, embody, or represent the nation that turned the politics of 1789 into the more lethal politics of 1794. In fact, the concept in question is better associated with Jean Bodin, not Thomas Hobbes. Hobbes's own conception of sovereignty was something like the opposite. For Hobbes, it was not the people that was the monarch, but the monarch that was the people. The key to this move was the idea of representation. Hobbes described the idea most famously in chapter 16 of his *Leviathan* (1651). "A multitude of men," he wrote, "are made *One* Person, when they are by one man, or one Person, Represented; so that it be done with the consent of every one of that Multitude in particular. For it is the *Unity* of

---

[155] [Hay du Châtelet], *Politics*, pp. 2–3.
[156] [Hay du Châtelet], *Politics*, p. 5.
[157] [Hay du Châtelet], *Politics*, pp. 5–6.

the Representer, not the *Unity* of the Represented, that maketh the Person One."[158] The use to which Hobbes put the idea of representation gave his theory of sovereignty a built-in democratic foundation that Bodin's concept of ruler sovereignty did not have, and, at the same time, precluded mixed government as an alternative to unitary sovereign power. In terms of Hobbes's logic, representation made every sovereign democratic and, inversely, every democracy representative (with the people, as a single entity, representing a multitude of people). It is well known that Montesquieu was not impressed by this theory of attributed action. "Hobbes's principle," he noted, "is very false: namely, that the people having authorised the prince, the actions of the prince are the actions of the people, so that the people cannot complain about the prince nor demand that he give any account for his actions because the people cannot complain about the people."[159] It is also well known that Montesquieu rejected Hobbes's claims about human vainglory and desire for dominion as the basis of his theory of how an authorised representative sovereign could use fear to keep these two primary human impulses in check. But Montesquieu's historical account of the origins and nature of modern monarchy allowed him to keep a modified version of Hobbes's idea of representation. By tying the concept of representation to the Roman-law principle of inheritance, and by showing how this principle had come to be applied to both the inheritance of fiefs and the inheritance of thrones, he was able to adopt Hobbes's concept of representative sovereignty, but to combine it with a number of subordinate, dependent, and intermediate powers whose existence was not directly dependent upon the sovereign itself.

The concept of monarchy contained in *The Spirit of Laws* was able to find room for the idea of an unaccountable representative sovereign without having to rely for its legitimacy either upon medieval notions of the monarch's two bodies, or upon more recent divine-right theories, or upon Hobbes's (or Locke's) analytically coherent, but historically implausible, contractual theory of authorisation. But however successful *The Spirit of Laws* might have been as a work of historical legitimation, it was less easy to see how Montesquieu's conception of monarchy could also find room for justice. Although Montesquieu began *The Spirit of Laws* by emphasising the need to "acknowledge relations of justice antecedent to the positive law by which they are established," many of his critics found the claim quite hard to reconcile both with his book's broader emphasis on human diversity and with his own acknowledgement that the picture of monarchy that

---

[158] Thomas Hobbes, *Leviathan* [1651], ed. C. B. Macpherson (Harmondsworth, Penguin, 1968), pt. 1, ch. 16, p. 220.

[159] Charles-Louis de Secondat, baron de Montesquieu, *Pensées*, ed. Louis Desgraves (Paris, 1991), no. 224, p. 253.

he had presented might seem, to some, to be more like a satire than a portrait.[160] For all the differences between them, almost all of Montesquieu's critics argued in favour of injecting a stronger moral dimension into the highly attenuated concept of justice that they associated with *The Spirit of Laws*, usually singling out those parts of the book dealing with honour, virtue, and climate to illustrate its moral shortcomings.[161] If monarchy was a form of government in which one person ruled along with a number of subordinate, dependent, and intermediate powers, it was quite hard to identify which of the parts of the system was ultimately responsible for maintaining justice. Part of the ambiguity had to do with the notion of justice itself and the extent to which, as Montesquieu construed them, the responsibilities of the sovereign went no further than maintaining those arrangements that gave monarchy its nature, leaving everything else to the formalities of the legal system and the various bodies of magistrates responsible for upholding legality. Although they differed from one another in many other respects, particularly in their respective treatments of the subjects of property and inequality, both Jansenists and more orthodox Catholics argued for a closer relationship between the respective claims of legality, morality, and justice.

Jansenism

The Jansenist theory of sovereignty had its origins in seventeenth-century discussions of papal power. "A multitude which cannot be reduced to unity is confusion," wrote Blaise Pascal, one of Jansenism's most devout adherents. "Unity," he continued, "which is not a multitude is tyranny." This, wrote François Guizot some two centuries later, "was the finest and most precise definition of representative government."[162] Pascal's formulation did not, of course, have anything in the first instance to do with representative government, even in Guizot's rather spiritual sense. It was aimed in-

---

[160] Montesquieu, *SL*, ed. Neumann, bk. 1, ch. 1, p. 2; bk. 3, chs. 5 and 6, pp. 23–4.

[161] For a recent overview of the critical response to Montesquieu's book, see Spector, *Montesquieu*, pp. 63–4.

[162] The passage can be found in Blaise Pascal, *Pensées*, ed. Brunschvicg, introd. Charles-Marc Des Granges (Paris, Garnier, 1958), *pensée* 871, p. 317, and in the translation of the Lafuma edition of the *Pensées* by John Warrington, ed. H. T. Barnwell (London, Everyman, 1960), *pensée* 848, p. 243. (I am grateful to Laurent Thirouin of the University of Lyon for directing me to it.) The passage is in François Guizot, *Histoire des origines du gouvernement représentatif en Europe*, 2 vols. (Paris, 1851), 1:93–4, and *The History of the Origins of Representative Government in Europe*, trans. Andrew R. Scoble, introd. Aurelian Craiutu (Indianapolis, Liberty Fund, 2002), p. 52 (I have modified the translation to restore the antithesis between "unity" and "multitude" in Pascal's formulation). See, too, Thomas Hare, *The Machinery of Representation* (London, 1857), pp. 37–8, and his *A Treatise on the Election of Representatives, Parliamentary and Municipal*, new ed. (London, 1861), p. 257 (both citing Guizot on Pascal).

stead at the government of the Catholic Church and was intended to explain both why the pope was not its absolute sovereign, and, in the context of the developing controversy over the content of Jansenius's *Augustinus*, why papal pronouncements on the putatively heretical propositions contained in that work were not necessarily authoritative for the church as a whole.[163] But the formulation was entirely compatible with the wider claims about the nature and limitations of sovereign power that became the hallmark of Jansenist legal and constitutional theory all the way through the eighteenth century. These, in turn, were connected to a strongly providential conception of the origins and nature of political power, one that set human affairs directly under the particular provisions made by the divine will. This aspect of Jansenist political theology has been somewhat neglected, in favour of either a rather secular rendition of Jansenist constitutional theory or one based very heavily on the figurist interpretations of scripture that were also a feature of Jansenist soteriology.[164] Figurism and providentialism could overlap, as they did in some of Jansenism's more millenarian moments, but the first was a derivation of the second. Without the providentialism, it is quite difficult to explain both the extraordinary persistence of Jansenist opposition to royal authority and, at the same time, its intense hostility towards almost every aspect of the modern world.

The key to the association between Jansenism and liberty was the idea of involuntary obligation. God, wrote Jansenism's most famous civil jurist, Jean Domat, in his *Treatise of Laws* of 1689, "having destined mankind for society, hath formed the ties which engage him to it."[165] Some of these engagements were voluntary, others involuntary. These latter, Domat stated, "are those under which God puts men without their own choice."

[163] For the deeper positions underlying the argument, see Thomas M. Lennon, *Reading Bayle* (Toronto, University of Toronto Press, 1999), pp. 42–80.

[164] See, on the one hand, Dale Van Kley, *The Jansenists and the Expulsion of the Jesuits from France, 1757–65* (New Haven, Yale University Press, 1975); *The Damiens Affair and the Unraveling of the Old Regime* (Princeton, Princeton University Press, 1984); "Pierre Nicole, Jansenism, and the Morality of Enlightened Self-Interest," in Alan Charles Kors and Paul J. Korshin, eds., *Anticipations of the Enlightenment in England, France and Germany* (Philadelphia, University of Pennsylvania Press, 1987); "The Jansenist Constitutional Legacy in the French Pre-revolution," in Keith Michael Baker, ed., *The Political Culture of the Old Regime* (Oxford, Pergamon Press, 1987), pp. 169–201; "The French Estates-General as Ecumenical Council," *Journal of Modern History* 61 (1989): 1–52; *The Religious Origins of the French Revolution* (New Haven, Yale University Press, 1996); "Christianity as Casualty and Chrysalis of Modernity: The Problem of Dechristianization in the French Revolution," *American Historical Review* 108 (2003): 1081–1103, and Dale Van Kley, ed., *The French Idea of Freedom* (Stanford, Stanford University Press, 1994); and, on the other, Catherine Maire, *De la cause de Dieu à la cause de la Nation. Le jansénisme au xviiie siècle* (Paris, Gallimard, 1998). For a concise overview, see William Doyle, *Jansenism* (London, Macmillan, 2000).

[165] Jean Domat, *A Treatise of Laws* [Paris, 1689], trans. William Strahan (London, 1722), ch. 2, §III, p. vi.

Among them, he wrote, were those arising from nomination to municipal office, or from becoming the guardian of an orphaned child, or from entrusting the management of one's affairs to a friend. Duty to the poor had the same involuntary character. The obligation that it entailed was as strong, however, as any of those arising from voluntary engagements.

> Thus, the condition of those who are members of society, who are destitute of the means of subsistence, and unable to work for their livelihood, lays an obligation on all their fellow members to exercise towards them mutual love, by imparting to them a share of those goods which they have a right to. For every man being a member of the society has a right to live in it: and that which is necessary to those who have nothing, and who are not able to gain their livelihood, is by consequence in the hands of the other members; from whence it follows, that they cannot without injustice detain it from them. And it is because of this engagement, that in publick necessities private persons are obliged, even by constraint, to assist the poor according to their wants.[166]

The Romans, Domat pointed out, "who have excelled all other nations in cultivating the civil laws," were "strangers to the knowledge of those principles."

> We have another very remarkable proof of it, in the idea which their philosophers gave them of the origin of the society of mankind, of which those principles are the foundation. For they were so far from knowing them, and from perceiving how they ought to form the union of men, that they imagined that men lived at first as wild beasts in the fields, without any communication, and without any tie to one another, until one of them bethought himself that it was possible to join them together in society, and began to civilize them for that purpose.[167]

The providential plan underlying human society was the expression of a divine will that governed the creation in particular ways, rather than, as with the Oratorian theologian Nicolas Malebranche, in terms of the internal coherence of a general will.[168] It lay behind the distinctions between nations, as well as those forming the many different occupations and activities to be found in every single nation. It applied as much to states and their rulers as it did to their members because it was providence, not human choice, that was the ultimate source of sovereignty and legality. Kings might be elected, or come to their thrones by inheritance, but the powers

---

[166] Domat, *Treatise*, ch. 4, §IV, p. xi.

[167] Domat, *Treatise*, ch. 1, §I, pp. i–ii, referring in a note to Cicero's *De inventionis*, bk. 1, §2 as evidence of the Romans' ignorance.

[168] On the different conceptions of providence arising from claims about whether God acted by way of particular or general wills, see Patrick Riley, *The General Will before Rousseau: The Transformation of the Divine into the Civic* (Princeton, Princeton University Press, 1986).

of life and death that they were entitled to exercise were not those that any human could authorise. As the Jansenist theologian Jacques-Joseph Duguet put it in the early eighteenth century, "we could hardly know" whether the "human origin of authority" was "usurped or lawful" if

> God had not taught us that he had ratified it, and that his providence has not only permitted the project and its inventors, but that he has render'd the power of government sacred by an immediate communication of His authority to those invested with it.[169]

But if government's power was sacred, its agents were still human. This was why they, too, were subject to the duties of office and the broader system of voluntary and involuntary engagements to which these offices belonged. As, following Domat, the author of a Jansenist pamphlet published during the arguments over Philip V of Spain's right to the French throne put it, voluntary engagements were no more or less binding than involuntary obligations.

> The first are those made by the will of a single person or by mutual consent. The second are those in which God has placed men without their own choice. These are the engagements of birth, of residence, of condition, etc., the duties of children, citizens, subjects, the prince, the responsibilities of town officials, or wards, etc.[170]

Rulers and magistrates were as subject to obligations as anyone else and had a duty to maintain all those aspects of society that provided for the needs of their members. These may well have included a wide variety of different occupations and conditions and, by extension, a great deal of inequality. But these aspects of the providential plan could not override the claims of either charity or legality, because legality was the divinely ordained framework that, as Pierre Nicole argued most memorably, allowed fallen human selfishness to mimic charity's injunctions.[171] "Properly speaking," wrote another Jansenist, the abbé Noël-Antoine Pluche, "it is to society in general, not to any single man, that every thing was given. Society alone is

---

[169] Jacques-Joseph Duguet, *Institution d'un prince ou traité des qualités, des vertus et des devoirs d'un souverain*, 4 vols. (Leiden, 1739), trans. *The Institution of a Prince, or a Treatise of the Virtues and Duties of a Sovereign*, 2 vols. (London, 1740), pt. I, ch. II, art. 1, pp. 11–2.

[170] [Secret], *Conférences*, p. 92.

[171] Cf. Pierre Nicole, "De la charité et de l'amour propre" [1673], reprinted most recently in Pierre Nicole, *Essais de morale*, ed. Laurent Thirouin (Paris, Presses universitaires de France, 1999). Domat simply repeated Nicole: "The fall of man not having freed him from his wants, and having on the contrary multiplied them, it hath also augmented the necessity of labour and commerce, and at the same time the necessity of engagements and ties; for no man being sufficient of himself to procure the necessities and conveniences of life, the diversity of wants engages men in an infinite number of ties without which they could not live." Domat, *Treatise*, ch. 9, §III, p. xx.

what can make man partake of the multiplicity of the bounties of the Creator."[172] This comprehensive characterisation of community entailed a strong commitment to the panoply of obligations, whether voluntary or involuntary, that it housed. "We see," wrote Domat, "in all these sorts of engagement and in all the others which we can imagine, that God forms them, and puts men under them, merely to employ them in the exercise of mutual love." It was this obligation to wish to others their true good that was "the principle and spirit of all those laws relating to engagements."[173] Almost all of the recurrent outbreaks of conflict between Jansenist magistrates and royal ministers during the eighteenth century are best understood from this point of view. Once the strong conviction about divine providence is put back in place, it is hard not to endorse the assessment of Jansenism that David Hume published in 1741. Superstition, he wrote, "is an enemy to civil liberty, and enthusiasm a friend to it." The Jansenists were "enthusiasts," and since enthusiasm was "the infirmity of bold and ambitious tempers," it was "naturally accompanied with a spirit of liberty."[174]

> The *Jansenists* are enthusiasts, and zealous promoters of the passionate devotion, and of the inward life; little influenced by authority and, in a word, but half catholics. The consequences are exactly conformable to the foregoing reasoning. The *Jesuits* are the tyrants of the people, and the slaves of the court: and the *Jansenists* preserve alive the small sparks of the love of liberty, which are to be found in the French nation.[175]

The strong conviction that human affairs were subject to the detailed plan of a providential order could, as Hume suggested, go hand in hand with a strong determination to maintain the array of obligations to which even royal sovereigns were bound. They were, after all, only human.

Public credit had no positive value in Jansenist political theology. Law's system, according to Jacques-Joseph Duguet, was "the most exorbitant usury" that had ever been devised.[176] Modern governments, he suggested, would be better advised to follow the practice of the rulers of imperial Rome. He proceeded to illustrate the point with a long quotation from

---

[172] Noël-Antoine Pluche, *Spectacle de la nature: or Nature Displayed. Being Discourses on such Particulars of Natural History as were thought most proper to excite the curiosity and form the minds of youth. Containing what belongs to man considered in society* [8 vols. (Paris, 1732–50)], 7 vols. (London, 1748), 6:3. On Pluche, see André Viala, "Les idées de l'abbé Pluche sur la société," in *La Régence*, Centre aixois d'études et de recherches sur le dix-huitième siècle (Paris, 1970), pp. 307–16; Denis Trinkle, "Noël-Antoine Pluche's *Le Spectacle de la Nature*: An Encyclopaedic Best Seller," *Studies on Voltaire and the Eighteenth Century* 358 (1997): 93–134.

[173] Domat, *Treatise*, ch. 4, §V, pp. xi–xii.

[174] David Hume, "Of Superstition and Enthusiasm" [1741], in Hume, *Essays*, ed. Miller, p. 78.

[175] Hume, "Of Superstition and Enthusiasm," p. 79.

[176] Duguet, *Institution of a Prince*, 2:448.

the sixth book of Tacitus's *Annals*, describing how the Roman emperor Tiberius Caesar had succeeded in enforcing Julius Caesar's law regulating the amount of land that each Roman citizen was entitled to hold by lending the plebeians large amounts of money at no interest at all to enable them to discharge their debts to their patrician creditors and retain possession of their land. A virtuous prince was, accordingly, advised to have a "great sum of money in reserve," using the resources of the state, as Caesar had done, to "diminish the value of interest and heighten the price of land."[177] It was quite easy for this position to be carried through to the period of the French Revolution. Thus one of the best-known figures within the Jansenist magistracy during the reigns of Louis XV and Louis XVI, the Parisian magistrate Robert de Saint-Vincent, was both an unequivocal opponent of the royal government *and* a supporter of a default on the debt. In a pamphlet published in 1781 he argued that while it might perhaps be preferable to increase taxation "in a great state, where the nation participates in the administration," as was the case in England, this was not desirable

> when a government is arbitrary and respects neither property nor the rights of the people and abuses the power entrusted it to destroy rather than to preserve. Then every means it uses to obtain resources are equally cruel and vicious.

In this case, he suggested, public credit was the lesser of the two evils because "the only danger would be a general bankruptcy that would bear solely upon the most well-to-do class," while additional taxation would affect "the most indigent class."[178] If the choice lay between ruining the rich and ruining the poor, then Robert de Saint-Vincent opted for ruining the rich. He was to remain true to his position in July 1789 when he threw in his hand with the baron de Breteuil's Ministry of the Hundred Hours in what was to become the last, abortive, attempt to rescue the established political order.[179] Other Jansenists certainly made different choices. But

---

[177] Duguet, *Institution of a Prince*, 2:453–4.

[178] [Robert de Saint-Vincent], *Observations modestes d'un citoyen sur les opérations de finance de M. Necker, et sur son Compte-rendu adressées à MM les pacifiques auteurs des Comment? des Pourquoi? Et autres pamphlets anonymes* (n.p., n.d).

[179] Pierre de Vaissière, *Lettres d' "aristocrates". La Révolution racontée par des correspondances privées* (Paris, 1907), p. 139. On Robert de Saint-Vincent's role, first in taking the lead in opposing the royal edicts of 19 November 1787 committing the state to an additional 420 millions' worth of debt ("on livre la fortune public, et on peut le dire, le sort de l'état, à des hommes sans pudeur, et dont l'avidité ne connoit pas de bornes") but, at the same time, granting civil rights to non-Catholics, and then, on 25 September 1788, in proposing the Paris parlement's ruling that the Estates-General should deliberate as it had done in 1614, see Guy-Marie Sallier, *Annales françaises depuis le commencement du règne de Louis XVI jusqu'aux états généraux*, 2nd ed. (Paris, 1813), pp. 115–37, 209 (p. 119).

their broad support for the confiscation of the property of the church in November 1789 and their later advocacy of a civil constitution for the French clergy were entirely consistent with earlier Jansenist conceptions of both the nature of the church and its government and the broader system of voluntary and involuntary obligations to which it, like every human institution, was subject. If, as it has been suggested, the French Revolution had "religious origins," these pointed rather more towards the communal politics of the period after 1789 than to a system of representative government that, at least as Sieyès envisaged it, was designed to block off exactly this possibility.[180]

Fénelon and His Legacy

The other alternative to Montesquieu's conception of monarchy effectively amounted to an endorsement of both the published and unpublished parts of his *History of the Troglodytes*. In keeping with the logic of the Troglodytes' adoption of both a royal government and then of commerce and the arts, this meant advocating a programme of political reform designed to promote and maintain equality and to secure the position of a powerful royal sovereign at the head of the whole edifice. But in place of Fénelon's programme of drastic taxation, public credit appeared to offer a less painful alternative. This, in practice, meant divesting the monarchy of its feudal legacy in order to extend the benefits of society to as many of its members as possible. The best-known and, in some respects, the most influential of these programmes of political reform was the marquis d'Argenson's *Considérations sur le gouvernement ancien et présent de la France*.[181] D'Argenson was the most intellectually prolific member of a remarkable family, whose commitment to equality and protection of an assortment of like-minded writers ran from the early eighteenth century up to 1848 and beyond.[182] He was an assiduous reader and conscientious diarist. His private jottings and papers make it a little easier to see why one of his contemporaries, the duc de Richelieu, called him the "secretary of state of Plato's republic."[183] "If today I were the favourite of the king, his prime minister, or were en-

---

[180] Cf. Van Kley, *Religious Origins of the French Revolution*.

[181] The best study of the political thought of the marquis d'Argenson is Nannerl O. Henry, "Democratic Monarchy: The Political Theory of the Marquis d'Argenson," (Ph.D. diss., Yale University, 1968); see, too, the same author's more concise overview in Nannerl O. Keohane, *Philosophy and the State in France* (Princeton, Princeton University Press, 1980), pp. 376–91.

[182] Some indication of the family's abiding concerns can be found in Elizabeth L. Eisenstein, *The First Professional Revolutionist: Filippo Michele Buonarroti (1761–1831)* (Cambridge, Mass., Harvard University Press, 1959), pp. 109–16.

[183] Cited in *Journal et Mémoires du Marquis d'Argenson*, ed. E.J.B. Rathéry, 9 vols. (Paris, 1859–67), 1:xxxi.

trusted with his finances and the most accredited of his ministers, as was Maximilian de Sully with Henri IV," d'Argenson noted in 1744,

> I would persuade his majesty to think solely, for ten years, of paying off his debts and of improving his estates, so that after those ten years he would be the greatest king on earth. . . . Every year he would keep the public informed of the progress made in reducing the state's debts and obligations; would reimburse the most onerous and dangerous of the venal offices; turn perpetual into life annuities; alienate the royal domain in perpetuity and burn its titles; authorise the repurchase of all feudal dues on the land, and a hundred other things: my system of democracy; increase the funds, establish a royal fiduciary bank to enjoy vast interest-free sums . . . keeping the army as a militia and the navy in the shipyards.[184]

His papers include a long manuscript, entitled "Political Reflections on Public Credit and Its Utility in a State Like France" ("Réflexions politiques sur le crédit public, et sur son utilité, dans un état tel que la France").[185] The work was written in 1734 or 1735, at the time of French involvement in the War of the Polish Succession. It was an unabashed defence of Law's system. Its startling thesis was that "a state that uses public credit and goes bankrupt every ten years will become much more powerful, despite its bankruptcy, than a similar state that makes no use of public credit."[186] Its argument echoed Law's. "When one is forced to contract debts," it began, "one should, as far as possible, try to avoid the most onerous. Properly examined, public credit is not a debt."

> It is, rather, the fabrication of a new kind of money. It is a form of value that is a companion to circulating coin and acts in the same way. It should be maintained, not extinguished. It is never a charge upon either the king or the state but is infinitely useful to them both. The king should be the debtor, or rather the faithful guarantor of a great treasury that costs him nothing to supply, that should last as long as the monarchy itself, and whose capital should never be reimbursed. It is therefore a kind of imaginary debt sanctioned by his will and he should take great care to ensure that it is preserved.[187]

The initial difficulty was to get this "imaginary debt" securely established. Here, the example of the Dutch was instructive. Although the Bank of Amsterdam had been established when the United Provinces was a republic, it owed little to the consent of the Dutch people. "They opposed it

---

[184] *Journal et Mémoires du Marquis d'Argenson*, ed. Rathéry, 4:107–9 (5 August 1744).

[185] Bibliothèque universitaire de Poitiers, Fonds d'Argenson, P. 60, chemise ix, Angleterre II.

[186] Bibliothèque universitaire de Poitiers, Fonds d'Argenson, P. 60, chemise ix, Angleterre II, fol. 4.

[187] "Réflexions," fol. 63.

furiously; there were seditious movements. The most rigorous punishments were needed to enrich a poor, brutal, ignorant people who would have stagnated in gross stupidity without the farsighted vision (*lumières perçantes*) and unshakeable firmness of her magistrates."[188] The implication was obvious. What the Dutch magistrates had been able to achieve was even more easily within the reach of a monarchy.

> If there is any country in which public credit can work to greatest effect and be most unshakeable, it is one that is subject to monarchical power. Everyone is in agreement that this form of government is the most perfect and, without going into a detailed examination of the reasons for this opinion, I need only say that it is because power is less subject to contradiction and decisions are more prompt.[189]

No one could refuse a king who decided to establish a system of public credit. The danger, of course, lay in its abuse. But even if it could be proved that bankruptcy was a certainty, this would still not be sufficient reason for deciding against public credit. "A bankruptcy of credit is a particular evil that a certain number of people will suffer. The cessation of all credit, caused by the stubborn folly of not using public credit at all, is a general evil that the whole body of the nation will suffer."[190] This was the lesson to be learned from Law's system. It had prevented a general credit crunch and, despite its failure, had doubled the tax intake while leaving the nation's agriculture, industry, and trade in a much healthier state than they had been in 1715.[191]

There was a close affinity between this defence of public credit and d'Argenson's own published views. In one of the few works that he published in his own lifetime—an anonymous *Letter* about a dissertation on commerce by the Italian marquis de Belloni that appeared in the *Journal oeconomique* of April 1751—d'Argenson introduced the slogan that was to become the hallmark of the opposition to what came to be known as the mercantile system. Belloni's advice to governments to use tariffs to promote industry was, d'Argenson argued, familiar and wrong. Such counsel was directed not at the good of commerce but at that of particular individuals, and, he claimed, all too frequently overrode the public good.

> The multitude should be left alone to go about its affairs (*Qu'on laisse faire la multitude*) and be allowed to disabuse us of such systems, to the great profit of society. It will teach us that the passage of merchandise from one state to another should be as free as water and air. All Europe should be one general,

---

[188] "Réflexions," fol. 43.
[189] "Réflexions," fol. 44.
[190] "Réflexions," fol. 68.
[191] "Réflexions," fols. 81 and 84.

common fair. The inhabitant of the nation that does the best will find the best and profit the most.[192]

One day, d'Argenson concluded, our nephews, disabused by experience, would laugh at the malady of those European nations presently attempting to force the principles of trade into a system. "They will place it on the same rank that we now assign to the Crusades and that we will soon come to give to the insanity of the European political balance."[193] This brought d'Argenson's idea of monarchy into line with the broader features of the abbé de Saint-Pierre's peace plan and Henri IV's Grand Design (it is worth noting that Saint-Pierre, like Voltaire, too, was also an admirer of Law's system, arguing in 1725 that, despite its failure, its positive effects could still be achieved by a more decentralised version of the same mechanisms).[194]

The key to d'Argenson's idea of monarchy (as, too, for Saint-Pierre, Dubos, and Voltaire) was the difference between what he called monarchy and royalty.[195] The distinction, which began with Bodin, was based on the difference between dominion and empire, or power based on ownership and power based on sovereignty. The feudal system involved a conflation of the two, which meant that the version of monarchy that it had spawned was simply a large-scale version of feudal ownership, which could, by extension, imply that the king was, in some sense, the real owner of the state.[196] Defining true monarchy, or what d'Argenson called royalty, required distinguishing the sovereign power involved in empire from the local power involved in dominion, so that the owners of property were subordinate to the sovereign, while the rights of sovereignty, including the right to dispense justice, could be differentiated clearly from those that pertained to property, particularly as these applied to the owners of feudal domains. The result was a closer association between sovereignty and justice than Montesquieu had made. Where Montesquieu used the distinction between dominion and empire to highlight the bifurcation of monarchy into two distinct entities—a single sovereign and a number of subordinate, dependent, and intermediate powers, responsible among other things for maintaining legality, if not justice itself—d'Argenson used

---

[192] "Lettre à l'auteur du *Journal oeconomique* au sujet de la dissertation sur le commerce de M. le marquis Belloni," *Journal oeconomique* (Paris, April 1751), pp. 107–17 (113–4). The whole of the letter, d'Argenson stated, was a commentary upon the words used by a merchant to Colbert: *laissez-nous faire* (p. 110).

[193] *Journal oeconomique* (April 1751), pp. 116–7.

[194] See his unpublished memorandum printed in Paul Harsin, *Crédit public et banque d'état en France du xvie au xviiie siècles* (Paris, Droz, 1933), pp. 133–53.

[195] Argenson, *Considérations* (1764), pp. 2–3.

[196] See, helpfully, Herbert H. Rowen, *The King's State: Proprietary Dynasticism in Early Modern France* (New Brunswick, Rutgers University Press, 1980).

a more conventional version of the same distinction to highlight the post-feudal character of absolute government and its ability to accommodate an office-based administrative system that could be separated off from the ownership of property, but which would still retain the unitary character of indivisible sovereignty.

The details of d'Argenson's idea of monarchy were presented in the main body of the *Considérations*. Its purpose, he wrote, was to show "that popular administration could be exercised under the authority of the sovereign without diminishing, but rather increasing, public power, so that it would be the source of the happiness of peoples."[197] The creation of such an administration entailed dismantling the apparatus of privilege, venality, and regulation that was the combined legacy of the feudal system and the financial expedients adopted to promote French external power. Instead of seeking grandeur and acquisitions abroad, d'Argenson argued, France should mine its untapped resources at home.

> We should focus our attention upon the countryside, upon internal trade—infinitely preferable to trade abroad—upon the amount of freedom and ingenuity (*génie*) to be left to the labour of citizens, upon the equality of goods, upon dwelling houses and population, upon the mainsprings of interest that are the cause of action or obligation—these are the subjects worthy of a truly politic government; they will produce true glory, even abroad, rather than a vain and sterile glory.[198]

The law of both the king and the nation, he asserted, was to be found in its entirety in the five Latin words *salus populi suprema lex esto*.[199] It implied a different system of government, a royal rather than an absolute monarchy, in which the principles of democracy were combined with the sovereign authority of a royal protector. "Democracy," d'Argenson wrote, "is as much the friend of monarchy as aristocracy is its enemy."[200] Achieving the kind of republican monarchy that he envisaged entailed separating the two attributes of sovereignty—force and justice—from the administrative system by decentralising administration onto a multitude of smaller units. The history of Spain and Portugal, d'Argenson observed, revealed a significant principle in politics. The smaller a state was, the better governed it was in comparison to a larger state with the same type of government. This was why Portugal had withstood better than Spain the ravages of empire and the influx of gold and silver.

---

[197] Argenson, *Considérations* (1784), pp. 9–10.
[198] Argenson, *Considérations* (1764), p. 21.
[199] Argenson, *Considérations* (1784), p. 195.
[200] Argenson, *Considérations* (1764), p. 148.

It is useful therefore to divide the cares, the goods, the districts, and each sphere of interest; the more carefully the object is treated, the more its mechanisms are quick and constant. But knowing how far this reduction should be taken is perhaps one of the first and most essential questions of the practical science of government.[201]

In this reformulation of the old problem of how far to carry the principle of divide and rule, d'Argenson emphasised the advantages of dividing authority to the point at which individual interests were too weak to challenge the authority of the central government but remained sufficiently strong to allow for the pursuit of individual utility. "Unity is strength; disunity produces weakness. Thus one can divide the parts of a state and subdivide spheres of authority up to the point at which they are able to govern themselves well but cannot cast a shadow over the general authority from which they emanate."[202] Managed successfully, the advantages would outweigh the disadvantages caused by the apparent dilution of authority.

> Labour performed by individuals for their own utility always seems less painful and considerable and is always better done. Work for the generality is executed by mechanisms that are too complicated and extensive to be perfect and, at the least, are always subject to slackness. The consequences of this principle go a long way in politics and are insufficiently reflected upon.[203]

A model of this kind of decentralised and office-based system of administration could, he suggested, be found in the Roman government of Gaul whose vestiges still survived in the *vigueries* of Provence and the municipal governments of the parts of the kingdom in which provincial estates still survived (*pays d'états*).[204] In this sense, d'Argenson's neo-Roman model of reform paralleled the office-based system of royal government advocated by his friends and political allies, Voltaire, the abbé de Saint-Pierre, and the abbé Dubos, during the three decades that followed the death of Louis XIV. Election to office, d'Argenson proposed, should become the basis of a decentralised administration made up of a network of district assemblies whose members would be elected from the municipal governments of the provinces in which they were located. These assemblies would, in turn, elect the members of a revitalised conciliar system responsible for giving counsel to the sovereign on matters related to the exercise of justice and the use of force both at home and abroad.[205] This did not mean that they would have any share of sovereign power. To be useful, monarchical au-

---

[201] Argenson, *Considérations* (1764), pp. 86–7.
[202] Argenson, *Considérations* (1764), pp. 30–1.
[203] Argenson, *Considérations* (1764), p. 275.
[204] Argenson, *Considérations* (1784), p. 117.
[205] Argenson, *Considérations* (1784), pp. 200–1, 220, 233.

thority should be enlightened, not shared.[206] But it did mean that every other kind of power should not depend on birth, apart from the single institution of the monarchy itself. Here, hereditary succession was a necessity (Poland exemplified the catastrophic consequences of its absence), but, d'Argenson argued, in matters of command over men, all inferior places should be subject to the choice of the sovereign or to election under the aegis of rules prescribed by the public authority.[207]

This principle applied as much to the ownership of land as to office. If Lycurgus's division of the land was a counsel of perfection that would necessarily be modified by differences in talent and fortune, this did not mean that inequality should be reinforced by the effects of inheritance. As d'Argenson commented, "every type of grandeur and innate fortune is vicious for the man who is satisfied with them and wrongly accepts them."[208] Property in land was usurpation secured by proscription. Its distribution was subject, as much as anything else, to the law of suitability (*le droit de convenance*), which, d'Argenson asserted, was the voice of reason and the source of public happiness and had, therefore, to take preference over the rights of titles and even that of possession.[209]

> Every day the interests of the state are confused far too much with those of individuals. It was once, for example, very important that sovereignty should not be shared, as it was under the first and second dynasties, among the members of the royal family. But as for the preservation of our much vaunted great fiefs, what difference does it make to the state whether they are dismembered or intact. . . . One should, by now, be persuaded that dismembering the great fiefs would be a precious good for the state or everything that I have said is no more than a long sophism. . . . Dividing the fiefs and royal domains would produce twenty different administrators able to replace sterility with abundance. Here the public interest is in opposition to a single family. Let the legislator choose after that.[210]

In the longer term, the new kind of monarchy that d'Argenson envisaged would have no room for anything other than a genuinely virtuous nobility. From this perspective, a postfeudal government would be one that was able to establish and maintain equality and prosperity by, as d'Argenson's compound of municipal administration and absolute monarchy implied, adding the political institutions of the ancients to the commercial, fiscal, and financial resources of the modern state.

---

[206] Argenson, *Considérations* (1784), p. 124.
[207] Argenson, *Considérations* (1784), pp. 128–9.
[208] Argenson, *Considérations* (1764), pp. 128–9.
[209] Argenson, *Considérations* (1764), p. 18.
[210] Argenson, *Considérations* (1764), pp. 307–8.

TRADE, THE SYSTEM OF RANKS, AND
THE ALTERNATIVE TO PUBLIC CREDIT

Montesquieu's own position was different. "I am not ignorant," he commented, "that men filled with two ideas, the one that commerce is the most useful thing in the world to a state, and the other, that the Romans had the best regulated government in the world, have believed that these people greatly honoured and encouraged commerce; but the truth is, that they rarely troubled their heads about it."[211] The remark was probably aimed at François Boureau Deslandes's *Essai sur la marine et le commerce* (Essay on Commerce and the Navy) or the abbé Gabriel Bonnot de Mably's *Parallèle des français et des romains* (Parallel between the French and the Romans), both of which, unlike d'Argenson's book, had been published, but it could equally have been applied to d'Argenson himself. Like almost everything published to promote reform in the decade before the War of the Austrian Succession, their works shared a common concern with combining ancient politics and modern commerce to promote French prosperity at home and power abroad. Montesquieu rejected this kind of combination. Monarchy and trade, he argued, were both modern. Trade had undergone many revolutions over the course of time and had acquired a range of financial instruments that had come to shield it from political interference. "We begin," he commented, "to be cured of Machiavelism, and recover from it every day. . . . What would formerly have been called a master-stroke in politics would be now . . . the greatest imprudence." This new situation meant that "though their passions prompt them to be wicked," men now had an "interest to be humane and virtuous."[212] In this sense, Montesquieu's argument paralleled the *Anti-Machiavel*, as, too, did his famous remark that "it is almost a general rule, that wherever we find agreeable manners, there commerce flourishes; and that wherever there is commerce, there we meet with agreeable manners."[213] But unlike Voltaire, Melon, d'Argenson, or the abbé de Saint-Pierre, Montesquieu also argued that there was only one kind of trade that was compatible with monarchy. This was trade based on luxury. The claim completed the argument implied by both the abandoned sequel of the Troglodyte history and the *Considerations* on the Romans. If luxury was an effect of inequality and if inequality was incompatible with republican rule, then monarchy was the only system of government that could live with them both.

As Montesquieu presented it, luxury served to neutralise the potentially divisive effects of inequality, not, as was usually argued, because the expen-

[211] Montesquieu, *SL*, bk. 21, ch. 14, p. 358 (Cambridge ed., p. 382).
[212] Montesquieu, *SL*, bk. 21, ch. 20, p. 366.
[213] Montesquieu, *SL*, bk. 20, ch. 1, p. 316.

diture of the rich supplied the income of the poor, but because of the way that it could become the basis of a tax regime founded upon a high-interest, high-price, but still competitive, trading economy. The way that it could was summarised in the second of the two commentaries on *The Spirit of Laws* that Montesquieu himself seems to have liked. This one was written in 1751 by a Bordeaux wholesale merchant named François Risteau.[214] As Risteau presented his argument, Montesquieu had shown that the combination of a single sovereign and a number of subordinate, dependent, and intermediate powers served to make territorial monarchies more suited to industry and trade than trading republics themselves. This, he went on to explain, was an effect of competition for funds in a society that was predicated upon display. Montesquieu had actually made the point somewhat telegraphically in a note on the subject of fashion that he had deleted from the final manuscript of *The Spirit of Laws*: "I would willingly go along here with the ideas of the author of *The Fable of the Bees* and would ask to be shown the sober citizens of any country who do them as much good as is done to certain trading nations by their coxcombs (*petits maîtres*)."[215] Bernard Mandeville (the author of *The Fable of the Bees*) had, in fact, produced an explanation of why, famously, "private vices" could be "public benefits" that could be associated either with the providentialism of Jansenist moral theory or with the more secular endorsement of modernity made by Voltaire or the abbé de Saint-Pierre.[216] Montesquieu's own position was both more historical and more directly connected to an analysis of the structure of markets produced by the unequal distribution of property and by the division of the economy into a trading and a nontrading sector.

Risteau's summary of his position was a reply to an attack on *The Spirit of Laws* by one of Montesquieu's critics, the abbé Joseph Delaporte. Like many others, Delaporte had taken issue with Montesquieu's rejection of virtue as the fundamental principle of monarchical government, arguing that he had mistaken the social inequality and extravagant ostentation prevailing in modern France for the nature of monarchy itself. A political system in which everyone, as in Fénelon's reformed kingdom of Salentum, was satisfied with what was necessary would, he argued, not only be one with more room for patriotism and the virtues commensurate with the glory of the prince and the state, but would also be a more effective trading

---

[214] François Risteau, *Réponse aux Observations sur l'Esprit des Loix* (Amsterdam, 1751), reprinted in Montesquieu, *Lettres familières* (Rome, 1773), from which subsequent citations arc taken.

[215] Montesquieu, *Pensées*, no. 1553, ed. Desgraves, p. 498; see, more generally, Pierre Rétat, "De Mandeville à Montesquieu: honneur, luxe et dépense noble dans l' 'Esprit des lois,' " *Studi Francese* 50 (1973): 238–49.

[216] On these readings of Mandeville, see Edward J. Hundert, *The Enlightenment's Fable: Bernard Mandeville and the Discovery of Society* (Cambridge, CUP, 1994), and Hont, "Luxury."

nation. According to Delaporte, Montesquieu's claim that trade in a monarchy "is generally founded on luxury" and in republics "is commonly founded on economy" was fundamentally misconceived; it was also the source of what Delaporte held was his mistaken endorsement of Cicero's opinion "that he did not like that the same people should be at once both the lords and factors of the whole earth."[217] There was no reason, Delaporte insisted, why a monarchy with a population of twenty million could not do both. Less waste and extravagance, he claimed, would enable France to make better use of its size, population, and geographical endowments to avoid the threat of competition from poorer countries able to produce manufactured goods at lower prices by building up a larger share of world trade through the sale of agricultural products and other bulk goods to other, less well-endowed nations. Greater frugality in the kingdom's political economy would, therefore, simultaneously provide more of a home for the social virtues and a solution to the "rich country–poor country" problem in world trade.[218]

In his reply, Risteau began by pointing out that Montesquieu had not meant to define trade founded on economy as "trafficking in those things necessary for life" or trade founded on luxury as "traffic in those things that have some relationship to luxury."[219] What was at issue was not the type of goods involved in trade, but the profit-making mechanisms in the two systems of trade and the way that these were connected to the levels of social equality and demand for credit in the two types of economy. Trade founded upon economy was trade based upon low profit margins and a high level of turnover; trade founded on luxury depended upon high profit margins and low turnover. "If it were otherwise," Risteau commented, "it would follow that there would be none other than goldsmiths, jewellers, precious stone dealers, makers of fine cloth and other merchants, artists and artisans of that sort undertaking trade founded on luxury." But this would make it hard to describe the activities of the six- to seven-hundred-strong French merchant fleet unless it were supposed that it was involved in trade founded upon economy. But, Risteau pointed out, the French trading

[217] Montesquieu, *SL*, bk. 20, ch. 4, p. 318. For a sensitive discussion of Montesquieu and Cicero in the broader context of his scepticism about the compatibility between republican government and the modern world, see Yoshie Kawade, "Ciceronian Moment: Republicanism and Republican Language in Cicero," *University of Tokyo Journal of Law and Politics 2* (2005): 13–28.

[218] For a broader discussion of the question, see Istvan Hont, "The 'Rich Country–Poor Country' Debate in Scottish Classical Political Economy," in Istvan Hont and Michael Ignatieff, eds., *Wealth and Virtue: The Shaping of Political Economy in the Scottish Enlightenment* (Cambridge, 1983), pp. 271–316, reprinted in his *Jealousy of Trade: International Competition and the Nation-State in Historical Perspective* (Cambridge, Mass., Harvard University Press), pp. 267–322.

[219] Risteau, *Réponse*, p. 328.

system was not like that of the Dutch, "who sail more cheaply than any other people of Europe." The Dutch system was a genuine example of trade founded upon economy. The abundant supply of funds, the relative absence of alternative outlets for investment, and their skill in keeping shipping costs as low as possible enabled them to undertake trading ventures in which the returns were only a little above the ordinary rate of interest. As Risteau put it, they were happy to earn small amounts but to do so continually.

> In those countries in which fashion has not reached a level at which it pushes people to have needs above their estates and their means, money is more abundant than elsewhere. It yields barely half the rate of interest that it does in monarchies where luxury reigns. It is to this reason, namely, the considerable quantity of money with no other outlet, that I would attribute that daring for great ventures that the author of *The Spirit of Laws* signals in republics and which is but rarely to be found in monarchies, where each individual is more anxious to establish a position above that of the merchant, to win men's favour and procure all the ease supplied by luxury . . . than to form new commercial projects.[220]

Trade in monarchies had, therefore, to be based not upon the number of enterprises but upon the level of profit generated by any particular undertaking. A wholesale merchant in an opulent country would not undertake anything unless assured of a higher profit than would be necessary in a country in which luxury had been banished and trade founded upon economy was the norm.

Montesquieu's conception of monarchy allowed luxury to offset inequality. It would do so, he also emphasised, in an entirely open economy, where prices were set by global markets for goods and money. As far as "money, notes, bills of exchange, stocks in companies, vessels, and, in fine, all merchandise" were concerned, "the whole world" was "composed of one single state, of which all the societies upon earth were members."[221] But competition between them did not mean that trade itself had to follow a single pattern. The internal structure of monarchy served to shape the character of its trade. Here, instead of the effects produced by equality, either by levelling down or levelling up, the dynamics of acquisitive emulation between the component parts of a rich, open, and highly stratified society would produce a number of different, but overlapping, markets to build up and maintain the wealth required for both domestic prosperity and external security. The pressure to keep up appearances and the relatively high levels of borrowing that this entailed would have the effect of crowding out funds

---

[220] Risteau, *Réponse*, p. 332.
[221] Montesquieu, *SL*, bk. 20, ch. 23, p. 328.

that might otherwise be available for the type of low-return, high-turnover trade based on broad, integrated markets that was the hallmark of the political economy of a trading republic. Profitable undertakings had, therefore, to meet and overcome the constraints imposed by the dynamics of acquisitive emulation generated by the social hierarchy. This placed a premium on fashion and on innovations designed not so much to cut costs as to raise profits to a level compatible with the erratic schedules of a low-turnover, high-cost manufacturing and trading system—either by opening up new markets, or by devising new processes, or by creating new products, or, more generally, by finding ways to keep up the momentum of innovation by a continuous process of technical or market or product substitution. As Montesquieu also emphasised, the panoply of venal offices created during the reign of Louis XIV formed a convenient link between the trade-based system of innovation and the family-based system of inheritance, allowing the aspirant rich to move from industry and trade into office and land, but maintaining the pressure upon the funds needed for further cycles of profitable innovation. The fact that the nobility was not involved directly in trade not only had the effect of leaving a level of society above the vagaries of the markets and prices, and of preventing positions of power and influence from being used for commercial advantage; it also had the further effect of generating a strong demand for private credit.

The intense demand for credit caused by the pressure of social emulation could then be combined with a fiscal system designed to tax expenditure on nonessential items to produce a large enough tax base to generate the income stream needed to meet the state's domestic and external expenditure. There was, therefore, a close connection between the way that Montesquieu went about calibrating luxury as the basis of a consumer-driven tax regime (using Plato's *Laws* to illustrate the idea) and his endorsement of private credit.[222] If necessities were zero on the scale that he envisaged, and double the level of the necessity was one (so that the subsequent geometrical progression would always be double plus one), then a calibrated sales tax could be used to tap luxury without jeopardising the pricing structure that trade based on luxury was required to adopt. The income produced by this kind of tax regime would make it unnecessary for the state itself to borrow money. "Some," Montesquieu commented (in a remark that was probably aimed at Jean-François Melon's famous claim that public credit was simply a matter of the left hand's lending to the right), "have imagined that it was for the advantage of a state to be indebted to itself."[223] Those who were of this opinion, Montesquieu argued, had confused commercial paper with the paper representing a state's debt. The

---

[222] The Platonic model is in Montesquieu, *SL*, bk. 7, ch. 1, p. 94.
[223] Montesquieu, *SL*, bk. 23, ch. 17, p. 394.

former signified real wealth, but the latter did not. It was, instead, a claim upon wealth that, if it was owned abroad, would generate an outflow of interest payments and lower the rate of exchange and, however it was owned, would add an extra level of taxation to the costs of producing real wealth as well as a built-in transfer of resources "to the indolent." These, Montesquieu concluded flatly, were "the inconveniences of public debts. I know of no advantages."[224]

Private credit, he argued, could do as much as a centralised system of government borrowing. If ten individuals were to convert their annual income of a thousand crowns each into an investment in the funds at 5 percent, then a state would be able to raise a sum of 200,000 crowns. But if they lent half their income to one another, the state would still have the same quantity of wealth at its disposal. It would be able to tax both their original expenditure and the expenditure generated by the credit made available to those who would not otherwise have been able to spend on the same scale.[225] Since, as Montesquieu also argued, taxes on goods, rather than persons or land, were "natural" to "moderate governments" because they represented less of a threat to property or liberty, and if these taxes were paid in the first instance by the seller before being wrapped up in the final price, then the trading sector would be the first in line to carry the costs of state expenditure before generalising them over the affluent part of society by way of its consumption. The only danger to which this virtuous circle might be subject was a high tax yield and the possibility that the influx of funds could tempt a government to embark upon costly and adventurous projects. It was, Montesquieu warned, a danger to which free states like Britain were particularly prone, because it would be the signal that the legislative and executive powers had begun to fuse.

Monarchy as such was less exposed to this kind of risk. Its grounding in indivisible hereditary property and the divorce between nobles and commercial activities built into its nature a powerful interest with a strong aversion to high taxation. The pressure to keep up appearances might lead some individuals to ruin themselves, but the openness of the elite would still allow them to be replaced, so that the flow of consumption-based tax revenue would not be impaired. More important, the ban on trade by nobles would set a floor underneath the costs of private credit. Since the sale of landed products would have to be carried out by intermediaries, credit would be built into the distribution and sale of primary goods right from the start.[226] Nobles would borrow against their future income, just as

---

[224] Montesquieu, *SL*, bk. 23, ch. 17, p. 394.

[225] Montesquieu, *SL*, bk. 23, ch. 17, p. 394.

[226] Recent research in eighteenth-century French economic history has served to confirm Montesquieu's insight: see Philip T. Hoffman, *Growth in a Traditional Society: The French*

wholesale and retail merchants would borrow against their future profits. The credit built into the agricultural sector would then be reinforced by the credit needed to maintain the expenditure and consumption patterns of the rich because the monetary flows produced by the sale of agricultural goods and the purchase of consumer goods could not be synchronised. Piecemeal entry into the nobility by way of venal office would also slow down the rate of increase of the trading sector and set a brake on the supply of capital available for commercial purposes. The result would be a structural demand for funds and an upward pressure on interest rates (Montesquieu had no time for the traditional claim that interest on money was usury). The trading sector would, as a result, be forced to seek high returns on its goods to cover the cost of its funds. It would, therefore, be obliged to adopt a pricing strategy that followed the product cycle, charging high prices for new or fashionable goods and cutting them ferociously when the product cycle turned, both to keep competitors from entering the market and to maintain the segmented structure of markets for products of different kinds.[227] Provided that the stream of small-scale innovation could be maintained and standardisation avoided (Montesquieu was extremely suspicious of the putative advantages of mechanisation), there was no reason to think that this product-cycle-driven way of promoting prosperity could not be generalised over the whole society. The strong demand for private credit would also function as a buffer between the domestic economy and the wider international market, allowing trade to be free, but keeping it relatively insulated from the possible disruption produced by exposure to variations in trade balances and monetary flows arising from strong dependence on foreign trade. Instead of the kind of homogeneity generated by broadening and deepening markets as the modernisers envisaged, Montesquieu advocated a different kind of economic system, one that was equally market-based, but which also fitted a system of rule made up of both a unitary centre and a number of subordinate, dependent, and intermediate powers. It was modern, but it was not unified. It was not quite so clear, however, whether it was also just.

Countryside, 1450–1815 (Princeton, Princeton University Press, 1996); Philip T. Hoffman, Gilles Postel-Vinay, and Jean-Laurent Rosenthal, _Priceless Markets: The Political Economy of Credit in Paris, 1660–1870_ (Chicago, 2000), trans. as _Des marchés sans prix. Une économie politique du crédit à Paris, 1660–1870_ (Paris, Editions de l'Ecole des Hautes Etudes en Sciences Sociales, 2001).

[227] See Michael Sonenscher, "Fashion's Empire: Theories of Foreign Trade in Early Eighteenth-Century France," in Robert Fox and Anthony Turner, eds., _Innovation and Markets in Eighteenth-Century France_ (London, Hambledon Press, 1998).

ᴄ᷎3᷎ᴄ

MORALITY AND POLITICS IN A DIVIDED WORLD

Montesquieu's Legacy

ACCORDING to the German philosopher Johann Gottfried Herder, "Montesquieu's noble, gigantic work" was "a *Gothic* edifice, according to the philosophical taste of its age," offering, he added, "*esprit*—and often no more than that."[1] The judgement was widely shared, as, too, were attempts to give Montesquieu's enigmatic book a stronger normative content. Before two generations had passed, it was possible to discover either that *The Spirit of Laws* explained why absolute government was uniquely compatible with the ancient Roman maxim *salus populi suprema lex esto* on which every state was based, or that its account of the Germanic origins of the English constitution had played a significant part in bringing the "ancient body" of the French monarchy to the edge of "total ruin," or that its several, entirely negative, allusions to James Harrington's *Oceana* were in fact designed to alert the attentive reader to Montesquieu's covert support for the agrarian that Harrington, like Fénelon and d'Argenson, had commended, and, more broadly, to his disguised endorsement of the continuing salience of the Greek, and particularly the Platonic, tradition in modern political thought.[2] The joke attributed to Helvétius, that the easiest way to recognise a fool was to come across someone who claimed to have understood Montesquieu, was quite well aimed. The Roman Montesquieu pointed towards unitary sovereignty and an office-based system of government and administration. His German counterpart implied weaker sovereignty and a balanced system of government, while his Greek incarnation suggested the merit-based hierarchy and egalitarian distribution of property of Fénelon's reformed kingdom of Salentum.

Most of the claims about the putatively Roman, German, or Greek arrangements underlying Montesquieu's political vision were, however,

---

[1] Johann Gottfried Herder, *Another Philosophy of History* [1774], trans. and ed. Ioannis D. Evrigenis and Daniel Pellerin (Indianapolis, Hackett, 2004), p. 78.

[2] The first characterisation can be found in [Le Roy de Barincourt], *Principe du droit fondamental des souverains*, 2 vols. (Geneva, 1788), 2:288. The second appears in Ferdinando Galiani, *Della moneta*, 2nd ed. (Naples, 1780), p. 413, reprinted in Ferdinando Galiani, *Della moneta e scritti inediti*, ed. Alberto Caracciolo and Alberto Merola (Milan, Feltrinelli, 1963), p. 343. The third is in Jean-Jacques Rutledge, *Eloge de Montesquieu* (London, 1786). See also Eric Nelson, *The Greek Tradition in Republican Thought* (Cambridge, CUP, 2003).

mainly confined to the internal organisation of states. It was more difficult
not to register the relatively strong approval of industry and trade pervad-
ing the overlapping antinomies between ancients and moderns, East and
West, republics and monarchies, as well as between the Romans and the
Germans, that gave *The Spirit of Laws* something like its internal architecture. But the bridge that industry and trade seemed to form between the
book's disparate parts compounded the uncertainty about what its final
message might be. In republics, property and trade went together. In monarchies, however, one kind of property had to be kept quite separate from
trade. If trade based on economy was most suitable for republics, and trade
based on luxury was best suited to monarchies, goods and money still circu-
lated within a global space. The strength of Montesquieu's analytical distinctions pulled against any more broadly synthetic conclusion about
where, in the last analysis, his moral and political allegiances could be
found. If modern Britain appeared to offer a model of liberty, prosperity,
and power, the prominence of Montesquieu's qualifying "prophecy" about
the long-term future of the English constitution added a further set of
questions about whether, in the end, his book really did have a positive
core. If the combination of trade and monarchy was modern, but if that
combination meant having to face the equally modern combination of war,
debt, and taxes by relying either on a government based on a principle of
false honour or on one with an unwritten constitution and a frenzied system of party politics, it was hard to avoid the conclusion that modernity's
foundations were precariously shallow.

    The word that now seems best able to capture both the subject-matter
of *The Spirit of Laws* and the moral and political values that it endorsed is
"civilisation."[3] It was coined in the context of the protracted argument over
the book's normative content that developed in the decade after its publication and was first used to refer to what, morally, was missing from the
modern world. Three of Montesquieu's readers played a prominent part
in this argument. The first was the financial administrator and political
economist François Véron de Forbonnais, the most prolific and analytically
sophisticated of the various writers about trade and politics brought together by the superintendent of commerce Jacques-Claude-Marie Vincent
de Gournay in the immediate aftermath of the War of the Austrian Succession.[4] The second was Jean-Jacques Rousseau. The third was Victor Ri-

---

[3] On the concept of civilisation, see Jean Starobinski, *Blessings in Disguise; or the Morality of Evil* [Paris, 1989], trans. Arthur Goldhammer (Cambridge, Polity Press, 1993), pp. 1–35, and the works listed in note 147 below.

[4] On Vincent de Gournay and his circle, see Simone Meyssonnier, *La balance et l'horloge* (Paris, Editions de la Passion, 1989); Antoin E. Murphy, *Richard Cantillon: Entrepreneur and Economist* (Oxford, Oxford University Press, 1986), ch. 15. On Forbonnais, see Gabriel Fleury, *François Véron de Forbonnais. Sa famille, sa vie, ses actes, ses oeuvres* (Le Mans, 1915); see,

queti, marquis de Mirabeau, whose best-selling book, *L'Ami des hommes* (The Friend of Mankind) contained the word that referred back, in a critical sense, to the unnamed subject-matter of *The Spirit of Laws*. It began to appear in 1756, soon after the publication of Rousseau's *Discourse upon the Origin and Foundation of the Inequality among Mankind* (as the contemporary English translation was entitled) and two years before Mirabeau announced his conversion to a new system of natural government that its advocates came to call Physiocracy (the rule of *phusis*, or nature).[5] Both Rousseau and Forbonnais played a part in the early critical reception of *The Spirit of Laws*, Rousseau as one of the hired pens of the wealthy tax-farmer Claude Dupin, whose three-volume *Observations sur un livre intitulé de l'Esprit des loix* was published late in 1750 or early in 1751, and Forbonnais as the author of an *Extrait du livre de l'Esprit des loix* that, along with a longer set of critical comments, was published in 1753. Although there were substantial differences in the premises on which their respective assessments of Montesquieu were based, there was nonetheless a significant convergence between the assessments themselves. Both Forbonnais and Rousseau argued that the existence of political society was radically incompatible with any strong idea of a single universal human society. This was not, in the first instance, a theological or moral claim. It was a claim about politics and the responsibilities of states to their members. Whatever their origins, internal structures, or broader purposes, states existed to enable their members to live. But this minimal function had, in the last analysis, to clash with any more general system of international reciprocity. No state could be a state if its members depended on another state for their survival needs. Each state had, therefore, to enable its members to meet those needs, irrespective of variations in the natural endowments with which they were equipped. Once there were states, both argued, trade would be distorted right from the start. The logic of self-preservation had to trump the logic of utility. All the neo-Gothic features of the modern world that Montesquieu had highlighted to indicate its capacity for stability and moderation could not disguise its fundamentally agonistic nature.

The claim chimed readily with the almost uninterrupted period of warfare of the middle of the eighteenth century and the bleak vista of Europe's rulers counterfeiting "the virtues of patriotism" to destroy the fruits of "a century of industry, virtue, and happiness" that could be found in the widely reprinted *Ode sur la guerre* (Ode on War) published in 1758 by one of Rous-

---

too, Eluggero Pii, "Montesquieu e Véron de Forbonnais. Appunti sul dibattito settecentescho in tema di commercio," *Il Pensiero politico* 10 (1977): 362–89.

[5] The best starting point for the subject of Physiocracy and its ramifications can now be found in Loic Charles and Philippe Steiner, "Entre Montesquieu et Rousseau. La Physiocratie parmi les origines intellectuelles de la Révolution française," *Etudes Jean-Jacques Rousseau* 11 (2000): 83–160.

seau's early patrons, the Lyonnais magistrate Charles Bordes.[6] But if Forbonnais and Rousseau both emphasised that a world made up of states was
a world prepared for war, their reactions to this fact were radically at odds.
For Forbonnais (as, more generally, for the Gournay group), the only way
out was to accept the logic of self-preservation and rely on the development
of industry and trade to keep one jump ahead of the game. Rich states,
Forbonnais argued, would always be able to maintain an advantage over
their poorer rivals, however much their growing domestic wealth might
seem to set limits on their international trading capacity. In the last analysis,
they would be able to use the power of public credit not only to meet their
external defence needs, but, if necessary, to force the international monetary
system to bend to meet their competitive requirements. A rentier-state, Forbonnais suggested, would still be very far from being a powerless state.
Rousseau's solution was the exact opposite. If the existence of states built
the logic of self-preservation into collective human life, then the only way
out was to block its capacity for escalation at its source. This meant redesigning states without, however, trying to go beyond the divided world to
which they all belonged. It meant, in the last analysis, that the only way to
neutralise the dynamics of collective self-preservation was to scale down the
units making up human society and to cut off their needs-based interdependence, thus creating room for a form of purely political cooperation that
the world as it was could not durably have. Once the logic of collective self-
preservation was in place, Rousseau emphasised in a famous letter to the
marquis de Mirabeau in 1767, there was no middle ground between "the
most austere democracy" and "the most perfect Hobbism."[7]

    The letter is usually taken to be an indication of the gulf between Physio-
cracy and Rousseau's political thought. But the distance between the system that the marquis de Mirabeau came to espouse after his self-styled
"conversion" by Physiocracy's intellectual founder, François Quesnay, and
the shadowy outlines of a federal republican system at which Rousseau
hinted in both his *Social Contract* and his *Emile* was actually not quite so
large as it may seem. The goal towards which their respective conceptions
of political society pointed was a world of largely self-sufficient states, able,
for this reason, to avoid the moral and political dilemmas arising from
an interdependent international system. For Frederick Melchior Grimm,
writing in 1767, Quesnay was "a decided cynic," just as Rousseau, for Im-

---

    [6] On Bordes and his poem, see Jean-Daniel Candaux, "Charles Bordes et la première crise
d'antimilitarisme de l'opinion publique européenne," *Studies on Voltaire and the Eighteenth
Century* 24 (1963): 315–44.
    [7] Jean-Jacques Rousseau to Victor Riqueti, marquis de Mirabeau, 26 July 1767, in Jean-
Jacques Rousseau, *Correspondance complète*, ed. Ralph A. Leigh, 52 vols. (Oxford and Geneva,
1967–98), 33:240. [Henceforth Rousseau, *CC*, ed. Leigh, followed by the volume and
page numbers.]

manuel Kant, was "that subtle Diogenes."[8] Both descriptions referred to the ancient Greek Cynic philosopher Diogenes of Synope, and to "the shortest way to morality" (as Kant put it) implied by the Cynic idea of self-sufficiency and the absence of moral dilemmas that it entailed. In this respect, Rousseau and the Physiocrats (as they came to be known by the time of the French Revolution) were on the same side, against Forbonnais and the Gournay group. But in another respect, Rousseau and Forbonnais were also on the same side, against the advocates of Physiocracy. This second pairing was a result of a division over whether or not it really was possible to get out of the logic of collective self-preservation in a world made up of states. Although their reasons were different, both Rousseau and Forbonnais argued that it was not, while the advocates of Physiocracy argued that it was.

When, in 1793 and again in 1795, Henri Grégoire, the regicide bishop of Blois, proposed that the French republic should issue a Declaration of the Rights of Nations (*déclaration du droit des gens*) to go along with its Declaration of the Rights of Man, he chose as the emblem of his draft declaration the epigraph (*Ex natura, ius, ordo & leges. Ex homine, arbitrium, regimen & coercitio*) that, in 1767, had been used to head Quesnay's manifesto-text, *Physiocratie*.[9] The choice fitted the book's subtitle, namely, "the natural constitution of the government most advantageous to the human race."[10] Grégoire also went to some lengths, in 1795, to highlight the difference between Quesnay and Fénelon. The latter's emphasis, he claimed,

---

[8] The phrases can be found (on Quesnay) in Maurice Tourneux, ed., *Correspondance littéraire, philosophique et critique de Grimm, Diderot, Raynal, Meister, etc.*, 16 vols. (Paris, 1877–82), 7:235, and (on Rousseau) in Immanuel Kant, *Lectures on Ethics* (Cambridge, CUP, 1997), p. 45.

[9] The text of Grégoire's speech to the Convention can be found in the *Moniteur*, an III, no. 217 (see the *Réimpression de l'ancien Moniteur*, 24:292–6), but there is a slightly fuller version in Guillaume N. Lallement, *Choix de rapports, opinions et discours prononcés à la tribune nationale depuis 1789 jusqu'à ce jour*, 21 vols. (Paris, 1818–23), 15:230–9. See L. Chevalley, *La Déclaration du droit des gens de l'abbé Grégoire 1793–1795* (Paris, n.d. [1911]); Robert Redslob, *Histoire des grands principes du droit des gens depuis l'antiquité jusqu'à la veille de la grande guerre* (Paris, 1923), pp. 288–9; Christian Louis Lange, "Histoire de la doctrine pacifique et de son influence sur le développement du droit international," *Académie du Droit International. Recueil des cours* 13 (1926): 171–426 (pp. 343–5); Boris Mirkine-Guetzévitch, "L'influence de la révolution française sur le développement du droit international dans l'Europe oriental," *Académie du Droit International. Recueil des cours* 22 (1929): 296–457 (pp. 309–15); Boris Mirkine-Guetzévitch, "La Révolution française et l'idée de renonciation à la guerre," *La Révolution française* 82 (1929): 255–68; Boris Mirkine-Guetzévitch, "La Révolution française et les projets d'union européen," *La Révolution française* 84 (1931): 322–35. On Grégoire, see Alyssa Goldstein Sepinwall, *The Abbé Grégoire and the French Revolution: The Making of Modern Universalism* (Berkeley and Los Angeles, University of California Press, 2005).

[10] Pierre-Samuel Dupont de Nemours, ed., *Physiocratie, ou constitution naturelle du gouvernement le plus avantageux au genre humain* [1767] (Leiden, 1768).

on the desirability of loving one's family more than oneself, one's country more than one's family, and the universe more than one's country had been carried through into the exaggerated republicanism of the very recent past.

> Reason has passed judgement both on those extravagant individuals who talked of a universal republic and on those deceitful men who made a profession of loving men set at a distance of two thousand years or two thousand leagues to avoid having to be just and good towards their neighbours: systematic, de facto cosmopolitanism is mere moral or physical vagabondage.[11]

It was Quesnay, Grégoire claimed, who had "proved convincingly that in the state of independence of nations, as for individuals, the right of appropriating what belongs to no one is limited to what can be appropriated by labour; that the right to do everything is subordinated to the condition of not doing harm to others."[12] The principle was negative, not positive, as Grégoire took the principle of "systematic, de facto cosmopolitanism" to be. But, since it took others' interests into account, it was still compatible with something more than selfishness. From this perspective, Physiocracy was, as its advocates stated repeatedly, a kind of alternative to the abbé de Saint-Pierre's peace plan. Unlike Saint-Pierre's plan, however, it was designed, in the very long run, to promote self-sufficiency and independence rather than lock states into an international trading regime under the aegis of a binding system of international arbitration. Unlike Saint-Pierre's plan, too, it was also designed to realise something like Sully and Henri IV's Grand Design without having to rely on an unattainable prior agreement between sovereign states. In analytical terms, this made Physiocracy an alternative version of Fénelon's reform programme (with the physical, not the moral, side of human nature doing the work, but with the same goal as its outcome) and, by extension, made the supporters of Physiocracy the opponents of the Gournay group, just as, a generation earlier, Fénelon's admirers were Montesquieu's opponents. This third alignment also made Physiocracy join up again with Rousseau within the broader framework supplied by Fénelon (*Telemachus*, it is worth noting, was, together with *Robinson Crusoe*, among the few books that Rousseau's model pupil Emile was expected to read).[13] For the Gournay group, trade was part of power politics. For Rousseau and the Physiocrats, the modern world had to find a way to keep them apart. It was not so much the ultimate goal that divided Rousseau from the Physiocrats, but whether it was possible to get there.

---

[11] Lallement, *Choix*, 15:233.

[12] Lallement, *Choix*, 15:234.

[13] See Patrick Riley, "Rousseau, Fénelon and the Quarrel between the Ancients and the Moderns," in Patrick Riley, ed., *The Cambridge Companion to Rousseau* (Cambridge, CUP, 2001), pp. 78–93.

François Véron de Forbonnais and the Limits of Trade

The starting point of this three-sided argument was the model of trade set out at the beginning of Jean-François Melon's *Political Essay on Commerce*. "Let it be supposed," Melon wrote at the very beginning of the book (in a chapter headed "Principles"), "that there are only three or four islands upon the face of the earth."[14] Each island would produce only one commodity, adapted to the nature of its soil. One would produce corn; the second wool; and the two others something else. The four islands would have to trade with one another to obtain what they did not have from one another's surpluses. But if one of the islands were to become "so improved as to produce a sufficient surplus of what groweth in the other islands," the effects on trade and policy would be dramatic. The key variable would the "island of corn." If it began to produce wool and other commodities, then the inhabitants of the other three islands would either have "to quit their islands, and go to work in the island of corn," or, if they understood their interest "as they ought," they would have to "compel the island of corn to sow the quantity that is necessary to feed them," and wipe out its capacity to produce their own commodities. But if corn managed to resist their "first attacks," then "the power of its product alone would subdue them." "Thus," Melon concluded, "corn is the basis of trade, because it is the necessary support of life, and the providing thereof, ought to be the first care of the legislature."[15] Producing more corn would produce more people. This did not necessarily have to occur in an absolute sense because one way of increasing population was "to know how to work at less expense" by raising productivity in both agriculture and industry. This was why the increase of population "was the second care of the legislature," and, by extension, why "money and its representation" were its third. Properly managed, the combination of agriculture, a productive population, and a range of monetary instruments would enable the rich island "to support the trade of those islands from which she hath nothing to fear and destroy the trade of the other islands whose competition may alarm her."[16]

Almost everything that Forbonnais published, beginning with his *Eléments du commerce* in 1754, was an elaboration of Melon's principles. The books that he produced after 1760, when Physiocracy's major texts began to appear (particularly his *Principes et observations oeconomiques* of 1767),

---

[14] Jean-François Melon, *Essai politique sur le commerce* [1734]. This and subsequent quotations are from the English translation, namely, Jean-François Melon, *A Political Essay upon Commerce* [1734], trans. David Bindon (Dublin, 1738), p. 1.

[15] Melon, *Political Essay*, pp. 2–4.

[16] Melon, *Political Essay*, pp. 4–10.

were even more emphatic in their endorsement of Melon's acceptance of the unavoidable nature of commercial rivalry. Two features of his early criticism of Montesquieu were carried through into these later works. The first was his rejection of Montesquieu's conception of monarchy and the significance that Montesquieu had attached to property and inheritance in giving monarchy its nature. In this, Forbonnais relied heavily on the abbé Jean-Baptiste Dubos's *Critical History of the Establishment of the French Monarchy in Gaul* and the skill with which Dubos had argued (and set out to demonstrate historically) that modern monarchies were a continuation of the office-based system of government that had been established in both republican and imperial Rome. However much the seventeenth-century system of venality might suggest otherwise, offices were not property in any of the usual senses of the term and had no necessary connection with inheritance. They were, instead, the component parts of systems of administration, making them particularly well suited to the government of the large territorial states that had grown up in Europe after the end of the feudal era. This office-based conception of monarchy (common to the abbé de Saint-Pierre, Voltaire, and the marquis d'Argenson as well as Dubos) made Montesquieu's distinction between the British monarchy and the monarchies of the European mainland untenable. Both, in fact, belonged to the same genus (the only difference was that, since the British peerage derived its entitlements from its membership of the House of Lords, it was a rather purer version of an office-based nobility than its European equivalents). This, in the second place, made Montesquieu's distinction between trade based upon economy as suitable to republics and trade based on luxury as suitable to monarchy equally untenable.[17] As Montesquieu himself had acknowledged, Britain had both. There was, therefore, good reason to challenge Montesquieu's endorsement of Cicero's maxim that the same nation should not be both lords and factors of the universe, and to opt, instead, for Melon.[18]

If the British monarchy was simply a variant of monarchy as such, then there was no reason not to adopt those of its attributes responsible for its

---

[17] François Véron de Forbonnais, *Elémens du commerce*, 2nd ed., 2 vols. (Leiden, 1754), 1:61, 70–1.

[18] "L'idée de conservation est dans chaque individu immédiatement attachée à son existence; ainsi l'occupation qui remplit son besoin le plus pressant lui devient la plus chère. Cet ordre fixé par la nature ne peut être changé par la formation d'une société qui est la réunion des volontés particulières. Il se trouve au contraire confirmé par de nouveaux motifs, si cette société n'est pas supposée exister seule sur la terre. Si elle est voisine d'autres sociétés, elle a des rivales; et sa conservation exige qu'elle soit revêtue de toutes les forces dont elle est susceptible. L'agriculture est le premier moyen et le plus naturel de se les procurer." Forbonnais, *Elémens du commerce*, 1:107–8.

prosperity and power. The difficulty was to be sure about what these were, particularly where the related subjects of war finance and public credit were concerned. The first, however, was certainly agriculture. Although Physiocracy is often associated with a strong bias towards agricultural development, it is actually more appropriate to apply the association to Forbonnais and the Gournay group. Forbonnais used Melon's model to highlight the political value of the English Corn Laws and to emphasise how much there was to learn from the calibrated system of subsidy that had been established in Britain to stabilise the damaging swings in grain prices caused by variations in harvest yields and, by doing so, to break out of the suboptimal levels of production that they caused.[19] Modern improvements in milling and grain storage (notably those pioneered by the agronomist Duhamel de Monceau) would make it possible to establish a decentralised network of public granaries, managed by religious communities (on pain of dissolution if they failed) and local military garrisons, to reinforce the stability of grain prices and, by doing so, supply a price-led incentive to agricultural improvement.[20] Although there was every good reason to reform guild regulations to widen entry into the urban trades and to promote the use of machinery in the production of manufactured goods (contrary to Montesquieu, Forbonnais argued that the disruption caused by new machinery was no more difficult to manage than the disruption caused by changes in fashion), it was vital to recognise that agriculture was a different case.[21] Promoting large-scale, capital-intensive agriculture, Forbonnais argued, was a self-defeating policy that would squeeze the market for capital, push up interest rates, generate rural unemployment, reduce domestic demand for manufactured goods, and force producers of manufactured goods to transfer their skills to other countries.[22] As Melon had indicated, no state could rely on commerce to maintain its power, unless its commerce were first based on a flourishing, skill-intensive, small-scale agricultural system. Cereals, champagne, camembert, and cognac, it might be said, were as vital to a state as the stream of innovations of urban industry.

As several of its reviewers noticed, the key chapter in the *Elements of Commerce* was the one on the circulation of money and the way that it built upon the theory of foreign trade, interest rates, and monetary circulation that had been set out by the seventeenth-century English writer on trade

---

[19] Forbonnais, *Elémens du commerce*, 1:113–24.

[20] Forbonnais, *Elémens du commerce*, 1:149–83. The best recent discussion of the subject is in Steven Laurence Kaplan, *Provisioning Paris* (Ithaca, Cornell University Press, 1984).

[21] Forbonnais, *Elémens du commerce*, 1:273, 276–7, 322, 325.

[22] Forbonnais, *Elémens du commerce*, 1:328.

and politics Sir Josiah Child (whose work Gournay himself translated).[23] The subject had a long history, stretching back to Aristotle's definition of money as a sign established by convention to circumvent the practical problems arising from both the nature of different kinds of goods and the varying circumstances of sellers and buyers in exchanging real wealth. Here, the physical properties of the sign took second place to its function as a counter—or *numéraire*—to compare relative values. But it was also possible to argue that money's function as a sign was a derivation of the properties that, in the first place, served to make it valuable (its colour, lustre, or sparkle, for example). This latter definition opened up a space for arguments favouring the creation of an artificial surrogate for money to offset the purely arbitrary association between its initial value and its subsequent commercial function (Law, for example, argued that since money began as a pledge, an artificial currency supported by a state's tax revenue was better adapted to meet the escalating needs of trade than metal coin). Forbonnais was entirely at home with all these aspects of the subject (the history of French public finance that he published in 1758 is still, in some respects, authoritative).[24] He included a balanced summary of the complex discussion of monetary policy that had taken place between Jean-François Melon and Jean-Baptiste Dutot after the failure of Law's system in the chapter of the *Elements of Commerce* dealing with monetary circulation (coming out in favour of Dutot's strong insistence upon the purely conventional character of money and accepting the limitations that this implied for creating a further, fiduciary, currency). He had no illusions about Law's system itself, but was still prepared to predict that in less than half a century the combination of military and economic pressure generated by Europe's unstable international system would make recourse to this kind of "political and commercial" bank occur again.[25]

Unlike several other members of the Gournay group, Forbonnais was not impressed by the wave of alarm about the size and potential effects of the public debt that developed in Britain after the War of the Austrian Succession. This found expression in the English country-party ideologue Henry St John, viscount Bolingbroke's *Some Reflections on the Present State of the Nation* in 1749 and, three years later, in the first edition of Hume's essay *Of Public Credit*, both of which appeared in French translation in the

[23] See Jacques-Claude Vincent de Gournay, *Traités sur le commerce de Josiah Child, avec les remarques inédites de Vincent de Gournay: Texte intégral d'après les manuscrits conservés à la Bibliothèque municipale de Saint-Brieuc*, ed. Takumi Tsuda (Tokyo, 1983), and Jacques-Claude Vincent de Gournay, *Mémoires et lettres de Vincent de Gournay*, ed. Takumi Tsuda (Tokyo, 1993).

[24] François Véron de Forbonnais, *Recherches et considérations sur les finances de France depuis l'année 1595 jusqu'à l'année 1721*, 2 vols. (Basel, 1758).

[25] Forbonnais, *Recherches*, 2:425.

same compilation of political discourses published in 1754 and 1756.[26] The arguments of the two works were initially quite similar. Bolingbroke, in his pamphlet, called for a voluntary default on the public debt as the necessary means for "the preservation of the commonwealth" since, as he put it, "the true owners of our political vessel" were the landowners, while the annuitants were no more than passengers on the British ship of state.[27] The first state to get rid of its debt, he argued, "will give the law to others, or be at least in a condition of not receiving it from one."[28] The scenario had an instant appeal in France and soon came to be incorporated into a version of the cult of Henri IV and Sully that was rather different from the one espoused by the abbé de Saint-Pierre. Where Saint-Pierre was a strong advocate of public credit, the emphasis here fell as much on Henri IV and Sully's success in eliminating the sixteenth-century French monarchy's debt as on their Grand Design. As Bolingbroke indicated, a bankruptcy carried out by a patriot king might be a genuinely virtuous act. Although Hume, in his essay, also called for a voluntary bankruptcy, he avoided this kind of claim right from the start and, in the later additions that he made to *Of Public Credit*, underlined the point that defaulting on the debt would destroy, not preserve, Britain's free constitution. But the piecemeal chronology of the changes that Hume made to reinforce his own grim message gave Bolingbroke's patriotic scenario a more immediate and durable impact (one indication of its appeal was the appearance of the comte d'Artois and his friends attired in full sixteenth-century regalia when France went to war in support of the American "insurgents" in 1778, starting off, it might be said, in much the same way as, in 1830, they were to end).[29] It was Bolingbroke's, not Hume's, idea of a patriotic coup against the nation's creditors that continued to be canvassed episodically all the way up to the French Revolution.

Forbonnais, however, did not take either Hume or Bolingbroke seriously. He wrote a memorandum to the French ministry stating that their warnings about public credit were best seen as Tory jeremiads (or possibly

---

[26] Henry St John, viscount Bolingbroke, "Some Reflections of the Present State of the Nation, Principally with Regard to her Taxes and her Debts, and on the Causes and Consequences of Them," in *The Works of the late Right Honourable Henry St. John, Lord Viscount Bolingbroke*, ed. David Mallet, 4 vols. (London, 1754), 3:143–79. It, with Hume's essay, appeared in a translation by Jacob Mauvillon in the first and second volumes respectively of *Discours politiques*, 2 vols. (Amsterdam, 1754 and 1756); Bolingbroke's "Reflections" first appeared in French as the *Testament politique de Milord Bolingbroke* (London, 1754).

[27] Bolingbroke, "Some Reflections," pp. 168, 174.

[28] Bolingbroke, "Some Reflections," p. 165.

[29] On the cult of Henri IV and Sully in the eighteenth century, see Marcel Reinhard, *La Légende de Henri IV* (Paris, 1935), and, on Bolingbroke in eighteenth-century France, see David Armitage, introduction to Henry St. John, viscount Bolingbroke, *Political Writings* ed. Armitage (Cambridge, CUP, 1997). On the episode involving the comte d'Artois, see Louis-Philippe, comte de Ségur, *Mémoires*, 3 vols. (Paris, 1825), 1:40.

even black propaganda) and not worth taking into consideration in French discussions of how far it might be appropriate to match the British funding system.[30] Nor was he prepared to adopt the kind of oversanguine prediction to be found in the very free adaptation of Josiah Tucker's *Remarks on the Advantages and Disadvantages of France and Great Britain*, published in 1754 under the name of Sir John Nicholls by another member of the Gournay group, Louis-Joseph Plumard de Dangeul (who was also Forbonnais's cousin). There, "Nicholls" had argued that the growing size of Britain's public debt and the rise in taxation required to fund it would, quite soon, force up British export prices to a level at which foreign trade would become untenable, thus making a bankruptcy unavoidable.[31] Forbonnais's own position was more sophisticated. As he recognised, the size of a public debt was far less important than the rate of interest and the level of taxation. The theory of public credit on which his view was based was a product of his broader theory of monetary circulation and the initial distinction that he made between "simple" or "natural" circulation and "compound" or "artificial" circulation.[32] Circulation of the first kind occurred when money functioned as a sign. But any interruption of commerce could give money a real set of attributes and a value of its own. In this guise, money itself would have a price (the rate of interest). Circulation, in the light of money's two functions, could be defined as "an unequal competition between commodities (*denrées*) and their signs, in favour of the signs."[33] Since money could become one of those commodities and not just a sign and could, as a result, be kept out of circulation if its holders received a favourable rate of interest, the only way to bring it back towards its natural function was to increase the available supply and, by doing so, to lower the rate of interest. Law's system had been one way of doing this, but it was "a useless and violent remedy" when other, natural, means were available.[34] These amounted to either the ownership of mines or foreign trade. Since the first was a pure contingency, this left foreign trade as the only way to promote and maintain domestic circulation and ensure that its "natural" form took precedence over "artificial" circulation. "Foreign trade," Forbonnais con-

---

[30] "Réfutation de quelques articles des Discours politiques de M. David Hume, traduits de l'anglois l'année dernière 1754," Bibliothèque de l'Arsénal, Mss. 4591, fols. 181 et seq. and 284 et seq. According to Forbonnais, "il est cependant aisé d'apercevoir dans Mr Hume un Tory outré. Son héros est feu Milord Bolingbroke, homme d'un mérite supérieur, mais qui lui-même étoit un Tory déterminé." (I have modernised spelling and capitalisation.)

[31] [Louis-Joseph Plumard de Dangeul], *Remarques sur les avantages et les désavantages de la France et de la Grande Bretagne* [1754], 3rd ed. (Leiden, 1754), pp. 349–50, 366–7, 378–9, 381–2, 396 (note a), 402–11.

[32] Forbonnais, *Eléments du commerce*, 2:143–8.

[33] Forbonnais, *Eléments du commerce*, 2:150.

[34] Forbonnais, *Eléments du commerce*, 2:165.

cluded, "is the only real internal interest of a state. That interest is the interest of the people and the interest of the people is the interest of the prince."[35] It was a long way from Fénelon, or even Montesquieu.

There were, however, limits to the development of foreign trade. Here, Forbonnais repeated the argument that Hume set out in his 1752 essay *Of commerce*.[36] Production for export would generate favourable trade and payments balances. These would produce an increase in the quantity of money in domestic circulation. Falling rates of interest would stimulate further production for export and a fresh injection of currency into the money supply. Although this additional volume was "indifferent in itself" to the country that received it, it was not indifferent "to the foreign country that buys the commodities."[37] That country would have a strong incentive either to look for alternative sources of supply, or to develop its own productive capacity, or to do without a commodity that had become too expensive. "It would seem," Forbonnais concluded,

> that foreign trade, whose object is to attract a continuing new supply of money, works towards its own destruction in proportion to the progress that it makes in trade of this kind, so that the state comes to be deprived of the very benefit attributed to circulation.[38]

Like Hume, too, Forbonnais did not take this to be an indication of the self-defeating character of foreign trade. If, he wrote, the quantity of signs really did increase to the point at which all a country's commodities were too dear, foreign trade would either revert to barter or simply become "null." But the rich country would still contain as many people as it was able to employ and feed. Its wealth "in finely crafted metals, diamonds, and rare and precious effects," not counting its other "more common movables," would "infinitely exceed" the quantity of money in circulation, and its people, "although without any foreign trade," would still be "very happy" for as long as their number remained in proportion to the produce of its land. The objective of the legislator would, in short, have been met because "the society that he would govern would be equipped with all the strength of which it was capable."[39]

---

[35] Forbonnais, *Eléments du commerce*, 2:222.
[36] On the discussion produced by Hume's essay, see Istvan Hont, "The 'Rich Rountry–Poor Country' Debate in Scottish Classical Political Economy," in Istvan Hont and Michael Ignatieff, eds., *Wealth and Virtue: The Shaping of Political Economy in the Scottish Enlightenment* (Cambridge, CUP, 1983), pp. 271–315, now in his *Jealousy of Trade: International Competition and the Nation-State in Historical Perspective* (Cambridge, Mass., Harvard University Press, 2005), ch. 3.
[37] Forbonnais, *Eléments du commerce*, 2:171–2.
[38] Forbonnais, *Eléments du commerce*, 2:172.
[39] Forbonnais, *Eléments du commerce*, 2:173.

But Forbonnais then proceeded to add a further step to Hume's conjectures. Although, he wrote, "the end point to which we have led a political body cannot, morally, be reached, it is still worth pursuing this hypothesis." Before reaching "a total interruption of its commerce with foreigners," a country could, "for a long succession of centuries," continue to compete for the right to draw in their money. Since, Forbonnais continued, money was both a sign and a measure, "the people that possess the most" would be "master of those who do not know how to reduce it to its just value," and, since the growth of the money supply in every country would have the effect of stimulating industry and increasing population, it would still be a matter of national interest for the rich country to be able to deprive its rivals of the means to become powerful.[40] Money made this possible. As Forbonnais had already shown, the progress of foreign trade would lead to an increase in the rich country's domestic money supply and bring money back towards its natural function as a sign. If this were offset by an aggressive policy of encouraging the holders of money to lend their funds to nations where money was mainly a measure of commodities, with a price of its own, the drift towards having to give up foreign trade could be stopped.

> They would lend it to the state and to wholesale merchants at a high rate of interest that would revert annually to the circulation of the creditor nation, depriving the other of the benefit of circulation. The workers of the debtor people would be no more than slaves allowed to work for a few days of the year to cover the costs of their mediocre subsistence; all the rest would belong to the master; and the tribute would be raised rigorously, whether that subsistence was comfortable or miserable.[41]

The outflow of currency produced by interest payments would make new investment in the debtor country more difficult because the relatively high level of local interest rates would squeeze profits before it squeezed wages. If, moreover, the creditor nation decided to do so, it could inject "a further disorder into the circulation of the debtor state by suddenly withdrawing its capital."[42] Finally, and in a more general sense, the imbalance in monetary flows between the debtor and creditor states would turn the exchange rate in favour of the creditor state, meaning, Forbonnais concluded, that "one should be intimately persuaded of the advantage of lending one's money to foreigners."[43] Since the rich creditor state would no longer need to maintain the price competitiveness of its now nonexistent exports, it could rely on the inflow of funds from its investments abroad to raise the

---

[40] Forbonnais, *Eléments du commerce*, 2:175, 176.
[41] Forbonnais, *Eléments du commerce*, 2:180–1.
[42] Forbonnais, *Eléments du commerce*, 2:181.
[43] Forbonnais, *Eléments du commerce*, 2:181–2.

price of its own currency and cover the cost of the goods that it still needed to import. From this perspective, trade was simply another branch of power politics.

The remorseless dynamics of capital flows and capital flights were, in the short term, the answer to foreign trade's long-term tendency towards autarchy. The idea of an irretrievably divided and competitive world underlying this vision became even clearer in Forbonnais's later *Principes et observations oeconomiques* (Economic Principles and Observations). The aim of this book was to refute the claim made by the advocates of Physiocracy that political societies could, in the long run, coexist in peace if they could be brought back to conditions in which the logic of collective reciprocity could be made to override the more dangerously unpredictable logic of collective self-preservation. To do so, Forbonnais broadened and deepened the argument of the *Elements of Commerce*. Even before the existence of money, he now argued, there was no way out of the logic of collective self-preservation. He began by presenting a very detailed description of how a society without money might work. It could have property, agriculture and manufacturing industry, domestic trade, a legal and fiscal system, and a government. All the activities associated with a society like that could, theoretically, be carried out without money. There could be barter, multiple storage facilities, officials to manage them, records of transactions, and promises of future transactions, as well as a decentralised system of public accounting to monitor and manage resource allocation. In circumstances like these, Forbonnais wrote, "the utility of society" should establish "no more dissension among mankind than beauty."[44] "Such," he continued, "might be the course followed by the commerce of the universe in the order established by nature."[45]

> The picture is grand, the thought sublime, but the fact, if it ever existed in this simplicity, can unhappily no longer exist unless the error of the millenarians were to come to pass.[46]

What ruled it out was the existence of more than one society. Once there was trade between societies, reciprocity was a possibility only on the basis of an unattainable equality, down to the last detail. To try to preserve it would simply have the effect of inadvertently favouring the less populous or less naturally well endowed society. In the physical as in the moral world, Forbonnais noted, "it is weakness that always produces jealousy."[47] A well-planted country, he observed, would never be the first to imagine reducing

---

[44] François Véron de Forbonnais, *Principes et observations économiques* (Paris, 1767), p. 53.
[45] Forbonnais, *Principes*, p. 53.
[46] Forbonnais, *Principes*, p. 53 (see, too, p. 145).
[47] Forbonnais, *Principes*, p. 54 (note b).

its consumption of foreign products or calculate that on some occasions it had given the produce of four acres of its own land in exchange for that of a single acre of a foreign country. But once the calculation had been made, there was no way back. The "fact of societies," as Forbonnais put it, ruled out the principles of "cosmopolitans."[48]

With this as his starting point, Forbonnais was able to sharpen his analysis of money. In place of the earlier distinction that he had made between money as a sign and money as a commodity, he now substituted one between money as a sign and money as "fictional real estate" (an *immeuble fictif*), or what would now be called an interest-bearing capital.[49] The new terminology, however, supported the same analysis. Circulation was a function of the rate at which a given quantity of money performed both roles. As a sign, it was a means of exchange; as capital, it produced interest. The higher the speed at which it could be made to switch from one role to another, the lower the rate of interest would be and the higher the level of prosperity that a state might reach. Here, everything would depend on the conduct of policy: towards taxation and expenditure, towards the owners of movable and immovable assets, and towards other societies. If, Forbonnais wrote, it was certainly not true that the state of war was natural to mankind, the fact of society still made it necessary to consider societies as living in a habitual state of suspicion and anxiety (*inquiétude*). This uneasiness, no less natural than sociability itself, was part of the reason for each society's cohesiveness (it was easy to foresee, Forbonnais noted, the price that Britain would have to pay in North America, now that Canada was no longer under French control).[50] The effect of this uneasiness was rivalry between nations, which could—and did—degenerate into jealousy, but would, nonetheless, further nature's goals, by stimulating the greatest possible growth in population and production. The uneven international distribution of money and goods was, however, "an invincible obstacle to the restoration of the natural order in Europe's general circulation."[51] The dynamics of foreign trade, monetary flows, and capital flight simply ruled out straightforward commercial reciprocity. The "real position of Europe" meant that "money, by reason of its double function as sign and real estate," was "the true motor of power."[52]

This, Forbonnais argued, was also why monetary, fiscal, and financial policies were vital to a state's competitive capacity, particularly under modern military and naval conditions. No nation, he wrote, "can be power-

---

[48] Forbonnais, *Principes*, p. 55 (note c).
[49] Forbonnais, *Principes*, pp. 107–8.
[50] Forbonnais, *Principes*, p. 113 (and note a).
[51] Forbonnais, *Principes*, pp. 116–7.
[52] Forbonnais, *Principes*, pp. 118–9.

ful abroad without public credit."[53] It was an unavoidable necessity. And, if it was not a blessing, it was still not an unmitigated evil. Although the paper issued by a state was not like commercial paper or the paper issued by private financiers because the capital that it represented was not redeemable at a specified time, it was still transportable and could be used as security for private credit. Nor, contrary to the authors of the jeremiads about the scale of public indebtedness, was the absolute size of a state's debt what mattered. Instead, since true public debts were perpetual debts, the combination of fiscal policy, state expenditure, and the international money market would determine how much a state could afford to borrow and the impact that this might have (via interest levels and money's dual functions) on general circulation. Trying to avoid these constraints—like Law on the one hand, but also like the advocates of Physiocracy, on the other—was simply naïve.

Physiocracy, or *The Natural and Essential Order of Political Societies*

Forbonnais's conception of an agriculturally based, commercially competitive, administrative monarchy was already established before Mirabeau and Quesnay began to publish the works that made them the "French economists" or, later, the Physiocrats. It combined Jean-François Melon's argument about the winning political strategy in a trade-based world with the system of royal government advocated by the abbé de Saint-Pierre, Voltaire, and the abbé Dubos. But the scale and scope of Forbonnais's attack on Physiocracy is an indication of the economists' own ambition. This was not simply a matter of presenting an alternative to actually existing political societies, an alternative whose content was flagged in the title of one of Physiocracy's key political texts, *L'ordre naturel et essentiel des sociétés politiques* (The Natural and Essential Order of Political Societies), written under Quesnay's close supervision by the former French colonial superintendent Pierre-Paul Le Mercier de la Rivière in 1763. It was also a matter of finding a way out of the logic of self-preservation that, as Melon had indicated in his *Political Essay on Commerce*, made "the island of corn" the winner in a world made up of states. The work of Forbonnais and, more generally, the Gournay group, simply served to indicate the magnitude of the problem. Taking Melon's logic as far as it would go laid out the prospect of a world made up of states, each armed to the hilt and able to withstand the worst effects of wars and trade blockades because of their flourishing agricultural systems, and all collectively equipped to fight one another into

[53] Forbonnais, *Principes*, p. 157.

a slower, but no less deadly, version of mutually assured destruction. "With a taste turned solely towards agriculture," noted the Swiss diplomat Georg Ludwig Schmid d'Auenstein, midway through the Seven Years War, "and with that wholly warlike system presently being introduced into Europe, we will soon be a band of Goths and Vandals."[54] If, as the subtitle of Quesnay's book announced, Physiocracy was the system of government that was most advantageous to the human race, it had to address this possibility. This was why the Physiocrats took Forbonnais, and the Gournay group as a whole, to be among their most deadly political enemies.[55] On its own, agriculture was the problem, not the solution.

Melon's model presupposed a property-based world, with the corn-producing island holding the most strategically vital asset. The Physiocratic way out was to accept the existence of property, but to circumvent its most divisive effects by devising a political system that, indirectly, would force its owners to subordinate self-interest to general utility. In this sense, Physiocracy was a less draconian, but more analytically subtle version of Fénelon's reform programme. "A few pages" of *Telemachus*, Mirabeau wrote in his *L'Ami des hommes*, "contain more sound politics (*saine politique*) than my whole book."[56] Although it preceded Mirabeau's "conversion" by Quesnay, the general orientation of *L'Ami des hommes* was carried through into Physiocracy. The means certainly changed, but the goal of a self-sufficient moral community remained the same. This, strongly moral, characterisation of Physiocracy may seem surprising. It is more usual to emphasise its rationalism, or the analytical novelty of Quesnay's "new science," or the incongruity of the Physiocrats' campaign for free trade under the odd banner of "legal despotism." None of these aspects of the economists' system is false. But they miss its more fundamental point. To contemporaries it was the moral side of Physiocracy that was the more immediately obvious. "No one, apart from the economists," wrote one of their fiercest critics,

---

[54] Georg Ludwig Schmid d'Auenstein, "De l'agriculture," in his *Traités sur divers sujets intéressants de politique et de morale* (n.p., 1760), p. 151. On Schmid, see, most recently, Vieri Becagli, "Georg-Ludwig Schmid d'Auenstein e i suoi *Principes de la législation universelle*: oltre la fisiocrazia?" *Studi Settecenteschi* 24 (2004): 215–52.

[55] See, for example, Mirabeau to Rousseau, 9 December 1767, in Rousseau, *CC*, ed. Leigh, 37:252–5, and Musée Arbaud, Aix-en-Provence, Fonds Mirabeau, 25, fol. 159, the chevalier de Mirabeau to Mirabeau, 11 October 1759, and fol. 414, the same to the same, 19 February 1761, where, as well as the hostility towards Forbonnais, Mme de Pompadour is described as Mirabeau's "worst enemy," and her advisor, the naval minister Berryer, as "ce vilain sac à charbon." The assessments were part of the still murky intrigues in which Mirabeau was involved during the period of the Seven Years War. On these, see Charles Laurent, *Les voyages en Bretagne du chevalier de Mirabeau* (Mayenne, Joseph Floch, 1983), pp. 101–3, 134, 140–1, 146, 189, 194.

[56] Victor Riqueti, marquis de Mirabeau, *L'Ami des hommes*, 3 vols. (Avignon, 1756–8), pt. II, ch. 4, p. 94 (or p. 268 in the Paris, 1883, ed. Albert Rouxel, reprint).

the abbé Gabriel Bonnot de Mably, "is simple enough to think that by paying dearly for our virtues, we will have them to the point of overflowing."[57] The point was put more sympathetically in a letter by the Basel political reformer and historian of humanity Isaak Iselin to one of his French correspondents in 1770. "Since your departure," he wrote, "I have been reading all six volumes of the *Physiocracy*."

> I am becoming all the more enthused by the respectable enthusiasts who are its authors. . . . I can well remember having fallen into the same way of thinking, but of not having dared to pursue it for fear of offending the respect that I believed was due to the ideas of my fellow citizens. But these truly generous men, real *viri fortes*, have restored my courage and taught me to regard both my own and my country's misfortunes with more fortitude. As each day passes, they have convinced me the more of what I wrote in my *History of Humanity*, namely, that true liberty can occur only in a monarchy in which enlightened reason has triumphed. . . . I would never have been so prejudiced against them if they, like the Wolffians, had not changed the meaning of several terms. Their idea of the tutelary power's coownership of property had a very Turkish air when it appeared under this kind of label. Nothing now seems to me to be more just. Their notion of despotism based on the natural and essential order of things seemed an odious and horrible idea. If they had presented it in its true light, I would have seen that it was my own original idea (*eigens Gedank*) as it was printed in my *History of Humanity*. They have certainly repelled a great many minds and will not find it easy to win them back. It is true that M. de Montesquieu gave monarchy so confused a notion that they may well have had good reasons for not using the word. The word royalty might have been more appropriate. Then, they would not have had to wrap up the baroque ideas of the famous president, whose chimerical qualities will come to be effaced by what is real in those of these wise men (*sages*).[58]

Iselin's characterisation of Physiocracy as "enthusiasm" (albeit "respectable" enthusiasm) and as Montesquieu's "baroque" conception of monarchy, revised and corrected by "enlightened reason" to become the setting in which "true liberty" really could exist, can be corroborated and developed in several related ways. Three subjects gave Physiocracy the strongly moral aspect that Iselin recognised. The first was the conception of human nature underlying the idea of the natural and essential order of political societies. The second was the place of property in human society. The third was the broader system that was designed to force what the Physiocrats

---

[57] Gabriel Bonnot de Mably, *Principes de morale* [1784], reprinted in his *Oeuvres*, 15 vols. (Aalen: Scientia Verlag, 1977), 10:296.

[58] Isaak Iselin to Jean Rodolph Frey, 14 April 1770. Iselin-Archiv, Staats-archives Basel, 47–56.

called the unnatural and retrograde order on which actually existing political societies were based to revert to one that was natural and progressive. Together, they amounted to a way of using Montesquieu's property-based conception of monarchy as the foundation of a radical and comprehensive programme of political reform at home and of an equally comprehensive system of international pacification abroad. The three subjects were already in place in Mirabeau's pre-Physiocratic *Ami des hommes*. It was Quesnay, however, who turned them into a system.

Physiocracy's starting point was an unusually intense version of the claim that the modern world was hurtling towards disaster (in this, Quesnay and Mirabeau were in agreement with Rousseau). The claim ran from one end to the other of all of Mirabeau's many published works (Quesnay himself actually published very little under his own name). One way or another, Mirabeau wrote in one of his very late works, the modern world had reached

> the period of indispensable revolutions, of the collapse and fatal end of the effects of modern politics and their entirely mercantile and fiscal principles. Absolute decadence, corruption, misery, and, eventually, the dispersal of existing political societies will be its necessary consequence.[59]

The only barrier against this terrifying prospect was Physiocracy. This made Mirabeau highly sceptical about the merits of every other reform project and hostile to any form of political upheaval unless (like the Swedish Revolution of 1772) it looked as if it might lead to the implementation of the Physiocratic programme. "The general clamour and my own reflections taught me, a long time ago, that we are living in the century of revolutions," he wrote to the Swedish noble Carl Fredrik Scheffer in 1772, after Gustavus III had seized power in Stockholm.

> My childhood saw the then novel phenomenon of three simultaneous state bankruptcies: the System, the South Sea Company, and the Bank of Venice. As an adolescent I saw two royal abdications, although there had been barely half a dozen since the beginning of the Christian era. So many revolutions, which, taken one by one, make—and will make—this century the age of crises of state, for the same reason that illness is a natural outcome of debauched excess, have, more than anything else, bound me to the study of what I regard as the sole anchor yet able to moor a humanity adrift in a sea of opinion, fragmented, demoralised, and exhausted by error.[60]

---

[59] Victor Riqueti, marquis de Mirabeau, *Entretiens d'un jeune prince avec son gouverneur*, 3 vols. (Lausanne, 1785), 3:318.

[60] Osvald Siren, "Ur Markis de Mirabeau's Brev till Greve Carl Fredrik Scheffer," *Lychnios* (1948–9): 51–84 (Mirabeau to Carl Fredrik Scheffer, 22 September 1772); see, too, Antonella Alimento, "La fisiocrazia in Svezia dopo il colpo di stato di Gustavo III attraverso la corris-

The Swedish Revolution was "truly heroic" and a model of the kind of drive to impose a plan of reform from above that Mirabeau himself seems to have toyed with. Other kinds of revolution were more dangerous. "We will see," he wrote to his brother at the beginning of French involvement in the American Revolution,

> whether insurrection against divine or human hierarchies is of our vintage or whether, in the general, necessary, and imminent revolution that threatens the whole of Europe, anyone else showed how to put societies gently back on their natural base and prevent Europe from experiencing what happened to the kingdoms of Mythridates and Masseniello.[61]

The huge amount of time and energy that Mirabeau put into promoting Physiocracy was driven by his conviction that it was the only alternative to social and economic catastrophe. The conviction itself was already visible in *L'Ami des hommes*. Physiocracy gave it both a firmer foundation and a wider scope.

Mirabeau began his first book with an account of the fundamental principles of human association. It would, he said, be brief because the principles to which he referred were "almost all familiar."[62] The first four pages of the work were, in fact, modelled on Cicero's *On Duties* ("the best work ever to come from human hands," as Mirabeau later told his brother) and the comparison between humans and animals with which it began.[63] The most useful distinction that could be made within the animal kingdom, Mirabeau wrote, was between "solitary" and "sociable" animals. Humans belonged to the latter class. "No truth is better demonstrated than one that rests upon facts. Everywhere where no more than two men have been seen, they have surely been found together in the same shelter or repair."[64] Solitary animals were instinctively aware that it was to their advantage to remain alone; sociable animals were equally guided by instinct towards their fellows. In this respect human instinct was like that of any other sociable creature.

---

pondenza di V. Riqueti de Mirabeau con C. F. Scheffer," *Annali della Fondazione Luigi Einaudi* 23 (1989): 297–369; Barbro Ohlin, "Du Pont de Nemours écrit à Carl Fredrik, comte de Scheffer," in Gunnar von Proschwitz, ed., *Influences. Relations culturelles entre la France et la Suède* (Goteborg, 1988).

[61] Musée Arbaud (Aix-en-Provence), Fonds Mirabeau 31 fol. 78, Mirabeau to the chevalier de Mirabeau, 28 August 1779.

[62] Mirabeau *L'Ami des hommes* (Avignon, 1756), pt. I, ch. 1, p. 1. Mirabeau also made it clear that he was building on the work of "les Auteurs politiques Protestans" who, he wrote, "sont les meilleurs" (p. 18). In this instance he was referring to Richard Cantillon.

[63] Musée Arbaud (Aix-en-Provence), Fonds Mirabeau 25, fol. 246, Mirabeau to the chevalier de Mirabeau, August 1760.

[64] Mirabeau, *L'Ami des hommes* (Avignon, 1756), pt. I, ch. 1, p. 2.

But, Mirabeau continued, human instinct was somewhat different from that of other sociable animals because it was also capable of becoming intelligence. All animals, he wrote, are "avid," but man was avid not only for the here and now, but also for the past and the future. "He is avid for everything; and while nature, on the one hand, compels him to unite with his fellows, intellect, on the other, instructs him that he is reliant upon his rival, on the natural enemy of all his pretensions."[65] The result of these two contradictory natural principles—one joining humans to their fellows, the other making them see other humans as their enemy—was, Mirabeau concluded, that laws concerning the division of goods were the first, and most indispensable, of all laws. "In a word, the division of goods is the first law of society and, so to speak, the trunk of every other law."[66] Laws concerning the division of goods first acknowledged and then moderated cupidity, setting up a sequence that made the whole structure of *L'Ami des hommes* an increasingly elaborate examination of the mechanisms required to prevent cupidity from overwhelming sociability.

Mirabeau made it clear that his target in doing so was luxury, or the Colbert-inspired system of industry, trade, and politics contained in Melon's *Political Essay on Commerce* and Hume's more recently published *Political Discourses*.[67] As he acknowledged at the beginning of the summary appended to his book, he took his cue from Montesquieu and the unusually emphatic endorsement of Stoic moral philosophy to be found in book 24 of *The Spirit of Laws*.[68] The aim of *L'Ami des hommes*, Mirabeau indicated, was to revive the morality of the Stoics, against the Epicureanism of Hume and Melon. "I wish to reawaken an old system of the mind denied by the heart," he wrote, "and come to preach Stoicism to those who are equally instructed in the vanity of the prejudices of vice as well as those of virtue."[69] But, in keeping with Cicero's rather mitigated Stoicism, this did not entail ignoring the part played by the passions in human life. The alternative to luxury was not frugality, but *faste*, or splendour—something that compelled admiration, not covetousness. In the third chapter of *L'Ami des hommes*, Mirabeau began by referring to "some men" who were "madly presumptuous" and others who were "uneasy and impatient" with the idea of any kind of yoke upon human passion. Both, he wrote, made no distinction between mankind and other animals except in terms of humans' more elaborately

---

[65] Mirabeau, *L'Ami des hommes* (Avignon, 1756), pt. I, ch. 1, p. 2.

[66] Mirabeau, *L'Ami des hommes* (Avignon, 1756), pt. I, ch. 1, p. 3.

[67] As Hume's French translator, the abbé Le Blanc informed him in 1757, Mirabeau "combat votre système sur le luxe, mais avec les égards dus à la supériorité de vos lumières": *The Letters of David Hume*, ed. J.Y.T. Greig, 2 vols. (Oxford, 1932, reprint, 1969), 1:137, note 2.

[68] Mirabeau, *L'Ami des hommes*, pt. III, pp. 167–9. See also Montesquieu, *The Spirit of Laws*, trans. Thomas Nugent [1750], 2 vols. (London, 1823) (hereafter *SL*), bk. 2, ch. 10. 2:33.

[69] Mirabeau, *L'Ami des hommes*, pt. II, ch. 5, p. 100.

structured physical organisation (the allusion was probably to the French exile Julien Offray de La Mettrie's recent and scandalous *Homme machine*). But of all the "deliria of the human mind," Mirabeau wrote, this was the one that least deserved attack. It did so not because its exponents were entirely right, but rather because none of them had seen the full implications of what they were saying. What, in fact, proved them right was not commerce or luxury, but the art of agriculture.[70]

Agriculture, Mirabeau asserted, was "the most sociable of all the arts."[71] It was sociable because, if property served to neutralize cupidity by dividing people from one another, agriculture could then be used to open up a space for moderation, temperance, and justice in human affairs. It was as much of an art as industry and trade, but an art that was able to assuage human need. It was also the product of the occupation of an extensive territory.[72] This, Mirabeau explained, was why it was possible to envisage the development of human society as a gradual process of separation and reunification, a process that was most pronounced in large territorial states where property was secured by a single sovereign authority.[73] Once it was clear "that sociability and cupidity exist and fight like two contrary elements in every man," the art of government would consist of "chaining down" the one in order to give free rein to the other.[74] Since cupidity could not be eliminated, it could, once relieved of its most pressing association with physical need, be diverted. "Cupidity is insatiable. Physical goods are limited; but moral goods are immense in number. Cupidity should therefore be directed towards these latter because it is only in this way that Peter's cupidity can be assuaged without affronting, envenoming, and fighting with that of Paul."[75]

Although, Mirabeau pointed out, governments cannot do much about physical goods like health, youth, strength, beauty, wealth, and dignities, they could exercise much more leverage on such moral goods as disinterest, honour, glory, generosity, probity, justice, fidelity, peace, charity, and love (namely, the virtues, "the general word for all the goods of this world") because "the power of government has greater scope over the moral than the physical."[76] Since men admire others' virtue, a government could use this propensity to divert cupidity into the desire for moral goods. "Recall the division that I made between sociability and cupidity. Every monetary distinction inclines us towards the latter, while every spur to honour and

---

[70] Mirabeau, *L'Ami des hommes*, pt. I, ch. 3, p. 24.
[71] Mirabeau, *L'Ami des hommes*, pt. I, ch. 3, p. 33.
[72] Mirabeau, *L'Ami des hommes*, pt. I, ch. 3, p. 25.
[73] Mirabeau, *L'Ami des hommes*, pt. I, ch. 3, p. 27.
[74] Mirabeau, *L'Ami des hommes*, pt. I, ch. 1, p. 6.
[75] Mirabeau, *L'Ami des hommes*, pt. II, ch. 3, p. 50.
[76] Mirabeau, *L'Ami des hommes*, pt. II, ch. 3, pp. 49–50.

consideration inclines us away from it and towards sociability."[77] Agriculture's capacity to lower the intensity of human avidity, thus leaving a space for governments to promote virtue, also made it possible to assign trade its rightful place in human affairs. Here, too, Mirabeau followed Montesquieu, citing his characterisation of trade with approval. "The spirit of commerce produces in men a certain feeling for exact justice, opposed on the one hand to banditry and on the other to those moral virtues that make it so that one does not always discuss one's own interests alone and that one can neglect them for those of others."[78]

Once trade was underpinned by agriculture, it was then possible to identify a way to neutralise the dynamics of competitive trade that Melon and Hume had argued were fundamental to the modern world. Bringing agriculture into the picture in the way that Mirabeau envisaged also required him to reverse the distinction that Montesquieu had made between trade based on economy as an attribute of republics and trade based on luxury as an attribute of monarchies. Republics, Mirabeau argued, were actually more adapted to the luxury trade, while large territorial monarchies were most suited to the trade in primary goods. Commerce in the most basic sense, he wrote, was simply "the useful and necessary relationship between any sociable being and his fellow."[79] In that sense as soon as there were two men, there was commerce. But even if commerce were understood solely as exchange, it could still be either *commerce de propriétaire*, involving the exchange of what was superfluous for what was necessary, or *commerce de mercenaire*, involving dealing in what someone else had produced and living off the profits produced by serving as an intermediary.[80]

Only this second type of commerce, Mirabeau claimed, had to be driven by monetary profit. The first type could rely on the built-in competitive advantage supplied by the development of agriculture, the growth of population, and the relatively low unit costs of the wage goods that a flourishing agricultural system would generate.

> Manufactured goods made in a very populous nation that has very little coin would be infinitely less expensive than anywhere else in the rest of a Europe flooded with gold and that would rush to get hold of them to resell them at a profit elsewhere.[81]

Promoting prosperity by freeing trade at home, thus raising agricultural output and reducing the relative wage costs of internationally traded goods,

[77] Mirabeau, *L'Ami des hommes*, pt. I, ch. 8, p. 136.

[78] Mirabeau, *L'Ami des hommes*, pt. IV, p. 61, citing Montesquieu, *Esprit des lois*, bk. 20, ch. 2 (trans. Cohler, Miller, and Stone [Cambridge, CUP, 1989]), p. 339.

[79] Mirabeau, *L'Ami des hommes*, pt. II, ch. 1, p. 5.

[80] Mirabeau, *L'Ami des hommes*, pt. II, ch. 1, p. 6.

[81] Mirabeau, *L'Ami des hommes*, pt. II, ch. 1, p. 11.

was the key to freeing trade everywhere. Once free trade had done its work at home, by raising agricultural productivity and reducing relative wage costs in the traded-goods sector so that indigenous industry could either match foreign competition or fall back upon a prosperous domestic market, a state could afford to open its borders in return for similar concessions from others. A government in this position, Mirabeau argued, would be the true friend of mankind because the agricultural autarchy that it had achieved meant that it would never have to solve the domestic problem of feeding its own population at the expense of the industry of other trading nations. Neutralising cupidity would enable a large territorial state to act in the interest of the whole human race. It would have no other interest than to use its power to promote a system of international cooperation and peace based upon free trade.

This, Mirabeau argued, was the only option left to the modern European states. Europe, he claimed, now faced a choice between continuing to pursue the self-defeating series of attempts that had been made to achieve universal monarchy and Henri IV and Sully's Christian republic, with France as its head. (It is worth noting that Mirabeau was very close to Montesquieu's bête noir, Marshal Belle-Isle, and, during the most disastrous period of the Seven Years War, even seems to have entertained hopes that he would join Belle-Isle in the French ministry.)[82] This, he emphasised, would not mean that France would rule Europe, since the "project for a Christian Republic was the deathblow to that of a universal monarchy. Europe's liberty was the plan's objective and equality was its basis."[83] Instead, he argued, France would be the state that would guide humanity towards true fraternity, substituting benign world leadership for the old chimera of universal monarchy.

My system is to envisage all humanity as a single family divided into several branches. The eldest branch in Europe ought to be France. She has shown all the others, for long enough, that even united against her they can fetter her only by fettering themselves. It is now time to make them learn that she wishes for no more than to be valued at her price, to be the arbiter of the world and promote its well-being as she does for her own people, extinguishing all

[82] See Laurent, *Les voyages en Bretagne*, pp. 82, 86–7, 89, and, for example, the following letters in Musée Arbaud, Aix-en-Provence, Fonds Mirabeau, 25: the chevalier de Mirabeau to Mirabeau, 11 October 1759, fol. 151; Mirabeau to the chevalier de Mirabeau, 29 October 1759, fol. 159; the same to the same, 9 September 1760, fol. 341, reporting that "le duc d'Ayen me disait l'autre jour, *il n'y a que vous qui puisse sauver l'état, et la plus saine partie du parlement le pense comme moi*" (Mirabeau's emphasis); and Mirabeau to the chevalier de Mirabeau, 19 October 1760, fol. 319.
[83] Mirabeau, *L'Ami des hommes*, pt. III, ch. 7, p. 157.

exclusive privileges, leaving only those supplied by nature and labour. This is the only universal monarchy that is not a dream.[84]

Unless, he warned, France became the arbiter of a world given over to free trade, the states of the modern world would destroy one another in their futile quest for the empire of the seas. Their populations would fall and their best inhabitants would emigrate to the New World, leaving those who remained to fight ferociously for pelts in the desert. "The project for fraternity between trading peoples, far from being an imaginary ideal, is the only one able to put cupidity back in its place."[85]

There was, moreover, a strategy for putting the Grand Design into effect. It would begin by promoting a system of alliances committed to free trade. Inevitably, that system would clash with the English Navigation Acts.[86] If the English refused to participate in the system of free trade, then France would promote a total embargo on English goods. This course of action was almost bound to end in war. But, Mirabeau argued, the state that was able to put itself in a position to promote a war to free trade would necessarily be the friend of mankind.

> Now, supposing that that prince, the friend of mankind, whose actions and opinions are all plainly to be seen and whose policies are in full public view, supposing that he might be forced to use the sword to support the common cause of humanity, can it be conceived that such a war would not become the common cause of all the allied powers? And then, once freed by a declaration of war from the shackles of justice that might otherwise prevent me even from imposing the yoke of humanity, I would not settle unless that treaty's basis was entry into the universal confraternity of trade.[87]

This was the only yoke that it was permissible to impose on one's neighbours and the only empire that it was useful and practicable to exercise over them. As Mirabeau emphasised, this was why his project was no castle in the air or a "warmed-up version of Plato and his republic" but, instead, an extrapolation of subsequent human arrangements in the light of the facts as they were.[88] "Peoples and sovereigns," he concluded,

> rivals for power and grandeur, I know the secret for infallibly making whoever of you is the first to believe me predominant, and this is that secret. Whoever most constantly takes the friendship of mankind as his standard and guide

---

[84] Mirabeau, *L'Ami des hommes*, pt. II. ch. 1, p. 33.

[85] Mirabeau, *L'Ami des hommes*, pt. III, ch. 5, p. 97.

[86] Mirabeau, *L'Ami des hommes*, pt. III, ch. 5, p. 99.

[87] Mirabeau, *L'Ami des hommes*, pt. III, ch. 5, p. 103.

[88] Mirabeau, *L'Ami des hommes*, pt. III, ch. 5, p. 103.

will reign over men's hearts and affections, which is the source of every kind of prosperity.[89]

That was the message of *L'Ami des hommes.*

From Friendship to Mankind to Political Economy

The mixture of war propaganda, crude power politics, and high moral principle contained in *L'Ami des hommes* made it an instant success. But eighteen months later Mirabeau was "converted" by François Quesnay and jettisoned the antithesis between sociability and cupidity that formed its analytical core. "I recall with the satisfaction of a man who has escaped from a shipwreck," he later wrote,

> how I, like so many others, was once a sort of Manichean and believed that I had found the principles of the good and the bad in sociability and cupidity. Happily, I have since come to know a true guide who placed me on the path from where I soon came to perceive the fixed and ineradicable outline of the physical law, the dazzling and certain light of the natural order.[90]

He explained his change of course in a remark about Montesquieu in his first attempt to collaborate with Quesnay, an essay entitled *Traité de la monarchie* (A Treatise on Monarchy), which he began to write at some time between 1757 and 1760.

> A few pages of the two political works of that illustrious writer are engraved in everything I have written. I often developed completely different consequences from his; I even took the liberty of contradicting him and could have done so more often had I wished. But I only ever established one principle that he did not see, namely, that *population depends solely upon subsistence goods.*[91]

He expanded upon this last claim in a letter to Rousseau in 1767, explaining that the argument of *L'Ami des hommes* had grown out of his reading of the *Essai sur la nature du commerce en général* (An Essay on the Nature of Commerce in General) by the Irish Jacobite exile, and onetime associate of John Law, Richard Cantillon (a work that he had read before its publication in 1755).[92] Following Cantillon, Mirabeau informed Rousseau, he had argued that riches were the fruits of the land, that human labour had the

---

[89] Mirabeau, *L'Ami des hommes*, pt. III, ch. 5, p. 110.

[90] Victor Riqueti, marquis de Mirabeau, *Lettres sur la législation, ou l'ordre légal dépravé, rétabli et perpétué*, 3 vols. (Berne, 1775), 3:728.

[91] A. N. M 778 (1), fol. 1.

[92] François-André-Adrien Pluquet, *Traité philosophique et politique sur le luxe*, 2 vols. (Paris, 1786), 2:328.

capacity to increase them, that the more humans there were, the more labour there would be and the more wealth it would be possible to create. He reproduced this account of the way that he had used Cantillon in a commemorative essay on the early-eighteenth-century economist Pierre de Boisguilbert, published in Stockholm in 1774.[93] The flaw in the argument of *L'Ami des hommes*, he acknowledged there, was its initial assumption that the way to promote prosperity was to promote population.

Quesnay, Mirabeau recorded, had told him that all this amounted to putting the cart before the horse. He now realised that Cantillon, "through his speculations and researches, had merely improved upon the error born in the last century by which trade was regarded as the principle of wealth."[94] What Quesnay had pointed out was that increasing population presupposed the existence of additional food supplies.

> He then had to explain his or, more exactly, nature's system. How the first men, whether hunters or shepherds, lived off the spontaneous products of nature, how the population of nations without agriculture is always still the same and their habitation always errant in order to forage for nature's successive products. How it was the industry of agriculture that made nations sedentary, how the growth of products which is a result of that art has always been the measure of the growth of population, how that growth in products derives solely from their quality as wealth, that quality of wealth from their exchange value, that exchange value from the consumption of those products, and how, therefore, the consumption of actual products is the source of a greater quantity of future products, the necessary basis of an increase in population.[95]

The Ciceronian framework of *L'Ami des hommes* had to be dropped. As another of the economists recalled, Quesnay was never impressed by Cicero. His favourite text was, instead, Demosthenes' grim warning to the Athenians, on the eve of the Persian Wars.

> You fear, Athenians, the expenditure of war. Very well! Philip will come: he will burn your houses; he will massacre your young people; he will carry off your women, your children and yourselves into slavery; and you will see the fruits of your economy.[96]

No state, the passage implied, could expect to be poor but free. The question was how to ensure that it could be rich but just.

---

[93] Reprinted in Jacqueline Hecht, ed., *Boisguilbert parmi nous. Actes du colloque international de Rouen* (Paris, Institute National d'Etudes Démographiques, 1989), pp. 379–443.

[94] Mirabeau to Rousseau, 30 July 1767, in Rousseau, *CC*, ed. Leigh, 33:261.

[95] Mirabeau to Rousseau, 30 July 1767, in Rousseau, *CC*, ed. Leigh, 33:262.

[96] Pierre-Samuel Dupont de Nemours, *The Autobiography*, ed. Elizabeth Fox-Genovese (Wilmington, Del., 1984), p. 272.

The new starting point was property. It was used, however, radically differently from the way that Mirabeau had used it at the beginning of *L'Ami des hommes*. There, Mirabeau had simply endorsed Cicero's claim that property was a check upon human avidity and the basis of the subsequent interaction between population growth, agricultural development, and free trade. Under Quesnay's guidance, property now came to be associated with a new technical vocabulary that made it possible to deal with it without having to refer either to ancient moral philosophy or, as with Montesquieu, to the strange modern afterlife of the Roman law. It was either "sterile" or "productive." It could be either "available" (*disponible*), "exchangeable," or "consumable." It could take the form of "primary advances," "annual advances," or "advances to reproduction." It could, in all these different guises, be represented by a single image, a *tableau économique*, setting out all the activities associated with its various functions, joined together by a zigzag-shaped set of intercrossing lines to represent the flows of income and expenditure connecting its several different kinds of owner. Quesnay's remarkably fertile imagination injected an impressively broad range of new conceptual terms into what his admirers began to call the "new science" of political economy and the prospect that it appeared to offer of dealing in a new way with the old subject of how power and justice could be reconciled. If Montesquieu's careful examination of Europe's Gothic past made it possible to begin to break the hold of Greece and Rome on modern Europe's political vocabulary, Quesnay's new technical vocabulary did something similar to property.

The new vocabulary soon earned the economists a reputation for unintelligible jargon. But it has also helped to disguise the more ambiguous evaluation of property underlying the new science. Where Mirabeau's initial position amounted to an endorsement of the moral purposes that landed property could be made to serve, the changes that he made under Quesnay's guidance introduced a more complicated assessment of its value and an even stronger claim about the moral purposes that it could be made to serve. This reassessment was a product of Quesnay's very different position on the principles of sociability and cupidity underlying *L'Ami des hommes*. By the time that he became famous as an economist Quesnay was nearly seventy years old. He was a prominent court physician, an early member of the Parisian Société des arts, and the author of a number of medical treatises dedicated to an assortment of powerful members of the French nobility; moreover (at least according to one set of memoirs), he had been the protégé of Louis XV's mistress, Mme de Pompadour.[97] Well before he became a Physiocrat, Quesnay seems to have made use of his

---

[97] For an interesting description of the faction-fighting in which Quesnay was involved, see Dupont de Nemours, *Autobiography*, ed. Fox-Genovese, pp. 250–8.

earlier medical investigations to produce a conception of human nature in which morality and physiology could be linked to one another in a way that was designed to address some of the difficulties arising in Christian moral theory from the radical separation between the physical and spiritual sides of human nature—a separation that was posited, in different ways, by René Descartes, Thomas Hobbes, and John Locke. This physiologically based conception of natural human aptitudes supplied a starting point for thinking about property both in terms of need, use, and consumption, as was common to all living creatures, and in terms of the more reflective uses and abuses to which it had come to be subject under the aegis of human intelligence. Physiocracy, or Quesnay's system, was designed to ensure that human intelligence would bring property back to its original, natural function, but at a level of prosperity that was far higher than anything created by simple animal use. As Quesnay presented it, the way to do so was to make the owners of the land pay for the whole expenditure of the state.

One indication of the physiological foundations of Quesnay's moral theory can be found in a treatise written by someone who had nothing at all to do with Physiocracy but was familiar with Quesnay's earlier medical work. This *Traité des sensations et des passions en général et des sens en particulier* (A Treatise on Sensations and Passions in General and the Senses in Particular) was the work of a physician from Rouen (and a corresponding member of the Berlin Academy) named Claude-Nicolas Lecat, now known mainly for his critical reaction to Rousseau's first *Discourse*. It was published initially in 1739 and, in revised form, in 1767. Its aim was to show that physical sensations and emotions (found, Lecat argued, in all forms of life) were the product of a complex set of physiological processes determined ultimately by a divinely created universal spirit that all living beings absorbed in respiration.[98] The presence of this spirit in the organs of the body meant, Lecat wrote, that the brain and the rational soul it housed were not, in the first instance, responsible for perceptions of sensation and emotion. As far as this function was concerned, the brain was no more than an echo of, or a clearinghouse (*bureau de correspondance*) for, perceptual information generated elsewhere.[99] The information itself had already been produced by the interaction between the various organs and the universal spirit that they contained. According to Lecat, their ability to generate perceptual information independent of the brain explains, for example, why, without any kind of reasoning, the sight of a meal excites hunger, not love.[100] Sensations and feelings had, therefore, quite a substantial cognitive content be-

[98] Claude-Nicolas Lecat, *Traité des sensations et des passions en général et des sens en particulier*, 3 vols. (Paris, 1767), 1:xxx–xxxi.

[99] Lecat, *Traité des sensations*, 1:lii.

[100] Lecat, *Traité des sensations*, 1:xliv.

fore they encountered the rational soul. Although, Lecat wrote, he was in many respects "a partisan and admirer of Locke," he could not accept his claim about the nonexistence of innate ideas.[101] All living creatures, he claimed, have an innate fear of danger and an aversion towards what threatens to harm or destroy them. These instinctive emotions were, in fact, a kind of knowledge generated, in a decentralised way, by the bodily organs.

In a note to the second edition of his treatise, Lecat claimed that his "new system" had been adopted by Quesnay in the second (1747) edition of the latter's *Essai physique sur l'oeconomie animale* (A Physical Essay on the Animal Economy).[102] He had, he added in a later passage, submitted the first edition of his *Treatise* in 1739 to the Parisian Academy of Surgery and had noticed that someone had underlined pages 128–9 of the text, leading him to fear that its secretary had disapproved of their content. He had been pleasantly surprised, he commented, to see, in the second edition of his *Essai physique*, that Quesnay had adopted "this new system describing the mechanisms of sensation and had substituted it for one involving traces imprinted on the brain that, in his first edition, he had given as the mechanism."[103] Its interest in this context lies in the light it throws on the concept of *évidence* that became a prominent feature of Physiocratic writing. If Lecat was not mistaken in noticing a similarity between his own system and the description of a decentralised linkage among sensations, passions, and cognition to be found in the second edition of the *Essai physique sur l'oeconomie animale*, then Quesnay's early medical and physiological work did have a bearing on his later publications as an economist. The kind of physiological mechanisms that he claimed were involved in the generation of knowledge and evaluations without reasoning have yet to be reconstructed in detail (soon after he died, the curious Protestant philosopher Antoine Court de Gebelin used Quesnay's physiology to make an ambitious argument about the natural origins of language and morality based on what he took to be the uniquely human capacity to make both vowel and consonant sounds, with the former expressing sensations and the latter ideas).[104] But Mirabeau, in a letter to Rousseau in 1767, clearly understood that *évidence* was simply the prereflective knowledge produced by the physical organs with which every living creature was endowed.[105]

---

[101] Lecat, *Traité des sensations*, 1:liii.

[102] Lecat, *Traité des sensations*, 1:xliv–xlv.

[103] Lecat, *Traité des sensations*, 1:152.

[104] Antoine Court de Gebelin, *Monde primitif, analysé et comparé avec le monde moderne, considéré dans l'histoire naturelle de la parole ou origine du langage et de l'écriture*, 9 vols. (Paris, 1775–82), 3: vi–vii, 284–5.

[105] François Quesnay, "Évidence" [1756], in *François Quesnay et la Physiocratie*, ed. Jacqueline Hecht, 2 vols. (Paris, Institut national de démographie, 1958), 2:397–426.

You do not understand our *évidence* and because of this you suspect us of a systematic spirit and of dreaming like the good abbé de Saint-Pierre. You believe that we seek to pursue the improvement (*perfectibilité*) of the human mind and to extend its limits. But far from wanting this, we want solely to bring it back to what is simple, to the primary notions of nature and instinct. All our laws can be reduced to conforming to the laws of nature with respect to the arrangements surrounding our labour and to the self-evident character of the right of property as it applies to the enjoyment of its fruits.[106]

This suggests that Mirabeau was able to drop the starting point of *L'Ami des hommes* because he had been given a new, physiologically driven version of natural human society, based on Quesnay's earlier investigations into the cognitive dimensions of sensation and emotion. As another Physiocrat, Guillaume-François Letrosne, put it,

It was by studying man's constitution, his needs and the means he has for meeting them, the laws of reproduction, the route followed by wealth as it is renewed annually from its origin to its consumption, its distribution throughout society, the nature of the various kinds of human labour and their effects, that he was able to grasp hold of the thread that, through a sequence of inferences and a perfectly integrated chain of reasoning, was to lead towards that science whose foundations he was the first to base on the physical laws of nature.[107]

The very simple set of human arrangements that the initial physical model implied could be used both as a kind of absolute standard against which later, acquired, arrangements could be set and, more importantly, as a kind of physical guide for tracking the sequence of income and expenditure involved in these more complicated social arrangements.

On Quesnay's premises, there was very little private property in natural society (at most it amounted to what was acquired by human effort for consumption and use). Nor, in any of his publications, did he spend much time on showing how private property of a more extended kind could have come into being. The fact of property was something that Quesnay simply took for granted (as too, it might be noted, did Montesquieu). Even if, as with Montesquieu's conception of monarchy, it began in violence and conquest, it was still possible to identify something in it that could make it just. Finding a way to do this meant, ultimately, that what the Physiocrats came to call the "legal despot" had to have a somewhat peculiar relationship to private property. It had to work against the grain of the existing

---

[106] Mirabeau to Rousseau, 30 July 1767, in Rousseau, *CC*, ed. Leigh, 33:256.
[107] Guillaume-François Letrosne, *De l'ordre social* (Paris, 1777), p. 447.

property regime without, however, undermining its productive capacity.[108] This was the point of the idea of a single tax on the net product. Since, as Fénelon (and, more famously, Locke) had earlier emphasised, all landed property was physically capable of producing many times more than was put into it, the fiscal system provided a way to force it to become as productive as possible. If the surplus produced from the land could be taken away peacefully from the actual owners of property and assigned to the various executive branches of the state by a single tax on landed income, the impact of that tax (on rents, agricultural production, expenditure, and investment) would gradually allow the original principle of justice underlying natural society to be restored. The art was to ensure that it was restored in such a way as to guarantee that it did not ruin landed property's capacity to continue to produce a surplus. The surplus would have to recur and, as population grew, would have to recur on an expanded scale. This meant allowing the actual owners to remain in possession of what they owned. But it also meant making the surplus (or net product) produced by the property they owned the sole source of the income needed by the military, legal, fiscal, and administrative agencies responsible for the executive functions of the state.

Property was therefore the cause of both the ruin and the recovery of the world. In a minimal sense, it was simply a product of the natural human effort involved in acquiring what was needed for use and consumption. In a more extended sense, however, it could be used to produce power and prosperity without having either to rely on an unattainable level of international commercial reciprocity, as with the abbé de Saint-Pierre, or, as with the Gournay group, to default into power politics. The secret (or "social art," as the economists called it) was to devise a way to prevent any interruption to the various flows of expenditure that property produced. Quesnay divided society into three, not two, classes: the landowners, the producers of agricultural goods, and the producers of manufactured goods. Despite the label of sterility attached to them, the members of the third class, the producers of manufactured goods, were as vital to the system as the other two. If expenditure of effort was the root cause of everything available to mankind, the sterile class was actually the key to the whole circulating mechanism. It was the only class that still continued to follow the original natural human propensity to spend in order to live, and was, therefore, a built-in source of demand for the products of the land. Its expenditure was the channel through which the landowners' consumption of manufactured goods would go back to the agricultural producers. The

---

[108] See Istvan Hont, "The Political Economy of the 'Unnatural and Retrograde' Order: Adam Smith and Natural Liberty," in Marion Barzen, ed., *Französische Revolution und Politische Ökonomie* (Trier, 1989), pp. 122–49, reprinted in his *Jealousy of Trade*, ch. 5.

larger it grew, the greater the pull of demand it would have on agricultural production and the greater the array of goods and services it would be able to make available both to the other two classes and to the state's own consumption requirements. The key was to ensure that the needs of the sterile class were catered for by domestic resources alone. As Quesnay emphasised in his *Encyclopédie* article on grain, this meant reversing standard assumptions about trade policy. Instead of exporting luxuries and importing necessities, a trading state should aim to do the opposite. That way, counterintuitively, it would never lose its independence.[109]

A two-class system would be either an agricultural society or a trading republic. A three-class system could grow in the right sequence if all the expenditure by the manufacturing sector reverted to the agricultural sector to become the starting point of further cycles of production and distribution. Managing the flow of expenditure was, therefore, the basis of the whole system. Taxing the owners of land would have the effect of forcing them into the monetary economy and would make their need for income the source of the direction of flow. The built-in demand for agricultural products from the sterile sector would prevent the flow from breaking down. Not taxing any sector of the economy but the landowners would have the double effect of raising demand for agricultural goods and of eliminating every obstacle between production by the agricultural sector and the reversion of all other forms of income to its source. The result would be a virtuous circle generated by rising rural productivity and a massively enlarged domestic market for manufactured goods. A state guided by this policy would become self-sufficient but would not lose its power. The longer-term effect of managing the flow of expenditure in this way would be to reduce existing levels of inequality. War and conquest might have destroyed the original, physically generated foundations of human society. But the inequality that had put an end to society in its first, natural, state could also be used to generate the resources required to bring the world back to its original foundational principles.

Just as Montesquieu had used a de facto system of property (the one that had developed in the wake of the conquest of Roman Gaul) to show how, over the course of time, it had been transformed into a system of government with an inbuilt capacity for stability, moderation, and prosperity, so the advocates of Physiocracy took an equally arbitrary set of property arrangements and set out to show how, under specified conditions, a de facto system could be brought back into alignment with justice. In the long term, the combined effects of the single tax on the net product (or what would be left over once provision for all the different types of advances to future

---

[109] François Quesnay, "Grains," in *François Quesnay et la Physiocratie*, 2:502 (*Maximes de gouvernement économique*, no. xiv).

production had been made) and the growing prosperity of all those parts of society that were not taxed at all would be a gradual, but continuous, reduction in absolute inequality. The fiscal system would put a ceiling on great wealth, while free trade would place a floor underneath great poverty. The rich would remain rich, but their share of total social wealth would still fall. Since, as Montesquieu had shown, luxury was a derivation of inequality, Physiocracy would put an end to luxury but still keep affluence. In Mirabeau's hands, the idea became the starting point for an ambitious and hugely energetic international campaign to put the new system into effect. His hyperbolic claim that the invention of language, the invention of money, and Quesnay's economic table were the three great landmarks of human history was an overstated indication of how the whole system was intended to work. As Forbonnais noticed, the keystone of the system was a rigid insistence upon the purely conventional character of money. The "great result," he noted, of the system set out in the *Philosophie rurale* (the most comprehensive statement of the economists' views, written by Mirabeau under Quesnay's guidance and published in 1763) was "to lead men to prohibit money from having the function of fictitious real estate" or, in a more modern idiom, capital.[110] If money could be kept to its role as a sign, it could be used to roll back all the distortions within and between societies that had come to form what the economists called "the unnatural and retrograde order" on which the modern world was based.

The way to do so was to rely on free trade. The remorseless effect of unremitting competition would push the existing unnatural order back onto its proper foundations by forcing every nation to give up on the legacy of its acquired endowments and revert to, or adopt, those that fitted it best. The starting point had to be grain, because if grain could be taken out of the equation of international competition, then the logic of collective reciprocity could begin to replace the logic of collective self-preservation. As Mirabeau put it in one of his last works, "you know what society is; utility is its motive and concord should be its bond."[111] Reviving reciprocity implied developing the productive power of agriculture as fully as possible so that, under conditions of free trade, the state with the most efficient agriculture would, in the first instance, become Europe's price-maker, but then, as other large territorial states acquired the same productive capacity, grain itself would gradually fall out of the international trading system. Melon's model would no longer apply. A state that had followed the entire Physiocratic programme would, as one of the economists put it, be one

---

[110] "On voit ici clairement le grand résultat; c'est de conduire les hommes à interdire à l'argent la fonction d'immeuble fictif": Forbonnais, *Principes*, p. 167.
[111] Mirabeau, *Entretiens*, 2:628.

that "would require nothing of others, because it would have known how to make its own existence independent."[112]

This was why free trade had to go before every other consideration. It would make commercial competition advantageous, not an extension of reason of state. No reason of state, Mirabeau emphasised floridly in one of the first of his publications to bear the marks of his collaboration with Quesnay, could ever override the principle of free trade in grain. "In sum," he wrote,

> absolute, general, indefinite freedom of trade in grain, in war as in peace, with enemies as with friends, with no reason whatsoever—even the safety of the whole empire—for provisioning oneself in any other way than bargain against bargain, cash in hand, without it ever being thought bad for an individual or a company to buy any amount whatsoever, is the principal pivot of agriculture. It is the prime divine and physical law of humanity and any intervention by any authority whatsoever in this area should be set, by a wise and enlightened people, on the same level as the crimes of burners of temples, poisoners of wells, and murderers of sovereigns and governments.[113]

This entailed following a radically different path from the one envisaged by Forbonnais and the Gournay group. Instead of the skill, variety, and labour-intensive activity involved in small-scale agriculture, everything had to be subordinated to raising agricultural productivity as speedily and effectively as possible.

This meant relying on the economies of scale of large-scale cereal production, substituting ploughs and livestock for human labour and using every advance in storage, milling, and transport as well as in agriculture itself to increase the unit output of the land. The self-sustaining character of the process had to be underpinned both by absolute free trade and by a tax regime that would allow markets to clear without any obstruction and, at the same time, would force the owners of land to seek the highest possible efficiency gains to offset the tax burden to which they would be subject. No tax could be allowed to interfere with the zigzag-shaped flows of goods and money from the land to the towns and back again. All those that did were simply subtracting resources from the pool of capital required to launch the next cycle of agricultural production. If the whole tax burden were placed entirely on the shoulders of the landowners, then they would be forced to increase the rents at which they leased out their land, so that

---

[112] Letrosne, *De l'ordre social*, p. 421.

[113] Victor Riqueti, marquis de Mirabeau, "Mémoire pour concourir au prix annoncé et proposé par la très louable société d'agriculture à Berne pour l'année 1759," in *Recueil de mémoires concernant l'oeconomie rurale par une société établie à Berne en Suisse*, vol. 1, pt. 2 (Zurich, 1760), pp. 227–311, 443–77 (p. 287).

their tenants would, in turn, be forced to innovate and seek the highest rates of return on their outlays. Cumulatively, the process would push the productivity of the land higher and higher, releasing larger and larger numbers of people into nonagricultural occupations while, at the same time, keeping the internationally traded goods sector competitive by way of a combination of the falling unit costs of wage goods and the rising demand for nonagricultural employment. In the very long term, the growth of population and the gradual subdivision of property would reduce existing differences between urban and rural society as agriculture came to be increasingly dominated by a combination of large-scale, mechanised cereal production and small-scale market-gardening, while urban industry would spill over into the countryside to produce a more stable balance in the distribution of occupations, activities, and mobility between them. In these circumstances, the "social circle," as Mirabeau called it, would be closed. Foreign trade would be largely unnecessary.

The change of course also entailed revising Montesquieu and, in particular, his concept of monarchy. In a lecture course on Montesquieu that he gave some years after his self-styled conversion, Mirabeau stated that the basic idea of *L'Ami des hommes* could be found in the tenth chapter of book 18 of *The Spirit of Laws*, entitled "Of the Number of Men in Proportion to Their Way of Procuring Subsistence." In it, Montesquieu had suggested that there was a ratio between population and production on uncultivated and cultivated terrains and a further set of ratios applicable to people who cultivated both the land and the arts. "What the author says here is quite right," Mirabeau commented. "At that time, one needed a great deal of wit and reflection to have seen so far, and someone I know rather well received many a fine compliment for saying the same thing after him in a manner that then pleased the public."[114] But in *L'Ami des hommes* Mirabeau (like most of his contemporaries) was highly critical of the connection that Montesquieu had made between changes in ratios like these and the idea of honour as the principle driving the scramble for preeminence that served to give a monarchy its prosperity and stability. "However fine and admirable the distinctions he sets out and however true they may well be," he wrote, "I am not sure whether he has not considered monarchies in a diseased state rather than their natural constitution."[115] In Mirabeau's pre-Physiocratic terms, monarchy (properly constituted) was the system

---

[114] "Ce que dit ici l'auteur est fort juste. Il fallait encore de son temps, bien de l'esprit et de la réflexion pour en voir jusqu' à là, et je connais d'assez près tel à qui l'on fit dans le temps de beaux compliments, pour avoir dit après lui la même chose d'une manière qui convient alors au public." Bibliothèque royale, Brussels. Mss. 20797, fol. 178. I am grateful to Loic Charles (Centre d'histoire de la pensée économique, Université de Paris I) for directing me to this source.

[115] Mirabeau, *L'Ami des hommes*, pt. 2, ch. IV, p. 74.

of government best able to maintain and promote sociability, or the human ability to behave morally without any coercion from the law. It was, if anything, better equipped to foster the virtues than any other kind of government but also, if anything, more exposed to decadence and decline if subjected to the decay of political virtue brought about by excessive self-regard.

Quesnay forced Mirabeau to adopt a different position. Montesquieu's account of the succession of governments, he wrote in the margins of the treatise on monarchy that Mirabeau began to write soon after the two began to collaborate, was simply "ideal." He advised Mirabeau to recast the treatise around three chapters. The first would deal with the society between men and women arising from the natural human appetite to produce and preserve children, and the human need for mutual assistance. Man, he wrote, knows that he cannot suffice for himself because if he is ill, he cannot attend to his need to subsist. The second chapter would then deal with the government of patriarchal societies according to natural law and history. The third would deal with the two types of society born of the "moral perversion" of brigand societies banded together to loot the wealth of these patriarchal societies. These were either military or ecclesiastical despotisms, in which authority was exercised by force or fraud, or they were monarchies.[116] Quesnay's medically inspired conception of natural human attributes supplied a very simple starting point (one not too far removed from Rousseau's description of the orangutan-like creatures of the beginning of his *Discourse on the Origin of Inequality*). Where Mirabeau's initial response to Montesquieu had been to try to reinstate a more conventional treatment of morality and politics, Quesnay's response was to reinforce Montesquieu's highly attenuated moral starting point. As Mirabeau noticed with some dismay, the revisions that Quesnay argued had to be made to the *Treatise on Monarchy* were couched in the idiom of seventeenth-century natural jurisprudence, forcing him (in a passage that he was told to excise) "to calculate according to the suppositions of that dry metaphysics whose pride eventuates in seeing humanity in its cradle as brute," and requiring him to adopt "a system that tends to replace the Creator by a fantastic idol called philosophy"—all of which (Mirabeau emphasised) was not at all compatible with his own "fashion of thinking."[117] Republics, Quesnay stated, were a late outcrop of despotic governments, emerging out of the primitive trading systems that humans had been forced to adopt

[116] A. N. M 778, "Traité de la monarchie," fols. 22–3. The whole text can now be found in Victor Riqueti, marquis de Mirabeau, and François Quesnay, *Traité de la monarchie*, ed. Gino Longhitano (Paris, L'Harmattan, 1999); see pp. 19–20 and pp. 176–80 for the passages in question.

[117] Mirabeau, *Traité*, ed. Longhitano, p. 37, note 50.

as the only way to survive in the conditions of physical desolation and scarcity created by prolonged exposure to despotic power.[118]

Quesnay's comments indicate that he took the family to be the only society that humans were naturally and generically able to establish. Anything else was the product of many more specific and local causal mechanisms. Where Mirabeau's objections to Montesquieu were largely moral, Quesnay's were more technical and analytical, aiming to reinforce rather than refute the concept of monarchy contained in *The Spirit of Laws*. Like Montesquieu he came out against the idea of a commercial nobility.[119] Unusually, he also accepted Montesquieu's argument about the positive effects of venal offices in stimulating industry and trade and as an avenue into the nobility that was independent of royal patronage.[120] However unflattering it might be for human nature, he noted, the idea of a poor nobility was simply incompatible with the respect accorded to great wealth. But he was particularly critical of Montesquieu's anxiety about monarchy's potential for despotism because, he argued, it was based upon a misunderstanding of the nature of sovereignty.[121] Sovereign power, according to Quesnay, was always representative. It was a power that was divine, even though those who exercised it were always established by human choice. But it could represent part of a society against the whole. If it did, it would be despotic. But it was never the rule of a single individual in any literal sense. As Quesnay put it in the unpublished entry on men (*Hommes*) that he wrote for the *Encyclopédie* (and which Mirabeau quoted extensively in the treatise on monarchy), it was never the case that a single human being could physically exercise sovereign power over millions of others. "Despotism," Quesnay commented, "is never anything other than a league between the sovereign and an organ (*corps*) of the state that has become more powerful than the sovereign itself. Monarchical despotism is a chimera. It has never existed and it is impossible that it can exist."[122] Despotism, according to Quesnay, was always either military, feudal, or clerical. It could, he claimed, be robust and durable. But to be so, it had to maintain its ability to represent a partic-

---

[118] Mirabeau, *Traité*, fol. 20, and ed. Longhitano, pp. 176–77.

[119] He made this clear in his *Encyclopédie* article on *impôts*. See *François Quesnay et la Physiocratie*, vol. 2, 1757c, p. 607.

[120] "Le premier fondement de la dignité de la noblesse est la richesse. Les grands du royaume sont de grands propriétaires libres. La pauvre noblesse figure mal. L'idée abstraite de la noblesse frappe peu les sens; les richesses loyales donnent considération et pouvoir. Si elles se séparaient de la noblesse, elles tiendraient bientôt le premier rang. Pour que la noblesse se soutienne en considération, il faut anoblir les riches et attirer les richesses dans la noblesse." Victor Riqueti, marquis de Mirabeau, "Bref état des moyens pour la restauration de l'autorité du roi et de ses finances," ed. Georges Weulersse, *Revue d'histoire économique et sociale* 6 (1913): 177–211 (here p. 185).

[121] Mirabeau, *Traité*, ed. Longhitano, p. 28.

[122] Mirabeau, *Traité*, ed. Longhitano, p. 110 and note 24.

ular part of society against the whole, either by maintaining superstition and ignorance if it was clerical, or by means of war and conquest if it was feudal or military.

The real threat to absolute monarchy, Quesnay argued, was not despotism but tyranny. Unlike despotism, tyranny was a short-term state. But it was also a state of acute political crisis.

> There is an intermediate period between monarchy and despotism that should not be confused and it is this that is the period of the greatest internal revolutions in states. It is the tyrannical government of the sovereign and his minister. It is true that this form of government is of no more than brief duration, but is the most worthy of reflection for a political thinker.[123]

For Quesnay, Montesquieu's description of despotism as a peril inherent in absolute monarchy was not only wrong but dangerous. By raising an imaginary spectre, particularly in his conjectures about the new militaristic "disease" affecting Europe, Montesquieu's warning about military despotism could have the effect of producing the much more real possibility of tyranny. Tyranny, Quesnay wrote, would always produce oppression, violation of the rule of law, and calls for the revival of the rights of the nation. In these circumstances, neighbouring powers would be likely to try to take advantage of the sovereign's weakness, producing either a slide towards full-blown military despotism or a collapse into civil war, military defeat, and conquest or, alternatively, the formation of a mixed, republican or aristocratic government, with all the potential for further division and conflict that they housed.

These latter scenarios, Quesnay argued, were much more likely to occur than military despotism.

> Thus monarchy does not always degenerate into military despotism, and there are no states in Europe susceptible to this last type of government, a type that is too destructive for kingdoms surrounded by powerful neighbours to be able to survive the destruction of agriculture and population caused by military despotism. Thus this form of despotism is possible only in states of an extraordinary extent, separated by vast deserts from other nations. Despotism is rarely a consequence of tyrannical monarchy. But revolutions of another kind are as redoubtable to the sovereign as they are inevitable, because it is only too well established from the history of the European states that tyrannical or arbitrary government cannot survive. This is why it should be studied with a great deal of attention and discernment by authors writing about the nature of governments. Above all, they should take care not to confuse these with military despotism as, by failing to distinguish absolute sovereignty from sovereignty

---

[123] Mirabeau, *Traité*, ed. Longhitano, p. 176, note 396.

that is dissolved and sovereignty that has been subjugated, M. de Montesquieu so crudely did.[124]

Monarchy, from Quesnay's perspective, was either *souveraineté absolue*, *souveraineté dissolue*, or *souveraineté subjuguée* (absolute sovereignty, sovereignty dissolved, or sovereignty subjugated). The point of Physiocracy was to identify and secure the institutional foundations of the first of these three conditions so that neither of the latter two could ever occur. As Quesnay put it in a note to Mirabeau,

> Monarchy is an organised body whose head continually changes, which makes this type of government extremely redoubtable, and experience proves its harmful effects only too well. It ought to be the organisation of the body that regulates the head. It is this organisation that has not yet been established securely, because monarchical government was originally a military government that seized hold of the civil and economical government.[125]

The kind of organisation that monarchy required was an extension of Montesquieu's dualism. There would be a sovereign (a legal despot) and a government, made up of a large number of subordinate, dependent, and intermediate powers, some elected and others appointed. The result, as Mirabeau put it, would be a monarchy ruling over a subordinate republic. In a monarchy, he wrote (again using a passage from Quesnay's unpublished *Encyclopaedia* entry on *Hommes*),

> distinct and separate orders, powerful because of their makeup, their privileges, and the habit of respect shown towards them by the population, are assigned the execution of each part of the law. Restrained in turn by one another and condensed and compressed by the sovereign power, they form as unchangeable a whole as any human institution can be.[126]

"Pure and simple monarchy," Mirabeau informed his brother after his conversion, "is, like a republic, a state that cannot last. Whoever considers the annals of humanity with any attention cannot find four successive reigns without revolutions in any country governed in that way. Monarchy therefore needs to be constituted by intermediaries."[127] As with Montesquieu, the authority of the state would be separated both from the day-to-day

---

[124] Mirabeau, *Traité*, ed. Longhitano, p. 177, note 396.

[125] Mirabeau, *Traité*, ed. Longhitano, p. 181, note 409.

[126] Mirabeau, *Traité*, ed. Longhitano, pp. 15–6. See, too, p. 48. Compare to François Quesnay, "Hommes,", in *François Quesnay et la physiocratie*, 2:540: "Sovereign monarchical power can subsist only through the authority of the laws and through the balance of the bodies of the state, each restrained in turn by the other; and by the laws that concern them and that limit and guarantee their rights."

[127] Mirabeau to the chevalier de Mirabeau, 15 July 1760, cited in Laurent, *Les voyages en Bretagne*, p. 210.

workings of its government and, more radically, from the natural liberty of its members. Since the state's fundamental laws were purely physical in origin, the role of the legal despot was simply to maintain the conditions that allowed them to work. The state would uphold justice but would leave the wider array of detailed local argument about questions of equity or expediency to the workings of polity, or *police*. It was Mirabeau, in fact, who revived the name for the kind of local court (*conseils de prud'hommes*) that came to be established to settle disputes in the urban trades of nineteenth-century France.[128]

As its critics noticed, Physiocracy implied a progression from a very thin moral beginning to a very thick moral ending. In this sense, the kind of sequence that the French economists envisaged was similar to the kind of historical and moral sequence to be found in the natural jurisprudence of Samuel Pufendorf and Richard Cumberland. But the emphasis on reforming actually existing societies made Quesnay's use of natural jurisprudence rather idiosyncratic. The kind of political society that he envisaged was not one based on a social contract. It would be ruled by law, but the law in question was physical and the rules that it supplied would be discerned by human intelligence, not made by human choice. The odd term "legal despot" referred to a sovereign who did not need to legislate because the law itself was, in quite a strong sense, already in place. The arrangements that the state was responsible for upholding could still be said to be contractual, but only in a highly metaphorical sense, since the kind of contract on which it was based was one between humans and the land. As another of the economists' supporters put it, this "pact between man and the land" was quite different from "a social contract whose execution cannot be guaranteed by any higher power."[129]

> The land has a duty towards the cultivator who nurtures and annually renews its fertility to supply full restitution of those annual expenses and the interest needed to maintain his productive establishment. It owes the landowner responsible for making it fit for cultivation both the enjoyment of an interest on his landed expenses so that his lot will be seen to be desirable and his efforts rewarded, as well as a fund that he cannot enjoy since he is obliged to use it to maintain and continue his undertakings. These are the conditions of the pact existing between man and the land, sealed and guaranteed by nature.[130]

---

[128] The term can be found in Mirabeau, *Entretiens*, 4:106–8. On the importance of this system of conciliation and arbitration, see Alain Cottereau, "The Fate of Collective Manufactures in the Industrial World: The Silk Industries of Lyons and London, 1800–1850," in Charles F. Sabel and Jonathan Zeitlin, eds., *Worlds of Possibilities: Flexibility and Mass Production in Western Industrialisation* (Cambridge, CUP, 1997), pp. 75–152.

[129] [André Roubaud], *Histoire générale de l'Asie, de l'Afrique et de l'Amérique*, 4th ed., 5 vols. (Paris, 1770–2), 3:974.

[130] Roubaud, *Histoire*, 3:924.

This kind of pact could not be found in "the arbitrary conventions of a vain social contract, whose reciprocal execution cannot be guaranteed by any higher power." The true basis of civil society was, instead, "the society formed between man and the land, with the land making its laws known by fulfilling, all by itself, the orders of a Providence that the land itself teaches you to glorify."[131]

The language may have been florid, but it helps to indicate the way in which Quesnay gave Mirabeau a more robust framework for thinking about how to reach the goal that he had set out in *L'Ami des hommes*. Although the means changed, the end remained the same. As Mirabeau emphasised in a work published in 1774, summarising a course of public lectures that he had given in Paris, it was still to substitute the logic of collective reciprocity for the logic of collective self-preservation.[132] Substituting the land and its products for the vaguer opposition between cupidity and sociability allowed Mirabeau to use the idea of guiding human avidity towards sociable ends that was the basis of the argument of *L'Ami des hommes*, but to anchor it to something measurable. Instead of trying to channel cupidity towards moral goods as he had done in his first book, Mirabeau was able to use Quesnay's technical insights into the flow of goods and money generated by agriculture to identify a way by which self-interest could be guided towards the same outcome. As Mirabeau pointed out in a late, unpublished essay on the marquis d'Argenson, "only property gives emulation to industry."

> Need, which accompanies labour imperiously, does not extend its power beyond what is strictly necessary. But peaceful and secure property attracts and fascinates self-love, which is ever quick to hope. Hope spurs on labour, and an expenditure of labour on what is more than strictly necessary produces abundance. This, in turn, stimulates further effort to share in its fruits, provoking offers of service, the birth of new desires, endowing these services and their effects with a value in exchange and, consequently, the quality of wealth.[133]

Human intelligence added desires to needs, and, unlike needs, desires were cumulatively limitless, marking, in this respect, an important difference between humans and animals.[134] Physiocracy was the art of channelling human desires towards collective prosperity and power. Since its foundation was physical and measurable, it had a secure basis for calculation in a way that was unavailable in the earlier opposition between sociability and

---

[131] Roubaud, *Histoire*, 3:925.

[132] Victor Riqueti, marquis de Mirabeau, *La Science ou les droits et les devoirs de l'homme* (Lausanne, 1774).

[133] A. N. M 752 (6), [Mirabeau], *Considérations sur le gouvernement de France par M. le marquis d'Argenson*, fol. 22.

[134] For a clear presentation of the difference, see Letrosne, *De l'ordre social*, p. 199, note 7.

cupidity. Measuring the uses and abuses to which landed property might be put repeated the role assigned to cupidity in *L'Ami des hommes* but gave real traction to a government armed with the power of a fiscal system to put society back on its proper foundations. "Praise be for our science," Mirabeau announced in his last major work, "for it invokes our invincible avidity, condemned by the vain declamations of so many other philosophers."[135] This was the theme of *L'Ami des hommes*. The new science was simply a better way to manage avidity. As Mirabeau emphasised in 1774, it had nothing to do with "the avid, odious, and senseless project of reducing nature to a republic" to be found in Pierre-Paul Thiry, baron d'Holbach's *Système de la nature* (The System of Nature), published, to his dismay, under the name of his near namesake, Jean-Baptiste de Mirabaud.[136] The whole purpose of the economists' new science, he added, was also directed against "the blasphemous system of a certain madman who imagined that tyranny was the Gordian knot of every society" (the allusion was probably to Simon Linguet's *Théorie des lois civiles* (A Theory of Civil Laws) and its argument that justice was best supplied by a sovereign who was the real owner of all the goods in its territory.[137] Nothing in the new doctrine, he emphasised, had led him to alter what he had written about the relationship between political economy and morality in *L'Ami des hommes*.[138]

In this sense, Physiocracy was the theoretical realisation of Mirabeau's initial idea. As with the system set out in *L'Ami des hommes*, it was designed to work progressively to detach human society from the self-defeating process of competing for money and power and, instead, reinstate reciprocal utility at a higher level of social organization and material prosperity than it had originally had in its first, natural state. For the Scottish moral philosopher Dugald Stewart, the teleological shape of the French economists' system made it look rather similar to the Stoic system of morality that Mirabeau himself had identified as his starting point. "The ethical system," Stewart noted, "of those ancient philosophers who held that virtue consists in following nature, not only involves a recognition of final causes, but represents the study of them, in as far as regards the ends and destination of our own being, as the great business and duty of life."

A still more remarkable illustration, however, of the influence which this species of evidence has over the belief, even when we are the least aware of its connection with metaphysical conclusions, occurs in the history of the French Economic System. Of the comprehensive and elevated views which at first suggest it, the title of *Physiocratie*, by which it was early distinguished, affords a strong

---

[135] Mirabeau, *Entretiens*, 1:507.
[136] Mirabeau, *La Science*, pp. 213–5.
[137] Mirabeau, *La Science*, p. 221.
[138] Mirabeau, *La Science*, p. 212.

presumptive proof; and the same thing is more fully demonstrated by the frequent recurrence made in it to the physical and moral laws of nature, as the unerring standard which the legislator should keep in view in all his positive institutions. I do not speak at present of the justice of these opinions. I wish only to remark, that, in the statement of them given by their original authors, it is taken for granted as a truth self-evident and indisputable, not merely that benevolent design is manifested in all the physical and moral arrangements connected with this globe, but that the study of these arrangements is indispensably necessary to lay a solid foundation for political science.[139]

For the economists themselves, however, the Stoic idea of living in accordance with nature was combined with a more strongly Christian emphasis on the ideas of sin, expiation, and recovery. This aspect of Physiocracy was signalled prominently by the recurrent references to the work of the seventeenth-century Oratorian theologian Nicolas Malebranche in several of the economists' major works. The whole of the second chapter of Malebranche's *Traité de morale* (A Treatise on Morality), describing how true virtue amounted to living in accordance with the divine order, appeared at the beginning of the *Philosophie rurale*, while a sentence from the same chapter ("the order is the inviolable law of minds; nothing is rightly regulated unless it conforms to it") became the epigraph of Lemercier de la Rivière's *Ordre naturel et essentiel des sociétés politiques*.[140] The quotations, it may be assumed, were intended to indicate something about the ultimate point of the whole system.

The association with Malebranche was not peculiar to Physiocracy. Hume also associated him with Montesquieu. "This illustrious writer," he wrote in a note referring to Montesquieu in his *Enquiry concerning the Principles of Morals*,

> supposes all right to be founded on certain *rapports* or relations; which is a system, that, in my opinion never will be reconciled with true philosophy. Father Malebranche, as far as I can learn, was the first that started this abstract theory of morals, which was afterwards adopted by Cudworth, Clarke, and others; and as it excludes all sentiment, and pretends to found everything on reason, it has not wanted followers in this philosophic age.[141]

---

[139] Dugald Stewart, *Elements of the Philosophy of the Human Mind*, 2nd ed., 2 vols. (Edinburgh, 1816), 2:497–9.

[140] Victor Riqueti, marquis de Mirabeau, *Philosophie rurale, ou économie générale et politique de l'agriculture, réduite à l'ordre immuable des lois physiques et morales, qui assurent la prospérité des empires* [1763] (Amsterdam, 1764), pp. xi–xxxiv. For a recent examination of the relationship between Malebranche and the economists, see Catherine Larrère, "Malebranche revisité: l'économie naturelle des physiocrates," *Dix-Huitième Siècle* 26 (1994): 117–38.

[141] David Hume, *An Enquiry concerning the Principles of Morals* [1751], ed. L. A. Selby-Bigge (Oxford, 1957), p. 197, note 1.

God, in Malebranche's theology, worked by way of general wills, since these best fitted the several attributes of a divinity.[142] This meant that the providential system was bound to produce effects that might seem partial or misplaced to human eyes (it rains, for example, on the sea as well as the land). But rational understanding of the broader system made its deeper purposes intelligible. Montesquieu, according to some of his readers, could be interpreted in this way.[143] So, more clearly, can Quesnay. Human misfortune and the inequality that it often involved, he wrote in the second edition of his *Essai physique sur l'oeconomie animale*, were part of a much more general system in which all those who had lived, were alive now, or were yet to be born were no more than a small part.[144] "A thousand natural causes," he observed, "inevitably and necessarily contribute to the creation of that inequality, and these causes are not at all subject to the moral order."[145] While a sovereign authority could repress the actions of those who wish to appropriate our goods or interfere with our liberty or lives, it could not, without disrupting the order of society, redress "disturbances" in the distribution of goods.[146]

But Physiocracy also had a further, more overtly moral dimension that was captured enduringly in the neologism that Mirabeau coined in *L'Ami des hommes*. The word "civilisation" has an obvious family resemblance to the terms "civility," "civil society," and "civil government."[147] It was first

---

[142] See Patrick Riley, *The General Will before Rousseau: The Transformation of the Divine into the Civic* (Princeton, Princeton University Press, 1986).

[143] See, particularly, Etienne-Géry Lenglet, *Essai, ou Observations sur Montesquieu* (Paris, 1792).

[144] As Mirabeau pointed out in a letter to his brother, this did not mean that "everything was for the good" (as the "real misfortune of the Jewish people" might be taken to be "a general good" since it provided evidence of the truth of revealed religion). That view of providence was incompatible with the idea of the Fall: "Somme totale, je ne puis admettre que tout soit bien dans le monde moral puis que cette idée est incompatible avec l'offense de Dieu qui est de foi et de sentiment intérieur dans notre conscience. Dieu a nécessité ses oeuvres physiques à l'obéissance et a réservé ses oeuvres morales, s'il est permis de parler ainsi pour l'affection. Il leur a en conséquence donné la liberté, et dans l'abus de cette liberté *tout est mal*": Musée Arbaud, Fonds Mirabeau, 25, fol. 257, Mirabeau to the chevalier de Mirabeau, 24 August 1760. For Rousseau's similar position, see Christopher Kelly and Roger Masters, "Human Nature, Liberty and Progress," in Robert Wokler, ed., *Rousseau and Liberty* (Manchester, Manchester University Press, 1995), pp. 53–69.

[145] François Quesnay, *Essai physique sur l'oeconomie animale*, 3 vols. (Paris, 1748), 3:370.

[146] Quesnay reproduced the passage in his essay entitled "Droit naturel," reprinted in François Quesnay, *Physiocratie*, ed. Jean Cartelier (Paris, Garnier-Flammarion, 1991), p. 75.

[147] For a general survey, see Jörg Fisch, "Zivilisation, Kultur," in Otto Bruner, Werner Conze, and Reinhart Koselleck, eds., *Geschichtliche Grundbegriffe*, 8 vols. (Stuttgart, 1972–97), 7:679–774, and, on the eighteenth-century concept itself, see Starobinski, *Blessings in Disguise*, pp. 1–35; Bernard Plongeron, "Affirmation et transformations d'une 'civilisation chrétienne' à la fin du xviiie siècle," in Jean-René Derré, Jacques Gadille, Xavier de Montclos, and Bernard Plongeron, eds., *Civilisation chrétienne. Approche historique d'une idéologie xviiie–xixe*

used, however, to criticise, rather than endorse, the behaviour and institutions to which those terms referred. Mirabeau coined the term in an unpublished treatise on civilisation, written before the publication of *L'Ami des hommes*. "If I were to ask most people of what civilisation consists," he wrote there, "they would reply, *the civilisation of a people is a softening of its manners, an urbanity, politeness, and a spreading of knowledge so that the observation of decencies takes the place of laws of detail.*"

> All of which merely shows me the mark, not the face, of virtue. Civilisation does nothing for society unless it gives it both the form and the content of virtue, and the corruption of humanity is born in the breast of societies softened by all the previously cited ingredients.[148]

Although, in the nineteenth and twentieth centuries, it became usual to set the French word *civilisation* against the German word *Bildung*, the meaning of the two words was, at the beginning, intended to be quite similar.[149] Just as the German Pietist word *Bildung* referred to the way by which something about the inner, spiritual side of human nature could come to be mirrored on the outside, so Mirabeau's coinage referred to the way by which genuine morality might come to inform the otherwise shallow veneer of civility and politeness to be found in modern life. As Mirabeau put it in *L'Ami des hommes*, "the natural circle running from barbarism to decadence by way of civilisation and wealth could be taken in hand by a skilful and attentive minister so that the machine could be put back into working order before it has reached its end."[150] In a sentence subsequently used to illustrate the dictionary definition of the term in the Jesuit *Dictionnaire de Trévoux*, he made the critical sense of the term quite explicit, bluntly asserting, against the apologists of luxury (whom he identified as Melon and Hume) that "religion is the mainspring (*premier ressort*) of civilisation."[151] It was, he added, the opposite of "the quest for luxury and a false civilisation."[152]

---

siècle (Paris, 1975), pp. 9–21 (p. 17); Bernard Plongeron, "Bonheur et 'civilisation chrétienne': une nouvelle apologétique après 1760," *Studies on Voltaire and the Eighteenth Century* 154 (1976): 1637–55; Bernard Plongeron, "Echec à la sécularisation des lumières? La religion comme lien social," in Michel Mat, ed., *Problèmes d'histoire du christianisme* (Brussels, 1984), pp. 91–126.

[148] A. N., M 780, No. 3², Victor Riqueti, marquis de Mirabeau, "Traité de la civilisation," fol. 3.

[149] On the German terms, see, helpfully, Raymond Geuss, *Morality, Culture, and History* (Cambridge, CUP, 1999), pp. 29–50.

[150] Mirabeau, *L'Ami des hommes*, pt. II, p. 176.

[151] Mirabeau, *L'Ami des hommes*, pt. I (Avignon, 1756), p. 136. Jacques Grés Gayer, "Barbare et civilisé d'après l'article 'instinct' du *Dictionnaire de Trévoux*," in Derré et al., eds., *Civilisation chrétienne*, pp. 47–62 (p. 57).

[152] Mirabeau, *L'Ami des hommes*, pt. 5, "Mémoire sur l'agriculture" (Hamburg, 1762), p. 51 (or, in the Avignon, 1760 ed., vol. 2, bk. 5, p. 29).

The prominence of the quotations from Malebranche in the preface to the *Philosophie rurale* (which Mirabeau wrote under Quesnay's supervision) suggests a way by which Mirabeau's neologism can be connected to the revised version of *L'Ami des hommes* that, substantively, is probably the best way to describe what Quesnay did by creating Physiocracy. The link was supplied by Malebranche's grand and baroque account of the nature and purposes of the Creation. Crudely summarised, the account went something like this.[153] God, in creating the world, had done so for a reason. But no reason could be an appropriate reason for a god unless it satisfied all the attributes of a divinity. Only something divine could be a good enough reason for the Creation. The reason for the Creation had, therefore, to be the Incarnation. But the Incarnation was predicated on the Fall. The ruin of the world was, therefore, the reason for the Creation. It was why God became a man and sacrificed himself to redeem the human race. But the Incarnation of God in Christ also had the further effect of equipping humans with the same human resources that Christ, as a man, had used to redeem humanity. The Incarnation and the Crucifixion added a moral dimension to the physical *évidence* available to every living creature because Christ's death was a human choice. The Incarnation and the Crucifixion enabled humans to know how to choose virtue. They enabled humans to know how to apply their intelligence to the basic information supplied by their physical senses and, by doing so, to make moral choices. Seen in this light, Physiocracy was the practical application of these theological insights. It was a humanly devised system of government that, by applying human intelligence to the natural clues supplied by a providential God, could give humanity the ability to make the right choices.

The world, as Malebranche presented it, was not the best of all possible worlds. But it was still one in which, because of the Incarnation, evil was surmountable. It was surmountable, moreover, in ordinary human terms because these were the terms that God had adopted in becoming human. The ruin of the world thus contained the key to the recovery of the world. That key was what Malebranche called the Grace of Christ, or the gift of being able to use the ordinary physical sensations and emotions associated with self-preservation and self-love as a guide to the more complex and abstract reasoning involved in moral choice. These were the only means that Christ had used to make the most significant moral choice of all. From this perspective, Malebranche was able to argue that the physical side of

---

[153] A clear rendition of Malebranche's theodicy (based, in the main, on his late *Réflexions sur la prémotion physique* [1715]) can be found in the vicomte d' Alès de Corbet, *De l'origine du mal, ou examen des principales difficultés de Bayle sur cette matière* (Paris, 1758). Most recently, see Donald Rutherford, "Malebranche's Theodicy," and Patrick Riley, "Malebranche's Moral Philosophy: Divine and Human Justice," in Steven Nadler, ed., *The Cambridge Companion to Malebranche* (Cambridge, 2000), pp. 165–89, 220–61.

human nature had a powerful positive dimension that had gone unrecognised in the stronger versions of Augustinian theology, particularly those developed in the seventeenth century by the Jansenists. This was one reason why he was able to defend the Protestant theologian Jacques Abbadie's claims about the close connection between self-love, rightly understood, and moral virtue.[154] The grace of Christ gave fallen humans the human means to know how to act morally and to play their part in the long, painful work of redemption in Christ and the Church. This, as Malebranche put it, was why the world as saved by Christ was a world of greater worth than the world as it had been at the Creation.

The connection between Malebranche and Physiocracy was probably generated by this insistence on both the unavoidable character of evil in human affairs and the human ability to find a way out. It was, as Quesnay emphasised in his *Encyclopédie* article on *évidence*, an ability grounded upon the application of human intelligence (whose origin, he wrote, was ultimately divine) to the perceptual information supplied by the physical world.[155] The combination of experience and intelligence amounted to a God-given human ability to put a ruined world right. From this perspective Physiocracy was a kind of theodicy, or a way of explaining how the evil in human affairs could be reconciled with the idea of an omnipotent, omniscient, and loving God.[156] The passage from Malebranche quoted in the *Philosophie rurale* was not just about how or what human beings might know, but about how they might know the right thing to do. It was about moral choice rather than knowledge as such. In one sense, the knowledge generated, in a decentralised way, by the bodily organs supplied a kind of answer. But it was an answer that was applicable to all living beings, not just to humans. Unlike plants or animals, however, humans could choose the kind of life they led. They could add culture and civilisation to mere natural survival. Physiocracy, from this perspective, amounted to recasting a well-established set of humanist themes concerning rationality, morality, culture, and civility into a new physical, moral, and theological system. Its point was to explain how it might be possible to enable a

---

[154] See Nicolas Malebranche, *Traité de l'amour de Dieu, en quel sens il doit être désintéressé* (Lyon, 1707).

[155] Quesnay, "Évidence," pp. 422–3. For Quesnay, perception on its own gave rise to quite complex instinctive knowledge. Thus, he wrote, animals were capable of recognising the law of noncontradiction (i.e., that something cannot be and not be the same thing), which was how a sheep knew where to go to escape a wolf: see [Anon.], *La petite encyclopédie, ou dictionnaire des philosophes* (Antwerp, 1772), p. 16, referring to the second edition of Quesnay's *Essai physique sur l'oeconomie animale*, 3:225–6, 263–4.

[156] The point is also made by Larrère, "Malebranche revisité," *Dix-Huitième Siècle* 26 (1994): 117–38. More generally, see Susan Neiman, *Evil in Modern Thought: An Alternative History of Philosophy* (Princeton, Princeton University Press, 2002).

world that, in a very deep-seated sense, had followed the wrong course to get back onto the right course and, by doing so, give humanity something like a second chance. The Physiocrats did, in fact, call the new system "humanism."[157]

ROUSSEAU AND PHYSIOCRACY

The link between the seventeenth-century concept of a divine general will and the more secular version of the concept that appeared first in *The Spirit of Laws*, then in Diderot's entry on *Droit naturel* in the *Encyclopédie*, and finally in Rousseau's *Social Contract* is now well known.[158] It is also well known that where Diderot used the term to refer to the general principles of morality recognised by all human beings, irrespective of their membership of any particular political society, Rousseau reverted to Montesquieu's usage.[159] The legislative power, Montesquieu wrote in the chapter on the English constitution in *The Spirit of Laws*, was "the general will of the state," while the executive power was "the execution of that general will."[160] Rousseau's definitions were identical. A general will was something that existed within, not between, societies. This left open the question of how societies could coexist. As with Mirabeau and Quesnay, Rousseau's answer began with Montesquieu, but, like them, too, he moved more decisively towards the idea of self-sufficiency. He endorsed Montesquieu's claim that liberty was not the "produce of all climates" and could not be attained by all peoples. "The more one reflects on this principle, established by Montesquieu," he commented, "the more sensible we become of its truth."[161] The "author of *The Spirit of Laws*," he noted too, had also explained why it was essential for the legislator to devise a system of govern-

---

[157] See *Ephémérides du citoyen*, 1765 (no. 1), p. 265: "L'amour général de l'humanité . . . vertu qui n' a point de nom parmi nous et que nous oserions appeler 'humanisme', puisqu' enfin il est temps de créer un mot pour une chose si belle et nécessaire."

[158] See Riley, *The General Will before Rousseau*, and, more recently, his "Rousseau's General Will," in Patrick Riley, ed., *The Cambridge Companion to Rousseau* (Cambridge, CUP, 2001), pp. 124–53.

[159] Robert Wokler, *Rousseau on Society, Politics, Music and Language* (New York, Garland Press, 1987), ch. 2; "The Influence of Diderot on the Political Theory of Rousseau," *Studies on Voltaire and the Eighteenth Century* 132 (1975): 55–111; Charles Porset, "L'inquiétant étrangeté de l'*Essai sur l'origine des langues*: Rousseau et ses exégètes," *Studies on Voltaire and the Eighteenth Century* 154 (1976): 1715–58.

[160] Montesquieu, *SL*, bk. 11, ch. 6, p. 153.

[161] Jean-Jacques Rousseau, *Du contrat social* [1762], bk. III, ch. 8, ed. Robert Derathé (Paris, 1993), p. 236 [abbreviated henceforth as *CS*]. English quotations are taken from J. J. Rousseau, *A Treatise on the Social Compact, or the Principles of Politic Law* (London, 1764) [abbreviated henceforth as *SC*], here, p. 130.

ment compatible with "some cause" that influences a people "in a particular manner," such as religion among the Hebrews and the Arabs, literature among the Athenians, commerce in Carthage and Tyre, navigation in Rhodes, war in Sparta, or public virtue in Rome.[162] Again like Montesquieu, he argued that the real threat to a political society was not "the abuse of laws by the government" but, as Montesquieu had emphasised in his examination of the English constitution, "the corruption of the legislature," which, Rousseau wrote, "is infallibly the consequence of its being governed by particular views."[163] He also argued that when the executive was not subordinate to the legislature and was, as a result, capable of usurping sovereignty, "this defect must be remedied by dividing the government," so that, as Montesquieu had indicated, again in the context of the English constitution, "all its parts would have no less authority over the subject, and yet their division would render them collectively less powerful to oppose their sovereign."[164] This applied particularly to the power to tax. Only a Plato or a Montesquieu, Rousseau wrote, was able to grasp the real complexity of devising a set of fiscal arrangements that could fit the three dimensions of assets, circumstances, and needs required by any equitable and proportional system of taxation.[165] Although he disagreed with Montesquieu on important technical details, he followed his counterintuitive argument (made once more in the context of his examination of the English constitution) about the way that liberty and taxation went hand in hand. In all these respects, Rousseau showed how carefully he had read Montesquieu during the time that he was employed as one of the assistants to the tax-farmer Claude Dupin's refutation of *The Spirit of Laws*.[166] There is no reason to think that his private reaction to Montesquieu's death ("He did not need so long a life to be immortal, but would that he had lived eternally to teach peoples their rights and duties") was not sincere.[167]

---

[162] Rousseau, *CS*, bk. II, ch. 11, pp. 214–5; *SC*, p. 86.

[163] Rousseau, *CS*, bk. III, ch. 4; *SC*, p. 110.

[164] Rousseau, *CS*, bk. III, ch. 7, pp. 235–6; *SC*, p. 129.

[165] Jean-Jacques Rousseau, *Discours sur l'économie politique* [1755], ed. Bruno Bernardi (Paris, Vrin, 2002), p. 76. On Rousseau's and Montesquieu's respective theories of taxation, see Céline Spector, "Théorie de l'impôt," in the same volume, pp. 195–221.

[166] On this phase of Rousseau's intellectual life, see Robert Shackleton, "Montesquieu, Dupin and the Early Writings of Rousseau," in S. Harvey, M. Hobson, D. J. Kelley, and S.S.B. Taylor, eds., *Reappraisals of Rousseau* (Manchester, Manchester University Press, 1980), pp. 234–49; Michel Launay, "Le *Discours sur les sciences et les arts*: Jean-Jacques entre Mme Dupin et Montesquieu," in Michel Launay, ed., *Jean-Jacques Rousseau et son temps* (Paris, José Corti, 1969), pp. 93–103; Anicet Sénéchal, "Jean-Jacques Rousseau, secrétaire de Mme Dupin," *Annales Jean-Jacques Rousseau* 36 (1963–5): 173–290; Jean-Pierre Le Bouler and Catherine Lafarge, "Catalogue topographique partiel des papiers Dupin-Rousseau dispersés de 1951 à 1958," *Annales de la société Jean-Jacques Rousseau* 39 (1972–7): 243–80.

[167] Rousseau to Jean Perdriau, 20 February 1755, in Rousseau, *CC*, ed. Leigh, 3:98.

Rousseau set out his more general view of Montesquieu's political thought in a famous passage in his *Emile*.

> The true principles of the law of politics have not been yet established, and I presume never will. Grotius, the master of this science, is but a child, and what is worse, he is reprehensible for his insincerity. When I heard this writer's praises sounded so high, and Hobbes loaded with infamy, I perceived that these two authors are very little understood. The truth is, their principles are exactly similar, and vary only in the expression. There is likewise a difference in their method. Hobbes builds his system on sophisms, and Grotius his upon the poets; in every thing else they agree.
>
>   The only modern capable of creating this great and useless science was the celebrated Montesquieu. But he avoided entering into a discussion of the principles of the law of politics; he was content with treating of the positive law under established governments; and there is nothing in the world more different than these two sciences.[168]

The phrase "the principles of the law of politics" (or *principes du droit politique*) was also the subtitle of Rousseau's *Social Contract*. Although he may have written it with his native Geneva in mind, it was also, as his summary of his book in *Emile* indicated, designed to supply the principles that Montesquieu's own work lacked. It did so, he stated in the book itself, because Montesquieu had not seen that a real measure of human virtue was a requirement of every type of legitimate government, if only because every type of government involved the use of sovereign power. A "certain celebrated author," Rousseau wrote, had "laid down virtue as the first principle of a republican government."

> For want, however, of making proper distinctions, this great genius hath been led into frequent mistakes, as well as want of precision; not having observed that, the sovereign authority being every where the same, the same principle must take place in every well constituted state; though it is true in a greater or less degree, according to the form of the government.[169]

The claim about the need to find a moral counterpart to simple political power brought Rousseau back to the question about the relationship between wealth and virtue that had been Montesquieu's starting point in his Troglodyte history. But Rousseau rejected Montesquieu's argument about monarchy's capacity to bypass the question. At the same time, however, he

---

[168] Jean-Jacques Rousseau, *Emile* [1762], bk. V, in *Oeuvres complètes* [hereafter *OC*], ed. Bernard Gagnebin and Marcel Raymond (Paris, Pléiade, 1969), 3:505. I have used the contemporary English translation, namely, *Emilius and Sophia, or a new system of education*, 4 vols. (London, 1763), 4:240.

[169] Rousseau, *CS*, bk. III, ch. 4, p. 227; *SC*, p. 112.

did not follow most of Montesquieu's critics in arguing that morality and government simply went hand in hand. Putting the human drive for self-preservation into a collective setting had, he argued, to be recognised for the highly complicated amalgamation that it really was. A political society could not be seen as a scaled-up version of a natural society because, as Rousseau argued in detail in the first part of his *Discourse on the Origin of Inequality*, it was not obvious that the natural human drive for self-preservation went along with any natural social capacity at all. The principle of self-preservation, which did lead some living creatures to live in societies—namely, self-love or *amour-de-soi*—applied straightforwardly to beings moved solely by instinct and, strikingly, to God (as one of his English readers noted, "Rousseau has chosen to deduce the infinite goodness of the Deity from his unlimited power, together with the principle of self-love, supposed essential to all sensible beings").[170] But it did not apply to humans in anything like the same straightforward sense. While, in their different ways, God and animals were both perfect, humans were not. They were, for better or worse, simply perfectible (the word was Rousseau's own). For humans, self-love applied to the self, and humans had all the natural equipment required to keep it that way. But they were simply not naturally equipped to manage the many comparisons and evaluations involved in living in society. Since these kinds of ability were not natural, they had to be artificial. But since societies were still made up of natural human beings, they still had to have some connection to how humans naturally were.

Many of Rousseau's contemporaries took the second *Discourse* to be a thinly disguised reworking of Thomas Hobbes's moral and political theory.[171] "Hobbes's book, the *Leviathan*, provided him with part of his ideas," wrote Voltaire's friend the marquis de Saint Lambert, "and those are the

---

[170] Nathaniel Forster, *A Sermon Preached at the Visitation of the Rev. Dr. Moss, Archdeacon of Colchester at St. Peter's Colchester, May 20, 1765 and before the University of Oxford, May 24, 1767* (Oxford, 1767), p. 9, citing Rousseau's *Emile*: "la bonté est l'effet nécessaire d'une puissance sans borne et de l'amour de soi, essentiel à tout être qui sent. Celui qui peut tout étend, pour ainsi dire, son existence avec celle des êtres. Produire et conserver sont l'acte perpétuel de la puissance; elle n'agit point sur ce qui n'est pas; Dieu n'est pas le Dieu des morts, il ne pourrait être destructeur et méchant sans se nuire. Celui qui peut tout ne peut vouloir que ce qui est bien." For the passage, see *Emile, ou de l'education* [1762], ed. Michel Launay (Paris, Garnier Flammarion, 1966), bk. IV, p. 367.

[171] See, for an overview, Raymond Trousson, *Jean-Jacques Rousseau jugé par ses contemporains* (Paris, 2000), and, more specifically, Béla Kapossy, "Virtue, Sociability and the History of Mankind: Isaak Iselin's Contribution to the Swiss and European Enlightenment" (Ph.D. diss., Cambridge University, 2003). Given Rousseau's involvement in its composition, his critics might have found some corroboration in the unusual endorsement of Hobbes in Charles Dupin, *Observations sur un livre intitulé "De l'esprit des loix"* (Paris, 1750), p. 13, but the description of the state of nature that it contained was very different from both Rousseau and Hobbes.

most reasonable."[172] As one of Rousseau's early critics commented, "Hobbes's man is brutal to the point of impiety; Rousseau's man is impious to the point of brutality. He is no more pious than impious; he is simply not moral at all."[173] In a weak sense, the charge had a point, because Rousseau, like Hobbes, began by making the standard sceptical move, dropping as many unverified assumptions about human nature as he could, before going on to try to identify the things that demonstrably did make humans human. But Rousseau set out to be even more sceptical than Hobbes had been, making it clear that his aim was to refute Hobbes by dropping what he took to be Hobbes's overly thick description of human nature. Montesquieu had followed the same procedure. But even Montesquieu, Rousseau went on to claim, had gone too far in presupposing that humans have a natural capacity for fear (in this respect, Rousseau really was nearer to Hobbes). There was no reason, Rousseau argued, to think that the dull uniformity of the original human habitat would have impinged in any surprising or alarming way upon the eternal present inhabited, in humanity's natural state, by solitary creatures with no ideas, no language, and no knowledge of themselves as selves at all. *Amour-de-soi* was a feeling, not knowledge. It was required for living but was not at all a cause of society. Fear, as Montesquieu had claimed, could not be the key to explaining how humans came to be social, first by comparing themselves to others and feeling their own inferiority and then, because of their joint recognition of the same feeling, coming to form the very first human bond.[174] Nothing at the beginning, Rousseau argued, would have made humans fearful.

If the initial sceptical move came from Montesquieu, the countermove was also aimed, in the first instance, at Montesquieu. It is well known that Denis Diderot chose to place Hobbes (personified by the figure of the "violent reasoner") at the centre of his *Encyclopaedia* article on natural law (*droit naturel*), written late in 1754 or early in 1755, soon after Rousseau had finished his second *Discourse* and at the same time as he was writing the entry on *économie (morale et politique)* for the *Encyclopédie* (the work that was published in 1758 as his *Discourse on Political Economy*).[175] It is not clear why Diderot chose to make Hobbes the central figure of his *Encyclopaedia* article, but it is likely that his decision was connected to the Prades affair and the suspicion about the similarity between Montesquieu and Hobbes's moral and political thought that it had raised. The Prades affair grew out

---

[172] Jean-François, marquis de Saint Lambert, *Oeuvres philosophiques*, 5 vols. (Paris, an IX), vol. 1, "Discours préliminaire," pp. 38–9.

[173] Jean-Bertrand Castel, *L'homme moral opposé à l'homme physique de Monsieur R***. Lettres philosophiques où l'on réfute le Déisme du jour* (Toulouse, 1756), p. 58.

[174] Montesquieu, *SL*, bk. 1. ch. 2, p. 4.

[175] The most recent investigation of the still-obscure chronology of these various works can be found in Rousseau, *Discours sur l'économie politique*, ed. Bernardi, pp. 7–36.

of a theology thesis submitted to the Sorbonne in November 1751 by the abbé Jean-Martin de Prades on the subject of human nature, or "the nature of the being on whose face God had breathed the spirit of life," as the thesis itself was entitled.[176] In setting out his description of human nature, Prades reproduced the argument at the beginning of the third chapter of the first book of *The Spirit of Laws*. "As soon as man enters into a state of society," Montesquieu had written, "he loses the sense of his weakness; equality ceases, and then commences the state of war."[177] War between nations, he continued, produced the law of nations and the political laws of particular governments, while war within nations produced the civil law. Prades, in his thesis, simply put Montesquieu into his own words to explain, as Montesquieu himself had done, the origins of the various types of positive law. But it was quite easy to associate his words, as well as Montesquieu's own, with Hobbes. In the annotations that he attached to his critical edition of *The Spirit of Laws*, the Dutch legal theorist Elie Luzac did just that. "There is," he commented on the beginning of Montesquieu's chapter, "too much Hobbesianism in this passage."[178] Montesquieu himself was well aware of the problem and went to some lengths to protect himself in the *Defence of the Spirit of Laws*, which he published in 1752, when the Prades affair was at its height. As Thomas Nugent, Montesquieu's English translator, put it in the summary of the *Defence of the Spirit of Laws* that he inserted at the beginning of his translation, Montesquieu's comments about justice at the very beginning of his book may well have seemed to be "directly levelled" at the eighteenth century's other great bugbear, Baruch Spinoza, but "he had Hobbes' system in his eye."[179]

The superficial similarity between Montesquieu and Hobbes created a problem for both Diderot and Rousseau. For Diderot the problem may, in the first instance, have been a practical one since both Prades and Montesquieu had been signed up as contributors to the *Encyclopédie*. But Diderot also had no theoretical sympathy at all with Hobbes, and the argument

[176] On the Prades affair, see the introduction by John Spink to Denis Diderot, *Suite de l'apologie de l'abbé de Prades*, in Denis Diderot, *Oeuvres complètes*, ed. Yvon Belaval et al., vol. 4 (Paris, Hermann, 1978), pp. 285–312, as well as his earlier article "Un abbé philosophe: l'affaire de J. M. de Prades," *Dix-Huitième Siècle* 3 (1971): 145–80. See, too, Jean-François Combes-Malavialle, "Vues nouvelles sur l'abbé de Prades," *Dix-Huitième Siècle* 20 (1988): 377–97; Franco Venturi, *La jeunesse de Diderot* [1939] (Geneva, Slatkine, 1967), pp. 192–236; and Thomas O'Connor, *An Irish Theologian in Enlightenment France: Luke Joseph Hooke, 1714–96* (Dublin, Four Courts Press, 1995), pp. 61–86.

[177] Montesquieu, *SL*, bk. 1, ch. 3, p. 5.

[178] Charles-Louis de Secondat, baron de Montesquieu, *De l'esprit des loix . . . Avec des remarques philosophiques et politiques d'un anonyme, qui n'ont point encore été publiées* [1763], 4 vols. (Amsterdam, 1764), 1:99.

[179] Thomas Nugent, "The translator to the reader," in Montesquieu, *The Spirit of Laws*, 2nd ed., 2 vols. (London, 1752), 1:v–vi.

that he developed in his article on *droit naturel* followed straightforwardly from this. It amounted to developing the moral theory that he had taken over from the third earl of Shaftesbury (whose *Inquiry concerning Virtue or Merit* he had translated in 1745). This was what he proceeded to do both in the *Apology* of Prades that he published in 1752 and in his article on *droit naturel* in the *Encyclopédie*. For Rousseau, however, the problem was more difficult, because he accepted Montesquieu's starting point. This ruled out Shaftesbury and, more broadly, moral sense theory. But reverting to Hobbes could not be the alternative, because this ruled out Montesquieu. The real alternative had to be something like Montesquieu's starting point, but one that, unlike fear, could get morality into human nature with some demonstrable degree of historical plausibility. There is no reason to think that Rousseau's objections to Montesquieu were not considered. They all amounted to the same, quite consistent charge that Montesquieu had not given politics, particularly modern politics, a moral foundation. The second *Discourse* can, in fact, be read as a conjectural history of humanity predicated on Montesquieu's claim about virtue's political irrelevance in a monarchy. Without virtue, wealth would be the only force underlying the dynamics of human association. The result would be a sequence of steps in which, as Rousseau put it,

> the establishment of the law and right of property was its first term; the institution of magistracy, the second; the conversion of legitimate into arbitrary power the third and last; so that the state of rich and poor was authorized by the first epoch, that of powerful and weak by the second, and the third by that of master and slave, which is the last degree of inequality, and the state to which all the others finally lead, until new revolutions either dissolve the government entirely, or bring it closer to legitimate institution.[180]

Virtues of some sort had, therefore, to be part of a "legitimate institution." Superficially, this put Rousseau on the same side as many of Montesquieu's other critics. But like Montesquieu himself, Rousseau did not begin with any strong assumptions about natural morality. Virtues were acquired, not innate. The difficulty is to describe what Rousseau thought that they were and how he thought that they might have been switched on.

The obvious candidate is the feeling of pity that Rousseau took over from Bernard Mandeville's *Fable of the Bees* as his alternative to Montesquieu's fear and the ability that pity gave to both humans and animals to perform an imaginative act of "identification" with others' suffering (like "perfectibility," "identification" was a word of Rousseau's own coinage).[181]

---

[180] Rousseau, *Discourse on Inequality*, in Jean-Jacques Rousseau, *The Discourses and Other Early Political Writings*, ed. Victor Gourevitch (Cambridge, CUP, 1997), p. 182.

[181] See Pierre Force, *Self-Interest before Adam Smith: A Genealogy of Economic Science* (Cambridge, CUP, 2003), pp. 25–7.

He introduced the subject in the context of an extensive assessment of Hobbes's moral theory in the first part of his second *Discourse*. Hobbes, he acknowledged, "very clearly saw the defect of all modern definitions of natural right." But Hobbes had not seen "that the same cause that keeps savages from using their reason, as our jurists claim they do, also keeps them from abusing their faculties, as he himself claims they do." He should, Rousseau continued, have realised that "savages are not wicked precisely because they do not know what it is to be good."[182] He had also not noticed that there was "another principle" which, "under certain circumstances," served to soften "the desire for self preservation even before the birth of *amour-propre*." This principle was pity, "a virtue all the more universal and useful to man as it precedes the exercise of all reflection in him and so natural that even the beasts sometimes show evident signs of it."[183] Since pity moderated self-love, the two natural qualities amounted to a presocial basis for morality. "It is from the co-operation and from the combination our mind is able to make between these two principles," Rousseau stated, "without it being necessary to introduce into it that of sociability, that all the rules of natural right seem to me to flow."[184] These rules, he acknowledged, were not as morally rich "as that sublime maxim of reasoned justice, *Do unto others as you would have them do to you*." They amounted instead to the "much less perfect, but perhaps more useful" maxim *Do your own good with the least possible harm to others*."[185] As with Quesnay's later abstentive moral theory, the injunction was largely negative, but, since others still played a part in the judgement, it was not entirely selfish.

Rousseau's useful maxim fitted the idea of a world before societies without any strain. But the kind of guidance that it could provide for the real world was still quite limited. Individuals might well be able to identify physical goods by means of their senses, and pity might well ensure that they did their own good with the least possible harm to others. But states do not have senses. If the size of a state's population could be taken as a measure of its internal well-being, it was still not enough to be a real guide to its survival needs. As Rousseau himself emphasised, in a world of states, there was no absolute standard against which these could be measured. However useful the maxim about doing your own good with the least possible harm to others might be, it could not override the limitless dynamics of international competition unless the state in question was insulated quite strongly from the outside world. "Every people who, by their situation, have no other alternative than commerce or war," Rousseau wrote in *The Social Contract*, "must necessarily be feeble." It was impossible, he contin-

---

[182] Rousseau, *Discourse on Inequality*, ed. Gourevitch, p. 151.
[183] Rousseau, *Discourse on Inequality*, ed. Gourevitch, p. 152.
[184] Rousseau, *Discourse on Inequality*, ed. Gourevitch, p. 127.
[185] Rousseau, *Discourse on Inequality*, ed. Gourevitch, p. 154.

ued, that "such a state can preserve its independency, but by its insig-
nificancy or its greatness."[186] The real alternative had to be autarchy. But
being collectively self-sufficient meant finding enough common motivation to be able to face the threat (or attraction) of another society while
remaining able to cohere. Rousseau struggled quite hard before he found
the right subtitle for *The Social Contract*, but the one that he settled upon
captured the nature of the problem very concisely.[187] Hobbes, Rousseau
argued, had certainly been right to see that reason could not, naturally,
have been available to get political principles into political societies. By the
time that it was available, it was already too late. But it did not follow that
he was also right about what those principles might be. Instead, it was
Montesquieu's interest in the passions as the source of the principles of
every type of government that had to be the starting point for a different
approach. Fear was not natural. *Pitié* and *amour-de-soi* were, but could not,
in themselves, be the load-bearing elements of the virtue required for every
system of government. Once there were states, humans were locked into
two sets of relationships—to other people as members of the state, but also
to other citizens as members of the sovereign. This was why they had to
be able to switch from one role to the other. If virtue had to be the principle
of every legitimate government, the first step had to be to explain where
it came from.

Virtue, for Rousseau, was an acquired human capacity. Its starting point
was another acquired human capacity, love. Rousseau spent the time that he
was employed by the royal tax-farmer Charles Dupin not only in studying
Montesquieu for the purposes of Dupin's refutation of *The Spirit of Laws*
but also in compiling material for a history of women (also aimed at Montesquieu) by Dupin's wife, Louise Dupin. This, too, seems to have played
a significant part in his later intellectual life. As with many other aspects
of his moral and political thought, Rousseau's treatment of love was very
close to Montesquieu's. Its basis, Rousseau suggested, was to be found in
another genuinely natural, but specifically female capacity, namely, *pudeur*
or modesty. Like *amour-de-soi* and *pitié*, modesty was a feeling that did not
arise from interaction with other humans. Whereas Montesquieu, in a
chapter entitled "Of Natural Modesty," defined modesty as "a shame of
our imperfections" common to both sexes (since, he wrote, "it is natural
for intelligent beings to feel their imperfections"), Rousseau confined the
natural emotion to women and, more specifically, to the beginning of sex-

---

[186] Rousseau, *CS*, bk. II, ch. 10, p. 211; *SC*, p. 76 (1764 translation, p. 78).

[187] On the various versions of the book's title, see the helpful note by Gourevitch in his
edition of the *The Social Contract and Other Later Political Writings* (Cambridge, CUP, 1997),
pp. 296–7.

ual maturity and the onset of menstruation.[188] "Attack and defence; audacity in men and modesty in women," he wrote, "are not, as your philosophers think, conventions but natural institutions that are easy to explain and from which all the other moral differences [in the sexes] can easily be deduced."[189] *Pudeur* was not a feeling that existed among children, who "are not naturally modest."

> Modesty is born only of knowledge of evil, and how can children who do not, and should not, have this knowledge have a capacity to experience the feeling that is its effect? To give them lessons of modesty and honesty would amount to teaching them that there are shameful and dishonourable things and give them a secret desire to know what these things might be. Sooner or later they will come to find out, and the very first spark to strike the imagination will surely accelerate the conflagration of the senses. Whoever can blush is already guilty; true innocence is not ashamed of anything.[190]

Modesty began with a women's awareness of her own sexuality and the beginning of sexual desire. Although Rousseau was careful to avoid giving a more detailed explanation of how a physical change could have a moral effect, he still went on to argue that it was part of an unusual providential system which (along with the tilt of the earth's axis and the seasons that it produced) had been designed to enable humanity to substitute reason and freedom for nature and instinct.[191] "The supreme being," he wrote, "sought to do the highest honour to the human race."

> By giving men inclinations without measure, he also gave them the law to regulate them, so that men could be free to command themselves. By allowing men immoderate passions, he joined reason to those passions to govern them. By giving women unlimited desires, he added modesty to those desires to contain them.[192]

---

[188] Montesquieu, *SL*, bk 16, ch. 12, p. 259. On this aspect of Rousseau's thought, see, especially, Paul Hoffmann, *La femme dans la pensée des lumières* (Paris, Editions Ophrys, 1977); Joel Schwarz, *The Sexual Politics of Jean-Jacques Rousseau* (Chicago, University of Chicago Press, 1984); and Yves Vargas, *Rousseau, l'énigme du sexe* (Paris, Presses universitaires de France, 1997).

[189] Jean-Jacques Rousseau, *Julie, ou la Nouvelle Héloïse*, in Rousseau, *OC*, 2:128.

[190] Rousseau, *Emile*, pt. 4, *OC*, 4:497–8.

[191] "If you ask me how it is possible that the morality of human life should be generated by a purely physical revolution, I shall reply that I have no idea. I am basing myself throughout on experience and do not seek to give an explanation of these facts. I do not know what the relationship might be between the seminal spirits and the affections of the soul, between the development of the sex and the feeling of good and evil, but I can see that the relationship exists," Rousseau wrote in a draft passage deleted before he published *Emile*: see the editor's introduction in Rousseau, *OC*, 4:lxxx.

[192] Rousseau, *Emile*, pt. 4, *OC*, 4:695.

The latter emotion made it possible to explain the human capacity for monogamy without having to make untenable assumptions either about female weakness and frailty on the one hand or about the part played by children in the formation of the family on the other (there was no reason, Rousseau pointed out, to assume that humans would naturally know that a brief sexual encounter would result in a helpless baby, nine months later). The modesty that signalled a woman's awareness of her own sexual desire was what made her beautiful, and it was this more than purely physical beauty that turned male sexual desire into love. As Rousseau indicated in both the *Essay on the Origin of Languages* and *Emile*, the self-reflective emotions involved in the process were what first turned humans into persons, equipped with the idea of a self.

Rousseau had no illusions at all about love's power. Since it was the first reflective emotion, it was also the starting point of *amour-propre*. While modesty was natural, love itself was not. Nor, by extension, was *amour-propre*. Both were the effects of interaction with others, with the latter being the pathological version of the former. This made it difficult to root out *amour-propre* without also removing love (the character of Wolmar in the *Nouvelle Héloïse* is an example of how strange this might look). Separating the two was, in a sense, what Fénelon's reform programme had been designed to do. But, however much Rousseau may have admired the ideal of pure love and what Fénelon had called "disappropriation" (the opposite, in other words, of the motivation underlying *amour-propre*), he was also a reader of Montesquieu.[193] Montesquieu had shown how *amour-propre* could be neutralised by an honour-based system of ranks. Rousseau did something similar with pride. Unlike Montesquieu's notion, however, it was intended to work between, rather than within, societies. But, as with Montesquieu, its starting point was still inequality. With Montesquieu, inequality gave rise to judgements about superiority and inferiority and the honour-based principle on which these were based. With Rousseau, it led to judgements about different societies. The fact of the variety of human languages would ensure that these would be skewed right from the start (it is important to remember that Rousseau's *Essay* was about the origin of languages, not just language). *Amour-propre* would turn into pride, which, in turn, would become patriotism, the love that could then be used to generate the collective motivation required to make Rousseau's original useful maxim work.[194] Music, language's first incarnation, would supply additional

[193] On this aspect of Fénelon's thought, see Jean Deprun, *La philosophie de l'inquiétude en France au xviiie siècle* (Paris, Vrin, 1979). For a recent discussion of Rousseau and Montesquieu, see Jean Ehrard, "Rousseau et Montesquieu: le mauvais fils réconcilié," *Annales de la société Jean-Jacques Rousseau* 41 (1997): 57–77.

[194] On the positive (but, in this rendition, rather Rawlsian) role of *amour-propre* in Rousseau's thought, see N.J.H. Dent, *Rousseau* (Oxford, Blackwell, 1988), ch. 2, and N.J.H. Dent

emotional motivation for social integration both because of its unique ability to signify human feelings and because of its inherently local character. Inversely, a civil religion would block the excesses to which national pride was prone by making the abstentive morality of the useful maxim a part of public life. If Physiocracy was a kind of theodicy, based upon a claim about how property could be used to put a ruined world right, Rousseau's political thought followed the same logic, with the passions awakened by the unnatural state of society performing something like the same redemptive role. Since Christ, for Rousseau, was simply a human, this made Rousseau's treatment of the kind of providentialist argument used in the theodicy problem come out as an even stronger version of "humanism" than Physiocracy itself.[195] An integrated and cohesive political society might be able to do its own good with the least possible harm to others because, from the inside, its own good might look, and feel, very good indeed.[196] As Rousseau himself acknowledged, he was a kind of Epicurean.

There was a substantial degree of continuity between the specifications of a political society that Rousseau set out in *The Social Contract*, written in the first instance as a guide towards a solution to the political conflicts in his native Geneva, and those that he supplied in 1771 to the Confederates of Bar (the Polish nobles who rebelled against Russian domination of Poland) in his *Considerations on the Government of Poland* (published only in 1782). If, as Rousseau put it, "the end of political society" was "the preservation and prosperity of its members," the way to get there had to come from within.[197] The first step had to be to clarify the technical vocabulary of political theory. This was what Rousseau did in *The Social Contract*. A political society, he wrote, was an artificial body that was once given the name city, or *civitas*, and was now called a republic. In a passive sense, its members gave it the name of state and, in an active sense, the name sovereign. As members of the state, the individuals who composed it were subjects; as members of the sovereign, they were citizens. It followed that not

---

and T. O'Hagan, "Rousseau on *Amour-Propre*," *Proceedings of the Aristotelian Society*, Supplement, 72 (1998): 57–74.

[195] For this aspect of Rousseau's thought, see Bernard Gagnebin, "J. J. Rousseau: Sur le péché d'Adam et le salut universel. Un document inédit," *Dix-Huitième Siècle* 3 (1971): 41–50. See, too, Giuliano Gliozzi, "Rousseau: mythe du bon sauvage ou critique du mythe des origines," in Chantal Grell and Christian Michel, eds., *Primitivisme et mythes des origines dans la France des lumières* (Paris, 1989), pp. 193–203 (201–2).

[196] For the Epicurean dimension of Rousseau's patriotism, see, particularly, Jean-Jacques Rousseau, "Lettre sur la vertu, l'individu et la société," ed. Jean Starobinski and Charles Wirz, *Annales de la société Jean-Jacques Rousseau* 41 (1997): 313–27, which can be compared to the description that Rousseau gave of a planned but unwritten work, entitled *La morale sensitive, ou le matérialisme du Sage* that he envisaged at the same period: see Rousseau, *Confessions*, ed. Bernard Gagnebin and Marcel Raymond (Paris, Pléiade, 1964), bk. 9, p. 409.

[197] Rousseau, *CS*, bk. III, ch. 9, pp. 241–2; *SC*, p. 105.

all subjects had to be citizens, and, as Rousseau pointed out in a note, there were up to five classes of subjects in Geneva but only two classes of citizens. (Sieyès's distinction between active and passive citizens, it is worth noting, was identical.) The active-passive distinction gave individuals two kinds of relationship. As members of the sovereign, they would have a relationship to private individuals; as members of the state, they would have a relation-ship to the sovereign. They would, therefore, have two roles, citizens as members of the sovereign and men as members of the state (women, noto-riously, were not citizens, because their authority was individual and moral, not collective and political—which was why, according to Rousseau, it was deep mistake to conflate the one with the other). Since both roles could apply to the same person, a political society had to establish and maintain a stable balance between the two. This was why virtue was required once a political society was in existence. The dual relationship produced by being a member of both a sovereign and a state made choices unavoidable and, as Rousseau went on to emphasise, only a general will that could be differentiated from every individual will could keep freedom of choice in place. Since society entailed dependence, not independence, the primacy of an internalised general will and an externalised system of legality was the only available way to insulate individual choices from dependence on any particular set of individual wills.[198]

Many of the more detailed features of Rousseau's political thought were designed to show how to make the choices as easy as possible. The first choice could not come from within, but had to come from without. "That function" Rousseau wrote, "which constitutes the republic, does not enter into its constitution" (Sieyès's later distinction between a constituting and a constituted power was similar).[199] This was the function of the legislator, a highly unusual external agent whose charisma (backed up by more than just an aura of divinity) would supply the motivation required to establish the initial unanimous choice. Subsequent choices were made less de-manding by the specifications of the conditions under which they would be made. A representative sovereign was ruled out. "The idea of represen-tatives is modern, descending to us from the feudal government, that most iniquitous and absurd form of government, by which human nature was so shamefully degraded," Rousseau noted, settling another score with Mon-tesquieu's honour-based conception of monarchy.[200] "The assembly of these representatives is called in some countries the third estate of the

---

[198] See, helpfully, Frederick Neuhouser, *Foundations of Hegel's Social Theory* (Cambridge, Mass., Harvard University Press, 2000), ch. 2, and his "Rousseau on the Relation between Reason and Self-Love," *Internationales Jahrbuch des Deutschen Idealismus* 1 (2003): 221–39.

[199] Rousseau, *CS*, bk. II, ch. 7, p. 204; *SC*, p. 69 (1764 translation, p. 67).

[200] Rousseau, *CS*, bk. III, ch. 15, p. 252; *SC*, p. 114 (1764 translation, p. 164).

nation," he also observed, "so that the particular interests of two orders are placed in the first and second ranks and the public interest only in the third" (here, too, Sieyès may not have had far to look).[201] If the sovereign was a general will, it could be represented only by itself (in the form of a law), never by a flesh-and-blood person. It was distinguishable both from the state, because it was active, and from the real wills of individuals, because it was general. But it did not have to have a continuous existence because, when it did exist, it was, by definition, all that it ever needed to be (Sieyès used the same formulation to refer to the nation). It would, therefore, have a fairly limited place in public life. As Rousseau indicated, it would be the sole source of new law. But citizens would neither initiate nor, in their public capacity, discuss projected legislation (the kind of private *cercles* that existed in Geneva were the way to give public opinion a presence). They would certainly have a right to a secret vote on proposed new laws, but "the right of voicing opinions, proposing, devising or discussing motions" would be something that a government "always takes great care to allow only to its own members."[202] The general will would then be known by way of simple majority votes (varying in size according to the importance of the subject at hand). Active citizenship was, in short, not quite as demanding as it might seem. The only regular requirement imposed by the sovereign on its members was the periodic vote on whether the present form of government should remain the same and whether its elected officials should remain in office.

Rousseau certainly ruled out representative sovereignty, but he did not rule out representative government. Government, he wrote, again following Montesquieu, was "an intermediary body established between the subject and the sovereign for their mutual correspondence."[203] As all the supporters of the system of gradual elections after 1789 later pointed out, what Rousseau called an "elective aristocracy" was simply his term for what they called "representative government." As they did too, Rousseau stipulated that an elective aristocracy had to have a democratic foundation (he was probably the first modern political thinker to say so explicitly). But, as he also indicated, democracy was simply the name of the sovereign before it chose a government. Since choosing a government involved giving rights and powers to some rather than to all, it had to be an act of government, not sovereignty, something that, as Rousseau pointed out, made it hard to see how a government could act before it had come into being. Democracy, however, met this unusual requirement. It had the unique advantage of enabling the sovereign to act like a government and choose the members

---

[201] Rousseau, *CS*, bk. III, ch. 15, p. 251; *SC*, p. 114 (1764 translation, p. 163).
[202] Rousseau, *CS*, bk. IV, ch. 1, pp. 260–1; *SC*, p. 122 (1764 translation, pp. 182–3).
[203] Rousseau, *CS*, bk III, ch. 1, p. 218; *SC*, p. 83 (1764 translation, p. 92).

of the kind of government that, as a sovereign, it had already specified.[204] But, like Sieyès later, this was as far as Rousseau was prepared to allow democracy to go. From time to time, the sovereign would decide whether the present form of government should remain the same, and, as a democracy, the people would then decide whether its present members should remain in office.

Beyond this, however, democracy was suitable for gods, not men.[205] Even in those circumstances in which it was essential, Rousseau was quite explicit in saying that a democracy did not have to be a single body, devoting the whole of the fourth chapter of book 4 of *The Social Contract* to a description of how the 400,000 or so members of the Roman republic had elected their rulers by way of an elaborate system of *comitia*, so that the citizenry as a whole never formed a single unitary entity. In this respect, Rousseau's description of the Roman system of government was something like a republican parallel to Montesquieu's version of monarchy, with an elected political hierarchy replacing the property-based system of ranks that made monarchy the kind of system of government it was. Since, as Rousseau emphasised (again following Montesquieu), only a relatively small republic could serve as the setting for the intense emotional compound required to make patriotism the basis of everyone's ability to internalise the general will, a real republic could dispense with a personified sovereign. This was why *The Social Contract* described a system of government suitable for Geneva, not France. But, as Rousseau went on to show in his *Considerations on the Government of Poland*, the same system could be scaled up to fit the dimensions of a large territorial state. The first step was to "give little thought to other countries, to be little concerned with commerce; but at home to increase both the food supply and consumers."[206] It would still, however, be difficult to rely on patriotism alone to maintain each member of the sovereign's capacity to internalise the general will. The larger the state, the smaller the government would have to be and the greater the level of virtue or self-denial both the government and the governed would have to have if the distinction between sovereignty and government was to be maintained.

Since Poland was a state of this kind, it could not have "the severe administration of small republics." But "the constitution of a large kingdom" could, Rousseau argued, still have "the solidity and vigour of a small republic."[207] The first prerequisite was to make the system of government a

---

[204] Rousseau, *CS*, bk. III, ch. 17.

[205] Rousseau, *CS*, bk. III, ch. 4, p. 228; *SC*, p. 92.

[206] Jean-Jacques Rousseau, *Considerations on the Government of Poland* [1782], in Rousseau, *The Social Contract and Other Later Political Writings*, ed. Gourevitch, p. 229.

[207] Rousseau, *Considerations*, ed. Gourevitch, p. 193.

federal one based upon the thirty-three palatinates into which the kingdom was divided. The second was what Rousseau, as Sieyès was to do later, called a system of "graduated promotions." This, he wrote, was "the strongest, most powerful" means to maintain liberty and, "if well implemented," would be "infallibly successful" in "carrying patriotism to the highest pitch in all Polish hearts."[208] All the "active members of the republic" would be divided into three classes. Eligibility for election to the Polish Diet would depend initially on some earlier form of public service in local administration. Eligibility for the second grade would require election to the Diet on three occasions. Membership of the Polish Senate would be drawn from this class of citizens. Finally, those who had been elected to the Senate on three separate occasions would be eligible to become guardians of the law, from whom the heads of the palatinates and other high offices would be drawn. Thus "after fifteen or twenty years of being continually tested under the eyes of the public" the "foremost positions of the state" would be filled by a suitably qualified combination of talent, experience, and virtue.[209] These, Rousseau went on to emphasise, would include the monarchy itself. "A hereditary crown prevents trouble," Rousseau observed, "but brings on slavery; election preserves freedom, but shakes the state with each new reign."[210] To avoid either possibility, he proposed that the Polish kings should be chosen by lot from among the thirty-three heads of the palatinates. The names of three candidates would be selected in this way, and one of them would then be elected by the Polish Diet to become king. With this form, Rousseau wrote, using a phrase that was rather similar to the one that Sieyès was to use in his public debate with Tom Paine in 1791, "we combine all the advantages of election with those of hereditary succession."[211]

This was not the first time that Rousseau made use of this formulation. It first appeared in one of the most famous of all his letters, the one he wrote to the marquis de Mirabeau on 26 July 1767. It was a product of an invitation to return to France and stay on one of Mirabeau's landed estates that Rousseau received in the autumn of 1766, at the height of his tribulations in England and his spectacularly public quarrel with Hume.[212] After

---

[208] Rousseau, *Considerations*, ed. Gourevitch, p. 238.

[209] Rousseau, *Considerations*, ed. Gourevitch, pp. 239–42.

[210] Rousseau, *Considerations*, ed. Gourevitch, p. 248.

[211] Rousseau, *Considerations*, ed. Gourevitch, p. 251. Sieyès later placed the words he used in his debate with Paine in quotation marks in a long manuscript entitled "Bases de l'ordre social," which he wrote at the time of the constitutional discussions of 1795. The text is printed in Pasquale Pasquino, *Sieyès et l'invention de la constitution en France* (Paris, Editions Odile Jacob, 1998), pp. 181–91 (see p. 191 for the passage in question).

[212] Mirabeau to Rousseau, 27 October 1766, in Rousseau, *CC*, ed. Leigh, 32:72–87. On the whole episode, see Jean Fabre, "Le Marquis de Mirabeau, interlocuteur et protecteur de

a delay of six months, Rousseau accepted the invitation, travelling to Mirabeau's country house at Bignon in the spring of 1767. It soon became clear,
however, that the invitation was not entirely disinterested. On 9 June,
Rousseau (replying, he said, to a passing word from his host) wrote Mirabeau a forthright letter, explaining that he would never, under any circumstance, publish or read anything (even the marquis's own works) likely to
reawaken his "extinct ideas" concerning politics.[213] Mirabeau was not dis-
couraged. He returned to the charge on 18 June, sending Rousseau his
most recent work, the *Elémens de la philosophie rurale* (Elements of Rural
Philosophy) accompanied by Le Mercier de la Rivière's recent *Natural and
Essential Order of Political Societies*.[214] Rousseau succumbed. But he did not
succumb in quite the way that Mirabeau hoped. On 26 July, he sent Mirabeau a long and devastating report on what, he stated, had been an extremely painful experience.[215] He had, he said, never been able to understand the *"évidence"* that was the basis of the economists' system of legal
despotism, and nothing in Le Mercier de la Rivière's work had seemed less
self-evident than the chapter dealing with the subject. Like the abbé de
Saint-Pierre's system, Rousseau wrote, the concept of *évidence* seemed to
assume that human reason had a continuous capacity for perfection. But
that assumption was groundless or, at best, could be maintained only if
natural and political laws were considered in abstraction. In any particular
government, made up of a variety of different elements, the self-evident
character of the laws of nature would necessarily disappear. No system of
rights and obligations deduced from the self-evident character of the natural order could be more than a fair-weather arrangement, doomed to collapse when its interlocking system of reciprocities was placed under strain.
What, Rousseau asked Mirabeau, would happen to your sacred rights of
property in periods of great danger or extraordinary calamity, when available revenue was no longer sufficient and the legal despot was forced to
have recourse to the ancient maxim *salus populi suprema lex esto?* The veil
would fall, and the impersonal system of rule called legal despotism would
become real despotism.

Rousseau," in *Les Mirabeau et leurs temps* (Paris, Société des Etudes Robespierristes, 1968),
pp. 71–90, and Reinhard Bach, "Rousseau et les physiocrates: une cohabitation contradictoire," *Etudes Jean-Jacques Rousseau* 11 (2000): 9–82.

[213] Rousseau to Mirabeau, 9 June 1767, in Rousseau, *CC*, ed. Leigh, 33:126.

[214] Mirabeau to Rousseau, 18 June 1767, in Rousseau, *CC*, ed. Leigh, 33:158–60.

[215] Rousseau to Mirabeau, 26 July 1767, in Rousseau, *CC*, ed. Leigh, 33:238–46. The letter
was subsequently reprinted in the fifth volume of a pirated edition of Rousseau's works published at some point after 1770, appearing again in the posthumous Geneva edition of his
collected works in 1782 as well as in a four-volume selection of his writing published in the
same year: see Jean-Jacques Rousseau, *Oeuvres. Nouvelle edition*, 5 vols. (Neufchâtel [Paris],
n.d.), 5:358–63; *Collection complète des Oeuvres de Jean-Jacques Rousseau* (Geneva, 1782),
24:572–78; Rousseau, *Pièces diverses*, 4 vols. (London, P. Cazin, 1782).

There were, Rousseau continued, two problems in political theory. The first was like trying to square the circle in geometry and consisted of trying to find a form of government in which the rule of law would stand above the rule of men. The economists, he suggested, had come to believe that it was possible to find such a system of government in the self-evident character of certain kinds of law. These latter might well exist in nature, but it did not follow that they existed in government. If they did, Rousseau argued, the laws in question would have to be found either in every type of government or in none. The simple truth was that the laws that the economists envisaged did not exist. The old republican idea of a government of laws, not men, could not be found. The only real alternative to the existing political order, he concluded, was extravagantly bleak.

> My opinion is that it is necessary to pass to the opposite extreme and suddenly set man as far above the law as he can be, consequently establishing arbitrary despotism, indeed the most arbitrary that is possible. I would like the despot to be God. In a word I can see no middle ground between the most austere democracy and the most perfect Hobbism. For the conflict between men and laws, giving rise to a continuous internal war in the State, is the worst of all political states.[216]

This, Rousseau continued, was why a second problem in politics was "to find in an arbitrary despotism a form of succession that is neither elective nor hereditary, or rather that is both the one and the other, so that, as far as is possible, it could be certain of avoiding either a Tiberius or a Nero."[217] But that "mad idea" was not something that he was prepared to pursue. He ended his letter by begging Mirabeau never to raise the subject of legal despotism again or send him any more books to read.

ROUSSEAU AND MABLY

The letter was Rousseau's final word on politics. But the episode had an epilogue that throws an intriguing light on their respective positions. Early in August 1767 Mirabeau replied to Rousseau in a long letter that, at least to his satisfaction, met the Genevan's objections and, at the same time, contained his well-known description of his conversion to Physiocracy by Quesnay. A few days later, he wrote again, asking Rousseau for permission to publish his letter, together with his own reply, in the economists' journal the *Ephémérides du citoyen*. Rousseau refused. But in December Mirabeau repeated the request, this time asking Rousseau whether he could use the

---

[216] Rousseau to Mirabeau, 26 July 1767, in Rousseau, *CC*, ed. Leigh, 33:240.
[217] Rousseau to Mirabeau, 26 July 1767, in Rousseau, *CC*, ed. Leigh, 33:240.

correspondence in the context of a reply to an attack on Le Mercier de la Rivière's book by the abbé Gabriel Bonnot de Mably. Mably, he wrote, was a man of upright manners and reputation, who had acquired a veneer of heterodoxy for "a very bad book on politics," and whose book on international relations, *Entretiens de Phocion*, or *Phocion's Conversations*, had gained him a high reputation in Switzerland for its "virtuous prose" (he had in fact won a prize for it from the Patriotic Society of Berne in 1763) and the patronage of the duchess d'Enville. He was, Mirabeau wrote, "so committed to the passions that he could not accept a system that had put an end to the puny, unsuccessful war that morality had waged upon them for so long, a system whose purely physical arrangement (*plan*) was designed to compress the ones by the others."[218] This time Mirabeau's request was successful. On 12 December, Rousseau agreed "with all his heart" to allow the correspondence to be published.[219]

Rousseau had known Mably and his brother, the abbé de Condillac, since the early 1740s.[220] They had a common interest in international relations and the problem of finding a way to get morality into politics (it was Mably who, during the period of the Seven Years War, entrusted Rousseau with the abbé de Saint-Pierre's papers, an initiative that led, in 1761, to the publication of Rousseau's version of Saint-Pierre's peace plan). Many of Mably's admirers took his most successful book, *Phocion's Conversations*, to be quite similar in content to Rousseau's own thought.[221] But even before they fell out in 1765 (after a very critical private letter by Mably on Rousseau's *Letters from the Mountain* was allowed to circulate publicly in Geneva), Rousseau made it clear that there was a significant difference between their respective approaches to international affairs.[222] Mably's works, he informed the prince of Wurtemberg, were "very good for their kind," but "one can sometimes find in them those principles of modern politics that it would be desirable for every man of your rank, including you, to condemn."[223] This was a rather more accurate assessment than his later accusation that *Phocion's Conversations* was a plagiarism of his own work (although it is quite possible that Mably did know something of the content of Rousseau's never published *Political Institutions*). Unlike Rousseau, Mably argued that it was possible for a large, territorial state to be just at

---

[218] Mirabeau to Rousseau, 9 December 1767, in Rousseau, *CC*, ed. Leigh, 34:230–2.

[219] Rousseau to Mirabeau, 12 December 1767, in Rousseau, *CC*, ed. Leigh, 34:237–9.

[220] On Mably, see, most recently, Johnson Kent Wright, *A Classical Republican in Eighteenth-Century France: The Political Thought of Mably* (Stanford, Calif., 1997).

[221] See, for example, the letters from Louis-Eugène, prince of Wurttemberg, to Rousseau of 22 May 1764 and from Pierre-Claude Moultou to Jacob-Henri Meister of 16 January 1777, in Rousseau, *CC*, ed. Leigh, 20:80–1; 40:121–4; 46:194.

[222] On Mably's letter on Rousseau, see Rousseau, *CC*, ed. Leigh, 23:87–9, 291–2.

[223] Rousseau to Louis-Eugène, prince of Wurtemberg, 26 May 1764, in Rousseau, *CC*, ed. Leigh, 20:93.

home and powerful abroad. This was most apparent in his *De la législation, ou principes des lois* (Of Legislation, or the Principles of Laws) of 1774 (the work that Mably described as his most considered political statement). Some two decades later, Pierre-Louis Roederer—in the second of the course of public lectures on the philosophical foundations of the new Declaration of the Rights of Man that he gave in Paris in the spring of 1793— described it as "no more than a long commentary on Rousseau's *Discourse on the Origin of Inequality.*"[224]

If it was (Mably never referred to Rousseau by name), it was certainly one based on substantially different conceptual foundations. In an essay published as an intervention in the great debate about the freedom of the grain trade during the 1760s (to which *De la législation* was also designed to contribute), Mably highlighted what he took to be wrong with the economists' physically based claims about the fundamental principles of human society by referring his readers for the correct account to a book entitled *De la sociabilité* (Of Sociability) by his friend the abbé François-André-Adrien Pluquet.[225] As an admiring reviewer of Pluquet's book pointed out in 1768 in the *Journal des beaux-arts et des sciences*, *De la sociabilité* was (although it also never mentioned his name) a point-by-point refutation of Rousseau's second *Discourse* (serving, Pluquet's reviewer claimed, to "console" rather than, as Rousseau had done, to "dismay" humanity).[226] It is easy to see why Pluquet entitled his reply to Rousseau *De la sociabilité*. It was designed to reinstate everything about the dignity of human nature that Rousseau, by denying that humans were naturally sociable, had discarded.

In most respects, Pluquet wrote, humans were no different from other animals. Like them, humans were vulnerable to attack from more powerful species; they needed to eat, to reproduce, and to unite to give one another security. But these qualities could not account for the ubiquity and durability of human association. Humans were united by more than fear or need because they remained united in conditions of calm and the absence of need. The reason was that, unlike animals, humans become restless and bored once their survival needs had been met, and translated this restlessness into creative and convivial activity.[227] These, according to Pluquet,

---

[224] Pierre-Louis Roederer, *Cours d'organisation sociale*, reprinted in his *Oeuvres*, ed. A. M. Roederer, 8 vols. (Paris, 1852–9), 8:145.

[225] "Je sais à quel degré de vertu on pourrait porter les hommes, en cultivant les principes de la sociabilité avec lesquels nous naissons, et que M. l'abbé Pluquet a développés avec autant de profondeur que de sagacité." Gabriel Bonnot de Mably, *Doutes proposés aux philosophes économistes sur l'ordre naturel et nécessaire des sociétés politiques* [1768], in his *Oeuvres*, 11:82–3. On Mably's links with Pluquet, see *Correspondance général d'Helvétius*, ed. Peter Allan, Alan Dainard, Jean Orson, and David Smith, 4 vols. (Toronto and Oxford, 1981–98), 1:312–5; 2:204–5.

[226] *Journal des beaux-arts et des sciences* 1 (Paris, 1768): 334–48.

[227] François-André-Adrien Pluquet, *De la sociabilité*, 2 vols. (Paris, 1767), 1:15–6.

were the qualities that made human society a genuine society. "It would seem," he wrote

> that nature has given physical needs so absolute an empire and so short a dura-
> tion only in order to make man keep his organs in a state suitable for satisfying
> the desire or need to know, so that the need to know might be said to be
> nature's principal object and physical needs a secondary objective; the plea-
> sures of the senses a means, and the knowledge that men acquire, and the
> satisfaction it procures, being the principal end of man's formation.[228]

This capacity to acquire and preserve knowledge was the basis of language and of humans' lordship of the earth. These showed, Pluquet argued, that nature had willed that the dominant power on earth would be guided by reason.

Mably transferred many of Pluquet's claims about human nature to poli-tics but also argued that these claims were the reasons why institutional design really did matter. "Self-love" (*amour-propre*), he wrote (flatly contra-dicting Rousseau), "is the bond that ought to unite us in society. If I did not love myself, how would I be capable of loving my fellow?"

> I can see with what admirable artifice the author of our existence has arranged
> the different needs to which he has subjected us to make us necessary to one
> another and to dispose our self-love towards a mutual benevolence. This is not
> all. He has endowed our souls with several social qualities, which, so to speak,
> are so many involuntary instincts, preceding all reflection, that make others'
> happiness dear to us and that encourage us, by the attractions of pleasure or
> the fear of pain, to approach one another, to unite, to love, to help, serve, and
> make reciprocal sacrifices.[229]

Self-love, he argued, was a stabilising force. It would be difficult, he pointed out, for anyone to accept any particular place in society or for any stable state of mutual interdependence to take hold if everyone had an equal mea-sure of the same qualities, inclinations, strength, and talents. But *amour-propre* had the effect of preventing anyone from complaining about the natural inequalities of ability present in any population, because it ensured that no one would willingly accept the idea that he or she might be inferior to someone else.[230]

Human passions, Mably claimed, were essentially sociable. But their vol-atility (gratitude, for example, could become servility, or need turn, patho-logically, into avarice) made them a perpetual threat to the development

---

[228] Pluquet, *De la sociabilité*, 1:83.
[229] Gabriel Bonnot de Mably, *De la législation ou principes des lois* [1774], reprinted in his *Oeuvres*, vol. 9, bk. I, ch. 1, pp. 28–9.
[230] Mably, *De la legislation*, bk. I, ch. 2, p. 62.

and survival of more general conceptions of morality. The shortest way to morality was, therefore, frugality. "Remember the noble simplicity with which Anacharsis the Scythian refused the rich presents of Hanno," he reminded his readers: " 'A rough hide serves to clothe me; I walk with bare feet; the ground is my bed and hunger makes me delight in the most frugal common fare. So, keep your presents for your citizens or your gods.' Could a man who had so few needs be wanting in any virtue?"[231]

Superficially, this made Mably quite like Rousseau, although both Rousseau's useful maxim and the patriotism motivating it were more clearly artificial and self-referential all the way through. As Mably presented it, frugality (or, as a second best, a rich government and a poor state) would serve to keep *amour-propre* in check, leaving room for the other social passions and, ultimately, for the improvement of human reason. "Unfortunately for the system of Hobbes," he wrote in a late, posthumously published, essay, "we are intelligent beings, which means that we have a reason that has to be the arbiter and judge of our various actions."[232] But reason (as his brother, the abbé de Condillac, had shown) developed slowly. This meant that although everyone was naturally sociable, there was no reason to expect that anything as abstract as the idea of the public good could have developed when human societies came into being. The public good, Mably argued, "is not a natural law."

> It is in truth a law of politics, which, by skilfully taking advantage of our needs, our social qualities, our weakness, our passions, and our tastes by a wise use of rewards and punishments, exists to teach the love that we have for ourselves that it is useful to moderate itself, to hide, to forget itself, and to attend to the self-love of our fellows and make their self-love the instrument of our own happiness.[233]

The art of the legislator, therefore, was to devise a setting in which both virtue and morality could survive by creating a system of government able to channel the stream of human passions towards the public good. As Dominique-Joseph Garat, the future interior minister of the first French republic, put it in a highly critical review of Mably's works,

> When one has been through the abbé de Mably's works with some attention, one can see that, in the whole history of the human race, he has been struck by one single thing, the constitutions of empires. With every people, whether ancient or modern, he looks for their constitution; all the authors he talks of are admired or dismissed in terms of what they had to say of constitutions;

---

[231] Mably, *De la legislation*, bk. I, ch. 2, p. 35.
[232] Gabriel Bonnot de Mably, *Du développement, des progrès et des bornes de la raison*, in his *Oeuvres*, 15:10.
[233] Mably, *Du développement, des progrès et des bornes de la raison*, p. 30.

according to him, there is only one sort of genius, the one that conceives of and executes a fine constitution; there is only one sort of happiness, which is to live and die in a free constitution.[234]

Although one of the major themes of virtually all of Mably's work was the need to establish a republican system of government, the kind of republic that he envisaged was quite different from the small-scale republican state needed to create and maintain the intensely inward-looking patriotic motivation that Rousseau had presented as the only viable alternative to personified representative sovereignty. Mably's republic was, instead, a very big territorial republic, modelled not so much on the ancient republics of Greece or Rome (morally admirable though they were) as on the huge federal republican system that, he argued, had once existed in Europe under Charlemagne. Although, he emphasised, the history of Greece and Rome was a vital source of information about the part played by property in human affairs because it contained the only surviving record of societies that had gone through the whole cycle of rise, growth, decline, and fall, the modern world was now far too heavily committed to a highly individuated property system for there to be any real possibility of finding a way back. The problem facing the modern world was, instead, to find a way to use the existing property regime to prevent a repetition of the cycle that had brought the ancient world to an end.

Mably had begun his own career by accepting the Machiavellian view that the cycle of rise and fall was largely governed by size and by the difficulties involved in maintaining a republican system of government when a republic's territory increased. His first book had been a parallel between modern France and imperial Rome based on the assumption that monarchy was the only regime compatible with a large territorial state. In this respect, his earliest work echoed the line of argument developed by Voltaire, the abbé de Saint-Pierre, and the marquis d'Argenson. But the War of the Austrian Succession led him to change his mind. The combination of modern standing armies, the system of public debt, and the fiscal regime that it entailed led him to abandon the standard view. The modern world, he now came to argue, was committed to property, money, and trade in a way that the ancient world had never been. Under these conditions, the centralised system of decision-making that was the hallmark of monarchy was no longer an advantage but a potentially fatal source of vacillation, inconsistency, and weakness. The system of absolute government that

---

[234] Dominique-Joseph Garat, *Mercure de France*, 6 March 1784, pp. 22–3. As another of Mably's critics noted (referring to his *Observations on the Government of the United States*), "the abbé has the idea that every law is or should be in the state constitutions": Filippo Mazzei, *Historical and Political Researches on the United States* [1788] (Charlottesville, University Press of Virginia, 1976), p. 141, note 1.

France had pioneered was the most pronounced example of the problem. From this perspective, Mably argued, the modern version of the cycle of decline and fall had begun with Henri IV and the consolidation of absolute royal sovereignty that had taken place in the early seventeenth century. The only way to prevent it from running its course was to devise a property-based system of republican government in a territory whose size and populousness would serve to make it largely self-sufficient.

As Mably presented it in 1751 in his *Observations sur les Romains* (Observations on the Romans), the problem of extent had been the nemesis of the ancient republics because none of them had been able to devise constitutions capable of accommodating the multiplicity of competing interests and the unequal distribution of goods generated by large political associations. As the Roman republic stumbled towards its final crisis, the Romans simply did not have the conceptual resources needed to identify the underlying causes of the divisions and conflicts driving it towards its fall. Among the many causes of their ruin, Mably wrote, all that the Romans could perceive was inequality and the corruption of manners that it brought in its wake. Accordingly, they could do no more than echo Cato the Censor's lament about the corrosive effects of luxury, imagining that the impotent example of the virtue of a few honourable men might be enough to stem the flood. But all that this moralistic declamation served to do was to create conditions for ambitious demagogues like the Gracchi to exploit popular misery. By the time of Caesar, Mably wrote, the only way to preserve the republic would have been to jettison the rule of law and do whatever was necessary to enable the republic to survive. Brutus, he observed, had been right to assassinate Caesar as a tyrant, but wrong to spare his allies and clients. His legalistic argument—that Caesar's allies were entitled as Roman citizens to the benefits of the rule of law because, although they were planning to commit acts of tyranny, they had not actually done so— was, Mably argued, incompatible with the survival of the republic. In some desperate circumstances, he observed, politics calls for the punishment of intentions or even the mere power to do harm. Yet, he warned, even had this more prudent policy been followed, the republic would probably still have fallen. There was no liberty left for the Romans to aspire to, unless some citizen, after making himself master of them all, had changed the form of the state from top to bottom and, by giving up all of Rome's conquests, had then gone on to compel the Romans to readopt the manners and poverty of their ancestors. Even if such a reform had been practicable, Mably commented, it was unlikely that any Roman citizen would have been virtuous enough to usurp sovereign power and use it in this way.[235]

---

[235] Gabriel Bonnot de Mably, *Observations sur les Romains* [1751], reprinted in his *Oeuvres*, 4:314–24, 356–8.

It is easy to see why Rousseau thought that Mably was rather too ready to adopt "principles of modern politics" that it would be desirable to condemn. The allusion was to Machiavelli and his advice about what Brutus should have done to his sons, which Mably had echoed. Although both Mably and Rousseau both argued that the alternative to the modern international system had to be federal in character, Rousseau himself never went on to suggest that the federation itself should become a state. It would, he wrote in the version of the abbé de Saint-Pierre's peace plan that he published in 1761, be a treaty-based system of alliances between sovereign states (nineteen on Rousseau's list), with no territory or government of its own and no permanent head. It would guarantee existing territorial boundaries as defined by the most recent relevant treaties and would underwrite all its members' forms of government, whether these were elective or hereditary. Although it would have a permanent congress and location, its seat would not be a capital city and its presidency would rotate at equal intervals from state to state. It would have no legislative power, but would simply take executive action on an ad hoc basis in the light of decisions by its members (each state would have one vote) and the financial quotas that they had agreed to supply. Any proposal to introduce a new regulation into the alliance would have to be approved by a simple majority and ratified by a majority of three-quarters five years later, after prior decisions by its member states. The sole purpose of the alliance would be to take military action against any state that violated a recognised boundary or threatened an established government.[236] It would, in short, exist simply to enforce Rousseau's useful maxim of doing one's own good with the least possible harm to others.

Mably's idea of a federal system was more closely related to France's position within the existing international system and the need, he argued, to create more room for morality in both. The federal system that he envisaged would be a real state, with its own territory, government, and capital city (so, too, it is worth noting, was the idea of a federal state, based on different moral premises, that could be found in Claude-Adrien Helvétius's posthumously published *De l'homme*).[237] Its component parts would be provinces, not separate sovereign states. It would be ruled by a republican system of government formed by the representatives of the several different estates to be found in any complicated political society and buttressed by a shared system of moral values and a strictly enforced agrarian. "Has na-

---

[236] The details summarise the five clauses of the alliance described in Jean-Jacques Rousseau, *A Project for Perpetual Peace* (London, 1765), pp. 19–20. For the original, 1761, version, see Rousseau, *OC*, 3:561–89.

[237] Claude-Adrien Helvétius, *De l'homme* [London, 1773], 2 vols. (Paris, Fayard, 1989), sec. IX, ch. 2, pp. 750–1. On Helvétius, see below, pp. 267–81.

ture made men to flee and devour one another?" Mably asked rhetorically in his *Phocion's Conversations*. "If she enjoins us mutual love, how wise would politics be in desiring that the love of one's country should prompt citizens to place the happiness of their republic in the misery of their neighbours?" It followed that the "virtue that is superior to the love of one's country is the love of mankind," the love that Rousseau ruled out.[238] This did not imply the kind of union that could be found in a single political society. But it did entail a capacity to establish and maintain systems of alliances similar to those that had once informed the ancient Greek Achaean League. Ordinary individuals, Mably pointed out, could do without friends and did not have to fear enemies because they enjoyed the protection of the magistrate. But states, he argued, did not enjoy such benefits. The law of nations was "but a slender safeguard to each particular society."[239] It had, therefore, to be reinforced by a positive system of durable alliances (which was why Mably entitled his very successful commentary on the modern, post–Westphalia Treaty system—a work whose first edition was sponsored by the marquis d'Argenson—*Le Droit public de l' Europe*, or *The Public Law of Europe*).[240] There also had to be a powerful, but just, state (one that had not succumbed to the illusory maxim that money was the sinew of war) to uphold the stability of this law-based international order, as the Spartan republic had once been able to do in the ancient world.

> Lycurgus, whose wisdom and abilities can never be sufficiently admired, was the man who first understood how much it concerns a state that would secure itself from the insults of its neighbours, to make the laws of that eternal union which nature has established between all mankind, the constant rule of their deportment towards them. He would have the love of one's country, which till then had been in Lacedemon unjust, fierce, and ambitious, to be refined by the love of mankind. His beneficent republic, now no longer making any use of its forces, but to protect weakness, and maintain the rights of justice, soon gained the esteem, friendship, and respect of all Greece, to which these sentiments gave a new taste for virtue.[241]

But maintaining justice abroad meant being just at home. This was the point of Mably's abiding concern with "the constitutions of empires."

"Nature," he wrote, "has not made man for the possession of wealth."[242] Nor, he wrote a few years later (again contradicting Rousseau), was prop-

---

[238] Gabriel Bonnot de Mably, *Phocion's Conversations or the Relation between Morality and Politics* [1763] (London, 1769), p. 136.

[239] Mably, *Phocion's Conversations*, p. 142.

[240] Gabriel Brizard, "Eloge historique de l'abbé de Mably" [1787], reprinted in his *Oeuvres*, 1:99, note b.

[241] Mably, *Phocion's Conversations*, p. 140.

[242] Mably, *Phocion's Conversations*, p. 166.

erty "the cause of the reunion of men into society." People came together "because they had social qualities and because their needs invited them to help and serve one another mutually."[243] As he presented it, the first systems of property would have been communal in character. Even when nations ceased to be nomadic and, under the pressure of growing population, were forced to adopt a settled way of life, agriculture would have continued under a system of common ownership. In the absence of any privately owned agricultural surpluses, there would have been no reason for the existence of avarice or ambition. But, Mably suggested, the idleness of some, or the partiality of the magistrates responsible for overseeing the allocation of goods, would have caused the communal system to break down. Private property probably began, he wrote, when the most hardworking members of the community asserted their own claims to justice, leaving the idle to fend for themselves and eliminating all public responsibility for the distribution of goods.[244] Privatisation had then provided reasons for avarice and ambition. Once entrenched, they could never be eliminated. Instead, they had to be used for the common good.

To do so, Mably argued, it was essential that the state itself had as few needs as possible so that it would offer nothing to tempt its citizens away from hardworking self-reliance. Mably strongly approved of the works of the English political moralist John Brown, telling the founders of the American republic that he knew nothing as "profound in politics" as the latter's *Estimate of the Manners and Principles of the Times*.[245] Like Brown, he argued that liberty could survive only in conditions of simplicity. "The art of the legislator consists in diminishing the needs of the state and not in increasing its revenue to meet its needs more easily," he wrote.[246] It followed that every "invention designed to increase the revenues of the state or the rights of the treasury (*fisc*) is a harmful invention and that, instead of relying upon money, political life ought never to have called for anything other than service."[247] Even if, he argued, the existence of property meant that nothing could be had for nothing, taxation should still be limited to direct taxation of landed income both because it was unjust for people without property to pay for the protection of goods that they did not own and because a land tax was the best way to prevent unnecessary government expenditure. Every magistracy, he emphasised, should be unpaid. Once a government was rich because the needs of its state were few, it could, if necessary, act benevolently by, for example, helping its citizens to repair

---

[243] Mably, *De la législation*, bk. 1, ch. 3, p. 69.

[244] Mably, *De la législation*, bk. 1, ch. 3, pp. 69–78.

[245] Gabriel Bonnot de Mably, *Observations sur le Gouvernement et les Lois des États-Unis d'Amérique* [1784], reprinted in his *Oeuvres*, 8:421.

[246] Mably, *De la legislation*, bk. 2, ch. 1, p. 120.

[247] Mably, *De la legislation*, bk. 2, ch. 1, p. 121.

damaged property, or maintaining a grain reserve to bridge poor harvest years, or, like the aristocratic government of the Swiss republic of Berne, paying for invalids to go abroad to take the waters if they could not afford to do so themselves.[248] The combination of a wealthy government and a frugal state was the key to the survival of public and private morality under conditions of generalised individual ownership.

Frugality had to be maintained by sumptuary laws and strict proscriptions of financial speculation. Nothing was more necessary, too, Mably argued, than for laws to regulate inheritance. In this respect, the laws of the early Roman republic were, he wrote, "admirable" both because they did not allow anyone's estate to pass into the hands of another family and because they placed strict limits on the faculty of making a will. The purpose of such legislation was not, he argued, to interfere with private property, but to ensure that it was always used in ways that were the most advantageous to society. It was an error, he added, to believe that the agrarian laws had destroyed the Roman republic. It followed that an agrarian was also an essential component of a modern system of justice. The rudiments of an agrarian that was suitable for the modern world could, he claimed, be found in Sweden, where there were strict limits on the amount of property that the members of each of the kingdom's four estates could own.[249] The number of estates could be increased (to seven or more) and the amount of property that each was entitled to own could be fixed, and, by this means, a basis could be found for a system of government compatible with the range of occupations and activities that a property-based society would have to contain. Service, not money, would be its ruling principle.

Importantly (and again in opposition to Rousseau), Mably argued that there was no obstacle to establishing and maintaining a system of this kind in a large territorial state. "It cannot be denied that the more a state is extended, the more easily abuses slip in," he wrote.

> But however vast an empire may be, neither the number nor the extent of its provinces amounts to an insurmountable obstacle to its policies, whether one wants to reform it or simply to maintain good order. Wherever they are, men have the same reason, the same needs, the same social qualities, and the same principle underlying the same passions, and this amounts to a great point of reunion. A skilful legislator, by giving different provinces the same laws, the same government, and the same interest would be able to form a single state with a regular mechanism and movement. By dint of art, he will be able to oppose the abuses that arise in an extensive society by establishing magistrates as vigilant as those of a small republic. All that is required to succeed in this

---

[248] Mably, *De la legislation*, bk. 1, ch. 4, pp. 109–19.
[249] Mably, *De la legislation*, bk. 2, ch. 2, pp. 139–46.

enterprise is to decompose, so to speak, a state and turn all its provinces into as many federated republics. Their union will be their strength abroad, and the small size of their territory will be their security at home.[250]

The model of this system of government, he added, was to be found in the empire established by Charlemagne.

> He began by dividing the lands of his dominions into a hundred different provinces. His secret was to give them individual assemblies open to every order of citizen. They were responsible for overseeing the needs of their district, for repressing abuses and maintaining respect for the laws. By way of this division, each province acquired the movement that could be imprinted upon it and the whole Empire acquired a new spirit and new manners.[251]

As Mably presented it, Charlemagne's empire was the archetype of an extensive system of republican government, headed by "a prince who was simultaneously a philosopher, a legislator, a patriot, and a conqueror."[252] Its constitutional core was a revived and more stable version of the ancient republican assemblies of the Franks. Under Charlemagne's aegis, and as the French people came to "possess a very extensive territory," each county of the empire came to depute a dozen representatives every autumn to a closed meeting on the Champ de Mars followed, in May, by a general assembly of the bishops, abbots, counts, lords, and deputies of the people, sometimes deliberating separately, sometimes as a single body, so that, as Mably put it, "there can be no doubt that the legislative power resided in the body of the nation," with the king as its executive head.[253] It is well known that Mably's image of Charlemagne as a patriot-king greatly appealed to Napoleon Bonaparte.[254]

Mably did not, however, expect France to play the part of a republican hegemon. He was appalled by the French government's decision in 1756 to form an alliance with the Holy Roman Empire. It confirmed his conviction that the corrupting combination of absolute government and public credit had eliminated the prospects for free government in France and would come to threaten the very survival of liberty in Europe as a whole. His fear was that the French alliance with Austria, instead of giving France a free hand to deal with Britain, amounted to a blank cheque to underwrite Habsburg ambitions in central, eastern, and southern Europe. France

---

[250] Mably, *De la legislation*, bk. 3, ch. 2, p. 286.

[251] Mably, *De la legislation*, bk. 3, ch. 2, pp. 286–7.

[252] Gabriel Bonnot de Mably, *Observations sur l'histoire de la France*, in his *Oeuvres*, 1:221.

[253] Mably, *Observations*, in his *Oeuvres*, 1:229.

[254] Napoleon read and annotated Mably's *Observations sur l'histoire de France* while at Auxonne: see Frédéric Masson, *Le Sacre et le couronnement de Napoléon* (Paris, 1908), pp. 63, 78.

would then be even more exposed to the paralysingly divisive domestic effects of the combination of war, debt, and taxation and acutely vulnerable to the possibility that the empire might ditch its French ally and side with an even more heavily indebted and desperate Britain, forced, by the severity of its domestic political dissensions, to solve its debt problem at the expense of the rest of Europe. "I would tremble for the liberty of Europe," Mably warned in one of the later editions of his *Droit public de l'Europe*, "if, instead of all those exchanges and cessions that can be read in our peace treaties, I were to see a people that was to force its enemies to reimburse its wartime expenditure and pay its debts."[255] He pinned his hopes for Europe's future on Prussia as the only power uncontaminated by the modern funding system that was also able to defend itself with a patriotic, quasi-feudal, militia system. "The reign of France, the house of Austria and England is over," he announced soon after France entered the American war. "For the good of Europe, it is to be desired that Prussian power, which we have seen take form, is able to maintain itself and come to be incontestably recognised."[256] Prussia would be Europe's only bulwark against despotism if the other states were to succumb to the Armageddon of a general bankruptcy.

Mably was no more confident about the prospects of the Americans. "Love of money necessarily suffocates love of liberty," he warned, "and the insurgents' bad laws will not be able to preserve their republic from the misfortune menacing it."[257] The best hope for liberty, he argued, would have been to leave the Americans to their own devices, forcing them to fight a long, bloody, but ultimately victorious war to establish their independence, while trapping Britain into a protracted military disaster in a distant country as the best way to promote a British revolution. A long-drawn-out war of liberation would have served to instil the military virtues in the nascent republic and reinforce the moral and political authority of the Continental Congress over the selfish proclivities of the individual states, thus protecting the vulnerability of their mainly farming and trading populations from ambitious and unscrupulous political leaders. Having achieved liberty too easily, the republic would, Mably wrote, have to find a surrogate for virtue to neutralise ambition. "The voice of justice, and above all benign justice, has a great empire over the spirit of citizens who are content with their lot and who are not moved by violent passions. But there are men whose atrocious souls can be contained only by terror."[258]

This was why, as a short-term expedient, he argued that the Congress should arm itself with a "body of troops" directly under its power, to be

[255] Gabriel Bonnot de Mably, *Le Droit public de l'Europe fondé sur les traités* [1748], 3 vols. (Geneva, 1776), 3:383.

[256] Gabriel Bonnot de Mably, *Notre gloire ou nos rêves* [1779], in his *Oeuvres*, 13:395.

[257] Mably, *Notre gloire*, p. 474.

[258] Mably, *Notre gloire*, p. 459.

assembled and used "according to the needs of the conjuncture." "I do not think," he added, "that this indispensable establishment will ever become dangerous, for as long as the delegates of the United States to the Congress enjoy this supreme magistracy for a limited and very short time."[259] Mably did not live (he died in 1785) to see his advice come home to roost in the country in which he expected it least, having long since given up on the recovery of liberty in France.

Rousseau's decision to allow Mirabeau to publish their correspondence is an indication that, despite their differences, they also shared a measure of common ground. The letters did not appear in the economists' house journal, the *Ephémérides du citoyen*, although it publicised them by printing a long (and very sympathetic) report written by their official censor, the royal historiographer Jacob-Nicolas Moreau.[260] Instead, they were published in 1768, as part of a pamphlet entitled *Précis de l'ordre légal* (An Outline of the Legal Order) and reprinted in the second, 1775, edition of a big book by Mirabeau entitled *Lettres sur la législation, ou l'ordre légal dépravé, rétabli et perpétué* (the title, *Letters on Legislation, or the Legal Order Depraved, Restored and Perpetuated*, was probably designed to indicate that the book's target was Mably's *De la législation* of 1774). In the account of his early life that he wrote in 1792, the pamphlet's editor, the economist Pierre-Samuel Dupont de Nemours, unhesitatingly associated Rousseau and Quesnay with two convergent theoretical projects. Quesnay, Dupont wrote, had embarked upon an ambitious project of political reflection designed to overturn the practice of abandoning "the government of nations" to "fortuitous combinations or blind routine."[261] That project had led to the development of the science of political economy, a science concerned not with the constitutions of governments but with those "economic laws which would be applicable to all constitutions." The "science of the social contract" belonged to Rousseau, while "that of political economy" had been created by Quesnay.[262] Dupont's annotations on his copy of the *Social Contract* (apparently made at two different stages of his life, in the 1760s and the 1790s) also acknowledged a measure of common ground. Although, according to Dupont, the highly attenuated notion of justice contained in Rousseau's second *Discourse* underestimated the range of moral capacities of the family-based communities of the state of nature (Mirabeau made the same point in his letter to Rousseau explaining what the Physiocrats understood by *évidence*), the precise distinction that he made between the sovereign,

---

[259] Mably, *Notre gloire*, p. 460.

[260] "Lettre de Monsieur M. Censeur royal à un Magistrat," *Ephémérides du citoyen* 9 (1768): 130–75.

[261] Dupont de Nemours, *Autobiography*, ed. Fox-Genovese, p. 238.

[262] Dupont de Nemours, *Autobiography*, ed. Fox-Genovese, pp. 238–9.

the state, and the government in the sixth chapter of book 1 of the *Social Contract* was the book's chief merit. "That merit," Dupont noted, "is very great and is a part of the science of political economy that belongs to Jean-Jacques and to him alone. But it is also the only part in which he had clear or true ideas."[263]

The judgement may have overlooked the substantial overlap between Rousseau's and Quesnay's respective theories of taxation (both took issue with Montesquieu's claim that redistributive taxation was best managed indirectly), but it also missed the real point of his letter to Mirabeau. In the last analysis, Rousseau argued, the distinction between the sovereign and the government was virtually impossible to maintain. Once there were states, there were also sovereigns. The fact that the sovereign might be a general will or a legal despot, and that a constitution could be designed very carefully to prevent it from becoming anything more, did not eliminate the possibility that it might still have to act in extraconstitutional ways. Once it did, there was nothing to prevent it from acting unjustly because the absence of any higher power was, by definition, what made sovereignty sovereign. This was the only, but fatal, flaw in Physiocracy. The economists' system was an ambitious and ingenious attempt to see how it might be possible to have something like the modern world, with its large territorial states, prosperity, and culture, but to avoid having its self-defeating commercial rivalry, its deep-seated domestic and international divisions, and its wars. Rousseau's verdict implied that the two aspects of modernity were inseparable. Nor was it possible to see a way out. As Rousseau acknowledged, he had come to a dead end.

---

[263] Jean A. Perkins, "Rousseau jugé par Du Pont de Nemours," *Annales de la Société Jean-Jacques Rousseau* 39 (1972–7): 171–95 (186).

ᴏᴼ4ᴼᴏ

INDUSTRY AND REPRESENTATIVE GOVERNMENT

Agriculture, Industry, and Inequality

IT IS now usual to claim that the French Revolution was a political revolution with social consequences. In the eighteenth century, it was equally usual to expect a social revolution with political consequences. Not everyone was willing to look forward to it as "the moment of the great revolution" with as much anticipation as the marquis de Mirabeau's protégé Antoine Court de Gebelin appears to have done at the time of the American war, or claim, as he put it, that "the restoration of the grand order was reserved for our century."[1] Even Mirabeau was stunned when another of his protégés, Charles Butré, announced that the order in question would not be based on agriculture. As Mirabeau commented acidly, Butré had discovered "by chance" that "man was not made to labour" because there was, apparently, "a higher order than the natural order."[2] But however unusual the prognosis may have been, the broader concern with scaling back the extremes of wealth and poverty and reverting to a more balanced interrelationship of agriculture, industry, and trade lay at the core of the eighteenth century's assessments of the nature and future of the modern world. The idea of a structural transformation of the public sphere that has captured so many historical imaginations in more recent times is a modern version of the same idea, echoing the eighteenth century's concern with rebalancing the relationship among absolute governments, centralised courts, capital cities, and the rest of society so that the human capacity for commerce—in the broad, eighteenth-century sense of the term—could be anchored to a genuinely reciprocal set of social arrangements. In its original version, the idea looked backwards, from the perspective of a world already taken to be too modern. In its modern version, the idea looks forwards, from the perspective of an old regime already taken to be too backward. The perspectives may have changed, but the telos is still the same.

In this respect, Physiocracy was simply a more analytically sophisticated version of the more widely shared view that the modern world's overcom-

---

[1] Antoine Court de Gebelin, *Monde primitif, analysé et comparé avec le monde moderne, considéré dans l'histoire naturelle de la parole or origine de langage et de l'écriture*, 9 vols. (Paris, 1773–82), 8:69.

[2] Mirabeau to Karl Friedrich von Baden, 17 August 1776, in Carl Knies, ed., *Carl Friedrichs von Baden Brieflicher Verkehr mit Mirabeau und Du Pont*, 2 vols. (Heidelberg, 1892), 1:90.

mitment to industry, trade, empire, war, and debt could not last. But a great deal more of what Pierre-Samuel Dupont de Nemours called the new science of political economy was also connected to the same concern. This was one reason why the American Benjamin Vaughan could still, in 1788, associate Fénelon, not Adam Smith, with what he took to be the basic principles of political economy.[3] Although it diverged fundamentally from both Rousseau and Physiocracy in this respect, much of the late eighteenth century's interest in the more positive aspects of public credit was centred upon the problem of finding a way to block the effects of inequality and overcentralised government that Fénelon had identified as the two great threats to modern political societies. Sir James Steuart's "rhapsody" about the levelling effects of a public debt was, in this sense, very Fénelonian. So, too, was the argument about using public credit to promote social justice by pushing up grain prices and wage levels that ran through the marquis de Casaux's *Considérations sur quelques parties du mécanisme des sociétés* (Considerations on Some Parts of the Mechanism of Societies) of 1784, a work that the younger Mirabeau set alongside those of the French economists and Adam Smith.[4] The same type of argument could also be found in the Swiss economist Jean-Frédéric Herrenschwand's *De l'économie politique moderne* (Of the Modern Political Economy) of 1786 with its claim that public credit was the only available tool to stabilise the modern combination of agriculture subordinated to industry or, as he put it, "the boldest system of political economy that the human race could ever have imagined for its survival."[5]

For Herrenschwand, the boldness of the modern system of political economy matched the precariousness of those whose livelihoods depended on manufacturing industry. Industry subordinated to agriculture supplied stability, because the basic human requirements for food, shelter, warmth, and clothing had to come first. Agriculture subordinated to industry exposed primary human needs to the volatility of markets, prices, and broader changes in patterns of international demand. Here, as Herrenschwand went on to demonstrate at some length, the more benign aspect of public credit's Janus face had a powerful appeal. The additional quantity of fiduciary instruments created by the modern funding system supplied a way to broaden and deepen domestic markets without having to rely upon the positive effects of foreign trade, while the largely domestic circulation of most of these instruments left a larger proportion of the available supply

---

[3] [Benjamin Vaughan], *New and Old Principles of Trade Compared* (London, 1788), p. vii, note, and above, p. 110.

[4] Philippe de Roux, *Le marquis de Casaux. Un planteur des Antilles inspirateur de Mirabeau* (Paris, Société française d'histoire d'outre-mer, 1951).

[5] Jean-Frédéric Herrenschwand, *De l'économie politique moderne. Discours fondamental sur la population* (London, 1786), p. 72.

of gold and silver coin to be used to fund residual imbalances in foreign trade. From this perspective, public credit could be used as an alternative to the Physiocrats' single tax on landed income to rebalance the relationship among agriculture, industry, and trade. In this guise, it presented the prospect of a more egalitarian and internationally cooperative future that did not require a direct fiscal assault on the accumulated legacy of inequality that Europe had inherited from its feudal and absolute pasts. This was the aspect of public credit that appealed so strongly to a host of now largely forgotten critics of the injustice of actually existing political societies and the inequality that they housed. Unlike many earlier neo-Machiavellians, they did not refer to ancient politics as the solution to modernity's problems. Instead, they referred to modern economics and the resources supplied by modern public credit. The late-eighteenth-century Anglo-Welsh political reformer David Williams's vast didactic poem *Egeria* (a conversation among Moses, Quesnay, and Sir James Steuart) is one monument to this largely forgotten tradition, best known now only in the work of Tom Paine. Instead of an agrarian law, Paine adverted consistently to the idea that the modern funding system, as exemplified by both the American continental currency and, later, the French *assignat*, had an unprecedented capacity to promote what, in one of his late works, he was to call "Agrarian Justice."[6]

In this evaluation, public credit was taken to have a transitional purpose. As with John Law's original system, it could be used to correct distributional problems arising from the misallocation of different kinds of property without having to call the ownership of property itself into question. As with Law, too, the point of having a public debt was, in the longer term, to be able to reduce or eliminate the legacy of previous borrowing. Once it had done its work, it would no longer be required. But the other face of public credit was at once more durable and less attractive. It did not look towards a more egalitarian and internationally cooperative future but instead presented an endless continuation of the world as it was. In this guise, public credit was war finance, and, for as long as there were wars, public debts would remain. This was the aspect of public credit that both Montesquieu and Hume singled out. The danger that it housed was not simply a

---

[6] David Williams, *Egeria, or Elementary Studies on the Progress of Nations in Political Economy, Legislation and Government* (London, 1803), and Thomas Paine, *Agrarian Justice, opposed to Agrarian Law and to Agrarian Monopoly: Being a Plan for Ameliorating the Condition of Man, Creating in Every Nation a National Fund* (London, 1797). On this aspect of Paine's thought, see Manuela Albertone, "Moneta e credito pubblico nel pensiero dell' abate Morellet: a proposito di aulcuni testi inediti," *Quaderni de storia dell'economia politica* 8 (1990): 47–106 (on Paine, see pp. 91–106). More generally, see my "Property, Community and Citizenship," in Mark Goldie and Robert Wokler, eds., *The Cambridge History of Eighteenth-Century Political Thought* (Cambridge, CUP, 2006).

matter of the way that the interest-bearing paper issued by states to fund their debts could also be used as securities to fund the costs of private borrowing, either for investment in agriculture, industry, or trade or for personal consumption. It was also a matter of the way that all these activities would be favoured by the strong emphasis on legality, constitutional propriety, and keeping faith with the state's creditors that served to make public credit secure. Hume's "violent death" scenario, like Steuart's "farce" or Guibert's image of modern political societies breaking like reeds under the blast of the icy north wind, indicated that too strong a commitment to public faith might destroy the state itself. The result was a double-bind. The more secure that public credit was, the more difficult it might be to maintain the very arrangements and values that helped to make it secure.

Both sides of the Janus-faced properties of public credit were carried through into the period of the French Revolution. From one point of view, it could be used to create a more balanced political economy, with, as Herrenschwand put it, industry dependent on agriculture. But from another, it could be made to consolidate the existing dependence of agriculture on industry. The alternatives pointed towards two rather different conceptions of trade and international relations. The first emphasised their cooperative and reciprocal character, while the second highlighted their competitive and divisive nature. The difference turned most directly on the status of manufacturing industry. In its natural place, it could fit into a world made up of separate nations and states, serving to cement relationships based on reciprocal utility. In its actual place, it underpinned the divisions of both domestic and international society. The best-known example now of these different assessments of manufacturing industry is the clash that took place over its status in the United States of America between republicans like Thomas Jefferson (and, in some measure, James Madison) and federalists like Alexander Hamilton. Both were supporters of commerce, but they disagreed very strongly about what its foundations should be. But the Jefferson-Hamilton split was not a peculiarity of American conditions. As another American observed, this time writing in the context of the French Revolution, it was a split that went back to Aristotle and Xenophon and had been opened up more recently by Montesquieu's distinction between trade based on luxury as suitable for monarchies and trade based on economy as suitable for republics. "The best republics," Aristotle was held to have said, "were those based on agriculture," while the arts, according to Xenophon, "corrupt the bodies of those practising them, require them to remain in the shade or by the fire, and leave them no time for either their friends or the republic."[7] Trade based on agriculture was morally and politi-

---

[7] [Thomas Waters Griffiths], *L'indépendance absolue des Américains des Etats-Unis prouvée par l'état actuel de leur commerce avec les nations européennes* (Paris, an VI/1798), pp. 137, 146.

cally different from trade based on urban industry. The one pointed towards the culture and civility of ancient Athens, the other to the splendour
and misery of imperial Rome. Time may have played a part in obliterating
the distinction, but the binary framework that it has left and the way that
this now seems to make every endorsement of commerce look "modern"
was also a result of a real theoretical shift.

The shift involved a reevaluation of the various types of social hierarchy
generated by agriculture, industry, and trade and the part that public credit
might be able to play in keeping them stable. This meant addressing both
aspects of the Janus-faced properties of public credit. Constitutional reform might make public credit more viable. But the more deeply entrenched it might become, the more necessary it would be to find extraconstitutional resources of authority and stability to limit its more perverse
effects. The eighteenth century's nightmare was not that public credit
would, in the first instance, promote social instability, but that the very
social stability that it would set in place would be self-defeating. The "bizarre social convention" that Sieyès imagined was one version of this kind
of argument. It would lead, he suggested, to a state of affairs in which some
members of society appeared to have agreed to spend all their time and
effort catering for the needs of a tiny, idle elite. In different ways, all the
various cataclysmic projections of the future that Guibert, Steuart, Raynal,
Bolingbroke, Brown, Mably, Mirabeau, or Lebrun set out were predicated
on the same kind of argument and the assumption that public credit favoured what, in eighteenth-century terms, was usually called epicureanism
or effeminacy.[8] Hume's "violent death" scenario spelled out the message.
Preferring a quiet life might, in some circumstances, turn out to be incompatible with political survival.

Living with the Janus-faced character of public credit meant recognising
its promise, but avoiding its menace. If its epicurean effects were unavoidable, this did not mean that it had to be discarded. Instead, it meant finding
a way to deal with the two different problems that it presented. The first
was legal and constitutional. This problem had been catered for by Montesquieu in the chapters of *The Spirit of Laws* dealing with the English
constitution. Constitutional government made public credit secure. The
second problem was social. In one sense, it had been catered for by Montes-

---

[8] On these themes in eighteenth-century thought, see Edward J. Hundert, *The Enlighten-
ment's Fable: Bernard Mandeville and the Discovery of Society* (Cambridge, CUP, 1994); Dale
Van Kley, "Pierre Nicole, Jansenism, and the Morality of Enlightened Self-Interest," in Alan
Charles Kors and Paul J. Korshin, eds., *Anticipations of Enlightenment in England, France and
Germany* (Philadelphia, University of Pennsylvania Press, 1987) pp. 69–85, and, classically,
Arthur O. Lovejoy, *Reflections on Human Nature* (Baltimore, Johns Hopkins University Press,
1961), and Jacob Viner, "The Role of Providence in the Social Order," *Memoirs of the Ameri-
can Philosophical Society* 90 (Philadelphia, 1972).

quieu's conception of monarchy, with its combination of a single royal sovereign and a number of subordinate, dependent, and intermediate powers. But the part played by property and inheritance in that conception of monarchy, and the way that the kind of honour-driven inequality on which it was based served to favour the more epicurean effects of public credit, ruled out a straightforward combination of the English constitution and Montesquieu's idea of monarchy. As Sieyès's "bizarre convention" indicated, a public debt would simply suck a noncommercial, but property-based, nobility into a centralised system of patronage. Putting together the two kinds of monarchy that Montesquieu had described had to involve establishing a different set of subordinate, dependent, and intermediate powers. Sieyès called the result a "monarchical republic" or "true monarchy." It amounted to redesigning both the constitutional and extraconstitutional aspects of modern political societies to enable them to accommodate both epicurean selfishness and patriotic selflessness, and, by doing so, to avoid having to make a choice among Spartan virtue, Athenian harmony, Roman grandeur, Christian simplicity, feudal chivalry, royal splendour, or any of the other great normative and political systems that the eighteenth century had inherited from its past. This, right from the start, was the note that Sieyès struck.

The third of the three pamphlets that he published in 1789 (but the first of the three that he actually wrote) began with a confident endorsement of modernity. "Enough others," he wrote in the first sentence of the *Views of the Executive Means Available to the Representatives of France in 1789*, "believe it to be necessary to ask earlier, barbarous centuries for laws suitable for civilised nations. We, however, will not lose ourselves in an uncertain quest for ancient errors and institutions. Reason is of every age. It is made for man and, especially when it speaks to him of his dearest interests, reason should be listened to with confidence and respect."[9] No one, he continued, would disdain "the recent productions of a perfected art" to meet the ordinary needs of life, or expect a modern watchmaker to base his art on anything other than "that part of mechanics that is the repository of the laws and observations of modern genius." The same, Sieyès asserted, applied to "social mechanics." If "the most trifling improvements in the arts of commerce and luxury" were welcomed with ardour, then "the progress of the first of all arts, the *social art*," deserved quite as much attention.[10]

Sieyès never set down the specifications of what, at various times, he referred to as "social mechanics," "the social art," "social science," or "the

[9] Emmanuel-Joseph Sieyès, *Vues sur les moyens d'exécution dont les représentants de France pourront disposer en 1789*, 2nd ed. (Paris, 1789), p. 1. (I have modified the translation, based on the first edition, in *Sieyès: Political Writings*, ed. Michael Sonenscher [Indianapolis, Hackett, 2003], p. 4).

[10] Sieyès, *Vues*, p. 2 (*Political Writings*, ed. Sonenscher, p. 5).

science of the social art." Some of his language was quite strongly resonant of Rousseau. "The sovereign, simply by being what it is, is always what it should be," wrote Rousseau.[11] "The nation is all that it can be, simply by virtue of being what it is," wrote Sieyès.[12] The distinctions that he made between active and passive citizenship, between a constituting and a constituted power, and even between the Third Estate and the two other orders of the French Estates-General could all be found in Rousseau. But his decision to replace the term "social science" by "the science of the social art" in the second and subsequent editions of *What Is the Third Estate?* was, on the other hand, a reversion to an established Physiocratic term that captured the point of the fiscal and institutional arrangements required to put the unnatural and retrograde order of actually existing political societies back onto their natural and essential foundations. In the context of the late eighteenth century, the "science of the social art" meant something precise, but it was much less clear what "social science" might be. The younger Mirabeau reinforced the association between Sieyès and Physiocracy by telling the National Assembly on 18 August 1789 that the principles that Sieyès had set out in his draft Declaration of the Rights of Man were the same as those developed by his father and Quesnay.[13] In both cases, however, appearances are misleading. Sieyès's gestures towards Rousseau on the one hand and towards Physiocracy on the other put his political thought in the wrong context from the very start. They had the effect of suggesting more of a connection than he may have intended between his particular conception of representative government and the more orthodox eighteenth-century concern with rebalancing the relationship among agriculture, industry, and trade. As the debate between Sieyès and Tom Paine in 1791 indicated, it was quite easy to associate the idea of representative government with the broader idea of a more socially integrated and morally cohesive community.

The real setting to which Sieyès's political thought belonged was quite different. In a remote sense, it began with Colbert. The Colbert in question was not, however, the Colbert of statutorily organised trade guilds, detailed regulations for producing manufactured goods, royal inspectors of manufacturing processes, and giant royal enterprises like the Gobelins mirror works or the Sèvres porcelain manufactory, but the Colbert of small-scale, highly specialised industry and intricately interdependent regional economies centred on the great commercial and manufacturing cities of Paris,

---

[11] Jean-Jacques Rousseau, *Du contrat social* [1762], ed. Robert Derathé (Paris, 1993), p. 185: "Le souverain, par cela qu'il est, est toujours ce qu'il doit être."

[12] Emmanuel-Joseph Sieyès, *Qu'est-ce que le tiers état?*, ed. Champion, p. 68: "La nation est tout ce qu'elle peut être, par cela seul qu'elle est." Sieyès, *Political Writings*, ed. Sonenscher, p. 137.

[13] *Archives Parlementaires*, 8:453.

Lyon, Marseille, and Bordeaux. It was the Colbert of Jean-François Melon—or "Colbert-Melon," as Voltaire liked to call him—and the cluster of writers associated with the Gournay group. In a more immediate sense, it was also the Colbert of two of Louis XVI's best-known finance ministers, Anne-Robert-Jacques Turgot and Jacques Necker. This last pairing may seem surprising. It is more usual to set Turgot against Necker and to associate the former with Physiocracy and identify only the latter, the author of an *Éloge de Colbert* published in 1773 shortly before Turgot entered the ministry, as Colbert's true intellectual heir. In fact, their evaluations of manufacturing industry and its real contribution to social wealth were very similar, and it was Turgot, not Necker, who gave this anti-Physiocratic position its fullest analytical grounding, one that was carried through into the period of the French Revolution by Pierre-Louis Roederer in his *Course on Social Organisation*. Its starting point was a radical revision to Montesquieu's property-based conception of monarchy. Turgot did not drop property but added property in money to property in land to modify Montesquieu's idea of monarchy as a system of government made up of a single ruler and a number of subordinate, dependent, and intermediate powers. Capitalists—as Turgot, following established usage, called them—were as much of an intermediate power as the owners of land. What set Turgot and Necker apart had more to do with their policy towards the landowners and the grain trade (where Turgot remained closer to the original Physiocrats) and with their respective assessments of public credit. For Necker, a public debt was rather like Physiocracy's single tax on landed income. Once there was a public debt, a state would have a built-in mechanism that could be used to force the producers of manufactured goods to remain productive. Coupled with an English-style system of balanced government (as described by Necker's Genevan compatriot Jean-Louis Delolme), it could be used to offset the divisive effects of private property, not only in land, but also in money.[14] For Turgot, the disadvantages of public credit remained too strong, especially under an absolute government. The unitary character of sovereignty, even if modified by a subordinate network of provincial assemblies, ruled out something as divisive and as potentially damaging to productive investment as a public debt.

Sieyès built on both, accepting Turgot's argument about capital, as well as land, as one of the primary sources of wealth and Necker's moderate endorsement of public credit. Both had a place in the system of representative government. Although he never described in detail how the two could be fitted together, there is nonetheless a highly integrated description of

[14] See Jean-Louis Delolme, *The Constitution of England, or an Account of the English Government; in which it is Compared both with the Republic Form of Government and the Other Monarchies of Europe* (London, 1770). On Delolme's continuing relevance after 1815, see below, conclusion.

how they could be combined under the aegis of the dual system of political and nonpolitical representation that he envisaged. Here, it was not the British constitution that was the model, but British mass production and the way that it opened up to deal with the moral and political problems associated with inequality. Broader and deeper markets for mass-produced goods could, gradually, make what the eighteenth century had called luxury more widely available and, by doing so, could circumvent some of the more dangerously political problems associated with managing the transition to a more balanced society. In this sense, mass production made Physiocracy redundant. The argument appeared in Necker's *Treatise on the Administration of the Finances of France* of 1784 and was set out in detail in the *Traité d'économie politique* (Treatise on Political Economy), published in 1803 by the political economist Jean-Baptiste Say (whose early revolutionary career began under the aegis of Mirabeau and Sieyès). As Say noted, it was Jean-François Melon who had been the first to argue that, as Say put it, "the spirit of conquest and the spirit of commerce are incompatible."[15] His own *Treatise on Political Economy* took Melon's formulation as its starting point and set out to show, both theoretically and practically, how it might be possible to insulate trade more fully from the competitive dynamics of power politics than, two generations earlier, Forbonnais and the Gournay group had been able to do.

As Say presented it, Melon's political treatment of commerce began in midstream. By moving several steps back up the analytical sequence, Say was able to argue that the cumulative gains produced by rising productivity opened up a real range of policy alternatives to prevent commercial rivalry from defaulting into undiluted power politics. Here, as Say acknowledged very fully, he was simply following Adam Smith, with the additional advantage of being able to compare French and British industry a generation later. But, in the setting formed by the interim period between the Peace of Amiens of 1801 and Napoleon Bonaparte's coronation as emperor in 1804, the argument also followed Sieyès (Say, in a letter that he sent to Sieyès along with a copy of his *Treatise*, clearly intended the gesture to be part of a discussion based on shared premises, not simply a mark of deference towards a powerful patron).[16] Properly understood, what Melon had called "the spirit of commerce" could be redescribed as what Say called *industrie*, and, in this light, could be identified as the stabilising principle of representative government in much the same way as Montesquieu had

---

[15] Jean-Baptiste Say, *Politique pratique*, in Jean-Baptiste Say, *Oeuvres complètes*, vol. 5, *Oeuvres morales et politiques*, ed. Emmanuel Blanc and André Tiran (Paris, Economica, 2003), p. 594. The editors give Say's source as Jean-François Melon, *Essai politique sur le commerce* [1733] (Paris, 1761), p. 79. See Jean-François Melon, *A Political Essay upon Commerce* [1734], trans. David Bindon (Dublin, 1738), pp. 138–9.

[16] A. N. 284 AP 16, dossier 5, Say to Sieyès, 21 Messidor an XI.

earlier identified virtue and honour as the stabilising principles of republics and monarchies. In this sense, both Say and Sieyès used the same basic concept of representation. If the political system that Sieyès envisaged was based on representation, representation itself was based on *industrie*, or industry understood in the generic sense that Say, following Sieyès, gave to the term. The point of the claim was not so much to show how economics could be separated from politics, but to show how economics and politics could coexist but still remain separate. From this perspective, Say's *Treatise* ran parallel to Sieyès's system of representative government.

Sieyès recurrently referred to the years around 1770 as the time when he began to formulate his system. "Work (*travail*) favours liberty only in becoming representative," he wrote in an undated note.

> What seems to have been most applauded in France in Smith's work [*The Wealth of Nations*] is its first chapter on *the division of labour*. Yet there is nothing in his ideas that was not common among all those of my fellow citizens who took an interest in economic matters. . . . As for myself, I had gone further than Smith as from 1770. I saw not only that the *division* of labour in the same trade, namely, under *the same higher level of management*, was the surest way to reduce the costs and increase the quantity of products, I also envisaged the *distribution* of the great occupations or trades as the true principle of the social state. . . . Multiply the *means*, or the power, to satisfy our *needs*; enjoy more, but work less (*jouir plus, travailler moins*), this is what defines the natural increase of liberty in the social state. Thus the progress of liberty follows naturally from the establishment of *representative* work.[17]

He made the point in print in the *Views of the Executive Means*. "The more a society progresses in the arts of trade and production," he wrote there, "the more apparent it becomes that the work connected to public functions should, like private employments, be carried out less expensively and more efficiently by men who make it their exclusive occupation. This truth is well known."[18] Later, in a note written after the publication of the second edition of Say's *Treatise on Political Economy* in 1814, he again alluded to the period around 1770 as the time when the idea had taken shape. Here, the remark referred not so much to the representative character of the division of labour itself as to the related idea that *all* labour could be taken to be productive (the idea of what Say called "immaterial products," or what might now be called the service industries, as well as public goods and human capital, was one of the genuine innovations of his book). The remark was prompted by Say's observation, in the preface to the second edition of his *Treatise*, that he would prefer not to have used the term "political

---

[17] A. N. 284 AP 2, dossier 13 (sheet headed "travail").
[18] Sieyès, *Political Writings*, ed. Sonenscher, p. 48.

economy" to describe the book's subject-matter. Political economy appeared to deal only with physical goods or saleable products, whereas its real subject-matter encompassed utilities of every kind, including things like skills, medicine, or education that were neither physical nor necessarily bought and sold. This, Say commented, was why the word *onéologie* was actually a more comprehensive, but far too obscure, name for political economy. The neologism, derived from the Greek words *oneō* and *logos*, was deliberately ambiguous and could mean both the science of profiting, acquiring, or benefiting and that of gratifying, delighting, or enjoying. To Sieyès, it filled a real theoretical gap.

> Properly speaking, wealth consists of all existing values, but up to the present *onéologie* deals only with venal, or vendible, values. Ease, well-being, or, in a word, enjoyment (*jouissance*) is connected to many more goods than those that can be bought and sold, as well as to the large number of those that can be consumed without having been bought or sold at all. This observation alone serves to show that *onéologie* ought to cover a range that has yet to be noticed. Labour that anyone applies directly, and individual, collective, or public enjoyments (*jouissances*), indicate the immensity of the field of those elements of happiness that have yet to become the object of study. A good social state would combine things in such a way that those moral and physical enjoyments that are not bought or sold would still amount to a very considerable portion of each individual's well-being. Human industry and action seem to me to be very restricted if they are to be considered solely in terms of their vendible, or venal, products (see the analytical table of the universality of human enjoyment that I made more than forty years ago). The spectacle of a human society, considered in terms of general well-being, looks to me like a very poor thing if the individuals composing it are taken to be no more than a multitude of agents or instruments of vendible production, as if a political association has to be seen as no more than the formation of a great manufactory in which three classes of individuals—idle rentiers, active entrepreneurs, and laborious instruments—wage a silent war over how much of a share of the vendible product they will have. Production and consumption are correlates, even though they are rarely equal. Wealth that is destined to be sold, and even that part which could be sold even if it is not, amount to no more than the smallest proportion of consumption and production within the more general movement. *Onéologie* has not therefore been given all the extension that it should have as a *political science*. I spent some time on this point of view and made much progress in 1774 and the following years. It guided me in the project for establishing public festivals that I gave to the Committee on Public Education in 1793, etc. *Fata negarunt* [Fate ruled otherwise].[19]

[19] A. N. 284 AP 5, dossier 3^2 (sheet headed *onéologie*). The note is discussed by Murray Forsyth in his *Reason and Revolution: The Political Thought of the Abbé Sieyès* (Leicester, Leicester University Press, 1987), p. 57, but is dated too early (Say used the word *onéologie* only in

The festivals in question were intended to present a panorama of both the political and nonpolitical parts of human life. The fifteen, for example, to be celebrated annually in every canton included festivals marking the beginning and end of the agricultural year, a festival for domesticated animals (Sieyès envisaged something like an agricultural show, with prizes for the best horse or cow, and was rather irritated when the suggestion gave rise to complaints about materialism), festivals for the young, for marriage, maternity, and old age, for the improvement of language and the invention of writing, for the origin of commerce and the arts, for navigation and fishing, as well as for the rights of man, the primary assemblies, the sovereignty of the people, and popular elections.[20] They were *onéologie* on display. Almost everything involved in human well-being could be incorporated into this comprehensively enlarged notion of political economy and could, in addition, be connected to the equally comprehensive idea of the division of labour as a representative system. If industry was the underlying principle of representation, then the range of activities to which the slogan *jouir plus, travailler moins* could be applied was virtually limitless. It is likely that this was the broad idea underlying the "Treatise on Socialism" (*Traité*

---

the preface to the second, 1814, edition of his *Treatise*) and, unusually, is not described correctly (Sieyès was actually amplifying on, not rejecting, what Say had written). The original French passage runs as follows (I have modernised the spelling): "La richesse proprement dite se compose de toutes les valeurs existantes; mais l'onéologie jusqu'à présent ne considère que les valeurs vénales. L'aisance, le bien-être, la jouissance, en un mot, tiennent à beaucoup d'autres biens que les richesses vénales et même que les richesses aussi nombreuses qui se consomment sans avoir été vendues. Dans cette seule observation, on voit déjà que l'onéologie peut recevoir une étendue dont on ne s'est pas encore avisé. Le travail que chacun s'applique directement et les jouissances particulières, communes et publiques, ouvrent un champ immense d'éléments de bonheur qui n'ont point encore été l'objet de cette étude. Un bon état social combinerait les choses de manière que les jouissances morales et physiques qui ne se vendent point entreraient pour une portion considérable dans le bien être de chaque individu. L'industrie et l'action humaines me paraissent bien resserrés quand on ne considère que leur produit vénal (voir le tableau analytique que j'ai fait il y a plus de 40 ans de l'universalité de la jouissance humaine). Le spectacle d'une société humaine sous le rapport du bien être général me semble bien misérable quand on ne représente les individus qui la composent que comme une multitude d'agents ou d'instruments des seules productions vénales. Comme si une association politique n'était que la formation d'une grande manufacture, où trois classes d'individus, des rentiers oisifs, des entrepreneurs actifs et des instruments laborieux se font constamment une guerre sourde pour avoir la plus grande part au produit vénal. La production et la consommation sont des choses corrélatives, quoique rarement égales; les richesses destinés à être vendues; celles mêmes qui en seraient susceptibles, quoique ne l'étant pas, ne composent dans le mouvement général que la plus petite portion de la consommation et de la production. L'onéologie n'a donc pas reçu toute l'extension qu'elle doit avoir comme *science politique*. Je m'étais occupé de cette vue, avec beaucoup de suite, en 1774 et années suivantes. Elle m'avoit dirigé dans le projet d'établissement des fêtes publiques que j'ai donné au comité d'instruction publique en 1793 etc. *Fata negarunt*."

[20] The details were published in the *Journal d'instruction sociale* 4 (29 June 1793): 100–2 and pp. 150–1 on domesticated animals.

du socialisme) or, more elaborately, a "Treatise on Socialism, or on the *Goal* Given by Man to Himself in Society and of the *Means* He Has to Attain It" (*Traité du socialisme, ou du* but *que se propose l'homme en société et des* moyens *qu'il a d'y parvenir*) that Sieyès, at some time, seems to have envisaged.[21]

HELVÉTIUS

If the modified image of Colbert that ran from Melon and Voltaire to Turgot and Say formed the broad context from which this vision emerged, its more immediate intellectual setting is more difficult to establish. In a broad sense, it was formed by a number of related investigations into the separate origins of several different types of social distinction. These investigations, described in this and the following sections, supplied a framework for the concept of representative government that Sieyès developed. The key move that Sieyès made was to see how they could all be connected to his own very simple idea of representation and, with this as a starting point, to show how they could then be integrated into a unitary political system with a multiplicity of separate parts. The idea of representation as something generic, and of political representation as something specific allowed Sieyès to build on the system of gradual promotion that Rousseau had described and to apply it to a far more commercially developed society than Rousseau himself had ever been willing to envisage. The underlying properties of this kind of society were to be described most comprehensively in Jean-Baptiste Say's *Treatise on Political Economy* of 1803, which, in its turn, presupposed the endorsement of the idea of gradual promotion that Say had made in his earlier, now less well known, *Olbie, or an Essay on the Means of Improving the Morals of a Nation* of 1800. Together, they can be taken to be a description of what Sieyès's system might have looked like, had it ever taken root (interestingly, Say briefly pinned his hopes for its implementation not upon Napoleon I, but upon Russia's emperor Alexander I, the chief architect, and for a time, possible liberal standard-bearer, of the post-Napoleonic Holy Alliance).

An initial clue to the proximate intellectual origins of Sieyès's system can be found in a book published in 1772 by François-Jean, marquis de Chastellux. This was *De la félicité publique*, or *An Essay on Public Happiness* as its English translation of 1774 was entitled. There is some similarity between the way that Chastellux described the idea of representation and Sieyès's later concept of a representative system. "Mr. Rousseau," Chastellux wrote,

---

[21] A. N. 284 AP 3, dossier 1³.

has said that wherever the citizens become so numerous as to render it necessary to make the government representative, there can be no true liberty. I am, nevertheless, of the opinion that there will be no solid and lasting liberty and, in particular, no happiness, but among peoples where everything is done by representation. Observe this little republic, where each citizen is, as it were, all because the state is nothing; where, at one moment, he assumes the gown and at another, his military armour: a shallow politician, an incapable judge, and an undisciplined soldier; continually either a prey to faction, or exposed to the rage of war. Whereas an extensive society, in which every individual is united to each other by the same interests and the same laws, finds peace in the separation that it makes of its tasks (*dans le partage qu'elle fait de ses travaux*). In such a society, the soldier is not engaged in pleading the cause of the oppressed; nor is the magistrate in defending the ramparts. The labourer, unmolested, pursues the cultivation of his ground, while the judge watches over the political welfare of the state and the warrior repels its invaders. If the last appears to bear entirely the public burden, he is amply indemnified by salaries and honours.[22]

Chastellux was a friend and admirer of the royal tax-farmer Claude-Adrien Helvétius (he published a warm obituary notice of Helvétius after the latter's death in 1771).[23] According to another of his obituarists, the marquis de Saint-Lambert, Helvétius began his intellectual career in the circles associated with Fontenelle and Montesquieu, but began to move nearer to Voltaire after the publication of *The Spirit of Laws*.[24] The egalitarian preoccupation of his first major work, *De l'esprit*, or *Essays on the Mind* as its English translation was entitled, which appeared in 1758, was certainly nearer to the *Henriade* and the *Anti-Machiavel* than to *The Spirit of Laws*. But if *De l'esprit* was, in some sense, a reply to *De l'esprit des lois*, its more immediate target was Rousseau. The rather crude epistemology on which its argument was based (involving a claim that sense impressions and judge-

[22] François-Jean de Chastellux, *An Essay on Public Happiness* [1772], 2 vols. (London, 1774), 1:97–8. I have modified the translation against the original text, reprinted in François-Jean de Chastellux, *De la félicité publique*, ed. Roger Basoni (Paris, Presses universitaires de France, 1989), p. 176. Sieyès's papers indicate that he had read *De la félicité publique* and, at some time between 1772 and 1774, imagined a parallel "political and pessimistic book" that would be a "continuation of Chastellux," dealing with the causes of human misfortune (see A. N. 284 AP 2, dossier 3⁴). There is also some evidence that, before Chastellux's death in 1789, the two men were part of the same opposition circles associated with the duc d'Orléans in 1787–8: see A. N. 284 AP 7, dossier 2 and A. N. 284 AP 1, dossier 6.

[23] On Helvétius, see David Wootton, "Helvétius, from Radical Enlightenment to Revolution," *Political Studies* 28 (2000): 307–36, and Jean-Fabien Spitz, *L'Amour de l'égalité* (Paris, Vrin, 2000), pp. 55–78. Neither, however, deals with the muted argument between Helvétius and Rousseau.

[24] Jean-François, marquis de Saint-Lambert, *Essai sur la vie d'Helvétius* [1772], reprinted in his *Oeuvres philosophiques*, 5 vols. (Paris, 1801), 5:220–5.

ments were identical) led to a volley of accusations of materialism and a
court case that ended with the book's being banned. The point of the epistemology was not, however, to make a philosophical argument about
human knowledge, but to attack Rousseau's rejection of natural human
sociability. Like Rousseau, Helvétius rejected Montesquieu's claim that
monarchies did not need virtue. Unlike Rousseau, however, he also argued
that virtue could be combined with both self-liking and self-love (*amour-
de-soi* and *amour-propre*) without leading to the spiral of social and political
polarisation that Rousseau presented in his second *Discourse*. Properly understood, he suggested, it might lead to the kind of stable international
order envisaged by the abbé de Saint-Pierre, buttressed by a transformation
of actually existing monarchies into large federal republics. As Jeremy Bentham famously put it, Helvétius made "the cause of the people the cause
of virtue."[25] Sieyès himself never went very far in this direction. Nor did
he have much intellectual sympathy with the reductive epistemology on
which the argument of *De l'esprit* was based. But there is good reason to
think that the framework in which he began to think about the relationship
between occupational specialisation and human well-being was established
by Helvétius. Helvétius made only one appearance in the imaginary conversation among several famous philosophers that Pierre-Louis Roederer
published in 1797. But his intervention (saying that the best government
was one under which the people was happiest) was taken by "Sieyès" to be
the starting point of the principal question to be settled.[26] If Roederer can
be taken as a guide, Helvétius may have got the wrong answer, but he had
asked the right question.

As Helvétius presented it, feeling (meaning sense perception) was identical to judging. The crude epistemology underlying the claim makes it easy
to miss its point. The point had little to do with the origins and nature of
knowledge and a great deal more to do with Rousseau's claim, in the *Discourse on the Origin of Inequality*, that humans were not naturally sociable
because every human had all the natural capacities required for self-preservation. *Amour-de-soi* did not need others at all. The argument that Helvétius developed turned Rousseau's scepticism against himself.[27] Humans

---

[25] Jeremy Bentham, *A Fragment on Government* [1776], ed. Ross Harrison (Cambridge,
CUP, 1988), p. 51.

[26] Pierre-Louis Roederer, "Entretien de plusieurs philosophes célèbres, sur les gouvernements républicain et monarchique," in *Oeuvres du comte P. L. Roederer*, ed. A. M. Roederer, 8
vols. (Paris, 1852–9), 7:63, 70.

[27] The idea of the move was prefigured in an early note aimed at Rousseau's first *Discourse*,
"il y a des choses sur lesquelles on doit étendre le voile du pyrrhonisme, mais en fait de science
il faut être furieusement savant pour être pyrrhonien car il faudrait savoir tout ce que l'esprit
humain peut savoir pour prouver que ce savoir n'est rien": Albert Keim, *Notes de la main
d'Helvétius publiées d'après un manuscrit inédit, avec une introduction et des commentaires* (Paris,

might indeed have all the natural capacities required for self-preservation, but it was not obvious how they could know that they had them. If feeling was judging, they could certainly make first-order judgements. But there was no reason to assume that they could make second-order judgements to corroborate the primary judgements supplied by the senses. According to Helvétius, even the radically pared-down notion of evidence produced by Descartes's hyperbolic doubt still required corroboration. "For Descartes," he noted, "not having placed a sign, if I may be allowed the expression, at the inn of evidence, every one thinks he has a right of lodging his own opinion there." Left to their own devices, humans could not escape "the impossibility of finding proper signs to express the different degrees of belief they annex to their opinion."[28] Others had to supply the signs.

Helvétius's refutation of Rousseau was a reversion to Hobbes. He was quite explicit about this in his posthumously published *De l'homme* or, as its English translation was called, *A Treatise on Man, His Intellectual Faculties and His Education*. "Hobbes," Helvétius wrote there, in a chapter headed "Of Sociability," "has been reproached with this maxim, *the strong child is a bad child*." But this, he continued, was simply another version of the seventeenth-century French dramatist Thomas Corneille's dictum that "he who can do whatever he wills, wills more than he should," as well as the line by La Fontaine that "the best reason is the reason of the strongest (*la raison du plus fort est toujours la meilleure*)." "They who write the romance of man," Helvétius asserted (modifying an antithesis that Voltaire had applied to Locke), "condemn this maxim of Hobbes. They who write his history admire it, and the necessity of laws proves it to be true."[29] The maxim was designed to encapsulate what Hobbes, in his *De Cive*, had presented as the two primary human motivations for society. The first was need or want. The second was what Hobbes had called "vainglory." Both were selfish motivations, but, more important, the point of the maxim was that they were also self-defeating. The robust child might well enlist oth-

---

1907), p. 38. Helvétius made a more publicly critical assessment of Rousseau in his posthumously published *De l'homme*, 2 vols. (London, 1773), vol. 2, sec. 5.

[28] Claude-Adrien Helvétius, *De l'esprit* [1758], ed. François Châtelet (Verviers, Editions Gérard, 1973), First Discourse, ch. 1, p. 23, note 6. I have followed the contemporary translation published as Helvétius, *De l'esprit: or essays on the mind and its several faculties* (London, 1759), pp. 3–4, note c. When I have used terms from this translation, references to the page numbers are in parentheses in subsequent notes.

[29] Claude-Adrien Helvétius, *De l'homme* [London, 1773], trans. as *A Treatise on Man, his Intellectual Faculties and his Education*, 2 vols. (London, 1777), vol. 1, sec. 2, ch. 8, p. 132 and the starred note. Voltaire's original referred to those philosophers who had written "only the romance of the soul," while Locke gave it its "history": Voltaire, *Letters concerning the English Nation* [1733], ed. Nicolas Cronk (Oxford, Voltaire Foundation, 1994), pp. 98–9. For a broader overview of the interest in Hobbes in eighteenth-century France, see Yves Glaziou, *Hobbes en France au xviiie siècle* (Paris, Presses universitaires de France, 1993).

ers' help to be able to survive but would soon see that "dominion," not cooperation, was the easiest way to acquire the necessities of life. The desire for others' approval might equally well lead the same robust child to seek others' company, but if everyone were esteemed, no one would be more esteemed. This, Hobbes had argued, was why the real ties of society had to be maintained by a representative sovereign state and the fear that the overwhelming force of a political union could establish and maintain.[30]

Both Montesquieu and Rousseau had rejected Hobbes's starting point. Montesquieu, at the beginning of *The Spirit of Laws*, had made joint recognition of the visible signs of fear an initial cause of human association and, in making fear the principle of a despotic government, had separated it off from the broader range of emotional motivations underlying other, less brutally natural, forms of political rule. Rousseau went one step further by denying that humans had any natural reason to be fearful, still less any natural reason for enlisting others' help or seeking others' company for reasons of need or vainglory. These sceptical moves made it easier to open up more room for something other than Hobbes's state-centred solution to the problem of social stability because they pushed back Hobbes's two primary motivations for society to later stages in the sequence linking natural human attributes to acquired social and political arrangements. For Montesquieu, the ideas of primogeniture and indivisible inheritance had some similarity to Hobbes's idea of vainglory, but they were the historical result of the way that inheritance had come, fortuitously, to be connected to a property-based form of dispute settlement. For Rousseau, the reflective nature of the general will presupposed a nonnatural human capacity for self-reflection that, once it had come into being, could then be used to allow the acquired emotion of pride or *amour-propre* to be translated into patriotism and anchored to the emotional dynamics of family life. Helvétius went back to Hobbes's starting point but denied that it had to lead to Hobbes's outcome. "Interest and want," he wrote in *De l'homme*, "are the principles of all sociability."[31] But, he argued, the combination was not entirely self-defeating because it contained the seeds of the multiple forms of human association that made the division of labour work. The primary motivations underlying human association might well be, as Hobbes had claimed, need (or "want") and pride (or "interest"), not love, or language, or fellow feeling, but they could, nonetheless, give rise to stable, broadly egalitarian societies. Although there would still be states, they would not have to have the same primary responsibility for maintaining social stability as they did in Hobbes's political thought.

[30] Thomas Hobbes, *The Citizen: Philosophical Rudiments concerning Government and Society* [1642], ed. Bernard Gert (Indianapolis, Hackett, 1991), pp. 110–3.
[31] Helvétius, *Treatise on Man*, vol. 1, sec. 2, ch. 8, p. 133.

Going back to Hobbes meant rejecting the way that Rousseau had rein-
troduced Hobbes's two primary motivations for society at a later stage of
the conjectural history of his second *Discourse*. Need and *amour-propre*,
Rousseau argued, were not the original causes of human association, but,
once they fused, they would generate the spiral of escalating interdependence that led to the despotic outcome of the false social contract. Need
itself was not a natural motivation for society. In the warm, fertile setting
of the South, it would be easy enough for isolated individuals to find food
and shelter. In the less hospitable environment of the North, it would ac-
centuate human dispersal because a poor climate and an arid soil would
force individuals to move further apart to forage for food. Pride, too, began
as something that was generic to the human race because it was based on
comparisons between humans and animals. The "first movement of pride,"
Rousseau wrote, involved a human "considering himself in the first rank
of species," but it would not involve being able "to claim first rank as an
individual."[32] The kind of calculating capacity that enabled individuals to
outwit animals would also supply a basis for rudimentary human cooperation and the primitive linguistic skills required to enable individuals to hunt
together. The use of simple implements would also allow them to make
shelters and live in the relatively settled society of the family. The result
was the first acquisition of leisure and the conveniences it could provide.
Once acquired, they would soon become necessities, and, if the initial pleasure associated with their acquisition might soon be forgotten, the pain
involved in their loss would be no less intense. Isolated families could
survive quite well, but an accident like an earthquake or a flood might
force them into more extensive interaction with one another, giving
rise to more general language use. Only then would *amour-propre* begin.
Permanent proximity would lead to casual encounters, particularly among
the young. Once they began to make comparisons, they would "acquire
ideas of merit and beauty which produce sentiments of preference." Song
and dance, "true children of love and leisure," would lead to circumstances
in which everyone "began to look at everyone else and to wish to be looked
at himself, and public esteem acquired a price."[33] In his *Essay on the Origins
of Languages*, Rousseau added a geographical direction to the temporal sequence, so that it ran, by way of rising population and migration, from
the South to the North, and then, by way of conquest and colonisation,
proceeded to flow back again. By then, humanity was inside Hobbes's
state of nature.

---

[32] Rousseau, *Second Discourse*, in Jean-Jacques Rousseau, *The Social Contract and Other Later
Political Writings*, ed. Victor Gourevitch (Cambridge, CUP, 1997), p. 162.
[33] Rousseau, *Second Discourse*, ed. Gourevitch, p. 166.

Rousseau divided the state of nature into two distinct periods. The first consisted of societies made up of independent households and a reciprocal division of labour. The second consisted of societies made up of interdependent households and a social division of labour. This was where the passions that Hobbes had described as primary began to take hold. So long as men "applied themselves only to tasks a single individual could perform and to arts that did not require the collaboration of several hands," Rousseau wrote, they could live "free, healthy, good and happy" lives. But "the moment that one man needed the help of another" and "as soon as it was found to be necessary to be useful for one to have provisions for two, equality disappeared, property appeared, work became necessary," and "slavery and misery were soon seen to sprout and grow together with the harvests."[34] Then all the capacities for comparison, reflection, and calculation that humans had acquired would come into play. The switch from the first, good, division of labour to its second, bad, counterpart began with metallurgy. Although its origins were obscure, its effects were easy to work out. "As soon as men were needed to melt and forge iron, others were needed to feed them." Since the producers of agricultural goods now had to feed more than themselves, they had to make the land produce more. Metallurgy accordingly came to be applied to agriculture. "Thus arose on the one hand ploughing and agriculture, and on the other the art of working metals and multiplying their uses."[35] Once the land began to be cultivated, property followed. Anyone who might have tried to establish it right at the start, Rousseau wrote famously, would have been denounced as an impostor. But, he continued, "in all likelihood things had by then reached a point where they could not continue as they were" before "this last stage of the state of nature was reached."[36] Once there was property, "the first rules of justice necessarily followed."[37] But differences in needs and natural ability made it impossible to render each his own and still maintain equality. Some would produce more than others, while some goods were needed more than others. Even with the same amount of work, some would do well, while others would barely be able to stay alive. "Things having reached this point," Rousseau concluded, "it is easy to imagine the rest." He decided, nonetheless, to leave little to the imagination.

Looked at in another way, man, who had previously been free and independent, is now subjugated by a multitude of new needs to the whole of nature, and especially to those of his kind, whose slave he in a sense becomes even by

---

[34] Rousseau, *Discourse on Inequality*, in Jean-Jacques Rousseau, *The Discourses and Other Early Political Writings*, ed. Victor Gourevitch (Cambridge, CUP, 1997), p. 167.

[35] Rousseau, *Discourse on Inequality*, ed. Gourevitch, p. 169.

[36] Rousseau, *Discourse on Inequality*, ed. Gourevitch, p. 161.

[37] Rousseau, *Discourse on Inequality*, ed. Gourevitch, p. 169.

becoming their master; rich, he needs their services; poor, he needs their help, and moderate means do not enable him to do without them. He must therefore constantly try to interest them in his fate and to make them really or apparently find their own profit in working for his: which makes him knavish and artful with some, imperious and harsh with the rest and places him under the necessity of deceiving all those he needs if he cannot get them to fear him and does not find it in his interest to make himself useful to them. Finally, consuming ambition, the ardent desire to raise one's relative fortune less out of genuine need than in order to place oneself above others, instils in all men a black inclination to harm another, a secret jealousy that is all the more dangerous as it often assumes the mask of benevolence in order to strike its blow in greater safety: in a word, competition and rivalry on the one hand, conflict of interests on the other, and always the hidden desire to profit at another's expense; all these evils are the first effects of property, and the inseparable train of nascent inequality.[38]

From this point, the same self-defeating mechanisms that Hobbes had placed at the heart of his conception of the state of nature came into play. But since, for Rousseau, they were acquired, not primary, they could be overcome. An authentic social contract, engineered by a skilful legislator, offered the possibility of an alternative to the unitary power of a representative sovereign as the way out.

Helvétius's reply to Rousseau looked towards the same outcome but relied on Hobbes's own premises. It was based on a claim that the two initial motivations that led humans to associate were not as self-defeating as Hobbes had asserted. The key move was to put the two together and to show how the combination of need and vainglory would give rise to social differentiation and a multiplicity of different sources of self-esteem. If, according to Helvétius, feelings were judgements, but judgements required corroboration from others to be made secure, then humans were sociable despite themselves. The kind of sociability that this would entail would, however, be local and partial all the way through. But the very partiality of human association could become the basis of many different kinds of social distinction under the aegis of a government that helped to maintain them all. Helvétius could, accordingly, drop Rousseau's distinction between *amour-de-soi* and *amour-propre* (he seems to have made a point of using the two terms entirely indiscriminately) because it had no real purchase on explaining human motivation.[39] The distinction overlooked the way that humans were saturated by judgements right from the start. Rousseau's claim

---

[38] Rousseau, *Discourse on Inequality*, ed. Gourevitch, pp. 170–1.

[39] See, particularly, his discussion in *De l'esprit* of La Rochefoucauld's notion of *amour-propre*, which Helvétius recurrently renamed as *amour-de-soi*. Helvétius, *De l'esprit*, ed. Châtelet, First Discourse, ch. 4, pp. 44–6.

that the solitary humanoids of the first state of nature would be able to pick up the information required to meet their survival needs from animals simply transferred the problem to another level. Unless humans had the same kind of instincts that animals appeared to have (a claim that Rousseau never made), the real human problem was to find a way to make any judgement secure. If, Helvétius argued, humans were natural sceptics, then they would have been the most sociable of creatures. To illustrate the idea, he picked out the philosopher Carneades, the figure with whom Rousseau was sometimes identified and the symbol of the scepticism that, from Grotius onwards, modern natural jurisprudence was taken to have displaced. If, Helvétius argued, humans really were like Carneades, they would know how little trust they could place in either their own or others' judgements, and, tolerantly, would simply accept their common shortcomings.[40] But the need to find corroboration from others for one's own point of view ruled out the sceptic's inner serenity. Peace of mind and confirmation of the self underlying self-love (or *amour-de-soi*) had to come from the outside.

Two causes, Helvétius argued, served to stabilise this state of affairs. The first was vanity, or the pleasure associated with finding that others shared one's own judgement or individual point of view. The second was laziness, or the pain associated with struggling to maintain an independent judgement or individual point of view.[41] Both played a part in generating the two kinds of esteem that served to stabilise human judgements. The first was what Helvétius called "esteem upon trust," meaning the ordinary lip service paid to established judgements (that Newton, for example, was a great philosopher). The second was "felt-esteem" or the esteem "produced solely by the impression made on us by certain ideas."[42] The first kind of esteem did not need to rely on real knowledge or understanding. *Amour-propre* was satisfied when individual judgements coincided with the judgements of others. Felt-esteem, on the other hand, involved a real concern for truth. But indolence made it hard to avoid giving this kind of esteem to anything that looked too dissimilar to an already established set of beliefs. The result was a powerful tendency to conform. Vanity and laziness would ensure that individual judgements would coincide with prevailing notions of utility. "Each individual," Helvétius wrote, "judges things and persons by means of the agreeable or disagreeable impression that he receives from them. The public is simply an assemblage of individuals. It can never take anything other than its utility for the rule of its judgements." This point of view, he continued, "was the only correct way to think about the properties of the mind, to appreciate the merit of any

---

[40] Helvétius, *De l'esprit*, ed. Châtelet, First Discourse, ch. 1, p. 23, note 6.

[41] Helvétius, *De l'esprit*, ed. Châtelet, Second Discourse, ch. 4, p. 67.

[42] Helvétius, *De l'esprit*, ed. Châtelet, Second Discourse, ch. 4, pp. 67–8 (pp. 33–4).

idea, to fix the uncertainty of our judgements on a single point, and to explain the astonishing variety of men's opinions in matters of mind."[43] Humans were driven to find confirmation of their own judgements in the judgements of others but were able to find that confirmation only in judgements that fitted their own. The circularity of the process explained both the partiality of patterns of belief and the slow pace of human improvement. Only occasionally might a point of view that was at odds with prevailing norms come to be incorporated into ordinary private judgements. It would do so gradually and incrementally, as its utility became apparent. But general judgements about utility were always likely to be limited. The larger the number of local ties there were between particular sets of individuals, the greater the number of obstacles there would be to any more general capacity to evaluate utility.

The local and partial character of human judgements did, however, contain the possibility of a correcting mechanism. "Truth," Helvétius wrote, "is never engendered and perceived, but in the fermentation of contrary opinions."[44] Contrary opinions could simply coexist. But they could also produce change because of the various kinds of feeling to which they might give rise. Although all feelings were judgements, some feelings were still more powerful than others. Helvétius used four terms to describe feelings. In ascending order of intensity, these were sensations, sentiments, desires, and passions.[45] The first, a sensation, was simply an effect of nature, like a feeling of hunger or thirst. The second, or a sentiment, presupposed the existence of society because, as with the feeling of ambition or pride, or the love of luxury, it involved comparison. Memory kept a sentiment alive. The imagination, or a combination of different memories, did the same for a desire. A desire, or the third type of feeling, was a sentiment fixed by the imagination on an absent object, while the fourth type, or a passion, was a desire that dominated every other desire. A passion was, therefore, something that can be described as a sensation reinforced by a sentiment and compounded by a desire. It was something that could override every other type of feeling. "The despotic power, if I may be allowed the term," Helvétius wrote, "of a desire to which all the others are subordinate, is therefore in us what characterizes passion."[46] It was the type of feeling that could break out of the circle of conformity in which ordinary judgements were trapped. This, according to Helvétius, was why the passions were the great engine of change in human affairs. "Passions," he wrote, "are in the moral, what motion is in the natural world."

[43] Helvétius, *De l'esprit*, ed. Châtelet, Second Discourse, ch. 1, p. 55.
[44] Helvétius, *De l'esprit*, ed. Châtelet, First Discourse, ch. 9, p. 98 (p. 53).
[45] Helvétius, *De l'esprit*, ed. Châtelet, Fourth Discourse, ch. 2, pp. 388–9 (p. 250–1).
[46] Helvétius, *De l'esprit*, ed. Châtelet, Fourth Discourse, ch. 2, p. 389 (p. 251).

If motion creates, destroys, preserves, animates the whole, that without it every thing is dead, so the passions animate the moral world. It is avarice which conducts ships over the deserts of the ocean; it is pride which fills up valleys, levels mountains, hews itself a passage through rocks, raises the pyramids of Memphis, digs the lake Moeris, and casts the Colossus of Rhodes.[47]

It was therefore "to strong passions that we owe the invention and wonders of arts; and consequently they are to be considered as the germ productive of genius and the powerful spring that carries men to great actions."[48] Only a strong passion, Helvétius argued, "which being more enlightened than mere good sense, can teach us to distinguish the extraordinary from the possible, which men of sense are forever confounding." A strong passion would have the effect of fixing our attention "on the object of our desire," causing us "to view it under appearances unknown to other men."[49] This emotionally generated capacity to look at the familiar from a fresh point of view was what "prompted heroes to plan and execute those hardy enterprises which, till success has proved the propriety of them, appear ridiculous, and indeed must appear so to the multitude."[50] But, Helvétius observed, there were "few men of strong passions and but few capable of lively sentiments."[51]

The way that feelings could increase in intensity as they decreased in variety was the starting point of the other aspect of Helvétius's reply to Rousseau. If feelings were judgements, humans were naturally overwhelmed with judgements. They were trapped in a circular process in which the frequency and variety of first-order judgements forced them to rely on others for local and partial corroboration. The process explained the huge and often bizarre assortment of human conceptions of utility. But if the frequency and variety of feelings could be reduced, the intensity and accuracy of judgements could grow. The great changes that occurred in human history were, Helvétius argued, an effect of strong passions. But strong passions could also be an effect of specialised activity. Specialisation could have the effect of concentrating the mind and, by doing so, could work against the natural human propensity to conform. Since even the routine associated with doing the same thing could give rise to efforts to escape boredom by thinking against the grain of received ideas, specialisation could be the antidote to, rather than the cause of, the dynamics of competitive comparison that Rousseau had taken to be the force underlying inequality in all of its several dimensions. From this perspective, the

---

[47] Helvétius, *De l'esprit*, ed. Châtelet, Third Discourse, ch. 6, p. 240 (p. 149).
[48] Helvétius, *De l'esprit*, ed. Châtelet, Third Discourse, ch. 6, p. 240 (p. 150).
[49] Helvétius, *De l'esprit*, ed. Châtelet, Third Discourse, ch. 6, p. 245 (p. 153).
[50] Helvétius, *De l'esprit*, ed. Châtelet, Third Discourse, ch. 6, p. 245 (p. 153).
[51] Helvétius, *De l'esprit*, ed. Châtelet, Fourth Discourse, ch. 2, p. 389 (p. 251).

self-centred emotional spiral that Rousseau had described could be blocked. Selfishness or *amour-propre* would still be there, but it would be split up into a number of different sources of self-esteem. Strong passions concentrated the mind. As Helvétius presented it, the division of labour did, artificially, the one thing that humans were not naturally equipped to do. It forced them to pay attention. In this sense, it was an artificial antidote to the natural volatility of human judgements and the way to put strong passions to social purposes.

Helvétius combined this idea with another well-established claim about human nature. As well as having senses, humans also had hands. "If nature, instead of putting hands and flexible fingers at the ends of our wrists, had put horses' hooves instead," he wrote at the very beginning of *De l'esprit*, "who would not doubt that men, with no arts, no fixed abodes, no defence against animals and entirely taken up with the cares of getting food and avoiding wild beasts, would still be roaming the forests like errant flocks?"[52] But for "a certain kind of external organisation," the human faculties of memory and sensibility would have been entirely sterile, and no human society would ever have managed to go beyond the very simplest sort of community.[53] Since, however, humans were natural tool-makers, they could interact with the external environment in ways that went beyond the capacity of other living beings. This capacity for invention explained why humans could respond creatively to painful circumstances, and why, when pressed by either boredom or necessity (boredom, Helvétius emphasised, was a uniquely human emotion), some human judgements could be genuinely innovative. But if boredom and need pushed in favour of innovation, vanity and laziness pulled in favour of conformity. The answer was to put the two together. Some individuals might have an aptitude (or *génie*) for doing one thing rather than another. Simply enabling them to do what they did best would be the easiest way to allow them to meet their need for others' approval and enable them to avoid the discomfort of having to pit themselves too strongly against prevailing norms. Excellence and diversity could then go hand in hand. The kind of specialised activity involved in the division of labour would work with the grain of the human propensity to set passions above desires, desires above sentiments, and sentiments above sensations. Nor was there any reason to think that there were limits to how far the process of social specialisation might go. Aptitudes were acquired, not innate, and could, in principle, be learned by anyone. As Helvétius put it in a note written before he began to write *De l'esprit*, "every mind is fit for everything in the same proportion as it is fit

---

[52] Helvétius, *De l'esprit*, ed. Châtelet, First Discourse, ch. 1, pp. 19–20.
[53] Helvétius, *De l'esprit*, ed. Châtelet, First Discourse, ch. 1, p. 21.

for one thing."[54] Indirectly, the effects of specialisation might be useful and, as was always the case in matters of utility, public opinion would decide. Public opinion might often be wrong, particularly if it was distorted by the local and partial views produced by pockets of power and inequality, but in the long run specialisation might bring individual and general utility into alignment.

Helvétius paid a heavy personal price for *De l'esprit*. The huge controversy that it generated, the part that it was thought to have played in causing his death in 1771, and the salon kept by his widow until well into the period of the French Revolution all did something to keep its argument alive. The argument injected a stronger normative dimension into the picture of human diversity set out in Montesquieu's *Spirit of Laws*. The reason why morality seemed, as Helvétius put it, "scarcely to have left its cradle" was that "men having been forced to unite in society, and to give themselves laws, were obliged to form a system of morality before they had learnt from observation its true principles."[55] If society was simply a de facto by-product of interest and want, then the principles of morality were another subject altogether. They could, in the most general sense, be described as utility. But if utility really was the principle underlying every type of human association, then the fit between individual and general utility had to be based on equality. Here, too, Helvétius argued, Hobbes had been right. If, he wrote in *De l'homme*, "the superiority of mind consists principally, as Mr Hobbes remarked, in the knowledge of the true signification of words," and if, as he claimed he had shown in *De l'esprit*, "all men equally well organised are, as I have proved, endowed with a memory sufficient to exalt them to the highest ideas," then private judgement and general utility could, in the long run, come to coincide.[56] If, he wrote in *De l'esprit*, every discovery were to be made in every branch of knowledge, then "all would be science and every branch of wit (*esprit*) would be impossible, for we should have ascended up even to the first principles of things." We would then, he continued, "possess all the materials of politics and legislation" and be able to extract "from all histories the small number of principles, which being proper to preserve among mankind the greatest equality possible, would one day give birth to the best form of government."[57]

The goal to which the argument pointed was the exact opposite of Rousseau's second *Discourse*. For Helvétius, inequality was an effect of the un-

---

[54] The note reads "que tout esprit est propre à tout dans la même proportion où il est propre à une chose": Keim, *Notes de la main d'Helvétius*, p. 28.

[55] Helvétius, *De l'esprit*, ed. Châtelet, Second Discourse, ch. 23, p. 184 (p. 112).

[56] Helvétius, *Treatise on Man*, vol. 1, sec. 2, ch. 9, p. 151, referring back to *De l'esprit*, Third Discourse, ch. 3.

[57] Helvétius, *De l'esprit*, ed. Châtelet, Fourth Discourse, ch. 3, p. 395 (p. 256).

avoidably premature character of human association, and, in the long run, specialisation might bring it to an end. Existing inequalities might one day give way to a more general system of human well-being, particularly if the prosperity of the large territorial states of the modern world could be combined with the smaller-scale political units and patriotism of the ancients. A large country like France, Helvétius suggested in *De l'homme*, might be divided into thirty provinces or republics, making it impossible for any one of the parts of the federal system of government to dominate the others.[58] The guarded, but comprehensive, treatment of the subject of luxury that he set out at the beginning of *De l'esprit* prefigured this broader message. After setting out the various arguments for and against luxury, Helvétius made it clear that both positions presupposed the existence of inequality, and that it was this that was the real subject at issue. Without inequality, he argued, there would be no luxury, even in a very rich society. There would instead be what, in *De l'homme*, he called "national luxury."[59] "In the hive of human society," he continued there, "to preserve order and justice, and to chase away vice and corruption, it is necessary that all the individuals be equally employed and forced to concur equally in the general good, and that the labour be equally divided among them."[60] It followed that the equality of the ancients could be combined with the opulence of the moderns without having to give rise to the moral and political dilemmas associated with the subject of luxury. But, apart from a brief, later allusion to David Hume's 1752 essay entitled *Idea of a Perfect Commonwealth* in his *De l'homme*, Helvétius did not have much to say about how the small units making up a federal system of government would manage their political and economic relationships, or how the federation itself might be able to maintain both opulence and equality in tandem.[61] Significantly, at least from the point of view of Helvétius's presence in Roederer's imaginary philosophical conversation, Hume's essay also contained a plan for a system of gradual promotion (or for "refining" democracy, as Hume put it) that was somewhat similar to the one that Rousseau set out in his proposals for a reformed Polish system of government.[62]

Rousseau saw the point of Helvétius's argument very well. Helvétius's master, he wrote in the critical summary of *De l'esprit* that he included in

[58] Claude-Adrien Helvétius, *De l'homme* [London, 1773], 2 vols. (Paris, Fayard 1989), vol. 2, sec. IX, ch. 2, pp. 750–1. See, too, Helvétius, *Treatise on Man*, vol. 2, sec. IX, ch. 2, p. 278.

[59] Helvétius, *Treatise on Man*, vol. 2, sec. VI, ch. 5, p. 84.

[60] Helvétius, *Treatise on Man*, vol. 2, sec. VI, ch. 5, p. 88.

[61] Helvétius, *Treatise on Man*, vol. 2, sec. IX, ch. 2, p. 275.

[62] On Hume's proposals to "refine the democracy," see David Hume, "The idea of a perfect commonwealth" [1753], in Hume, *Essays: Moral, Political and Literary*, ed. Eugene F. Miller (Indianapolis, Liberty Press, 1985), p. 528.

his *Julie or the New Eloisa*, was Plato.[63] From this perspective, *De l'esprit* was a passion-based version of the combination of justice and the division of labour of Plato's *Republic*. As Rousseau summarised its argument, Helvétius had claimed that "all mankind are by nature susceptible of passions strong enough to excite in them that degree of attention necessary to a superiority of genius."[64] It followed that the character of any mind could be shaped by the education that it received, and that a society could be arranged in ways that fitted the purposes underlying its existence. Rousseau disagreed, arguing that societies should be arranged to fit different individual aptitudes, not that aptitudes should be arranged to fit social utility. Helvétius replied in kind. "M. Rousseau," he wrote in *De l'homme*, batting back the label that had been applied to himself, "being a too close imitator of Plato, has, perhaps, frequently sacrificed precision to eloquence."[65] He made a point of highlighting the similarity between Rousseau's thought and the moral-sense theory of the third earl of Shaftesbury. The affinity between the two, he suggested, was a product of their common commitment to the idea of the natural goodness of man. "No individual," Helvétius replied, "is born good or bad. Men are the one or the other according as a similar or opposed interest unites or divides them." Since self-love was "the necessary effect of our sensations," it followed that, "whatever the Shaftesburyians may say," our love for others was an effect of "the same faculty."[66]

It was not an entirely convincing reply. Even Helvétius did not go so far as to describe Rousseau straightforwardly as a moral-sense theorist, but, by insinuating that he was, he avoided the real point of Rousseau's argument. It was one that centred on the gradual emergence of the reflective mechanisms involved in the formation of the self, and on how, once one person had enough provisions for two, this would lead to a state of affairs in which individual survival needs would be locked into a system of social cooperation that favoured the rich, the propertied, and the powerful and, because it did, had to rely on hypocrisy to be able to work. The picture of the division of labour that Helvétius presented was quite compatible with the picture of the division of labour in Rousseau's first social state. The difficulty was to see whether it really could be taken beyond that point without having to bring back Hobbes's state-centred solution. This was the trap into which one of Helvétius's admirers, the future minister of the interior of the first French republic, Dominique-Joseph Garat, fell (he was

[63] Jean-Jacques Rousseau, *Julie, ou la Nouvelle Héloïse* [1761], in Rousseau, *Oeuvres complètes*, ed. Bernard Gagnebin and Marcel Raymond, vol. 2 (Paris, Pléiade, 1964), pt. V, letter 3, p. 565.

[64] Rousseau, *Julie*, in Rousseau, *Oeuvres*, 2:564–5. I have quoted from the contemporary translation, *Julia*, 3 vols. (Edinburgh, 1773), vol. 3, letter 137, pp. 150–1.

[65] Helvétius, *Treatise on Man*, vol. 2, sec. 5, p. 2.

[66] Helvétius, *Treatise on Man*, vol. 2, sec. 5, ch. 1, pp. 10–1.

to suggest, later, that Sieyès had superseded Hobbes).[67] In his entry in 1778 to a prize competition commemorating the career of the sixteenth-century French chancellor Michel De l'Hôpital, Garat argued that the development of the division of labour and the refinement of manners that it would produce would generate so strong a feeling of social revulsion about the misery of the poor that it would then be easy for a reforming royal sovereign to promote equality.[68] The argument fell fairly effortlessly into the difficulty that Rousseau had highlighted. The problem with representative sovereignty was not simply its power to do harm, but its power to do good.

A real reply to Rousseau had to accept more of his argument about the origins of inequality, but go on to show that inequality itself did not matter, or, if it did, that it could still be managed in ways that were consonant with justice. In *De l'homme*, Helvétius referred to one possible way of doing this. "The imagination of the people of the North," he wrote in a note rejecting the idea of environmentally generated differences between southern and northern nations that were a prominent feature of both Montesquieu's and Rousseau's conjectural histories, "is not less vigorous than those of the South. Compare the poems of Ossian to those of Homer."[69] For Rousseau, leisure gave the imagination room to develop. Once it also had surplus goods at its disposal, it could be deployed to work out how useful it might be for one person to have provisions for two and begin the gradual process of human self-enslavement. From Rousseau's perspective both began in the South. Although there were many other reasons for the widespread interest in Ossian and his putative poems in the second half of the eighteenth century, one of them had a great deal to do with the possibility that the picture of a primitive northern nation that Ossian presented also opened up a way to refute Rousseau on something like his own terms.[70]

Turgot

Ossian had a particular appeal to Rousseau's critics because it appeared to offer a sentimentalist alternative to the sentimentalist argument of the second *Discourse*. This made it easier to engage with Rousseau without having to fall back on more orthodox moral and political theory or rely on simply

---

[67] See Sieyès, *Political Writings*, ed. Sonenscher, pp. xlv–xlvi.

[68] See Dominique-Joseph Garat, *Éloge de M. de l'Hôpital, chancelier de France* (Paris, 1778).

[69] Helvétius, *Treatise on Man*, vol. 2, sec. 5, note 5, p. 61.

[70] The classic study of Ossian in France is by Paul Van Tieghem, *Ossian en France*, 2 vols. (Paris, 1917). For a recent overview, see Howard Gaskill, ed., *The Reception of Ossian in Europe* (London, Thoemmes Continuum, 2004), and, for other sorts of interest in Ossian, Fiona Stafford, *The Sublime Savage: James Macpherson and the Poems of Ossian* (Edinburgh, Edinburgh University Press, 1988).

dismissing Rousseau as a Hobbist. France's future controller general of finances, Anne-Robert-Jacques Turgot, was one of the spurious poet's early translators (as, too, were Diderot and one of Rousseau's other intellectual opponents, the literary critic and translator of William Robertson, Jean-Baptiste-Antoine Suard).[71] Some of the elements of the picture of the kind of stratified, but nonoriental, society that "Ossian" presented were carried through into the argument of the *Réflexions sur la formation et la distribution des richesses* (Reflections on the Formation and Distribution of Wealth) that Turgot published in 1766. There, Turgot set out to describe the multiple origins of the formation of wealth and to show that, if inequality had a number of separate, causally unrelated, starting points, it did not have to be projected forwards towards the single despotic outcome that Rousseau had presented. If, as Rousseau had argued, inequality began when one person had enough provisions for two, then describing the origins of a number of different types of inequality could be used to reinforce the idea that formal political and legal equality could coexist with real economic and social inequality without producing the kind of fusion of the rich, the propertied, and the powerful into a single dominant interest that Rousseau had described. If this was the case, then a multiplicity of social hierarchies could supply several somewhat different standards of judgement and subject the claims of justice to a number of different evaluations and competing points of view. Inequality might still matter, but it would not have to matter in quite the same way or end up by compromising justice itself. Nor, as Turgot emphasised privately, would justice have to entail the kind of self-interested egalitarianism that Helvétius had set out in *De l'esprit*.[72]

Turgot began the *Reflections* by attacking the idea of egalitarian reciprocity. "If the land were distributed among all the inhabitants of a country in such a way that each person had exactly, and no more than, what was needed for food," he wrote, "it is obvious that, everyone being equal, no one would have been willing to work for anyone else."[73] In conditions of real equality no one would have had the means to pay for anyone else's labour because everything that was produced would have been consumed by the producers themselves. Nor, Turgot continued, could this

[71] See his (anonymous) "Lettre adressée aux auteurs du *Journal étranger*," in *Journal étranger*, September 1760, pp. 3–16, reprinted in Anne Robert-Jacques-Turgot, *Oeuvres*, 5 vols. (Paris, 1913–9), ed. Gustave Schelle, 1:624–7. More generally, see Van Tieghem, *Ossian en France*, 1:103–35. Van Tieghem's own concern with romanticism and its origins meant that he missed the connection between Rousseau, the critics of his second *Discourse*, and the interest in Ossian (see *Ossian en France*, 1:216–9).

[72] For Turgot's scathing assessment of *De l'esprit* (which he compared unfavourably to Rousseau's own *"folies"*), see Turgot, *Oeuvres*, ed. Schelle, 3:636–41.

[73] Anne-Robert-Jacques Turgot, *Réflexions sur la formation et la distribution des richesses* [1766], ed. Joël-Thomas Ravix and Paul-Marie Romani (Paris, Flammarion, 1997), §i, p. 157.

state of affairs ever have really existed. Before it became privately owned, the land would have had to be cultivated because there would otherwise have been no reason to have divided it. If this were the case, then the cultivators of the land would probably have produced as much as they could without stopping at what was simply required for survival. Even if strict equality really had existed, Turgot added, it could not have lasted. No single piece of land could cater for all physical needs. Some types of land were better suited for supplying wood for heating or linen for clothing, while others were better for cereals or livestock. Reality, in short, was quite resistant to equality.

But reality was also quite compatible with the division of labour. Here, Turgot moved decisively away from the needs-based idea of the division of labour that both Rousseau and the Physiocrats had followed. Rousseau had argued that dependence on others for survival would, ultimately, lead to despotism. The Physiocrats had replied by claiming that legal despotism and a single tax on landed income could block that outcome. Rousseau, in his letter to Mirabeau, countered by arguing that the legal despot could not be separated from the whole system. In the last analysis, the needs of the state were also part of a self-centred system and, in emergency, its needs, too, would have to be met. Trying to block inequality in the way that the Physiocrats envisaged would simply lead to the greatest inequality of them all. Turgot turned his back on the whole argument but still did not move towards the kind of egalitarianism that Helvétius had envisaged. Instead, he developed an argument based on two different kinds of inequality. One kind of inequality was connected to human needs. But another kind was connected to the human desire for things that were decorative and ornamental. Although, Turgot argued, both kinds of inequality were compatible with the division of labour, they would not reinforce one another in the cumulative way that both Rousseau and the Physiocrats had argued that the combination of inequality and the division of labour was bound to do. The two kinds of inequality might, instead, cancel one another out. The result would not be equality. But the two kinds of inequality produced by the needs-based and money-based divisions of labour could still produce both upward and downward mobility within a stable social system.

Turgot first outlined the development of inequality as it had been described by both Rousseau and the Physiocrats. This sequence followed the logic of human needs. Meeting even the simplest of physical needs involved many different tasks. Wheat had to be turned into flour and then into bread. Wool had to be spun, woven, cut, and sewn. "If the same man whose land was to produce all these different things had to make them undergo all these different processes to meet his needs, it is certain that he would

succeed very badly," Turgot pointed out.[74] Just as reality favoured the exchange of the products of one type of land for those of another, so it also
favoured the exchange of the products of one type of work for those of
another. "Everyone gained from this arrangement, because each individual
who specialised in one kind of work succeeded much better in doing it."[75]
But, Turgot continued, it would still be the case that the cultivator would
occupy the key position in this interdependent network. Physical necessity
meant that humans had to eat before they wore shoes. Like Melon's corn-
producing island, "the cultivator can, absolutely speaking, do without the
work of the other workers, but no other worker can live unless the cultivator enables him to live." The work of the cultivator was, therefore, the
primary bond of society. "What his work produces beyond his personal
needs is," Turgot emphasised, "the sole source of the income that all the
other members of society receive in exchange for their work."[76] The surplus
generated by agriculture would be the first form of capital and would be
used to pay the wages or stipends, as Turgot called them, of the stipendiary
class. As population grew and private property became entrenched, the
initial split between agricultural producers and stipendiary manufacturers
would give way to a three-sided division among landowners, agricultural
producers, and the manufacturing sector. This first model of the development of the division of labour pointed towards the combination of the legal
despot and the single tax on landed income that Quesnay and Mirabeau
had established.

At this point, however, Turgot dropped the Physiocratic sequence. The
Reflections on the Formation and Distribution of Wealth has an awkward structure. After setting out and developing one proposition, Turgot went on to
introduce another, so that the work as a whole has three different analytical
components introduced at different stages of the whole argument. The
first of these centred on agriculture. The second centred on money, while
the third focussed on capital. After dealing with the first, Turgot back-
tracked to the second. This way of thinking about wealth was probably
supplied by the abbé Ferdinando Galiani's Della moneta of 1751, a work to
which Turgot referred soon after the publication of the Reflections.[77] "There
is," he wrote a quarter of the way through the Reflections, "another way of
being rich without having to work and without possessing land, which I
have not yet spoken of." This consisted of "living off the income of one's
money or from the interest drawn from money that is lent."[78] Money, he

[74] Turgot, Réflexions, §iii, p. 158.
[75] Turgot, Réflexions, §iv, p. 159.
[76] Turgot, Réflexions, §v, p. 160.
[77] Anne-Robert-Jacques Turgot, "Valeurs et monnaies" [1769], in Turgot, Réflexions, ed.
Ravix and Romani, p. 286.
[78] Turgot, Réflexions, §xxix, p. 174.

went on to argue, was not necessarily a part of the needs-based sequence that both Rousseau and the Physiocrats had presupposed. It did not have to be understood as a purely artificial sign that had been adopted by agreement in order to compare values and facilitate exchange. Gold and silver, Turgot suggested, could have become a universal money "without any arbitrary convention among men, without any law, but simply by the nature of things." They were not, "as many people have imagined, signs of value," because they had a value of their own.[79] Metals already had real utility before they were used in exchange: "their brilliance made them sought after for ornamentation and decoration (*parure*); their ductility and solidity made them more suitable for vases than earthenware."[80] They would be traded for these reasons before they came to be used to measure and compare the value of different types of goods. But once they began to be used as a measure of value, their own value would grow. "It is impossible," Turgot wrote, "that the eagerness with which everyone now sought to exchange their superfluous goods for gold or silver rather than for any other good would not have greatly increased the value of these two metals in exchange."[81]

Once there was money, the division of labour could also begin. Here, the sequence did not have to follow the one that both Rousseau and the Physiocrats had described. The initial decorative value of gold and silver made them exchangeable, but their acquired function as a measure of value gave them a further use that reinforced their initial attractiveness. Acquiring precious metals made sense, not just because they looked good but also because they had a real, additional use. The dual value that money came to have made it easier for buying and selling to become separate in space and time, which, in turn, made occupational specialisation a real possibility. "The use of money," Turgot wrote, "has greatly facilitated the separation of various tasks among the different members of society."[82]

> The more that money came to stand in for everything else, the more each individual, by devoting himself to the type of culture or industry that he had chosen, could rid himself of every care in meeting his other needs and think only of getting as much money as he could by selling his fruits or industry, certain in the knowledge that, with this money, he could have all the rest. It is thus that the use of money has prodigiously hastened the progress of society.[83]

Money made the division of labour work. But the leads and lags involved both in the separation between buying and selling and in the division of

---

[79] Turgot, *Réflexions*, §xliii, p. 183.
[80] Turgot, *Réflexions*, §xlii, p. 182.
[81] Turgot, *Réflexions*, §xlv, p. 184.
[82] Turgot, *Réflexions*, §xlviii, p. 186.
[83] Turgot, *Réflexions*, §xlviii, p. 186.

labour itself also supplied a mechanism for capital formation. Having money made it possible to save money. Once it had been saved, it could be used to increase the capacity to produce agricultural or manufactured goods. Once there was money, the needs-based sequence could be combined with the monetary-driven sequence under the more general aegis of the idea of capital.[84]

The idea of capital, which appeared halfway through the book, formed the third component of the analysis. "All the types of work involved in agriculture, industry, and commerce," Turgot observed, "require advances."[85] In every kind of work, the worker had to have tools of some kind, materials for the work at hand, and an ability to live until the product of the work was exchanged or sold. The simplest kinds of advance were purely natural.

> The first cultivator took the seeds that he sowed from the plants produced by the earth itself and, until the harvest came round, lived from hunting, or fishing, or gathering wild fruits; he captured or trapped animals wandering in the woods; he subjected or tamed them and made use of them, first for his own food, then to assist him in his work.[86]

Domesticated animals were the first real capital. At a time when there was still a large amount of unowned and uncultivated land, Turgot continued, one could have livestock without being a landowner. It was likely that the nations that had first begun to cultivate the land were those that had come across animals that were relatively easy to tame and had been able to give up the wandering and agitated life of hunting peoples. The pastoral life was more settled and provided more leisure. It offered more opportunity to study differences in terrain and the natural processes that formed the basis of the supply of food for livestock. It was perhaps for this reason, Turgot observed, that the Asian nations had been the first to cultivate the land, while those of America had remained hunters for so much longer.

If domesticated animals were one kind of capital, slaves were another. Either or both could be exchanged for land. If someone with a large amount of land wanted to increase its output, exchanging some of it for cattle or slaves would lead to higher production on the rest. Once there was money, the process would continue at a more rapid pace. Money itself could be substituted for livestock or slaves and used to buy in the goods required to increase the output of the land. The result would be a new way to measure the value of land. The price of a piece of land could be set against the amount of revenue that it would produce in a year, so that its

---

[84] Turgot, *Réflexions*, §§xlix–l, pp. 186–7.
[85] Turgot, *Réflexions*, §lii, p. 188.
[86] Turgot, *Réflexions*, §liii, p. 189.

purchase price could then be seen as a multiple of its annual revenue. Land whose purchase price was ten or twenty times its annual revenue would be less expensive than land with a thirty- or forty-year purchase. The yield on this capital could then be compared to the yield that other ways of using capital might produce. The returns might be higher and might come in more quickly, but the risks of loss might also be greater. The calculation would also have to include an assessment of the opportunity costs involved in using the capital in one way rather than another. There were, Turgot noted, five different ways of using capital. The safest investment would be in the land because the land itself would still be there, even if its revenue dried up. Lending money to wealthy individuals was almost as safe, but the capital might be lost if the individual in question became insolvent. Investments in agriculture, manufacturing industry, or trade might produce higher short-term returns, but might also carry higher risks. The rate of return from the land would set a floor under the returns from different kinds of investment. But as direct investment in the land increased and the number of years' purchase rose, the returns from the four other types of investment would become more attractive. The movement of capital from one type of investment to another would set a ceiling on prevailing rates of interest. This, Turgot observed, was the correct definition of circulation, the term that had been a prominent feature of the analyses of money and trade produced by Forbonnais and the Gournay group. "It is this continuous advance of, and return on, capitals," he wrote, "that constitutes *what should be called the circulation of money*, that useful and fertile circulation which gives life to all the work of society, which maintains movement and life in the political body, and which is very rightly compared to the circulation of blood in the animal body."[87]

This step allowed Turgot to establish a position midway between the strongly trade-based theory of prosperity and power developed by Forbonnais and the Gournay group and the strongly price-driven theory developed by Quesnay and Mirabeau. The key variable in Turgot's concept of circulation was the rate of interest, or the ratio between the available supply of monetary capital and the level of effective demand for money for investment. This meant that the solution to the long-term survival of a trade-based society was not, as Forbonnais had argued, trade itself, but the rate at which money could be converted into capital, either by saving directly or, in a more indirect sense, by saving on the expenditure involved in producing goods. From Turgot's point of view, the solution to the "rich country–poor country" problem was the savings rate, not the dynamics of capital flows and capital flights. The same point of view also applied to Physiocracy. Simply establishing a competitive advantage in the unit costs of pro-

---

[87] Turgot, *Réflexions*, §lxviii, p. 201.

ducing agricultural goods and, by doing so, reducing the price of internationally traded goods was not, in itself, a solution. Favourable trade and payments balances, Turgot argued, might well give rise to an increase in the amount of money in domestic circulation, and, if the circulation of goods and money were not obstructed by the wrong kind of fiscal system, this might well make a larger supply of money available for improvements in productivity in the next cycle of production. But this, in itself, would not necessarily prevent a trading economy from falling behind. The additional amount of money in circulation might actually cause interest rates to rise, not to fall, because the rise in prices produced by the increase in the supply of money might cause demand for cash to grow, leaving less money available to be lent, thus producing a credit squeeze. As Turgot emphasised, the value of money in circulation and the value of money in capital formation were driven by two entirely different principles. The first was a function of the supply of available cash. The second was a function of the total supply of available capital and the ease with which it could be converted into money. "It is these accumulated savings," he wrote, "that are offered to borrowers, and the more there are, the lower the rate of interest will be, unless the number of borrowers were to increase in proportion."[88]

This made the domestic determinants of the rate of interest—not the size of the trade or payments balances or even the amount of the net product—the fundamental engine of prosperity. It could be seen, Turgot wrote, as a kind of economic thermometer or "as a kind of level below which all work, all agriculture, all industry, and all trade would cease."[89] Like the sea, the lower it was to fall, the more land it would make available for cultivation, but the higher it was to rise, the larger the number of previously viable enterprises it would submerge. The rate of interest, Turgot argued, was a better proxy than population for measuring the general level of well-being of a society. A populous society, contrary to what Rousseau had claimed, was not necessarily a prosperous society. But one that was able to put its wealth to productive use was likely to be both. The rate of interest also had an even more far-reaching significance. The information that it supplied could be used to rebut the whole tradition, including both Rousseau and the Physiocrats, that had taken its cue from Fénelon and had highlighted the dangerously unbalanced character of the modern combination of trade, industry, and centralised government. "The spirit of thrift (*économie*) in a nation," Turgot noted, "tends without interruption to increase the sum of its capitals, to add to the number of lenders, and to reduce the number of borrowers." The habit of luxury, however, "does

---

[88] Turgot, *Réflexions*, §lxxix, p. 212.
[89] Turgot, *Réflexions*, §lxxxix, p. 217.

the exact opposite."[90] Since, he pointed out, the rate of interest had been falling in Europe over several centuries, it had to be concluded "that the spirit of thrift has been more general than the spirit of luxury."[91] Contrary to many received ideas, the great wealth of the modern world was not a synonym for luxury but an effect of the long-term excess of savings over consumption. The rich, Turgot commented, might well live beyond their means. But the proportion of the rich in any society was far outweighed by the much larger proportion of those who wanted to be rich, since, "in the present state of things, where all the land is occupied," the only way to get rich was to earn more or spend less.[92] This, Turgot argued, was what had actually happened. The relatively low level of prevailing interest rates was a sign that modernity's prosperity was an effect of its parsimony, not its prodigality.

This focus on the level of interest rates had a number of implications for policy. Here the two different types of division of labour, one generated by needs and the other by decoration and ornamentation, supplied a framework. It meant that two sets of individuals were able to live without having to work. The first were the landowners because they could lease out their land in return for a rent. The second were the owners of money because they could lend it out at interest. Both appeared to be in a position to supply the tax revenue required for the expenditure of the state. Articles simply bought for consumption, like furniture, jewellery, gold and silverware, paintings, or statues, all had a value, and, in a rich nation, the sum of those values could be quite considerable. They could all, if necessary, be converted into money and, in this sense, form a reserve that could be tapped for public use. But this did not mean that the wealth of the capitalists was as available (*disponible*) as the wealth of the landowners. All landowners, as Turgot put it, could be capitalists, but not all capitalists had to be landowners. Only the income of the landowners was income that was really available. The capitalists might, in a personal sense, be available because, like the owners of land, they did not play any direct part in the production and distribution of wealth, but their property was still part of the broader process of circulation. Landed property, however, retained its productive capacity irrespective of whether its products were actually circulating at any particular moment in time. Taxing capital would have the effect of reducing its supply and of pushing up interest rates. Taxing the land would still leave all its physical properties intact. "In a word," Turgot concluded, "the capitalist who lends money has to be considered as a merchant of a commodity that is absolutely necessary for the produc-

[90] Turgot, *Réflexions*, §lxxx, p. 212.
[91] Turgot, *Réflexions*, §lxxxi, p. 212.
[92] Turgot, *Réflexions*, §lxxxi, p. 212.

tion of wealth and that cannot be too low in price." It would, he stressed, be as unreasonable to burden his trade with a tax as it would be to lay a tax on the manure used to fertilise the land.[93] It followed that the whole tax burden had to fall upon the shoulders of the landowners. Theirs was the only truly available wealth and the only kind of wealth that a government could tax without interfering with the supply of capital to agriculture, industry, and trade.

The conclusion aligned Turgot with Physiocracy. But, as the marquis de Mirabeau understood, Turgot's recognition of the independent status of money and capital ruled out a straightforward reversion to needs and utility as the long-term goal of a genuinely Physiocratic transformation of society. The two types of division of labour underlying the formation and distribution of wealth that he identified brought him nearer to Forbonnais and the Gournay group. But instead of relying on the dynamics of foreign trade and the international capital markets for prosperity and power, Turgot highlighted the need to rely on domestic savings and investment and the ceaseless conversion of capital into money and money into capital to reach the same goal. Taxing the landowners would mean that the price of land would include the prevailing level of tax rates. This would reduce the rate of return on direct investments in the land and prevent demand for land from pushing up the general level of interest rates. This, in turn, would have the effect of making investments in agriculture, manufacturing industry, and trade more attractive. But the security and stability of landed investments would still set a ceiling on the movement of capital into other types of investment. Inequality would not go away, but it did not have to be connected particularly strongly to the ownership of land. Nor, if the long-term movement of interest rates was any guide, was it true that inequality had been increasing. Instead, the effects of the two different types of division of labour had been to neutralise one another, leaving a fairly stable hierarchy of ranks in place. If, as Montesquieu had claimed, monarchy was a system of government made up of a single ruler and a number of subordinate, dependent, and intermediate powers, then, after Turgot, it was possible to think about the nature and composition of those intermediate powers in a considerably different way.

CHASTELLUX

Chastellux amplified on this new emphasis on the multiple sources of inequality. The broad argument of the *Essay on Public Happiness* that he published in 1772 began with Helvétius. The "sole end of all government,"

---

[93] Turgot, *Réflexions*, §xcv, pp. 222–3.

Chastellux wrote, was "the greatest happiness of the greatest number of individuals."[94] One could evaluate this, he argued, by measuring the range of goods available to both individuals and states. Individuals had needs, but so, too, did states, and the two could often clash. Making an assessment of the well-being of both was the province of "the science of economics." The first step (one that probably took its cue from a chapter in *De l'homme* dealing with the employment of time) was to answer the question "[H]ow many days in the year, or hours in the day, can a man work without either incommoding himself or becoming unhappy?" The second was "how many days must a man work in the year, or how many hours must he work in the day, to procure for himself that which is necessary to his preservation and his ease?"[95] Once these upper and lower limits were defined, it would then be possible to establish

> how many days in the year, or how many hours in the day, may remain for this man to dispose of: that is to say, how many may be demanded of him, without robbing him either of the means of subsistence or welfare: so that, now, the whole matter rests upon an examination, whether the performance of that duty, which the sovereign exacts from him, be within, or beyond the time which each man can spare from his absolutely necessary avocations.[96]

The idea presupposed the existence of a division of labour based on equality. As Chastellux put it, "we must imagine that every part of the labour, exercised throughout the state, is equally divided amongst a set of individuals." If everyone worked in one way or another, it would then be possible to measure the amount of time an individual had available for his own welfare and "what time he hath left upon his hands to be disposed of in the service of his sovereign."[97] This remaining time, Chastellux wrote, was what properly should be called the *net revenue*. It did not have any necessary connection with the agriculture and the land, but was simply time that was really available for public service. If the sovereign were to encroach on the time required for the subject's "own proper use," then the "fruits of all his industry and culture" would fall into decay, to the ultimate detriment of both.[98] This broad model did not presuppose any distinction between different types of wealth or make any discrimination between productive and

---

[94] Chastellux, *Essay*, 2:112, 124, 180. This translation of "le plus grand bonheur du plus grand nombre d'individus" is given in the third of the three passages in which the phrase occurs.

[95] Chastellux, *Essay*, 1:44. Compare to Helvétius, *Treatise on Man*, vol. 2, sec. viii. ch. 2, pp. 196–201 ("Of the employment of time").

[96] Chastellux, *Essay*, 1:44–5.

[97] Chastellux, *Essay*, 1:45

[98] Chastellux, *Essay*, 1:46.

unproductive labour. It implied, as Chastellux put it, "a new system of science, hitherto unknown."[99]

> The examination of nature and of her fixed, immutable and necessary laws, should be the first foundation of all knowledge, the *initium sapientiae*. From these primary notions of nature, one might proceed to her principal productions and, at length, to her circumscribed and individuated operations. *Andrology*, or the knowledge of man in general, would serve as the basis to medicine, natural history and morality, and these would give birth to politics, which would prove to be the result of all the others. It is then that an absolute *Physiocracy* would arise, a government founded on the powers of nature and the energy of her action.[100]

It was Say's *onéologie* under an earlier name.

Having established this broad framework, Chastellux did not, however, set out to show how it could be applied. The aim of the *Essay on Public Happiness* was, rather, to indicate the distance between the analytical construct and every actually existing political society. As with Helvétius, the emphasis fell on the unavoidably premature character of human association and the many different versions of utility that this entailed. "We generally err," Chastellux noted, "by considering things too abstractedly, and by squaring our notions with certain expressions, which are frequently no more than figures, or abridged formularies, serving to collect our ideas."[101] This propensity to rush to judgement lay behind most human conflict. The way out was not to set the passions against the interests, because the two were usually synonymous, but to identify a form of government capable of neutralising the human capacity for conflict. The largely fabulous monarchies of ancient Egypt, Chastellux acknowledged, did offer some grounds for believing that "whatever the nature of man may be, good laws and excellent administration can suppress the propensities to war."[102] Conjecture could explain how the combination of land that was irrigated by the Nile and the relatively limited demand for housing and clothing that went along with Egypt's climate could have produced the civilisation responsible for building the Pyramids, but it also confirmed the parameters of the general model, because the great ancient monarchies were the exception, not the norm. Agriculture in the ancient world was never capable of producing a durable enough surplus to meet the needs of both states and their members in a sustainable way. Its recurrent failure to meet the demands generated by rising population meant that most of the political societies of antiq-

---

[99] Chastellux, *Essay*, 1:142–3 (p. 195).
[100] Chastellux, *Essay*, 1:143 (p. 195)
[101] Chastellux, *Essay*, 2:115 (p. 372).
[102] Chastellux, *Essay*, 1:29.

uity were a product of the migrations and settlements produced by the precarious balance between population and subsistence goods. This, Chastellux emphasised, revealed a significant fact. "It is that all the governments of antiquity, except the great ancient monarchies, the origin of which we are ignorant of, owe their birth to a town, to a city."[103]

> The more individuals are disseminated over the surface of the earth, the more are they occupied in procuring their subsistence, either by the chase, or the cultivation of the ground; the less, also, do they want a legislation. On the other hand, the more they are united, the more the circumstances which draw them to each other, are multiplied, and the more are they constrained to have recourse to treaties and conventions. The result, therefore, is that the first want of every society, must have been the want of a polity and that all governments began by being no more than a simple polity. In this instance it, particularly, appears that language serves to explain facts, and not that facts serve to explain the language. *Politeia* amongst the Greeks, and *civitas* amongst the Romans, signified originally only the government of a city, although they were, afterwards, supposed to mean everything which appertained to an administration in general and, in the present times, by the word 'polity' may be understood the government of men, in opposition to the term 'administration', which, rather, signifies the government of properties.[104]

Ancient governments ruled both people and property. Only the moderns had managed to find a way to separate the two. It followed that history had to be the real guide for thinking about politics, not the abstractions produced by both Rousseau and the Physiocrats. Chastellux highlighted the fundamental similarity between them, describing both as "some modern semi-politicians" (*certains demi-politiques modernes*) who, like Thomas Hobbes, had succumbed to "vain sophisms" about the "unity and plenitude of power" either "in a single man or in an assembly of the people" before going on to dismiss the system of legal despotism and *évidence* as "frivolous ideas."[105] "Let it not be doubted," he wrote, "that agriculture should be the first object of legislators and property the leading principle of agriculture."[106] If this were the case, then human societies really would have passed through a sequence of natural stages. The "first expenses, whether of money or labour," would have led to small-scale human associations. These initial outlays would have established the first right of property, and property in turn "would not have failed to have introduced plenty and variety

---

[103] Chastellux, *Essay*, 1:123.

[104] Chastellux, *Essay*, 1:123–4.

[105] Chastellux, *De la félicité publique*, ed. Basoni, pp. 495–6. The passage in question is from a postscript to the 1776 edition, published after the English translation.

[106] Chastellux, *Essay*, 1:126.

of productions, from whence must have arisen commerce, and from commerce must have proceeded riches." Then, "the necessity of public markets" and the advantages of places located on river banks or the shores of the sea "must have given rise to cities." Cities, being "the simple consequence of an agrarian government, must have received from it, their manners and their laws." If this really had been the case, then the laws and governments of states would have reflected their agrarian origins, and, "perhaps, the word glory would not have been known in any language."[107]

But, Chastellux emphasised, "the contrary to this has been the case" (which did not, he added, mean that he was "a sectary of Hobbes").[108] Human history had not followed a natural order. Although it was not clear whether this was an effect of an oversupply of natural resources, which made intensive agriculture unnecessary, or an oversupply of population, which made agriculture inadequate, or simply because of the obvious advantage of using force, not labour, to acquire goods, it was still impossible to discover "that states have been indebted for their origin to cultivators." They seemed, "on the contrary," to have been founded by "robbers and vagabonds." The result was "that cities were the first rudiments of nations, and that the political government (*le gouvernement de police*) served as the chief principle in the constitution of states."[109] Since this was how things really had happened, the quest for origins was futile, at least for political purposes. "If a municipal administration, and simple forms of polity," were "the first governments of every state," then it was pointless "to seek, in the infancy of states, the seeds of their future grandeur," still less "to amuse ourselves in the vain hope of finding the principles of a universal monarchy on a walled hillside."[110] In this sense, Chastellux argued, "the plan of a government founded upon agriculture" was "an absolutely new idea, existing only in opinion or on paper." The "political system of government" of the ancients was, in fact, the "irreconcilable enemy of property."[111] Ancient history was a history of "perpetual convulsions, censures, reformations, divisions of land, distributions of corn, arbitrary taxes and, in short, all property hazarded in every one of these political quarrels." The reason was obvious. Those "respectable philosophers" who aimed to interest humanity "in those two important objects, their subsistence and their happiness," simply needed to remember that "at all times when alterations in the constitution of the state and the fortunes of individuals were necessarily involved together," the result had been more frequent "quarrels and sedi-

---

[107] Chastellux, *Essay*, 1:126–7.
[108] Chastellux, *De la félicité publique*, ed. Basoni, pp. 132–3. (The passage is not in the English translation.)
[109] Chastellux, *Essay*, 1:127–8 (p. 189).
[110] Chastellux, *Essay*, 1:130 (p. 190).
[111] Chastellux, *Essay*, 1:129–30 (p. 190).

tions." It was only when factional conflicts had come to be centred upon "privileges and dignities" rather than property itself that it had become easier to appease them.[112]

This, Chastellux argued, was why the politics of the moderns offered more grounds for hope than those of the ancients, and, in the second place, why it was a profound political mistake to follow the Machiavellian idea of reverting to first principles in periods of crisis.[113] The mistake applied particularly to "those profound contemplators, who secluding themselves from their fellow-creatures, are assiduously employed in framing laws for them, and the most frequently neglect the care of their domestic, and private concerns, to prescribe to empires that form of government to which they imagine that they ought to submit."[114] It was a fairly transparent allusion to the facts of both Mirabeau's and Rousseau's private lives. Chastellux drove the point home by comparing such "contemplators" to the figure of a debtor sitting in a debtors' gaol in the engraving by William Hogarth. The imprisoned debtor was writing a great work entitled *A New Scheme for Paying the Debt of the Nation*.[115] What was needed, Chastellux argued, was a different set of analytical procedures to make it easier to avoid using arbitrary assumptions about human nature as the basis of extravagant political systems (the remark was aimed at both Rousseau and the Physiocrats). "Now, I consider," he wrote, "human reason as armed with two instruments, and these are contemplation and experiment."

> It is astonishing, that mankind should have been almost constantly mistaken in the use of these two instruments. The physical system hath been submitted to contemplation, and the political system to experiment. The laws of nature have been founded on ingenious, but extravagant conjectures; the laws of society have been founded on particular facts.[116]

State-of-nature theory would not do. "We live in a metaphysical age," Chastellux observed, in which every writer on politics "now ascends to the origin of society." If the subject was commerce, "he introduces three properties, or if it must be so, three islands, one of which produces corn, another wine, another hemp, etc."[117] But this kind of attempt to think back to some presocial state was purely speculative. If it was difficult, Chastellux wrote, "to define what human nature has fixed, relative to the state of society," it was certainly "frivolous and useless to propose these questions: 'Are men in a state of mutual and perpetual war?'; 'are they born the friends or

[112] Chastellux, *Essay*, 1:130 (p. 190).
[113] Chastellux, *Essay*, 1:184, note 1 (p. 217, note 2).
[114] Chastellux, *Essay*, 2:172 (pp. 396–7).
[115] Chastellux, *Essay*, 2:172, (p. 396, note 1).
[116] Chastellux, *Essay*, 1:140 (p. 194).
[117] Chastellux, *Essay*, 2:288.

the enemies of each other?' "[118] The questions simply presupposed too much. If the state of nature meant "the most brutal state existing," then this "could be said to reign not more amongst the savages than in our forests and fields." If it meant "all which is in the order of nature," then there was "a state of nature as peculiar to the city as to the country, to the tradesman as to the husbandman, to the man that launches into society, as to him that buries himself in solitude."[119] Presuppositions about human nature simply distorted political science. In this light, Chastellux suggested, the purpose of political science had to be to "engage in observations purely historical, and studious researches after facts, and the principles by which they were occasioned."[120] These he called "general facts" or "facts infinitely more certain than those which have been so sedulously transmitted to us, and which, like grains of dust, could have no weight, unless united in a single mass."[121]

The facts of human history revealed the gulf between the political societies of the ancients and those of the moderns. The ancient world had been unable to separate government from administration, or the government of men from the government of properties. The ubiquity of slavery, the political importance of public granaries, and the recurrence of conflict over the distribution of land were the clearest indications of this state of affairs. The moderns, however, had been freed from the close association between property and politics. The barbarian invasions and the fall of the Roman Empire had been the great turning point in human history. "The history of the world," Chastellux wrote,

> doth not appear to have presented us with more than two grand epochs, two very distinguished generations of the human species: the propagation of one generation arose from their prosecutions of tillage, and from those emigrations which are the consequences of a simple and natural multiplication; it was thus that the Phoenicians peopled Europe and Africa. The other generation, issuing forth in arms, and, as it were, by enchantment, from the bosom of the ice, and the recesses of the desert, approached to devour the labours of the former generation, like those swarms of locusts, which, whilst none can tell from whence they come, consume, in one night, the subsistence of a whole people.[122]

In the first age of the world, new political societies were formed "by emigrations and colonies," but in its second age, "by invasions and conquests." The difference had given rise to "two principles of government absolutely

[118] Chastellux, *Essay*, 1:xi (p. 122).
[119] Chastellux, *Essay*, 1:xvi–xvii (pp. 123–4).
[120] Chastellux, *Essay*, 1:v (p. 119).
[121] Chastellux, *Essay*, 1:40 (p. 147).
[122] Chastellux, *Essay*, 2:6.

opposite to one another" and an "entirely new organization of political societies, not unlike to those organisations which the philosophers attribute to the universe, where one part is active and the other part is passive; where one part gives and the other part receives the form. *Novus rerum nascitur ordo* [A new order is born]."[123]

This new order was the feudal system. As Chastellux acknowledged, Montesquieu had been the first to highlight its bearing on modern systems of government. But, he added, Montesquieu had also been "successfully refuted."[124] The real explanation of the origins of modern monarchy, Chastellux suggested, was to be found in the system of personal vassalage, "a vassalage independent of properties," underlying the Frankish system of dispute settlement and the way that this non-property-based social hierarchy had been grafted onto an already-established system of military benefices in Roman Gaul.[125] In this light, Montesquieu's assertion of the purely German origins of modernity had to be modified by the continuing influence of Rome's original system of republican government. The Romans had established an office-based system of rule. The Germans had made it possible to separate office from property. In embryo, this separation of authority from property held out the prospect of a further separation of government from administration that Chastellux identified as the real difference between ancient and modern systems of government. The great cities of the modern world were the one living legacy of its ancient past. But the feudal system supplied a way to go beyond the property-driven political conflicts of the urban governments of the ancient world. Feudal privilege supplied a level of authority that could counter the property-based politics of the ancient system of municipal government, allowing the two to coexist as relatively separate social hierarchies. This sort of separation, Chastellux argued, might have been possible in the later Middle Ages, in what he described as the second epoch of the feudal system. Once the original Roman military benefices had become hereditary and public office had acquired a durable character, it might then have been possible to substitute election for inheritance and turn the original system of feudal government into something like "that government of property and representation, that free and half-democratical government," that was now to be found in modern Britain.[126]

Again, however, the actual had ruled out the possible. As well as the independent status of the church and the resultant conflation of religion with politics, it had been the New World that had held the Old World

---

[123] Chastellux, *Essay*, 2:8.
[124] Chastellux, *Essay*, 2:8.
[125] Chastellux, *Essay*, 2:16, note c.
[126] Chastellux, *Essay*, 2:59–60.

back. The invention of the compass and the conquest of America had, at
the time of the Renaissance, made gold and silver "the real kings of Europe."[127] "The commerce of the moderns," Chastellux observed, "is not
established either to favour the communication of commodities, or to facilitate their exchange. It has sprung from avarice. It has arisen amidst the fury
of war and the bitterness of national hatred. It has taken for its principle, a
spirit of exclusion and domination and it has but too strenuously maintained it in our days."[128] It had all too easily defaulted into conquest. "Immense countries, weak and ignorant people were as baits to the ambition
of the maritime nations; and thus it is that men return to their first propensity, the desire of invading and of obtaining all by violence, rather than by
labour."[129] But the long-term effects of trade had, nonetheless, tilted the
balance of power decisively away from poor but populous nations. The
moderns, Chastellux claimed, following Hume, were not only more populous than the ancients, they were also more prosperous and more powerful.
This, he suggested, was the main reason not to expect any reversion to the
politics of the ancients. Using the model that he had set out at the beginning of the book, he argued that a rich country would always have more
resources at its disposal to withstand military threats from poorer, more
populous countries. If "the labour of a nation was divided amongst all the
individuals," the nation with the highest per capita productivity would be
able to make a larger proportion of its wealth and population available for
defence.[130] Adding money to the hypothetical argument did not change its
outcome. Other things being equal, "the truly powerful nation is the nation
which, consuming specifically more, or labouring specifically less than another nation, can at a crisis, either recur to a saving of their subsistence or
an augmentation of their labour."[131] As with Turgot, savings, investment,
and the uses to which capital could be put were the real key to external
power and security.

Unlike Turgot, however, Chastellux had no real confidence in the capacity of a unitary system of government to manage the combination of a
subsistence-based division of labour founded on agriculture and a money-
based division of labour founded on industry and trade. In his view, the
idea of taxing the landowners as the way to meet all the costs of the state's
expenditure was sheer political fantasy. The compatibility between the agricultural and manufacturing sectors of society was complicated by the existence of a large landowning sector whose expenditure was devoted mainly

---

[127] Chastellux, *Essay*, 2:133.
[128] Chastellux, *Essay*, 2:290.
[129] Chastellux, *Essay*, 2:373.
[130] Chastellux, *Essay*, 2:264–5.
[131] Chastellux, *Essay*, 2:270.

to conspicuous consumption. This ruled out Turgot's model of capital circulating from one class of assets to another under the aegis of a fiscal system that was designed to offset the attractions of landed income. As Chastellux presented it, the way of life of the landowners meant that it was simply not possible to convert large numbers of the manufacturing population into soldiers without undermining the whole system of expenditure and consumption on which the modern, postfeudal order was based. This was one reason why standing armies had become the norm. Their existence had allowed the relationship among landed expenditure, urban industry, and agricultural production to remain viable. But if standing armies had helped to stabilise the relationship between the agricultural and manufacturing sectors, the extra costs of the most recent wars were bound to subject this distribution of population and resources to an additional strain. The state's demand for resources in wartime had to compete with the landowners' need to maintain their patterns of consumption. As a result, a much greater proportion of the costs of modern warfare would fall on the agricultural sector. Directly or indirectly, it would be the agricultural sector, the one that contained the largest number of the poorest members of society, that would have to carry much of the burden of the state's external security.

This, Chastellux argued, was why public credit was a vital resource for modern European states. It was the only way to protect the agricultural sector, and the poorest part of the population, from having to shoulder a disproportionate share of the costs of fighting wars. The alternatives were both unappealing. Eliminating conspicuous consumption (which was Fénelon's solution) was one kind of solution. Leaving the agricultural sector to carry the costs of war would simply ratchet up the gap between the rich and the poor. In both cases, the alternatives to public debt were either a revolution from above or one from below because the accumulated wealth and power of the landowning sector were too deeply entrenched to be easily modified. "Rich particulars," Chastellux pointed out, were on the "same level with sovereigns or the state."[132] They consumed but did not produce. The luxury of the moderns was not simply "the use of property" but had become "a kind of right."[133]

> Hence it happened that whilst there was a necessity for employing a great number of men in new professions, the rich preserved the privilege of purchasing the labour of the people in competition with the state. Luxury, magnificence and pleasure have preserved the greater part of their agents, and the government, having been obliged to purchase the labour of the lower people at the expense of the lower people, this labour has been thrown back as an

[132] Chastellux, *Essay*, 2:318.
[133] Chastellux, *Essay*, 2:321-2.

additional load on the cultivators and on all the artisans who concur with them either in the production or in the preparation of subsistence. Thus, nations have been crushed because the burden which should have been divided between all, has been borne only by those classes of citizens most useful to the state. Thus war has augmented the general labour, which is already an evil, and it has augmented it in an unequal and oppressive manner, which is a still greater evil.[134]

Nor, given the practical difficulties associated with switching from one occupation to another, was it easy for a society with a highly developed division of labour to convert populations from civil to military occupations. Although, Chastellux argued, these problems were generic, they were particularly acute in France. The combination of venal office and private finance meant that the French financial system was far less efficient than its British or Dutch counterparts in tapping available wealth to fund the costs of war. The intermittent periods of peace that accompanied the eighteenth century's wars had come at a high price. A "fresh war has arisen within the bosom of states," one that was "more ruinous than bloody" and "more troublesome than terrifying," but that had turned the question of the size and distribution of taxation into a permanent source of conflict between "nations and their sovereigns."[135]

In these circumstances, public credit was a real blessing. Nor, Chastellux argued, was it as fraught with danger as its critics had claimed. He singled out Hume's description of the various possible deaths of public debt for particular criticism, repeating Forbonnais's suggestion that Hume's essay *Of Public Credit* had been clouded by Tory prejudice. "He is pleased to reduce matters to an absurdity by supposing that there is no end to borrowing, and that the state owes all the revenue of particulars," Chastellux commented. Despite its size, he argued, the cost of funding the British public debt was still only a small fraction of gross national income. Wars, he continued, were costly undertakings, and the only obvious alternative to borrowing money to meet their costs was to rely on plunder. Nor was there any evidence at all that public credit had undermined British prosperity. "Neither population, nor agriculture, nor manufactures, nor great roads, nor magnificent establishments, nor, in short, anything seem to be wanting." The facts were actually "a terrible argument in the hands of the sceptics in politics." Although they certainly showed that Hume was wrong, they could also be used to claim that everything was right. Chastellux was not prepared to go that far. The debt, he argued, was a real burden, but one that had been carried largely by Ireland and Scotland. The

---

[134] Chastellux, *Essay*, 2:322–3.
[135] Chastellux, *Essay*, 2:300–1.

British ban on Irish imports, in particular, had been designed to keep up English rents to make it easier to fund the costs of war. Once Scotland's and Ireland's undeveloped resources were available, they would release large additional amounts of wealth. But even without them, Hume's jeremiads were still entirely misplaced, while his suggestion that it would be preferable to keep funds in the public treasury was equally undesirable. "A canal, a seaport, a great road, the cultivation of a barren waste are worth a hundred times more than ten millions locked up in coffers," Chastellux argued. The general conclusion was that "the national debt was not so great an evil as has been imagined; in short, that its reimbursement is not absolutely necessary, nor even the most important object of a good administration." It could indeed be a source of stability because of the multiplicity of interests that had come to be vested in the state's debt.[136] As one of his admirers put it, Chastellux had succeeded in "drawing a salutary remedy from the poison itself."[137]

The most immediate purpose of the whole argument was to indicate that the modern combination of war and debt had, in a quite literal sense, bought time for a gradual process of institutional reform. The escalating costs of war and the political difficulties associated with raising the taxes needed to fund existing levels of debt were, Chastellux argued, powerful structural obstacles to further cycles of international conflict. The failure to consolidate the Maupeou coup in France in the last years of the reign of Louis XV revealed the limits of absolute power. Individuals might still be sent to the Bastille, but the reversion to the institutional status quo at the beginning of the reign of Louis XVI indicated that it was not as easy to do the same thing either to "sovereign courts, or the estates of a province, or proprietors who declare that it is impossible for them to pay anything."[138] War was most likely to occur in the East, where the Ottoman Empire was "tending towards its dissolution" and would, Chastellux predicted, soon be swallowed up by Russia. In the longer term, however, the Russian Empire would also disappear, and "from its vast ruins, free and happy states will arise, as once there issued from the entrails of a bull those swarms of bees, the honey of which supplied mankind with sweet and wholesome nourishment."[139] Like many of his contemporaries, Chastellux argued that the French loss of Canada would soon lead to intense conflict between Britain and her American colonies. The longer it lasted, the more it would weaken British influence in Europe and undermine an empire

[136] Chastellux, *De la félicité publique*, ed. Basoni, pp. 494–7. (The passage is not in the English translation.)

[137] Dominique Audibert to Chastellux, Marseille, 23 January, 1786. Archives Chastellux, dossier 171.

[138] Chastellux, *Essay*, 2:308.

[139] Chastellux, *Essay*, 2:285.

already overstretched by Britain's increasing involvement in India.[140] The period of peace that seemed to be likely was, Chastellux suggested, an opportunity to begin to close "the wounds of humanity."[141]

Jacques Necker and Burke's Paradox

Events were soon to show how mistaken Chastellux had been. But a great deal of the more fundamental argument of the *Essay on Public Happiness* was incorporated directly into Jacques Necker's first major publication, an *Éloge de Colbert* (In Praise of Colbert) published in 1773, and was repeated in his two most important later works, *De l'administration des finances de la France* (On the Administration of the Finances of France) of 1784 and *De l'importance des opinions religieuses* (Of the Importance of Religious Opinions) of 1788. As the title of the third book suggests, Necker had no sympathy at all with the sort of religious scepticism to be found in both Helvétius and Chastellux. But he did share their concern with inequality and endorsed Chastellux's scepticism about the political viability of establishing the kind of complementary relationship between agriculture and industry that Turgot had envisaged. Turgot's misfortunes during his brief ministry served to underline the point. This was one reason why Necker took over Chastellux's claim that public credit, in conjunction with the kind of "government of property and representation" that Chastellux associated with modern Britain, was the only available means to offset inequality's most divisive effects.[142] His diagnosis of the problem followed on directly from what Chastellux had written. Its starting point was the problem of private property. "Imagine for a moment," Necker wrote in his *Of the Importance of Religious Opinions*, "the next generation assembled in an ideal world, not knowing, before living on earth, who would be born to parents blessed with all the favours of fortune and who would be afflicted by misery from the very cradle."

> They would be instructed in the principles of civil law; they would be told about the suitability of laws of property and presented with a picture of the disorder that would be the inevitable effect of a continuous variation in the distribution of goods. Then all those making up the new generation, all equally uncertain of the chance reserved for them by the hazards of birth, would sign up unanimously to the events awaiting them and, at such a moment, when all the relationships of society exist as pure speculation, one might say that the individual interest and the public interest are genuinely one and the same.

[140] Chastellux, *Essay,* 2:295–7.
[141] Chastellux, *Essay,* 2:299.
[142] Chastellux, *Essay,* 2:59–60.

But that identity ceases to exist when each individual, arriving on earth, takes possession of his lot.[143]

Here, neither Helvétius nor Rousseau could offer much guidance. "It can be seen in the light of the preceding reflections," Necker continued, "that political society as a project and political society in action present themselves for observation as two different epochs. But because those epochs are not separated by any obvious limit, they are almost invariably confused in the minds of political moralists."

> He who believes in the union of individual interests and the public interest and who celebrates that harmony, has considered society only in terms of its primitive and general plan. He who, on the contrary, thinks that everything is wrong and lacking in accord because there are great differences in power and fortune, takes society only in terms of its present movement and rotation. Both these two misapprehensions have been consecrated by famous authors. Someone drawn on by a lively imagination, strongly affected by present objects, could not fail to have been struck by the inequality of conditions, while the philosopher transported by his abstractions beyond the circumference of societies could not fail to see only the principles and relationships that determined the first formation of the civil laws.[144]

The idea of property as it might have been distributed if it had been transported from another planet and property as it had actually been distributed by human history first appeared in the *Éloge de Colbert*.[145] Necker's analysis of history's real effects was equally consistent. Agriculture, equity, and population growth would have gone hand in hand, he wrote in 1773, "in a society where the goods of the earth were collected in common and shared out equally."[146] But private property ruled out equality. Once property was established, he wrote in 1784, "all those, who work for their livelihood, are subjected to the imperious will of men of property and are forced to be satisfied with receiving a salary adequate to the common necessities of life."[147] Competition for work and the daily recurrence of urgent subsistence needs made these circumstances unavoidable. "Every age and every country present the same spectacle and there is no exception nor mitigation of that species of slavery, but in those few states where the form of

---

[143] Jacques Necker, *De l'importance des opinions religieuses* [1788], reprinted in his *Oeuvres*, vol. 12 (Paris, 1821), p. 35.

[144] Necker, *De l'importance des opinions religieuses*, pp. 36–7.

[145] Jacques Necker, *Eloge de Colbert* (Paris, 1773), p. 72.

[146] Necker, *Eloge*, p. 21.

[147] Jacques Necker, *De l'administration des finances* [1783], 3:93. In this and subsequent citations, I have used the English translation, *A Treatise on the Administration of Finances of France*, 3 vols. (London, 1785), 3:95–6.

government leaves some political rights in the hands of the people, the enjoyment of which has an influence over its consideration and furnishes it some means of resistance."[148] As he had indicated more explicitly in the *Éloge de Colbert*, it was only in England, where the people was "the owner of a value that it can dispense to the rich and force them into moderating their rights," that the progress of luxury had been blocked. Along with the relatively precarious bargaining power that Britain's extensive trade and vast empire gave to her wage-earners, the British people's capacity "to elect or not elect" their members of Parliament was the only real brake on inequality.[149]

The very productivity of manufacturing industry, Necker emphasised, made the process cumulative. What "one hundred thousand workmen" might once have been able to produce in the previous century could now be produced by eighty thousand. The work of the extra twenty thousand could now be allocated to "new pieces of workmanship" whose results would simply add to "the enjoyments and luxury of the wealthy." Here, Necker followed Rousseau. It was wrong, he wrote, to think that luxury led to the progress of sciences. Instead, "it is rather to the progress of sciences of every sort that we ought to impute the increase of luxury."[150] Once it was possible to do a year's work in a month, inequality was bound to grow. The durability of many new products also meant that they could be passed from one generation to the next, making the progress of inequality even more inexorably cumulative. Barring an unlikely reversion to Spartan austerity, Necker observed, the only real obstacle to this process was "the inconstancy of taste and the empire of fashion." Were it not for the fact that "wealthy men were not continually busied in altering what was done the day before," affluent persons would "soon be led to spend their incomes entirely contrary to the good of society." Instead of "that kind of expense which finds occupation for the greatest number of men," they would spend their wealth on more domestic servants, more horses, bigger parks or gardens, and "every kind of expense the most adverse to population and to the strength of the state."[151]

As Necker put it in the *Éloge de Colbert*, "the important service rendered by the trades, arts, and manufacture" was "to favour the increase of population by blocking, but without constraint, the excess of subsistence goods that the landowners hold in their hands and that they have the right to dispose of as they wish."[152] Fashion helped to reinforce this corrective

---

[148] Necker, *Administration*, 3:96.
[149] Necker, *Eloge*, p. 133.
[150] Necker, *Administration*, 3:99.
[151] Necker, *Administration*, 3:101–2.
[152] Necker, *Eloge*, p. 21.

mechanism. The competitive desire to replace what was old by what was new, irrespective of purely utilitarian criteria, helped to counteract the potentially limitless accumulation of subsistence goods in the hands of the landowners. The stabilising effects of fashion could be reinforced still further, Necker commented, if luxury were to become more widely available. If, he wrote, "the disproportion of property was less considerable, the number of individuals who might attain to the enjoyment of objects of mere convenience would be increased and the number of those who are now able to spend a great part of their income on splendid superfluities would diminish in proportion."[153] The task of the administrator was to manage public finance in ways that were consonant with this end. Just as Physiocracy was a system designed to work against the grain of the actually existing distribution of landed property in order to promote a long-term rearrangement of the distribution of goods, so the administrative system that Necker envisaged was designed to work against the grain of the actually existing distribution of capital in order to promote a gradual rebalancing of the relationship between the propertied and the propertyless by broadening and deepening capital markets.

This, as Necker put it, meant limiting the growth of "the circumscribed class of annuitants (*capitalistes rentiers*) who are almost all to be found in the great cities" by promoting competition in capital markets and increasing the velocity of the circulation of wealth.[154] Even before Turgot's short ministry began, Necker made it clear that he thought that the modified version of Physiocracy that Turgot had set out in his *Reflections on the Formation and Distribution of Wealth* was still too ambitious a framework for trying to manage a property-based society. Once property and money existed, Necker argued, no system of administration could ever have enough reliable information about the mechanisms underlying price formation and the allocation of resources to be able to rely upon a single tax to calibrate both the state's fiscal needs and the costs of the advances required by agricultural producers, the new primary investments by landowners, the scale of landowners' own consumption, and the amounts that might then be available for paying taxes.[155] The same uncertainty applied to the grain trade. It was simply impossible, Necker argued, to rely on prices as a proxy for the availability of supply and leave markets to allocate basic subsistence goods without making any provision at all for administrative involvement. The right to live, he commented, was as much of a right as the right to property, and although it might well be true that under conditions of "perfect liberty" the two would go together, it was simply absurd to accept that

---

[153] Necker, *Administration*, 3:105–6.
[154] Necker, *Administration*, 3:108.
[155] Necker, *Eloge*, pp. 23–4.

"one or two centuries" might be required "to see its effect."[156] Although he
never referred directly to Turgot in any of his publications, Necker proceeded to shift the focus of government responsibility to the other side
of Turgot's argument about the relationship between interest rates and
investment, turning that relationship into the only available tool that an
administrator could use. If direct action by way of the fiscal system was too
crude an instrument to use to correct existing inequalities, this left the
indirect effects of changes in interest rates and the money supply as the
administrator's only reliable resource.

Necker amplified on Turgot's definition of circulation, emphasising the
extent to which interest rates were a function of effective supply and demand, not simply the broader supply of available capital. Part of a country's
money supply, Necker observed, was used in daily transactions to buy and
sell "the necessaries and luxuries of life." Government, he commented,
"has no sort of influence over it, neither should it wish to have any."[157] The
part of circulation of relevance to government was the quantity of money
that was superfluous to everyday consumption needs. It was this "overplus,"
Necker wrote, "that may be applied to useful speculations and is laid out
either in the loans made by the state or by individuals or in all sorts of
enterprises." This was the circulation relevant to both public and private
credit. Circulation of this kind was "that which collects into the hands of
moneyed men from all parts of the kingdom all the specie unnecessary to
those multiplied operations that are the result of the expenses of the state
and of the collective inhabitants of the kingdom."[158] The greater the number of hands in which this money was tied up, the larger the number of
obstacles there would be to its circulation. Cumbersome administrative
procedures, multiple tasks without adequate managerial supervision, inade-
quately financed agencies, complicated fiscal and accounting systems, overcentralised decision-making, and narrowly restricted systems of appointment and promotion were all likely to make circulation slower and less able
to meet any effective demand for funds than it might optimally be.

Britain's real advantage, Necker argued (anticipating recent historiography), had rather less to do with its constitution than with the efficiency of
its government and, more particularly, with the way that the combination
of its public institutions and country banks helped to make money speedily
available as capital. "The cause of this surprising facility of making loans,
of which England has in the last war [of American independence] given

---

[156] Necker, *Eloge*, pp. 32–3, 38.
[157] Necker, *Administration*, 3:270.
[158] Necker, *Administration*, 3:272.

examples more striking than ever, must not," Necker wrote, "be solely attributed to the extent of the public confidence."[159]

> I am convinced that with the same public credit that kingdom would not have been able to make these loans if the wonderful activity of the circulation of specie had not existed; or, in order to explain this idea more distinctly, if the money paid into the royal exchequer in consequence of these loans, and immediately after distributed among the various departments charged with the public expenses, had not quickly returned into the hands of moneyed men, who were thereby enabled to lend it again the following year.[160]

The widely used practice of issuing banknotes and other kinds of promissory paper, the small size of the British Isles, the fact that London was simultaneously a seaport, a capital city, the chief trading centre, and the site of almost all foreign exchange operations, as well as the large number of provincial deposit banks, all had as much to do with the stability of both public and private credit and the low level of British interest rates as did the system of government itself. In France, Necker observed, the proceeds of loans floated by the government remained in circulation for two or three years before returning, by way of taxation and interest payments, to the original lender. In Britain, "the same return is accomplished . . . in the course of one year."[161] It was not surprising, therefore, that irrespective of the political risks associated with absolute government, interest rates in Britain were lower than in France, just as the amount of cash in circulation in Britain was also lower than in France. It followed that a well-conceived programme of fiscal and administrative reform might go a long way towards closing the gap.

The reformed system of royal government that Necker envisaged was very similar to Turgot's. Although he dropped the idea of a single tax on the net product, he kept the institutional structure of the tax regime that Turgot had advocated. A network of elected provincial assemblies would take over responsibility for the allocation, assessment, and collection of direct taxation, while the tax-farms and other private agencies responsible for the collection of taxes on consumption and for military, naval, and other public expenditure would be replaced by government agencies (*régies*) managed on bureaucratic lines. Both sets of reforms would have the effect of freeing the royal government from the uncertainty and costs of trying to manage government income and expenditure from the centre and, by doing so, would bring the ratio between projected revenue and real

---

[159] Necker, *Administration*, 3:274–5. Compare to John Brewer, *The Sinews of Power: War, Money and the English State* (London, Collins, 1989).

[160] Necker, *Administration*, 3:275.

[161] Necker, *Administration*, 3:277.

collection costs into line with those that existed in Britain. Necker's promotion of a public discount bank (the Caisse d'escompte) also followed the logic of Turgot's analysis of the self-correcting character of private capital markets. Variations in the supply of funds for different types of investment would lead to variations in asset prices and changes in relative rates of return on capital, causing a gradual rotation of capital from one type of investment to another. The discount bank would simply help to speed up the process and, by leaving a larger pool of capital in circulation, would encourage general interest rates to fall to lower levels than they might otherwise have done.

The different policies that Necker and Turgot adopted towards the grain trade were an effect of their different assessments of public credit. Turgot was perfectly at ease with encouraging capital formation and promoting private credit, but, like both Hume and Steuart, he recognised that public credit was a different kind of entity. Unlike private credit, public credit has no inbuilt limitations. Real people can borrow only up to their ability to pay. But states are sovereign entities, not real people. The international capital markets might be able to set limits on the amounts that states can borrow by pushing up interest rates to levels at which debt service becomes impossible, but within a state's own boundaries borrowing and lending would still simply turn into taxing and spending. At some point, technical problems would become political problems. Turgot's policies were designed to prevent this possibility from arising. Freeing the grain trade and relying on the tax revenue supplied by the landowners meant opting for economic growth and rising tax revenue to meet the costs of external defence. Necker's alternative amounted to deferring the political risk of conflict over taxation by managing the financial risk involved in public credit. There was no need, he argued, to adopt the dangerous political course of trying to transfer the whole burden of taxation onto the landowners, or to apply the equally dangerous policy of unlimited free trade in grain as an incentive to boost the productivity of the land. Piecemeal reform made Turgot's rigid principles unnecessary, because the same goal could be reached more gradually.

Necker's gamble was predicated on the assumption that it might be possible to separate politics from administration for long enough to be able to face the next major European war with more economic power. He had no illusions about how much financial breathing space there might be, but his calculation was that the relatively lower levels of agricultural and manufacturing productivity in France could be raised to match those existing in Britain, where the tax burden was already higher. The country with the highest per capita output was, he argued, always likely to be the winner in both economic and military competition if it could also keep its tax levels lower than those of its rivals. A high-productivity, high-tax economy was, in the long term, bound to lose out to one with the same level of productivity but with a lower tax burden, because the price levels of a high-tax regime would lead to a rising tide of cheaper imports. This, Necker suggested, was what might happen to Britain.[162] Combining a high per capita output with a relatively lower per capita rate of taxation would still yield an income stream that, in absolute terms, would be able to meet the costs of the additional borrowing that a further major war was bound to produce. If the war simply maintained the international status quo, the balance of economic and political power would begin to shift towards France, and the gradual decline of both public and private confidence across the Channel might then lead to "a crisis in England whose effects could not be calculated."[163]

Events again had the last word. The hypothetical English crisis was pre-empted by two real political crises in the United Provinces and the Austrian Netherlands and the prospect of another European war soon after the War of American Independence had ended. This possibility cut across French domestic politics just at the time that the monarchy's financial problems were threatening to produce a new cycle of conflict over the abiding problems of debt finance and taxation. French support of the Dutch patriots against the Prussian- and British-backed house of Orange ruled out a repetition of the show of force towards the magistrates of the French parlements that Louis XV had adopted in 1770 and 1771. Opting in 1787 for the partial debt default that the abbé Terray had engineered in 1771 amounted to attacking the financial resources of France's Dutch allies and handing them on a plate to Prussia and Britain. The same problem applied to the Belgian opposition to Joseph II. The high-level infighting and pro-longed political uncertainty within the French royal government between 1787 and 1789 were, at least in part, a product of this conjuncture. By the time that the royal government decided to exercise its authority, it was already too late.[164] But, as one of the new regime's political opponents put it in 1796, things might have gone differently. "At that time," he wrote (referring to the period that preceded the fall of the Bastille), "you had a king and a government that you have since stigmatised as arbitrary, des-potic, and tyrannical and caused it to disappear."

> Suppose that there is nothing exaggerated in these qualifications and that, using its despotism, that government, instead of assembling the Estates-Gen-eral to fill the deficit and provide for its needs, had decided to issue a paper currency, you could not disagree that it did not have the power and that, if it

---

[162] Necker, *Eloge*, pp. 121–6.
[163] Necker, *Eloge*, p. 115.
[164] See, particularly, Munro Price, *The Fall of the French Monarchy* (London, Macmillan, 2002).

had wished, it could also have taken back everything that its creditors held from the domains of the crown and then gone on to declare those domains to be national property (*biens nationaux*), just as it could have confiscated the property of the clergy and ordered their sale, thus making them the security and basis of the paper currency that it had put into circulation.[165]

The imaginary history simply turned the French Revolution into a royal revolution with the same outcome.

But the imaginary history is also an indication of the real political difficulties left over after the Bastille fell. After the revolution, the king's debt became the nation's debt. This meant that taxing and spending would have to play as much of a part in the political life of the new regime as it had done in the old. Barring an end to war, it was also likely that the nation's debt would continue to grow. This meant that the usual way of thinking about the relationship between public credit and political liberty had been reversed. Usually, public credit was associated with the politics of necessity. Governments borrowed money in wartime emergencies to fund the additional costs of facing external threats. The same logic applied to debt default. The huge costs of warfare might well force states to borrow money to defend themselves, but the resulting combination of rising taxation and conflict over the distribution of the tax burden might, in the next war, force them to default. What necessity had created, necessity might also have to destroy. This was the basis of Hume's "natural death" of public credit. After 1789, however, the imperative was reversed. Necessity now applied to maintaining public credit. The result was a political paradox. Instead of the possibility that political liberty and public credit might, ultimately, be incompatible, the new French regime was committed to them both.[166] The argument of Burke's *Reflections on the Revolution in France* followed the logic of the paradox to its final conclusion. Relying on public credit to secure political liberty meant, he argued, applying the politics of necessity to all the established institutions of the old French regime, leaving all the domestic political arrangements of the French state exposed to the measures usually reserved for international power politics. From this perspective, it was not so much the unitary sovereignty of the nation that, in itself, was a cause of political instability, but the failure to block recurrent appeals to the politics of necessity as the only way to preserve the nation's sovereignty. As Mirabeau came to see, Sieyès's political failure opened the way towards the eighteenth century's long-predicted revolution and to a real-life reali-

---

[165] [Anon.], *Lettres à l'auteur du Quotidienne, par un de ses abonnés* (Hamburg, 1796), p. 22.

[166] For a helpful way in to the subject, see Ferenc Feher, *The Frozen Revolution: An Essay on Jacobinism* (Cambridge, CUP, 1987), pp. 30–48; and, for the financial aspects of the debt problem, François Crouzet, *La Grande Inflation. La Monnaie en France de Louis XIV à Napoléon* (Paris, Fayard, 1993).

sation of the scenario that Burke was only the most recent to rehearse. One by one, Burke argued, all of France's ancient institutions would be swallowed up by the new regime's overriding need to preserve its financial stability. The argument turned Hume's "natural death" scenario into a sequence of increasingly desperate attempts at emergency resuscitation. If Hume was right, Burke's argument implied, regime change alone could not eliminate the possibility that France would have to face a choice between Steuart's "farce" and Steuart's "rhapsody."

Joseph Fauchet and Pierre-Paul Gudin de la Brenellerie

Two pamphlets published at almost the same time as Burke's own work indicate how difficult it was to find a way to deal with the paradox. One opted for republican austerity, the other for a representative meritocracy as solutions to the problem. Both were written towards the end of 1790, when the institutional shape of the new regime was almost in place.[167] The first, written by the future French ambassador to the United States of America, Joseph Fauchet, was a violent attack on the new regime from a strongly republican point of view. The second, written by Pierre-Paul Gudin de la Brenellerie, a life-long friend and intellectual ally of Pierre-Samuel Dupont de Nemours, was a defence of the same regime from the standpoint of the modified version of Physiocracy that Turgot had developed. Both, in different ways, relied on Rousseau for the framework of their respective arguments. Fauchet's pamphlet, entitled *Le despotisme décrété par l'assemblée nationale* (Despotism Decreed by the National Assembly), was the more overtly polemical of the two. He began with an ironic rehearsal of the standard view of Montesquieu. The "wise men" making up the National Assembly had, he wrote, "finally justified Montesquieu's much disputed assertion that virtue is not the principle of monarchical government."[168] They had gone even further than Montesquieu by making gold, not honour, the underlying principle of the new regime. The principle applied to the new electoral system, the king's civil list, the power of the

---

[167] A review published in the 18 December 1790 issue of the *Journal de la société des amis de la constitution monarchique* (no. 1, pp. 20–30) makes it likely that the first of these pamphlets, *Le despotisme décrété par l'assemblée nationale*, was published only late in 1790. Gudin de la Brenellerie's *Supplément au Contrat Social* (Paris, 1791) was reviewed in the 12 February 1791 issue of the same journal (no. 9, pp. 3–5) but was approved by the French censor in November 1790.

[168] [Joseph Fauchet], *Le despotisme décrété par l'assemblée nationale* (London, 1790), p. 5. Some biographical information on Fauchet can be found in the edition of his *Mémoire sur les Etats-Unis d'Amérique* [1795], ed. Carl Ludwig Lokke, *Annual Report of the American Historical Association for the Year 1936*, 3 vols. (Washington, 1938), 1:85–123.

executive, and the continued existence of the old regime's standing army. As, Fauchet continued, "the Genevan legislator" (Rousseau) had shown, there were two kinds of social contract, and, by preserving the monarchy, the French had opted for the wrong one.[169] The idea of monarchy that Fauchet had in mind was a modified version of the false social contract of Rousseau's second *Discourse*. "As soon as men had properties," he wrote, "they also knew war."

> Whoever was the most agile, the most robust, who killed the most enemies, or who gave the best counsel was placed at the head of those of his party. It was easy to feel the advantage of having him as a chief, and each time that society faced any danger it became usual to have recourse to him.[170]

At first this power was temporary, often lasting no longer than the time of a battle. But as societies grew, wars also increased and the number of combatants grew. Treaties began to be known, and, to avoid confusion, military chiefs began to be entrusted by those they commanded "to represent the two warring peoples and to speak, act, and settle in their name." Gradually this power to represent a people on the outside moved to the inside. "The habit of respect gave rise to the habit of obedience," and the habit of obedience was all too easy to exploit.[171] What began as a people's trust in its leader gradually turned into the leaders' rule over their people, and, Fauchet commented, "since this has been going on for a long time, an Aristotle, a Grotius, and every Machiavellian would claim that this has always been the case and is lawful."[172]

Nothing, Fauchet emphasised, was illegitimate about the process, but its outcome was still despotic. Property led to war. War led to representation, and representation led to despotism. Usurpations and crimes might later occur, but these simply reinforced the initial sequence. Nothing that the National Assembly had done, Fauchet argued, diverged from its logic. Nor, apart from the Declaration of the Rights of Man, was there any indication that the National Assembly could see the real danger of the political system that it had established. Both Roman history and modern history showed that the idea of a limited monarchy was simply an oxymoron. As Rousseau had pointed out, even the best of kings still had the power to be wicked.[173] It followed that if France did not become a republic, then its people would be well advised to add the cry of "Long live slavery" (*Vive l'esclavage*) to those of "*Vive la Nation*" and "*Vive le Roi*."[174] There was no reason, Fauchet

---

[169] [Fauchet], *Despotisme*, p. 13.
[170] [Fauchet], *Despotisme*, p. 8.
[171] [Fauchet], *Despotisme*, p. 9.
[172] [Fauchet], *Despotisme*, p. 10.
[173] [Fauchet], *Despotisme*, p. 17.
[174] [Fauchet], *Despotisme*, p. 25.

emphasised, to refer back to the republics of the ancient world for models of republican rule. The "colossus of despotism" that now straddled the two worlds was beginning to crumble, opening a way for all the nations of the globe to take the "fraternal peoples of the United States of America as their model."[175] In France, this would mean abolishing the monarchy and replacing the standing army by a republican militia. The resulting reduction in public expenditure could be used to promote equality and maintain the combination of frugality and patriotic spirit that, under extremely adverse conditions, had secured the liberty of the Swiss, Dutch, and English republics in Europe's relatively recent past. If the spirit that had enabled these republics to overcome adversity continued to exist, Fauchet argued, size did not matter. Republics declined only if they pursued self-aggrandisement.[176] Expansion magnified inequality, while self-sufficiency kept natural differences in ability under control. Even in a republic, Fauchet noted, everyone could not be equally powerful, but they could, "as one of our modern philosophers has said, all be equally free."[177] Perhaps surprisingly, he associated these strong republican views with some of the leading members of the National Assembly, referring by name to "the eloquent Barnave," "the courageous and unshakeable Lameth," the "patriot d'Aiguillon," and those "austere Romans, Menou, Robespierre, Biauzat, Camus, and Dubois de Crancé," as "incorruptible friends of the people" whose "love of true liberty" matched his own political views.[178] Mirabeau, Sieyès, and Roederer were not mentioned at all.

The second of the two pamphlets was considerably more substantial. It was entitled *Supplément au Contrat Social* (Supplement to the Social Contract) and was the work of a Parisian man of letters with a Genevan family background named Pierre-Paul Gudin de la Brenellerie. Gudin was a close friend of the late eighteenth century's most successful playwright, Pierre-Augustin Caron de Beaumarchais, as well as of Dupont de Nemours (like Rousseau, Gudin noted, all three were watchmakers' sons).[179] He had, early in 1789, published an *Essai sur l'histoire des comices de Rome, des Etats-Généraux de France, et du Parlement d'Angleterre* (described by Jeremy Bentham as the work of a "very intelligent author"), and the later work was a shorter, more analytically explicit version of the historical argument of the earlier one.[180] Both books were intended to indicate the compatibility between

---

[175] [Fauchet], *Despotisme*, p. 13.

[176] [Fauchet], *Despotisme*, pp. 49–50, 53, 55–6.

[177] [Fauchet], *Despotisme*, p. 13.

[178] [Fauchet], *Despotisme*, pp. 60–1.

[179] Pierre-Paul Gudin de la Brenellerie, *Histoire de Beaumarchais*, ed. Maurice Tourneux (Paris, 1888), pp. 5–6.

[180] Jeremy Bentham, *Political Tactics* [1791], ed. Michael James, Cyprien Blamires, and Catherine Pease-Watkin (Oxford, Clarendon Press, 1999), p. 91. On Gudin, see Roger Barny,

Rousseau's political thought and the modified version of Physiocracy that Gudin took over from the work of Turgot and Dupont de Nemours and, by doing so, to show how the sovereignty of the general will could be maintained in a large, populous, and socially divided state like France.

In this setting, the emotional internalisation of the general will that was possible in a small state like Geneva was replaced by a more neutral identification of its status and content with the public interest or common good. Here, Rousseau's Polish system of graduated promotion to political office was joined to the modified version of Physiocracy that Gudin adopted from Turgot and Dupont de Nemours. Together, they allowed Gudin to apply the political theory of the *Social Contract* to the problem of restoring economic and social stability in a large territorial state. "I will often cite this excellent work, the clearest, most methodical, and the best that has been done on the political constitution of states," he wrote (referring to the *Social Contract*) in his *Essay on the History of the Roman Comitiae, the French Estates-General, and the English Parliament* of 1789. "Whoever seeks instruction should read and think about it. No one has better laid down the natural order of society. No one has better set out its principles or better understood its metaphysics."[181] As its title indicated, the whole work was intended to be a guide to the members of the forthcoming French Estates-General, using Rousseau's conceptual vocabulary to make a comparative analysis of representative institutions. The focus was therefore on government and on the extent to which the Comitiae of the Roman republic, the French Estates-General, and the English Parliament had been able to establish and maintain the general will (as Gudin, following Rousseau, called it) and, at the same time, prevent its abuse by any particular part of society. Unsurprisingly, the Estates-General came off worst. Its division into three separate orders and the increasingly glaring discrepancy between the size and wealth of the Third Estate and the privileges of the other two orders meant, Gudin argued, that the Estates-General was still threatened by the recurrent stalemate and unscrupulous exploitation of political deadlock that had marred its history. "The Third Estate," Gudin wrote, "meets all the needs of the kingdom by way of agriculture; it enriches it by trade; it makes it honoured for its literature and fine arts that, even now, it is almost alone in cultivating successfully in France; it defends it with excellent troops."

> It has no need of the other two orders, which will be able to make themselves useful and rid themselves of the restlessness that torments them only by turn-

---

L'éclatement révolutionnaire du Rousseauisme (Besançon and Paris, Les Belles Lettres, 1988), pp. 28–53.

[181] Pierre-Paul Gudin de la Brenellerie, *Essai sur l'histoire des comices de Rome, des Etats-Généraux de la France et du Parlement de l'Angleterre*, 3 vols. (Philadelphie [i.e., Paris], 1789), 1:10 (note 1)

ing to those same activities that they affect to disdain and that are all the more worthy of respect since they are the real foundations on which the whole state, and even the entire social order, are based.[182]

Although every individual would be a member of a state, sovereignty would still, as Gudin put it, have to be "circumscribed." Slavery had done this for the Romans. Taxation, he argued, performed the same function for the moderns. Both reduced membership of the sovereign to a fraction of the total membership of the state (although the fraction was much larger in the case of the moderns). The multiple subdivisions of both the Roman Comitiae and the English electoral system reduced the likelihood that sovereignty would ever come to be divided into permanent majorities and minorities, leaving the general will intact. In both the Roman republic and modern Britain the legislature and the executive were kept separate by the different ways by which their respective membership was selected. Both political systems were also equipped with a number of different veto points to keep the various governmental powers separate. Gudin was particularly insistent about the desirability of establishing what he called "a regulator" (in the sense of the governor or balance wheel of a watch) to maintain the consistency and continuity of political decision-making.[183] In Rome, this had been the original function of the people's tribunes. In Britain, it was maintained by both the monarch and the House of Lords and, in France, by the parlements. The danger, as history showed, was when the regulator began to stray beyond its purely negative function and started to encroach on the active powers of government. Once this began to happen, the government would start to allow sovereignty to leak into political life (which, as Gudin put it, was "the radical vice that destroys every constitution"), making deep-seated divisions between majorities and minorities more difficult to avoid.[184]

The problem could still, however, be managed if the calibre of political leadership remained high. Gudin was, accordingly, quick to endorse what Rousseau had written about the Roman system of graduated promotion. "The only permanent condition," he wrote, quoting Rousseau, "should be that of a citizen." Every other condition should be subject to election, making every position, again as Rousseau had put it, "a state of trial."[185] With the Romans, ten or eighteen years of military service were necessary before it was possible to practise the law, the prerequisite for election to one of the republic's inferior magistracies. These, in turn, gave eligibility for election to the republic's highest offices and, in a more general sense, served

[182] Gudin, *Essai*, 2:171–2.
[183] Gudin, *Essai*, 1:37, 100, 107.
[184] Gudin, *Essai*, 1:35.
[185] Gudin, *Essai*, 1:53.

to "set the state on its base," as Rousseau had put it, with the same kind of pyramid shape that Roederer was later to associate with Sieyès's system of representative government.[186] Although no actually existing system of government fitted all these requirements, Gudin singled out the British system as the best available model both because of the multiplicity of checking mechanisms built into political decision-making and because its agriculture, industry, and trade were no longer subject to the legacy of Europe's feudal past. The same, however, was not the case in France. There, the power and way of life of what Gudin called the "super-proprie-tors" (meaning the residue of the dual system of feudal land ownership with its separate owners of land's "direct" and "useful" demesnes) still rep-resented a substantial obstacle towards the more balanced interrelationship of agriculture, industry, and trade to be found in modern Britain.

The *Supplément au Contrat Social* was largely an amplification of the prin-ciples underlying the earlier, historical work and, since Rousseau "had worked only for small states," an adaptation of his principles to the larger setting of postrevolutionary France.[187] Three aspects of the earlier work were given greater prominence. The first was the need to "circumscribe" the membership of the sovereign.[188] The second was the abiding need for a "regulator," analogous to the tribunes in the Roman republic and the multiple veto points of the English constitution, to block the National Assembly's already visible drift towards adding administration to legisla-tion and, by doing so, to reinforce the still-embryonic system of decentral-ised departmental and municipal administration.[189] The third was the need to establish a comprehensive system of graduated promotion. Interestingly, Gudin made no reference at all to Mirabeau's attempt to establish a differ-ent version of the same system in December 1789 and gave no sign that anyone other than Rousseau had described the idea. He went to some lengths, however, to explain how the system would differ from the indirect elections that had been used to elect deputies to the Estates-General. There, parish or district assemblies had elected deputies to assemblies of the *bailliages* or *sénéchaussées*, which, in turn, had elected the membership of the Estates-General. The result, he suggested, had often been that the representatives and represented did not know one another at all.[190] Gradu-ated promotion, Gudin argued, would have the opposite effect. As with Rousseau's recommendations for Poland, the sequence of steps would begin either with military service or with teaching. Neither would be al-

---

[186] Gudin, *Essai*, 1:54, 107.
[187] Gudin, *Supplément*, p. 3.
[188] Gudin, *Supplément*, pp. 8–12.
[189] Gudin, *Supplément*, pp. 25–6, 29–37, 284–7.
[190] Gudin, *Supplément*, pp. 21–2.

lowed to become a professional career but would instead be the prerequisites for eligibility for election. If, Gudin argued, Rousseau's Polish system were applied to France, then two million men would become teachers or serve in the army and, after a period of ten years' service, would become eligible for election to one or other of the existing total of some 384,000 municipal offices. These officials would then be eligible for election to the 6,000 or so district offices, and they, in turn, could then be candidates for election to one or other of the 3,300 departmental positions. Eligibility for election to national office would, however, be open to everyone who had served in a lower capacity, both to ensure that promotion would be based on more than mere seniority and to prevent collusion among elected officials to keep themselves in place.[191] Outgoing officials would revert to being simple citizens, but would remain eligible for election to office at the same or a higher level, which would also add to the pool of eligible candidates for national office. Voting itself, however, would remain direct. The right to vote would be limited to taxpayers (which was how sovereignty would be "circumscribed"), who would be the owners of real, usually landed, property. Since, as Turgot had shown, a government could not tax capital as readily as the land's net product without interfering with circulation, and since the owners of capital were also likely to be the owners of urban or rural property, it was not necessary to have a separate tax on capital to admit its owners into political life. The line dividing active from passive citizens, Gudin wrote, would run between those who were able to provide for their own subsistence, "at least for a period of time," and those who could not.[192] The ultimate goal of Gudin's version of the system of graduated promotion was still to shift the balance of economic and political power back towards the natural developmental sequence of Physiocracy.

Gudin made a point of emphasising how widely predicted the French Revolution had been, citing the passage about the impending state of crisis and the century of revolutions that Rousseau had included in his *Emile*, as well as a letter from Frederick the Great to Voltaire of 1767 suggesting that the growing burden of the French and Austrian public debts would soon lead to the end of the independence of the Catholic Church and the confiscation of the property of the monastic orders. He also summarised the contents of Mably's *Droits et devoirs du citoyen*, written, he said, at the time of the Maupeou coup of 1771, to point out (as Keith Baker has shown more recently) the astonishing similarity between Mably's idea of a "managed" revolution and the events of 1787–8.[193] The standard response,

---

[191] Gudin, *Supplément*, pp. 61–2, 79–83, 297–301, 304–14.

[192] Gudin, *Supplément*, pp. 9–11.

[193] See Keith Michael Baker, *Inventing the French Revolution: Essays on French Political Culture in the Eighteenth Century* (Cambridge, CUP, 1990), ch. 7.

Gudin commented, had been to treat predictions like these as the work of Cassandras.[194] Against those who accused the philosophers of fomenting the revolution, he argued that they had actually been trying to forestall it.

> [C]ertain that it would be unavoidable, they tried to find the means to allow it to happen without the nation's undergoing those terrible convulsions that had bloodied almost all those revolutions that occurred in France or any other state and which, too often, served to make them entirely pointless.[195]

He emphasised the fundamental similarity among various proposals for political representation and fiscal decentralisation contained in the reform plans of Turgot, Necker, and the marquis d'Argenson. The revolution had happened, he concluded, because "nothing had been done about their proposals to forestall a revolution that they had foreseen."[196] The danger now, he warned, was that the dynamics of reform would spin out of control. Every legislature was exposed to the risks of making precipitate decisions, and prevailing economic circumstances were an open invitation to potentially dangerous attempts to speed up the process of reform. The existing combination of the idle rich and the propertyless poor was a political powder keg that only a more equitable distribution of property could defuse. "The greatest problem in politics," Gudin wrote, repeating the warning issued by Necker and Jacques-Henri Meister, was "to find a way to avoid having those who are idle or those who have no property in a state."[197] A gradual redistribution of property, by way of the abolition of substitutions and entails as well as the creation of a system of partible inheritance, had to be the main long-term goal of the new French regime. "To tame man's ferocity and develop his intelligence it was necessary to awaken his cupidity, to attach him to agriculture, commerce, and the arts by showing him the prospect of the riches and all the pleasures that they can provide."[198] It was a long way from Rousseau, but it still captured the nature of the problem that both Rousseau and the Physiocrats had addressed.

Gudin reinforced the argument by outlining the broader structural changes that were taking place in the world economy. These, he suggested, were likely to reinforce existing inequalities unless corrective action were taken. The supply of bullion from Mexico, Peru, and Brazil that had once underpinned the growth of Europe's foreign trade was beginning to dry up. The emergence of the United States of America was bound to add to the demand for the gold and silver coin used to settle trade balances across

[194] Gudin, *Supplément*, pp. 124–8.
[195] Gudin, *Supplément*, p. 130.
[196] Gudin, *Supplément*, p. 135.
[197] Gudin, *Supplément*, p. 159.
[198] Gudin, *Supplément*, p. 158.

international borders. In a more local sense, the institutional changes taking place in France were also bound to have a deep effect on the economic relationship between Paris and the rest of France. There was no longer a large royal court, and many of the major institutions of government—notably the huge jurisdiction of the parlement of Paris, as well as the major private financial institutions, the fiscal tribunals, and the five-yearly assemblies of the French clergy—had all disappeared. The massive inflows of money and other financial instruments into the capital generated by all these institutions had fallen, but the population of Paris still remained the same. The result was that the balance of payments had begun to move against the capital as it continued to import the materials and subsistence goods required by its population, but now faced a dwindling supply of income to fund its daily and weekly expenditure on imports from the rest of France.[199] In the long term, Gudin acknowledged, the process was likely to lead to a rebalancing of the economic and demographic relationship between Paris and the other French urban centres. In the short term, however, it presented a more worrying prospect. "The more populous a country becomes and the more it becomes covered with towns, market towns, or large villages," he wrote, "the more it tends towards liberty. But the less populous it becomes and the fewer and poorer that towns become, the more large landed property tends to grow and the more likely it is that slavery and feudalism are ready to be reborn."[200]

Both Gudin's and Fauchet's analyses make it easier to see why the problem of sovereignty came to loom so large in revolutionary politics. Emphasising the nation's sovereignty, as Fauchet did, made it harder to accept its divisions. Recognising the nation's divisions, as Gudin did, made it harder to see how to maintain its sovereignty. The difficulties were registered very well in the short political career of Antoine-Joseph Barnave, the man whom Joseph Fauchet associated with his own republican principles. Barnave was the most energetic opponent of the system of graduated promotion that Gudin in one way, and Mirabeau, Roederer, and Sieyès in another, supported. The unitary character of the nation, he argued in December 1789, ruled out the divisive hierarchy that Mirabeau proposed. But the difficulty of reconciling the nation's sovereignty with its various constituent interests led to an abrupt change of course. The key turning point was the subject of France's colonial empire and the possibility that the collapse of the French empire in the Caribbean would undermine the trade and industry required to maintain the new regime's financial stability. Were this to happen, Barnave argued, the economic and political influence of the landowners might, as Gudin also suggested, become predominant. Necessity, he now claimed,

[199] Gudin, *Supplément*, pp. 212–26.
[200] Gudin, *Supplément*, pp. 185–6.

meant that liberty had, for the time being, to go hand in hand with empire, even an empire based on slavery. As the royalist *Journal de la société des amis de la constitution monarchique* noted with some pleasure in May 1791, "the discussion [in the National Assembly] related to the colonies offered a new spectacle." Fauchet's heroes, Barnave and Lameth, were now to be seen "in coalition with the right," while the abbé Sieyès was now "in coalition with the largest number of the Jacobins."[201]

Barnave's notes, written largely in 1792 and 1793, indicate something of the thinking associated with this change of course. "Nature," he wrote in one fragment, "has established jealousy and reciprocity among men. The one leads them to oppose others' well-being as something harmful to their own; the other leads them to favour the well-being of others as something that reacts with their own." The two capacities led to two broad systems "in morality, politics, political economy, foreign policy, and even in agriculture," one based on jealousy and the other on reciprocity. Physiocracy was the most comprehensive example of the latter. "The modern doctrine, based principally on the writings of the sect called the economists," Barnave noted, "has adopted the system of reciprocity in all its applications."[202] The prestige that still surrounded their system had, he noted, played a major part in "the disasters of the colonies."[203] By promoting too speedy an end to the French colonial empire, the supporters of reciprocity were running the risk of simply replacing one kind of jealousy by another. Putting an end to empire meant playing into the hands of the kingdom's landowners and substituting one exclusive interest for another. For Barnave, a political society had to be able both to counter jealousy and to favour reciprocity. Echoing the argument that the Scottish moral philosopher Adam Ferguson had made in his *History of Civil Society* of 1767 against Montesquieu's honour-based concept of monarchy, Barnave advocated a strategy that was designed to favour the emergence of an elite based on public service, particularly service in the recently established National Guard headed by his new political ally the former marquis de Lafayette. A municipality, as one of Lafayette's political allies put it in 1791, was simply the name of a natural human community, with as much of a natural right to the use of armed force as any single individual.[204] The National Guard could, from this point of view, become a new source of moral authority,

---

[201] *Journal de la société des amis de la constitution monarchique* 23 (21 May 1791): 7.

[202] Antoine-Joseph Barnave, "Etudes sur l'homme," in his *Oeuvres complètes*, ed. Bérenger de la Drôme, 4 vols. (Paris, 1843), 3:13–4.

[203] Barnave, "Sur les économistes," in Barnave, *Oeuvres*, ed. Bérenger de la Drôme, 2:63.

[204] Louis-Ramond de Carbonnières, *Opinion énoncée à la société de 1789 sur les loix constitutionnelles* (Paris, 1791), p. 44. Compare Barnave's claim about jealousy and reciprocity as the dual motivations underlying human societies to Adam Ferguson, *An Essay on the History of Civil Society* [1767], ed. Fania Oz (Cambridge, CUP, 1995), pp. 7–29.

and, once a stable, service-based political elite had emerged, the empire could then be allowed to unravel without jeopardising domestic economic and political stability. But if trade were to dry up too soon, the economic power of the landowning former nobility would destroy what had been achieved after 1789. "France," Barnave wrote, "situated between two oceans, placed so to speak at the centre of commercial Europe, was destined to arrive at a high level of industry and moveable wealth, but the immense extent of her territory was bound to ensure that the preponderance of the aristocracy would last for a long time."[205] In the short term, the need to neutralise the power of the landowners made the survival of the French colonial empire a matter of necessity and, by extension, justified any way that could be found to bring the revolution to an end. The argument was echoed by another self-proclaimed republican, the self-styled "orator of the human race," Anacharsis Cloots.[206]

The war and the formation of the republic in 1792 magnified the problem of maintaining political liberty and financial stability in just the way that Burke had predicted. The Jacobin solution, presented by Robespierre and Saint-Just to the republican Convention in the spring of 1793, was to opt decisively for the standard system of republican government.[207] The new French republic would be governed by a scaled-up version of the small and great councils that had been the hallmark of republican government in Italy, the Netherlands, and the Swiss republics for many hundreds of years. The whole republic would form a single electoral unit and elect the membership of its legislative and executive councils without any of the divisions produced by different local electoral constituencies and property qualifications. The non-Jacobin alternative was set out in the draft republican constitution presented to the Convention by the former marquis de Condorcet, and in the calibrated system of catering for municipal, departmental, and national majorities and minorities that it contained. Condorcet's proposal, with its emphasis upon the blocking power built into the component parts of the republic's government and the number of different veto points that this would produce, was given quite extensive discussion in the latter part of Pierre-Louis Roederer's *Course on Social Organisation*, a course of public lectures that Roederer gave at the Parisian

---

[205] Barnave, "Introduction à la révolution française," in Barnave, *Oeuvres*, ed. Bérenger de la Drôme, 1:75.

[206] A helpful thumbnail sketch of Cloots's thought can be found in Richard Tuck, *The Laws of War and Peace* (Oxford, Oxford University Press, 1999).

[207] The focus on the idea of sovereignty in the studies of Jacobinism and its origins by François Furet, Lucien Jaume, or even Patrice Gueniffey in his *La politique de la terreur: essai sur la violence révolutionnaire 1789–94* (Paris, Fayard, 2000) has made it easy to overlook the very conventionally republican character of the institutional arrangements proposed by Robespierre and Saint-Just in the spring of 1793.

Lycée in the spring of 1793.[208] The broad theoretical framework for the government of a large, socially stratified republic that he presented was intended both to counter what Robespierre and the Jacobin leadership were proposing and to reinforce Condorcet's alternative proposal with the help of some of the less politically unmentionable aspects of Sieyès's idea of representative government.

PIERRE-LOUIS ROEDERER

As its general title indicated, Roederer's lecture course took its cue from Sieyès's initial insight into the double-bind produced by adding a debt to a state. A republican constitution might well supply a framework for securing civil and political liberty, but something more was required to secure the constitution itself. This was why it was necessary to examine the whole "organisation" of society and why what Sieyès had called "social science" had to identify the deeper potential sources of constitutional stability. The lecture course had two targets. The first consisted of those who took agriculture, manufacturing industry, and trade for granted and assumed that a government's chief responsibility was simply to keep them in place. This part of the argument was aimed at those, like Tom Paine, Jacques-Pierre Brissot, Etienne-Gabriel Clavière, and perhaps even Condorcet himself, who underestimated the relatively precarious and historically contingent properties of the modern world.[209] Constitutional government itself, Roederer emphasised, was dependent on the kind of "social system" that had

---

[208] On Condorcet, see, particularly, Ian McLean and Fiona Hewitt, eds., *Condorcet: Foundations of Social Choice and Political Theory* (London, Edward Elgar, 1994), and Emma Rothschild, "Condorcet and the Conflict of Values," *Historical Journal* 39 (1996): 677–701. The most recent biography is by David Williams, *Condorcet and Modernity* (Cambridge, CUP, 2004). On Roederer, see most recently, Ruth Scurr, "Social Equality in Pierre-Louis Roederer's Interpretation of the Modern Republic, 1793," *History of European Ideas* 26 (2000): 105–26, and her "Pierre-Louis Roederer and the Debate on the Forms of Government in Revolutionary France," *Political Studies* 52 (2004): 251–68.

[209] The best starting point for understanding the economic and political thought of these individuals remains Gary Kates, *The Cercle Social, the Girondins, and the French Revolution* (Princeton, Princeton University Press, 1985). See also Patrice Gueniffey, "Cordeliers and Girondins: The Prehistory of the Republic?" in Biancamaria Fontana, ed., *The Invention of the Modern Republic* (Cambridge, CUP, 1994), pp. 86–106; James Livesey, "Agrarian Ideology and Commercial Republicanism in the French Revolution," *Past & Present* 157 (1997): 94–121; Richard Whatmore, "Commerce, Constitutions, and the Manners of a Nation: Etienne Clavière's Revolutionary Political Economy, 1788–1793," *History of European Ideas* 22 (1996): 351–68; Mark Philp, "English Republicanism in the 1790s," *Journal of Political Philosophy* 6 (1998): 235–62, and, for a helpful way into the thought of Tom Paine, see the introduction by David Wootton to David Wootton,ed., *Republicanism, Liberty and Commercial Society 1649–1776* (Stanford, Stanford University Press, 1994).

come into being and the many, apparently natural, arrangements that it housed. This, he explained, was why Sieyès's term "social science" had to encompass the related subjects of morality, politics, and political economy, or the whole subject-matter of the natural and political theory of post-Grotian natural jurisprudence.[210] The other part of Roederer's argument was aimed at those who simply rejected the premises on which the modern world was based. Here, he singled out Diderot (who, like many of his contemporaries, he mistakenly took to be the author of *Code de la nature*, or *Nature's Code*, which had in fact been published in 1751 by an obscure financial official named Etienne-Gabriel Morelly) and the abbé Gabriel Bonnot de Mably for particular attention.[211] While the first target consisted of the advocates of an egalitarian system of property distribution, the second consisted of the advocates of a system of common ownership. The aim of the lecture course, Roederer announced, was to make it possible to come to a verdict on the competing claims of those who stood for the preservation of public wealth and equal rights by way of the inequality of fortunes, on the one hand, and, on the other, those "levellers of fortunes whose leaden cylinder would compress land that should be cultivated, suffocate or mutilate the germs of production that should be developed, and, consequently, harm every interest and every right."[212] Real equality might have been the core value of the ancients. Real inequality, but formal legal and political equality, had to be those of the moderns. The problem was to explain how the two could be reconciled and, by doing so, identify the extraconstitutional sources of constitutional stability. The pivotal figure in the argument that Roederer proceeded to develop was Rousseau. In the heated political context of the constitutional debates taking place in the spring of 1793, Roederer set out to identify the theoretical convergence between Rousseau and Sieyès and, by doing so, to rescue Rousseau from Robespierre (whom he attacked openly in the tenth of his lectures) by separating off Rousseau from Mably.[213]

It was a daring move. To carry it off, Roederer went straight to the heart of Rousseau's denunciation of inequality, picking out the most famous pas-

---

[210] Pierre-Louis Roederer, *Cours d'organisation sociale*, in Roederer, *Oeuvres*, 8:130. On the early history of the concept of "social science," see, most recently, Martin S. Staum, *Minerva's Message: Stabilizing the French Revolution* (Montreal, McGill-Queen's University Press, 1996), and Keith M. Baker, "The Early History of the Term 'Social Science,'" *Annals of Science* 20 (1964): 211–26, and Brian W. Head, "The Origins of *'la science sociale'* in France, 1770–1800," *Australian Journal of France Studies* 19 (1982): 115–32.

[211] Something overlooked in Norman Hampson, "Mably and the Montagnards," *French History* 16 (2002): 402–15.

[212] Roederer, *Cours*, p. 134.

[213] Robespierre's proposed additions on property to the republic's Declaration of the Rights of Man were, Roederer stated, "une véritable logomachie": *Cours*, p. 245.

sage of Rousseau's second *Discourse* for extended commentary. "How many crimes, wars, murders, how many miseries and horrors mankind would have been spared," Rousseau had written, if, to the first man "to whom it occurred to say, *this is mine*," someone had replied, "beware of listening to this impostor; you are lost if you forget that the fruits are everyone's and the earth no-one's."[214] Roederer set out to explain both why Rousseau was right and yet why the age-old assertion about the fundamentally communal character of property was still compatible with a great variety of different types of private ownership and a large amount of inequality. To do so, he developed the substance of an argument that he had earlier set out in a memorandum in 1788 calling for the abolition of the customs barriers surrounding the province of Lorraine, and in a pamphlet entitled *De la députa-tion aux Etats-Généraux* (On Deputation to the Estates-General) that he had published in 1789. The argument made detailed use of the account of the origins of different types of inequality that Turgot had set out in his *Reflections on the Formation of Wealth*, buttressed by the analysis of land, labour, and capital contained in Adam Smith's *Inquiry into the Nature and Causes of the Wealth of Nations* and his *Theory of Moral Sentiments*, as well as what Roederer knew about an as yet unpublished commentary on the latter work by Condorcet's wife, Sophie de Grouchy (according to Roederer, Sieyès, in whose hands he had seen it in 1790, "had been astonished by it").[215] He began by construing what Rousseau had written in terms of an elaborate metaphor. If the earth was no one's, then all the land, buildings, and other immoveable goods that it contained could be described as being held on deposit by their owners. Since the counterpart to a deposit was a pledge, everyone had an entitlement to property's fruits. Exercising the pledge meant redeeming some or all of the deposit.[216] The metaphor, with its connotations of trusteeship (or, less happily, pawnbroking), then had to explain why the depositaries, or the owners of real property, really would have to honour the pledge issued to the depositors and, by doing so, make property's fruits available to everyone. To do so, Roederer used a combination of Turgot's account of the multiple origins of inequality and the moral psychology of Helvétius and Adam Smith.

---

[214] Rousseau, *Discourse on Inequality*, ed. Gourevitch, p. 161.

[215] Roederer, *Cours*, p. 194.

[216] "Nous verrons . . . en un mot, si ce qu'on appelle la propriété territoriale, celle des capitaux placés en exploitations agricoles, et l'industrie qui les fait valoir, son autre chose que des dépositaires des fruits de la terre chargés de distribuer ces fruits entre toutes les classes ouvrières et capitalistes de la société, qui, de leur côté, sont nantis de toutes les richesses mobilières, de toutes les facultés industrielles que l'amour des jouissances rend nécessaires aux propriétaires de subsistances, et pour lesquelles seules ils en font naître au delà de leurs besoins": Roederer, *Cours*, p. 134 (see, too, pp. 153, 154–5, referring explicitly to the passage in Rousseau, and p. 239).

Specialisation, Roederer argued, began with conveniences, not luxuries. He went back to Montesquieu's choice of modernity's starting point in the Germanic invasions of the Roman Empire to explain how the process had occurred. The move enabled him to avoid having to deal directly with the sequence that Rousseau had presented in his second *Discourse*. (Rousseau's "favourite error," Roederer commented elsewhere in his lecture course, was that the social state did not make men better or happier and, in its historical account of the origins of the family, depended on the unproven assumption that the humanoids of the original natural state were solitary herbivores, not carnivores, thus eliminating the possibility that women might have depended on men to carry out the various hunting or snaring tasks required for the meat that they needed in late pregnancy and immediately after childbirth).[217] Conquest gave the conquerors a surplus that could be used to provide their serfs with subsistence goods while they made them conveniences like furnishings. Once the furniture-producing serfs had accumulated a surplus of their own, they would not need the capital supplied by the landowners. The landowners would then be able to use the funds that had been released to improve their land. "Thus," Roederer emphasised, "in Europe, and everywhere where there is a large amount of inequality of property ownership, agriculture depends on manufacturing industry."[218] The same process of capital accumulation and capital release would then apply to the functions of the middleman. Once they had accumulated a surplus, traders and merchants would not have to depend on goods and credit supplied by either the manufacturers or the landowners. This, in turn, left the manufacturers with larger amounts of available capital. "Thus," Roederer concluded, "three sorts of property are necessary for the fecundity of the land, the ownership of the soil and two kinds of capital, and, since it requires three types of work to be combined and, so to speak, stipulated among those undertaking them for the exploitation of the land— agricultural, manufacturing, and mercantile work—it also requires the capital to be divided among the three types of work."[219] The question that this arrangement raised was whether it was compatible with the more fundamental purposes of social organisation itself.

Every society, Roederer argued, faced three kinds of risk. There were those produced by natural disasters and famine, those produced by acute domestic economic and social inequality, and those produced by external threats and war. No political society, he stated, could eliminate all three. Physiocracy in its original guise had been designed to deal with the first.

---

[217] Roederer, *Cours*, pp. 168 (on the herbivore-carnivore distinction) and 256 (on Rousseau's "favourite error").

[218] Roederer, *Cours*, pp. 140–1.

[219] Roederer, *Cours*, p. 143.

It had subordinated everything to the goal of self-sufficiency, and, since industrial productivity based on a solid agricultural foundation looked, self-evidently, like the winning ticket, it had been a gamble on the probability that the favourite in the race towards autarchy really would win (the metaphor was Roederer's). But by backing the favourite so strongly, the economists had played into the hands of the levellers. They, rightly, had recognised the domestic risks arising from inequality and its affront to human dignity and had been given a voice by Mably, the economists' most determined opponent. As Roederer conceded, levellers like Robespierre were advocates not of indigence, but of "the possession of a necessary amplitude." But it was still the case that their system opened a door to the third kind of risk. Although, Roederer argued, every redistributive project carried domestic political risks, these were not the only reason for relying on more natural redistributive mechanisms like replacing primogeniture by equal, partible inheritance. The risk to domestic society that every redistributive project carried was the power that emphasising the purely conventional character of property would place in the hands of the state. If citizens were to become liable in their persons and not, as Rousseau had argued, in their property for failing to meet their civil and political obligations, then their lives and liberty would be directly subject to the state's power. But this danger was still less potentially fatal than the manifest harm that levelling projects would do to external security. "Less production," Roederer warned, "means less population; less population means less armed force."

> France feeds one man for every five *arpents* (or acres) of land. In this respect, she is ahead of Germany and Spain. But England, Switzerland, and Holland have the advantage over France in terms of the same production-population ratio. We have to reach parity on the one side without falling back on the other. If the Greeks overcame the Persians, if the Romans conquered the world, and the Franks vanquished the Roman, none of these examples are conclusive against the utility of populousness. First, the invention of gunpowder, by entirely changing the art of battle, has removed a great deal of the power of individual valour and made sheer numbers a necessary resource. Second, since every belligerent people has now reached more or less the same degree of softness, the advantage that savage manners once gave to some relatively young peoples over others who were older and corrupt no longer applies, which is another reason for seeking the advantage of numbers.[220]

In the last analysis, the risks of war had to set limits on the feasibility of eliminating the two other kinds of risk. If the broad features of the social organisation of modernity had come into being to preserve and reinforce

---

[220] Roederer, *Cours*, p. 152.

liberty and security, then in contradistinction to what the Swiss political economist Jean-Frédéric Herrenschwand had written, the wealth and populousness generated by industry, agriculture, and trade (in that order of causation) housed the least risk.

If property was held on deposit but its fruits were available on pledge, then Roederer still had to explain why the depositors were able to rely on the depositaries to supply them with goods. Here, Roederer reverted to the modernist defence of luxury. The answer, he stated, was that there was "a law of nature, more imperious than any human law, that ordered it thus," meaning, he continued, "that law which makes man pursue ever newer enjoyments (*les jouissances toujours nouvelles*), which the perfectibility of his mind and perhaps his own volatility make known to him wherever his wit may reach, and which habit turns into necessity as soon as it has been tasted."[221] As the final phrase suggests, the most striking line in Voltaire's poem *Le Mondain* (The Man of the World)—"luxury, that necessary superfluity"—had a long afterlife. The vaguely epicurean picture that Roederer presented raised the further question of how the pursuit of pleasure and ever-newer *jouissances* could be kept stable. Here, he stated, there were three broad positions. There were those who argued that the only guarantee of social conventions had to be a very independent, strong, and powerful government, reinforced by a publicly imposing religion. Necker, he said, was an apologist of this "religious and monarchical system." There were also those who claimed that human arrangements were largely self-supporting, and that, as in a theatre, where a single hushing sound could impose silence, or in a church, where a single sign could make everyone fall to their knees, a human society could, if its individual members had very similar interests and values, simply govern itself. Tom Paine, Roederer claimed, was a good example of this position. Helvétius, he went on to say, occupied a position midway between the two. It was one that accepted the need for government, but recognised the "important point" that the more that government could be limited without harm to the social order, the better guaranteed that social order would be.[222]

The part played by the passions in the self-centred system that Helvétius had developed fitted the economic arrangements of modernity. But it was also more fundamentally grounded. The "organisation of the human body and its complexion," Roederer emphasised, "are not only the origin and instrument of the passions, but also one of their governors (*régulateurs*) and movers (*mobiles*). Thus a general system of human actions would, essentially, be the outcome of physiological and anatomical knowledge."[223] One

[221] Roederer, *Cours*, p. 153.
[222] Roederer, *Cours*, pp. 180–1.
[223] Roederer, *Cours*, p. 182.

day, he speculated, chemistry might reveal all the secrets of the inner life of human beings and allow morality and politics to have the same degree of certainty as geometry. That day, however, was still far off.[224] The more immediate task was to identify the part played by the passions in giving cohesion to a social organisation based on many different types of occupations and property. Roederer followed Helvétius in dividing the passions into two kinds. Physical passions were a product of present sensibility and external sensation. The very transparency of the human skin made it easy to identify and interpret their presence.[225] Moral passions, on the other hand, were a product of the uniquely human capacity for foresight, which Roederer illustrated by using Pascal's famous example of the fear of death and the oddly paradoxical character of a feeling associated with a state that involved no feeling.[226] This latter type of passion pushed the subject of the human imagination to the centre of the discussion and led Roederer to begin an extended examination of the moral theory of Adam Smith's *Theory of Moral Sentiments*.

Smith, he stated, was "a more powerful adversary" than anyone else of the system of self-interest developed by "Pufendorf, Mandeville, Hobbes, La Rochefoucauld, and, above all, Helvétius."[227] Closer inspection, however, suggested that Smith and Helvétius actually had a great deal in common. "It is easy to prove," Roederer announced, "that these two systems come very near to one another, and it even seems to me that, instead of contradicting one another, they round each other off (*se complètent*)."[228] As Smith himself had said, sympathy was an "immediate emanation of self-liking (*amour-de-soi*) and sensibility" and could be described as the "older sister" of self-interest.[229] This meant that "there is in sympathy what is called self-interest, just as there is self-interest in what is called sympathy."[230] If this was the case, then Smith could be combined with Helvétius to produce a more robust moral theory than Helvétius alone had supplied. Roederer saw the more immediate point of Smith's argument very well. All sympathy's power, he stated, came "uniquely" from the imagination, the same source that Rousseau had picked out as the key to explaining the origins of inequality.[231] As Roederer also saw, Smith's aim had been to refute Rousseau. The push that, according to Rousseau, the imagination would give to the idea of a self and then to evaluating that self's social

---

[224] Roederer, *Cours*, p. 182.
[225] Roederer, *Cours*, p. 135.
[226] Roederer, *Cours*, p. 183.
[227] Roederer, *Cours*, p. 186.
[228] Roederer, *Cours*, p. 189.
[229] Roederer, *Cours*, p. 187.
[230] Roederer, *Cours*, p. 191.
[231] Roederer, *Cours*, p. 187.

standing would, according to Smith, be offset by the pull exercised both by the self-correcting capacity of an imaginatively based and internalised impartial spectator, and by the real physical and demographic limits on the consumption of necessities. However unequal a society might be, it could still produce an adequate range of moral standards and would still contain no more than a determinate number of stomachs and a finite capacity for the consumption of necessities.

If the wealth of modern societies was the key to their ability to maintain external security and the relatively limited notion of justice that this implied, it was less easy to see how the mechanisms involved in the production and distribution of that wealth could be reconciled with any more extensive notion of justice. Here, Smith's moral theory appeared to contain an unacceptably naturalistic endorsement of the distinction of ranks. As Roederer described it (quoting Smith himself), sympathy supplied "the principle or at least the sanction for, and legitimation of, social distinctions."[232] It meant, according to Roederer, that "the law of sympathy is the principal cause of the inequalities existing among men in society," and, by extension, that there was "a natural and primitive law that was opposed to a government's being exempt from having a rich, powerful, crowned head (*chef*)."[233] In the context of the constitutional debates then taking place in the republic's Convention, this was a step too far. As Roederer described Smith's moral theory, the naturalistic terms in which it was couched also had the disadvantage of conflating wealth, power, and consideration in ways that were morally and politically unacceptable. "It should be remembered," he stated, "that in his [Smith's] system he recognises a *natural principle* of the inequality of conditions among men." But, Roederer replied, "sympathy does not motivate the love of power and wealth; wealth in itself is not a principle of social inequality any more than all the powers might be."[234] Wealth and power, Roederer argued, were means, not ends. More wealth meant more necessities; more power meant greater security. The problem was to ensure that the means met the ends.

It may not have been the most acute interpretation of Smith's moral theory (and it may also have been deliberately designed to protect Rousseau from Smith in order to be able to use Rousseau for other, more immediately polemical purposes), but it brought Roederer back to Sieyès and, more specifically, to the idea of society as a combination of means and ends that, as Roederer put it, had been given so "perfect" an analysis in the introduction to the draft Declaration of the Rights of Man that Sieyès had submit-

[232] Roederer, *Cours*, p. 200.
[233] Roederer, *Cours*, p. 188.
[234] Roederer, *Cours*, p. 200.

ted to the National Assembly in 1789.[235] According to Sieyès as Roederer summarised him, all individuals have both needs and the means to meet those needs. Since both attributes were generic to the human race, they were the basis of equality. All individuals could also be either means or obstacles to one another. The former implied concord, the latter conflict. The state of nature favoured the latter, but the state of society favoured the former. Society could equip itself with the means to prevent individuals from obstructing one another and, by doing so, enable them to use one another as means. It had, therefore, to have common means. These, whether they were supplied by one or many or all, would apply to the whole society. If they did not, they would not be common. As Roederer presented it, union led to concord, rather than, as in his earlier description of Tom Paine's idea of social organisation, concord's giving rise to union.[236]

If, as Roederer argued, all political societies faced three types of risk, their ability to face externally generated threats to their survival had to come first. But, under modern conditions of war and debt, neutralising that risk could leave governments exposed to the two other forms of risk, namely, an inability to deal with natural disasters, or the political stasis produced by deep-seated social divisions. Representative government, as Sieyès had construed it, supplied a way to meet the first type of risk without then having to face the others. Roederer went on accordingly to highlight the similarity between what Sieyès and Hobbes had written about natural rights. "It is therefore neither absurd nor reprehensible, neither against the dictates of true reason," Hobbes had written in his *De Cive*, "for a man to use all his endeavours to preserve and defend his body and the members thereof from death and sorrows." It was "the first foundation of natural right." But, Hobbes continued, "it is in vain for a man to have a right to the end, if the right to the necessary means be denied him." Nature gave everyone a right to everything, but it was a right that could hardly be exercised in the state of nature. "For the effects of this right," Hobbes wrote, "are the same, almost, as if there had been no right at all. For although any man might say of every thing, *this is mine*, yet could he not enjoy it, by reason of his neighbour, who having equal right and equal power, would pretend the same thing to be his."[237] Political society, not natural society, had to be the way to secure the right. This was the point of Roederer's metaphor about land's being held on deposit and its fruits' being available

---

[235] Roederer, *Cours*, p. 137.

[236] Roederer, *Cours*, pp. 230–1 (which can be compared to his characterisation of Paine on pp. 180–1 as someone who subscribed to the belief that it was possible to "unite citizens' interests so tightly and enlighten their minds so powerfully on the advantages of that union that society would exist because of the strength of the association itself").

[237] Roederer, *Cours*, p. 231, quoting Hobbes, *De Cive*; see Hobbes, *The Citizen*, ed. Gert, 1, §7, 8, 9, 10, pp. 115–7.

on pledge to everyone. It allowed him to align what Rousseau had written about property in his second *Discourse* with Hobbes and Sieyès and set it against Mably and Robespierre, on the one hand, and, less emphatically, against Paine and the advocates of a purely self-sustaining social system, on the other. But it also ruled out what Roederer took to be the excessively naturalistic explanation of the origins of inequality of Smith's *Theory of Moral Sentiments*. Reconciling the egalitarian premises of Hobbes's and Sieyès's starting point with the inequality of modern social organisation led Roederer to make use of a modified version of Helvétius's theory of the passions.

The point of the move was to suggest that, once basic survival needs had been met, judgements based on taste would offset inequality's potential for producing social envy. Here, Roederer turned to the findings of modern physiology, referring to Toussaint Bordenave's *Essai sur la physiologie* (Essay on Physiology), a frequently reprinted popularisation of the work of the Swiss physiologist Albrecht von Haller (whose *Elements of Physiology* Bordenave had translated in 1769), to argue that humans were naturally equipped with internal as well as external senses, with the former being the generic name given by Bordenave to memory, imagination, attention, and judgement.[238] All pleasures and pains, Roederer claimed, were not of the same nature. Some were attached to our interest in self-preservation, but others were not. Some were connected to our needs, but others were simply attached to sensations themselves. These latter were responsible for all the aesthetic judgements that went along with the external senses, but were not vital for existence. "The internal senses," Roederer stated, "are the inner sentinels of the animal economy, placed at the seat of our needs, or rather are the organs of our needs, while the external senses are the organs of sensations that both do and do not pertain to our needs."

---

[238] See Toussaint Bordenave, *Essai sur la physiologie, ou physique du corps humain*, 4th ed., 2 vols. (Paris, 1787), 1:111–2: "Outre la sympathie des parties du corps entre elles, il y a encore une sympathie réciproque entre l'âme et le corps. L'âme étant agitée dans son principe, elle produit, par l'action des sens internes, des mouvements sympathiques et particulières à certaines parties, selon l'espèce d'affection de l'âme: ainsi le souvenir d'une chose hideuse excite des nausées; la terreur cause la pâleur, les palpitations, les tremblements des lèvres; l'imagination plus ou moins vive détermine des mouvements différents, etc. . . . De même les passions de l'âme, que l'on peut rapporter en général à l'amour ou à la haine, excitent dans le corps des mouvements automatiques, indépendants de la volonté. Réciproquement le corps agit sur l'âme: telle affection du corps cause telle idée; l'aspect des choses extérieures excite des passions dans l'âme; une impression faite sur le corps pendant le sommeil ou pendant la veille, est suivie d'un sentiment interne; la santé du corps contribue à la tranquillité et à la bonne disposition de l'âme, et elle est affectée par les moindres dérangements du corps." Interestingly, Bordenave relied quite heavily on Quesnay's *Essai physique sur l'économie animale* in speculating about the part played by the nerves and a "vital principle" in the interaction between the soul and the body (see Bordenave, *Essai*, 1:94–5, 103–4, and, on Malebranche, Quesnay, and the internal senses, 2:241–2, 247).

Smelling the scent of a rose is to have an agreeable sensation by way of the
sense of smell; hearing a harmonious tune is to have an agreeable sensation by
way of the sense of hearing. But sensations of this kind are not at all necessary
for existence or even useful for self-preservation; they affect only the eyes, the
ears, or the brain and affect the brain only by way of the eyes and ears. After
experiencing them, one may *desire* them, but the desire whose object they are
is neither very urgent nor very durable. Eating, drinking, or tasting the enjoyments of love, on the other hand, involve having not only agreeable sensations
but those required for existence or health. They give rise to enjoyment not
only by way of the senses of taste or touch, but by way of the internal organs
of the stomach and generation.[239]

The needs for action after rest, or rest after action, were examples of needs
arising from our internal organisation, independent of the external senses.
These needs were not the result of any particular sense but a product of "a
sentiment common to all the parts of our being, to all our organs." They
were the result of our mobility (*mobilité*) and force of inertia (*inertie*) and
their constant action and reaction upon one another. Memory, imagination, and the other internal senses turned novelties into habits and made
the idea of physical necessity something that could never be fixed. But they
also supplied a bedrock of evaluation that could offset the more volatile
judgements made by the external senses. This, Roederer argued, meant
that it was not only our faculty for enjoyment but our habitually formed
need for certain types of enjoyment that gave rise to those "lively and constant desires named *passions*, which are the motivators of the great human
determinations and the principle of the moral passions." The principle of
the passions, he concluded, was "less in the external than the internal organs."[240] Behind the ideas, feelings, and knowledge generated by the external senses lay a deeper level of determination generated by the internal
senses of memory, imagination, attention, and judgement.

The two different sources of the passions meant that they could, as
Roederer put it, be "graduated," and, if the more volatile and ephemeral
passions involved in aesthetic judgements could be anchored to the more
deep-seated passions supplied by the internal senses, modern social organisation would have an internal source of stability that would make limited
government viable.[241] As Roederer put it when he began his examination
of the passions, moral passions were more plastic than physical passions.
"Power, wealth, and consideration are the nets that bring them together,
the reservoir that holds them, the barrier surrounding them, etc. Give one

[239] Roederer, *Cours*, p. 225.
[240] Roederer, *Cours*, p. 225.
[241] Roederer, *Cours*, p. 206.

of these instruments the power of the other two, and the other two will soon be abandoned. Give to consideration alone what belongs to wealth and power, or tie power and wealth to consideration alone, and you will make love of consideration the dominant virtue, citizens' only moral passion."[242] The way to do so was to ensure that consideration came first, so that having an interest in consideration would be the first of a number of means used to maintain "the graduation of the passions."[243] It would be very easy, Roederer suggested, "to place the enjoyments to which interest tends at the very end of the road (*à l'extrémité de la carrière*) to which the public good summons the assistance of citizens," just as it would be easy to "graduate that motive" by acting obliquely and indirectly on sensibility itself. "These truths," he added, "are the basis of a theory of legislation that might appear paradoxical," which was why they needed to be spelled out in detail.[244]

The remark pointed towards the same kind of argument that the advocates of the system of graduated promotion had used in 1789. But Roederer had to cut off the lecture course before he could present a full version of the theory of legislation in question. He turned first to an examination of the theory of human understanding both to finish off his presentation of the moral elements of society and to indicate the power of "several principal agents that ought to be used for the graduation of human passions."[245] Here, he made extensive use of Rousseau's *Essay on the Origin of Languages* and, in particular, of Rousseau's examination of music and painting to show how they could be used to shape the moral dimension of social life. The political side of the argument began with a hint in the very first lecture that the course would focus on "various systems of political organisation," notably "the federative system, so justly rejected in France," and the system of "unity and indivisibility." The opposition between them, Roederer added, "could be reduced to not very much."[246] By the time that he came back to the subject in his tenth lecture, however, the situation in Paris had become very dangerous. As the divisions in the Convention widened during the month of May 1793, Roederer could not do much more than hint at the similarity between Rousseau's idea of an "elective aristocracy" and Sieyès's notion of "representative government" and highlight the congruence between the notion of the separation of powers embedded, but not named, in Condorcet's draft republican constitution and the more strongly

[242] Roederer, *Cours*, p. 205.
[243] Roederer, *Cours*, p. 206.
[244] Roederer, *Cours*, p. 206.
[245] Roederer, *Cours*, p. 206.
[246] Roederer, *Cours*, p. 139.

vertical separation of powers of Sieyès's constitutional theory.[247] He also hinted at the broader idea of a system of gradual promotion by advocating a lower age of political majority (eighteen instead of twenty-five) and by presenting a very positive view of the idea that apprenticeship in manufacturing industry should begin with the life of an itinerant journeyman (*compagnonnage*), and that future army officers should begin by living in barracks and eating ordinary soldiers' food.[248] Unsurprisingly, he made no reference at all to the more directly political applications of the idea, leaving it to hang over the imaginary conversation among several famous philosophers that was the last, undelivered, lecture of the whole course. But the idea resurfaced, not only in Roederer's subsequent career, but in the work of Jean-Baptiste Say.

JEAN-BAPTISTE SAY

Jean-Baptiste Say's first publication was a pamphlet entitled *Olbie, or an Essay on the Means of Improving the Morals of a Nation*. It was written as an entry to a prize competition organised by the French Institute in 1798 but was published in 1800, soon after the coup that Sieyès organised to bring Napoleon to power. As Say noted in his foreword, the work was intended to appear at a time when "two men whose eminent talents and morality are undisputed" had become responsible for "the project of founding the stability of the republic on the observation of the rules of morality."[249] *Olbie* (from the Greek word *olbios*, meaning happy or beatific) was an imaginary community designed to show how this could be done. Its aim was to show how ethics (*morale*) or "the science of manners" (*moeurs*) could be applied to morality (*moralité*) to enable men "to procure all the happiness compatible with their nature."[250] Applying *morale* to *moralité* to produce *moeurs*, or "the constant habits of a person or a nation in the conduct of life," meant ensuring that individual and general utility would coincide. Although Say made it clear that *Olbie* presupposed an already-established moral theory

---

[247] Roederer, *Cours*, pp. 302 (on Rousseau), 249–52 (on Condorcet).

[248] Roederer *Cours*, pp. 134 (on knowledge and ignorance as the only legitimate criteria distinguishing full citizens from the others), 177 (on the age of political majority), 267 (on apprenticeship).

[249] Jean-Baptiste Say, *Olbie, ou essai sur les moyens de reformer les moeurs d'une nation* (Paris, an VIII/1800), pp. ix–x. On Say, see, most recently, R. R. Palmer, *J.-B. Say: An Economist in Troubled Times* (Princeton, Princeton University Press, 1997); Evelyn L. Forget, *The Social Economics of Jean-Baptiste Say: Markets and Virtue* (London, Routledge, 1999); Richard Whatmore, *Republicanism and the French Revolution: An Intellectual History of Jean-Baptiste Say's Political Economy* (Oxford, Oxford University Press, 2000).

[250] Say, *Olbie*, p. 2.

(its aim, he wrote, was simply to show how it could be applied), the utility-based framework that he outlined owed something to Helvétius as well as to Rousseau's criticism of Helvétius.[251] "Men," Say noted, "are what one makes them," although, he added, this did not mean that Helvétius was right in thinking "that their faculties are the same (*pareilles*) on leaving nature's hands."[252] Different natural aptitudes led to different activities and occupations. But the people of Olbie had found a way to prevent the division of labour from turning into a stratified system of power.

Part of the solution was a proper theory of political economy, a subject that Say reserved for his next publication (he limited himself here to the remark that "a judicious distribution of general wealth" could only be "the fruit of a good system of political economy").[253] The other part was the way that the people of Olbie were governed. All the powers of their government arose from the people, but all the potential for virtue or corruption lay at "the summit of power." Morality at the apex would determine the morality of the whole "social pyramid."[254] If material well-being (*aisance*) was the first precondition of any free state, the Olbiens also had the advantage of no longer living under institutions that sustained religious prejudice. Here, Say followed what Rousseau had written about the incompatibility between Christianity and political society.[255] He also followed Rousseau in describing the way that the people of Olbie had become moral. In this context, the key text was not the *Social Contract* but the *Considerations on the Government of Poland*. The Olbiens had effectively put Rousseau's Polish system into practice by establishing a system of government in which virtue was made to be "profitable" as well as "loveable" and vice was "harmful" as well as "hideous." As Say put it, quoting from the section of Rousseau's *Considerations on the Government of Poland* that described the system of graduated promotion, the Olbiens had established a system of government in which "virtue opens all the doors that fortune sees fit to close."[256] In Olbie, power and money were disconnected.

The subordination of wealth to justice was most apparent in the Olbiens' tax regime. Necessities were exempted from all taxation. But since it was impossible "in the state of civilisation" to draw a clear line separating necessities from conveniences and luxuries, a flat tax was bound to be arbitrary and would favour an even more arbitrary distribution of wealth unless the

---

[251] Say, *Olbie*, notes A and B, pp. 81–2.

[252] Say, *Olbie*, p. 3, note 1.

[253] Say, *Olbie*, p. 10.

[254] Say, *Olbie*, p. 6.

[255] Say, *Olbie*, pp. 9–11, 82–96.

[256] Say, *Olbie*, pp. 17–8. See Jean-Jacques Rousseau, *Considerations on the Government of Poland* [1782], in Rousseau, *The Social Contract and Other Later Political Writings*, ed. Victor Gourevitch (Cambridge, CUP, 1997), §13, para. 26, p. 248.

rate of taxation increased in proportion to higher levels of revenue. The Olbiens used a geometric scale to fix tax payments so that each additional fraction of income was matched by a proportionate increase in the tax rate. Taxes applied to all income, not that produced by any single type of property. The resulting tax regime meant that individuals were left with an incentive to better their own circumstances, but the state still took a further proportion of their additional income. Since, "in the state of civilisation," wealth generated wealth and it was always more difficult to make the first hundred écus than the first hundred thousand francs (an increase in earning power, Say noted, of 333:1), the Olbiens' geometrically increasing tax rate (similar in structure, although Say did not refer to it, to Montesquieu's treatment of luxury in *The Spirit of Laws*) allowed individual and general wealth to grow together, but still ensured that equity was maintained.[257]

This progressive tax regime called for a strong and respected government. The first step that the people of Olbie took towards establishing one had been to create a system of public examinations. Active citizenship depended upon passing an examination in the principles of political economy. Every citizen who had pretensions "to fill the functions of nominating the first magistrates" or follow "the road towards great office" had to pass this initial test.[258] Here, as with Roederer, the model was China and its mandarins. The second step had been to revive the Athenian and Roman practice of the census. Since some of the Olbiens had "the means to subsist legitimately without having to work," each citizen was further obliged to declare his habitual occupation, and this duly registered occupation became part of a person's legal identity and had to accompany all signed public documents and legal deeds.[259] As a further disincentive to idleness, the Olbiens also set about enclosing all rural property with hedges, so that livestock could put out to pasture without having to be tended by shepherds. In Olbie, agriculture took precedence over the pastoral life. But agriculture was not combined with a militia in the standard republican way. Since standing armies were part of "the present political system, even in times of peace," the Olbiens also required their soldiers to perform public works and, like the Romans, build roads, bridges, canals, and amphitheatres.[260] Through the requirement that all the people of Olbie have a useful occupation, "it became possible to prevent the love of gain from becoming the only stimulus encouraging men to work."[261] An excessive love of wealth, Say emphasised, had been the cause of the ruin of Phoenicia and Carthage,

---

[257] Say, *Olbie*, pp. 24, 101–3.
[258] Say, *Olbie*, pp. 25–6, 104.
[259] Say, *Olbie*, p. 27.
[260] Say, *Olbie*, pp. 24, 105.
[261] Say, *Olbie*, pp. 28–9.

as well as Venice and Holland in more recent times. When the influence of money on a nation became "immense," he noted, its politics became "narrow, exclusive and even barbarous."[262] Adam Smith supplied corroboration. "Commerce," Say wrote, quoting Smith, "which ought naturally to be, among nations, as among individuals, a bond of union and friendship, has become the most fertile source of discord and animosity." While the "violence and injustice of the rulers of mankind" was "an ancient evil" to which no remedy could be found, the "impertinent jealousy of merchants and manufacturers who neither are, nor ought to be, the rulers of mankind" was a development of "the present and the preceding century." Like Smith, Say argued that "the mean rapacity, the monopolizing spirit of merchants and manufacturers" had to be kept out of public life.[263]

Again as in China, this meant acknowledging the value of the sciences, fine arts, and letters. It also meant recognising that virtue was more than just the love of liberty, as Rousseau mistakenly had claimed.[264] Prudence and the domestic virtues were those cultivated in Olbie. They saved for their old age by way of mutual savings clubs. The range of rewards and punishments surpassed those recommended by "the famous Beccaria" and applied to every position of responsibility. Only those who could prove their worth were eligible for any public post. "Every writ of nomination bore the candidate's titles to have been shown preference, and mention was made of all the functions that he had performed previously, and, so that the public could be the judge of the merit of his titles, each appointment to public office was printed in the roll of appointments published by the government, whose every article could be reprinted and discussed everywhere."[265] Since, in a republic, "many positions are given directly by the people," and since these positions were "the source of all the others," it was a matter of great importance to ensure that every choice was well informed.[266] To ensure that the Olbiens were able to make the right choices, recreational societies open to all citizens were established in every canton and arrondissement. These were not political clubs like those that had existed in France after 1789, but meeting places for private citizens, with gardens and seating arrangements for small, social gatherings. There, the inhabitants of an arrondissement would be able to bring their families, play billiards or *boule*, read the newspapers, and talk about current events. In this way, they would get to know one another, so that those at the base of the pyramidal system would be able to make informed electoral choices.

---

[262] Say, *Olbie*, p. 106.

[263] Say, *Olbie*, p. 106, quoting Adam Smith, *Wealth of Nations*, vol. 1, bk. 4, ch. 3, p. 493.

[264] Say, *Olbie*, pp. 31–2, 111.

[265] Say, *Olbie*, p. 37.

[266] Say, *Olbie*, p. 37.

The result would be a system of virtuous administration, in which the power of money would be offset by the equally powerful rewards available to merit and morality.

Olbie, Say emphasised, was a society that was able to produce all the goods "that, in a rich and industrious nation, contribute to the well-being of its citizens."[267] The sort of goods that were usually called luxury were available to everyone, but their consumption was confined to what the soil and industry of Olbie produced.[268] In any society, Say noted, the range of goods that could be classed as real luxuries was rather small. These were goods that were prized but had no utility at all. Producing them, he emphasised, was genuinely harmful. If, for example, the rich acquired a taste for gold braid, this would not mean that they would reduce their consumption of ordinary items of clothing. Instead, the result would be that part of the workforce would be unavailable to produce what everyone ordinarily consumed, causing higher prices and reducing the purchasing power of the poor. The high prices and low living standards of the fashion-based silk industry of Lyon was, Say argued, a telling example of the problems generated by the failure to develop the production of goods that had a more general utility.[269] Contrary to the old argument about the way that the expenditure of the rich gave employment to the poor, conspicuous consumption reinforced inequality. In Olbie, the money that had once been used to buy fine things had come to be used "to give life to manufacture and to impart value to industry and talent that was dying of misery, with no profit to society or glory for the nation."[270] The high wages produced by full employment also changed the relationship between men and women. Some aspects of the old morality "of our ages of chivalry" and its recognition of women's distinctive virtues (chastity and gentleness) were revived, while the elimination of dowries and the introduction of divorce made marriage a matter of choice.[271] Although there were no trade guilds, women had their own self-financed corporations to promote charitable work, and some trades (hairdressing, dressmaking, ribbonware, musical-engraving, and cooking) were reserved for them.[272] In Olbie, chivalry and industry went together.

Olbie also had a meritocratic elite. In addition to their responsibility for recording every citizen's occupation, the censors were also "guardians of manners."[273] There were nine of them, each elected by one of the republic's

---

[267] Say, *Olbie*, p. 123.

[268] Say, *Olbie*, p. 124.

[269] Say, *Olbie*, pp. 124–6.

[270] Say, *Olbie*, p. 43.

[271] Say, *Olbie*, p. 46.

[272] Say, *Olbie*, pp. 52–5.

[273] Say, *Olbie*, p. 59.

provinces for renewable periods of two years at a time, and drawn from
those who had reached the age of retirement after distinguished careers in
public or private life. Candidates for the office were proposed by an electoral jury and elected by a second one. If the juries disagreed, they would
switch roles so that the nominating jury became the electing jury until a
successful election occurred. Unlike the Spartan ephors or the Roman censors, Olbie's censors had no political influence. They could not bar anyone
from holding office or order anyone to be removed from a public position.
They could, however, issue public reprimands and impose modest fines
(equal to an individual's tax payments) on those they decided had performed badly. Their decisions were made in secret and were not subject to
the formalities of the courts of law. Instead, three of the nine censors were
drawn by lot to deal with particular cases and were required to come to a
unanimous verdict. As with the Chinese, the censors' verdicts became part
of the public record, with two great registers, a book of merit and a book
of blame, containing the results of their decisions.[274] The censors were also
responsible for awarding the many prizes and honours distributed on the
public holidays and theatrical festivities celebrated in Olbie. These honours
were awarded mainly to the obscure and persevering rather than the great
and powerful. The same policy applied to the Olbiens' many monuments.
Few of them referred to purely political achievements, partly because understanding political duties called for abstract knowledge and an extended
use of reason, but mainly because political achievements were largely an
effect of the observation of private and social duties.[275] Accordingly, there
was only one Pantheon for great men, but many others to celebrate the
more ordinary virtues. Hundreds of monuments and temples—built not
only in cities but on roadsides and boulevards, and in public gardens—
celebrated ordinary virtues, making both the urban and rural environments
a vast didactic display. Useful maxims, taken mainly from the works of
Benjamin Franklin, helped to reinforce the moral message (Say had published a translation of Franklin's *Way to Wealth* in 1795).[276] Instead of learning to prize glory and conquest, the Olbiens were taught, for example, not
to put off to tomorrow what they could do today, and that it cost more to
feed one vice than two children.[277] With virtues like these, Say concluded,
a nation would not only be the "happiest" but would also be "the richest
and most powerful on earth."[278]

[274] Say, *Olbie*, pp. 60–3, 128.
[275] Say, *Olbie*, p. 75.
[276] Whatmore, *Republicanism and the French Revolution*, p. 117. On the earlier French interest in Franklin, see Jessica Riskin, *Science in the Age of Sensibility: The Sentimental Empiricists
of the French Enlightenment* (Chicago, University of Chicago Press, 2002), pp. 114–6.
[277] Say, *Olbie*, pp. 64–78, 132.
[278] Say, *Olbie*, p. 73.

Say turned to the subject of how a nation really could become rich and powerful in his *Treatise on Political Economy* of 1803.[279] In the letter that he wrote to Sieyès to accompany a copy of his book, Say emphasised the extent to which he had made use of the ideas of his predecessors, "above all, Smith," but he also drew Sieyès's attention to "those new parts" of the book that, he said, had not yet been treated properly, notably "the development of the phenomenon of production and consumption and the theory of real and relative dearness (*cherté*)," and invited him to give these his critical attention.[280] He was, in other words, quite clear about the originality of what posterity has come to know as Say's law. He began the book by positioning his own work in a line of descent that ran from Turgot to Smith, midway between "the most severe morality" of the Physiocrats, on the one side, and the exaggerated concern with trade balances to be found in the work of the Gournay group and Sir James Steuart, on the other.[281] The principles it contained would, he emphasised, form "a general plan of administration" that could be followed under a wide range of governments. Echoing what Smith had also argued against the Physiocrats, Say emphasised that even a poor system of political economy could, as in Britain, produce good results if it were followed consistently.[282]

Say turned political economy into what he was later to call *onéologie*. Everything that was not already abundant (like light or air) could be made available for human use. Giving something a use gave it a value, which was why any utility-creating activity could be described as industry, and why industry, in this broad, generic sense, was the master category of political economy. The *Treatise on Political Economy* was an anatomy of what industry was and of how its component parts were articulated. Industry consisted of three types: agriculture, manufacture, and commerce. Each type housed three operations: theory, application, and execution. All the work involved in both sets of types was productive. "Work," as Say put it, "is not productive because it is work. It is productive because it produces."[283] Since all the various types of property involved in producing utilities could be borrowed and lent as well as bought and sold, the three types of industry and the three kinds of operation that they housed could all generate an income, either as the wages of manufacture, the interest of capital, or the rent of

---

[279] A review in the 26 Thermidor an XI and 14 and 24 Vendémiaire an XII (7 and 17 October 1803) issues of the *Moniteur*, notably the third instalment (pp. 99–100), highlighted what Say had written on British industry.

[280] A. N. 284 AP 16, dossier 5, Say to Sieyès, 21 Messidor an XI (10 July 1803).

[281] Jean-Baptiste Say, *Traité d'économie politique*, 2 vols. (Paris, 1803), 1:xviii–xxii, 155, note 1. (In what follows, references throughout are to this first edition).

[282] Say, *Traité*, 1:xxix–xxx, xxxii.

[283] Say, *Traité*, 1:125.

the land. But the price of products and the price of what Say called the sources of production (meaning land, labour, and capital) would move in an inverse relationship to one another. "The sources of production," he argued, "as far as their value is concerned, go on one side of the scales; the products go on the other."

> The reason why the value of products moves in the opposite direction to that of productive services is very simple. Production is simply a great exchange, where the various productive services *are given* and products *are received*. If, in this exchange, one receives *more*, it is as if one has given *less*, and if one receives *less*, one gives *more*.[284]

This was what Say meant by relative and absolute dearness (*cherté*). To explain the point, he used the example of the knitting frame. Once it had been invented, the same supply of labour, land, and capital would produce twice as many stockings as before, meaning that the same quantity of productive services had been exchanged for double the quantity of products. In other words, either the various factors of production had been paid double what they had been worth before, or, inversely, the product was worth half as much as it had been before.[285] The perpetual oscillation produced by productivity was a self-correcting mechanism, increasing the total value of the utilities produced at time t, but reducing the value of those required for further cycles of production at time $t + 1$. The mechanism ruled out the possibility of a general surplus of production over consumption. As Say famously put it, the *"extent of the demand for the means of production in general* does not depend, as too many people have imagined, on *the extent of consumption.*"

> Consumption is not a cause; it is an effect. It is necessary to buy in order to consume. Now, you can buy only with what you have produced. Is the quantity of products demanded determined by the quantity of products that have been created? Without any doubt. Anyone can consume what he has produced in any way he wants, or use his own product to buy another. The demand for products in general is therefore always equal to the sum of products.[286]

It followed that "the best means of creating outlets for products is to increase them, not to destroy them." If this was self-evident, Say concluded, "what should be thought of those systems that encourage consumption to favour production?"[287] Production could sometimes exceed consumption,

[284] Say, *Traité*, 2:79–80 (the italics in this and subsequent citations are Say's own).
[285] Say, *Traité*, 2:80.
[286] Say, *Traité*, 2:175–6.
[287] Say, *Traité*, 2:176.

but the surplus could simply be added to the store of accumulated capital. There might also be local gluts. But the perpetual oscillation between the value of outputs and the value of inputs would supply enough information for the owners of different types of assets to shift resources from one branch of industry to another. This, Say argued, was why "I cannot conceive that the products of a nation's industry in general can ever be too abundant, because the one provides the means for the other to buy."[288]

The broader significance of the argument is worth emphasising. It meant that no part of society had any claim to special status in either economic or political terms. Neither the landowners, on the one side, nor the merchants and manufacturers, on the other, were any more vital to the power and prosperity of society as a whole. The generic term "industry" encompassed them all. The multiple systems of ranks that it housed were all, in one way or another, compatible with the wealth and the long-term stability of a large territorial state. This made the question of whether or not to favour agriculture over manufacturing industry, or vice versa, redundant. It also made it easier to see how to prevent economic policy from defaulting into power politics. The competitive character of trade could not be avoided. But the key to maintaining a state's competitive capacity lay at home, not abroad. The perpetual oscillation between the value of outputs and the costs of inputs produced enough information to guide the future allocation of resources without requiring the additional support of taxes or tariffs. There was no need either to rely on a single tax on the landowners to keep the economic machine in motion or to rely on public credit and the broader financial resources of the state to keep production and consumption in balance. Public credit, like the grain trade, could then be treated as something exceptional. The fact that grain was a basic item of popular consumption meant that there would sometimes be exceptional circumstances in which free trade would have to be suspended.[289] The fact that wars sometimes occurred meant that governments would have to borrow money. But the broader rules, or what Say called "general facts," would continue to apply.[290] The exceptions were just that. This was why the arrangements that Say had outlined in his *Olbie* mattered. The pyramid-shaped moral and political system that it contained was designed to ensure that the people of Olbie really could see the difference between the exceptions and the norms.

---

[288] Say, *Traité*, 2:179.

[289] Say, *Traité*, 1:311.

[290] On "general facts," see Whatmore, *Republicanism and the French Revolution*, pp. 141–2, 146–8.

The whole argument of the *Treatise* was designed to show that improvements to productivity were the key to maintaining the self-correcting character of the whole economic system. The more that industry was divided, the more it could be made to produce. Here Say simply followed Smith, emphasising the way that the division of labour reduced lost productive time, increased workers' competence, and favoured technical improvements. Although some kinds of industry, like agriculture, were less susceptible to the process than others, free competition would transfer the resulting efficiency gains from the producers to the consumers. Ultimately, this meant that all markets would have to become truly global, because only then would it be possible for every service and every branch of the wholesale and retail trades to specialise. It also meant that finely crafted luxury goods would have to give way to mass production because only mass-produced goods could be manufactured on a scale commensurate with the costs of maintaining a highly developed divison of labour. The only limit was the availability of capital.[291] Like Helvétius, Turgot, Roederer, and Condorcet, Say was careful to avoid the sequence that informed Rousseau's account of the origins of inequality. Nor, like Quesnay, did he go back to force and violence to explain the origins of the unnatural and retrograde order on which the modern world was based. Helvétius had rejected Rousseau by going back to Hobbes. Turgot had referred to decoration and ornamentation to suggest the multiple origins of inequality, and Roederer had followed up on this argument. Condorcet, in his posthumously published *Historical Outline of the Progress of the Human Mind*, pointed towards temporary differences in male and female mortality. The death of an adult before the children of a household were old enough to form families of their own would, he suggested, leave a surplus that could be either consumed or saved and put to productive use.[292] Say was prudently agnostic. Explaining how humans might have been able to accumulate enough products to be able to produce more products was, he wrote, "a difficulty that man has not been given the power to resolve."[293] It was enough to accept the fact that surpluses did exist, and that humans, more than animals, were natural hoarders and, unlike animals, had been able to devise ways to make the goods that they hoarded durably and collectively available.[294]

---

[291] Say, *Traité*, 1:35, 74.
[292] Antoine-Nicolas Caritat de Condorcet, *Sketch for a Historical Picture of the Progress of the Human Mind* [1795], trans. June Barraclough, introd. Stuart Hampshire (London, 1955), p. 6.
[293] Say, *Traité*, 1:83.
[294] Say, *Traité*, 1:90.

Say emphasised that there were no shortcuts to the accumulation of capital. It was slow and cumulative because everyone always also had to live and work. But once it began to take hold, it had the potential to increase the productive power of industry to unprecedented levels. As in *Olbie*, concentrations of wealth and power were the only real obstacles towards keeping the growth of production ahead of the growth of consumption. Happily, the "mad profusion" of the kind of expenditure that once had gone on follies like Versailles was a thing of the past, while the abolition of substitutions and entails as well as the revival of partible inheritance and the division of property could be relied on to correct excessive concentrations of wealth. Unlike the revolutions of the ancient world, Say noted, "modern revolutions" had actually favoured "the progress of opulence."[295] Industry, as much in agriculture and trade as in manufacturing, had acquired a dual structure, with a small core of large units surrounded by a much larger number of smaller units, and the stability of this structure formed a durable obstacle to excessive concentrations of wealth and power.[296] Nor was it necessary, Say also argued, to have to rely solely on real net savings to ensure that the growth of production kept ahead of the growth of consumption. It was not the case, as both Turgot and Smith had claimed, that the relatively lower levels of European interest rates of the past century or so were entirely an effect of thrift. It was equally likely, Say suggested, that rising productivity had played as much of a part. Rising productivity led to higher real incomes and reduced the real costs of capital goods (wallpaper, Say noted, was a good example of how it produced both outcomes).[297] The greater availability of disposable income and the lower costs of capital goods had both increased the pool of financial resources available for investment, and European interest rates had broadly tracked these developments. Enforced frugality was, therefore, largely unnecessary, and, where it had occurred because of "the economic system of a great number of governments," it had been the poor who had had to pay the price.[298] The broader message was clear. Productivity produced productivity, and there was no limit to how far it could go.

Say made a particular point, especially in the first edition of the *Treatise on Political Economy*, of highlighting the broader significance of British mass production (well captured, he noted in an earlier article, by the kind of life described by the English word "comfortable," a word that he thought

[295] Say, *Traité*, 1:97.
[296] Say, *Traité*, 1:104–5, 122–3.
[297] Say, *Traité*, 1:98–101.
[298] Say, *Traité*, 1:98.

ought to be added to every French dictionary).²⁹⁹ Say clearly liked its connotations. "I live in one of the richest regions of France," he wrote in 1824.
"Yet of twenty houses there are nineteen in which, on entering them, I see
... none of the things that the English call *comfortable*."³⁰⁰ The point was
not lost on his political opponents. "There are, in English Epicureanism,"
wrote the very royalist newspaper *Le Catholique* in 1826, "terms that are
unknown in continental dictionaries."

> *Fashionable, comfortable, respectable* designate, in three words, that crude sybarit-
> ism that offers everything to itself as an end and absorbs all the activity of
> mind of whosoever seeks to find it. Here, the insolence of luxury can be seen
> repudiating that elegance of manner to which a fund of generosity of soul and
> amiability of character still continues to hold. Sumptuous abodes and elegant
> furnishings stand in for grace of soul. Everything is sumptuous; nothing is
> grand or noble or majestic in aspect. It is civilisation in miniature, whose re-
> sults can be compared to the products of that elegant artifice which does hon-
> our to the industry of its manufacturers, all of whom are doubtless enlightened
> men, but who are still bereft of any real cultivation of mind. It is civilisation
> for egoists, whose only aspiration is to enjoy the pleasures of the table and the
> most material goods of life.³⁰¹

The modern doctrine of "industrial utility" (or, it might be said, Jean-
Baptiste Say misliked) served "to equate civilisation with a hive of industrious bees or a republic of ants."³⁰²

For Say, however, living comfortably took the exclusiveness out of luxury. "The English," he wrote in the *Treatise*, "who are less successful than
the French in the arts of taste, in architecture, painting, or sculpture, generally surpass them in that choice of forms, designs, and colours from which
the industrial arts derive their profits."³⁰³ They were now fully in possession
of that part of industry that consisted of applying acquired knowledge to
the needs of life, and had been able to give the products of their manufacturing industry the "irresistible appeal of convenience."³⁰⁴ The result had
been that they were able to avoid the routine involved in excessive standardisation, on the one hand, and the caprice associated with social snob-
bery, on the other. In France, a mahogany furniture set would certainly

²⁹⁹ Jean-Baptiste Say, "Boniface Véridick à Polyscope, sur son projet de théâtre pour le
peuple," *La Décade philosophique* 10 (10 Germinal an IV/21 March 1796): 38–44, cited in
Whatmore, *Republicanism and the French Revolution*, p. 124.

³⁰⁰ Cited in Palmer, *J.-B. Say*, p. 77.

³⁰¹ [Anon.], "De l'influence des doctrines matérielles sur la civilisation moderne," *Le Catholique* 3 (1826): 304.

³⁰² *Le Catholique* 3 (1826): 306.

³⁰³ Say, *Traité*, 1:133.

³⁰⁴ Say, *Traité*, 1:133.

look more splendid and have more variety than its English counterpart. Each household would want a slightly different form, or more bronze ornamentation or sculpture. But the result was that "fine furniture is in use only among a very small number of well-off people," while in England, "barely a household is so poor that it cannot afford a mahogany table."[305]

> In England, no one has any caprice about small things. All the dining tables, front doors, or ironware used for the same sort of thing are made alike or limited to a small number of different varieties. What do English consumers want? That each item does what it should and is of good quality. Consequently, they are soon of the same mind about forms and materials and, having settled on their point of view, have little desire to change it. Hence large-scale production is possible, and the majority of products can all, so to speak, be drawn from the same mould. The division of labour can be taken to its furthest extent, something that can happen only when it is a matter of creating a large number of similar products. The result is that these products are generally better made, better fitted together, better finished, and incomparably less expensive.[306]

True industrial improvements were, therefore, "those that tend to spread the use of products that are within the reach of the greatest number, to improve them and make them more common through their low prices."[307] The corollary to this shift of emphasis was that broader and deeper domestic markets were a more stable foundation for durable prosperity than foreign trade. As in Olbie, prosperity was largely a matter of being self-sufficient. In themselves, exports were simply a "less advantageous" supplement to internal consumption.[308] The real utility of foreign trade had little to do with trade and payments balances in themselves and much more to do with the pressure to innovate and raise productivity that open markets would maintain.

Say made it clear that public debts were liabilities, not assets. Every kind of public loan took capital or portions of capital out of productive use and diverted it towards consumption. But he could not ignore the fact that the scale of consumption involved in modern warfare made public debts unavoidable. "No country, in the situation in which modern states now stand, with the enormous expenses that war entails," he wrote, "can support a war by the sole means of the current resources that its people might be able to supply." Public credit was now both "a means of defence and, unfortunately, a means of attack." It was a "new weapon, more terrible than gunpowder," that every power had to use lest it risk falling back into a

---

[305] Say, *Traité*, 1:137.
[306] Say, *Traité*, 1:136.
[307] Say, *Traité*, 1:138.
[308] Say, *Traité*, 1:154–5. On Sieyès's views on foreign trade, see above, ch. 1, note 139.

"manifest inferiority" once one of them had begun.[309] Say went back to
Melon's claim that public credit was simply the right hand lending to the
left, and, as Montesquieu and Hume had done before, listed all the putative
advantages of public credit and rejected them each, one by one.[310] By 1803,
however, Hume's solution was no longer available. Public credit was a part
of every modern state, and its stability had come to depend on the constitutions of their governments. "Where the public authority is vested in a single individual," Say wrote, "it is next to impossible that public credit should
be very extensive: for there is no security, beyond the pleasure and good
faith of the monarch."

> When the authority resides in the people or its representatives, there is the
> further security of a personal interest in the people themselves, who are credi-
> tors in their individual and debtors in their aggregate character and, therefore,
> cannot receive in the former without paying in the latter. This circumstance
> alone would lead us to presume, at a time when no great undertaking can be
> completed without great expense, and when no great expense can be supported
> without loans, that representative governments will acquire a marked prepon-
> derance in the scale of national power, simply on account of their superior
> financial resources, without reference to any other circumstance.[311]

He was, of course, right. But even here the conclusion was qualified. Representation made public credit secure, but representation itself could not prevent public credit from ballooning upwards. The technicalities of debt management like sinking funds, or, by implication, even the multiple hierarchies
of a society like Olbie, could not block the upward spiral. Public credit, Say
continued, provided so easy a way to dissipate great capital sums that "several commentators (*publicistes*)" had still concluded that it was fundamentally
harmful.[312] A government whose power depended on public credit would
find itself involved in every political interest. It would conceive of "gigantic
enterprises" crowned sometimes with glory, sometimes with shame, but always ending in exhaustion. A weak government, on the other hand, would
be held to ransom by the great powers. It would have to pay them to fund
their wars and pay them again to remain at peace, opening its purse to
preserve an independence that it would still lose, or lending them its funds,
only to find itself a victim of a debt default.[313] These, he warned, were not
"gratuitous assumptions," but he left his readers to work out their implications.[314] It is easy enough to identify Geneva or Holland with the small

[309] Say, *Traité*, 2:518–20.
[310] Say, *Traité*, 2:520–5.
[311] Say, *Traité*, 2:526–7.
[312] Say, *Traité*, 2:528.
[313] Say, *Traité*, 2:528–9.
[314] Say, *Traité*, 2:529.

states described in the second scenario. The context of the Peace of Amiens in which Say wrote the first edition of the *Treatise* makes it less clear whether the warning contained in the first scenario referred to Britain or to France. In subsequent editions, Say singled out Britain. "It is impossible to avoid a precipice," he wrote in the fifth edition, "when the road leads nowhere else."[315] But in the light of Say's well-documented misgivings about Napoleon, the ambiguity still left room for France.[316] Either possibility was compatible with the advantages and disadvantages of public credit. Its very nature meant that it could never lose its Janus face.

[315] Jean-Baptiste Say, *A Treatise on Political Economy* [1836], ed. Munir Quddus and Salim Rashid (New Brunswick, Transaction Books, 2001), p. 487. On Say's later views, see Gareth Stedman Jones, "National Bankruptcy and Social Revolution: European Observers on Britain, 1813–1844," in Donald Winch and Patrick O'Brien, eds., *The Political Economy of British Historical Experience* (London, 2002), pp. 61–92.

[316] On Say's ambivalence towards Napoleon, see Whatmore, *Republicanism and the French Revolution*, pp. 136–7, 182–3, 191, and Palmer, *J.-B. Say*, p. 46. Say dedicated the second edition of the *Treatise* to the Russian tsar Alexander I.

CONCLUSION

SAY'S misgivings about Napoleon were soon confirmed. On 18 May 1804, Napoleon was proclaimed emperor of the French and on 2 December 1804 received Charlemagne's sword and crown at the famously stage-managed coronation ceremony inaugurating the new reign. Three weeks before the coronation, the now imperial Senate ratified the plebiscite of the French people that made "the imperial dignity" hereditary in "the direct, natural, legitimate, and adoptive descent of Napoleon Bonaparte and the natural and legitimate descent of Joseph and Louis Bonaparte," as specified by the earlier proclamation establishing the empire. Once again, it was Pierre-Louis Roederer who introduced the legislation. Once again, too, it was Montesquieu who supplied the framework of his speech. "The order of succession was not established for the sake of the reigning family," Roederer said, quoting book 26, chapter 16, of *The Spirit of Laws*, "but because it is the interest of the state that there is a reigning family."[1] Nothing in 1789, he continued, had been written or published to oppose the idea of "a monarchical republic or a republican monarchy." This, finally, had been what the constitution of the Year VIII had established. The question now was to decide whether the monarchical part of the system should become hereditary. Here again, it was Montesquieu who gave the argument its structure. A "vast empire," Montesquieu had written, could be governed only by a single individual. But, where Montesquieu had argued that it was bound to be governed despotically, Roederer now argued that he was wrong. Montesquieu had claimed that a monarchical state had to be medium-sized. If it were too small, it would be a republic. If it were too large, "the nobility, possessed of great estates, far from the eye of the prince, with a private court of their own and secure, moreover, from sudden executions by the laws and manners of the country, might throw off their allegiance." Were these circumstances to arise, Montesquieu added, the only way to preserve the state was "the sudden establishment of unlimited power." But doing so would signal the end of monarchy. "The rivers," Montesquieu warned, rehearsing the same image that he had earlier applied to imperial Rome, "hasten to mingle their waters with the sea; and monarchies lose themselves in despotic power."[2]

---

[1] Pierre-Louis Roederer, *Oeuvres de comte P. L. Roederer*, ed. A. M. Roederer, 8 vols. (Paris, 1853–9), 7:264–5, referring to Montesquieu, *The Spirit of Laws*, trans. Thomas Nugent [1750], 2 vols. (London, 1823) (hereafter *SL*), bk. 26, ch. 16, (2:74).

[2] Montesquieu, *SL*, bk. 8, ch. 17, p. 121, as cited by Roederer, *Oeuvres*, 7:269.

Present circumstances, Roederer claimed, ruled this prospect out. Today, he argued, it would actually be easier to govern an empire the size of Charlemagne's than, in the age of Charlemagne, it would have been possible to govern a relatively small-sized state like France in the age of Louis XV. In part this was a matter of relative population densities, levels of economic development, and improvements in the means of communication. But it was also a matter of "the artifice of hierarchies and balances of power, now perfected by experience."[3] These, Roederer stated, "make it possible to govern much greater multitudes more surely" than had ever been possible in the past. The kind of wealthy magnates (*principaux*), he continued, that Montesquieu had described had been largely eliminated by partible inheritance, while present-day political magnates ruled over no more than "the little divisions of France." The multiplicity of hierarchies meant, too, that the power of some magnates would be balanced by others holding authority of a different kind. This meant that "courts beyond the prince's court" were no real danger, and, if any were formed, the time that would be needed to turn intrigue into real disobedience would be much shorter than "the instant" required to ensure that disobedience would be followed quickly by repression.[4]

It would be easy to conclude from what Roederer said that, in the last analysis, the secret police, not the "artifice of hierarchies," would be the real source of imperial stability. The veiled threat may have been aimed at the empire's royalist and republican enemies, but the difference between legitimate and illegitimate power that it suggests was arguably less simple. Roederer's equivocation about whether the revolution had produced a monarchical republic or a republican monarchy captured something more fundamentally ambiguous about the idea of representative government. It was an equivocation about sovereignty and about where, according to the relevant noun, it was taken to be located. According to one noun, it was located at the bottom of the social pyramid. According to the other, it was located at the top. The idea of representation was compatible with both. The Napoleonic Empire, with its periodic plebiscites, its indirect elections, and its improvised amalgamation of the various types of distinction that France had inherited from its assorted pasts (Rome's Senate, Charlemagne's nobility, Louis XIV's court), captured the ambiguity quite well. If, as Sieyès argued in 1795, everything was representative in the social state, it still remained the case that one kind of representation referred to states, which were singular, while another kind of representation referred

---

[3] Roederer, *Oeuvres*, 7:269.
[4] Roederer, *Oeuvres*, 7:269.

to their members, who were plural.[5] The problem of keeping them separate, yet part of the same system, still remained.

From the vantage point of the early nineteenth century, it looked like an ambiguity built into representative government. As the American diplomat Alexander Hill Everett noted sardonically about the government of Restoration France, "the difficult problem presented itself, to invent a system of popular representation in which the people should not be represented." Somewhat surprisingly, he continued, "they appear to have succeeded, at least for the moment, better than could have been reasonably expected."[6] The same point emerged from a different part of the political spectrum. "It is said," wrote the royalist Joseph de Maistre, "that the people are sovereign; but over whom?—over themselves, apparently."

> The people are thus subject. There is surely something equivocal if not erroneous here, for the people who command are not the people who obey. It is enough, then, to put the general proposition, 'The people are sovereign', to feel that it needs an exegesis. This exegesis will not be long in coming, at least in the French system. The people, it will be said, exercise their sovereignty by means of their representatives. This begins to make sense. The people are a sovereign which cannot exercise sovereignty.[7]

The charge was echoed in 1817 by a French constitutional theorist named Jean-Pierre Pagès, who was later to edit Benjamin Constant's *Cours de droit politique* (Course on Political Law). "Thus," Pagès wrote,

> that system of representation which has come to us from feudal government would be impracticable in a nation that has the energy of youth, a consciousness of its manners, its strength, its love of country, and that would seek to enjoy the freedom to which it is entitled. But it is wonderful for peoples who have fallen into softness, corruption, avidity, and egoism because it denies them the possibility of completing the process of their depravation and of succumbing to anarchy through licentiousness. In states like these, representatives

---

[5] See Sieyès's speech to the Convention of 20 July 1795, reprinted in Paul Bastid, *Les discours de Sieyès dans les débats constitutionnels de l'an III* (Paris, 1939), and, more broadly, Sieyès, *Political Writings*, ed. Michael Sonenscher (Indianapolis, Hackett, 2003), pp. xvi–xxii, xxvi–xxvii. For a helpful historical overview of the ambiguities surrounding the concept of sovereignty, see James J. Sheehan, "The Problem of Sovereignty in European History," *American Historical Review* 111 (2006): 1–15.

[6] Alexander Hill Everett, *Europe: or a General Survey of the Present Situation of the Principal Powers; with Conjectures on their Future Prospects* (Boston, 1822), p. 52. On Everett, see the biographical entry in Cathal J. Nolan, ed., *Notable U.S. Ambassadors since 1775: A Biographical Dictionary* (Westport, Greenwood Press, 1997).

[7] Joseph de Maistre, *Study on Sovereignty*, bk. 1, ch. 1, cited in Jack Lively, ed., *The Works of Joseph de Maistre* (New York, Macmillan, 1963), p. 93.

are harmful only to kings. With respect to the people, they are like viziers in whom its idleness can find repose from all political care.[8]

The obvious alternative was to establish more direct political representation. "Direct elections alone are what constitute a true representative system," wrote Benjamin Constant in the *Mercure de France* in January 1817, invoking the authority of Jacques Necker's "courageous, eloquent, and profound" *Dernières vues de politique et de finance* (Last Words on Politics and Finance) and the attack on the Constitution of the Year VIII that it contained.[9] "The spirit of a republican constitution," Necker had written there, "is undoubtedly to attribute to the people . . . all the political rights that it can exercise with order." But, despite its republican patina, the constitution that Sieyès had drafted ruled this out. "Good faith should require it to be agreed," Necker continued, "that one should cease to give the name republic to a form of government in which the people would be nothing, nothing other than by fiction."[10] The system of indirect representation that was the most prominent feature of Sieyès's system gave the people a right that, according to Necker, it would find to be "a matter of perfect indifference."[11] However much praise might be lavished on the new system for eliminating hereditary distinctions of every kind, it was doomed to die of apathy because it had no real connection to the people it purported to represent.

> The prime utility of participation by the people in the nomination of its magistrates and its legislators is to form a continuous, more or less tight link between the leaders of a state and the whole mass of its citizens.
>
> Destroy that relationship, whether by divesting the people of the only political right that it can exercise or by changing that right into a simulacrum, a simple fiction, and there will no longer be a republic or it will exist only in name.[12]

There was no substitute, Necker argued, for "the free, direct elections that form the essence of a republic."[13]

---

[8] Jean-Pierre Pagès, *Principes généraux du droit politique dans leur rapport avec l'esprit de l'Europe et avec la Monarchie constitutionnelle* (Paris, 1817), pp. 483–4.

[9] Cited in Benjamin Constant, *Recueil d' articles. Le Mercure, La Minerve et La Renommée*, ed. Ephraïm Harpaz, 2 vols. (Geneva, 1972), 2:38 and 39 (note 3). On Constant's views on Sieyès, see Norman King and Etienne Hofmann, "Les lettres de Benjamin Constant à Sieyès avec une lettre de Constant à Pictet-Diodati," *Annales Benjamin Constant* 3 (1988): 89–110.

[10] Jacques Necker, *Dernières vues de politique et de finance* [1802], in Jacques Necker, *Oeuvres*, 12 vols. (Paris, 1821), 11:15–6.

[11] Necker, *Dernières vues de politique et de finance*, p. 16.

[12] Necker, *Dernières vues de politique et de finance*, p. 21.

[13] Necker, *Dernières vues de politique et de finance*, p. 94.

From this perspective, the slide from republic to empire was largely an effect of the absence of direct elections. But from another perspective, the very features of the French republic that Necker singled out were taken to be likely to lead to the same despotic outcome, irrespective of the kind of electoral system on which political power was based. According to English political economist Thomas Malthus in his *Principles of Political Economy* of 1820, the real problem facing modern France was the absence of a system of ranks. "On the effects of a great sub-division of property," he wrote there, "a fearful experiment is now making in France."[14] Although, he conceded, "the state of property in France appears at present to be favourable to industry and demand," there was no reason to think that this state of affairs would last. Continued population growth and partible inheritance were likely, "at the end of a century," to lead to "extraordinary poverty and distress. In this state of things, with little or none of the natural influence of property to check at once the power of the crown and the violence of the people, it is not possible to conceive that such a mixed government as France has now established can be maintained."[15] Nor, for the same reasons, was a republic likely to be any more viable. Instead, Malthus argued, France would revert to a more durable version of the Napoleonic regime. The "state of property above described would," he suggested, "be the very soil for a military despotism."

> If the government did not adopt the Eastern mode of considering itself as the sole territorial proprietor, it might at least take a hint from the Economists, and declare itself co-proprietor with the landlords, and from this source (which might still be a fertile one, though the landlords, on account of their numbers, might be poor), together with a few other taxes, the army might easily be made the richest part of the society; and it would then possess an overwhelming influence which, in such a state of things, nothing could oppose. The despot might now and then be changed, as under the Roman emperors by the Praetorian guards, but the despotism would certainly rest upon very solid foundations.[16]

As Alexander Hill Everett noticed, there was a substantial degree of similarity between the broader argument about the dynamics of population and inheritance underlying Malthus's prognosis and the earlier argument of Rousseau's *Discourse on the Origin of Inequality* (Malthus, it is worth remembering, certainly knew his Rousseau well). "It is somewhere observed by

---

[14] Thomas Robert Malthus, *Principles of Political Economy* [1820], 2nd ed. (London, 1836), p. 376.

[15] Malthus, *Principles*, p. 377.

[16] Malthus, *Principles*, p. 378.

Rousseau," Everett wrote, "that he had passed his life in reading voyages and travels."

> This fact does not tend, I think, to diminish the surprise which judicious and reflecting men have generally felt at finding so powerful a writer maintain that man is by nature an isolated and independent being, and that his situation is more eligible in this his natural condition, than it is in the artificial and unnatural one of society.[17]

The "startling paradox" of Malthus's system, and the challenge that it presented to "all our best and noblest natural sentiments," as well as to "the benevolent and social instincts of our nature," made Malthus look rather like Rousseau and, by extension, made his prediction about France's future look quite similar to Rousseau's earlier warning about the long-term survival of Europe's monarchies.[18] The point was not lost in France, where in his *Traité de législation* (Treatise on Legislation) of 1826 Jean-Baptiste Say's son-in-law, Charles Comte, set out to rework the intellectual legacy of Helvétius, Bentham, and Rousseau in the light of Malthus's examination of the dynamics of population, property, and inheritance in order to explain why the demographic behaviour of the various components of a stratified industrial society would still, without further political reform, leave what had come to be called the social question unanswered.

The ambiguity was also apparent in another evaluation of the system of representative government. This one was the work of an obscure admirer of Napoleon Bonaparte named Charles-Jean-Baptiste Bonnin, who had welcomed Bonaparte's escape from the island of Elba with a pamphlet entitled *De la révolution européenne* (On the European Revolution) predicting that the restored imperial regime would finally put an end to patriotism, "that particular virtue of nations" with its propensity to turn each people into strangers to one another, and replace it by the more noble spirit of humanity, when nations "come to feel that they are no more than the members of a great family, governed by similar laws and institutions and guided by the same spirit."[19] Later, in a work written during a period of imprisonment for his Bonapartist sympathies, Bonnin singled out Sieyès's draft Declaration of the Rights of Man of 1789 as the text that, he asserted, best embodied the principles of what he, following Sieyès, called "social science" (Mably and Montesquieu, Bonnin claimed, were its two most authoritative exponents). He also had no hesitation about reinforcing Sieyès's text by including a further set of articles dealing with the conditional nature of

---

[17] Alexander Hill Everett, *New Ideas on Population with Remarks on the Theories of Malthus and Godwin* [1822], 2nd ed. (Boston, 1826), p. 29.

[18] Everett, *New Ideas on Population*, pp. vi, viii, 124.

[19] [Charles-Jean-Baptiste Bonnin], *De la révolution européenne* (Paris, 1815), p. 195.

the right to private property, which he took over (without mentioning his name) from Robespierre's draft Declaration of the Rights of Man of 1793.[20] It was, in its way, an inadvertent corroboration of the abbé Morellet's irritated annotations to *What Is the Third Estate?* and his complaint that in the most famous of all his political pamphlets Sieyès had made no explicit provision for the special status of private property, particularly property in land.[21]

The ambiguity grew out of the mixture of inclusiveness and exclusiveness that was the hallmark of Sieyès's pyramid-shaped system of representative government and the uncertainty about the part played either by internal constitutional arrangements or by external social distinctions in setting limits to the scale and scope of sovereign power. If, as Roederer claimed in 1804, "the artifice of hierarchies" ruled out despotic government from modern France, it was still not easy to see why some hierarchies might be more acceptable than others, and how those that were could be insulated from those other kinds of distinction (wealth, birth, or occupation) that were more strongly embedded in prevailing economic and social arrangements. The same problem arose from the opposite direction. If representative government was the generic name of the government of the moderns, it was hard to specify how it could be relied upon to avoid getting entangled with one or other of the local or partial interests (including that of its own members) that it represented, or how it could be prevented from adopting some local or partial conception of the public good. The ambiguity played itself out, first under the empire and then under several further regimes. The restored monarchy, and the many competing claims for restitution and retribution that it brought in its wake, also brought back the full range of problems about public credit, taxation, and representation that the eighteenth century had faced. Once again, constitutional government appeared to be the way to make public credit secure, but public credit appeared to be the way to make constitutional government insecure.

Unsurprisingly, the many uncertainties built into the idea of representative government continued to apply. Uncertainty about the location of sovereignty entailed uncertainty about the nature and status of intermediate powers. Uncertainty about these entailed further uncertainty about the composition and distribution of the wealth on which both might be expected to rely. Uncertainty about these entailed yet further uncertainty

---

[20] [Charles-Jean-Baptiste Bonnin], *Lettres sur l'éducation écrites en octobre et en décembre 1823, dans sa prison, par le publiciste C.-J.-B. Bonnin, sur l'éducation de sa fille* (Paris, 1825), pp. 195–9, 281–305, 329.

[21] See the edition of Emmanuel-Joseph Sieyès, *Qu'est-ce que le tiers état?* published in 1822, four years after Morellet's death in 1819, and the notes at pp. 85 and 173 for Morellet's reservations about what he took to be Sieyès's perfunctory gestures towards the private ownership of landed property.

about the size and constitutional shape of the kind of state that might be able to house them all. The difficulties were registered quite well in the different intellectual and political trajectories followed by the various advocates of what came to be called "industrialism," a label that could be applied to texts as apparently dissimilar as Johann Gottlieb Fichte's *Closed Commercial State* of 1800 and Henri de Saint-Simon's *Reorganisation of European Society* of 1814 because it captured some of the uncertainties about size, social structure, and forms of government that had to be faced once it became clear that the Jacobin hope of rolling back the eighteenth century's debt-driven combination of political and economic rivalry had failed (Jean-Baptiste Say, it is worth remembering, dedicated the second edition of his *Treatise of Political Economy* to Russia's emperor Alexander I, the chief architect of Europe's Holy Alliance).[22] In this sense, the nineteenth century's problems were still Montesquieu's problems. As Tocqueville went to some lengths to show, the names might have changed, but the things themselves were still the same.

The problems that Montesquieu had highlighted three generations earlier found their most immediate expression in arguments about the nature and attributes of the Restoration nobility. In the most straightforward sense, these centred on the question of whether the restored nobility was entitled to restitution of its lost property rights or, if not, to compensation for what it had lost. In a deeper sense, they centred on the more fundamental question of whether or not a monarchy needed a nobility. "Nonetheless," wrote Charles Théremin, one of Sieyès's former admirers, in 1817, "the doctrine that without a nobility there can be no throne is heard being preached everywhere, and Montesquieu did indeed say that monarchy cannot survive without a nobility."

> But it is one thing to have a feudal nobility endowed with privileges that it holds entirely of itself and quite another thing to have a national and political nobility, with privileges that it holds entirely from the king and exercises solely for the general utility. Thus, even if one agrees with Montesquieu that a mon-

---

[22] The parallel was made in an article by the royalist political philosopher Ferdinand, baron d'Eckstein, "De l'industrialisme," *Le Catholique* 5 (1827): 241, as a description of Fichte's *Der geschlossen Handelstaat* (The Closed Commercial State) [Stuttgart, 1800], by way of contrast to the "industrialisme de l'aune et de la toise" (p. 232) of the Saint-Simonians, Say, and Charles Comte. For some indications of the wider setting, see Anthony Pagden, ed., *The Idea of Europe from Antiquity to the European Union* (Cambridge, CUP, 2002). On Jean-Baptiste Say's *Treatise* and the idea of a reformed Russia under Alexander I as a potential alternative to the rival versions of "the spirit of conquest" represented by Napoleon I, on the one hand, and by the allied coalition, on the other, see the (increasingly forlorn) hopes expressed by Say's friend, the Swiss republican Frédéric-César de la Harpe, in Jean-Charles Biaudet and Françoise Nicod, eds., *Correspondance de Frédéric-César de la Harpe et Alexandre I*, 3 vols (Neuchâtel, La Baconnière, 1978–80), 2:58–9, 75, 79, 90–1, 171, 384–5, 536.

archy cannot survive without a nobility, it does not follow that this nobility has to be a feudal nobility, because there is another kind of nobility, namely, one made up of the peerage.[23]

Here, as with Benjamin Constant, it was the British political system that was the reference point, and it was the argument made by one of Montesquieu's critics, the Genevan exile Jean-Louis Delolme, about the precociously postfeudal system of royal government that had been established in England after the Norman Conquest, that now supplied a framework for making a parallel between 1789 and 1066. According to Delolme, in his *The Constitution of England* (a work first published in 1770), the genuinely despotic government that the Normans had established ruled out the kind of subordinate, dependent, and intermediate powers that Montesquieu had associated with monarchy.[24] English-style political and civil liberty had developed in opposition to the crown, rather than, as in the European mainland, in opposition to a feudal nobility. In Britain, the long sequence of conflicts between the crown, on the one side, and the nobles and commoners, on the other, had given rise to an office-based system of political representation, as against the property-based system of representation that Montesquieu had identified with monarchy. Instead of inheritance and the part that it played in giving monarchy its nature, modern, postfeudal monarchy, including its nobility, was entirely based on office. This, according to Théremin, was why the period of the French Revolution now meant that the type of political system that had developed in Britain after 1066 was a real possibility for both France and the rest of Europe after 1789. From this vantage point, the pendulum had begun to swing back from Montesquieu towards Voltaire. The outcome of the French Revolution appeared to corroborate Delolme's suggestion that Montesquieu's "prophecy" really had been mistaken.[25]

A more wide-ranging example of the continuity can be found in a curious transatlantic dialogue that took place soon after the end of the Napoleonic Wars and the formation of the Holy Alliance. The protagonists were the retired American diplomat Alexander Hill Everett, on the one side, and, on the other, a former Danish administrator of German origin named Conrad Georg Friedrich Elias von Schmidt-Phiseldeck who, between 1813 and 1818, had been director of Denmark's National Bank. The individuals themselves are now barely known. But the arguments that they rehearsed

[23] [Charles Théremin], *De la noblesse féodale, et de la noblesse nationale* (Paris, 1817), pp. 27–8.

[24] Jean-Louis Delolme, *The Constitution of England, or an Account of the English Government; in which it is Compared both with the Republic Form of Government and the Other Monarchies of Europe* (London, 1770) (here, I have used the London, 1821 printing), chs. i–iii, pp. 5–41.

[25] Delolme, *Constitution of England*, ch. xviii, pp. 340–59.

had first been made by Alexander Hamilton, on the one side, and by Immanuel Kant, on the other. In this sense, the dialogue can be used to describe the way that the long discussion of the Janus-faced attributes of public credit was carried through into the nineteenth century. Both parties to the dialogue argued that what Everett called Europe's "age of revolutions" would, in the long term, give rise to a European federal union.[26] Both also argued that that the union in question would be based on the modern system of representative government. But their respective conceptions of both a federal system of government and the kind of mechanisms of political representation that it would involve were still substantially different. As Everett put it, representation could mean either "democracy made easy" or "democracy rejected."[27] His own position was a development of the first formulation, while Schmidt-Phiseldeck's followed the second. The difference was connected to different assessments of the post-Napoleonic international system and the various forms of trade and industry that it would house. In a more narrow sense, it was also connected to two quite different assessments of public credit. For Everett, representative government and the modern funding system were the two great engines of what he called, unequivocally, "civilisation," or "the progress of industry, wealth and knowledge."[28] For Schmidt-Phiseldeck, the modern funding system was the last vestige of "the overgrown system of European politics" that only representative government could cure.[29] The dialogue remained within the same framework that, four generations earlier, had given the muted argument between Voltaire and Montesquieu its shape, with the idea of representative government now standing in for the idea of monarchy. Just as the monarchies of the moderns could be taken to be either the perfection or the negation of the republics of the ancients, so representative government could be taken to be either the realization or the nemesis of democracy. It could be either a republican monarchy or a monarchical republic because it was not clear whether, in Montesquieu's language, its nature called for either the equality of the former or the inequality of the latter, and, if its underlying principle was industry, whether this entailed either more, or less, inequality.

Schmidt-Phiseldeck's book, entitled *Europe and America*, was published simultaneously in German, French, English, Dutch, Danish, and Swedish in 1820. The broad framework of its argument was supplied by a passage

[26] Everett, *Europe*, p. 18. On the phrase, see above, chapter 1.

[27] The two phrases can be found in Alexander Hill Everett, *America or a General Survey of the Political Situation of the Several Powers of the Western Continent with Conjectures on their Future Prospects* (Philadelphia, 1827), p. 81.

[28] Everett, *Europe*, p. 9.

[29] Conrad Friedrich von Schmidt-Phiseldeck, *Europe and America* [1820], ed. Thorkild Kjærgaard (Copenhagen, Rodos, 1976), p. 185.

from Immanuel Kant's *Critique of Judgement* of 1790 and the distinction between good and bad social hierarchies that Kant had suggested there. Kant did so in the context of a discussion of the methodology of taste and an argument about the way that taste could never be learnt from a determinate set of precepts. It had, instead, to be acquired through the study of what he called "those prior forms of knowledge that are called *humaniora*." A foundation course in the humanities (meaning the opposite of theology, or even natural theology) was appropriate, he wrote, "presumably because *humanity* means on the one hand the universal *feeling of participation* and on the other the capacity for being able to *communicate* one's innermost self universally, which properties taken together constitute the sociability that is appropriate to humankind, by means of which it distinguishes itself from the limitation of animals."[30] The two aspects of humanity did not, he emphasised, come naturally. The first presupposed a social contract and the equality that went along with the right to participate in public life. The second presupposed a capacity for communication among all the various social gradations lying between what Kant called "the most polished" and "the most unrefined" parts of a nation.

> The age as well as the people in which the vigorous drive towards forming a social compact which transforms a nation into a lasting community, and which impulse had to contend with the considerable difficulties that embrace the weighty problem of uniting freedom (and thus also equality) with coercion (more from veneration and submission to laws voluntarily enacted than from a sense of fear): such an age and such a people had first to invent the art of a reciprocal communication of ideas between the most polished and the most unrefined portion of the nation; to pay attention to the several gradations that exist between the enlightened and cultivated state of the former and the natural simplicity and originality of the latter, and in this way to discover the mean between the highest possible cultivation and man in a contented state of nature, which alone constitutes the true scale for taste as a universal human sense and which is not to be governed by any general rules.

The model, Kant argued, would remain relevant however advanced a society became. A later age, he wrote, would "always be further from nature" and, without having "enduring examples of it," would scarcely be in a position to form a concept of "that happy union of the lawful constraint of the highest culture with the force and correctness of a free nature, feeling its own worth, in one and the same people."[31] It was Kant's version of the

---

[30] Immanuel Kant, *Critique of the Power of Judgement* [1790], ed. Paul Guyer (Cambridge, CUP, 2000), pp. 229–30. I have modified the translation by the contemporary English version and the clearer political dimension that it brings out as published in Schmidt-Phiseldeck, *Europe and America*, pp. 229–31.

[31] Kant, *Critique*, ed. Guyer, p. 230.

problem of how to reconcile natural, political, and national majorities that Roederer discussed in 1796.[32] Although Sieyès never wrote anything comparable, his own interest in the multiple social hierarchies generated by a fully commercial society and his explicit rejection of applying the empirical inductive procedures of the natural sciences to moral and political problems converged with the same set of ideas and, by extension, go some considerable way towards explaining the widespread interest in his thought in the German-speaking world.[33] From Kant's perspective, inequality would be overridden by the combination of judgement and respect for judgment involved in what he called "the true scale for taste as a universal human sense."

For Schmidt-Phiseldeck, writing in 1820, no existing European state was likely to attain Kant's "happy union." Instead, he noted, it was "perhaps reserved for America at some future time to realise this idea."[34] This was as much an effect of Europe's disadvantages as of America's advantages and their deep-seated roots in Europe's past. Here, the eighteenth-century concern with Europe's unusual historical trajectory continued to resonate. "The plough," Schmidt-Phiseldeck wrote, "was held in the greatest veneration by all the nations of the ancient world who are celebrated in history." But the Scythian and German tribes "whom the migration of nations seated on the ruins of the Roman universal empire" had not been among these. "Amongst them, war alone, the chase and every exercise wherein strength and courage and contempt of death could be evinced were held in esteem."[35] Such limited agriculture as they practised was restricted to the tiny plots of land around their huts and was left to the care of their slaves or prisoners of war under the supervision of their womenfolk. Only their southerly migrations into the Roman provinces had brought them into contact with "the conveniences and ornaments of civilized life." There, the recurrent alternation between warfare and leisure, the slave-based system of agriculture, and the fortified cities and castles of the barbarian invaders favoured the activities of "the workman and the artist who embellished their existence," and this, in turn, gave rise "between the nobility, who were originally free, and the vassal peasant" to "an intermediate class with its several gradations and a restless desire of aspiring to those ranks of society which possess a pretended pre-eminence."[36]

The diagnosis may have owed something to Montesquieu, or to William Robertson and Adam Smith, but the prognosis owed rather more to the bleaker assessment of modernity's predicaments that the eighteenth cen-

---

[32] See above, pp. 83–4.

[33] On this latter aspect of Sieyès's thought and its resonance in the German-speaking world, see Sieyès, *Political Writings*, ed. Sonenscher, pp. xvii–xviii, note 30.

[34] Schmidt-Phiseldeck, *Europe and America*, p. 231 (note).

[35] Schmidt-Phiseldeck, *Europe and America*, p. 77.

[36] Schmidt-Phiseldeck, *Europe and America*, pp. 78–9.

tury passed on to the nineteenth. The first symptom that required treatment was Europe's overdeveloped manufacturing industry and its precarious dependence on "the supplying of artificial wants."[37] Unlike Say,
Schmidt-Phiseldeck had no confidence at all about the self-correcting
character of modern industry. The combination of a growing manufacturing sector and spreading mechanisation might, he argued, have remained
stable "as long as productive industry was limited to particular states which
supplied the rest of the world with their manufactures." But the general
diffusion of knowledge and the "partly erroneous zeal" of governments
had ensured that "every branch of industry, without regard to climate or
situation," had come to be domesticated in every state.[38] Europe was now
locked into the accumulated effects of its earlier choices and was condemned to have to find resources for a huge population of specialised workers, whose acquired skills, as well as the obstacles placed in their path by
the rising entry costs of acquiring capital, ruled out the possibility of occupational flexibility. Agriculture, too, had paid a price for manufacturing
industry's growth. It was becoming too small in scale to maintain its productivity, and, as a result, an increasing proportion of the rural population
was trapped in conditions of overpopulation, debt, and forced sales. Both
sets of problems favoured emigration to the New World. There, the combination of local natural endowments, the political institutions of the
United States, as well as the more recent collapse of Spain's colonial empire
were likely to produce a more balanced process of economic development
and a society that would become increasingly self-sufficient. "Europe, existing in her present shape," Schmidt-Phiseldeck warned, "cannot do without America." But America, he continued, "has no occasion for Europe and
her communication with the latter in the reciprocal way of trade must
necessarily cease."[39]

The probability that it would was a severe threat to the stability of Europe's public finances. Europe's trade and finance, Schmidt-Phiseldeck argued, had developed together. Trade had underpinned private credit, and
private credit had played a key role in building up the financial resources
that had been used to fund the costs of Europe's wars and the drive to
world domination that they had brought in their wake. But what might
once have been a virtuous circle was now certainly vicious. The long period
of interdependence between trade and finance that had begun with the
discovery of the New World would soon come to an end. "Europe cannot
exist without America, shall she remain as she is at present," Schmidt-
Phiseldeck wrote.

[37] Schmidt-Phiseldeck, *Europe and America*, p. 80.
[38] Schmidt-Phiseldeck, *Europe and America*, pp. 81–2.
[39] Schmidt-Phiseldeck, *Europe and America*, p. 92.

For the European was centuries ago, and continues to be, monarch of the terrestrial globe, sovereign by the superiority of his intelligence, by the extent of his external possessions, by the produce of his still more extended commerce, and by the tribute which he attracts to himself from every corner of the earth, of all the splendid treasures which inanimate nature can boast of, and of all that the industry of millions of beings working only for his purpose, can accomplish.[40]

Conquest and commerce had gone hand in hand. But the stability of both empire and trade rested, in the last analysis, on the flow of bullion that Europe had been able to import from the New World. The real value of gold and silver coin had made it possible to maintain the stability of "that intolerable number of representative means of payment" that, otherwise, would "threaten to burst asunder all the ties of civilized life."[41] Gradually, however, the recurrent injections of additional real value into the money supply on which Europe had relied would begin to dry up. Industrialisation in North America would be matched by economic development in the South, turning the whole Western hemisphere into a huge, self-contained common market. The result would be massive price deflation in Europe's own economy, as gold and silver rose in relative value against the prices of both agricultural and manufactured goods. Prevailing nominal prices would command smaller future quantities of real goods, generating growing pressure on both public and private credit and increasing the temptation to hoard. Europe's complex social structure appeared to rule out any modification to existing political and economic arrangements. But America's rise to autarchy appeared to rule out their survival.

Europe's only course of action, Schmidt-Phiseldeck argued, was to imitate the Americans and opt for self-sufficiency. "But this will only be the case," he emphasised,

> provided the future policy of Europe considered as a body, allows each of her members to prosecute their several aims for as long as they come under an universal system of legality, without injury to the rights of others, upon a basis of unshackled competition, and freed from the provocations and chicanes of jealousy and egoism.[42]

Trade would become separate from power politics. But to maintain the distinction between "unshackled competition" and "the provocations and chicanes of jealousy and egoism," Europe would have to become "one grand state."[43] This would not involve becoming "actually united under

---

[40] Schmidt-Phiseldeck, *Europe and America*, p. 93.
[41] Schmidt-Phiseldeck, *Europe and America*, p. 95.
[42] Schmidt-Phiseldeck, *Europe and America*, p. 131.
[43] Schmidt-Phiseldeck, *Europe and America*, p. 132.

one central power," but it would still mean that Europe would have to govern herself "upon the principles of one common interest, and one public spirit, as far as regards her relation to other parts of the world." It would also mean that the members of the union "would be ever ready to uphold the natural fundamental laws of every organized union by opposing the strength of all to the aggressions of a few."[44] There were, Schmidt-Phiseldeck argued, reasonable grounds for thinking that a "European state-union" was now a possibility. After passing through "all the deformities of phantastic constitutions," Europe, it now seemed, would persist "in a representative form of government." Unlike the republics, monarchies, and empires of the past, representative governments looked inwards, not outwards. As Schmidt-Phiseldeck put it,

> it appears peculiar to this constitution to direct its attention to the internal welfare and the secret defects of the state, and, at the same time, to oppose a salutary counterpoise to the natural tendency of the government which is directed towards abroad.[45]

This focus on domestic concerns would give an impetus towards the elimination of legal and religious discrimination, put an end to different types of fiscal privilege, and abolish guild restrictions and every form of rural serfdom. It would also favour more uniformity in legal systems, in monetary and fiscal policy, and in the basic units of measurement involved in economic and administrative life. Most important of all, it would allow the European states to bring their standing armies down to a size commensurate with a more stable international system. They would, Schmidt-Phiseldeck wrote, still have their own permanent officer corps to train and exercise their national armies, but the bulk of Europe's military personnel would be supplied by compulsory periods of military service. The resulting peace dividend would begin to release the resources required to enable Europe "to resume the forsaken track."[46] Europe's new internal orientation, Schmidt-Phiseldeck suggested, would be reinforced by a different kind of colonial policy, aimed at promoting settlements in the territories presently occupied by the Ottoman Empire. There, he wrote (picking up an old theme in European thought), "we trust that considerable armies will be made use of, for the last time."[47]

The most pressing reason for the European union was, however, public debt. The structural transformation of monetary flows produced by America's rise to autarchy would increase the costs of debt service. The taxes

---

[44] Schmidt-Phiseldeck, *Europe and America*, p. 132.
[45] Schmidt-Phiseldeck, *Europe and America*, pp. 136–7.
[46] Schmidt-Phiseldeck, *Europe and America*, p. 149.
[47] Schmidt-Phiseldeck, *Europe and America*, pp. 148–9.

presently required to fund interest payments would absorb larger and larger shares of private income, making it increasingly difficult for states to honour their debts. In these circumstances, all the major states would be faced with a choice between either maintaining nominal interest rates and paying in a depreciated currency, on the one hand, or cutting nominal interest rates and opting for a bankruptcy, on the other. But the latter course of action, Schmidt-Phiseldeck warned, would destroy Europe's economy by ruining the private credit on which it had come to be based.

> It is only since money has circulated in such abundance as to afford the means of universal exchange and of satisfying every species of service, in its smallest ramifications, that the division of labour has so wonderfully progressed and through which alone the present prosperity of manufactories and fabrics, and the perfection of their productions, could have been attained. Every stoppage in this main spring would cause a retrograde movement in the animated productions of civil society, or even bring them to a total stagnation.[48]

This left currency devaluation as the only viable option. But devaluing the currency of one state was likely to trigger a spiral of competitive devaluations unless it was coordinated. This, Schmidt-Phiseldeck argued, was why "the regulation of the relative value of money" had to become a common concern of all the European states, and why "a measure of this nature is the only one capable of giving birth to a uniformity of the pecuniary standard throughout Europe, so suitable to the occasions of the age."[49] If, he wrote, "there is no prospect of re-establishing the balance in the income and expenditure of the most European states," then "no other remedy can be applied but to make a timely and voluntary renunciation of the existing institutions and with wise circumspection and vigorous hand, even to proceed to the formation of new ones."[50] Representative government, he went on to argue, had a real capacity to "hinder the chaotic distraction of the transition and deprive the new social formation from bearing the stamp of a revolutionary origin."[51]

The new Europe would have less government. Paid royal officials would be replaced by unpaid elected representatives. Standing armies would be replaced by "the sedentary army of the country."[52] Although the administration of justice and national defence would have to remain the responsibility of central governments, responsibility for tax assessment and collection, welfare provision, the maintenance of public amenities, and law

---

[48] Schmidt-Phiseldeck, *Europe and America*, pp. 165–6.
[49] Schmidt-Phiseldeck, *Europe and America*, p. 168.
[50] Schmidt-Phiseldeck, *Europe and America*, p. 186.
[51] Schmidt-Phiseldeck, *Europe and America*, p. 185.
[52] Schmidt-Phiseldeck, *Europe and America*, p. 187.

enforcement could all be "left to the different communities, as being the nearest concerned." All that was required was that care should be taken to ensure that "by an energetic and proper subordination of the several powers, which the French term *hiérarchie des pouvoirs*, individual ebullitions did not derange the motion of the whole."[53] The transformation, Schmidt-Phiseldeck emphasised, would be slow and painful because it would take place under the difficult conditions generated by America's emancipation from Europe's economic tutelage and against the competing claims of the many entrenched interests left over from the age of feudal privilege and mercantile empire. But, under determined and courageous leadership, it would gradually remove government from any involvement in the affairs and private actions of individuals, leaving room, Schmidt-Phiseldeck wrote, for government "to gain in proportion in moral grandeur and in the veneration of the people."[54] If, even then, "a reduction of the national debt were the only means of giving birth to a better order of things," it was still likely to be the case that "it would be effected under a representative constitution, not without considerable public and private distraction, but yet without producing those consequences, which under other circumstances, such decisive measures would most probably develop."[55] From this perspective, Hume's scenario of the eventual "natural death" of public credit continued to apply, but it would now be managed by a number of different representative governments, locked together within a broader "European state-union" (or a *europäische Bund*, as Schmidt-Phiseldeck entitled another of his books). The new framework would supply a nondespotic outcome to what Kant had called Hume's "heroic medicine."[56] In time, as Schmidt-Phiseldeck indicated by his quotation from Kant, it would lead to the kind of integrated set of social gradations that Kant had counterposed to the divisiveness of the wrong kind of social hierarchy, or, in Sieyès's vocabulary, would allow the "adunation" produced by political institutions to be matched by the "assimilation" produced by morality.[57]

From another perspective, however, it was already too late. Here, the problem was not the presence but the absence of public debt, and the likelihood that Europe would soon be united under the aegis of Russia, the one state whose military power did not depend on public credit. This was the point of view set out by the American diplomat Alexander Hill Everett in his *Europe, or a General Survey of the Present Situation of the Principal Powers*, a work published in 1822, partly in reply to what Schmidt-Phiseldeck had

[53] Schmidt-Phiseldeck, *Europe and America*, p. 189.
[54] Schmidt-Phiseldeck, *Europe and America*, p. 190.
[55] Schmidt-Phiseldeck, *Europe and America*, pp. 194–5.
[56] Immanuel Kant, *The Contest of the Faculties*, in Immanuel Kant, *Political Writings*, ed. Hans Reiss (Cambridge, CUP, 1991), p. 189.
[57] Sieyès, *Political Writings*, ed. Sonenscher, p. x.

written.[58] The broader framework of his argument had already been outlined in a short, imaginary conversation between Montesquieu and Benjamin Franklin that Everett published in the April 1821 issue of the *North American Review*. There "Franklin" took issue with "Montesquieu" on broadly democratic premises. In every country, he argued, "effective power is attached to the possession of property." Where property was "very equally divided among the members of society," political power was also "equally divided and the government is in substance democratic." Where the opposite occurred, government, too, would follow. As "Franklin" put it,

> It would seem therefore, Mr. President, that in attributing the establishment of hereditary ranks, titles and magistracies to the necessity of protecting certain individuals distinguished by birth, wealth and honours from the jealousy of the people, you have exactly inverted the natural order of causes and effects. Wealth is the real essence of aristocracy and itself affords security to rank and titles.[59]

It may not have been a very subtle rendition of Montesquieu, but the broader point was quite clear. Property was "the principal element of political power," and the more widely it was distributed, the more stable a society was likely to be. "Such a supposition," Everett continued, "cannot be treated as chimerical because it is actually realised in the United States."[60] Provided, he argued in his book on Europe, that there were no obstacles in the way, the different types of property involved in agriculture, trade, and manufacturing industry could all be relied upon to complement one another to produce something like the combination of mobility and stability implied by Say's law (Everett, in a letter to Say himself, did, in fact, endorse what he called Say's principle "that an excess of production is impossible").[61] The broader framework was set out as a simple general model. "It may be shown by mathematical demonstration," he wrote, "that when every description of property is entirely unfettered by artificial institutions, there will exist of necessity the greatest variety in the amount of individual estates that is possible in the nature of things."

> Suppose, for example, that a hundred persons are playing at a game of skill for a sum of a hundred thousand dollars and that their skill is respectively in the ratio of an ascending series of numbers from one to a hundred. Their shares in the sum at stake at the close of the game will be in the same proportion,

---

[58] Everett, *Europe*, pp. 433–8.

[59] Alexander Hill Everett, "Dialogue on the Principles of Representative Government, between the President de Montesquieu and Dr. Franklin," *North American Review*, April 1821, pp. 346–65 (p. 351).

[60] Everett, "Dialogue," pp. 351, 352.

[61] Everett to Say, 18 February, 1824, printed in Jean-Baptiste Say, *Mélanges et correspondance d'économie politique*, ed. Charles Comte (Brussels, 1843), p. 657.

and will stand in relation to each other, as 1, 2, 3, 4, etc. to 100; and this is the greatest possible variety which can be effected by the division of this sum among a hundred persons. This is the image of a society where the whole of the common property is thrown into a general stock, from which each individual member draws his share, according to his talents and his industry.[62]

Partible inheritance and the vagaries of individual behaviour would ensure that the rules of the game remained the same. In the absence of artificial obstacles, capital would simply circulate from one branch of production to another and the prodigious productivity of manufacturing industry would allow the game to be played and replayed at ever higher levels of wealth and population.

In itself, public credit would simply accelerate the process. The "vast creation of public debt, which is certainly one of the most remarkable phenomena of modern times," was something that paralleled the broader "progress of industry, wealth and knowledge, or in a word of civilisation."[63] It would favour that progress because it would lead to a continuous transfer of wealth away from the landed residuum of Europe's feudal past. As Everett put it,

> Now this prodigious creation of artificial capital operates to a very great extent, if not to its full nominal amount, as a transfer or cession of property from the landed proprietors to the industrious and mercantile classes. Those loans are realised in the form of rents [i.e., annuities] and are ultimately a charge upon the land and its owners; while in the hands of the capitalists the securities that represent them are the equivalent to money.[64]

Whatever the purposes for which it might have been called into existence, public credit would reinforce the availability of capital. But its positive effects required real legal and political equality. This, Everett argued, was why they were not yet to be found in Britain, despite the many merits of the British system of government. There, the political power and influence of Britain's landowners and the combined effects of the British corn laws and tariff policy meant that the tax burden would continue to fall disproportionately on industry and trade. This, he suggested, was why Hume's scenario continued to apply. "The coolest and most sagacious political philosopher that perhaps ever appeared in Europe," he wrote, "pointed out more than half a century ago an approaching crisis in the financial affairs of that country. This crisis has come on more slowly than he anticipated and the period at which he predicted that it would arrive has already passed." But this did not mean that it would never happen.

[62] Everett, *Europe*, pp. 44–5.
[63] Everett, *Europe*, pp. 9, 32.
[64] Everett, *Europe*, p. 32.

It has been perceived that the delay has not been owing to incorrectness of the principles on which the prediction was founded—that the danger is still as certain as ever, unless something is done to prevent it—and that the crisis will be only the more dreadful when it arrives, from the slowness of its advances.[65]

Elsewhere, however, circumstances were different. France, in particular, no longer had any appreciable public debt, and, contrary to what Malthus had written, the huge redistribution of property that had taken place during the period of the revolution did not favour despotism. It would, instead, lead to the emergence of a "natural aristocracy" of "talents, wealth and virtue" that stood at odds with the mixed system of government that had been established at the Restoration. "A country without artificial inequalities in the distribution of property and personal privileges," Everett observed, "is substantially republican."[66] Had the allied powers been able to recognise this and follow a different policy at the Vienna Congress, they would have set out to promote a rapid revival of French financial prosperity to allow the new French regime to recover from the disaster of the revolution. Their failure to do so had weakened France still further and now left Europe exposed to despotism from another direction.

According to Everett, Europe would be united, but under a backward Russian military despotism. The eighteenth-century scenario that his compatriot Robert Walsh had once applied to Napoleonic France now applied to Russia. The huge military and financial effort involved in defeating Napoleonic France had, Everett argued, left all the European states exposed to the power of the one state whose military capabilities did not depend on the resources supplied by the modern funding system. In the medium term, he suggested, this would mean that Europe would be united under Russian military power, although Britain would be able to remain independent both by avoiding involvement in European affairs and by relying on her empire to maintain the precarious stability of her economy. The world

---

[65] Everett, *Europe*, pp. 19–20. For other versions of the same idea, see Gareth Stedman Jones, "National Bankruptcy and Social Revolution: European Observers on Britain, 1813–44," in Donald Winch and Patrick O'Brien, eds., *The Political Economy of British Historical Experience* (London, 2002), pp. 61–92. Early-nineteenth-century European discussions of the long-anticipated, but never-realised, "British revolution" and, by extension, of the underlying properties of the "English constitution" and its potential for reform have not been given as much attention as equivalent discussions in the eighteenth century. Benjamin Constant's famous lecture on ancient and modern liberty is one starting point (see above, p. 49). Another might be the intellectual trajectory followed by the Genevan political reformer Etienne Dumont, whose late *Souvenirs sur Mirabeau et sur les deux premières assemblées législatives* (published after the revolutions of 1830) can be read as a final settling of accounts with Sieyès's system and an endorsement of the utility-based alternative that Dumont came to find in Bentham. On Dumont, see particularly Jean Bénétruy, *L'Atelier de Mirabeau. Quatre proscrits genevois dans la tourmente révolutionnaire* (Geneva, Alexandre Jullien, 1962).

[66] Everett, *Europe*, pp. 46–7.

would then be dominated by three great powers: Russia, Britain, and the United States. In the longer term, however, representative government would prevail. In part this was because Russia's nobility was already locked into western European patterns of consumption, however hostile it might still be to western European patterns of political thought. A "tragedy of Racine or a case of champagne," Everett commented, "is a stronger argument in favour of liberal ideas than any to be found in the *Minerva* or the *Constitutional*."[67] In part, too, it was because even the most militarised despotism would be unable to avoid the pressure to promote prosperity generated by the international capital markets. In the longer term, trying to maintain the principles enshrined in Europe's Holy Alliance (which, Everett assumed, would also be the basis of the Russian-dominated European union) would turn out to be self-defeating. As Everett pointed out, the emperor of Austria might well, as he had recently done, borrow a large sum of money from an American financier to attack the principles of liberty in Italy, but its effect would be, on the one hand, to throw "the weight of an amount of property equal to the loan into the scale of the general mercantile interest of Europe and the world" and, on the other, to charge "the expenses of keeping this capital in existence upon the landed proprietors of the Austrian Empire." The example was generally applicable. Public debt would, in this way, dig the graves of liberty's own grave-diggers. It was, Everett concluded, "one of the most singular instances perhaps that could be produced of an effect 'counter-working its cause.' "[68]

The model of the future was to be found in the government of the United States. As Everett put it in a third work, *America or a General Survey of the Western Continent*, which he published in 1827, the "great problem in politics" was "to discover the form of government which best combines the security that can only be enjoyed in large states, with the acknowledgement and exercise of the right of self-government inherent in the people." The two principles of representation and federation underlying the American union had supplied the answer. Together, Everett wrote, their object was not, "as some affirm, *democracy rejected*, but *democracy made easy*."[69] Taking his cue from the strong endorsement of both public credit and manufacturing industry made earlier by Alexander Hamilton, he went on to argue that the combination of representative government and a prosperous economy would, in the not too distant future, produce the world's most powerful state.[70] "By the middle of the next century," he suggested, the

---

[67] Everett, *Europe*, p. 31.

[68] Everett, *Europe*, pp. 33–4.

[69] Everett, *America*, pp. 80–1.

[70] For Everett's views on Hamilton (combined with equally fulsome praise of Madison, Adams, and, in some measure, Jefferson), see *America*, pp. 106–14.

population of America would reach some "three hundred millions" (which was quite a good guess) and, after a further hundred years, climb to "the sum of twelve hundred millions." Even by the end of the nineteenth century, however, the population, geographical extent, and form of government of the United States would make it the greatest power on earth.

> Superior in each and all of these particulars to the whole European commonwealth taken together, the United States at the close of this century will outweigh very much in political importance, the combined power of its members; and instead of having any thing to apprehend from their injustice or violence, will be naturally courted by them all as a useful friend and ally, and will have it in their power to exercise a very beneficial influence upon their institutions and policy.[71]

Everett's argument supplied some of the more bullish American background to Friedrich List's *National System of Political Economy* and, at the same time, offered a less morally demanding long-term vision of Europe's future than the one that Schmidt-Phiseldeck had set out.[72] From the perspective that Everett presented, it was the New World that had finally removed the spectre of decline and fall from the Old. But for the European discovery of America, Everett concluded, "the Christian nations" would probably have continued "to ravage one another as before, with constant wars, until some one military state should have arisen sufficiently active and successful to subjugate the rest." This had been "the history and termination of the European civilisation of a former epoch," and, if one looked back at the European nations "at the point at which they stood about the middle of the seventeenth century," there was no reason to think that, projecting forwards from the time of the Westphalia peace settlement, the moderns would have been any more likely to have avoided the cycle of decline and fall than the ancients had been.[73] The difference had been America, and, from Everett's point of view, it was a difference that would continue to apply.

It is a familiar story. It is certainly more familiar than the one projected forwards by Conrad Schmidt-Phiseldeck. Both, however, had their origins in the eighteenth century's earlier projections of Europe's future. One conception of that future looked back to Henri IV's Grand Design and the kind of republican monarchy that would fit its broadly egalitarian structure.

---

[71] Everett, *America*, pp. 136–66, 349.

[72] On List, see Istvan Hont, *Jealousy of Trade: International Competition and the Nation-State in Historical Perspective* (Cambridge, Mass., Harvard University Press), pp. 148–54, and for the American background to List's thought, see Friedrich List, *Outlines of American Political Economy* (Philadelphia, 1827), and Keith Tribe, *Strategies of Economic Order: German Economic Discourse 1750–1950* (Cambridge, CUP, 1995), pp. 32–65.

[73] Everett, *America*, p. 336.

Another looked back to Europe's feudal past and the kind of monarchical republic that would fit its broadly hierarchical structure. After 1776, the two frameworks crossed the Atlantic. For James Wilson, one of the new republic's founders, the United States was the real incarnation of Henri IV's Grand Design. "Here," he wrote, "the sublime system of Henry the Great has been effectually realized, and completely carried into execution."[74] For Alexander Hamilton, the new union was best seen as a better-designed version of the system of government that Montesquieu had called monarchy, with America's hierarchy of districts, states, and national government forming a constitutionally organised and republican equivalent to the strange historical process that, for Montesquieu, had turned feudal government into its royal aftermath.[75] In this sense, Hamilton's idea of a federal union was a republican version of Necker's (or Chastellux's) idea of monarchy. The dialogue between Everett and Schmidt-Phiseldeck a generation later was a continuation of the same argument, with the former echoing Hamilton's assessment of public credit's positive attributes and the latter rehearsing Kant's assessment of its primary association with war. The system of representative government that the abbé Sieyès envisaged fitted into the same intellectual space. Where Everett highlighted representative government's affinity with general equality and social prosperity, Schmidt-Phiseldeck highlighted its compatibility with material inequality and moral authority. Sieyès's system was designed to be compatible with both. It was the eighteenth century's most elaborate attempt to find a way to deal with both the promise and the menace of public debt. From the vantage point of the twenty-first century, it now seems clear that the promise has far outweighed the menace, and that the horizons of debt-induced political expectation now stretch far beyond anything that the eighteenth century envisaged. Perhaps they always will. Sieyès's system was predicated on the possibility that they might not, and that neither a monarchy nor a republic as these had been standardly understood would be able to face the difficulties that might lie at the horizon's edge. The fact that they have not occurred may make Sieyès's subsequent reputation as an obsessive constitutional tinkerer seem well deserved. But it may also make what came instead of the deluge, as well as the deceptively familiar nineteenth-century ideologies of liberalism, conservatism, socialism, communism, nationalism, or federalism, a more historically open-ended subject than we think.

[74] James Wilson, *Works*, ed. Robert Green McCloskey, 2 vols. (Cambridge, Mass., Belknap Press, Harvard University, 1967), 1:261.

[75] Alexander Hamilton, James Madison, and John Jay, *The Federalist*, 17, ed. Terence Ball (Cambridge, CUP, 2003), pp. 78–9.

BIBLIOGRAPHY

PRIMARY

Manuscript and Periodical Sources

Although most of the sources on which this book is based were published in the eighteenth or early nineteenth century, I have made use of manuscripts from the collections listed below. References to articles in eighteenth- or early-nineteenth-century periodical journals, such as the *Annual Register, Le Catholique, Le Courier de Provence, La Décade philosophique, Le Véridique, ou Courier universel, Gazette nationale, ou Le Moniteur universel, Ephémérides du citoyen, Journal d'économie publique, Journal d'instruction sociale, Journal oeconomique, Journal de la société des amis de la constitution monarchique, Journal de Trévoux, Journal des beaux-arts et des sciences, Journal Encyclopédique, Mercure de France, Monthly Review, North American Review, Nouvelles politiques nationales et étrangères*, as well as to the multivolume *Archives Parlementaires*, appear under the names of individual authors below, and in the footnotes to the text.

Argenson papers: Bibliothèque universitaire de Poitiers, Fonds d'Argenson.
Chastellux papers: privately owned (I am grateful to the descendants of the family for the opportunity to consult them).
Dupont de Nemours papers: Hagley Museum and Library, Delaware, Winterthur Mss.
Forbonnais papers: Bibliothèque de l'Arsénal, Paris, Mss. 4591.
Iselin papers, Staatsarchiv, Basel, 47–56.
Mirabeau papers: Archives Nationales, Paris, M 752, 778, 780; Musée Arbaud, Aix-en-Provence, Fonds Mirabeau; Bibliothèque royale, Brussels, Mss. 20797.
Rabaut Saint-Etienne papers: Archives Nationales, Paris, F⁷ 4774⁸⁶.
Roederer papers: Archives Nationales, Paris, 29 AP.
Sieyès papers: Archives Nationales, Paris, 284 AP.
Zimmermann papers: Nieder Sachsische Staatsarchiv, Hanover.

Printed Sources

Adams, John Quincy. *Writings*. Edited by Worthington Chauncey Ford. 2 vols. New York, 1913.
Andrews, John. *An Essay on Republican Principles and on the Inconvenience of a Commonwealth in a Large Country and Nation*. London, 1783.
Argenson, René-Louis de Voyer de Paulmy, marquis d'. "Lettre à l'auteur du *Journal oeconomique* au sujet de la dissertation sur le commerce de M. le marquis Belloni." *Journal oeconomique* (Paris), April 1751, pp. 107–17.
———. *Considérations sur le gouvernement ancien et présent de la France*. Amsterdam, 1764.
———. *Journal et Mémoires du Marquis d'Argenson*. Edited by E.J.B. Rathéry. 9 vols. Paris, 1859–67.

[Aubert de Vitry, François-Jean-Philibert]. *Jean-Jacques Rousseau à l'assemblée natio-nale*. Paris, 1789.

Auguis, Pierre-René. *Les révélations indiscrètes du xviiie siècle*. Paris, 1814.

Barante, Prosper de. *Des communes et de l'aristocratie*. Paris, 1821.

[Barincourt, Le Roy de]. *Principe du droit fondamental des souverains*. 2 vols. Geneva, 1788.

Barnave, Antoine-Joseph. "Etudes sur l'homme." In his *Oeuvres complètes*, edited by Bérenger de la Drôme, vol. 3. 4 vols. Paris, 1843.

———. "Introduction à la révolution française." In his *Oeuvres complètes*.

———. "Sur les économistes." In his *Oeuvres complètes*, vol. 2.

Bentham, Jeremy. *A Fragment on Government* [1776]. Edited by Ross Harrison. Cambridge, CUP, 1988.

———. *Political Tactics* [1791]. Edited by Michael James, Cyprien Blamires, and Catherine Pease-Watkin. Oxford, Clarendon Press, 1999.

Bertolini, Stefano. "Analyse raisonné de *l'Esprit des lois*" [1754]. In Montesquieu, *Oeuvres posthumes*. Paris, 1798.

Biaudet, Jean-Charles, and Françoise Nicod, eds. *Correspondance de Frédéric-César de la Harpe et Alexandre I*. 3 vols. Neuchâtel, La Baconnière, 1978–80.

Bielefeld, Jacob Friedrich von. *Institutions politiques* [1760]. New ed. 3 vols. Leiden and Leipzig, 1768.

Bolingbroke, Henry St John, viscount. "Some Reflections of the Present State of the Nation, Principally with Regard to her Taxes and her Debts, and on the Causes and Consequences of Them." In *The Works of the late Right Honourable Henry St. John, Lord Viscount Bolingbroke*, edited by David Mallet, 3:143–79. 4 vols. London, 1754.

———. *Testament politique de Milord Bolingbroke*. London, 1754.

———. *Discours politiques*, 2 vols. Amsterdam, 1754 and 1756.

———. *Political Writings*. Edited by David Armitage. Cambridge, CUP, 1997.

Bonnin, Charles-Jean-Baptiste. "Sur l'établissement d'une noblesse" [1808]. Re-printed in his *Doctrine sociale ou principes universels des lois et des rapports de peuple à peuple déduit de la nature de l'homme et des droits du genre humain*. 2nd ed. Paris, 1821.

———. *Considérations politiques et morales sur les constitutions*. Paris, 1814.

[———]. *De la révolution européenne*. Paris, 1815.

[———]. *Lettres sur l'éducation écrites en octobre et en décembre 1823, dans sa prison, par le publiciste C.-J.-B. Bonnin, sur l'éducation de sa fille*. Paris, 1825.

Bordenave, Toussaint. *Essai sur la physiologie, ou physique du corps humain*. 4th ed. 2 vols. Paris, 1787.

Brizard, Gabriel. "Eloge historique de l'abbé de Mably" [1787]. Reprinted in Mably, *Oeuvres*, vol. 1. 15 vols. [Paris, 1794–5]. Aalen, Scientia Verlag, 1977.

Brougham, Henry, Lord. *Historical Sketches of Statesmen who Flourished in the Time of George III*. 6 vols. London, 1843.

Burke, Edmund. *Speech on presenting to the House of Commons on the 11th February, 1780 a plan for the better security of the independence of Parliament, and the economical reformation of the civil and other establishments*. In Edmund Burke, *Works*, 2:275–6. London, 1899.

———. *Reflections on the Revolution in France* [1790]. Edited by J.G.A. Pocock. Cam-bridge, Mass., and Indianapolis, Hackett, 1987. Edited by J.C.D. Clark. Stanford,

Stanford University Press, 2001. Edited by Frank M. Turner. New Haven, Yale University Press, 2003.

———. *A Letter to a Noble Lord* [1796]. In Edmund Burke, *Further Reflections on the Revolution in France*, Edited by Daniel E. Ritchie. Indianapolis, 1992.

———. *Thoughts on the Cause of the Present Discontents*. In Edmund Burke, *Works*, vol. 1. 12 vols. London, John C. Nimmo, 1899.

Carbonnières, Louis-Ramond de. *Opinion énoncée à la société de 1789 sur les loix constitutionnelles*. Paris, 1791.

Castel, Jean-Bertrand. *L'homme moral opposé à l'homme physique de Monsieur R***. Lettres philosophiques où l'on réfute le Déisme du jour*. Toulouse, 1756.

Cerisier, Antoine-Marie. *Le destin de l'Amérique, ou dialogues pittoresques dans lesquels on développe la cause des événements actuels, la politique et les intérêts des puissances de l'Europe relativement à cette guerre et les suites qu'elle devrait avoir pour le bonheur de l'humanité*. London, 1780.

Chalmers, George. *An Estimate of the Comparative Strength of Great Britain During the Present and Four Preceding Reigns*. 2nd ed. London, 1794.

Chastellux, François-Jean de. *De la félicité publique* [1772]. Edited by Roger Basoni. Paris, Presses universitaires de France, 1989.

———. *An Essay on Public Happiness* [1772]. 2 vols. London, 1774.

Chénier, Joseph-Marie. *Épître sur la calomnie*. Paris, an V/1796.

———. *Le Docteur Pancrace*. Paris, an V/1796.

Condorcet, Antoine-Nicolas Caritat de. *Bibliothèque de l'homme publique*. Paris, 1790–1.

———. *Sketch for a Historical Picture of the Progress of the Human Mind* [1795]. Translated by June Barraclough. Introduced by Stuart Hampshire. London, 1955.

Constant, Benjamin. *Recueil d'articles. Le Mercure, La Minerve et La Renommée*. Edited by Ephraïm Harpaz. 2 vols. Geneva, 1972.

———. *Oeuvres complètes. Correspondance générale III*. Edited by C. P. Courtney, Boris Anelli, and Dennis Wood. Tübingen, Max Niemeyer Verlag, 2003.

Corbet, vicomte d'Alès de. *De l'origine du mal, ou examen des principales difficultés de Bayle sur cette matière*. Paris, 1758.

Court de Gebelin, Antoine. *Monde primitif, analysé et comparé avec le monde moderne, considéré dans l'histoire naturelle de la parole ou origine du langage et de l'écriture*. 9 vols. Paris, 1773–82.

[Currie, James]. *A Letter, Commercial and Political addressed to the Right Honourable William Pitt: in which the Real Interests of Britain in the Present Crisis are Considered, and Some Observations are Offered on the General State of Europe*. 3rd ed. London, 1793.

Dalrymple, Sir John. *An Essay towards a General History of Feudal Property in Great Britain* [London, 1757].

[Dangeul, Louis-Joseph Plumard de]. *Remarques sur les avantages et les désavantages de la France et de la Grande Bretagne* [1754]. 3rd ed. Leiden, 1754.

Delolme, Jean-Louis. *The Constitution of England, or an Account of the English Government; in which it is Compared both with the Republic Form of Government and the Other Monarchies of Europe*. London, 1770.

Desaubiez, M. *Système de finances et d'économie publique applicable aux divers gouvernements de l'Europe et du Nouveau Monde* [London, 1780]. Paris, 1826.

[Desprès, Jean-Baptiste-Denis]. "Essai sur la marquise de Pompadour." In Nicole du Hausset, *Mémoires de Madame du Hausset, femme de chambre de Mme de Pompadour*, edited by Quintin Crauford. Paris, 1824.

Domat, Jean. *A Treatise of Laws* [Paris, 1689]. Translated by William Strahan. London, 1722.

———. "Of the nature and spirit of laws and their different kinds." In Jean Domat, *The Civil Law in its Natural Order*. 2 vols. London, 1722.

Duguet, Jacques-Joseph. *Institution d'un prince ou traité des qualités, des vertus et des devoirs d'un souverain*. 4 vols. Leiden, 1739. Translated as *The Institution of a Prince, or a Treatise of the Virtues and Duties of a Sovereign*. 2 vols. London, 1740.

Dumont, Etienne. *Recollections of Mirabeau and of the two first legislative assemblies of France*. London, 1832.

Dupin, Charles. *Observations sur un livre intitulé "De l'esprit des loix"*. 3 vols. Paris, 1750.

Dupont de Nemours, Pierre-Samuel. *The Autobiography*. Edited by Elizabeth Fox-Genovese. Wilmington, Del., 1984.

———, ed. *Physiocratie, ou constitution naturelle du gouvernement le plus avantageux au genre humain* [1767]. Leiden, 1768.

Eckstein, Ferdinand, baron d'. "De l'influence des doctrines matérielles sur la civilisation moderne." *Le Catholique* 3 (1826).

———. "De l'industrialisme." *Le Catholique* 5 (1827).

Everett, Alexander Hill. "Dialogue on the Principles of Representative Government, between the President de Montesquieu and Dr. Franklin." *North American Review*, April 1821, pp. 346–65.

———. *New Ideas on Population with Remarks on the Theories of Malthus and Godwin* [1822]. 2nd ed. Boston, 1826.

———. *Europe: or a General Survey of the Present Situation of the Principal Powers; with Conjectures on their Future Prospects*. Boston, 1822.

———. *America or a General Survey of the Political Situation of the Several Powers of the Western Continent with Conjectures on their Future Prospects*. Philadelphia, 1827.

[Falkenskjold, S. O.]. *Mémoires authentiques et intéressants, ou histoire des comtes Struensee et Brandt*. London, 1789.

[Fauchet, Joseph]. *Le despotisme décrété par l'assemblée nationale*. London, 1790.

[———]. *Mémoire sur les Etats-Unis d'Amérique* [1795]. Edited by Carl Ludwig Lokke. In *Annual Report of the American Historical Association for the Year 1936*. 3 vols. Washington, 1938.

Fénelon, François de Salignac de la Mothe-. *Les Aventures de Télémaque, fils d'Ulysse* [1699/1715]. Edited by Albert Cahen. 2 vols. Paris, 1927.

———. *Télémaque*. Amsterdam, 1725.

———. *The Adventures of Telemachus, the Son of Ulysses*. 3rd ed. 2 vols. London, 1720.

———. *The Adventures of Telemachus, Son of Ulysses*. Edited and translated by Patrick Riley. Cambridge, CUP, 1994.

———. *Démonstration de l'existence de Dieu, tirée de la connaissance de la nature*. Paris, 1713.

———. *A Demonstration of the Existence and Attributes of God*. London, 1720.

———. "Sentiments on the balance of Europe." In *Two Essays on the Balance of Europe*. London, 1720.

Ferguson, Adam. *An Essay on the History of Civil Society* [1767]. Edited by Duncan Forbes. Edinburgh, 1966. Edited by Fania Oz. Cambridge, CUP, 1995.

Ferrand, Antoine. *L'esprit de l'histoire, ou lettres politiques et morales d'un père à son fils*. 3rd ed. 4 vols. Paris, 1804.

Fichte, Johann Gottlieb. *Der geschlossen Handelstaat* [Stuttgart, 1800]. Translated as *L'état commercial fermé*. Lausanne, L'Age d'homme, 1980.

Fiévée, Joseph. *Des intérêts et des opinions pendant la révolution*. Paris, 1809.

Forbes, Sir William. *An Account of the Life and Writings of James Beattie*. 2 vols. Edinburgh, 1806.

Forbonnais, François Véron de. *Extrait du livre de "l'Esprit des loix"*. Amsterdam, 1753.

———. *Elémens du commerce*. 2nd ed. 2 vols. Leiden, 1754.

———. *Recherches et considérations sur les finances de France depuis l'année 1595 jusqu'à l'année 1721*. 2 vols. Basel, 1758.

———. *Principes et observations économiques*. Paris, 1767.

Forster, Nathaniel. *A Sermon Preached at the Visitation of the Rev. Dr. Moss, Archdeacon of Colchester at St. Peter's Colchester, May 20, 1765 and before the University of Oxford, May 24, 1767*. Oxford, 1767.

Galiani, Ferdinando. *Della moneta*. 2nd ed. Naples, 1780.

———. *Della moneta e scritti inediti*. Edited by Alberto Caracciolo and Alberto Merola. Milan, Feltrinelli, 1963.

Garat, Dominique-Joseph. *Éloge de M. de l'Hôpital, chancelier de France*. Paris, 1778.

Gentz, Friedrich. *Essai sur l'état actuel de l'administration des finances et de la richesse nationale de la Grande Bretagne*. London, 1800.

Girardin, Stanislas. *Discours et opinions. Journal et souvenirs*. 4 vols. Paris, 1828.

Gournay, Jacques-Claude Vincent de. *Traités sur le commerce de Josiah Child, avec les remarques inédites de Vincent de Gournay: Texte intégral d'après les manuscrits conservés à la Bibliothèque municipale de Saint-Brieuc*. Edited by Takumi Tsuda. Tokyo, 1983.

———. *Mémoires et lettres de Vincent de Gournay*. Edited by Takumi Tsuda. Tokyo, 1993.

Gravina, Jean-Vincent. *Esprit des loix romaines*. 3 vols. London, 1766.

[Griffiths, Thomas Waters]. *L'indépendance absolue des Américains des Etats-Unis prouvée par l'état actuel de leur commerce avec les nations européennes*. Paris, an VI/1798.

Grotius, Hugo. *De jure belli ac pacis* [1625]. Translated by Jean Barbeyrac as *Le Droit de la guerre et de la paix*. Amsterdam, 1724.

Gudin de la Brenellerie, Pierre-Paul. *Essai sur l'histoire des comices de Rome, des Etats-Généraux de la France et du Parlement de l'Angleterre*. 3 vols. Philadelphie [i.e., Paris], 1789.

———. *Supplément au Contrat Social*. Paris, 1791.

———. *Histoire de Beaumarchais*. Edited by Maurice Tourneux. Paris, 1888.

Guffroy, Armand-Benoît-Joseph. *Lettre en réponse aux observations sommaires de M. l'abbé Sieyès sur les biens ecclésiastiques*. Paris, n.d. [but late 1789 from internal evidence].

Guizot, François. *Histoire des origines du gouvernement représentatif en Europe*. 2 vols. Paris, 1851.

Guizot, François. *The History of the Origins of Representative Government in Europe.* Translated by Andrew R. Scoble. Introduced by Aurelian Craiutu. Indianapolis, Liberty Fund, 2002.

Guyne, François. *Traités de la représentation du double lien et de la règle "Paterna Paternis, Materna Maternis" par rapport à toutes les coutumes de la France* [1698]. Paris, 1773.

Haller, Karl Ludwig von. *Restauration de la science politique ou théorie de l'état social naturel.* 4 vols. Paris and Lyon, 1824–61.

Hamilton, Alexander, James Madison, and John Jay. *The Federalist*, 17. Edited by Terence Ball. Cambridge, CUP, 2003.

———. *The Federalist.* Edited by J. R. Pole. Indianapolis, Hackett, 2005.

Hausset, Nicole du. *Mémoires de Madame du Hausset, femme de chambre de Mme de Pompadour.* Edited by Quintin Crauford. Paris, 1824.

[Hay du Châtelet, Philippe]. *The Politics of France.* 2nd ed. London, 1691.

Helvétius, Claude-Adrien. *De l'esprit* [1758]. Edited by François Châtelet. Verviers, Editions Gérard, 1973.

———. *De l'esprit: or essays on the mind and its several faculties.* London, 1759.

———. *De l'homme.* 2 vols. London, 1773.

———. *De l'homme* [London, 1773]. 2 vols. Paris, Fayard, 1989.

———. *A Treatise on Man, his Intellectual Faculties and his Education.* 2 vols. London, 1777.

———. *Correspondance général d'Helvétius.* Edited by Peter Allan, Alan Dainard, Jean Orson, and David Smith. 4 vols. Toronto and Oxford, 1981–98.

Herder, Johann Gottfried. *Another Philosophy of History* [1774]. Translated and edited by Ioannis D. Evrigenis and Daniel Pellerin. Indianapolis, Hackett, 2004.

Herrenschwand, Jean-Frédéric. *De l'économie politique moderne. Discours fondamental sur la population.* London, 1786.

Hobbes, Thomas. *Elements of Law Natural & Politic* [1640]. Edited by Ferdinand Tönnies. Introduced by M. M. Goldsmith. London, Cass, 1969.

———. *The Citizen: Philosophical Rudiments concerning Government and Society* [1642]. Edited by Bernard Gert. Indianapolis, Hackett, 1991.

———. *Leviathan* [1651]. Edited by C. B. Macpherson. Harmondsworth, Penguin, 1968.

———. *Writings on Common Law and Hereditary Right.* Edited by Alan Cromartie and Quentin Skinner. Oxford, Oxford University Press, 2005.

Hume, David. "Of Civil Liberty" [1741], "Of Superstition and Enthusiasm" [1741], "Of Public Credit" [1752], and "The idea of a perfect commonwealth" [1753]. In David Hume, *Essays: Moral, Political and Literary*, edited by Eugene F. Miller. Indianapolis, Liberty Press, 1985. "Of Civil Liberty" [1741]. In Hume, *Political Essays*, edited by Knud Haakonssen. Cambridge, CUP, 1994.

———. *An Enquiry concerning the Principles of Morals* [1751]. Edited by L. A. Selby-Bigge. Oxford, 1957.

———. *Discours politiques.* 2 vols. Amsterdam, 1754 and 1756.

———. *The History of England.* 6 vols. London, 1778.

———. *The Letters of David Hume.* Edited by J.Y.T. Greig. 2 vols. Oxford, 1932, reprinted 1969.

Jefferson, Thomas. *Notes on the State of Virginia* [1781]. Edited by William Peden. Chapel Hill and London, University of North Carolina Press, 1982.

———. *Papers* Edited by Julian P. Boyd et al. 31 vols. to date. Princeton, Princeton University Press, 1950–.

Kant, Immanuel. *Critique of the Power of Judgement* [1790]. Edited by Paul Guyer. Cambridge, CUP, 2000.

———. *Toward Perpetual Peace* [1795]. In Immanuel Kant, *Practical Philosophy*, translated and edited by Mary Gregor. Cambridge, CUP, 1996.

———. *The Conflict of the Faculties* [1798]. Translated and edited by Allen W. Wood and George Di Giovanni. Cambridge, CUP, 1996. Also translated as *The Contest of the Faculties*, in Immanuel Kant, *Political Writings*, edited by Hans Reiss. Cambridge, CUP, 1991.

———. *Lectures on Ethics*. Cambridge, CUP, 1997.

Keld, Christopher. *An Essay on the polity of England: with a view to discover the true principles of government, what remedies might be likely to cure the grievances complained of, and why the several provisions made by the legislature, and those recommended by individuals have failed*. London, 1785.

Lacretelle, Pierre-Louis. *Sur le Dix-Huit Brumaire. A Sieyès et à Bonaparte*. Paris, an VIII.

Lallement, Guillaume N. *Choix de rapports, opinions et discours prononcés à la tribune nationale depuis 1789 jusqu'à ce jour*. 21 vols. Paris, 1818–23.

Law, John. *Money and Trade, Considered with a Proposal for Supplying the Nation with Money* [1705]. In his *Oeuvres complètes*, edited by Paul Harsin. 3 vols. Paris, 1934.

[———]. *The Present State of the French Revenues and Trade, and of the Controversy betwixt the Parlement of Paris, and Mr. Law*. London, 1720.

Lebrun, Charles-François. *La voix du citoyen*. Paris, 1789.

Lecat, Claude-Nicolas. *Traité des sensations et des passions en général et des sens en particulier*. 3 vols. Paris, 1767.

La légion d'honneur en 1819. Par un membre de l'ordre. 2nd ed. Paris, 1819.

Lemontey, Pierre-Edouard. *Histoire de la régence et de la minorité de Louis XV* [1816]. 2 vols. Paris, 1832.

Lenglet, Etienne-Géry. *Essai, ou Observations sur Montesquieu*. Paris, 1792.

Lerminier, Edmond. *De l'influence de la philosophie du xviiie siècle sur la législation et la sociabilité du xixe siècle*. Brussels, 1834.

Letrosne, Guillaume-François. *De l'ordre social*. Paris, 1777.

A letter to Lord North, on his Re-Election into the House of Commons. London, 1780.

Lettres à l'auteur du Quotidienne, par un de ses abonnés. Hamburg, 1796.

Lezay, Adrien. *De la faiblesse d'un gouvernement qui commence et de la nécessité où il est de se rallier à la majorité nationale*. Paris, an V.

Linguet, Simon-Nicolas-Henri. "De la société en général. Révolution singulière dont l'Europe est menacée." *Annales politiques, civiles et littéraires du dix-huitième siècle* 1 (1777): 83–103.

———. *Political and Philosophical Speculations on the Distinguishing Characteristics of the Present Century*. London, 1778.

List, Friedrich. *Outlines of American Political Economy*. Philadelphia, 1827.

Lourdoueix, Honoré de. *De la restauration de la société française*. 3rd ed. Paris, 1834.

Mably, Gabriel Bonnot de. *Le Droit public de l'Europe fondé sur les traités* [1748]. 3 vols. Geneva, 1776. Also in *Oeuvres*, vols. 5–7. 15 vols. [Paris, 1794–5]. Aalen, Scientia Verlag, 1977.

———. *Observations sur les Romains* [1751]. Reprinted in his *Oeuvres*, vol. 4.

———. *Phocion's Conversations or the Relation between Morality and Politics* [1763]. London, 1769.

———. *Observations sur l'histoire de la France* [2 vols., 1765; 3 vols. 1789]. In *Oeuvres*, vols. 1–3.

———. *Doutes proposées aux philosophes économistes sur l'ordre naturel et nécessaire des sociétés politiques* [1768]. In *Oeuvres*, vol. 11.

———. *De la législation ou principes des lois* [1774]. In *Oeuvres*, vol. 9.

———. *Notre gloire ou nos rêves* [1779]. In *Oeuvres*, vol. 13.

———. *Principes de morale* [1784]. In *Oeuvres*, vol. 10.

———. *Observations sur le Gouvernement et les Lois des États-Unis d'Amérique* [1784]. In *Oeuvres*, vol. 8.

———. *Du développement, des progrès et des bornes de la raison*. In *Oeuvres*, vol. 15.

Mackintosh, James. *Vindiciae Gallicae*. London, 1791.

———. "The Administration and Fall of Struensee." Originally published in the *Edinburgh Review*, 1826. Republished in Sir James Mackintosh, *Miscellaneous Works*. London, 1851.

Maddock, Henry. *The Power of Parliaments Considered, in a Letter to a Member of Parliament*. 2nd ed. London, 1799.

Madrolle, Alphonse de. *La sagesse profonde et l'infaillibilité des prédictions de la révolution qui nous menace*. Paris, 1828.

Maistre, Joseph de. *Study on Sovereignty*. In Jack Lively, ed., *The Works of Joseph de Maistre*. New York, Macmillan, 1963.

Malebranche, Nicolas. *Traité de l'amour de Dieu, en quel sens il doit être désintéressé*. Lyon, 1707.

———. *Réflexions sur la prémotion physique* [1715].

Malthus, Thomas Robert. *Principles of Political Economy* [1820]. 2nd ed. London, 1836.

[Margon, Guillaume Plantavit de la Pause de]. *Lettres de Monsieur Filtz-Moritz sur les affaires du temps et principalement sur celles d'Espagne sous Philippe V et les intrigues de la princesse des Ursins, traduites de l'anglois par Monsieur de Garnesai*. 2nd ed. Amsterdam, 1718.

Marmontel, Jean-François. *Oeuvres posthumes. Régence du duc d'Orléans*. 2 vols. Paris, 1805.

Maximes du droit et d'état, pour servir de réfutation au mémoire qui paraît sous le nom de Monsieur le duc du Maine, au sujet de la contestation qui est entre lui et Monsieur le Duc, pour le rang de prince du sang. N.p., 1716.

Mazzei, Filippo. *Historical and Political Researches on the United States* [1788]. Charlottesville, University Press of Virginia, 1976.

Meister, Jacques-Henri. *Des premiers principes du système social appliqués à la révolution présente*. Paris, 1790.

———. *Souvenirs de mes voyages en Angleterre*. 2 vols. Zurich, 1795.

———. *Souvenirs de mon dernier voyage à Paris* [Paris and Zurich, 1797]. Reprinted and edited by Paul Usteri and Eugène Ritter. Paris, 1910.

Melon, Jean-François. *Essai politique sur le commerce* [1734].

———. *A Political Essay upon Commerce* [1734]. Translated by David Bindon. Dublin, 1738.

———. *Opere*, I and II. Edited by Onofrio Nicastro and Severina Perona. Sienna and Pisa, 1977 and 1983.

Mignet, François. "Eloge historique de M. le comte Roederer." *Mémoires de l'académie royale des sciences morales et politiques de l'Institut de France*, 2:lv–xclxxxix. Paris, 1839.

———. *Notices et mémoires historiques*. 2 vols. Paris, 1843.

Mirabeau, Victor de Riqueti, marquis de. *L'Ami des hommes*. 3 vols. Avignon, 1756–8. Reprint, ed. Albert Rouxel, Paris, 1883.

———. "Mémoire pour concourir au prix annoncé et proposé par la très louable société d'agriculture à Berne pour l'année 1759." In *Recueil de mémoires concernant l'oeconomie rurale par une société établie à Berne en Suisse*, vol. 1, pt. 2, pp. 227–311, 443–77. Zurich, 1760.

———. *Philosophie rurale, ou économie générale et politique de l'agriculture, réduite à l'ordre immuable des lois physiques et morales, qui assurent la prospérité des empires* [1763]. Amsterdam, 1764.

———. "Dialogues entre un enfant de sept ans & son mentor, par Mr B." *Ephémérides du citoyen* (1769), pt. 6.

———. *La Science ou les droits et les devoirs de l'homme*. Lausanne, 1774.

———. *Lettres sur la législation, ou l'ordre légal dépravé, rétabli et perpétué*. 3 vols. Berne, 1775.

———. *Entretiens d'un jeune prince avec son gouverneur*. 3 vols. Paris, 1785. 4 vols. London and Paris, 1785.

———. "Bref état des moyens pour la restauration de l'autorité du roi et de ses finances." Edited by Georges Weulersse. *Revue d'histoire économique et social* 6 (1913): 177–211.

Mirabeau, Victor de Riqueti, marquis de, and François Quesnay. *Traité de la monarchie*. Edited by Gino Longhitano. Paris, L'Harmattan, 1999.

Mitford, William. *The History of Greece*. 3rd ed. 6 vols. London, 1795.

Montesquieu, Charles-Louis de Secondat, baron de. "Mémoire sur les dettes de l'état" [1717]. In Montesquieu, *Oeuvres complètes*, edited by Roger Caillois, 1:66–71. 2 vols. Paris, 1949.

———. "Réflexions sur la Monarchie Universelle" [1734]. In his *Oeuvres complètes*, ed. Caillois, 2:19–38.

———. *Considérations sur les causes de la grandeur des romains et de leur décadence* [1734]. Edited by Jean Ehrard. Paris, Garnier-Flammarion, 1968. Edited by Françoise Weil and Cecil Courtney. Oxford, Voltaire Foundation, 2000.

———. *De l'esprit des lois* [1748] and (with comments by Elie Luzac) *De l'esprit des loix . . . Avec des remarques philosophiques et politiques d'un anonyme, qui n'ont point encore été publiées* [1763]. 4 vols. Amsterdam, 1764.

———. *The Spirit of Laws*. Translated by Thomas Nugent [1750]. 2 vols. London, 1823.

———. *The Spirit of Laws*. Translated by Thomas Nugent. London, 1750. Edited by Franz Neumann. New York, Hafner Publishing Company, 1949.

Montesquieu, Charles-Louis de Secondat, baron de. *The Spirit of the Laws.* Edited and translated by Anne Cohler, Basia Miller, and Harold Stone. Cambridge, CUP, 1989.

———. *The History of the Troglodytes.* Chelmsford, 1766.

———. *Reflections on the Causes of the Rise and Fall of the Roman Empire.* Oxford, 1825.

———. *Lettres persanes.* In his *Oeuvres complètes,* vol. 1, edited by Jean Ehrard and Catherine Volpilhac-Auger. Oxford, Voltaire Foundation, 2004.

———. *The Persian Letters.* Translated by George R. Healy. Indianapolis, Hackett, 1999.

———. *Correspondance.* In his *Oeuvres complètes,* 3 vols. Paris, Editions Nagel, 1950–5.

———. *Pensées.* Edited by Louis Desgraves. Paris, Robert Laffont, 1991.

Moreau, Nicolas-Jacob. "Lettre de Monsieur M. Censeur royal à un Magistrat." *Ephémérides du citoyen* 9 (1768): 130–75.

Munter, D. *A Faithful Narrative of the Conversion and Death of Count Struensee, late Prime Minister of Denmark.* London, 1773.

Murhard, Friedrich, ed. "Europa im Jahre 1823." In *Allgemeine Politische Annalen,* 10:3–142. Stuttgart and Tübingen, 1823.

Necker, Jacques. *Eloge de Colbert.* Paris, 1773.

———. *De l'administration des finances* [1783].

———. *A Treatise on the Administration of Finances of France.* 3 vols. London, 1785.

———. *De l'importance des opinions religieuses* [1788]. Reprinted in his *Oeuvres,* vol. 12. 12 vols. Paris, 1821.

———. *Dernières vues de politique et de finance* [1802]. In his *Oeuvres,* vol. 11.

Nicole, Pierre. "De la charité et de l'amour propre" [1673]. Reprinted most recently in Pierre Nicole, *Essais de morale,* edited by Laurent Thirouin. Paris, Presses universitaires de France, 1999.

Nugent, Thomas. "The translator to the reader." In Montesquieu, *The Spirit of Laws,* 1: v–vi. 2nd ed. 2 vols. London, 1752.

Pagès, Jean-Pierre. *Principes généraux du droit politique dans leur rapport avec l'esprit de l'Europe et avec la Monarchie constitutionnelle.* Paris, 1817.

Paine, Thomas. "From Mr. Thomas Payne to M. Emanuel Syeyes." In *Sieyès: Political Writings,* edited by Michael Sonenscher, pp. 165–6. Indianapolis, Hackett, 2003.

———. *Agrarian Justice, opposed to Agrarian Law and to Agrarian Monopoly: Being a Plan for Ameliorating the Condition of Man, Creating in Every Nation a National Fund.* London, 1797.

Pascal, Blaise. *Pensées.* Edited by Brunschvicg. Introduced by Charles-Marc Des Granges. Paris, Garnier, 1958. Translated by John Warrington. Edited by H. T. Barnwell. London, Everyman, 1960.

Pellissery, Roch. *Le Caffé politique d'Amsterdam, ou entretiens d'un françois, d'un hollandais et d'un cosmopolite sur les divers intérêts économiques et politiques de la France, de l'Espagne et de l'Angleterre.* 2 vols. Amsterdam, 1776.

———. *Lettres de M. de Pellissery, prisonnier onze an et deux mois à la Bastille et treize mois à Charenton.* Paris, 1792)

Petit, Michel-Edmé. *Le procès des 31 mai et 2 juin, ou la défense des 71 représentants du peuple.* N.p., n.d. [but Paris, 1795].

La petite encyclopédie, ou dictionnaire des philosophes. Antwerp, 1772.

Plowden, Francis. *The Constitution of the United Kingdom of Great Britain and Ireland, Civil and Ecclesiastical.* London, 1802.

Pluche, Noël-Antoine. *Spectacle de la nature: or Nature Displayed. Being Discourses on such Particulars of Natural History as were thought most proper to excite the curiosity and form the minds of youth. Containing what belongs to man considered in society* [8 vols. Paris, 1732–50]. 7 vols. London, 1748.

Pluquet, François-André-Adrien. *De la sociabilité.* 2 vols. Paris, 1767.

———. *Traité philosophique et politique sur le luxe.* 2 vols. Paris, 1786.

Pollock, Joseph. *Letters of Owen Roe O'Nial.* Dublin, 1779.

[Pownall, Thomas]. *A Memorial most humbly addressed to the Sovereigns of Europe, on the Present State of Affairs between the Old and New World.* 2nd ed. London, 1780.

Pufendorf, Samuel. *Le Droit de la nature et des gens.* Translated by Jean Barbeyrac. 2 vols. Amsterdam, 1712.

Quesnay, François. *Essai physique sur l'oeconomie animale.* 3 vols. Paris, 1748.

———. "Évidence," "Grains," "Hommes," "Impôts." In *François Quesnay et la Physiocratie,* edited by Jacqueline Hecht, vol. 2. 2 vols. Paris, Institut national de démographie, 1958.

———. "Droit naturel." Reprinted in François Quesnay, *Physiocratie,* edited by Jean Cartelier. Paris, Garnier-Flammarion 1991.

Ramsay, Andrew Michael. "Discours de la Poésie Épique et de l'Excellence du Poème Télémaque." In Fénelon, *Télémaque,* pp. xxxviii–xxxix. Amsterdam, 1725.

Raynal, Guillaume-Thomas-François. *Histoire philosophique et politique des établissements européens dans les Deux-Indes* [1772]. 10 vols. Geneva, 1781.

———. *A Philosophical and Political History of the Settlements and Trade of the Europeans in the East and West Indies.* Translated by J. O. Justamond. 6 vols. Reprinted New York, 1969.

Réflexions d'un allemand impartial sur la demande de la garantie de la pragmatique impériale. N.p., 1732.

Réflexions d'un cosmopolite. N.p., n.d. [1733].

Risteau, François. *Réponse aux Observations sur l'Esprit des Loix.* Amsterdam, 1751. Reprinted in Montesquieu, *Lettres familières.* Rome, 1773.

Robinet, Jean-Baptiste-René. *Dictionnaire universel des sciences moral, économique, politique et diplomatique, ou Bibliothèque de l'homme d'état et du citoyen.* 30 vols. London, 1772–83.

Roederer, Pierre-Louis. *Questions proposées par la commission intermédiaire de l'assemblée provinciale de la Lorraine, concernant le reculement des barrières, et observations pour servir de réponse à ses questions* [1787]. In *Oeuvres du comte P. L. Roederer,* edited by A. M. Roederer, vol. 7. 8 vols. Paris, 1853–9.

———. "Lettre de Roederer à Adrien Lezay sur Chénier." *Journal d'économie publique* 2, no. 13 (10 Nivôse an 5/21 December 1796): 175–86.

———. "Querelle de Montesquieu et de Voltaire sur les deux principes du gouvernement monarchique et du gouvernement républicain." *Journal d'économie publique,* 10 Nivôse an 5/30 December 1796. Reprinted in his *Oeuvres,* 7:55–61.

Roederer, Pierre-Louis. "Entretien de plusieurs philosophes célèbres, sur les gouvernements républicain et monarchique." *Journal d'économie publique*, 20 Prairial-lan 5/8 June 1797. Reprinted in his *Oeuvres*, 7:61–71.

———. "Premier mémoire sur la constitution politique de la Chine." In his *Oeuvres*, 8:97–104.

———. *Cours d'organisation sociale*. In his *Oeuvres*, 8:129–305.

———. *De la propriété considérée dans ses rapports avec les droits politiques*. Paris, 1819.

———. *De la propriété*. 3rd ed. Reprinted in his *Oeuvres*, 7:335–48.

———. *The Spirit of the Revolution of 1789 and Other Writings of the Revolutionary Epoch*. Edited by Murray Forsyth. Aldershot, Scolar Press, 1989.

Roland, Manon. *Appel à l'impartiale postérité*. 2 vols. London, 1795.

[Roubaud, André]. *Histoire générale de l'Asie, de l'Afrique et de l'Amérique*. 4th ed. 5 vols. Paris, 1770–2.

Rousseau, Jean-Jacques. *Discours sur l'économie politique* [1755]. Edited by Bruno Bernardi. Paris, Vrin, 2002.

———. *Lettre à M. d'Alembert sur les spectacles* [1758]. Translated as *A Letter from M. Rousseau of Geneva to M. d'Alembert of Paris concerning the effects of Theatrical Entertainments on the Manners of Mankind* (London, 1759).

———. *Julie, ou la Nouvelle Héloïse* [1761]. In Rousseau, *Oeuvres complètes*, edited by Bernard Gagnebin and Marcel Raymond, vol. 2. Paris, Pléiade, 1964.

———. *Du contrat social* [1762]. Edited by Robert Derathé. Paris, 1993.

———. *Emile, ou de l'éducation* [1762]. Edited by Michel Launay. Paris, Garnier Flammarion, 1966.

———. *Emile* [1762]. In Rousseau, *Oeuvres complètes*.

———. *Emilius and Sophia, or a new system of education*. 4 vols. London, 1763.

———. *A Treatise on the Social Compact, or the Principles of Politic Law*. London, 1764.

———. *A Project for Perpetual Peace*. London, 1761.

———. *Considérations sur le gouvernement de Pologne* [1772]. Edited by Barbara de Negroni. Paris, 1990.

———. *Julia*. 3 vols. Edinburgh, 1773.

———. *Considerations on the Government of Poland* [1782]. In Rousseau, *The Social Contract and Other Later Political Writings*, edited by Victor Gourevitch. Cambridge, CUP, 1997.

———. *Pièces diverses*, 4 vols. London, P. Cazin, 1782.

———. *Collection complète des Oeuvres de Jean-Jacques Rousseau*. Geneva, 1782.

———. *Oeuvres. Nouvelle édition*. 5 vols. Neufchatel [Paris], n.d.

———. *Extrait du projet de paix perpétuelle*. In Rousseau, *Oeuvres complètes*, 3:561–89.

———. *Confessions*. Edited by Bernard Gagnebin and Marcel Raymond. Paris, Pléiade, 1964.

———. *Correspondance complète*. Edited by Ralph A. Leigh. 52 vols. Oxford and Geneva, 1967–98.

———. "Lettre sur la vertu, l'individu et la société." Edited by Jean Starobinski and Charles Wirz. *Annales de la société Jean-Jacques Rousseau* 41 (1997): 313–27.

———. *Discourse on Inequality*. In Rousseau, *The Discourses and Other Early Political Writings*, edited by Victor Gourevitch. Cambridge, CUP, 1997.

Russo, Vincenzio. *Pensieri politici* [1799]. Reprinted by the Biblioteca Nazionale Vittor Emmanuele III and the Fondazione Giangiacomo Feltrinelli. Naples and Milan, 2000.

Rutledge, Jean-Jacques. *Eloge de Montesquieu*. London, 1786.

Sainte-Beuve, Charles-Augustin. *Causeries de lundi*. 12 vols. Paris, 1852–7.

Saint-Hyacinthe, Claude Thémiseul de. *Entretiens dans lesquels on traite des entreprises de l'Espagne, des prétentions de Mr. Le chevalier de Saint George et de la renonciation de sa majesté catholique*. The Hague, 1719.

Saint-Lambert, Jean-François, marquis de. *Essai sur la vie d'Helvétius* [1772]. Reprinted in his *Oeuvres philosophiques*, 5:220–5. 5 vols. Paris, 1801.

———. *Oeuvres philosophiques*. 5 vols. Paris, an IX.

Saint-Pierre, Charles-Irénée Castel, abbé de. "Réflexions sur l'Anti-Machiavel de 1740." In his *Ouvrajes de politique et de morale*, vol. 16. 16 vols. Rotterdam, 1739–41.

[Saint-Vincent, Robert de]. *Observations modestes d'un citoyen sur les opérations de finance de M. Necker, et sur son Compte-rendu adressées à MM les pacifiques auteurs des Comment? des Pourquoi? Et autres pamphlets anonymes*. N.p., n.d.

Sallier, Guy-Marie. *Annales françaises depuis le commencement du règne de Louis XVI jusqu'aux états généraux*. 2nd ed. 2 vols. Paris, 1813.

Say, Jean-Baptiste. "Boniface Véridick à Polyscope, sur son projet de théâtre pour le peuple." *La Décade philosophique* 10 (10 Germinal an IV/21 March 1796): 38–44.

———. *Olbie, ou essai sur les moyens de reformer les moeurs d'une nation*. Paris, an VIII/ 1800.

———. *Traité d'économie politique*. 2 vols. Paris, 1803.

———. *Mélanges et correspondance d'économie politique*. Edited by Charles Comte [1834]. Reprinted in Jean-Baptiste Say, *Cours complet d'économie politique pratique*. Paris, 1843.

———. *A Treatise on Political Economy* [1836]. Edited by Munir Quddus and Salim Rashid. New Brunswick, Transaction Books, 2001.

———. *Politique pratique*. In Jean-Baptiste Say, *Oeuvres complètes*, vol. 5, *Oeuvres morales et politiques*, edited by Emmanuel Blanc and André Tiran. Paris, Economica, 2003.

Schmid d'Auenstein, Georg Ludwig. "De l'agriculture." In his *Traités sur divers sujets intéressants de politique et de morale*. N.p., 1760.

Schmidt-Phiseldeck, Conrad Friedrich von. *Europe and America* [1820]. Edited by Thorkild Kjærgaard. Copenhagen, Rodos, 1976.

[Secret, Pierre]. *Conférences d'un anglois et d'un allemand sur les lettres de Filtz-Moritz*. Cambrai, 1722.

Ségur, Louis-Philippe, comte de. *Mémoires*. 3 vols. Paris, 1825.

Sieyès, Emmanuel-Joseph. *Essay on Privileges* [1788]. In *Sieyès: Political Writings*, edited by Michael Sonenscher. Indianapolis, Hackett, 2003.

———. *Qu'est ce que le tiers état?* [1789]. With annotations by André Morellet. Paris, 1822.

———. *What Is the Third Estate?* [1789]. In *Sieyès: Political Writings*, ed. Sonenscher.

———. *Vues sur les moyens d'exécution dont les représentants de France pourront disposer en 1789*. 2nd ed. Paris, 1789.

Sieyès, Emmanuel-Joseph. *Quelques idées de constitution applicable à la ville de Paris en juillet 1789*. Paris, 1789.

———. "The explanatory note of M. Syeyes, in Answer to the Letter of Mr Payne." In *Sieyès: Political Writings*, ed. Sonenscher, pp. 166–73.

———. *Opinion de Sieyès sur plusieurs articles des titres IV et V du projet de constitution de l'an III*. Paris, 1795.

———. *Emmanuel Sieyès. Politische Schriften*. Edited by Konrad Engelbert Ölsner. N.p., 1796).

———. *Emmanuel Joseph Sieyès, Ecrits politiques*. Edited by Roberto Zapperi. Montreux, Editions des archives contemporaines, 1989.

———. *Des Manuscrits de Sieyès*. Edited by Christine Fauré, Jacques Guilhaumou, and Jacques Valier. Paris, Honoré Champion, 1999.

———. "Bases de l'ordre social." In Pasquale Pasquino, *Sieyès et l'invention de la constitution en France*, pp. 181–91.

Smith, Adam. *An Inquiry into the Nature and Causes of the Wealth of Nations* [1776]. Edited by R. H. Campbell, A. S. Skinner, and W. B. Todd. 2 vols. Indianapolis, 1981.

Steuart, Sir James. *An Inquiry into the Principles of Political Oeconomy* [1767]. Edited by Andrew Skinner. 2 vols. Edinburgh and Chicago, 1966.

Stewart, Dugald. *Elements of the Philosophy of the Human Mind*. 2nd ed. 2 vols. Edinburgh, 1816.

Sullivan, Francis Stoughton. *Lectures on the Constitution and Laws of England: with a Commentary on Magna Charta, and Illustrations of Many of the English Statutes*. London, 1776.

Sumner, Charles. *Prophetic voices concerning America*. Boston, 1874.

[Théremin, Charles]. *De la noblesse féodale, et de la noblesse nationale*. Paris, 1817.

Tourneux, Maurice, ed. *Correspondance littéraire, philosophique et critique de Grimm, Diderot, Raynal, Meister, etc.* 16 vols. Paris, 1877–82.

Turgot, Anne-Robert-Jacques. "Lettre adressée aux auteurs du *Journal étranger*." In *Journal étranger*, September 1760, pp. 3–16. Reprinted in Turgot, *Oeuvres*, edited by Gustave Schelle, 1:624–7. 5 vols. Paris, 1913–9.

———. *Réflexions sur la formation et la distribution des richesses* [1766]. Edited by Joël-Thomas Ravix and Paul-Marie Romani. Paris, Flammarion, 1997.

———. "Valeurs et monnaies" [1769]. In Turgot, *Réflexions*, ed. Ravix and Romani.

[Vaughan, Benjamin]. *New and Old Principles of Trade Compared*. London, 1788.

Voltaire, François-Marie Arouet de. *La Henriade* [1723]. Paris, Garnier, n.d.

———. *Letters concerning the English Nation* [1733]. Edited by Nicolas Cronk. Oxford, Voltaire Foundation, 1994.

———. *Lettres philosophiques* [1734]. Edited by Raymond Naves. Paris, Garnier, 1962.

———. "Of John Law, Melon and Dutot. On commerce and luxury" [1738]. Reprinted in Voltaire, *Dialogues and Essays, Literary and Philosophical*, pp. 183–93. Glasgow, 1764.

———. *Correspondance*. Edited by Theodore Besterman. 13 vols. Paris, Pléiade, 1964.

[Walsh, Robert]. *A Letter on the Genius and Dispositions of the French Government, including A View of the Taxation of the French Empire*. 3rd ed. Philadelphia, 1810.

Williams, David. *Egeria, or Elementary Studies on the Progress of Nations in Political Oeconomy, Legislation and Government*. London, 1803.

Wilson, James. *Works.* Edited by Robert Green McCloskey. 2 vols. Cambridge, Mass., Belknap Press, Harvard University, 1967.

Yorke, Henry Redhead. *Letters from France in 1802.* 2 vols. London, 1804.

Young, Arthur. *Letters on the French Nation.* London, 1769.

———. *Political Essays Concerning the Present State of the British Empire.* London, 1772.

———. *Travels in France* [1792]. Edited by Constance Maxwell. Cambridge, CUP, 1929.

SECONDARY

Albertone, Manuela. "Moneta e credito pubblico nel pensiero dell' abate Morellet: a proposito di aulcuni testi inediti." *Quaderni de storia dell'economia politica* 8 (1990): 47–106.

Alimento, Antonella. "La fisiocrazia in Svezia dopo il colpo di stato di Gustavo III attraverso la corrispondenza di V. Riqueti de Mirabeau con C.F. Scheffer." *Annali della Fondazione Luigi Einaudi* 23 (1989): 297–369.

Azouvi, François, and Dominique Bourel. *De Königsberg à Paris. La Réception de Kant en France (1788–1804).* Paris, 1991.

Bach, Reinhard. "Rousseau et les physiocrates: une cohabitation contradictoire." *Etudes Jean-Jacques Rousseau* 11 (2000): 9–82.

Baker, Keith M. "The Early History of the Term 'Social Science.'" *Annals of Science* 20 (1964): 211–26.

———. *Inventing the French Revolution: Essays on French Political Culture in the Eighteenth Century.* Cambridge, CUP, 1990.

Barny, Roger. *L'éclatement révolutionnaire du Rousseauisme.* Besançon and Paris, Les Belles Lettres, 1988.

Barraclough, Geoffrey. "Europa, Amerika und Russland in Vorstellung und Denken des 19. Jahrhunderts." *Historische Zeitschrift* 203 (1966): 280–315.

Barton, H. Arnold. *Scandinavia in the Revolutionary Era 1760–1815.* Minneapolis, University of Minnesota Press, 1986.

Bastid, Paul. *Les discours de Sieyès dans les débats constitutionnels de l'an III.* Paris, 1939.

———. *Sieyès et sa pensée.* 2nd ed. Paris, Hachette, 1970.

Becagli, Vieri. "Georg-Ludwig Schmid d'Auenstein e i suoi *Principes de la législation universelle*: oltre la fisiocrazia?" *Studi Settecenteschi* 24 (2004): 215–52.

Bénétruy, Jean. *L'Atelier de Mirabeau. Quatre proscrits genevois dans la tourmente révolutionnaire.* Geneva, Alexandre Jullien, 1962.

Blackburn, Robin. *The Overthrow of Colonial Slavery.* London, Verso, 1988.

Blaufarb, Rafe. *The French Army 1750–1820: Careers, Talent, Merit.* Manchester, Manchester University Press, 2002.

Bobbio, Norberto. *La teoria delle forme di governo nella storia del pensiero politico.* Turin, 1976.

Boivin-Champeaux, L. *Notices historiques sur la Révolution dans le Département de l'Eure.* Évreux, 1868.

Bongie, Laurence L. "Voltaire's English, High Treason and a Manifesto for Bonnie Prince Charles." *Studies on Voltaire and the Eighteenth Century* 171 (1977): 7–29.

Bonney, Richard, ed. *Economic Systems and State Finance*. Oxford, Oxford University Press, 1995.

———. *The Rise of the Fiscal State in Europe: 1200–1815*. Oxford, Oxford University Press, 1999.

Bredin, Jean-Denis. *Sieyès. La clé de la Révolution française*. Paris, Editions de Fallois, 1988.

Brewer, John. *The Sinews of Power: War, Money and the English State, 1688–1783*. London, Collins, 1989.

Campbell, Peter R., ed. *The Origins of the French Revolution*. London, Palgrave, 2006.

Candaux, Jean-Daniel. "Charles Bordes et la première crise d'antimilitarisme de l'opinion publique européenne." *Studies on Voltaire and the Eighteenth Century* 24 (1963): 315–44.

Carcassonne, Elie. *Montesquieu et le problème de la constitution française au xviiie siècle*. Paris, 1927.

Charles, Loic, and Philippe Steiner. "Entre Montesquieu et Rousseau. La Physiocratie parmi les origines intellectuelles de la Révolution française." *Etudes Jean-Jacques Rousseau* 11 (2000): 83–160.

Chérel, Albert. *Fénelon en France au xviiie siècle*. Paris, 1916.

Chevalley, L. *La Déclaration du droit des gens de l'abbé Grégoire 1793–1795*. Paris, n.d. [1911].

Childs, Nick. *A Political Academy in Paris, 1724–1731: The Entresol and Its Members*. Oxford, Voltaire Foundation, 2000.

Chrétienne, Valérie. *Charles-François Lebrun (1739–1824)*. 2 vols. Lille, Atelier national de reproduction de thèses, 1998.

Clark, Henry C., ed. *Commerce, Culture, and Liberty: Readings on Capitalism before Adam Smith*. Indianapolis, Liberty Fund, 2003.

Cobban, Alfred. *The Social Interpretation of the French Revolution*. Cambridge, CUP, 1964.

Combes-Malavialle, Jean-François. "Vues nouvelles sur l'abbé de Prades." *Dix-Huitième Siècle* 20 (1988): 377–97.

Connell, Philip. "British Identities and the Politics of Ancient Poetry in Later Eighteenth-Century England." *Historical Journal* 49 (2006): 161–92.

Cottereau, Alain. "The Fate of Collective Manufactures in the Industrial World: The Silk Industries of Lyons and London, 1800–1850." In Charles F. Sabel and Jonathan Zeitlin, eds., *Worlds of Possibilities: Flexibility and Mass Production in Western Industrialisation*, pp. 75–152. Cambridge, CUP, 1997.

Crouzet, François. *La Grande Inflation. La Monnaie en France de Louis XIV à Napoléon*. Paris, Fayard, 1993.

Cuche, F-X., and J. Le Brun, eds. *Fénelon Mystique et Politique (1699–1999)*. Paris, Honoré Champion, 2004.

Daniel, Stephen H. *The Philosophy of Jonathan Edwards: A Study in Divine Semiotics*. Bloomington, Indiana University Press, 1994.

———. "The Ramist Context of Berkeley's Philosophy." *British Journal for the History of Philosophy* 9 (2001): 487–505.

Dauphin-Meunier, A. "Les dernières années du marquis de Mirabeau." *Le Correspondant*, January 1913.

De Dijn, Annelien. "Aristocratic Liberalism in Post-Revolutionary France." *Historical Journal* 48 (2005): 661–81.

Dent, N.J.H. *Rousseau*. Oxford, Blackwell, 1988.

Dent, N.J.H., and T. O'Hagan. "Rousseau on *Amour-Propre*." *Proceedings of the Aristotelian Society*, Supplement, 72 (1998): 57–74.

Deprun, Jean. *La philosophie de l'inquiétude en France au xviiie siècle*. Paris, Vrin, 1979.

Dessauer, Frederick E. "The Constitutional Decision: A German Theory of Constitutional Law and Politics." *Ethics* 57 (1946): 14–37.

Desserud, Donald. "Commerce and Political Participation in Montesquieu's Letter to Domville." *History of European Ideas* 25 (1999): 135–51.

Dickey, Laurence. "*Doux-commerce* and Humanitarian Values: Free Trade, Sociability and Universal Benevolence in Eighteenth-Century Thinking." *Grotiana*, n.s., 22–3 (2001–2): 271–317.

Dickson, P.G.M. *The Financial Revolution in England: A Study in the Development of Public Credit, 1688–1756*. London, Macmillan, 1967.

Doyle, William. *The Oxford History of the French Revolution*. Oxford, Oxford University Press, 1989.

———. *Origins of the French Revolution*. 3rd ed. Oxford, Oxford University Press, 1999.

———. *Jansenism*. London, Macmillan, 2000.

Dunbar, Louise Burnham. "A Study of 'Monarchical' Tendencies in the United States from 1776 to 1801." *University of Illinois Studies in the Social Sciences* 10 (1922): 1–164.

Dybikowski, J. *On Burning Ground: An Examination of the Ideas, Projects and Life of David Williams*. Studies on Voltaire and the Eighteenth Century, 307. Oxford, Voltaire Foundation, 1993.

Ehrard, Jean. "Actualité d'un demi-silence: Montesquieu et l'idée de souveraineté." *Rivista di storia della Filosofia* 4 (1994): 9–20.

———. "Rousseau et Montesquieu: le mauvais fils réconcilié." *Annales de la société Jean-Jacques Rousseau* 41 (1997): 57–77.

Eisenstein, Elizabeth L. *The First Professional Revolutionist: Filippo Michele Buonarroti (1761–1831)*. Cambridge, Mass., Harvard University Press, 1959.

Ellis, Harold A. *Boulainvilliers and the French Monarchy: Aristocratic Politics in Early Eighteenth-Century France*. Ithaca and London, Cornell University Press, 1988.

Elster, Jon. *Alchemies of the Mind: Rationality and the Emotions*. Cambridge, CUP, 1999.

Eötvös, József. *The Dominant Ideas of the Nineteenth Century and Their Impact on the State* [1851–4]. Translated by D. Mervyn Jones. 2 vols. Boulder, Colo., Social Science Monographs; Highland Lakes, N.J., Atlantic Research and Publications Inc.; distributed by Columbia University Press, 1996 and 1998.

Eyck, F. Gunther. "English and French Influences on German Liberalism before 1848." *Journal of the History of Ideas* 18 (1957): 313–41.

Fabre, Jean. "Le Marquis de Mirabeau, interlocuteur et protecteur de Rousseau." In *Les Mirabeau et leurs temps*, pp. 71–90. Société des Etudes Robespierristes. Paris, 1968.

Farr, Evelyn. *Before the Deluge: Parisian Society in the Reign of Louis XVI*. London, Owen, 1994.

Fauré, Christine. "Sieyès, lecteur problématique des lumières." *Dix-Huitième Siècle* 37 (2005): 225–41.

Feher, Ferenc. *The Frozen Revolution: An Essay on Jacobinism.* Cambridge, CUP, 1987.

Ferguson, Niall. *The Cash Nexus: Money and Power in the Modern World 1700–2000.* London, Allen Lane, The Penguin Press, 2001.

Fichtner, Paul Sutter. *Protestantism and Primogeniture in Early Modern Germany.* New Haven and London, Yale University Press, 1989.

Fisch, Jörg. "Zivilisation, Kultur." In Otto Bruner, Werner Conze, and Reinhart Koselleck, eds., *Geschichtliche Grundbegriffe*, 7:679–774. 8 vols. Stuttgart, 1972–97.

Fleury, Gabriel. *François Véron de Forbonnais. Sa famille, sa vie, ses actes, ses oeuvres.* Le Mans, 1915.

Forbes, Duncan. *Hume's Philosophical Politics.* Cambridge, CUP, 1975.

———. Introduction to Georg Wilhelm Friedrich Hegel, *Lectures on the Philosophy of World History.* Cambridge, CUP, 1975.

———. "Sceptical Whiggism, Commerce and Liberty." In Andrew S. Skinner and Thomas Wilson, eds., *Essays on Adam Smith*, pp. 179–201. Oxford, Oxford University Press, 1975.

Forbes, Duncan. "Natural Law and the Scottish Enlightenment." In Roy H. Campbell and Andrew S. Skinner, eds., *The Origins and Nature of the Scottish Enlightenment*, pp. 186–204. Edinburgh, John Donald, 1982.

Force, Pierre. *Self-Interest before Adam Smith: A Genealogy of Economic Science.* Cambridge, CUP, 2003.

Ford, Worthington Chauncey, ed. *The Writings of John Quincy Adams.* New York, 1913.

Forget, Evelyn L. *The Social Economics of Jean-Baptiste Say: Markets and Virtue.* London, Routledge, 1999.

Forsyth, Murray. *Reason and Revolution: The Political Thought of the Abbé Sieyes.* Leicester, Leicester University Press, 1987.

———. Introduction to Pierre-Louis Roederer, *The Spirit of the Revolution of 1789 and Other Writings of the Revolutionary Epoch*, edited by Murray Forsyth. Aldershot, Scolar Press, 1989.

Fukayama, Francis. *The End of History and the Last Man.* New York, Free Press, 1992.

Furet, François. *Interpreting the French Revolution* [1978]. Cambridge, CUP, 1981.

Furet, François, and Ran Halévi, eds. *Orateurs de la révolution française.* Paris, Gallimard, 1989.

Gagnebin, Bernard. "J. J. Rousseau: Sur le péché d'Adam et le salut universel. Un document inédit." *Dix-Huitième Siècle* 3 (1971): 41–50.

Gaskill, Howard, ed. *The Reception of Ossian in Europe.* London, Thoemmes Continuum, 2004.

Geuss, Raymond. *Morality, Culture, and History.* Cambridge, CUP, 1999.

Giesey, Ralph E. "The Juristic Basis of Dynastic Right to the French Throne." *Transactions of the American Philosophical Society*, n.s., 51 (1961): pt. 5.

Glaziou, Yves. *Hobbes en France au xviiie siècle.* Paris, Presses universitaires de France, 1993.

Gliozzi, Giuliano. "Rousseau: mythe du bon sauvage ou critique du mythe des origines." In Chantal Grell and Christian Michel, eds., *Primitivisme et mythes des origines dans la France des lumières*, pp. 193–203. Paris, 1989.

Goldstein, Jan. *The Post-Revolutionary Self: Politics and Psyche in France, 1750–1850*. Cambridge, Mass., Harvard University Press, 2005.

Gueniffey, Patrice. "Cordeliers and Girondins: The Prehistory of the Republic?" In Biancamaria Fontana, ed., *The Invention of the Modern Republic*, pp. 86–106. Cambridge, CUP, 1994.

———. *La politique de la terreur: essai sur la violence révolutionnaire 1789–94*. Paris, Fayard, 2000.

Guilhaumou, Jacques. "Fragments d'un discours sur Dieu: Sieyès et la religion." In *Mélanges Michel Vovelle*, pp. 257–65. Aix-en-Provence, Publications d'Université de Provence, 1997.

Gwyn, William B. *The Meaning of the Separation of Powers: An Analysis of the Doctrine from Its Origin to the Adoption of the United States Constitution*. Tulane Studies in Political Science, 9. New Orleans, 1965.

Hammond, Paul Y. "The Political Order and the Burden of External Relations." *World Politics* 19 (1967): 443–64.

Hampson, Norman. "The Origins of the French Revolution: The Long and the Short of It." In David Williams, ed., *1789: The Long and the Short of It*. Sheffield, Sheffield Academic Press, 1991.

———. "Mably and the Montagnards." *French History* 16 (2002): 402–15.

Hanley, Sarah. "The Monarchic State in Early Modern France: Marital Regime, Government and Male Right." iIn Adrianna E. Bakos, ed., *Politics, Ideology and the Law in Early Modern Europe: Essays in Honor of J.H.M. Salmon*, pp. 107–26. Rochester, University of Rochester Press, 1994.

———, ed. *Les Droits des femmes et la loi salique*. Paris, Indigo, 1994.

Hardman, John. *French Politics 1774–1789: From the Accession of Louis XVI to the Fall of the Bastille*. London, Longman, 1995.

Hardy, James D., Jr. *Judicial Politics in the Old Regime: The Parlement of Paris during the Regency*. Baton Rouge, Louisiana State University Press, 1967.

Hare, Thomas. *The Machinery of Representation*. London, 1857.

———. *A Treatise on the Election of Representatives, Parliamentary and Municipal*. New ed. London, 1861.

Harling, Philip, and Peter Mandler. "From 'Fiscal-Military' State to Laissez-Faire State." *Journal of British Studies* 32 (1993): 44–70.

Harsin, Paul. *Crédit public et banque d'état en France du xvie au xviiie siècles*. Paris, Droz, 1933.

Haslam, Jonathan. *No Virtue like Necessity: Realist Thought in International Relations since Machiavelli*. New Haven, Yale University Press, 2002.

Head, Brian W. "The Origins of '*la science sociale*' in France, 1770–1800." *Australian Journal of France Studies* 19 (1982): 115–32.

Hecht, Jacqueline. ed. *Boisguilbert parmi nous. Actes du colloque international de Rouen*. Paris, Institut National d'Etudes Démographiques, 1989.

Henry, Nannerl O. "Democratic Monarchy: The Political Theory of the Marquis d'Argenson." Ph.D. diss., Yale University, 1968.

Hirschman, Albert O. *The Passions and the Interests: Political Arguments for Capitalism before Its Triumph*. Princeton, Princeton University Press, 1977.

———. *Essays in Trespassing: Economics to Politics and Beyond*. Cambridge, CUP, 1981.

———. *Rival Views of Market Society and Other Recent Essays*. New York, Viking, 1986.

Hoffman, Philip T. *Growth in a Traditional Society: The French Countryside, 1450–1815*. Princeton, Princeton University Press, 1996.

Hoffman, Philip T., Giles Postel-Vinay, and Jean-Laurent Rosenthal. *Priceless Markets: The Political Economy of Credit in Paris, 1660–1870*. Chicago, 2000. Translated as *Des marchés sans prix. Une économie politique du crédit à Paris, 1660–1870*. Paris, Editions de l'Ecole des Hautes Etudes en Sciences Sociales, 2001.

Hoffmann, Paul. *La femme dans la pensée des lumières*. Paris, Editions Ophrys, 1977.

Holbo, Christine. "Imagination, Commerce and the Politics of Associationism in Crèvecoeur's *Letters from an American Farmer*." *Early American Literature* 32 (1997): 20–46.

Hont, Istvan. "The Rhapsody of Public Debt: David Hume and Voluntary State Bankruptcy." In Nicholas Phillipson and Quentin Skinner, eds., *Political Discourse in Early Modern Britain*, pp. 321–48. Cambridge, CUP, 1993.

———. *Jealousy of Trade: International Competition and the Nation-State in Historical Perspective*. Cambridge, Mass., Harvard University Press, 2005.

———. "Luxury." In Mark Goldie and Robert Wokler, eds., *The Cambridge History of Eighteenth-Century Political Thought*. Cambridge, CUP, 2006.

Horstmann, Rolf-Peter. "The Role of Civil Society in Hegel's Political Philosophy." In Robert B. Pippin and Otfried Höffe, eds., *Hegel on Ethics and Politics*, pp. 208–40. Cambridge, CUP, 2004.

Hundert, Edward J. *The Enlightenment's Fable: Bernard Mandeville and the Discovery of Society*. Cambridge, CUP, 1994.

Iannini, Christopher. " 'The Itinerant Man': Crèvecoeur's Caribbean, Raynal's Revolution, and the Fate of Atlantic Cosmopolitanism." *William and Mary Quarterly* 61 (2004): 201–34.

Jaume, Lucien. *La Révolution française et le Jacobinisme*. Paris, Fayard, 1989.

———. *Echec au libéralisme*. Paris, Kimé, 1990.

———. *L'individu effacé, ou le paradoxe du libéralisme français*. Paris, Fayard, 1997.

Jones, Colin. "The Great Chain of Buying: Medical Advertisement, the Bourgeois Public Sphere and the Origins of the French Revolution." *American Historical Review* 101 (1996): 13–40.

———. *The Great Nation: France from Louis XIV to Napoleon 1715–99*. London, Allen Lane, 2002.

Kaiser, Thomas E. "The Abbé Dubos and the Historical Defence of Monarchy in Early Eighteenth-Century France." *Studies on Voltaire and the Eighteenth Century* 267 (1989): 77–102.

Kaplan, Steven Laurence. *Provisioning Paris*. Ithaca, Cornell University Press, 1984.

Kapossy, Béla. "Virtue, Sociability and the History of Mankind: Isaak Iselin's Contribution to the Swiss and European Enlightenment." Ph.D. diss., Cambridge University, 2003.

Kates, Gary. *The Cercle Social, the Girondins, and the French Revolution*. Princeton, Princeton University Press, 1985.

Kawade, Yoshie. "La liberté civile contre la théorie réformiste de l'état souverain: le combat de Montesquieu." In Caroline Jacot Grapa, Nicole-Jacques Lefèvre, Yannick Séité, and Carine Trevisan, eds., *Le Travail des Lumières. Pour Georges Benrekassa*, pp. 203–23. Paris, Champion, 2002.

———. "Ciceronian Moment: Republicanism and Republican Language in Cicero." *University of Tokyo Journal of Law and Politics* 2 (2005): 13–28.

Keim, Albert. *Notes de la main d'Helvétius publiées d'après un manuscrit inédit, avec une introduction et des commentaires*. Paris, 1907.

Kelley, Donald R., and Bonnie G. Smith. "What Was Property? Legal Dimensions of the Social Question in France." *Proceedings of the American Philosophical Society* 128 (1984): 200–30.

———. Introduction to Pierre-Joseph Proudhon, *What Is Property?* [1840]. Cambridge, CUP, 1994.

Kelly, Christopher, and Roger Masters. "Human Nature, Liberty and Progress." In Robert Wokler, ed., *Rousseau and Liberty*, pp. 53–69. Manchester, Manchester University Press, 1995.

Kelly, Duncan. "Carl Schmitt's Political Theory of Representation." *Journal of the History of Ideas* 65 (2004): 113–34.

Keohane, Nannerl O. *Philosophy and the State in France*. Princeton, Princeton University Press, 1980. [See also Henry, Nannerl O.]

Kervegan, Jean-François. "Souveraineté et représentation chez Hegel." In Jean-Pierre Cotten, Robert Damien, and André Tosel, eds. *La représentation et ses crises*, pp. 243–62. Besançon, Presses Universitaires Franc-Comtoises, 2001.

Kidd, Colin. *Subverting Scotland's Past*. Cambridge, CUP, 1993.

King, Norman, and Etienne Hofmann. "Les lettres de Benjamin Constant à Sieyès avec une lettre de Constant à Pictet-Diodati." *Annales Benjamin Constant* 3 (1988): 89–110.

Klaits, Joseph. *Printed Propaganda under Louis XIV: Absolute Monarchy and Public Opinion*. Princeton, Princeton University Press, 1976.

Knies, Carl, ed. *Carl Friedrichs von Baden Brieflicher Verkehr mit Mirabeau und Du Pont*. 2 vols. Heidelberg, 1892.

Koselleck, Reinhart. *Critique and Crisis: Enlightenment and the Pathogenesis of the Modern Society*. Cambridge, Mass., M.I.T. Press; Leamington Spa, Berg Press, 1988.

———. *The Practice of Conceptual History*. Stanford, Stanford University Press, 2002.

Labbé, François. "La Rêve Irénique du Marquis de la Tierce. Franc-maçonnerie, lumières et projets de paix perpétuelle dans le cadre du Saint-empire sous le règne de Charles VII (1741–1745)." *Francia* 18 (1991): 47–69.

Labourdette, Jean-François. *Vergennes. Ministre principal de Louis XVI*. Paris, Editions Desjonquières, 1990.

Laisney, Louis. "Un Normand qui a influé sur les destinées de la France de Louis XV à Louis XVIII. Charles François Lebrun (1739–1824)." *Revue du département de la Manche* 15 (1973): 121–240.

Lange, Christian Louis. "Histoire de la doctrine pacifique et de son influence sur le développement du droit international." *Académie du Droit International. Recueil des cours* 13 (1926): 171–426.

Laquièze, Alain. "Benjamin Constant et les lectures à l'Athénée royal consacrées à la constitution anglaise." *Annales Benjamin Constant* 23–4 (2000): 155–71.

Larrère, Catherine. "Malebranche revisité: l'économie naturelle des Physiocrates." *Dix-Huitième Siècle* 26 (1994): 117–38.

Launay, Michel. "Le *Discours sur les sciences et les arts*: Jean-Jacques entre Mme Dupin et Montesquieu." In Michel Launay, ed., *Jean-Jacques Rousseau et son temps*, pp. 93–103. Paris, José Corti, 1969.

Laurent, Charles. *Les voyages en Bretagne du chevalier de Mirabeau*. Mayenne, Joseph Floch, 1983.

Laursen, John Christian. "David Hume and the Danish Debate about Freedom of the Press in the 1770s." *Journal of the History of Ideas* 59 (1998): 169–72.

———. "Spinoza in Denmark and the Fall of Struensee, 1770–1772." *Journal of the History of Ideas* 61 (2002): 189–202.

———. "Luxdorf's Press Freedom Writings: Before the Fall of Struensee in early 1770s Denmark-Norway." *The European Legacy* 7 (2002): 61–77.

Le Bouler, Jean-Pierre, and Catherine Lafarge. "Catalogue topographique partiel des papiers Dupin-Rousseau dispersés de 1951 à 1958." *Annales de la société Jean-Jacques Rousseau* 39 (1972–7): 243–80.

Leclercq, Henri. *Histoire de la Régence pendant la minorité de Louis XV.* 3 vols. Paris, Honoré Champion, 1923.

Lemaire, André. *Les lois fondamentales de la monarchie française*. Paris, 1907.

Lennon, Thomas M. *Reading Bayle*. Toronto, University of Toronto Press, 1999.

Lieberman, David. "The Legal Needs of a Commercial Society: The Jurisprudence of Lord Kames." In Istvan Hont and Michael Ignatieff, eds., *Wealth and Virtue*, pp. 203–34. Cambridge, 1983.

Livesey, James. "Agrarian Ideology and Commercial Republicanism in the French Revolution." *Past & Present* 157 (1997): 94–121.

Lochernes, M. Frederick. *Robert Walsh*. New York, 1941.

Lombard, Alfred. *L'abbé Dubos, un initiateur de la pensée moderne*. Paris, 1913.

Lovejoy, Arthur O. *Reflections on Human Nature*. Baltimore, Johns Hopkins University Press, 1961.

Lusenbrink, Hans-Jurgen, and Alexandre Mussard, eds. *Avantages et désavantages de la découverte de l'Amérique: Chastellux, Raynal et le concours de l'Académie de Lyon de 1787*. Saint-Etienne, Université de Saint-Etienne, 1994.

Lüthy, Herbert. *La banque protestante en France de la révocation de l'édit de Nantes à la Révolution*. 2 vols. Paris, 1959–61.

Macdonald, James. *A Free Nation Deep in Debt: The Financial Roots of Democracy*. New York, Farrar, Straus and Giroux, 2003.

Maire, Catherine. *De la cause de Dieu à la cause de la Nation. Le jansénisme au xviiie siècle*. Paris, Gallimard, 1998.

Manin, Bernard. "Checks, Balances and Boundaries: The Separation of Powers in the Constitutional Debate of 1787." In Biancamaria Fontana, ed., *The Invention of the Modern Republic*, pp. 27–62. Cambridge, CUP, 1994.

Margerison, Kenneth. "P. L. Roederer: Political Thought and Practice during the French Revolution." *Transactions of the American Philosophical Society* 73 (1983): vii–166.

Martin, Jean. "Quatorze billets inédits de Mirabeau à Etienne Dumont et à Du Roveray." *La Révolution française* 78 (1925): 289–311.

Masson, Frédéric. *Le Sacre et le couronnement de Napoléon*. Paris, 1908.

McCoy, Drew R. *The Last of the Fathers: James Madison and the Republican Legacy*. Cambridge, CUP, 1989.

McLean, Ian, and Fiona Hewitt, eds. *Condorcet: Foundations of Social Choice and Political Theory*. London, Edward Elgar, 1994.

Meinecke, Friedrich. *Machiavellism: The Doctrine of Raison d'Etat and Its Place in Modern History* [1924]. Translated by D. Scott. Edited by W. Stark. London, Routledge, 1957.

Meyssonnier, Simone. *La balance et l'horloge*. Paris, Editions de la Passion, 1989.

Miller, Peter. *Defining the Common Good: Empire, Religion and Philosophy in Eighteenth-Century Britain*. Cambridge, CUP, 1994.

Mirkine-Guetzévitch, Boris. "L'influence de la révolution française sur le développement du droit international dans l'Europe oriental." *Académie du Droit International. Recueil des cours* 22 (1929): 296–457.

———. "La Révolution française et l'idée de renonciation à la guerre." *La Révolution française* 82 (1929): 255–68.

———. "La Révolution française et les projets d'union européen." *La Révolution française* 84 (1931): 322–35.

Montier, Amand. *Robert Lindet*. Paris, 1899.

Moras, Joachim. *Ursprung und Entwicklung des Begriffs der Zivilisation in Frankreich, 1756–1830*. Hamburg, 1930.

Morel, Henri. "Les 'droits de la nation' sous la régence." In *La Régence*, pp. 249–62. Centre aixois d'études et de recherches sur le dix-huitième siècle. Paris, Armand Colin, 1970.

Murphy, Antoin E. *Richard Cantillon: Entrepreneur and Economist*. Oxford, Oxford University Press, 1986.

Nakhimovsky, Isaac. "Voltaire, Frederick the Great, and the *Anti-Machiavel* in Historical Context." M.Phil. diss., Cambridge University, 2002.

Neiman, Susan. *Evil in Modern Thought: An Alternative History of Philosophy*. Princeton, Princeton University Press, 2002.

Nelson, Eric. *The Greek Tradition in Republican Thought*. Cambridge, CUP, 2003.

Neuhouser, Frederick. *Foundations of Hegel's Social Theory*. Cambridge, Mass., Harvard University Press, 2000.

———. "Rousseau on the Relation between Reason and Self-Love." *Internationales Jahrbuch des Deutschen Idealismus* 1 (2003): 221–39.

Nolan, Cathal J., ed. *Notable U.S. Ambassadors since 1775: A Biographical Dictionary*. Westport, Greenwood Press, 1997.

Norberg, Kathryn. "The French Fiscal Crisis of 1788 and the Financial Origins of the Revolution of 1789." In Philip T. Hoffman and Kathryn Norberg, eds., *Fiscal Crises, Liberty, and Representative Government 1450–1789*, pp. 253–98. Stanford, Stanford University Press, 1994.

North, Douglass C. *The Rise of the Western World: A New Economic History*. Cambridge, CUP, 1973.

———. *Institutions, Institutional Change, and Economic Performance*. Cambridge, CUP, 1990.

North, Douglass C., and Barry Weingast. "Constitutions and Commitment: The Evolution of Institutions Governing Public Choice in Seventeenth-Century England." *Journal of Economic History* 49 (1989): 803–32.

O'Brien, Patrick K. "Fiscal Exceptionalism: Great Britain and Its European Rivals from Civil War to Triumph at Trafalgar and Waterloo." *Working Paper 65/01*, Department of Economic History, London School of Economics, October 2001.

O'Connor, Thomas. *An Irish Theologian in Enlightenment France: Luke Joseph Hooke, 1714–96*. Dublin, Four Courts Press, 1995.

Ohlin, Barbro. "Du Pont de Nemours écrit à Carl Fredrik, comte de Scheffer." In Gunnar von Proschwitz, ed., *Influences. Relations culturelles entre la France et la Suède*. Goteborg, 1988.

Pagden, Anthony, ed. *The Idea of Europe from Antiquity to the European Union*. Cambridge, CUP, 2002.

Palmer, R. R. *J.-B. Say: An Economist in Troubled Times*. Princeton, Princeton University Press, 1997.

Pappas, John. "La Campagne des philosophes contre l'honneur." *Studies on Voltaire and the Eighteenth Century* 205 (1982): 31–44.

Pascal, François. *L'économie dans la terreur: Robert Lindet 1746–1825*, Paris, SPM, 1999.

Pasquino, Pasquale. *Sieyès et l'invention de la constitution en France*. Paris, Editions Odile Jacob, 1998.

Perkins, Jean A. "Rousseau jugé par Du Pont de Nemours." *Annales de la Société Jean-Jacques Rousseau* 39 (1972–7): 171–95.

Perkins, Merle H. *The Moral and Political Philosophy of the Abbé de Saint-Pierre*. Geneva, Droz, 1959.

———. "Voltaire's Concept of International Order." *Studies on Voltaire and the Eighteenth Century* 36 (1965).

Perkins, Merle J. "Montesquieu on National Power and International Rivalry." *Studies on Voltaire and the Eighteenth Century* 238 (1985): 1–95.

Perrot, Jean-Claude. *Une histoire intellectuelle de l'économie politique*. Paris, Ecole des Hautes Etudes en Sciences Sociales, 1992.

Phillipson, Nicolas, and Quentin Skinner, eds. *Political Discourse in Early Modern Britain*. Cambridge, CUP, 1993.

Philp, Mark. "English Republicanism in the 1790s." *Journal of Political Philosophy* 6 (1998): 235–62.

Pii, Eluggero. "Montesquieu e Véron de Forbonnais. Appunti sul dibattito settecentescho in tema di commercio." *Il Pensiero politico* 10 (1977): 362–89.

Pitkin, Hannah Fenichel. *The Concept of Representation*. Berkeley and Los Angeles, University of California Press, 1967.

Plongeron, Bernard. "Affirmation et transformations d'une 'civilisation chrétienne' à la fin du xviiie siècle." In Jean-René Derré, Jacques Gadille, Xavier de Montclos, and Bernard Plongeron, eds., *Civilisation chrétienne. Approche historique d'une idéologie xviiie–xixe siècle*, pp. 9–21. Paris, 1975.

———. "Bonheur et 'civilisation chrétienne': une nouvelle apologétique après 1760." *Studies on Voltaire and the Eighteenth Century* 154 (1976): 1637–55.

———. "Echec à la sécularisation des lumières? La religion comme lien social." In Michel Mat, ed., *Problèmes d'histoire du christianisme*, pp. 91–126. Brussels, 1984.

Pocock, J.G.A. *The Machiavellian Moment: Florentine Political Thought and the Atlantic Republican Tradition* [1975]. 2nd ed. Princeton, Princeton University Press, 2003.

———. "Hume and the American Revolution: The Dying Thoughts of a North Briton." In his *Virtue, Commerce, and History: Essays on Political Thought and History, Chiefly in the Eighteenth Century*, pp. 125–41. Cambridge, CUP, 1985.

———. *Barbarism and Religion.* 4 vols. Cambridge, CUP, 1999–2005.

Porset, Charles. "L'inquiétant étrangeté de l'*Essai sur l'origine des langues*: Rousseau et ses exégètes." *Studies on Voltaire and the Eighteenth Century* 154 (1976): 1715–58.

Postigliola, Alberto. "Sur quelques interprétations de la 'séparation des pouvoirs' chez Montesquieu." *Studies on Voltaire and the Eighteenth Century* 154 (1976): 1759–75.

———. "En relisant le chapitre sur la constitution de l'Angleterre." *Cahiers de Philosophie Politique et Juridique* 7 (1985): 7–28.

Price, Munro. *The Fall of the French Monarchy.* London, Macmillan, 2002.

———. "Mirabeau and the Court: Some New Evidence." *French Historical Studies* 29 (2006): 37–75.

Procacci, Giovanna. *Gouverner la misère: la question sociale en France (1789–1848).* Paris, Seuil, 1993.

Przeworski, Adam. "Institutions Matter?" *Government and Opposition* 39 (2004): 527–40.

Radrizzani, Ives, ed. *J. G. Fichte. Lettres et témoignages sur la révolution française.* Paris, Vrin, 2002.

Rahe, Paul A. "The Book That Never Was: Montesquieu's *Considerations on the Romans* in Historical Context." *History of Political Thought* 26 (2005): 43–89.

Redslob, Robert. *Histoire des grands principes du droit des gens depuis l'antiquité jusqu'à la veille de la grande guerre.* Paris, 1923.

Reinhard, Marcel. *La Légende de Henri IV.* Paris, 1935.

Renaut, F. P. *La question de la Louisiane 1796–1806.* Paris, 1918.

Rétat, Pierre. "De Mandeville à Montesquieu: honneur, luxe et dépense noble dans l' 'Esprit des lois.' " *Studi Francese* 50 (1973): 238–49.

Richter, Melvin. *The Political Theory of Montesquieu.* Cambridge, CUP, 1977.

Riley, James C. *The Seven Years War and the Old Regime in France: The Economic and Financial Toll.* Princeton, Princeton University Press, 1986.

Riley, Patrick. *The General Will before Rousseau: The Transformation of the Divine into the Civic.* Princeton, Princeton University Press, 1986.

———. "Malebranche's Moral Philosophy: Divine and Human Justice." In Steven Nadler, ed., *The Cambridge Companion to Malebranche*, pp. 220–61. Cambridge, CUP, 2000.

———. "Rousseau, Fénelon and the Quarrel between the Ancients and the Moderns." In Patrick Riley, ed., *The Cambridge Companion to Rousseau*, pp. 78–93. Cambridge, CUP, 2001.

———. "Rousseau's General Will." In Patrick Riley, ed., *The Cambridge Companion to Rousseau*, pp. 124–53. Cambridge, CUP, 2001.

Riskin, Jessica. *Science in the Age of Sensibility; The Sentimental Empiricists of the French Enlightenment.* Chicago, University of Chicago Press, 2002.

Robertson, John. *The Case for the Enlightenment; Scotland and Naples 1680–1760*. Cambridge, CUP, 2005.

Root, Hilton L. *The Fountain of Privilege: Political Foundations of Markets in Old Regime France and England*. Berkeley and Los Angeles, University of California Press, 1993.

Rosanvallon, Pierre. *Le Moment Guizot*. Paris, Gallimard, 1989.

Rothkrug, Lionel. *Opposition to Louis XIV: The Political and Social Origins of the French Enlightenment*. Princeton, Princeton University Press, 1965.

Rothschild, Emma. "Condorcet and the Conflict of Values." *Historical Journal* 39 (1996): 677–701.

Roux, Philippe de. "Le marquis de Casaux. Un planteur des Antilles inspirateur de Mirabeau." *Société d'histoire des colonies françaises*, 1951.

Rowen, Herbert H. *The King's State: Proprietary Dynasticism in Early Modern France*. New Brunswick, Rutgers University Press, 1980.

Rutherford, Donald. "Malebranche's Theodicy." In Steven Nadler, ed., *The Cambridge Companion to Malebranche*, pp. 165–89. Cambridge, CUP, 2000.

Saguez-Lovisi, Claire. *Les lois fondamentales au xviiie siècle. Recherches sur la loi de dévolution de la couronne*. Paris, Presses universitaires de France, 1983.

Schechter, Ronald, ed. *The French Revolution*. Oxford, Blackwell, 2001.

Schmidt, James. "Inventing the Enlightenment: Anti-Jacobins, British Hegelians and the *Oxford English Dictionary*." *Journal of the History of Ideas* 64 (2003): 421–43.

Schofield, Norman. " 'The Probability of a Fit Choice': American Political History and Voting Theory." In Keith Dowding, Robert E. Gooding, and Carole Pateman, eds., *Justice and Democracy*, pp. 59–78. Cambridge, CUP, 2004.

Schuyler, Robert Livingston. *Josiah Tucker: A Selection from His Political and Economic Writings*. New York, Columbia University Press, 1931.

——. *The Fall of the Old Colonial System*. Oxford, Oxford University Press, 1945.

Schwarz, Joel. *The Sexual Politics of Jean-Jacques Rousseau*. Chicago, University of Chicago Press, 1984.

Scurr, Ruth. "Social Equality in Pierre-Louis Roederer's Interpretation of the Modern Republic, 1793." *History of European Ideas* 26 (2000): 105–26.

——. "Pierre-Louis Roederer and the Debate on the Forms of Government in Revolutionary France." *Political Studies* 52 (2004): 251–68.

Sénéchal, Anicet. "Jean-Jacques Rousseau, secrétaire de Mme Dupin." *Annales Jean-Jacques Rousseau* 36 (1963–5): 173–290.

Sepinwall, Alyssa Goldstein. *The Abbé Grégoire and the French Revolution: The Making of Modern Universalism*. Berkeley and Los Angeles, University of California Press, 2005.

Sewell, William H. *A Rhetoric of Bourgeois Revolution: The Abbé Sieyès and "What Is the Third Estate?"* Durham, N. C., Duke University Press, 1994.

Shackleton, Robert. "Montesquieu's Correspondence." *French Studies* 12 (1958): 330–1.

——. "Montesquieu, Dupin and the Early Writings of Rousseau." In S. Harvey, M. Hobson, D. J. Kelley, and S.S.B. Taylor, eds., *Reappraisals of Rousseau*, pp. 234–49. Manchester, Manchester University Press, 1980.

Sheehan, James J. "The Problem of Sovereignty in European History." *American Historical Review* 111 (2006): 1–15.

Siren, Osvald. "Ur Markis de Mirabeau's Brev till Greve Carl Fredrik Scheffer." *Lychnios* (1948–9): 51–84.

Skinner, Quentin. *The Foundations of Modern Political Thought*. 2 vols. Cambridge, CUP, 1978.

———. "The State." In Terence Ball, James Ball, and Russell L. Hanson, eds., *Political Innovation and Conceptual Change*, pp. 90–131. Cambridge, CUP, 1989.

———. *Visions of Politics*. 3 vols. Cambridge, CUP, 2002.

Skocpol, Theda. *States and Social Revolutions*. Cambridge, CUP, 1979.

Smith, Jay M. *The Culture of Merit: Nobility, Royal Service, and the Making of Absolute Monarchy*. Ann Arbor, University of Michigan Press, 1996).

Sola, Giorgio. "Classe dominante, classe politica ed élites." *Il Pensiero politico* 36 (2003): 464–84.

Sonenscher, Michael. "The Cheese and the Rats: Augustin Cochin and the Bicentenary of the French Revolution." *Economy and Society* 19 (1990): 266–74.

———. "The Nation's Debt and the Birth of the Modern Republic: The French Fiscal Deficit and the Politics of the Revolution of 1789." *History of Political Thought* 18 (1997): 64–103, 267–325.

———. "Fashion's Empire: Theories of Foreign Trade in Early Eighteenth-Century France." In Robert Fox and Anthony Turner, eds., *Innovation and Markets in Eighteenth-Century France*. London, Hambledon Press, 1998.

———. "Enlightenment and Revolution." *Journal of Modern History* 70 (1998): 371–83.

———. "Republicanism, State Finances and the Emergence of Commercial Society in Eighteenth-Century France—or from Royal to Ancient Republicanism and Back." In Martin Van Gelderen and Quentin Skinner, eds., *Republicanism: A Shared European Heritage*, 2:275–91. 2 vols. Cambridge, CUP, 2002.

———. "Property, Community and Citizenship." In Mark Goldie and Robert Wokler, eds., *The Cambridge History of Eighteenth-Century Political Thought*. Cambridge, CUP, 2006.

Spector, Céline. "Théorie de l'impôt." In Jean-Jacques Rousseau, *Discours sur l'économie politique* [1758], edited by Bruno Bernardi, pp. 195–221. Paris, Vrin, 2002.

———. *Montesquieu. Pouvoirs, richesses et sociétés*. Paris, Presses universitaires de France, 2004.

Spink, John. "Un abbé philosophe: l'affaire de J. M. de Prades." *Dix-Huitième Siècle* 3 (1971): 145–80.

———. Introduction to Denis Diderot, *Suite de l'apologie de l'abbé de Prades*. In Denis Diderot, *Oeuvres complètes*, edited by Yvon Belaval et al., 4:285–312. Paris, Hermann, 1978.

Spitz, Jean-Fabien. *L'Amour de l'égalité*. Paris, Vrin, 2000.

Stafford, Fiona. *The Sublime Savage: James Macpherson and the Poems of Ossian*. Edinburgh, Edinburgh University Press, 1988.

Starobinski, Jean. *Montesquieu par lui-même*. Paris, Seuil, 1956.

———. *Blessings in Disguise; or the Morality of Evil* [Paris, 1989]. Translated by Arthur Goldhammer. Cambridge, Polity Press, 1993.

Stasavage, David. *Public Debt and the Birth of the Democratic State: France and Great Britain, 1688–1789*. Cambridge, CUP, 2003.

Staum, Martin S. *Minerva's Message: Stabilizing the French Revolution.* Montreal, McGill-Queen's University Press, 1996.

Stedman Jones, Gareth. "National Bankruptcy and Social Revolution: European Observers on Britain, 1813–1844." In Donald Winch and Patrick O'Brien, eds., *The Political Economy of British Historical Experience*, pp. 61–92. London, 2002.

Stettner, Walter F. "Sir James Steuart on the Public Debt." *Quarterly Journal of Economics* 59 (1945): 451–76.

Stone, Bailey. *The Genesis of the French Revolution: A Global-Historical Interpretation.* Cambridge, CUP, 1994.

———. *Reinterpreting the French Revolution: A Global-Historical Perspective.* Cambridge, CUP, 2002.

Stone, Lawrence, ed. *An Imperial State at War.* London, Routledge, 1993.

Swann, Julian. *Politics and the Parlement of Paris under Louis XV.* Cambridge, CUP, 1995.

Taylor, George V. "Non-capitalist Wealth and the Origins of the French Revolution." *American Historical Review* 72 (1967): 469–96.

Tillet, Edouard. *La constitution anglaise, un modèle politique et institutionnel dans la France des lumières.* Aix-en-Provence, Presses Universitaires d'Aix-Marseille, 2001.

Tilly, Charles. *Coercion, Capital, and European States AD 990–1990.* Oxford, Oxford University Press, 1990.

———, ed. *The Formation of National States in Western Europe.* Princeton, Princeton University Press, 1975.

Treitschke, Heinrich von. *History of Germany in the Nineteenth Century.* Translated by Eden and Cedar Paul. 7 vols. London, 1916.

Tribe, Keith. *Strategies of Economic Order: German Economic Discourse 1750–1950.* Cambridge, CUP, 1995.

Trinkle, Denis. "Noël-Antoine Pluche's *Le Spectacle de la Nature*: An Encyclopaedic Best Seller." *Studies on Voltaire and the Eighteenth Century* 358 (1997): 93–134.

Trousson, Raymond. *Jean-Jacques Rousseau jugé par ses contemporains.* Paris, 2000.

Tuck, Richard. "The Modern Theory of Natural Law." In Anthony Pagden, ed., *The Languages of Political Theory in Early Modern Europe.* Cambridge, CUP, 1987.

———. "Grotius and Selden." In J. H. Burns and Mark Goldie, eds., *The Cambridge History of Political Thought, 1450–1700.* Cambridge, CUP, 1991.

———. *Philosophy and Government, 1572–1651.* Cambridge, CUP, 1993.

———. *The Laws of War and Peace.* Oxford, Oxford University Press, 1999.

Turner, Frederick Jackson, ed. *Correspondence of the French Ministers to the United States 1791–1797.* 2 vols. [Washington, 1904]. New York, Da Capo Press, 1972.

Vaissière, Pierre de. *Lettres d' "aristocrates". La Révolution racontée par des correspondances privées.* Paris, 1907.

Van Kley, Dale. *The Jansenists and the Expulsion of the Jesuits from France, 1757–65.* New Haven, Yale University Press, 1975.

———. *The Damiens Affair and the Unraveling of the Old Regime.* Princeton, Princeton University Press, 1984.

———. "Pierre Nicole, Jansenism, and the Morality of Enlightened Self-Interest." In Alan Charles Kors and Paul J. Korshin, eds., *Anticipations of the Enlightenment in England, France and Germany.* Philadelphia, University of Pennsylvania Press, 1987.

———. "The Jansenist Constitutional Legacy in the French Pre-revolution." In Keith Michael Baker, ed., *The Political Culture of the Old Regime*, pp. 169–201. Oxford, Pergamon Press, 1987.

———. "The French Estates-General as Ecumenical Council." *Journal of Modern History* 61 (1989): 1–52.

———. *The Religious Origins of the French Revolution*. New Haven, Yale University Press, 1996.

———. "Christianity as Casualty and Chrysalis of Modernity: The Problem of Dechristianization in the French Revolution." *American Historical Review* 108 (2003): 1081–103.

———, ed. *The French Idea of Freedom*. Stanford, Stanford University Press, 1994.

Van Tieghem, Paul. *Ossian en France*. 2 vols. Paris, 1917.

Vargas, Yves. *Rousseau, l'énigme du sexe*. Paris, Presses universitaires de France, 1997.

Venturi, Franco. *La jeunesse de Diderot* [1939]. Geneva, Slatkine, 1967.

Venturino, Diego. *Le Ragioni della tradizione, nobilità e mondo moderno in Boulainvilliers (1658–1722)*. Turin, 1993.

Viala, André. "Les idées de l'abbé Pluche sur la société." In *La Régence*, pp. 307–16. Centre Aixois d'Etudes et de Recherches sur le Dix-huitième Siècle. Paris, 1970.

Vile, M.J.C. *Constitutionalism and the Separation of Powers*. 2nd ed. Indianapolis, Liberty Fund, 1998.

Viner, Jacob. "Power versus Plenty as Objectives of Foreign Policy in the Seventeenth and Eighteenth Centuries" [1948]. Reprinted Jacob Viner, *Essays on the Intellectual History of Economics*, edited by D. A. Irwin. Princeton, Princeton University Press, 1991.

———. "The Role of Providence in the Social Order." *Memoirs of the American Philosophical Society* 90 (Philadelphia, 1972).

Vishniak, Mark. "Justifications of Power in Democracy." *Political Science Quarterly* 60 (1945): 351–76.

Volpilhac-Auger, Catherine. "Tacite et Montesquieu." *Studies on Voltaire and the Eighteenth Century* 232 (1985).

———. "Tacite en France de Montesquieu à Chateaubriand." *Studies on Voltaire and the Eighteenth Century* 313 (1993).

Waddicor, Mark H. *Montesquieu and the Philosophy of Natural Law*. The Hague, Martinus Nijhoff, 1970.

Weil, Françoise. "Les lectures de Montesquieu." *Revue d'histoire littéraire de la France* 57 (1957): 494–514.

Whatmore, Richard. "Commerce, Constitutions, and the Manners of a Nation: Etienne Clavière's Revolutionary Political Economy, 1788–1793." *History of European Ideas* 22 (1996): 351–68.

———. *Republicanism and the French Revolution: An Intellectual History of Jean-Baptiste Say's Political Economy*. Oxford, Oxford University Press, 2000.

Whitaker, Arthur P. *The United States and the Independence of Latin America, 1800–1830*. 2nd ed. New York, Norton, 1964.

Williams, David. *Condorcet and Modernity*. Cambridge, CUP, 2004.

Wokler, Robert. "The Influence of Diderot on the Political Theory of Rousseau." *Studies on Voltaire and the Eighteenth Century* 132 (1975): 55–111.

Wokler, Robert. *Rousseau on Society, Politics, Music and Language*. New York, Garland Press, 1987.

Wootton, David. Introduction to David Wootton, ed., *Republicanism, Liberty and Commercial Society 1649–1776*. Stanford, Stanford University Press, 1994.

———. "Helvétius, from Radical Enlightenment to Revolution." *Political Studies* 28 (2000): 307–36.

———. "Liberty, Metaphor and Mechanism: 'Checks and Balances' and the Origins of Modern Constitutionalism." In David Womersley, ed., *Liberty and American Experience in the Eighteenth Century*. Indianapolis, Liberty Fund, 2006.

———, ed. *The Essential Federalist and Anti-Federalist Papers*. Indianapolis, Hackett, 2003.

Wright, Johnson Kent. *A Classical Republican in Eighteenth-Century France: The Political Thought of Mably*. Stanford, Calif., 1997.

Zweig, Egon. *Die Lehre vom Pouvoir constituant*. Tübingen, 1909.

INDEX

Unless otherwise stated, references to Mirabeau in subentries to this index (e.g., civilisation, Mirabeau on) indicate Victor Riqueti, marquis de Mirabeau, rather than his son, Honoré Gabriel, comte de Mirabeau.